The Media WITHDRAWN Student's Book

The Media Student's Book is a comprehensive introduction for students of media studies. It covers all the key topics and provides a detailed, lively and accessible guide to concepts and debates. This fourth edition, newly in colour, has been thoroughly revised, re-ordered and updated, with many very recent examples and expanded coverage of the most important issues currently facing media studies. It is structured in four main parts, addressing key concepts, media practices, media debates, and the resources available for individual research.

Individual chapters include: Interpreting media • Narratives • Genres and other classifications • Institutions • Questions of representation • Ideologies and power • Industries • Audiences • Advertising and branding • Research • Production organisation • Production techniques • Distribution • Documentary and 'reality TV' • Whose globalisation? • 'Free choices' in a 'free market'?

Chapters are supported by case studies which include: Ways of interpreting • *CSI: Miami* and crime fiction • J-horror and the *Ring* cycle • Television as institution • Images of migration • News • The media majors • The music industry, technology and synergy • Selling audiences • Celebrity, stardom and marketing • Researching mobile phone technologies • Contemporary British cinema.

The authors are experienced in writing, researching and teaching across different levels of pre-undergraduate and undergraduate study, with an awareness of the needs of those students. The book is specially designed to be easy and stimulating to use with:

- marginal notes, definitions, references (and even jokes), allied to a comprehensive glossary
- follow-up activities, suggestions for further reading, useful websites and resources plus a companion website supporting the book at www.routledge.com/textbooks/0415371430
- references and examples from a rich range of media forms, including advertising, television, films, radio, newspapers, magazines, photography and the internet.

Gill Branston is a Senior Lecturer and Director of Undergraduate Studies in the School of Journalism, Media and Cultural Studies at Cardiff University. **Roy Stafford** is a freelance lecturer, writer and examiner in media education and training.

What reviewers said of previous editions:

The Media Student's Book

Fourth Edition

GILL BRANSTON

and

ROY STAFFORD

Routledge
Taylor & Francis Group

LONDON AND NEW YORK

First published 1996
by Routledge

Reprinted 1996 (twice), 1997, 1998

Second edition first published 1999
Reprinted 2000, 2001, 2002

Third edition first published 2003
Reprinted 2003, 2004

This fourth edition first published 2006
by Routledge
2 Park Square, Milton Park, Abingdon, Oxon OX14 4RN

Simultaneously published in the USA and Canada
by Routledge
270 Madison Ave, New York, NY 10016

Routledge is an imprint of the Taylor & Francis Group, an informa business

Typeset in Garamond by Keystroke, Jacaranda Lodge, Wolverhampton
Printed and bound in Great Britain by Scotprint, Haddington

British Library Cataloguing in Publication Data
A catalogue record for this book is available from the British Library

Library of Congress Cataloging in Publication Data
Branston, Gill.
    The media student's book / Gill Branston and Roy Stafford. – 4th ed.
      p. cm.
    Includes bibliographical references and index.
      1. Mass media. I. Stafford, Roy. II. Title.
    P90.B6764 2006
    302.23–dc22   2005027571

ISBN10: 0–415–37142–2 (hbk)
ISBN10: 0–415–37143–0 (pbk)

ISBN13: 9–78–0–37142–1 (hbk)
ISBN13: 9–78–0–37143–8 (pbk)

Contents

CONTENTS

CONTENTS

Illustrations

Every effort has been made to contact copyright holders of the images within the book. This was not possible in all cases. If there are any oversights, these will be remedied if the rights holder contacts Routledge.

Acknowledgements

Thanks to Stephen Castles, Sue Crockford, Elisabeth Grawe, Sara Gwenllian-Jones, Anne Hubbard, John Jewell, Fiona Johnson, Nick Lacey, Colin Larcombe, Wing-Fai Leung, Justin Lewis, Paul Mason, Donald Matheson, Gary Merrill, Sarah Mumford, Sarah Perks, Chris Powell, John Robinson, Wowo Wauters, Granville Williams, Andy Willis, Tana Wollen.

To the readers of and contributors to *in the picture* magazine.

To Rebecca Barden and Moira Taylor, again, for their rare combination of enthusiasm and patience during the many processes of making this fourth, even more complex edition, especially given changes to their working conditions. The highly charged final stages of production ('The tsunami image is a fake!' 'Who has the rights to the Abu Ghraib image?' etc.) were as stimulating and ultimately satisfying as ever this time; also thanks to the input of Julene Knox and Anna Hines.

To Lucy Branston, Alistair Bryan, Lauren Bryan, Ruby Seago, Marion Pencavel and Rob Seago for many virtues and suggestions. Some of these unfortunates had to tolerate the authors yet again during the process of authoring, 'above and beyond the call of duty'.

Finally, and emphatically, yet again, none of this would have been possible without the help and questions of the students, teachers and media practitioners with whom we have worked over many years.

Introduction

Media studies is now an established area of work in schools, colleges and higher education in many countries. This book has always tried to work with the ways in which it *both*

- relates very intimately to the sharpest contemporary cultural pleasures, and
- has to draw on a range of sometimes difficult theories to debate these experiences.

It's been very gratifying to work on the fourth edition – and to be able to use colour. In this Introduction we give the rationale for writing a book like this one and briefly outline changes to it since its first appearance in 1996.

Modern media . . .

We have all grown up in environments saturated with media experiences. In countries with reliable and widespread electricity supplies, these experiences are interfused with everyday life itself, especially through television, radio and technologies such as mobile phones or the internet. One theorist wrote some time ago that 'TV now escorts children across the globe even before they have permission to cross the street' (Meyrowitz 1985: 238). This seems far truer today. 'The media' are utterly familiar and one of our aims is to penetrate this familiarity and make them somewhat 'strange', so as not to take them at their own face value.

This familiarity and embeddedness of media, the easy pleasures as well as the terrors that they trade in, and the expectations which all these factors arouse, create problems for any textbook. The media compete for your attention, and perhaps your sense of what knowledge is, and how it is to be presented. Television, from children's programmes, through educational television, to the vast range of broadcast material, has probably taught you a great deal, in vivid ways which books cannot hope to emulate.

The everyday quality of modern technologies combines dazzling and disturbing capacities. It is now possible, using professional digital imaging, to make it seem as though Humphrey Bogart and Scarlett Johansson are playing a scene together, or that the Earth can 'morph' into an apple before our eyes; to broadcast such scenes simultaneously across continents; and to accompany them with music created entirely by computer.

Figure 0.1 A media image which would have been unthinkable twenty years ago, showing the underwater epicentre of the 2004 tsunami. It can be circulated around the globe, almost instantaneously, through the internet, news programmes, etc. It uses imaging technology which can represent the unseeable. And can possibly help to avoid the worst effects of such natural disasters in future. (Taken by Survey Ship HMS *Scott*.)

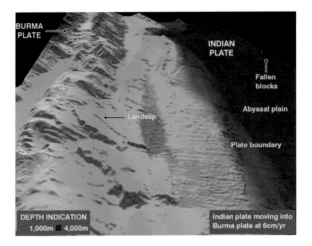

It is also possible for amateurs to make short 'films' with mobile camera phones, for example. (One of us was 'filmed' in this way by a student, while lecturing on documentary.) This is a huge opportunity which did not exist ten years ago. But it has a darker side. Just a few examples: parts of the media love to report 'happy slapping' films, where assaults are staged and then recorded onto mobile phones. Paedophile use of the internet is well documented. Terrorist groups such as Al-Qaeda have made short videos of attacks on enemy troops, as well as of the torture and even execution of hostages, and circulated these through the internet. Occasionally, as with US soldiers' footage of the torture of prisoners, such evidence finds its way into news and documentary programmes, a quite new set of connections for media.

One of the things *The Media Student's Book* tries to do is to locate such different potentials within debates and theories which can help us understand them, and the ways they get treated by the media.

The internet has been touted, like many earlier technologies, as a kind of utopian space where information about 'the universe and everything' is readily available and all questions can be answered. For the moment this seems partly true, for those with access. Wikipedia, the lively encyclopedia free to those online, is another resource which

Figure 0.2 A mobile phone camera used to record the escape of commuters from one of the London Underground bombs, 7 July 2005.

was not available ten years ago. You may also have quite sophisticated experience of interactive learning through computers, at home and at college, and 'smart' ways of working through trial and error problem-solving, pattern recognition and strategic thinking, often honed in computer games.

. . . and the study of modern media

The ease of use of technologies – 'just push the button' – can make theories and histories seem irrelevant, though they are not.

- Technologies are not equally distributed, nor are they accessible or affordable for everyone – not even bloggers or games players.
- The internet is not always reliable. Certainly print publishers face more legal scrutiny (in the possible use of libel laws for example) than some websites.

Yes, the technologies can be terrific – exciting and disturbing at the same time. But we hope you enjoy the sections on their histories, distribution and ways of working, rather than feeling those chapters to be diversions from the delights of celebrating 'virtual reality'. However convincingly you have Humphrey and Scarlett together in the same frame, however much information is at your fingertips on the internet, you can't rely on virtual decisions about what dialogue they will speak, or how they will be lit, framed and directed to move. Nor can you make full use of the internet without some sense of what information you need, and what information from it is likely to be reliable.

So we try here to develop other skills, which TV and games will not generally open up. Sometimes this results in a conceptual guide, including quite complicated arguments where necessary, in longish chapters. But we know you will need to make connections between ideas and to exploit the possibilities of following links, as on a website. So you'll find plenty of cross-references and key terms, shown in **bold**, which can be traced through the Glossary or marginal notes. Information is offered in different-sized chunks and formats. In some ways the book resembles a tool box – of concepts, histories, debates, guides to production and so on. We hope you'll like and use the definitions, jokes, photos and quotes in the margins, as well as the case studies and activities.

Some students have problems in media studies because of its terminology. Words which have fairly straightforward meanings in everyday life (like 'sign' or 'closed') take on rather different ones within this subject. This can be confusing and we've tried, wherever possible, to warn you of likely misunderstandings.

The development of media studies has been often 'driven' by developments in higher education. From the 1960s onwards, many academics, trying to get modern media taken seriously as objects for study, had to present arguments in very specialised language. Along with an excitement with theoretical developments such as structuralism and semiotics, which seemed to promise radical political possibilities, this produced a very difficult set of theoretical terms. These were especially difficult for those who had not been involved in the years of struggling through, applying and familiarising themselves with them.

Now the dust has settled, the real gains of some of these approaches can be brought into study of the media. Some are already part of 'style' reporting and other culturally directed parts of the media, as more media graduates begin work there. Other parts of what has become almost the official language of the subject in higher education are less relevant now, and often depend on such a huge amount of study that we have left them out.

The likely readerships of this book

Media studies is still a fairly young subject area and the syllabuses – the official definitions – offered by the various examining bodies are still being developed. Indeed, given the nature of the field of enquiry, they will always be changing. We've tried to cover all the basic concepts you will encounter and quite a few of the debates or issues addressed by media A levels, by Access courses and many undergraduate modules as well. Media theories have directly influenced work in many other subjects including sociology, English and cultural studies; media production practice increasingly spills over into art, design and photography, and most degree courses try to incorporate some media material, if only via 'images of the subject area', since that is what most students will have before entering higher education.

Our 'target audience' includes many different groups of students, so don't be surprised if you find things that aren't on your syllabus. Dip into them anyway – we hope you'll find that they increase your understanding of the key concepts (and they may well be required or will be enriching for the next course you take).

We haven't included any model essay answers because no one particular syllabus is targeted and we would rather try to support your basic curiosity and understanding of concepts and debates than add to a growing plagiarism industry. We've suggested a wide range of 'activities', some very simple and others more complex. Most of these you can pursue on your own. We hope they are all enjoyable and worthwhile in their own right rather than dry 'exercises'.

What's different about this fourth edition?

This edition, like all the others, has involved us in a complete rethink of the whole subject area. Much has happened since 1996, not least the transformation in media technologies. As a readership, most of you have become used to living in the world of digital media. For you, the 'revolutionary' move from analogue to digital is now just part of history and so we have decided to remove our separate Technologies chapter. But although most media production has gone digital, distribution remains analogue in many cases and we focus on newspapers and cinema in the revised chapters 7 and 13, 'Industries' and 'Distribution'. The official 'switch-off' for UK analogue television in 2012 has major consequences for several media industries and you'll find references to it throughout the book.

We know that you like our references to more recent material and we have introduced new topics (from 'podcasting' and 'blogging' to the 2004 tsunami) explored across chapters, in case studies, sometimes in shorter embedded case studies and even activities. Just some examples:

- Images of migration
- *CSI: Miami* and crime fiction
- Japanese horror movies
- Jamie Oliver's series on school dinners
- Free newspapers
- Documentary theory as it applies to *Big Brother* and to Michael Moore
- Blogging and news
- Mobile phone technology
- Celebrity, stardom and marketing
- Thrillers.

We've tried to help you with developments at the cutting edge of the field. For example:

- Terms such as 'stereotyping' and 'representation' are now quite problematic, given the different stages of the representation of different groups, the proliferation of images of them, and a rigidity in the ways the terms are 'taken for granted'. These changes and debates are embodied in the new Chapter 5 'Questions of representation' and case study.
- This was one of the first textbooks to look critically at the notion of 'postmodernism', which seemed to be everywhere a few years ago. Though the term is still used, rather loosely, it has lost some of its authority, and also some of the meanings we were critical of. **Modernity** is now regularly used in its place, a welcome move. So that chapter has gone, and this has allowed slightly longer sections on other issues.
- **Globalisation** continues to be a crucial area, and is again updated as one of the key 'media debates' chapters. A new case study on 'Images of migration' is also useful for understanding a fast-changing world.
- The retitled and revised Chapter 16 '"Free choices" in a "free market"?' helps you engage with some of the central debates focusing on media economics and the activities of media organisations and regulators.

How the book is organised

There are several types of material in the book. The main chapters carry the key theoretical ideas, histories and concepts which are explained and contextualised in general terms. These often include 'embedded case studies', shorter than the separate case studies, but a great help in explaining and applying concepts as we go along. The separate case study chapters allow us to explore applications of theory or more specialised theoretical points in detail.

Case studies are distinguished by page design. Chapters use a single column with extra material in the margin, but case studies are presented in two columns without marginal notes, and on four-colour text design. We expect you will need to keep 'dipping in' to the main chapters, but that you might read the case studies straight through.

Finding material

The book isn't organised like a 'set text' – there is no correct way to use it. Instead, it is designed for your support, so it is important that, whatever you need, you can find it easily. At the start of all chapters and case studies is a list of main headings. In chapters the appropriate headings are repeated in a computer-style menu at the top of each page. 'Running heads' at the top of each page always let you know where you are.

If you want to find a key term, look in the Glossary for a quick definition and in the Index for specific page references. The first time a key term appears in a chapter it will be presented in bold type.

References and other conventions used

As all media researchers will tell you, good references are invaluable, in fact a part of academic honesty. They provide evidence of the origins of material and they point to further sources which could be used. We've adopted a number of strategies. Whenever we quote another writer, we place a name and a date in the text, e.g. (During 2005). This refers you to a book written by Simon During and published in 2005. The full reference (which includes title and publisher) is then given at the end of the chapter or case study. You should learn to list these full references, for any books you use, at the end of your essays. The lists at the end of the chapters include the sources we have used and perhaps some other material we think relevant. Some of our sources are quite difficult, both to obtain and to read, so we don't always expect you to go to them direct. At the end of the book we have included a 'selected' list of important (and accessible) texts, which we recommend you to look at. We also list useful websites, and occasionally DVDs and videos.

The titles of films, television and radio programmes, newspapers and magazines are usually given in italics. Again, this is a convention that you might usefully copy, especially if you word-process your work. It makes it much easier to read essays. We have given the country of origin and the date of release of films to help you find them in reference sources. We have tried to use film examples that are well referenced, so, even if you've never heard of them, you should be able to find out more, often via the internet.

The two of us 'combined' have worked, over the years, in both further and higher education, and in media education generally. We 'entered the field' because we enjoyed popular culture in all its forms and recognised its cultural and even political importance in the contemporary world. We still feel that media studies should be challenging and fun. Whatever your interest – passing an exam or simply understanding the culture you inhabit – enjoy reading and working with the book and do let us know, by writing to the publishers, about your ideas for improving it. Even better, email us direct with your comments: gill.branston@ntlworld.com; roy@itpmag.demon.co.uk

Reference

Meyrowitz, Joshua (1985) *No Sense of Place: The Impact of Electronic Media on Social Behaviour*, New York: Oxford University Press.

Part I
Key Concepts

Media scrum at Barcelona Football Club © Jordi Cotrina/El Periodico

1 Interpreting media

- **Semiotic approaches**
- **Structuralism**
- **Denotation and connotation**
- **Debates**
- **Content analysis**

- **Case study of the two methods in action: 'violence' and the media**
- **References**
- **Further reading**

The media are not so much 'things' as places which most of us inhabit, which weave in and out of our lives. Their constant messages and pleasures seem to flow around and through us most of our waking lives, so there's little problem with immediate understanding or enjoyment of them. Yet many feel that a key part of the modern world is formed by the processes and assumptions involved in all this.

In this chapter we will focus on two approaches to media texts. Each of these is best used with an awareness of the other one. *Semiotic approaches* have utterly changed the ways media studies tries to interpret individual 'texts', as we call our objects of study whether adverts, blogs, films or photos. *Content analysis*, on the other hand, tries to explore what seem to be patterns or omissions across many of these 'texts'.

Old joke: 'If you want to know anything about the nature of water, you don't ask a fish.' How does this apply to our relations with modern media? What are the problems of trying to get a view from outside 'the water'?

Semiotic approaches

Modern media are often thought of as a kind of conveyor belt of meaning between, or in the middle of, 'the world' and audiences, producing **images** 'about' or 'from' this or that debate, event or place. Sometimes this involves news, or the hidden secrets of celebrities, or far reaches of the galaxy. **Semiotics**, however, does not assume that the media work as simple channels of communication, as 'windows on the world'. Instead they are seen as actually *structuring* the very realities which they seem to 'describe' or 'stand in for'. Meaning is socially produced, whether through words, colour, gesture, music, fashion, etc.

You need to spend a bit of time with these sections. The semiotic terms you'll be trying out are not explicitly used, all the time, in media analysis.

The word 'media' comes from the Latin word 'medium' meaning 'middle'.

A Tory MP commenting on a Labour Party conference: 'Tony Blair wearing a red tie: what greater signifier could there be than that?' (4 October 2000).

Many of them have been hugely qualified in recent years, as they have been more widely applied. And as the role of the media has changed. Some would argue that it is so interfused into daily life that interpretative approaches alone need to be heavily qualified. Nevertheless, interpretative and indeed semiotic approaches are rightly very much part of the subject area, and indeed of mainstream media and fashion, with their frequent discussions of style differences, deconstruction, signs and 'spinning', or making things and events *signify*. You may find you already know more about them than you at first imagine! Or that you've always wondered why media studies is peppered with terms such as '**construct**' and 'signify'.

When the media were first seriously studied, in the late 1950s, existing methods from literary, social science and art criticism were applied to them. Value was set on 'good dialogue', 'convincing characters' and 'beautiful compositions'. But it soon became clear that simply to discuss a film or television programme by such methods was not enough. People began to question the critical terms used and to ask: 'good' or 'convincing' or 'beautiful' according to what criteria? For whom? At the same time semiotics and the accompanying theories of **structuralism** were brought into play. They asked radical questions about how meanings are constructed in different languages and cultures. These approaches tried to 'hold off' older questions of the value of different stories or images in order to explore the ways that meaning is constructed. This can be hard when first encountered.

Semiotics is also called 'semiology', and we can define it as the study of **signs**, or of the social production of meaning by sign systems, of how things come to have *significance*. Drawing largely on the work of the linguists Saussure, Peirce and **Barthes**, semiotics argues that verbal language is just one of many systems of meaning. Other systems include gesture, clothing, architecture, etc. which can be studied like verbal languages.

Roland Barthes (1915–80) French linguist who pioneered semiotic analysis of cultural and media forms. Most famous for *Mythologies* (1972, originally published 1957), a collection of essays wittily applying his theories to ads, wrestling, Greta Garbo's face and so on. (See later for Saussure and Peirce.)

But how do these languages, or sets of representations, work? At the time when semiotics was first developed, there were two main models for understanding language/representations:

- language as a *reflection* of the world, where meaning itself is already fixed ('the Truth') and lies in events, people, objects waiting for language to try to 'get at' or 'express' it (in 'realistic' photographic or film styles, for example)
- language as based in the *intentions* of the 'author', that is, language as predominantly the way in which we each express ideas, feelings which are unique to ourselves (this approach would value eccentric styles of writing or photography, as being 'individual').

Of course there is a lot of point to both these positions (language does try to 'capture' and communicate the real outside the speaker, *and* language use is always unique and individual). But semiotics rejected both these models and made a third emphasis:

- Language is both *constructed* and *inherited*, by people using it within existing cultures, to produce meanings. Things and events in themselves do not have inherent meaning. Of course they exist. But neither they, nor the ways we describe or photograph or even perceive them, are ever *experienced* as 'raw' or 'unmediated'. It is the ways that cultures, through their changing use of language, have 'agreed' to perceive, and then to name, things and processes that determine how they get defined or valued. And this social 'agreement' means we can never produce completely private languages of our own, however characteristic our individual language use will be, whether in words or dress or the photos we take.

Semiotics uses the term *signs* to describe the ways that meanings are socially produced. Signs have several characteristics:

- First, a sign has physical form, called the **signifier**. This might be a haircut, a traffic light, a finger print. It might be a word – though as signifiers words offer meaning in two main ways. The *signifiers* or physical forms are sometimes marks on paper (R-O-S-E), sometimes sounds in the air (the spoken word 'rose'). See Figure 1.1.

- Second, a sign refers to something other than itself. This is called the **signified** and it is important to grasp that it is a concept, not a real thing in the world. Though it's hard to separate the sounds of 'rose' when you hear them from your concept of a rose, semiotics *emphasises* this distinction. Indeed, it adds a third term, that of the **referent**, which is what both the signifier and the signified refer to: real roses, in all their different colours and shapes, which will inevitably differ from the single, rough and ready concept any one of us conjures up when we see or hear the word.

- Third, semiotics emphasises that our perception of reality is itself *constructed* and *shaped* by the words and signs we use, in various social contexts. By dividing the world into imaginative *categories*, rather than simply labelling it, language crucially determines much of our sense of things. The most famous example is snow. English mostly uses only a few nouns – snow, slush, sleet – to signify different snowy conditions. But the Inuit (Eskimos), in a much closer relationship to it, have a language which makes detailed distinctions between kinds of snow – 'light', 'soft', 'packed', 'waterlogged', 'shorefast', 'lying on surface', 'drifting on a surface' and so on). (See Hall 1997: 22–3 and the general issues of translation it raises.)

Try to apply semiotic theory to the process called 'signing' for hearing-impaired viewers on television, where meanings are signified through gesture. What seem to be the reasons for the choice of particular signed gestures?

rose
or
ROSE

Figure 1.1 Rose.

Obscure joke to test how you're doing so far: Umberto Eco, semiotics professor, once said 'I would still earn my living as a semiotician even if it was called something else.'

Britain, an island with 'island weather', has a large number of terms associated with rain – showers, drizzle, squally, mist, cats and dogs, tipping down, etc. See how many of these signifiers you can list, then plot them on a graph for light/heavy, etc.

These categories, into which media languages divide the world, work by means of **differences**, such as those between kinds of snow or rain. Dissident social movements work partly through putting terms into new relationships and thus attempting to *re-signify* processes. A famous example is the change from the signifier 'terrorist' to the signifier 'freedom fighter' and later 'hero of liberation' for Nelson Mandela. This re-signified identical activities during the years of anti-apartheid struggle in South Africa by putting them into different relationships to 'apartheid'.

The term 'western' is an example of a powerful mythical construct. Before the eighteenth century it simply signified a direction on a map – the opposite of east. But as West European colonial power spread, 'the West' came to signify a group of people supposedly unified by residential geographies, traditions and 'shared civilisation'. It also exists as part of a binary: 'the West and the rest', signifying 'the only kind of modernity'. (See Bennett et al. 2005: 372–4.)

> Many meaning systems work with dual oppositions as a central part of their structure: God and the Devil or Good and Evil in religions; Yin and Yang in Taoist thought; male/female in most social orders. Popular stories and entertainments often work through related formal 'pairings' or oppositions: black/white (hats in early westerns); night/day; East/**West**; brunette/blonde and so on.

Emphasis on differences as key to meaning-making was one which semiotics shared with structuralism. To understand this properly, we need to explore it a little.

Structuralism

This is a set of ideas and positions which broadly emphasised two positions.

First, structuralism argued that all human social order is determined by large social or psychological structures with *their own* irresistible logic, independent of human will or intention. **Freud** and **Marx** in the nineteenth century had begun to interpret the social world in this *structured* way. Freud argued that the human psyche (especially the unconscious mind) was one such structure. It makes us act in ways of which we're not aware, but which are glimpsed in the meanings of certain dreams, slips of the tongue and so on. Marx argued that economic life, and particularly people's relationship to the means of production (do they own them, or do they work for the owners of them?), was another, which determines political sympathies and dominant power structures.

Second, and later, structuralism argued that meanings can be understood only within these systematic structures and the differences or distinctions which they generate. For example, structuralist **anthropology** might study how a culture organises its rules on food as a system:

Sigmund Freud (1856–1939) Austrian founder of psychoanalysis or the theory and practice of treating neuroses. Theories of 'normal' unconscious mental processes have been suggested from its procedures.

Karl Marx (1818–83) German philosopher and journalist, analysing and seeking to overthrow by revolutionary means the emerging industrial capitalist order of nineteenth-century Europe.

- by rules of exclusion (the English see eating frogs and snails as a barbaric French custom)
- by signifying oppositions (savoury and sweet courses are not eaten together in most western cuisine)
- and by rules of association (steak and chips followed by ice cream are OK; steak and ice cream followed by chips are not OK).

Only within such rules would particular combinations or menus be valued, or seen as 'wrong', or as rebellious, or eccentric.

ACTIVITY 1.1

Jot down other examples of these structures in other food systems you know, for example Chinese or Indian food.

- Can you list any such oppositions or rules of combination in the way you and your friends dress?
- Does your school or college operate any such rules, for example around the length of hair, or hoods, or jewellery which may or may not be worn?

Lévi-Strauss was a structuralist anthropologist whose work greatly influenced semiotics. He emphasised the importance of **structuring oppositions** in **myth** systems and in language (also sometimes called **binary oppositions** because the qualities can be grouped into pairs of opposites). These produce key boundaries or differences within cultures, usually with unequal weight or value attached to one side of the pairing. **Saussure** applied this to the ways that language produces meanings, often through defining terms as being the opposite of other terms: black/white; hot/cold; etc. We have learnt to grasp very quickly that the word 'man', for example, means different things in different contexts: it can be opposed to 'boy', or to 'woman', or to 'god', or even to 'beast'. So 'woman' is almost always defined in relation to 'man', or 'femininity' in relation to its differences from 'masculinity'.

However, we learn to associate words, and media products, *with* each other, as well as to differentiate them. **Genre** is an inseparable part of understanding how meanings are encountered in practice and its blend of *repetition and difference* is key to understanding broader areas of meaning-making (see Chapter 3).

Claude Lévi-Strauss (b. 1908) French anthropologist (*not* the inventor of the jeans). Most active from the 1950s, studying myths, totems and kinship systems of tribal cultures in North and South America.

Ferdinand de Saussure (1857–1913) French linguist who pioneered the semiotic study of language as a system of signs, organised in 'codes' and 'structures'. Others, such as the Russian theorist Volosinov, have suggested the term 'decoding' tends to treat language as a dead thing, rather than a living and changing *activity*.

PURE SMIRNOFF. THE DIFFERENCE IS CLEAR.

Figure 1.2 Branding and advertising depend largely on successfully claiming 'binary' difference for some products and brands from other, often very similar, ones. The distinction claimed for this vodka, as opposed to its competitors, is constructed visually by embodying contrasts of gender (male/female), history (pre-human/human), biology (human/non-human) and posture (crouching/upright).

Example: Titanic

Working with semiotic terms may involve first trying to see which elements seem to be in systematic opposition. For example, the narrative of *Titanic* (US 1997) works partly by differences such as upper deck/lower deck; upper class/lower class; American/European, which are worked through in signifiers of types of music, of dress, of colours, of sets, of characters, etc.

In many semiotic interpretations a further step is to explore the extent to which one side of an opposition (or binary, as it's sometimes called) is

Figure 1.3 How many of the structuring oppositions of the film are visible here?

always valued less than the other. In this case, the lively, egalitarian 'lower deck/lower class' passengers, represented by Jack/DiCaprio, are valued more highly by the film than the upper classes on the upper decks. This set of oppositions is part of why Rose/Winslet's development and decisions through the plot are given more than romantic weight. The character is constructed as throwing in her lot with a more democratic future through this system of difference. (You might like to think about the connotations of these characters' names here – see p. 18.)

Another example is advertising campaigns. In planning meetings there will often be 'brainstorming' sessions where the qualities which will be attributed to the product (or the celebrity to be associated with it) are contrasted, in a classic list of binary oppositions, to qualities which are 'not-Levi's' or 'not-BMW'.

This structuralist emphasis on oppositions helps explain semiotics' insistence that signs are fully understood only by reference to their difference from other signs in their particular representing system or code. For example, once colour became possible in cinema or photography, the potential of black and white changed. It then could signify differently to produce a photo or a film in black and white (like *Schindler's List* (US 1993)) since black and white can then signify 'seriousness' or 'pastness' or even just quirkiness.

You need to grasp the extent to which visual and verbal representations are composed of such material signs, working partly through differences, but also partly through associations with each other, especially via genre and other ways of classifying into groups. Signs have relationships among themselves, as well as in the ways they represent the world. Words can rhyme or be punned upon; colours can be echoed (or 'rhymed'?) across a film, a pop video, an ad.

Some post-structuralists take these 'constructionist' positions even further. They argue that no shared meanings are possible because everything is understood *only* through difference. It's important to note, however, that meaningful differences (e.g. black/white) differentiate things that *share* certain qualities: here they are both parts of the colour spectrum. See Andermahr *et al.* (2000).

Denotation and connotation

Signs, then, signify or name or **denote** different aspects of our experience or of the world. The word 'red' denotes a certain part of the colour spectrum, *differentiated* by language from other parts (such as 'blue' or 'pink') of what is in fact a continuous spectrum. But signs also **connote**, or link things. They may link things by association with broader cultural concepts and values, or with meanings from personal history and experience. Let's take the ways that colours are signified.

The word 'red' *denotes* or classifies one part of the colour spectrum. Broadly (merging sometimes into pink, purple or orange of course) it can be used to describe blood, fires, sunsets, blushing complexions. This perhaps indicates why, in certain cultures, the colour and the word have

'To an optimist the glass of water is always half full, to a pessimist, half empty.'

Another example: over the last 30–40 years the signifier for 'dense tropical forest' has changed from 'jungle' to 'rainforest'. What are the connotations of the two terms? Why do you think the change has occurred?

gathered *connotations* of fierceness, passion, danger. In *Pretty Woman* (US 1990) there is a scene where Vivien/Julia Roberts wears a red, quite formal dress (after her multicoloured hooker's gear in the first scene, and before a black, even more formal, dress in a later scene). At this point in the film it could plausibly be argued that the red dress signifies a growing confidence and passion in her feelings about her relationship with Edward/Richard Gere. But 'red' does this both by means of its 'passionate' *associations*, and also partly through its deliberate *difference* from her other costumes in that film – and from the cultural awareness of readers that red is unlikely in this film to denote 'communism' or 'STOP' or 'danger' – as it might in other fictional structures. A splash of red around the mouth of a polar bear (in 'nature' documentaries) changes its meaning to that of ruthless hunter, and is perhaps shocking for viewers used to a very different signification: the white bears' cuddly role in hundreds of stories and the Christmas Coca-Cola ads.

The word 'gold' again *denotes* or marks off both a part of the colour spectrum and a particular metal. But it has historically developed much wider *connotations* within certain cultures, deriving partly from its being prized for jewellery, special ceremonies and as a currency. These surface in such phrases as 'golden opportunity', 'good as gold' and so on. In cigarette ads, within serious health regulation, which minimises what can be claimed, it is used to signify 'Benson & Hedges quality'.

- What is your favourite font? Why? What are its resonances for you?

The US flag, the 'Stars and Stripes', originally signified or *denoted*, in the abstract way that flags do, the union of the different states after the Civil

Figure 1.4 Italian street stall, 2005. An instantly recognisable font gives these very Italian greetings a 'twist' or new connotation.

A powerful signifier and ways it has been used/acquired connotations

Figure 1.5 'This spectacular "blue marble" image is the most detailed true-color image of the entire Earth to date. Using a collection of satellite-based observations, scientists and visualizers stitched together months of observations of the land surface, oceans, sea ice, and clouds into a seamless, true-color mosaic of every square kilometer . . . of our planet.' (Thanks to NASA for use of this image and description.)

1 When images of Earth were first beamed back from space, it became easier to conceive of the planet as one whole system. This became an enormous resource for environmental politics, though the image itself was taken as proof both of Earth's beauty and uniqueness, but also of the relative insignificance of humankind – two very different connotations. Signs, however apparently simple, are always open to different claims on meaning. A similar shot was also used as the final image of the global disaster eco-blockbuster *The Day After Tomorrow* (US 2004) where the astronauts viewing it comment that 'the air has never looked so clean . . .'

2 Likewise 'anti- choice' campaigners often use ultra-sound images of a foetus in a globe-like womb. These work to marginalise the pregnant woman's discourse: no such single, vivid, image could be used to sum up the variety of painful reasons for which she might have to seek an abortion. For some, the globe-like image may suggest a 'natural' or even 'divine' inevitability that any pregnancy should go ahead, whatever the circumstances, or whoever the father.

War (1861–5) between the North and the slave-owning South. There are now fifty stars, representing the number of states; the red stripes represent the original thirteen British colonies and the blood of the revolutionary war of independence against the British. Its *connotations*, as emblem of the activities of one of the most powerful nations on the planet, are now clearly very different for those who support and those who oppose particular US policies.

Figure 1.6 RAC logos, Royal Automobile Association

ACTIVITY 1.2

Look at the logos for the RAC (Royal Automobile Club, now selling services to motorists but originally an exclusive social and sports club) in Figure 1.6.

- Describe as precisely as you can how the badges and logos have changed over the years.
- What kind of connotations seem to be attempted in the latest logo? How?
- Can you describe the connotations of the different kinds of lettering?
- How would you compare the lettering or font with, say, logos like that of Coca-Cola?

Different kinds of signs

Charles Sanders Peirce
(1839–1914) American pioneer of semiotics, usually quoted for his distinctions between different kinds of sign: iconic, indexical, arbitrary and symbolic.

Let's look in more detail at how semiotics has explored visual representation systems, as well as words. A key distinction is made (initially by **Peirce**) between **iconic**, **indexical**, **arbitrary** and **symbolic signs**. Verbal language, spoken and written, is mostly composed of *arbitrary* signifiers in the sense that there is no necessary resemblance between the black marks on the page – 'daffodil' – and those plants in the rest of the world that have been named 'daffodil'. Any pronounceable combination of letters could have been originally decided on to signify 'daffodils' (as is clear if you know a language other than English).

Iconic signifiers, on the other hand, always resemble what they signify. There is a physical similarity between a photo, or a good drawing of a daffodil, and most people's sight of those flowers, and for this reason the photo is called an iconic signifier.

The term *indexical* is used to describe signifiers that act as a kind of evidence: smoke from a fire, sweat from effort, spots from measles, and so on. Or to use the distinction of analogue and digital, thermometers or sundials are indexical signs of heat or of time passing, whereas digital technologies (translating music into number signals, which are then reassembled) act like arbitrary signs.

The term *symbolic* is used of visual signs (not words, which are always 'arbitrary' signifiers) that are arbitrarily linked to referents. Flags are nearly always symbolic, since they have to try to unite so much in one sign. The diamond hats often worn by monarchs are called crowns, and symbolise monarchy as well as being indexical signifiers of wealth.

Figure 1.7 Road signs, Department of Transport

Thirty years ago the road sign used to warn drivers to take care near a school was the image of the 'torch of learning' (see Figure 1.7a): it was meant to stand as symbol of the place where that learning happened. But this conventional, symbolic meaning became unfamiliar, and the sign was changed to the 'two children crossing' sign (see Figure 1.7b), i.e. to a more iconic sign.

Such distinctions are especially useful in drawing attention to the ways that photographs, film, television images and so on, though often seeming to be a record or even a trace of the real, are in fact as constructed as verbal (arbitrary) accounts. They only *seem* like 'a window on the world'.

Codes and the social nature of signs

So signs, far from 'naturally' just 'labelling' the real world, are never as 'natural' as they seem. Photos are framed, lit, edited, however dramatic the events they 'capture'. The choice of 'green' for the traffic sign meaning 'GO' could be replaced by 'pink', if that were the agreed colour for 'GO'.

But it's worth emphasising the broad cultural or social *agreement* (or even *force*) needed for meaning to be produced – as well as its arbitrariness or slipperiness. We learn to read signs in relation to wider systems of meaning, to which the term **codes** is often given. These have

Icon originally referred to visual emblems or portraits of saints, rather than their written or spoken names. Confusingly, though, global stars such as Tom Cruise are sometimes called 'icons', partly to suggest that they are like saints in a very visual culture.

Of course digital media alter the indexicality of photographic evidence, or what can be assumed as its visual authority. Any photo can be *suspected* of fakery. It means more value must be given to the reliability of the *institution* which is circulating the photo.

The only exceptions to the indexicality of words are those called 'onomatopoeic', ones whose sound when spoken resembles what it signifies: like 'rumble' or 'hiss'.

Figure 1.8 An eloquent kind of *evidence* of numbers on one of the demonstrations against the 2003 US air strikes against Afghanistan.

- It is *constructed*, insofar as the angle and positioning of the camera, and choice of lens, enable the huge scope of the image.
- But this construction is in order to provide *a kind of evidence* – of a visibly huge demonstration.

We could almost say 'definite evidence' for institutional, as well as textual reasons. A digital fake on this topic, with so much other evidence, elsewhere, of the size of the march, for the front page of a newspaper, is highly unlikely. (See Chapters 4 and 14 for further discussion of these areas.)

to be broadly *shared*. Roland Barthes began exploration of this area, using terms such as 'rhetoric', 'myths' and 'mythologies'. Stuart Hall used the term 'codes' both for the 'professional assumptions' of production (see Chapter 12 below) and for wider sets of values with which they connect. So a cosmetics ad may depend on the accepted ways to light 'glamorously' the face of a woman widely considered beautiful, and could be said to express the 'dominant code' that all women should be glamorous and beautiful for men (Rose 2001: 89). Later in this book we use more politically emphatic words such as 'ideologies' and 'discourses', and discuss the important struggles for meaning which they signal. For one of the dangers in using the word 'code' is that it can make communication always sound like a conspiracy on the part of the mysterious 'encoders'.

Paradoxically, it is because signs have to be employed by us, the 'readers' or 'users', to produce meanings at all that they are inherently unstable. In this process, of being socially used and often shared by many people, the meanings of signs are neither fixed nor single, but **polysemic**, or capable of having several meanings. The Union Jack has stood as symbol of the unity of the United Kingdom, and by extension the monarchy that rules it. But for republican groups in Wales, Ireland or Scotland, or for punk fashions or opponents in war, it is used and understood in quite other ways. Fan studies have looked at the ways that fans will often produce versions of favourite media products (such as Buffy or Dr Who) on the internet which are wildly different from those officially circulated.

Figure 1.9 'Cool Britannia'? Part of the moves to re-signify 'Britishness' in the 1990s.

ACTIVITY 1.3

Look at Figure 1.9. What would be an equivalent image of Britishness now? Did you see any photos which tried to represent 'Britishness' differently in the weeks after the London bombs of 2005? How successful were they in what you think they were trying to achieve?

One way in which control is attempted over ambiguity or *polysemy* of visual images, especially for news purposes, is through the use of captions or voice-over commentary. Semiotics calls this **anchoring**, a process which tries to select and therefore control the meanings which could legitimately be made by a reader. Think of it as similar to the way that an anchor tries to limit the movements of a boat or ship in the sea. It's less directly related to news 'anchors', though it's worth thinking of the power those figures have to frame or secure interpretations of news stories in some directions and not others.

Such shifting cultural 'agreements' mean that signification is never 'secure' or fixed. Such shifts mean also that struggles can take place over signification, over how a sign is to be 'officially' read. For example:

- In the 1960s the centuries-old negative connotations of the word 'black' in US culture were challenged by the US Civil Rights movement with the slogan 'Black is Beautiful'.

The word 'polysemy' – 'having many meanings' – comes from the Greek words *poly* meaning 'many' and *semeion* meaning 'sign'.

See the excellent DVD *Outfoxed* (2004) on the ways this kind of 'anchoring' works for the Fox News Channel.

ACTIVITY 1.4

Take three photos, either from the press or your family album.
- Devise captions for them which will anchor their connotations very differently from the way in which the original press or family album setting had done.

- The words 'cool', 'wicked', 'hectic' and 'bad' have, in some contexts, completely lost or even reversed their previous meanings in the last few years: a 'slippage' has occurred as slang terms have entered more mainstream circulation.

Figure 1.10 Road sign, Elderly People, Department of Transport

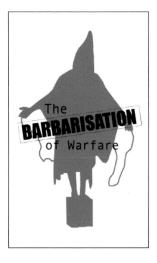

Figure 1.11 A stylised version of a notorious soldier's photo of US torture of Iraqi prisoners at the Iraq prison camp Abu Ghraib. So well known did the original photo become that its mere outline circulated as an iconic image, to signify 'Abu Ghraib atrocities' in certain contexts.

ACTIVITY 1.5

- Cut out a few pictures at random from a paper or magazine.
- Cut out the same number of phrases, again at random, from the same sources.
- Mix them all up and pick out, face down, one picture, and one phrase, at random.

See whether the phrase, even though randomly chosen, seems to have a kind of authority as 'caption' anchoring the meaning of the picture. However wild, most captions can seem to make a kind of sense of the picture.

- The traffic sign for 'Caution, older people crossing the road' signified by stooped, stereotypical figures of 'the old' has been objected to (a 'struggle over the sign' began) by some groups of older people.
- Television and print news rooms sometimes debate how they should describe certain acts: are they performed by terrorists? Or by a resistance movement? Is an announcement about redundancies to be worded as 'massive job losses', 'letting go' certain workers, 'rationalisation', 'downsizing' or 'slimming down the workforce'?
- Think how else particular events could be signified through different word or image choices. You might build up a collection of pictures and alternative words for further news work.

Overall, semiotics has been enormously useful in rethinking the key social activity of meaning-making. But semiotic and post-structuralist emphases have often contributed to a crippling sense of powerlessness in the face of modern political and social developments. Language and representation have been emphasised as being *only* untrustworthy, slippery, commercially corrupt, and their relationship to the rest of the real world consistently downplayed.

ACTIVITY 1.6

Look at the front and back covers of this book, and of a book you consider very different.
- What do you think the designers were trying to signify? What particular signs and connotations are your evidence?
- Is there any 'slippage' between what seem to have been their intentions and the meanings you take from the designs?

ACTIVITY 1.7

Make notes on the next news headlines or lead stories you encounter with an eye to their verbal construction. You might also choose visual 'framings': which of many possible photos of a celebrity or politician has been chosen?

Debates

- Semiotic approaches spread partly through some vivid detailed readings of individual images, which were easy to use in teaching and debate. But this raises questions about the representativeness and **replicability** of its analyses. How representative of ads in general, for example, are those chosen by Williamson (1978) or Barthes (1972)? Would someone else have come up with the same conclusions?

- Semiotics has developed an elaborate, even over-elaborate, terminology. Sometimes this is confusing or unnecessary (see Rose 2001: 97–8 for helpful comments).

- Semiotics rightly lays heavy emphasis on meaning as constructed. But does this sometimes *over*-emphasise the arbitrariness of signs, and *under*-emphasise the extent to which they have to be shared, to have associations, in order to produce meaning at all? This has important implications for the way in which some semioticians scornfully dismiss such notions as 'identification' (based on a sense of what is held in common) or 'empathy' and, following on from that, the kinds of politics and responses based on such involvements.

- How far can such slippery matters as 'interpretation' and 'meaning' be objectively and scientifically mapped? This certainty is often implied by the tone and vocabulary of some semioticians' writing. 'Codes', for example, with its roots in signals technologies, often seems to imply a very simple notion of communication. Better to say that 'texts' offer a *meaning potential*, not a fixed 'code' to be cracked once you've learnt it, like semaphore or traffic signs. We're now likely to have a more relaxed sense that 'textual analysis [is] an educated guess at some of the most likely interpretations that might be made of [a] text' (McKee 2001). This still describes a difficult process, needing educated approaches.

- Does semiotics' heavy emphasis on 'meaning' ignore the extent to which pleasure, irrational play with texts, and the often mischievous misreadings of audiences come into the picture? Despite the idea of 'polysemy', semiotics has been fairly uninterested in how audiences actually engage with texts.

Replicability unambiguous quality of a research method, so that 'different researchers at different times using the same categories would [interpret] the images in exactly the same way' (Rose 2001: 62).

Figure 1.12 Many uses of the word 'spin' or even of PR are critical of powerful organisations and the ways they protect their interests.

'Spin' is a word with several powerful meanings. They range from PR (public relations) and general communication skills through to conscious lying and/or the use of contradictory or empty statements. ('Spin doctor', instead of 'press officer', certainly evokes 'witch doctor' and dark powers, such as those associated with Alistair Campbell or Peter Mandelson.)

Q Note four recent examples of the term, and say how it is being used. Does it resemble 'signification' as we've been considering it?

Figure 1.12 shows unpaid Greenpeace volunteers fitting solar panels to the medieval-style roof of Deputy Prime Minister John Prescott's house, to draw attention to the gap between official rhetoric on climate change, and how little is being done to hit the targets for household energy efficiency (as well as to Prescott's lifestyle). The action tried to alter perceptions of government inaction through a 'publicity stunt'.

Q Would you call it spin? If not, is this because you sympathise with the aims of Greenpeace?

It's always worth considering:
1 What is being 'spun' (rather than the simple fact that a stunt or a press release is being used)? Is a small campaign using limited resources in an imaginative way, or is a wealthy government department justifying some unpopular measure or, indeed, trying to communicate a worthwhile measure which needs arguing for? Often what is objected to is a certain muffled official use of language ('issues' will be spoken of, rather than problems or conflicts, for example).
2 Is the word 'spin' being used to mean 'lying'? Or is it objecting to *any* kind of attempt at 'getting meanings across imaginatively'?
3 Is the assumption in attacks on 'spin' that there is some eternal truth of factual information which 'we' could get at if only this work of signifying or making meaning weren't going on?
4 Does this fit with a cult of 'sincerity' and 'openness'? Is it perhaps nostalgic for a time of simpler, more authoritatively given meaning? John Tulloch (2005) makes interesting points on 'spin' and the ways it is used.

One term which has the potential to help us think about the relationship between signifiers and audiences is **mode of address**. Coming out of linguistics, it refers to the ways a text seems to 'speak to' its audience, or 'who it thinks we are'. A good comparison: in everyday encounters, our way of addressing a teacher, a friend, a bank manager incorporates a (different) 'position' for each of those people in what we are saying: as someone being treated respectfully, with intimacy or with caution. The further implication is that when *we* are addressed in certain ways (as 'naughty children', as newly 'grown-up', etc.) we 'play along' and may partly even assume or perform the identity thus constructed for us, at least temporarily.

If your course involves practical work you will be expected to think carefully about how to address the audience for it. In academic work you will have to learn how to address an essay to an imagined audience: how much knowledge are you supposed to assume they have? How much 'proof' (references etc.) do they need of the statements you make?

ACTIVITY 1.8

Take a current affairs programme, e.g. *Newsnight*, and make notes on its mode of address. Look at such signifiers as title sequence; studio set-up, if any; voices, accents, dress, demeanour of the presenters; whether the programme openly takes a position on its subject; use or avoidance of 'you', 'us', etc. by the presenter.

Q How would you summarise these signs to describe its mode of address overall? Respectful? Boisterous and irreverent? A mix of the two?

Such textual work suggests that modes of address:
- are linked to assumptions about audiences, and the desire to attract or maximise them, or to target specialised ones
- may also reinforce or even help to *create* these assumed identities, by defining and informally 'teaching' them, and the performances which sustain them.

Content analysis

Other, rather different approaches to texts are often called **empirical**. This describes research using observable evidence or experience as its material, and seeking to avoid bias as far as possible. *Content* or *quantitative* analysis is a major empirical method. It works by counting the frequency of relevant elements in a clearly defined sample of texts, and then analysing those frequencies (see Rose 2001: 56). You might want to explore, for example, how often the word 'immigrant' is used to mean the same as 'asylum seeker' in a sample of newspapers. Content analysis (perhaps using LexisNexis software) could help you to do this.

The selected quantities (of, e.g., newspapers or ads) must first be 'coded'. This means that a set of descriptive categories or labels are attached to them, such as 'headlines involving the word "asylum seeker"'. These should be unambiguous, such that 'different researchers at different times using the same categories would code the images in exactly the same

Empirical: relying on observed experience as evidence. A controversial term, often caricatured to imply an approach opposed to any kind of theory and relying on sense experience or simplistic 'quantity' of information and facts alone.

Figure 1.13 The question 'What's missing?' is a key one whenever you consider or when you are compiling statistical or quantitative surveys.

way' (Rose 2001: 62). This is meant to make the process replicable (see above). It's a useful method because, as one set of researchers into magazine photos commented, 'It does allow . . . discovery of patterns that are too subtle to be visible on casual inspection and [also allows] protection against an unconscious search through the magazine for only those which confirm one's sense of what the photos say or do' (Lutz and Collins in Rose 2001: 89).

Closer textual interpretation of individual texts is often needed at other stages of a research project, if there are enough resources. For example, counting will tell whether one side in a conflict has been interviewed many more times than its opponents. The tempting assumption is that this side has been advantaged. But it needs to be checked: the style of the interviews might be generally hostile. Likewise the frequency with which words, or even pairings of words, are used will not give you the tone of the usage, or its combination with photos etc., for which textual analysis is needed.

ACTIVITY 1.9

Conduct a simple content analysis research into motor car TV ads.

Count how many car ads there are on any one or more TV channels on any Friday or Saturday night between 8p.m. and 10p.m. (when large male audiences are assumed).

How many of these take place in deserted, remote country roads? How many show gridlock or traffic jams? Use textual approaches to suggest what is the tone of these ads – openly fantasising? Humorous, in ways which 'magic away' experiences of gridlock? Or are they very serious about the product, signified as 'hero'?

A less obvious but important area for such methods is the systematic *absence* of certain terms or topics in media coverage. Jay Katz (1999) reminds us that many news items fail to give the gender of actors in particular stories, such as the fact that it is overwhelmingly males who commit road rage offences, or school shootings in the US. By simply headlining 'school killers' such stories miss the chance to discuss important issues, which question the naturalised link between masculinity and violent behaviour.

Content analysis is popular also partly because numbers, unlike languages, form a universal 'currency'. They can be read, increasingly, by computers, even when their author is not there to explain them. Such analysis is seen as more 'scientific', more full of 'hard facts', than other approaches. Though this is only partly true, it does, as a result, operate as a powerful, often well-funded model of research into audiences.

CASE STUDY OF THE TWO METHODS IN ACTION: 'VIOLENCE AND THE MEDIA'

Unfortunately a jump is often made from quantitative or content analysis research findings to media speculation about 'obvious' evidence of the supposed effects of the media. The **violence debate**, for example, is full of 'countings'. Rightly concerned when horrible murders, raised numbers of rapes and assault, etc. take place, campaigners then make the huge leap of arguing that these might be prevented by censoring 'violence in the media'. This often means *countable* 'acts of violence' in the media and ignores broader political questions *as well as* closer textual ones. For example:

- the problem of defining the 'violence' that is to be counted. It may seem quite a simple thing to decide what to count as 'violence' or 'violent acts' on TV, rap music or in computer games. Yet the question of what, in our culture, gets *perceived* as 'violence' is a huge one. Some kinds of activity are labelled 'violent' and others aren't: the latter are sometimes called 'restraining' or 'keeping the peace' – or 'boys will be boys', for example.
- the differences between the many *kinds* of media representations that get counted. Is the 'violence' in a *Tom and Jerry* cartoon or a computer game the same as the violence seen in a news bulletin?

It is crucial to emphasise for quantitative research that what matters is the quality of the questions asked and the conclusions drawn. This can be more difficult for visual or audio-visual forms than for printed ones.

As with any media text, *the counting of elements that can be counted* is a circular process, which sometimes ignores the ways semiotic codes and resonances of meaning are combined, let alone what audiences might be doing with the 'texts'. In the case of film or television, for instance, research would have to combine the 'act of violence' with interpretative questions for individual texts, for example:

- its place in the narrative
- the stance that the audience is *invited* to take up in relation to it (by camera movement, positioning, editing, costume, lighting, set design, etc.)
- the likely audience which can be assumed from how the text is circulated (Sky Sports prime time? small local campaign group leaflet?) and therefore likely interpretations for it

- casting (e.g. is a sympathetic star or celebrity involved?)
- intertextual reference (is a joke being made about another text which somewhat changes the status of the 'act of violence', as often happens in *The Simpsons?*)
- the historical stage of its genre (e.g. is it a horror film/game, whose twenty-first-century audiences are likely to be blasé about special effects around violent death?)
- the full social context in which it 'plays' (e.g. are guns widely available and seen as normal possessions, as in the US? Is a sense of the gendering of violent behaviour (see Katz 1999) included?).

Barker and Petley (2001) have some striking discussion on the question of violence and the media.

ACTIVITY 1.10

Take a recent film or television programme that was called 'violent'. Decide what genre it is part of. Go through the above list and decide:

- What is its 'message' about violence?
- How would you argue this (see checklist above)?
- How might this strike: (1) an audience experienced in its genre; (2) an audience not experienced in its genre?

Finally, it's worth noting that certain vivid representations of violence may have not negative but positive effects in the revulsion they invite us to feel, for example at certain kinds of assault, or military power, or bullying.

ACTIVITY 1.11

Think back to the most horrifying or frightening moment in a media text that you have ever experienced.
- How does it fit the discussion above?
- Why was it so horrifying for you? Did it evoke, for example, your own experience of bullying or abuse?
- Did anyone else in the audience share your feeling?
- What kind of text, what kind of genre, was it part of? Fairy tale? Cartoon? News? Game?
- Did this make a difference to how you experienced it?

'if we want to know how fictions gain hold of our imaginations so that they . . . become a part of our "real" lives . . . we have to pay attention to . . . properties of aesthetic form and emotional affect. . . . these . . . produce or imply meanings which we may well find at odds with the ostensible "messages" [obtained through] counting stereotypes, themes, or plot outcomes' (Gledhill 1997: 343).

Media studies valuably emphasises that the meanings of representations are never 'given' but are always going to be constructed, slippery and contestable. This goes against the trend of some to present meanings as 'natural' and 'obvious', or to blame 'spin' for any ambiguities.

We've tried to present two different kinds of approach, which need to work more closely together. Even the most close-textured analysis of a single text needs to think about how typical that text is, and of its audience. Equally, even the best-funded content analysis needs to be aware of the complexities of the texts it's summarising, and of how audiences' possible responses complicate matters.

Bear these questions in mind as you test out these approaches. The rest of this book takes them into much wider arenas of power and battles to secure (or 'spin') one meaning for a word, a flag, a slogan, over others. One of the exciting challenges of this subject area is to hold a balance between appreciating audiences' often subversive interpretations, and exploring how texts themselves offer some meanings and pleasures, and try to cut off or marginalise others.

References

Andermahr, Sonya, Lovell, Terry and Wolkowitz, Carol (2000) *A Glossary of Feminist Theory*, London and New York: Hodder Arnold.

Barker, Martin and Petley, Julian (eds) (2001) *Ill Effects*, London: Routledge.

Barthes, Roland (1972) *Mythologies* (originally published 1957), London: Paladin.

Bennett, Tony, Grossberg, Lawrence and Morris, Meaghan (eds) (2005) *New Keywords: A Revised Vocabulary of Culture and Society*, London and New York: Blackwell.

Gledhill, Christine (1997) 'Genre and gender: the case of soap opera', in Stuart Hall (ed.) *Representation: Cultural Representations and Signifying Practices*, London, Thousand Oaks and New Delhi: Sage.

Hall, Stuart (ed.) (1997) *Representation: Cultural Representations and Signifying Practices*, London, Thousand Oaks and New Delhi: Sage.

Katz, Jay (1999) *Tough Guise*, Amherst, Mass.: Media Education Foundation video.

Kitzinger, Jenny (2004) 'Audience and readership research', in *The Sage Handbook of Media Studies*, London: Sage.

McKee, Alan (2001) 'Introduction: interpreting interpretation', *Continuum: Journal of Media and Cultural Studies*, 15, 1.

Rose, Gillian (2001) *Visual Methodologies*, London: Sage.

Tulloch, John (2005) 'The persistence of spin', *Media Education Journal*, 34.

Williamson, Judith (1978) *Decoding Advertisements: Ideology and Meaning in Advertising*, London: Marion Boyars.

Further reading

Bignell, Jonathan (1997) *Media Semiotics: An Introduction*, Manchester and New York: Manchester University Press (from which several activities in this chapter are adapted).

Corner, John (1998) *Studying Media: Problems of Theory and Method*, Edinburgh: Edinburgh University Press (esp. Introduction and Chapters 3 and 6).

Eagleton, Terry (1983) *Literary Theory: An Introduction*, Oxford: Blackwell (esp. Chapter 3).

Tolson, Andrew (1996) *Mediations: Text and Discourse in Media Studies*, London and New York: Arnold.

Other resources

Outfoxed – Rupert Murdoch's War on Journalism, DVD dir. Robert Greenwald, ring 01223 830111 for availability.

CASE STUDY: WAYS OF INTERPRETING

- **Images from photojournalism**
- **Content analysis**
- **Voices and sound images**
- **References and further reading**

This case study takes photojournalist and digital images and tries to give you confidence in analysing them, using semiotic, along with more traditional, compositional approaches. We also suggest ways of analysing sound 'images'. We have deliberately not analysed a set of moving audio-visual images because this is so hard to do adequately on the page. But Chapter 11 below contains many of the terms you will need for this, and the method of applying them is similar to that outlined here.

Images from photojournalism

Many, if not most, of the still images we see in the media are advertising or celebrity related. They are constructed and then carefully chosen in planning meetings, and shot in studios, and specially chosen locations, whether real or digitalised.

The thrill of photojournalism for many is that, though 'constructed' in several ways, it seems 'caught', evidence, a kind of trace of the real (see Chapter 14 Documentary and "reality TV"'). This is why readers are sometimes disappointed when they learn that news photos have been digitally 'doctored'.

We can learn much about the analysis of *all* images by focusing on news shots. Don't forget that even while seeming so real, a trace of an actual event, they have also involved choices, and themselves been chosen (i.e. constructed) out of scores of others because of how they work within meaning systems, or

the resonances of other images. Let's explore this idea. It need not work consciously for the photographer, but we can see its results. For example, mother and child victims of famine or disaster often seem to be chosen because they resemble the Madonna and child Jesus from countless western religious paintings.

We will briefly consider four ways in which the resonance of one famous photo has worked. When you analyse such photos, consider the sets of 'codes' at play, which are both 'textual' and meaning-related:

- *photographic and technical codes* such as lighting; camera angle; use of colour or black and white; distance from subject; kind of focus; any evidence of whether amateur or professional photographer; post-shooting techniques which have exaggerated certain qualities of the image, by airbrushing if a digital image, for example. Of course you will have to describe some of these approximately: you can rarely know exactly what film stock or other processes have been used, though you may be able to find out. The date of the image may suggest whether digital effects have been used.

- other *codes related to broad cultural and aesthetic frames of reference*: the choice of what to include and what to leave out via framing, for example; why *this* framing decision was made, rather than others which were possible; how has the whole composition been arranged; are any verbal elements used to 'anchor' an otherwise ambiguous image?

- *codes of intertextuality*: what other images might this photo connect with, consciously or not, for its readers?

In textual analysis of any image, you need to observe its formal or rhetorical strategies, especially:

Q how does it seem to address its readers?

- Examine the areas of composition, framing, colours, choice of words, if any (verbal elements are always worth focus), setting, lighting, key signifiers, references to other texts (intertextuality).

Focus on the question:

- What is my evidence for arguing that the text is addressing its readers in a particular way?

Figure 1.14 On 19 February 1945, towards the end of the Second World War, 30,000 US troops invaded the Pacific island of Iwo Jima. After four days, 5,563 dead and 17,000 wounded, they took their two targets: Mount Suribachi and one of the island's two airfields. As they captured the main ridge of Suribachi, Joe Rosenthal took several photos of the US flag being planted. This one was awarded the Pulitzer prize, and became the inspiration for a popular film, several monuments, stamps and thousands of other images. See Evans (1997).

The photo in Figure 1.14 is at one and the same time

- *an iconic sign*. It is an analogue, not digital, photograph of real people: the sign visually resembles its referent and as such is vivid in ways that written accounts cannot be. Some seem to feel it is authentic in ways words cannot be.
- *an indexical sign*. The sky, light and shadows in the scene seem to act as a kind of evidence of 'outdoors' – given that the photo is not one from the era of digitalisation.

Its composition is striking. It has some of the qualities of classical painting and sculpture, with a triangular form at the centre providing energetic tension between the flag's tilt to the left and the men's bodies, straining to the right. As Barker speculates, 'the flag at the apex somehow doesn't overshadow the men who plant it. Instead it seems to reach to the sky, to rise above them and crown their efforts' (Barker 1991). It is also not a victoriously, or easily, flying flag – it is only partly unfurled (see Chapter 6 on the ways a displayed flag can signify: national institutions rarely allow their flag to trail on the ground). The amount of space given to the sky is clearly part of this sense of the men straining towards something bigger than themselves, and sky (or heavens) for some readers may have religious signification.

The group of male soldiers has a monumental quality (indeed, the photo was later the model for a sculptured monument in Washington). Their helmets (we cannot see their faces, or age, or degree of beauty, or skin colour: two of them were Native Americans), and their apparent obliviousness to the camera (no eye contact) emphasises their anonymity. Perhaps this opens space for our wonderings about them, as well as avoiding any clear signifiers of ethnic or class origin, so they can be more easily read as signifying simply 'American soldiers'.

Though the photo's pose echoes classical norms, it also works difference within this repetition of 'classical' codes. For example, it contains signifiers of the difficulty of this masculine enterprise – the man whose hand is trying but just failing to grasp the flagpole. This

Marines raise flag on Iwo Jima, Feb. 23, 1945

Figure 1.15 One of the many ways this image was woven into patriotic discourses of the US and the Second World War. The US Post Office originally rejected the idea of a stamp because, they said, 'no living person can appear' on one. On the day of issue in 1945 people stood in queues stretching city blocks to buy one (www.iwojima.com).

difficulty seems graded through the group, so the stance of the soldier on the right seems one of absolute certainty and effort. The rubble and wreckage at their feet seems to signify the damage of war (and, for those involved, the thousands of deaths on the island) out of which this flag rises. It seems crucial that the framing has chosen to include this debris.

Rosenthal had taken a photo a few minutes earlier of a group of some sixteen US soldiers waving their rifles triumphantly to camera around the fully flying US flag but this perhaps connected too well with the codes of the holiday snap, or family album to work as the famous shot did, with more tragic resonance.

In periods of intense patriotism Figure 1.16 seems near to a 'closed text', strongly encouraging only one reading: 'heroic American firemen struggle to raise the flag in the aftermath of a terrorist attack on New York'. Yet like any image this is polysemic; it cannot guarantee that it will be read in only one way. We can just about imagine that a member of Al-Qaeda might read it differently, in an extremely deviant reading; or that some of the firemen laid off after 'Ground Zero' might make a 'negotiated' or ambiguous reading (see Chapter 6 below) or that female fire-fighters might reflect on the overwhelmingly masculine image of their job.

Once you have seen the celebrated Iwo Jima image it is easy to speculate that the photographer here was prompted by the way the firemen's position, from a

Figure 1.16 Firemen at the World Trade Center, '9/11', caught in an action which both resembles and differs from that of the Iwo Jima group.

particular angle, echoed the earlier shot. This time the flag raising produces the thrill of repetition with difference:

- They are civilian workers, not soldiers, though perhaps the uniforms and air of fatigue resonate with the 'front line' feel.
- They are men who do not appear to work like a unified military unit. The signifiers of uncertainty in their faces and the pose of the man on the left, as well as their denim overalls, helmets, etc., are a marked contrast to, as well as an echo of, the earlier shot.
- They are all 'white'. Oddly enough, in an era when much imagery is aware of the need to try to be representative by including members of other

groups, this perhaps adds to the 'authentic' 'captured' quality of the shot.

- Finally, instead of the open sky of Iwo Jima, the dusty wreckage of the World Trade Center is the background to their efforts. This qualifies and undercuts the confidence of a simply 'gung-ho' patriotic reading. It is rather like the debris in the foreground of the original.

Figure 1.17

The digital image above, Figure 1.17, made as part of a 9/11 digital archive, makes explicit the links we're suggesting.

The next image, Figure 1.18, which refers to 'Iwo Jima' is by the celebrated British cartoonist Steve Bell. He often makes his political comments by referring to classical paintings and 'remaking' them in cartoon form, where of course 'anything can happen', unlike photojournalism which is a kind of trace of the real. Bell captions or 'anchors' the cartoon with a verbal pun, 'Raising the standard of international justice, Mazar-i-Sharif', and writes a copyright sign at top side left (thereby staking authorship claims over it, especially important for political artists in preventing misuse of their copyrighted images). He takes the Rosenthal image as a 'classic' but changes its key signifiers to produce an oppositional reading of the patriotism so firmly embedded in the other three pictures.

- The stars and stripes of the flag have been altered. Flags are symbolic signs, in Peirce's sense of being abstract. In the 'Stars and Stripes' the stars signify

These are both relatively 'smooth', unblurred photos. Readers often understand the 'blurring' as indicating a photo is 'truthful-because-not-polished-looking'. This is partly because pieces of dangerously obtained photojournalism, both still and moving, are necessarily blurred: there's an *indexical* link between the event and the photo, if you like. But this blur can be faked or constructed, as in several notorious examples of 'arranged' war footage or, more recently, in television codes such as the deliberately awkward, documentary 'snatched'-looking filming of *ER*.

Here we enter fascinating areas of how we read 'realist' codes: what do we take as (indexical) evidence that something 'really' happened? To some extent (and especially in an era of computer-fakeable imagery) we have to rely on evidence from outside the photo, or 'text', to answer these questions, for example evidence of the trustworthiness of the institution which produced and circulated it (see Chapter 14 'Documentary and "reality TV"').

Figure 1.18 Steve Bell, Mazar-i-Sharif, 29 November 2001: a cartoonist's comment on controversial US treatment of prisoners during the attacks on Afghanistan after 11 September 2001.

the number of states in the US; the red stripes are less easily agreed on: most say they signify the blood of those who made a violent revolution against the British for independence in the eighteenth century. In the days after 11 September, however, the 'star-spangled banner' was a symbol of national mourning, and then of more traditional defiance to enemies. Bell, two months and many US bombings later, makes the stripes seem to be made of dripping blood, and the stars of the skull and crossbones of death, or piracy.

- Though the bodies echo the original pose, they are clearly not all American, judging from the signifiers of uniforms and turbans.
- Finally, instead of the debris and wreckage which the men seem to 'come out of' (both compositionally and ideologically) in Rosenthal's photo, here the ghastly damage of war – human bodies – is strewn all around the foreground, the middle ground and into the distance.

Content analysis

Content analysis cannot often offer the subtle interpretations which semiotic and compositional approaches can. But it is less speculative, indeed it tries to be objective and as such is a very good way of checking out the 'hunches' which are often the starting point for exciting research. The two approaches together can provide real insights into media imagery.

Figure 1.19 gives an example, which you might try to apply. Hunter Davies (2005), a writer on football, had a feeling that the best football coverage was to be found in the broadsheet papers, not the tabloid press (or 'red-tops' as they're now often called). 'But have I made up this wisdom, based on . . . glimpses of one or two papers? Yeah, actually.' So to check it, he employed a postgraduate, on work experience in his office, to analyse every national newspaper's sports pages for a typical Monday, one with no big international match to skew the coverage. The question was: which devoted the most space to football?

Figure 1.19   National dailies, Monday 6 December 2004

Newspaper	Total number of pages	Number of sports pages	% of total devoted to sports	Number of football match reports	% of sports coverage devoted to football	Second most covered sport	Third most covered sport
Guardian	126	32	25	17	51	racing (13%)	rugby union (11%)
Daily Star	72	27	38	39	70	racing (12%)	greyhounds (7%)
Daily Mail	88	23	26	17	58	rugby union (12%)	athletics (10%)
Sun	88	41	47	38	85	racing (4%)	cricket (4%)
Daily Mirror	80	36	45	40	85	racing (6%)	rugby union (3%)
The Times	120	40	33	44	60	rugby union (8%)	cricket (3%)
Daily Express	80	20	25	23	59	racing (10%)	rugby union (9%)
Independent	108	22	20	12	60	rugby union (13%)	racing (11%)
Daily Telegraph	44	12	27	19	40	rugby union (20%)	racing (10%)

Source: Hunter Davies, 'The Fan', *New Statesman*, 14 February 2005, pp. 58–9

As always with content (or quantitative) analysis, what you find always partly depends on what you ask, and how aware you are of its limitations. So Davies asks: 'what do you mean by space? Tabloid pages have fewer words, bigger pictures, bigger headlines than broadsheet pages . . . Pages also contain adverts, and sometimes a mixture of sports. So we had to count column inches.' They also counted how many first person columns by players there were, and how much coverage of Premiership as opposed to other leagues.

But to supplement this quantitative work, they also give a qualitative, more subjective account of such aspects of coverage as:

- how opinionated different papers are: e.g. do they include abuse and 'rude quotations' such as 'the ref was full of bull'?
- how witty and amusing the coverage is – a very subjective area!

ACTIVITY 1.12

Take six issues of your favourite magazine. Apply one of the content analysis methods outlined in Chapter 1 in order to discover what proportions of it consist of:

- adverts
- celebrity coverage
- a mix of those two and
- what the average of these is across the magazine issues you chose.

You might then combine this with an assessment of how many of the images are hostile or sympathetic towards the celebrities involved – which will involve *qualitative* methods.

Voices and sound images

'Images' need not always be visual, or printed. Sound is coded, and signifies in ways as complex as visual images, though after decades of developed analysis the visual image is more readily recognised as 'made up'. Sound is difficult to discuss: we can't offer you a sound 'text' on this page, for one thing. We have had to ignore music, sound effects, etc., though these, in the background, can be key to how voices signify within films and television (try it with your own voice). But to ignore sound, for audio-visual media, can mean that a whole dimension is missing from analysis and appreciation.

Imagine: you can't see a person, but you can hear their voice. What does this tell you about them?

- Pitch: is the voice 'high' or 'low'?
- Volume: 'loud' or 'quiet'?
- Texture: 'rough' or 'smooth', 'soft' or 'hard'?
- Shape: 'round' or 'flat'?
- Rhythm or cadence: does the voice rise and fall or keep a continuous pace and tone? Recently an upward inflection at the end of sentences, making them sound like questions, has spread like wildfire across the English-speaking world, some say from Australian soap operas.

Other key components of voices will also be in play:

- accent, which usually refers to pronunciation (and often rhythm, cadence) and inflection. British voices are particularly characterised by accents: flattened or 'extended' vowels, missed consonants, etc.
- dialect: everyone in the UK speaks a dialect, a sub-language. This differs from so-called 'standard English', also called 'received pronunciation' or 'BBC English', which is better described as the dialect of the southern English upper middle class. Dialects have differences of vocabulary ('wicked'), syntax and pronunciation, and dialect and accent together are often read as key signifiers of class origin. Think of Sean Connery's Scottish accent in his performance of James Bond, an English public school Establishment figure in the original novels and some film versions. Or why the particular voice-over for the British series of *Big Brother* was chosen, and how it signifies – pace, gender, accent,

dead-pan delivery, etc. What difference would it have made to the hugely successful *Jamie Oliver's School Dinners* series (Channel 4 2005) if a female, upper-class voice-over had been used?

ACTIVITY 1.13

Take a cassette recorder and a good-quality external microphone, and tape several different people talking in a variety of situations (classroom, pub, at home). Play back the recordings and try to ignore what they say. Just listen to the sound of the voices.

- Can you recognise any of the codes listed above?
- Use them to describe the sound of any one voice.
- Can you relate the sound to the age or gender of the person? Surprisingly, some 'old' voices sound 'young' and vice versa. Perhaps it is other vocal qualities which suggest someone is old or young?

Unlike that of most of the voices we encounter at college or at home, the technical quality of radio voices has been 'coded' by radio technologies. What we hear is a reproduction of the original voice, dependent on:

- the acoustics of the studio: a room with hard, shiny surfaces will produce a harsh, 'bright' edge to the voice; a studio with absorbent surfaces will soften the voice
- the choice of microphone
- the engineer's processing of the signal, for example in an echo chamber.

These institutional and technical codes are tremendously important. Radio 5, for example, has a different mode of address to its listeners from Radio 4, partly through the voices of the presenters and callers, especially those with distinctive regional accents. Also the ways the Radio 4 and Radio 5 engineers process the voices are different. Maybe you imagine the studios of the two stations differently, just from the sound of the voices in them.

Star presence across a range of media involves not just looks, but also voices and the work of processing them for sound tracks.

A voice is understood by most audiences as less constructed, more authentic than visible appearance, as a 'trace' off the body: size, gender, even smoking habits (see Branston 1995).

Examples:

1 From the 1930s to the 1950s the irritation of many British audiences with the upper-class voices in British films was expressed around 'the two types of people in our films – the Cockney and the Oxford accent type'.

2 Later, the Scottish accent and brusque delivery of lines by Sean Connery as James Bond in 1962 were crucial signifiers of the more classless 'modern' social world of 'Bond-as-scripted-and-performed-in-the-Broccoli-films', compared to the upper-class 'John-Buchan-type-hero-in-the-Cold-War' agent of Fleming's novels (see Branston 2000). The voice is arguably as important to this early reinvention of Bond as Connery's working-class, rugged star image. Both contrast with the different beauty and smoother 'trans-Atlantic' voice of the Pierce Brosnan performance. How do the voice and star image of Daniel Craig alter the character?

3 It's been argued that the powerfully controversial written journalism of Julie Burchill has not led to television or radio success because of the light, unauthoritative quality of her voice.

We hope that these brief ideas about a 'semiotics of sound' will help you think about voices in audio-visual as well as purely audio-forms. It may also help you with recording voices for your own productions.

ACTIVITY 1.14

Run up and down the array of stations on your radio dial. Stop briefly at each voice you hear.

- Do you recognise the station immediately? Through a combination of codes?
- Does BBC local radio use more recognisably 'local' voices? Are commercial stations more likely to be staffed by presenters with an all-purpose 'music radio' voice?
- Why do you think this might be so?

This takes us into realism debates. Just like the blurred photographic image, the overlapping of voices on discussion programmes on radio (i.e. everyone talking at once) often signifies 'authentic lively debate' – and of course can be constructed, or faked, as can other aural signifiers.

References and further reading

Barker, Martin (1991) 'Iwo Jima: the photograph as symbol', *Magazine of Cultural Studies*, autumn.

Branston, Gill (1995) 'Viewer, I listened to him . . . voices, masculinity, *In the Line of Fire*', in Pat Kirkham and Janet Thumim (eds) *Me Jane: Masculinity, Movies and Women*, Lawrence and Wishart.

Branston, Gill (2000) *Cinema and Cultural Modernity*, Buckingham: Open University Press.

Crisell, Andrew (1994) *Understanding Radio*, 2nd edition, London: Routledge.

Davies, Hunter (2005) 'The fan', *New Statesman*, 14 February.

Evans, Harold (1997) *Pictures on a Page: Photojournalism, Graphics and Picture Editing*, London Pimlico.

Rose, Gillian (2001) *Visual Methodologies*, London: Sage.

Wells, Liz (ed.) (2000) *Photography: A Critical Introduction*, 2nd edition, London and New York: Routledge.

Wilby, Peter and Conroy, Andy (1994) *The Radio Handbook*, London: Routledge.

2 Narratives

- **General theories of narrative**
- **Narration, story and plot**
- **Narratives in different media**
- **Institutions and narratives 1: broadcasting and soaps**
- **Institutions and narratives 2: computer culture**
- **References and further reading**

- Making stories, or **narratives** is a key way in which meanings and pleasures are organised and made vivid both in and outside the media.
- Both factual and fiction forms are subject to this kind of shaping. Even the word 'history' comes from the Greek word for narrative: *historia*.

Most of us spend a lot of time telling stories: gossiping about friends; telling jokes; filling family photo albums to tell a story, with appropriate events (rarely photos of stays in hospital) and highly constructed characters (the 'proud graduate', never the 'debt-ridden student' at the happy ending of one 'story'). All cultures make stories, as involving and enjoyable ways of creating sense and meanings. Two points about systematic study of narrative in modern media:

- Narrative theory suggests that stories in whatever media and whatever culture share certain features.
- But particular media are able to 'tell' stories in different ways.

It is worth adding that you will hardly ever encounter a story separate from expectations about it, usually about how it fits with **genres** and their audiences.

Bear this in mind as you try out this chapter, and try to read it along with Chapter 3.

General theories of narrative

This chapter explores the main narrative theories used in media studies. These offer explanations of the devices and conventions governing how stories (fictional or factual) are organised into sequence, and the invitations these may make to audiences to become involved in some ways, but not

Like most semiotic approaches, these isolate texts from their context and use, for the purpose of analysis. In fact very few of us see a film or TV story without any knowledge of its genre or star, or without expectations set up by reviews.

Joseph Campbell (1904–87) influenced by Carl G. Jung (1875–1961), who argued that certain myths and symbols represent 'archetypal' patterns which have been central to human existence (e.g. the anima or 'feminine' side of men etc.).

'Once upon a time it was a small gathering of people around a fire listening to the storyteller with his tales of magic and fantasy. And now it's the whole world . . . It's not "domination" by American cinema. It's just the magic of storytelling, and it unites the world' (Steven Spielberg, *Variety*, 7 December 1993, p. 62).

Vladimir Propp (1895–1970) Russian critic and folklorist whose influential book on narrative, translated as *Morphology of the Folk Tale*, was first published in 1928.

others. Like much media studies, this suggests that quite ordinary activities are powerfully taken for granted, and often connected to dominant sets of values.

Of course there are other ways of thinking about the telling and writing of stories, especially if you are on a scriptwriting course, focusing on the production rather than analysis. One name which frequently comes up is that of **Joseph Campbell**, an anthropologist interested in myths, or ancient stories which can be argued to be shared across cultures. He is said by film-makers such as George Lucas to be a key influence on films such as the *Star Wars* series.

The publication of *Hero with a Thousand Faces* (1949) established Joseph Campbell as a comparative mythologist, arguing that 'eternal' myths or stories are shared by all cultures. Some have suggested that his fashionable theories:

- flatten important differences between the ways myths and stories are used in various cultures
- are used to give high cultural and quasi-religious meanings to commercially powerful products such as *Star Trek* or Lucas's *Star Wars* films.
- conveniently avoid offending lucrative global audiences by not being too specific about exactly which 'god' or religion is being invoked.

(Hollywood loves to give 'universal' rather than commercial accounts of the global sales of its big budget films.)

Most of media studies, however, is not involved in trying to *produce* stories – a wildly unpredictable process: crazy to think it can be reduced to a formula. It tries to *understand* them, especially in terms of their possible social roles. A good definition of narrative for these purposes (which applies to both fiction and non-fiction forms) is given by Branigan, who argues it is '*a way of organising spatial and temporal data into a cause-effect chain of events with a beginning, a middle and end that embodies a judgement about the nature of events*' (1992: 3; original italics).

Important theorists have included **Propp**, Barthes, Todorov and Lévi-Strauss, who often worked with myths, novels and folk tales to explore how narrative *structures or shapings* act within particular cultures. Here are the bare bones of these influential **structuralist** approaches to narrative.

Propp, in the 1920s, examined hundreds of examples of one kind of folk tale to see whether they shared any structures. He argued that whatever the surface differences (i.e. whether the stories dealt with poor woodcutters or youngest princes) it was possible to group its characters and actions into:

- eight character roles (or 'spheres of action' as he called them, to indicate how inseparable are character and action: think about it)
- thirty-one functions (such as 'a prohibition or ban is imposed on the hero' or 'the villain learns something about his victim') which move the story along, often in a highly predictable order. For example, 'the punishment of the villain' always occurs at the end of a story. What is apparently the same act can function in different ways for different narratives. For example, the 'prince' may build a castle (or a spaceship) as:
  - preparation for a wedding
  - defiance of a prohibition
  - solution of a task.

Roles or spheres of action, Propp argued, make sense of the ways in which many different figures (witch, woodcutter, monster, etc.) can be reduced to eight character roles – not the same as the actual characters since one character can occupy several roles or 'spheres of action'. These are:

1 the *villain*
2 the *hero*, or character who seeks something, usually motivated by an initial lack – of money, or a mother, for example. ('Hero' is one of those terms that does not mean the same within theory as it does in life outside, where 'hero' usually refers to a male, and 'heroic' has moral connotations of 'admirable' or 'good'. Here the words are closer to describing someone who actively carries the events of a story, whether Bridget Jones or Bart Simpson.)
3 the *donor*, who provides an object with some magic property
4 the *helper*, who aids the hero
5 the *princess*, reward for the hero (though see above) and often object of the villain's schemes
6 her *father*, who rewards the hero
7 the *dispatcher*, who sends the hero on his way
8 the *false* hero.

The very terms 'prince' and 'princess' are much more than job descriptions. They come to us loaded with narrative expectations and connotations.

Diana, Princess of Wales, had her life repeatedly narrativised in different media. An early narrative 'ended' at her wedding in 1981, working as a classic fairy tale. Her 'lack' (unhappy childhood, desertion by her mother, desire to 'fit in', few formal educational qualifications) was resolved by the magical transformation of 'becoming a princess' – the 'happy ending'. At the time this was signified by the kiss on the balcony of Buckingham Palace, repeated over and over in the media. (See Geraghty 1998.)

Figure 2.1 The kiss

Such work on stories is inevitably bound up with the times which produced them. Propp's original study worked with fairy tales told in times when many women died in childbirth, and the role of ('wicked') stepmothers could be a shared reference point for audiences. Now the hero can often be a female character, like Lara Croft, especially since the word 'heroine' (Propp's 'princess') designates a character who hangs around looking decorative until the hero sweeps her away.

Yet fairy tales, or versions of them, are still familiar to us. Think of the immensely profitable Disney animated versions, or the *Shrek* films (US 2001 and 2004) which comment so neatly on Disney; the *Star Wars* series, *Harry Potter* or *Lord of the Rings* books and films, with their stories of male initiation, good versus evil and so on. Other stories, from real life, can be given fairy-tale shapings – think of the 'royal soap opera' or countless celebrity 'rags to riches' tales.

Propp's approach tried to uncover structures beneath the apparent differences of widely circulated, popular forms. It reminds us that, though characters may seem very 'real', they must be understood as *constructed characters*. Though played by actors who are cast for their resemblance to how we might imagine the character, they have *roles to play for the sake of the story* and often get perceived very quickly, by audiences, in these roles – as 'hero', 'villain', 'helper' and so on. Even though most people are not aware of these roles, we tend to feel it very sharply when the person we thought was the hero or helper turns out to be the villain, as in *The Usual Suspects* (US 1995) or in *Psycho* (US 1960) where, to the shock of its first audiences, the female hero (and star) is killed off a third of the way through the film, and the shy young man who seemed to be a helper turns out to be something very different. Other media forms also construct villains – perhaps you are a fan of American wrestling with its over-the-top melodramatic oppositions of 'good' and 'evil'?

Other narrative forms, such as the *Mahabharata* from Indian culture, or western musicals and 'women's films' take pleasure in much less

Though the *Big Brother* format began with unknown participants, the celebrity form has quickly followed. This may be because of the need for the players to have narrative functions (villain, helper, princess, etc.) by means of editing, choice of camera angles, tasks, etc., as well as by initial 'casting' from thousands of applicants.

With 'celebrities' these roles can be much more quickly assumed, since they already have existing 'images' or reputations of one kind or another, or have even played 'villains' etc.

'In the movies of African film maker Sembene Ousmane . . . the influence of an oral tradition – associated with the "griot" storytellers who, in some African cultures, would, at public gatherings, recount the many tales that bound the community together – creates narrations that seem more like layers of music and song, moving around space rather than forward through history' (Corrigan and White 2004: 218).

The TV serials of Doordarshan (the Indian national TV service) are epic narratives spanning not just centuries but thousands of years. In ninety-one segments, they are intended for weekly Sunday morning viewing in India but the video tapes are gold box packaged for home and export audiences.

action-driven or puzzle-driven narratives. Instead they use convoluted patterns (often circular) and several climaxes. Spectacle, fantasy and humour are given real narrative weight – for example in musical and '**Bollywood**' forms.

ACTIVITY 2.1

- Check that you can identify narrative roles in your favourite fictional media text.
- Try watching a non-fiction form (such as the news) for the way media language will attribute narrative roles and thus construct 'characters'. Even in weather forecasts 'characters' will often be made of natural forces: winds, isobars and so on may be called 'the villain' or 'to blame'; a warm front is 'coming to the rescue'.
- Does language used to describe illness or disease (such as cancer or AIDS) often construct it in dramatically villainous terms?

Todorov, another structuralist, argued that all stories begin with an '**equilibrium**' where any potentially opposing forces are 'in balance' – the 'once upon a time' moment. This is disrupted by some event, setting in train a series of other events, to close with a second, but different 'equilibrium' or status quo. His theory may sound just like the cliché that every story has a beginning, a middle and an end. But it's more interesting. His 'equilibrium' labels a state of affairs, a status quo, and how this is 'set up' in certain ways and not others. 'Workers today decided to reject a cut in pension funds', for instance, begins a news story with an apparent disruption to an equilibrium (of contented workers and fair management) but in fact we know about only one side of that 'balance'. We don't know what kinds of trade-off were offered, after what length of negotiations, etc. How, where and when *else* any story (especially a news story) could have begun are always good questions to ask.

Tzvetan Todorov, Bulgarian structuralist linguist (b. 1939) publishing influential work on narrative from the 1960s onwards.

Princess Diana's life, in its second period, was often 'told' by the media as a 'new story' which begins with the question: what does her presence in the British Royal Family mean? What kind of 'disruption' to that set-up was she: breath of fresh air or neurotically selfish, like 'Fergie'? The *Panorama* interview can be seen as an attempt by her to 'tell her own story': this time, as one of moral virtue. (See Geraghty 1998.)

For specialists: the five codes are the action or proairetic; the enigma or hermeneutic; the semic; the symbolic; and the cultural or referential code.

Barthes suggested that narrative works with five different **codes** which activate the reader to make sense of it. This is an intricate theory, using deliberately unfamiliar terms, and Barthes is not at pains to make it accessible. We have opened it out a little to apply it to *CSI: Miami* in the case study. Particularly interesting is his suggestion that an 'enigma code' works to keep setting up little puzzles to be solved (and not only at the beginning of the story), to delay the story's ending pleasurably: e.g. how will Tom Cruise get out of this predicament? What is in the locked room? How does *x* really feel about *y*?

The film *Memento* (US 2000) experiments with narrative by having as hero a man who has lost his short-term memory and who uses notes and tattoos to remind himself of the past he painfully reconstructs as he hunts his wife's killer.

- If you haven't seen the film, try to sketch how such a narrative might proceed. What are its difficulties, and its pleasures?

'Scripts', in this context, are 'shared expectations about what will happen in certain contexts, and what is desirable and undesirable in terms of outcome' (Durkin 1985: 126). See Chapter 5 for more discussion.

Narrative pleasures and involvements still matter, however much may be given away in film (or other media) publicity. See the urgent notices about 'spoilers': 'WARNING: STORY AND PLOT REVEALED' or the established convention that even serious discussion should not reveal the ending.

An action code will be read by means of accumulated details (looks, significant words) which invoke (and reinforce) our knowledge of what are often highly conventional **'scripts'** of such actions as 'falling in love' or 'being tempted into a robbery'. Barthes is important for this early attempt at building the possible involvement of readers and their culturally formed expectations into a model of how narratives 'work' textually. And more than this, he considers not just how the narrative works 'internally' but also how it evokes for its reader connections to the world outside the text – cultural references etc.

Such structuralist approaches have been applied not just to individual fictions but also to non-fiction forms such as major news stories, to see whether narrative drives 'set up' certain expectations and puzzles, look for (and in fact construct) tidy 'beginnings' and 'endings', etc. This widespread process can mean that complex historical and political explanations are structured out of the storytelling.

CASE STUDY: APPLYING TODOROV TO NEWS

I

Important events such as wars finish. But narratives don't just come to a halt – they *end*, in a way which 'rounds things off', assigns blame and praise, etc. (the 'new equilibrium'). The news media have often structured the end of wars so as to leave out stubborn elements that in fact don't end but go on happening: soldiers' and civilians' injuries and post-traumatic stress syndrome, the continuing arms trade which feeds wars, etc. So deep are the satisfactions of 'the ending' that newsrooms will try hard to find signifiers which suggest a return to normality – very like the 'and so they all lived happily ever after' of the fairy tale.

Sometimes it will take the shape of a correspondent making his way (it's usually a male reporter) into the now-said-to-be-liberated war zone: like the BBC's John Simpson entering Kabul in November 2001; sometimes footage like the tumbling of the statue of Saddam Hussein in 2003 with reporters' comments like 'It is absolutely, without doubt, a vindication of the strategy'; and 'This war has been a major success' (see www.information clearinghouse.info/article284 on the probable faking of the statue incident, and Cromwell and Edwards (2005) on the aftermath of this 'ending').

In the past the sign of wars happily concluding have been: ships sailing back; soldiers talking of their pleasure at a job well done; and eventually the welcome home by the women and children. This sense of an ending is much more difficult to achieve for such a nebulous process as the announced 'war against terrorism' and the horrors of the occupation of Iraq.

2

Almost as soon as the death of Diana, Princess of Wales, was known, interpretations of its ending sought to 'seal' versions of Diana. Internet messages tried to 'fix' the meaning of the car accident into conspiracies. 'Sick' jokes and critical questions played up her privilege and often frivolous lifestyle, ending in a drink driving accident. Others claimed her saintliness, in the flowers and messages on the site of the Paris car crash, outside Harrods, Buckingham Palace, etc.

Since then there have been attempts to shift the role of other 'characters' in the story, such as Prince Charles, moving from 'villain' to 'hero', in his role as father to 'Will' and 'Harry', and in the 2005 legitimising by marriage of his long affair with Mrs Camilla Parker-Bowles. In the process some see him as, in turn, the victim of a cold and ruthless British Royal Family – which occupies the villain function in this version.

Figure 2.2 Impromptu 'shrine' to Diana outside Harrods store which is owned by the father of her companion the night she was killed.

Paradigm: a class of objects or concepts.

Syntagm: an element which follows another in a particular sequence. Imagine choosing from a menu. Paradigmatic elements are those from which you choose (starters, main courses, desserts). The syntagm is the sequence into which they are arranged. Sometimes these structures are treated as 'horizontal' (across time) and 'vertical' (along values) aspects of narratives.

'Western heroes have usually restricted themselves to a pitiably narrow range of activities. They can't daydream, or play the fool, or look at flowers, or cook . . . or . . . make mistakes' (Tompkins 1992).

Q Do you think this binary is still as firmly in place as in the 'classic western'?

Lévi-Strauss argued that an abiding structure of *all* meaning-making, not just narratives, was a dependence on **binary oppositions**, or a conflict between two qualities or terms. He was less interested in the order in which events were arranged in the plot (called **syntagmatic** relations) than in looking 'beneath' them for deeper or **paradigmatic** arrangements of themes. Though this theory can be applied to individual stories and can act as a useful 'way in', strictly speaking it should be applied to *sets* of narratives, as in the western genre, or across some news stories. Writers suggested that the different sheriffs, outlaws, schoolmarms, Native Americans, etc. of hundreds of westerns could be usefully analysed in Proppian narrative terms (Native Americans as thrilling 'villains' whose motives were often withheld, for example). They could also be seen as organised, over time, according to systematic oppositions, among others:

homesteaders	Native Americans
Christian	pagan
domestic	savage
weak	strong
feminine	masculine
garden	wilderness
inside society	outside society

For the fighting in Afghanistan (and the earlier Gulf War of 1991) structuring oppositions might include:

east	west
barbarism	civilisation
feudal	modern

Figure 2.3 *In Without Knocking*, 1909, Charles Russell, a painting which can be seen as celebrating the ways a rupture of these oppositions is embodied in certain cowboy actions. It is a structure of excitement which flows into western films, and which cinema is well suited to dramatising.

despotism	democracy
fundamentalism	freedom
backward 'dirty' weapons	modern 'clean' weapons ('surgical strikes' etc.)
good	evil

Narration, story and plot

The term **narration** describes *how* stories are told, how their material is selected and arranged in order to achieve particular effects with their audiences. This partly involves how much knowledge we are allowed to have – think of the importance of 'secrets' in soap operas.

Plot and **story** are key terms here. Bordwell and Thompson (2004) take Russian formalist theory but use the sometimes confusing English terms. They define story as consisting of 'all the events in a narrative, both explicitly presented and inferred'. The plot, on the other hand, is 'everything visibly and audibly present in the film before us; in other words those highly selected parts of the story which the narrative puts before us'. You can think of the story as something you are able to assemble at the end of the narrative. It would include routine events, like washing, which we assume carry on happening during many stories, but would be tedious as part of the plot. It may also include material we only find out by the end of the story, having been busy trying to piece things together throughout, such as the identity of a key figure in *The Usual Suspects* (US 1995). Figure 2.4 provides a helpful graph of another complex narrative.

The study of narration and narrative is called narratology.

A useful distinction developed by Russian theorists in the 1920s was that between *syuzhet* (**plot**) and *fabula* (**story**). The Russian words are sometimes used, partly because the meanings of the two English terms are often slippery, and get confused with each other.

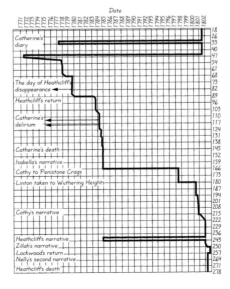

Figure 2.4 The narrative structure of the well-known novel *Wuthering Heights* shown as a graph. Much is revealed about Heathcliff's childhood towards the end of the narrative, by which time he seems almost monstrous: the insight into his treatment in childhood suddenly swings our sympathies right round, back to him for a while.

ACTIVITY 2.2

Q Can you see how 'flashbacks' (via characters talking about earlier parts of their lives, diaries discovered, etc.) adjust the delivery of the story so as to manipulate audience interest and sympathy?

Entertaining cheats are possible: *Sunset Boulevard* (US 1950) and *Desperate Housewives* (US 2004) tell their stories through a first-person narrator who is dead in the story's 'present', and who only gives some of their knowledge to the viewer. *The Usual Suspects* (US 1995) relies for its surprise on a long, misleading flashback.

Q If you've seen *The Others* (2001), did you feel it 'cheated' successfully?

Other writers have explored this area in terms of the knowledge which the 'reader' has, compared to that of the characters: is it the same or more? When more, when less? How much more? How has this been contrived? For example, we should feel at the end of a good detective story or thriller that we have been enjoyably puzzled, so that the 'solution', our piecing together of the story in its proper order out of the evidence offered by the plot, will come as a pleasure. We should not feel that the plot has cheated; that parts of the story have suddenly been revealed which we couldn't possibly have guessed. The innocent secretary cannot, at the last minute, suddenly be revealed to have been a poisons expert.

Another part of the construction of narratives involves the 'voice' telling the story. A first-person narration will use 'I' as the voice of the teller, and should not give the reader access to events which that 'I' could not have witnessed or known of. A third-person or impersonal narration however refers to a story which seems to 'get itself told', as in 'Once upon a time there was a prince . . .'. It's often called the voice of the omniscient narrator, since in theory it knows everything to do with the story. Though cinema and many television or video narratives begin with a literal 'voice-over' telling us the story from a personal point of view, they usually settle into the mode of impersonal narration, voiceless and just seeming to unfold before us.

This voice is often that of one of the *characters* in a story, a hugely underestimated area of narrative study. Characters 'work' on the basis of appearance, clothing, gestures, star image, etc. and often embody 'typical' traits, especially if they are only needed for background actions. Corrigan and White point out how, although movies aim to create broadly realistic characters, most of them are a blend of ordinary and extraordinary features (rather like stars). This makes for characters that are 'recognisable in terms of our experiences and exceptional in ways that make us interested in them. . . . Even [with] . . . characters [like] the . . . heroine of *Alien* (1979) understanding them means appreciating how that balance between the ordinary and extraordinary is achieved' (2004: 224).

One way of trying out your knowledge of these theories is by looking in detail at how ads work, since a lot of effort has normally been put into

---

ACTIVITY 2.3

How do you think the balance between the ordinary and the extraordinary is achieved in the case of 'Ripley/Sigourney Weaver'?

How in the case of your current favourite movie character?

---

constructing their short, easy-to-read narratives. Non-narrative ads of course won't do this, often consisting simply of a set of claims about a product (a supermarket listing its best prices) or setting up a glamorous mood linked to the product, as in many car ads. But if using narrative form, an ad will

- group its events in cause and effect order
- even in a few seconds, create a sense of characters, action and perhaps enigma codes through economical use of signs and typifying traits – blonde hair, certain glances, etc.

ACTIVITY 2.4

Look at a few ads from television. Ask yourself of each:

- Is this a narrative? Does it 'begin' rather than just 'start', and 'end' rather than 'stop'?
- How do I know? Are the people in it constructed as 'characters'? How is this done?
- Or is it simply a list of claims or prices, or an image of a situation in which the product seems attractive?

Ads work as Propp suggests: the same traits both build a sense of characters as like 'real people' and are crucial for the action, the furthering of the plot. Casting will work with its own 'cues' to the audience: blonde hair, a certain accent, height, star image, etc. will all imply certain (different) characters and consequences within particular narrative (or generic) contexts.

There will be a discernible 'hero' who carries the plot along (though often you may feel that in the ordinary sense of the word the 'hero' is usually the product). There will be, as Todorov suggests, some sense of an initial situation, which is disrupted or altered and then happily resolved – usually, of course, through the magical intervention of the product being sold.

1912: Point of view and narrative: two polar bears read a newspaper headline about the sinking of the *Titanic*. One says to the other: 'What happened to the iceberg?'

You will also probably be able to distinguish the *story* as you can reassemble it, having gone through a narrative, and the *plot* which has kept you surprised or held throughout it. Even if flashback is not used, try to imagine the same events told differently, from the point of view of another character, for example, or with different amounts of time, and therefore emphasis, given to different segments of the narrative.

Narratives in different media

These broad structures, which seem to govern all story-making and storytelling, have to work differently in different media, and for different cultures. This is worth bearing in mind if you're involved in a project which asks you to *choose* a medium in which to make a story: what can *x* medium do (strip cartoon, say, or radio) that *y* cannot, and vice versa? These differences are partly due to the nature of different media and technologies, as well as the audiences who use and enjoy them.

Stories in words

There's no space to deal with literary or verbal narratives, but Activity 2.5 focuses on the different methods they use compared to audio-visual or other forms.

ACTIVITY 2.5

See if you can storyboard this sentence from the Harry Potter book, *Harry Potter and the Philosopher's Stone* (Book 1) (Rowling 1997: 191) so as to convey exactly what it says so economically: 'In years to come, Harry would never quite remember how he had managed to get through his exams when he half expected Voldemort to come bursting through the door at any moment.'

Photography

This might seem an odd example of a narrative form, since it deals in frozen moments of time (like stained-glass windows or drawings). But often the impact of a powerful news or advertising photo lies in what it makes us imagine has gone before or is about to happen. In this sense narrative is often signalled, depending on angle, information given, construction of imagined characters – and whether or not black and white film stock is involved. The difference between black and white and colour often signals 'pastness' and 'presentness' in the story.

Look for ads which use the black and white/colour contrast in the way suggested.

How do they set in play narrative expectations and knowledge?

Comic strips and animation

Comic strips (and by extension animation films and serials) tell their stories by a compelling combination of

- words (including thought bubbles);
- line drawings. These can streamline and exaggerate characters and events more than even the highest-budget movie. You never have to worry about spots on the star's face or problems with lighting in comic strip and animation;
- flashpoint illustrations of key moments involving extreme angles and exaggerations.

Comic strips and animations often represent a world which differs from our own: think of the four-fingered, yellow-skinned inhabitants of *The Simpsons*, with their unlikely 'local media', slapstick comedy, babies that never grow up, far flung storylines and painfree violence. But most viewers

Figure 2.5 'Every picture tells a story?' Or, more powerfully, they often suggest one. The context for this photo: some time before the First World War (1914–18) two fishermen walked into a studio in Aberdeen and asked for their photo to be taken. The resulting image is so striking it invites story construction. It's fascinating to speculate about what their relationship is, whether or not we assume they are gay.

Figure 2.6 Film-makers in the last thirty years have tried to copy the dynamism and drama of comic books, their inventive styling and melodramatisation of narrative. ("Batman" #610 © 2004 DC Comics. All Rights Reserved. Used with Permission.)

ACTIVITY 2.6

What difference does this 'speed' and clarity or capacity for exaggeration make to the kinds of narratives which can be told in animation?

Do you think *South Park* and *The Simpsons* tell different kinds of stories partly because of their different styles of animation? How would you apply this to films such as *The Incredibles* (US 2004) which are heavily marketed on off-screen star voices?

realise and enjoy this exaggeration/difference and also enjoy the ways that narratives (let alone particular lines of dialogue) are like our world. They can relate in bitingly satirical ways to real-life political or cultural issues, unlimited by budget constraints. They conform to the narrative tricks of many soaps, including the convenient meeting place for characters, gossip, etc. – here the Quickie Mart.

Cinema

Like video and audio recordings, this is a 'time-based' medium, manipulating time and space, as well as images or words alone. The average feature film length of about two hours, with audiences seeing it all at one sitting, can give it some of the intensity of a short story. It may lead to an experience different from that of longer fictions like soaps, serials or novels, read or viewed over days, weeks, even years, woven into our lives while we do other things in between. Chapter 12 will explore further the ways we have become accustomed to stories being partly 'told' via conventions of setting, editing, sound, framing, camera positioning, etc. in both cinema and television.

But for now, look at the image from *Days of Heaven* (US 1978) in Figure 2.7 and think about how it uses space.

Radio

Radio uses sounds and silence, and this affects the way it can handle narrative. It has to construct the illusion of space between characters, and time between segments, through the use of voices, noises, sound effects and silence. It will not devote much time to features on which cinema might want to linger, as evidence of how the movie has spent its resources (say the display of visual special effects or of costumes). Characters cannot stay silent for long periods of time (like the Tim Roth character, mostly

Figure 2.7 Look at what this expresses just through framing – the workers in relation to the sky, the corn, the land; how the owner's large house discreetly but definitely overlooks the whole operation – and how the camera gives all this to its viewers as a lovely, classically 'three part' image. And we haven't even begun to think about how the story is carried by music, or costume, or individualised actors and their script.

In recent big budget films, note the attempts made to lure audiences into buying the game, the DVD, etc., in order to see, in more detail, the rich settings and fast-cut action which are often only glimpsed in the movie.

silent, dying 'onstage' in *Reservoir Dogs* (US 1992)), since they would seem to have 'disappeared'. Since radio's signifiers are relatively cheap and easy to produce, it is free to construct the most bizarre and exotic stories, from time travel to a play about memories flashing through the head of a drowning woman.

If you are a fan of *The Hitchhiker's Guide to the Galaxy* (originally BBC Radio 1978) you might like to compare how its narrative is shaped in radio, television, film, novel and computer game forms, partly because of their different budget strictures. Most noticeably, and important for a two-hour motion picture, the film makes more use of a conventional plot than is present in the original. This change is accompanied by major changes in character motivation.

Q   Did you feel that the demands of a two-hour movie have led to a more conventional plot than in the radio original? Does this necessitate changes in character motivation, which were relatively absent in the original? And do we thereby lose many of the minor eccentric characters in favour of much more emphasis on the central ones?

Q How did very successful BBC comedy sketch series *The League of Gentlemen* adapt its narrative for cinema release in *The League of Gentlemen's Apocalypse* (UK 2005)?

ACTIVITY 2.7

Look at your favourite scene from a recent movie on DVD/video.
How would you represent it:
● on radio?
● in written form?
● in comic strip form?

Institutions and narratives 1: broadcasting and soaps

Differences between the ways stories get told in different media are partly, then, to do with the material (sound, celluloid, computer screens, line drawings, image and sound, spoken or written words alone) of that medium. But they are also to do with *institutional* or *industrial* demands. The box below takes one example: the differences in how 'closed' or single and 'open' or serial narratives tend to work in those different media institutions, 'cinema' and 'broadcasting'.

Soaps can be defined as open-ended, multi-strand serial forms, broadcast across fifty-two weeks of the year. They developed first on US radio in the 1930s as a cheap way of involving housewives, whose buying choices the detergent manufacturers (and other businesses) wanted to influence. It seemed an ideal form both for commercial television in the 1960s, keen to sell the promise of audiences' regular attention to advertisers, and for the BBC to revive in 1985 with *EastEnders*, wanting to boost its early evening audiences. This was partly in the hope that they would stay with the channel all evening, and also to help the BBC produce evidence of large audience numbers when making its arguments for the level of the next licence fee. Major soaps have acted like big news programmes, and major serials as 'flagship programmes', which helped to **brand** channels.

Though soap opera is one of the most familiar and discussed forms of media, it is not just 'one thing'. Even on British terrestrial television there are Australian, US, Welsh, Scottish and other soaps, made within different kinds of broadcasting institutions (**public service broadcasting**, commercially funded, etc.). These in turn divide into

'Closed' narrative e.g. films in cinema

1 'Tight' reading involved; audience aware it's watching a complete story and therefore reading with the likely end in mind.

2 Relatively few central characters; 'depth' of audience knowledge often set up, with even interior voice-overs giving characters' thoughts, hallucinations, etc.

3 Characters arranged in a 'hierarchy' (central, cameo, supporting roles, extras, etc.).

4 Often with audience invited to make 'verdicts' on them, identifying narrative roles, as in hero, villain, victim.

5 Time usually very compressed: typical two hours of screen time constructs events as happening over months, years, sometimes centuries.

6 Time and events are usually special to this particular story, and need have no resemblance to the viewer's world, though specific reference is possible as are flashbacks and even flashforwards.

7 Reader or viewer usually has evidence about the characters only from this single text – plus star, publicity and genre expectations (though synergy and the prevalence of sequels complicate this).

'Open' narrative e.g. television and radio soap opera

1 Casual reading, without the sense of an ending; soaps proceed as though they could go on for ever – even when one is terminated.

2 Many more characters, naturalistically represented and producing a multi-strand plot.

3 Characters not usually in a marked hierarchy but shift in and out of prominence (partly to suit the production needs of the serial).

4 Characters shift also in and out of narrative function. Today's villain may be next week's helper or even hero.

5 Time usually corresponds to 'real world time' within the segments of each episode, though across it time is compressed, as in cinema. Flashbacks rare.

6 The differences between time in the serial and outside are blurred. Episodes may make broad reference to real-life events going on at the same time, such as elections or Christmas.

7 Audiences are assumed to have different kinds of memory, and knowledge of a long-running soap. Magazines, television, the press often speculate about actors' contracts, and thus the fate of characters.

8 The same audience can be assumed to watch the film from beginning to end.	8 Each episode has to try to address both experienced and new viewers.
9 Often elaborate visual image, and music as integral part of the narrative.	9 Relatively rare use of music, especially in British soaps, and relatively simple visual image.

high- and low-budget products, and have different relationships to documentary forms, to ideas of glamour, to sitcom, romance, regional identities and also to male audiences.

Listen to *The Archers* or BBC Asian Network's radio soap *Silver Street*, and see if the same need for a meeting place applies, even though sets and their costs are not as relevant as they are for TV.

Nevertheless, we can generalise: one of British soap's attractions for its producers has been that costs can be kept down, partly because narrative can be centred on a few key or 'nodal' locations (e.g. the hotel, pub, launderette or café). These are meeting places, one of the staples of the narrative, and also key to soaps' economies and production needs. Since a soap usually has to go out for two or three nights a week, many storylines are necessary, so that particular ones can swing in and out of prominence, allowing:

- time for rehearsals, and for actors' holidays, pantomime contracts, pregnancies, illnesses, etc.
- a wide appeal through several stories happening at once so as to involve different sections of the audience. If you're impatient with one 'strand', you know that another, which interests you more, will probably be along in a minute or so. The meeting places give both a chance for storylines to meet and switch, and also coherence and the feeling of 'community' so central to soap's pleasures.

Soap narratives may also change as a result of attempts to shift the composition of their audiences — and advertisers. Over the last few years several soaps have moved 'upmarket' in terms of their sets, costumes, situations and some character types, as part of the attempt to sell more expensive ad slots addressing more affluent audiences. After the success of *Brookside*, other soaps tried to attract male audiences to this traditionally female form by means of 'tough' storylines and characters, as in *The Bill*, which falls between a soap (continuous production, never a 'closed' ending to an episode) and a series (self-contained storylines each week, as in *ER*). Serials (including 'classic' serials) and 'mini-series' (often a pilot project) are other narrative forms designed to meet particular scheduling needs.

Soaps have also often covered controversial themes in order to aggregate audiences. In October 2001 *EastEnders* dealt with child abuse via Kat being discovered as the mother of Zoe (a character until then treated as her sister in the series) as a result of in-family abuse when Kat was a very young adult. Blanket publicity and coverage of this storyline, in the press, on television, etc., on the morning of the revelatory episode stressed the care taken by the programme-makers with this topic, in contacting the Samaritans, NPSCC, etc. What was then interesting was how skilfully the narrative itself was written and performed so as to maintain the involvement of an audience who, in the simplest sense, 'knew what was going to happen'.

ACTIVITY 2.8

If you hear that any other such controversial, well-'flagged' episodes are coming up, record it and try to see how its narrative turns are kept interesting for audiences who broadly know their outcome. Stop the tape and ask yourself 'How would I end this scene? What lines would I write?' Then see how it has in fact been achieved.

Consider this comment on the difficulties which *EastEnders* seemed to encounter in 2004–5, when it went to four days a week.

> You need to restrict it to three nights a week and not run repeats on terrestrial TV. It's too disposable – there's the feeling that it's everywhere and it doesn't matter if you miss an episode. . . . They need to show people doing nothing; they can't seem to do small plotlines, only big. The audience like the adrenalin rush of the big ballistic plots, but it can't be sustained; people want to watch friends talking in a pub. . . . Bringing people back is always a sign of bankruptcy. Returning characters take all the storylines and the new characters are excluded. Den [Sharon's father in the serial] should never have been brought back – it was a symptom of desperation.
>
> (Paul Abbot, TV writer of *Shameless*, *State of Play*, etc., quoted in Jeffries 2005)

How true do you think his comments are? Would you apply any of them to your favourite soap?

Soap operas often work in terms of secrets, of knowledge sometimes kept from all other characters – but not the viewer.

Q How does this shape the pleasures of narrative suspense for viewers? What pleasures might take its place?

It also seems that soap has actual advantages over more prestigious drama forms in its long-runningness (*Coronation Street* has been running since 1960!). This means that the long-term, often invisible consequences of 'social issues' (such as rape, unemployment, child abuse, the trauma of serving in a war) can be dealt with and resurface for a particular character over many years – as in real life. This gives it certain advantages over single narratives such as 'issue films' or plays. Of course soap opera also has limitations to its realism: when have you ever heard characters in a television soap discussing political campaigns or election issues, and naming politicians or even rival television soaps, as most of us do?

Radio, because it is cheaper to produce, can work differently. In *The Archers*, November 2001, for example, a young character complained 'I'm missing *Hollyoaks* for this'. And foot and mouth disease in 2001, with its disastrous consequences for farming, was mentioned by the end of the week in which it was first reported. This might have been more difficult for a television soap. Why?

ACTIVITY 2.9

Make notes on an episode of your favourite soap.

- How many storylines does the episode contain?
- To which sections of the audience do you think they try to appeal?
- If it's on a commercial channel, what do the ads before, during and after suggest about the expected audience?
- Which are the main storylines? The same as a few weeks ago? Changed? Why?
- How is time managed in the episode?
- How many sets are used? Why have these places been chosen?
- Are there any rumours circulating about the fate of particular characters or actors, in the press, on television or in fanzines?
- How does your knowledge of these affect your viewing? Does it add to your pleasure? How?
- How does the soap story try to address both experienced and new viewers? How are repeated use of characters' names, repeated updatings of the storylines and so on managed so as to inform new viewers, yet not bore regular ones?
- Is it making reference to a current news issue? If so, in what way?

Institutions and narratives 2: computer culture

I

It's hard to generalise about 'computer games' since there are so many kinds: sports games, racing games, MMPORGs (Massively Multiplayer Online Role-Play Games – *EverQuest* etc.), single-player fantasy adventure RPGs (Role Playing Games), first-person shooters and some others where narrative form is of little or no consequence. Single-player adventure games generally move towards a climactic challenge which completes the main quest, as in classic narrative theory, whereas in multiplayer online games (like Ultima Online) the forking-path narrative structure, in which player choices continually direct and create the direction of the narrative, is obviously much more extreme and open-ended.

New cognitive skills developed by games playing include trial and error problem solving, pattern recognition, strategic thinking. These are directly transferable not just to many intelligence tests, but to twenty-first-century techno-warfare. Indeed, games technology partly came out of the Pentagon, and some games experts are currently helping the Pentagon develop 'network warfare'.
See http://www.ict.usc.edu/~gordon/NILE04.PDF.

ACTIVITY 2.10

If your favourite computer game does involve storytelling, how does it construct its narrative(s) and attempt to draw you in?

What does the story centre on? How much focus is there on themes such as vigilantism, torture, violence?

Are you drawn in by the game's sumptuous special effects? Or is the construction of character and story also key to games which you find 'satisfying' or immersive?

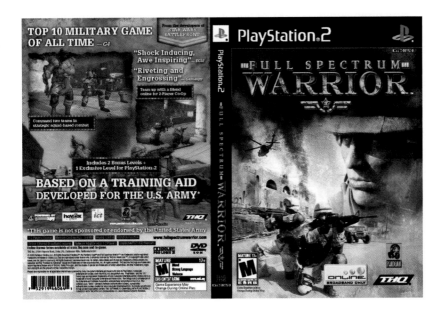

Figure 2.8 A computer game ('strategy game plus tactical shooter elements') which advertises its military connections. Look up the term 'Full Spectrum Dominance' on Google.

On plans for the release of *The Godfather* video game, autumn 2005

'[The creative director] Campbell's approach is not to re-create the narrative of *The Godfather* but to place players inside a cohesive 1930s New York, where they create their own stories alongside that of the Corleone family. [He explains] "Our game, your experience is a line that snakes round the movie and intersects with what we think are all the best parts . . . You're in conversation with Sonny and he suddenly gets that phone call and rushes out. Tom Hagen urges you to follow him (Marlon Brando, months before his death, James Caan and Robert Duvall all recorded new dialogue for the game) and you leap into a car in pursuit . . . Sonny has to die. My challenge is to create a game where you . . . stumble into these classic scenes and suddenly realise where you are" . . . Campbell plays around the existing story – but never with it.'

(Simons 2005)

2

Contemporary Hollywood cinema is mostly produced by huge conglomerate companies which own many of the spin-off computer games, music tracks, clothes, videos, CDs, etc. which their films may help to market. It's been suggested (see Branston 2000) that we are getting used to new narrative possibilities as a result of two related developments:

- these commercial links between 'blockbuster movies' and the products they often publicise (see Chapter 9 'Advertising and branding', and its case study)

- many people's increasing cultural familiarity with the ways that computers allow us to retry possibilities – in games and drafts of essays, as well as hypertext novels, where readers can select their own route by clicking on active links to new text which changes the story. These experiences may be producing new kinds of narrative.

For example: not only do blockbuster films such as the *Star Wars* series function, narratively, so as to resemble an extended games or toy ad, with the same kinds of action puzzles, spectacle, suspenseful situations etc. – in other words, as a kind of ad for the game which the same corporation will try to sell you – but they also have a 'prequel/sequel' narrative aspect which resembles the possibility we now experience with computers, of going back over previous ground in a story or project, and 'replaying' it.

This has happened before of course. Every new version of Charles Dickens's *A Christmas Carol* uses the structure. But crucially this nineteenth-century vision of 'replaying' was for moral and religious purposes – of repentance and a 'second chance'. Much contemporary cinema seems fascinated simply by the possibility of having a games-like control over the way the 'narrative' turns out. This is part both of Hollywood blockbusters and of less mainstream cinemas. *Groundhog Day* (US 1993) and *Sliding Doors* (UK 1998), as well as *Possible Loves* (Brazil 2001) or *Vanilla Sky* (US 2001), rerun their romantic and comic narratives rather like a game or a tape; *eXistenZ* (Canada/France/UK 1999) explicitly moved between the reality levels of movies and games; *Antz* (US 1999) had the mental landscape of a multi-level game; and *Run Lola Run* (Germany 1998) plays the same 'story' several times, suggesting that small differences are crucial ones. Though not all of these share the corporate marketing connections of blockbusters, they are interested in new possibilities for narrative which seem to be related to widespread audience experience of computers.

You may yourself use phrases which express your experience of computer games and other media technologies: 'I wanted to just rewind the whole incident', 'Fast forward please', 'Cut', 'Beam me up Scottie'.

ACTIVITY 2.11

Explore the process of how you 'read' a film or ad for narrative developments in your next viewing.

- Then note how it relates to the kinds of knowledge usually available before entering a cinema or renting a video or watching ads.
- Have you ever seen a film or ad with no generic knowledge (e.g. via a poster in the cinema foyer, friends' comments) of what to expect?

This takes us to Chapter 3 'Genres and other classifications', and how all such narrative expectations are prepared, and played with.

References and further reading

Barthes, Roland (1977) *Introduction to the Structural Analysis of Narratives*, London: Fontana.

Bordwell, David and Thompson, Kirstin (2004) *Film Art: An Introduction*, 7th edition, New York: McGraw-Hill.

Branigan, Edward (1992) *Narrative Comprehension and Film*, London: Routledge.

Branston, Gill (2000) *Cinema and Cultural Modernity*, Buckingham: Open University Press.

Campbell, Joseph (1949) *The Hero with a Thousand Faces*, reprint Myrkos, 1972.

Corrigan, Timothy and White, Patricia (2004) *The Film Experience An Introduction*, Basingstoke: Palgrave Macmillan.

Cromwell, David and Edwards, David (2005) *Guardians of Power: The Myth of the Liberal Media*, London: Pluto Press.

Durkin, Kevin (1985) *Television, Sex Roles and Children*, Milton Keynes: Open University Press.

Field, Syd (1994) *Four Screenplays: Studies in the American Screenplay*, New York: Dell.

Geraghty, Christine (1991) *Women and Soap Opera*, London: Polity Press.

Geraghty, Christine (1998) 'Story' in 'Flowers and tears: the death of Diana, Princess of Wales', *Screen*, 39, Spring.

Jeffries, Stuart (2005) 'I love *EastEnders* so much', *Guardian*, 25 April.

Lévi-Strauss, Claude (1972) 'The structural study of myth', in R. and F. De George (eds) *The Structuralists from Marx to Lévi-Strauss*, New York: Doubleday Anchor.

Propp, Vladimir (1975) *The Morphology of the Folk Tale*, Austin: University of Texas Press.

Rowling, J.K. (1997) *Harry Potter and the Philosopher's Stone (Book 1)*, London: Bloomsbury.

Simons, Ian (2005) 'Modern times', *New Statesman*, 25 April.

Todorov, Tzvetan (1977) *The Poetics of Prose*, Oxford: Blackwell.

Tomkins, Jane (1992) *West of Everything: The Inner Life of Westerns*, Oxford: Oxford University Press.

CASE STUDY: *CSI: MIAMI* AND CRIME FICTION

- • **Crime fiction**
- • **Plot/story**
- • **Todorov**
- • **Applying Propp**
- • **Applying Barthes**
- • **Applying Lévi-Strauss**
- • **Narratives, institutions, ideologies**
- • **References**
- • **Further reading**

Stories centring on crimes and how they are solved are an interesting way into narrative theory since they have at their very centre the painstaking reconstruction of 'another story' – 'what really happened'. This reconstructing involves the same kinds of speculation (attempts to assess character and motivation, likely actions and unlikely ones, 'the evidence') which we as 'readers' are carrying out on the detective fiction itself and, indeed, on many stories. Here we will try to:

- • apply the main theories of narrative to the first episode of *CSI: Miami*
- • explore the relation of genre expectations to how we become involved with narratives
- • suggest how its narrative works in relation to dominant values and ideologies.

Crime fiction

The group that is usually called 'crime fiction' most often deals with the *solving* of crimes. One possible division of these narratives would be into those we could call the whodunit, the howdunnit and even the whydunnit.

But even given these nuances, usually the focus will be on solving rather than exploring crimes. Their broader social causes, or the experience of committing them, or of being tried and punished for them, are

ACTIVITY 2.12

List a few stories which you think illustrate these different enigma structures. Try to apply to them narrative theories from Chapter 2 to show how they *differ.*

examples of possible areas related to crime which are usually broached by other genres, such as 'the prison film', horror, the drama-documentary, or the courtroom drama.

We'll focus here on the first episode of the CBS series *CSI: Miami*, one of the *CSI* (crime scene investigation) series separately located in New York, Miami and Las Vegas. But you should be able to apply these suggestions to most episodes. Though we're focusing on narrative, it is through genre expectations that most audiences make sense of series like *CSI*. These are flagged in publicity, casting and opening sequences.

Let's consider crime narratives in a bit more detail. Most of them in fact deal with detection. It doesn't take a Sherlock Holmes to deduce that 'detective fiction' usually involves a detective, but it also usually involves a junior, and an interest in the relationship between them, often as great as the crime they have

One of the pleasures of earlier forms, such as the Sherlock Holmes stories (written between 1887 and 1893), or series like TV's *Inspector Morse* (1987–2000), is that though we can never be as brilliant as Holmes/Morse, we can catch up through Dr Watson/Lewis – and also enjoy the satisfaction of feeling that we will never be as 'slow' as the latter. (See Brunsdon 1998 on Morse.)

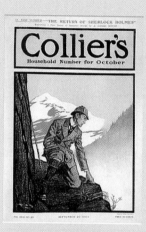

Figure 2.9 The aloof, 'above the world' image of Sherlock Holmes, his 'deerstalker' hat suggesting a certain class identity. More usually it is the foggy streets of Victorian London which challenged his stalking capacities.

Q Are there any similarities and differences to Horatio, or other contemporary TV detectives?

Q How might the uses of computer games techniques (fast accurate zooms, flashbacks, etc.) lessen the narrative need for a character like Watson?

to solve. There may also be a fascination with the place where the detectives are based, whether foggy nineteenth-century London, the Botswana of Precious Ramotswe and her No. 1 Ladies Detective Agency, or the Chicago of V.I. Warshawski.

The most common narrative in the genre is focused on a single detective, and there are two major strands:

1 one focused on the English 'gentleman' detective, from Sherlock Holmes to Inspector Morse, but also involving a few 'gentlewomen' such as Miss Marple. Holmes often worked in the dark of nineteenth-century London. The resonant imagery of fog often makes his stories border on the horror genre (even when set around the Baskerville country estate). In such a setting, Holmes worked like a 'beacon of intelligence' or 'a doctor who will cure the ills of society'.

2 the other strand, from the 1920s, was centred on a more 'hard-boiled' US detective, not a gentleman, much more vulnerable than the Holmes figure, especially to the sexually available women he encountered. He was often involved in dubious connections and methods, and often voiced telling criticisms of the social order. This figure has influenced British crime writers such as Ian Rankin (though see http://www.mysteryguide.com/hard-boiled.html for a sense of the complexity of the groupings).

Q Can you see traces of these two traditions in any of the detectives in *CSI: Miami*?

Figure 2.10 Horatio and Eric: any resemblance to Sherlock Holmes and Watson? Any differences?

The other increasingly popular strand within 'detective fiction' is the 'police procedural', involving a team of police and a focus on the working process of solving the crime in methodical, often weary and footslogging ways. In the case of *CSI*, the frustrating work of investigation is replaced by a reliance on an almost magical high-tech scientific method, often referred to in specialised language and acronyms. The terminology itself has a special section in the CSI website.

Q How far are the relationships between the members of the team still of interest in this kind of detective story?

Plot/story

Let's look at 'The golden parachute', the first episode of *CSI: Miami*, via a summary or synopsis of its plot, and then consider how this has been arranged, or plotted, so as to differ from the crime story, which we can reconstruct by the end.

Note: the word 'synopsis' on many websites refers to a trailer-like teasing summary of the beginning of the narrative. A true synopsis summarises all the happenings in a text, and has to give away endings or uses 'spoilers'. This is the only way to understand the whole work of the narrative, for which the ending is crucial.

Synopsis: 'The golden parachute'

Pre-title sequence: two men fishing in swampland witness a plane crash. The Miami CSI team arrive, including Horatio Caine, in charge, and his junior Eric. There is a question as to which section of the police force is in charge of the investigation. They find a body from the crash. Eric thinks it is alive, Horatio tells him it is not.

Title sequence: spectacular shots of the Florida Everglades and stylised 'hi-tech' montages of images of the main characters at work.

Megan Donner arrives, once boss of the team but now returning after a six-month absence following the death of her husband. There's a brief argument between her and Horatio about who has jurisdiction in this case – the 'Feds' or CSI. Different approaches to detection arise, which resurface throughout the episode. A small entry wound is found in the upper torso of the first body, that of the pilot. The two 'fishermen' are interviewed and ask for a reward. The team discover substitute parts in the plane; they decide they need to find whoever shot the pilot. They find an empty brief case; and, alive, Sommer, the head of the insurance firm whose managers were on the plane. They take Sommer to hospital. A woman's body is found five miles away. It's that of Christina, senior accountant of the firm, and the second passenger out of her seat (deduced from absence of seat belt burn on the body). Her hands are hurt: first of several swift flashbacks to the possible scene of her death. Horatio visits her mother and they talk: Christina 'battled depression' in high school and was 'so good at keeping secrets'.

Horatio reveals to colleagues that the management team were going to Washington to appear before the SEC (Security and Exchange Commission) on charges of fraud. Calleigh discovers that the door opened in flight. Other research shows the exit door pins were tampered with. 'Let's find out who worked on that plane.' They find the (Hispanic) worker who filed down the pins, but deduce that the door was opened from the inside: they release him.

Sommer is interviewed in hospital. He claims not to recall anything, then says that he was in his seat (though he has no seat belt burns) and that Christina had been drinking and behaving oddly, hinting she killed herself. He seems puzzled at a mention of gunshot. They fingerprint him and make tests on Christina's hair which reveal that she used anti-depressants and tried to kill herself six months ago. The aircraft's black boxes seem to be missing. Sommer's fingerprints are all over the aircraft door. Horatio and Megan try to reconstruct what happened and decide there was a struggle, with Christina hanging on to the door. Sommer is discovered to have checked himself out of hospital.

Eric and Tim ask the fishermen/poachers for items they accuse them of looting from the crash site. They retrieve the black box from a tank of baby alligators. The box gives them the last few moments of cockpit sounds. These are manipulated to discover seventeen seconds of struggle, but no sound of a bullet fired. They search Christina's apartment. Ballistics expert Calleigh has discovered there was no bullet but that a substandard bolt killed the pilot. Horatio notices the fire extinguisher is missing and speculates that Sommer used it to force Christina off the plane.

The team discovers that the plane's door had substandard parts. Copies of subpoenas reveal that the plane was taking insurance company executives to an SEC hearing over fraud allegations. The woman whose body was found miles from the crash was a whistleblower (exposing corruption in the company). The company chief is later found hanged.

Horatio talks again with Christina's mother. He reads out the beginning of a letter she had written exposing the fraud, over shots of the team working. The episode ends with Horatio thinking of the whistleblowing woman, and mentally 'saluting' her, as her words 'without the truth we ourselves are powerless' act as voice-over.

Discussion

That took a long time! But hopefully it gave you a chance to see how the arrangement of the plot(ting) differed from the story, which we are able to reconstruct by the end. It offers pleasures which the straightforwardly told story would not have done. Always ask yourself 'How else could this have been done?' when analysing the arrangement of a narrative.

Q   When is the earliest story event dealt with in the plot?

A   Christina's suicide attempt (revealed via analysis of a piece of her hair) six months before, as she wrestled with her feelings around revealing the fraud.

Q   What other events are deliberately 'delayed' or altered for the sake of narrative pleasure?

A   The delay in finding the black box keeps us speculating in the absence of 'firm' evidence.

The discovered brief case could have been full of revealing documents. Christina's body could have been found first, along with trails to this full knowledge. The team look for clues to a gunman for a good part of the episode, which turns out to be a red herring, as does the quarrel about who is in charge of the investigation: CSI or 'the Feds' (though this contributes to 'character' another key pleasure of narratives; more later).

Red herring: something that draws attention away from the central issue, as in 'Talk of a new factory is a red herring to take attention away from redundancies.'

The expression (dated to the late 1800s) alludes to dragging a strong-smelling smoked herring across a trail to cover up the scent of a hunted animal and throw off tracking dogs (adapted from www.answers.com).

ACTIVITY 2.13

Q   Can you find any other delays or red herrings in the episode summary? To help focus on plotting and time shifts, make notes on moments when your chosen text goes into 'real time' (i.e. when the length of time taken by events on screen corresponds almost exactly to the length of time they would take in real life).

Q   When do these shifts happen, and why do you think they happen?

Q   Would you say this episode handles a whodunit, a howdunnit, or a whydunnit puzzle?

Todorov

Todorov's theory can be applied to this episode. But the 'once upon a time' moment, when opposing forces are 'in balance', is disrupted very fast, indeed it hardly lasts the length of the title sequence. The interesting question of where else it could have started has already been broached. To start with the 'disruption' being Christina's mental struggle as she decides to 'blow the whistle' would place the story in a different genre or group of fictions, and set up different expectations and enigmas. It might be the start of a corporate crime thriller or an 'issue' drama, with a strong interest in corporate corruption. And the new equilibrium (crime solved, a kind of justice done) is fragile, as always with series and serials: we know they'll need a new story for next week!

Q What values are confirmed in the final equilibrium?

A Though the issue of corporate corruption is raised, it is narrativised so as to be 'at the side' of the investigation. And the suicide of the 'villain' perhaps softens the verdict on those misdeeds – much more than an arrest would have done.

Applying Propp

Propp's much earlier theory, perhaps because it is so broad, can still be applied. The characters here do indeed fall into certain character roles (hero, helper) though to a limited extent, and there is indeed 'solution of a task' which, along with 'punishment of the villain', coincides with narrative closure. But you may argue that suicide as 'punishment' softens the character to such an extent that we're not really invited to think of him as a villain. And the 'hero' sometimes seems like the whole team, even if Horatio is clearly in charge, and picked out for narrative interest.

Applying Barthes

Barthes argued (in 1970) that a text (from the Latin word meaning 'tissue') was not one thing, but a weaving together of different strands and processes, some of them 'internal' to the story, some making connections to its 'outside' or the rest of the real. Few now would find the theory as striking as it seemed when first published, but it is still interesting to consider in how many different ways readers are given access to stories.

Barthes suggested that narrative works with five codes, which together 'activate' the reader. The two codes which are 'internal' to the text are:

- the 'enigma (or hermeneutic) code', which sets up and usually solves major puzzles. Here the main one occurs at the start of the episode: why did this plane crash? At least two kinds of pleasure are involved: it can be as enjoyable to 'know' the answers as it is to have those predictions confounded by the twists and surprises of the narrative. Of course this does not apply to all genres (think of musicals).

- the action (or 'proairetic') code, which makes complex actions 'readable' through small details so we don't need to have everything spelt out. Here the sight of the stretcher with Sommer on it signals a whole sequence of 'taking into hospital', so it is no surprise we next see him in a bed.

Then there are codes that point out of a story, and relate it to the rest of the culture:

- the semic code, which involves all the connotations built up around the characters and their actions. These stem from culturally recognisable discourses and patterns of meaning, such as those around 'powerful professional women' for *CSI: Miami*. (Barthes and other deconstructive writers were relatively uninterested in the questions of 'character' that arise for fans of this series who conduct heated debates around Horatio and whether he is too infallible, controlled, impassive to be satisfying as a 'character', for whom flaws and a personal life are required.)

- the symbolic code, which embodies the substitution of a small or concrete thing for a bigger, abstract one. The unrealistic darkness of the team's labs perhaps works in a symbolic way, as in *film noir*, to suggest the *moral* darkness of the world into which they're throwing the *light* of scientific investigation.

- the cultural or referential code, which anchors the text in its historical context, and points out of it towards that. In this episode there are lines like 'Most whistleblowers are women', which signal a contemporary fact, as well as using a contemporary word for someone who exposes corruption. 'The Dolphins' is an even more specific reference to a Miami football team. Of course there is also much audio-visual footage of the Florida setting, familiar to both those who live there and those worldwide who watch US TV and movie fictions.

Applying Lévi-Strauss

Lévi-Strauss is less interested in the chronological plotting of a single story (though that is how his 'syntagmatic' group has come to be used) than in repeated elements and their systematic relationship, usually across many stories. He called these the 'paradigmatic' aspect of myths. Nevertheless, the 'binary oppositions' into which these can sometimes be arranged are often applied to individual stories as a useful way into their value systems. A Lévi-Straussian approach to the *CSI* series overall might locate it within the abiding binary 'crime/law and order' and ask:

Q How does it embody this binary – through contrasts of characters, settings, actions?

Q How does it fit into broader US TV treatments of that binary?

Rapping (2003), for example, argues persuasively that there has been an overall shift in such US TV. The progressive 'defence attorney' crime fictions of the 1960s and 1970s, often featuring compassionate fighters for the underdog, were replaced in the early 1990s with series focused on heroic chasers and prosecutors. This is due partly to the rightward shift of US politics, but also to the difficulty of presenting defence attorneys sympathetically after their role in several high-profile trials of the very wealthy, like OJ Simpson (see the jaded view of the law in *Murder One* (1995–6) and *LA Law* (1986–94)).

We might also point to the ways that the different detection methods of Megan and Horatio (she insisting on staying strictly with the evidence; he often citing a 'gut feeling' for an idea) are consistently opposed, and relate to a much broader historical contrast of the same kind in many crime fictions.

Narratives, institutions, ideologies

Branigan's (1992: 3) formulation of narrative as 'a way of organising spatial and temporal data into a cause-effect chain of events with a beginning, a middle and end that embodies a judgement about the nature of events' sums up a lot of what this case study tries to apply to narrative in general. And Rapping's argument helps us locate the series ideologically.

But *CSI: Miami* is also a specific TV series, or rather franchise (not a novel or a single film) in a hugely competitive market. This shapes how it tells its stories. For example, it is shown mostly on advertising-funded TV channels, so you probably noticed that parts of it suddenly included a few seconds of spectacular aerial views, unmotivated by the story's needs. These offer themselves to the purchasing network as possible 'ad breaks', allowing people a few seconds to return from the ads back to the narrative. Equally the episode can be watched without these sections interrupting things, an advantage where different regulatory regimes means that ads do not interrupt programmes as often as on some US networks.

The show also deploys audio-visual narrativity: it tells the tale differently from the language forms which most of our theorists considered. For example, the opening sequence is an excitingly choreographed combination of music, cutting and the plane crash, which smoothly and shockingly culminates in the fuselage hitting the water, almost as the fishermen's lines do. As well as opening the narrative, it promises *how* it will be told – smartly, smoothly, slickly but also so as to provide thrills and an exotic locale.

ACTIVITY 2.14

How do you feel the title music works in setting up expectations of the narrative to follow? Why do you think it was chosen? Which track would you choose?

Though it's mostly the Florida Everglades setting that is used here, in other episodes Florida more broadly offers:

- a potentially big Hispanic audience
- narratives centring on border-crossings, smuggling, drugs, refugees, etc.
- a circling round the seedy, glamorous and bizarre aspects of its often sordid 'entertainment industries'
- audience genre knowledge of 'gangsters going south for the sun'
- overall the 'wet heat' atmosphere of fetid swamps, with their moral connotations (see the film *Wild Things* (US 1998), especially the title sequence, for similar resonances).

In fact the series was shot in LA; the non-laboratory settings are often anonymous hotel rooms (especially the now generically horror-laden bathroom) or the sprawling housing of the Miami suburbs.

The use of **CGI** (computer-generated imagery) and ingenious 'body' effects for some of the laboratory scenes likewise form a kind of spectacular visual 'pleasure', which is offered in especially vivid ways by film, TV and computer games. The body effects originate in horror, and have spread to 'medical procedurals' like *ER* and *Casualty* (see Jacobs 2003) in recent years. The science-related CGI effects in many ways substitute for the 'Dr Watson' function, the

---

ACTIVITY 2.15

Jot down what different kinds of narrative might work best in each of the three locations of the *CSI* series: New York, Las Vegas and Florida. How would you use the audio-visual potential of the different settings?

---

character who needs fairly simple things explained. Here, the visuals will do that explaining. Maybe, in narratives where the emphasis of the puzzle has shifted away from actually 'catching the bad guy', the effects stand in for the excitement of the now missing chase.

However, it has also been suggested that this flashing hi-tech science is the hero or star of the show, literally the 'light in the darkness' of many scenes. (This is much more the case than in the British equivalent, *Waking the Dead* (BBC 2000–) though the website screensaver uses this element.)

Figure 2.11 The British equivalent: *Waking the Dead* (BBC 2000–). Similarities? Differences?

But it produces the problems of impoverished characterisation, which many fans complain of. The characters (especially Horatio) are said to rarely make mistakes and show little emotion. The little speeches of the forensic surgeon to each corpse, 'Hello you . . .', seems the licensed space where some emotion can be expressed. Moreover, the series is notably bereft of car chases and shoot-outs.

This blankness could be argued to be part of the hard-boiled tradition, and Horatio's manner is softened in the discussions with Christina's mother and in his mental 'salute' to the whistleblower at the end.

Overall, however, time spent on developing such interiority, or doubts, is generally limited, partly because the team spend so much more time 'dishing out exposition' to explain the technical terms, than showing emotion or having complex lives, in or outside work, or indeed, arguing about the broader issues (here, corporate capitalist corruption) raised by particular crimes.

'We subtly develop the characters. Every so often I get a call from Billy [William Petersen, who plays Gil Grissom in the Las Vegas version] saying "You're turning the show into a soap opera" and I tell him we're not' (McLean 2005).

ACTIVITY 2.16

What do you feel about such narrative directions in any of the CSI series? Is it becoming a 'soap opera'? What might be the advantages of that in a police series? You might consider Cagney and Lacey (CBS 1982–8) and NYPD Blues (ABC 1993–2005) as well as The Bill (ITV), examples of crime detection narratives with this different kind of weighting.

ACTIVITY 2.18

Take this, or any other episode of the CSI series and time how much of it is devoted to shots of the technology they use, without dialogue. Consider in what other ways the central crime could have been handled by the script.

'Such is the trust placed in CSI by its viewers, it has had a discernible effect on applications to study forensic science, among women especially. It has also got US juries demanding higher – perhaps too high – standards of proof from real crime scene investigators' (McLean 2005).

ACTIVITY 2.17

Q How do you feel the character of Horatio works in relation to these debates?

Have you seen the Dead Ringers 2005 parody: CSI Balamory? On which elements does it focus? If you haven't seen it, try to script a possible parody.

The exaltation of hi-tech science as that which will save us, with its supposedly infallible accuracy and enlightenment, is the reason for this. McLean (2005) speculates that the reasons for its swift popularity was that it was 'very black and white – the evidence never lies – it was comforting in a grey world'. But this means that the series lacks a whole aspect of real-life crime investigations – failure to conclude a case, or even the making of mistakes, with horrendous results for those convicted. These parts of the representation and narrativisation of science in CSI: Miami are among the most ideologically powerful and limiting parts of its workings.

References

Branigan, Edward (1992) *Narrative Comprehension and Film*, London: Routledge.

Brunsdon, Charlotte (1998) 'Structure of anxiety: recent British television crime fiction', *Screen*, 39: 3.

Jacobs, Jason (2003) 'Genre and context', in *Body Trauma TV: The New Hospital Dramas*', London: BFI, pp. 17–53.

McLean, Gareth (2005) 'CSI: Tarantino', *Guardian*, 11 July.

Rapping, Elayne (2003) 'The return of the attorney-hero: politics and justice in the prime time courtroom', in *Law and Justice as Seen on TV*, New York: New York University Press, pp. 21–47.

Further reading

Brown, S. (2003) *Crime and Law in Media Culture*, Buckingham: Open University Press.

Cohen, Stan (2002) *Folk Devils and Moral Panics*, 3rd edition, London: Basil Blackwell.

Cooke, Les (2001) 'The police series', in Glen Creeber (ed.) *The Television Genre Book*, London: BFI, pp. 19–23.

Ditton, Jason and Farrall, Stephen (eds) (2001) *The Fear of Crime*, Aldershot: International Library of Criminology.

Sparks, Richard (1992) 'Television, dramatisation and the fear of crime', in *Television and the Drama of Crime: Moral Tales and the Place of Crime in Public Life*, Milton Keynes: Open University Press, pp. 78–98.

Other resources

http://www.itpmag.demon.co.uk/Downloads/TVCrime.pdf.

www.allyourtv.com.

ww.moviefreak.com.

CSI series are available either in boxed sets or sometimes as Channel Five repeats. See websites like www.tvtome.com for details of other episodes etc.

3 Genres and other classifications

- Genres and classification
- Repertoires of elements
- Examples of elements and their fluidity
- Status, 'art' and genres
- Genres, escapism and verisimilitude

- Other kinds of classification
- Conclusion
- References
- Further reading

Genres and classification

All media output is classified by:

- its makers
- its marketers, reviewers and official classifiers or censors
- its 'consumers'.

Marketers, critics, and academics use rather different terms for groups of films. *Choices* (rental shop) *DVD Guide*, April/May 2005, quoted forty-three titles for release:
action 7; comedy 11; children's 3; drama 11; thriller 4; horror 6; action thriller 1.

These classifications (horror or thriller? 'R18' or 'PG'? 'art' or 'schlock'?) have material effects on the ways we encounter, enjoy and understand media. They shape the status of works and their ability to get made at all, and then to withstand marginalisation. This chapter focuses on 'genre' and other ways of grouping or framing texts and thereby creating expectations and evoking familiarities.

'**Genre**' is simply a French word for 'type' or 'kind', as in biological classifications of plants and animals (mammals, reptiles, etc.). In fact its biological association is useful as it helps us think about how genres change, mutate, produce hybrids – like species. Genre is one of many forms of **classification**, rather like *maps*. Road maps always have to leave many features out, and to emphasise only some features of a landscape in order to be useful. Gardeners classify plants into 'weeds' and 'proper plants' when of course, by another system of classification, like botany, all of these are 'plants'.

The anthropologist Mary Douglas studied the ways some substances are classified as 'dirt', which she defined as 'matter out of place', highlighting the extent to which a notion of 'dirt' is partly based on taboo or classification systems.

'Genre' is often taken to imply cut-and-dried, simple boundaries: 'just another' horror or western. 'Once you've seen one, you've seen them all.' But in fact there is always both **repetition and difference** at play in genre products.

An example: a lightbulb joke depends on the same kinds of knowledge and expectations for its audience as any genre product. Unless you've never heard one before, when you hear the question you know that a joke is involved (a genre aiming to produce laughter) and are therefore likely to begin thinking in certain directions rather than others for the answer. In other words, you operate a kind of classification of it – as *not* being a serious question, as *likely* to involve certain kinds of play. If you enjoy lightbulb jokes, part of your pleasure is that you both sort-of-know and don't-quite-know what to expect from it. In other words, a *system of expectation* is set up around it, one which involves both repetition and difference, and which depends on you knowing a generic classification ('joke'). The repetition is of the bare framework of elements: a lightbulb, a group of people about whom certain stereotypes exist, a number which relates the two amusingly. The difference lies in *how* the particular

Q   How many folksingers does it take to change a lightbulb?

A   Six. One to change the bulb and five to sing about how good the old one was.

Q   How many Real Men does it take to change a lightbulb?

A   Real Men aren't afraid of the dark.

Q   How many mystery writers does it take to change a lightbulb?

A   Only one, and they usually give it a surprising twist at the end.

ACTIVITY 3.1

Zap through the channels on your television or radio. Look at title sequences.
- How quickly are you able to tell what kind of programme or music is on offer? In seconds?
- How were you able to tell? What kinds of differences are signalled through music, colours, kinds of dialogue, voices, pace of editing, costume, lighting, etc.?

Try turning down the sound on the title sequence of a television genre and substituting another kind of music.
- What difference does this make?
- Can you tell gardening or cookery programmes from motor racing coverage just by the title music, for example? Or by the kinds of voices used?

connections between those elements will be made *this* time. As the genre becomes established, play can be made with its conventions. Part of the pleasure is often in O.T.T. references to well-known stereotypes.

'Genre' describes the ways that companies producing and trading in media goods try to minimise risk by grouping and selling their products through established expectations. Economically this helps to predict expenditure in the costly and volatile media business, which requires some **standardisation** of production. This was true of the 'production line' of the Hollywood studio system (from around 1925 to 1950) and is still true of many 'in-house' productions of the BBC and ITV. Television companies need predictable annual income, whether from the licence fee (BBC) or from selling advertising space (ITV) or from selling ad space plus subscription fees (cable and satellite companies).

If output can be settled into broadly familiar groupings – for example, TV into 'light entertainment', 'news' or 'current affairs'; films into thrillers, romantic comedies, etc. – then economies of scale can operate. This means that because of the sheer scale of repeated production, similar sets, scriptwriters, key actors, etc. can be profitably reused, rather than made or searched for afresh for each media product. It also means that output can be predicted and therefore advertised, marketed, contracted in advance and so on. And it means advertisers can be assured they have access to certain audiences and scheduling times. Traditionally British soap operas such as *EastEnders* and *Coronation Street*, for example, have promised large audiences since they have been key to building a channel's 'audience share' in the early evening. The long-running *Coronation Street*'s capacity to do this made it worth Granada building a permanent set and employing a serial historian to avoid embarrassing mistakes in the storyline for loyal viewers.

Standardisation has a double meaning. It can signify 'sameness'; but can also denote the maintenance of standards, in the sense of quality: worth bearing in mind in the debates around 'sameness' and 'difference' in media and cultural studies.

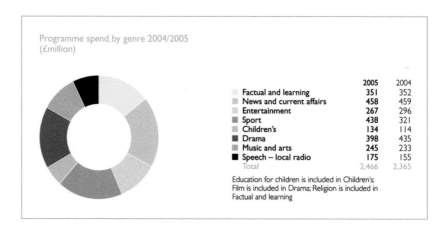

Programme spend by genre 2004/2005
(£million)

	2005	2004
Factual and learning	351	352
News and current affairs	458	459
Entertainment	267	296
Sport	438	321
Children's	134	114
Drama	398	435
Music and arts	245	233
Speech – local radio	175	155
Total	2,466	2,365

Education for children is included in Children's; Film is included in Drama; Religion is included in Factual and learning

Figure 3.1 BBC TV 'Programme spend by genre' chart, BBC Governors' Annual Report 2005

But recent developments – in cinema since the break-up of the studio system (in the late 1950s), and in broadcasting since the founding of Channel 4 in 1982 and then cable and satellite broadcasting – have fragmented 'the audience' and led to attempts to target ever more specialised, small audience segments or niches of potential audience. The term '**narrowcasting**' distinguishes these advertising-led developments from an older media ecology where fewer channels (just BBC and ITV for UK television) had the power to 'broad-cast' to larger audiences. Media forms have consequently become more and more **cross-generic** or **hybrid**, as audiences have grown accustomed to a huge amount of media output, so that different kinds of music, television and film clash and mix genres: **docusoaps**, drama-documentary, the comedy and 'reality' documentary mix of *The Office* (BBC 2002–3) or horror and comedy in the *Scream* series, and so on. This phenomenon is sometimes known as **intertextuality**, reflecting the variety of ways in which media and other texts interact with each other, rather than being unique or distinct.

Nevertheless, even if media products are mixed – cyber-punk, comic horror – these mixtures still involve *familiar* genres or categories. Indeed, a key part of thinking all this requires an awareness that these familiar

Niche originally meant a little nest or recess in a wall; **niche marketing** now refers to attempts to reach specialised but highly profitable groups of potential consumers with particular media products or aspects of products.

Hybridity: term originally used of the crossbreeding of plants. Here it describes media products mixing different sets of cultural values, technologies and/or formal properties: e.g. '**cross-over** hits' in pop music; '**drama-documentary**'. See 'subgenre' below.

Intertextuality: the variety of ways in which media and other texts interact with each other, rather than being unique or distinct. It is different from 'allusion', which is a more conscious referencing by one text of another.

Figure 3.2 Vampire-horror-action-comedy-teen-school series: the hybrid that is *Buffy the Vampire Slayer*.

classifications are themselves never simple, or simply standardised. Though such mixings are sometimes called 'postmodern', genre films have *always* involved some kind of 'hybridity' and were never 'pure' thrillers or romances or horror films. Hollywood (and earlier nineteenth-century cultural forms) always tried to attract as many audience segments as possible – often by lacing a 'male' genre with a romance element. *Casablanca* (US 1942), for example, plays with romance in combination with the elements of a political thriller and a male central character.

There are, of course, provisional boundaries – but these can mutate, to come back to the original meaning of 'genre'. Every film is slightly different in the way it plays the possibilities of its inevitable mixings and overlaps (see Altman 1999 and also Neale 2000, 2002 for interesting discussion). And to complicate matters further, some critics use the term 'cycle' to describe brief but fairly intense periods of production within a genre when individual films share a particular approach – the Dracula 'cycles' of the horror film for example (see our case study of *The Ring*). Don't treat these divisions as legally binding, or intimidating classifications. But do take from them a sense of the fluidity of the term 'genre'.

Repertoires of elements

Genre in media studies is often used only to refer to popular fictional forms. Documentary, for example, even though arguably a genre with its own conventions, audience expectations, etc., is left out of most major treatments of genres, including Neale (2000, 2002) (see Chapter 14). Thus genre becomes often another word for entertainment forms, and one way of dismissing these is to assert that 'They're all the same' or 'If you've seen one, you've seen them all'. For the owners of media industries, standardised practices are indeed a profitable part of making genre products. But this should not necessarily lead to the negative emphasis by reviewers and even viewers on 'sameness', 'repetition' or 'standardisation'. This underestimates the differences which are *always* involved in even the most repetitive-seeming genres.

Audiences understandably seek the pleasures of the familiar. We enjoy the ritual and reassurance involved in knowing *broadly* what 'might happen' in a particular media text. Yet genres are not all the same. Different genres appeal to different audiences, and to different tastes within the same viewer. And further, there are mixes or hybrid forms of these. But even the output within separate genres is not the same as other industrial products. You may hope that each tube of your favourite toothpaste will be the same, but you do not want absolute repetition in cultural products.

Whereas hybrid genres are produced by the interaction of different genres to produce fusions, such as romantic comedies or musical horror films, subgenres define a specific version of the genre by refining it with an adjective, such as 'spaghetti western' (see Corrigan and White 2004: 297).

'Taste classifies, and classifies the classifier', Bourdieu (1984: 6), leading theoretician of taste, class and cultural status.

If a work belongs to a 'high' cultural form such as tragedy, painting, classical music, then the words for audience expectations will often be 'codes', 'conventions', 'traditions', 'archetypes'. If it belongs to a more 'popular' cultural form, the language may involve 'stock formulas', 'clichés', 'a staple diet', 'recipe for success', 'stereotypes', 'churned out'. The factory and the kitchen provide highly classed and gendered terms for the inferior sets of ranking.

Watch out for this difference in the next reviews you read. Jot down the key terms used.

Even the apparently most repetitious form – the 'cover' version in pop music, where an artist makes his/her 'repeat' of an already well-known song – sells precisely on its blend of the familiar and the new. And 'new' here includes new audiences who don't remember the older version. Their response is part of the novelty.

An important development in thinking about entertainment genres has been to put them into the context of audiences' understandings and activities. Genres are no longer seen as sets of fixed elements, constantly repeated, but as working with '**repertoires of elements**' or fluid systems of learnt conventions and expectations. These are shared by makers and audiences, who are *both* active on *both* sides of meaning-making. The maker can rely on certain kinds of audience familiarity to play with, and the audience looks forward to playing within the stabilities. These conventions, and the expectations they can invoke, include the areas of:

- *narrative* – how the stories in a genre usually begin and conclude, what kinds of characters are at the centre of the fiction, etc.
- *audio-visual codes of signification* (for which the terms **iconography** or *mise en scène* are sometimes used), which would include settings (the western's classic landscape; the hi-tech arena of SF), costumes, lighting and even certain stars' physical presence.
- *a relationship to the rest of the real world*, including perceptions of how realistic the genre is seen to be, and how it handles the ideological values of the area it covers (e.g. war, **romance**, crime).

Iconography: a term from art history, originally referring to books of the fifteenth and sixteenth centuries guiding artists as to the correct colours, gestures, facial expressions, etc. with which to encode Christian doctrine. Since cinema and television work with *moving, audio-visual* images, the term 'signification' (see Chapter 1) is probably more useful.

Examples of elements and their fluidity

Let's take what is often called romance, or 'chick flick' (and is part of the hybrid form 'romcom'). Like many much used commercial and theoretical terms, these confuse different elements. Romance originally referred to

The term *convention* is usually understood negatively, as a set of rules which will simply reinforce and repeat normative values. But conventions, precisely in order to survive, need to be able to adapt and shift. Critics of entertainment forms often imply that each product should be utterly different. But if any story, or video game, or melody, were *utterly* different from all others, we would have no means by which to understand it.

For example *Reservoir Dogs* (US 1992) was praised for its 'difference' and 'originality'. But these qualities were to some extent dependent on generic conventions. It played with and against the expectations of the male-centred action adventure film, almost in arthouse ways. It involved: a crime; intense relationships, exclusively between men; gory violence. Within this 'sameness' or familiarity, the pacing and arrangement of the elements from the repertoire could be experienced as 'difference': the unusual plot and story shape, the importance given to a quirky kind of dialogue, the handling of violence, the very individual use of pop music and so on.

medieval tales of knights, honour, battle – and the (often adulterous) love of characters like Lancelot and Guinevere. 'Romantic', as we now understand it, inherits feelings (of longing, of unrequited or troubled love, etc.) from the love strands in these earlier 'romances'.

Romantic comedy refers to a hybrid form, which mixes comedy and romance situations. And chick flick usually refers to a film defined by its primary audience ('chicks'??) and called 'women's fiction' when it takes book form. The *narrative* will often start with the arrival into the life of the female 'hero' of a male who interests her romantically. This sets in play situations involving, for example, the nature of intimate or sexualised relations between men and women, or expectations about being single and thirty, or how to combine work and marriage, etc. The narrative will often proceed by means of intimate conversations and encounters, coincidences, mistakes and so on, delaying and thus intensifying the audience's desire for the couple(s) to 'get it together' (though often desire is prolonged by this not happening). *Ideologically* it is suggested (see La Place 1987 for summaries) that the particularly close and caring attention paid to the woman by the hero provides female readers and viewers with a fantasy escape from the often inattentive men they are actually involved with. This figure is sometimes called the 'maternal male' and it may come as a surprise that if you look again at apparently macho figures such as Rhett Butler in *Gone With the Wind* (US 1939) they often act out these feelings at points in the script. Here Rhett is literally shown as more maternal than Scarlett. Mostly the 'maternal' relating to her is via a special and

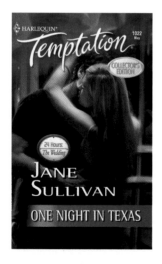

Figure 3.3 Though the tall dark mysterious man (a Mr Big?) is still present, are there changes to other promises in this cover of a Harlequin novel (the US equivalent of Mills and Boon)?

Figure 3.4 The surprisingly maternal Rhett Butler.

endlessly sympathetic understanding of her nature – such as mothers are traditionally supposed to have – along with a sexualised attraction/attractiveness.

Such intimacy was signalled in some of the *audio-visual conventions* of these 'women's films': less use of fetishised shots of women's bodies than in male-centred genres; much use of close-ups, especially focused on the eyes, of male and female actors; certain styles of intimate acting, voice and dialogue; and a particular kind of music – sweeping chords, piano and string sections of the orchestra – amplifying the key romantic moments (though see 'Genres, escapism and versimilitude' below). Also often deployed were lavish or fashionable clothes and 'utopian' domestic settings, often with 'tie-ins' to clothing and household advertising – see the parody of such marketing in *The Truman Show* (US 1998).

ACTIVITY 3.2

Q How far does this list of audio-visual conventions apply to your favourite romance? How are elements played with, or perhaps ignored? For example, is there more display of the male body now? More open discussion of sex and desire? More combination with different genres, such as the social satire?

Male genres have traditionally had higher status, in terms of budgets and critical esteem. They have been perceived and marketed as:

- more 'real', taken as guaranteed through reference to real battles, uniforms, generals, the training undertaken by actors etc. in combat films

- less emotional, though in fact they deal with *different kinds* of emotion.
- not escapist. Yet action adventure, for example, allows its audiences fantasy escapes from the complication and the mundaneness of the world of the everyday – the world from which the shark hunt takes the men in *Jaws* (US 1975), for example. However, it is usually more traditional 'feminine' genres (romance, musical) which get *classified* as 'escapist'.

It seems a shame that this avoidance of the emotional aspect of combat films, for example, means there is little discussion of some of its central pleasures: the space it allows for expression of male bonding and closeness, in the 'unit' of soldiers of very mixed background, as well as for expression of fears around physical fragility and the conditions of survival and trauma in war. These offer important connections to another kind of reality, that of justified fears.

The *Big Brother* format and generic links

Let's look at an example of a recent mixed TV form, often called '**reality TV**'. *Big Brother* has attracted large audiences worldwide over several series – an estimated 67 per cent of the UK population watched the first series at least once, and over 10 million viewers tuned in for the final episode (Hill 2002).

Big Brother is called a '**format**' by its makers, a category now often used in TV, and one which overlaps with 'genre'. Both *The Weakest Link* and *Who Wants to Be a Millionaire?* would belong to the genre 'quiz show' though their *formats* or set-ups differ. When a TV format is sold it can include everything from the presenting links, type of set, lighting, music, etc. – even the senior producer, who may be included as part of the contract. *Big Brother* lists nineteen countries on its part of the website for Endemol TV, which owns the format. *Pop Idol* (2002) was another example, with the twenty-part format sold to US Fox TV for a rumoured $1 million an episode after a hugely successful UK series.

Big Brother is like a genre in operating a loose '*repertoire of elements*', and in combining two distinct TV forms:

1 'reality television' (it is unrehearsed and unscripted, and uses surveillance camerawork)
2 game show

along with a third element:

3 audience involvement via interactive technology, including phone votes (hugely lucrative for the producing TV company) and live web broadcasts not shown on TV.

Figure 3.5 Endemol homepage.

Innovatively, its game show element has both teams and the individuals within them competing against each other; it uses highly selected contestants, willing to perform, and bright 'showbiz' or hi-tech lighting in the house.

Q How different would these shows be with low-key lighting?

Big Brother has proved to be a globally mobile structure. There is room for local cultural adaptations, involving e.g. the rules for voting contestants out; a choice of settings (celebrities in the jungle, in one adaptation); the coverage of nudity, sex, visits to the bathroom, jacuzzi; the use of celebrities coming into the house.

In all of this, whether you call it a genre or a format, the idea of a *'repertoire of elements'* which can be selected from or played in many ways, is very useful.

Status, 'art' and genres

In terms of the status ascribed to media works, 'art' is often a seal of approval, signifying a certain level of 'quality' and 'seriousness' and, commercially, the very important power of copyright. A question less often asked is: how do products succeed in getting categorised as 'art' or a 'quality' product? This is often a considered process, from the initial 'pitching' stages, which determine budgets, through decisions as to which genres have status and which do not, or whether key makers, cast members, etc. can be seen as 'authors' or 'serious stars', to audiences and preparing or framing products for particular kinds of reception.

However, 'art' is an unstable classification, heavily dependent on the investing decisions of big patrons like Maurice Saatchi. When the celebrity artist Tracey Emin lost her cat and put up 'lost cat' notices around her London neighbourhood they were taken down and treated as though they might become valuable works of art. Arguably this would have happened even if she'd written 'This is not a work of art' on them.

If a genre text can successfully claim 'artistic' or fully 'authored' status for itself then it may well occupy special media spaces. John Pilger, for example, can be seen as a documentary 'author'. He is allowed to make controversial documentaries on topics such as the invasion of Iraq; he is given comparatively large budgets to do so, but is usually announced in such a way as to distance the host television channel from too close association with his potentially awkward political positions. (And he is dependent on being commissioned in the first place.) The TV work of Russell T. Davies and Paul Abbott have similarly been allowed more 'artistic licence' than works by less celebrated authors.

Another example, from the level of reception. There is controversy over whether the BBFC (see p. 89) makes different classification decisions (on representing sexual activity, for example) depending on whether a text is considered 'art' and is therefore assumed to circulate in 'safer' environments, such as arthouse cinema, likely to involve different audiences from 'popular' cinema.

ACTIVITY 3.3

Q Thinking about it, do you agree there is an assumption that the audience for one genre (e.g. soap opera) could never enjoy other genre products (e.g. documentary)? Perhaps you would 'confess' to enjoying a much ridiculed form, such as *Footballers Wives* or *Celebrity Big Brother?* Or to boredom with a popular form? Or to liking a text at the 'serious' end of the cultural range: a documentary or a foreign film, perhaps categorised by your friends as arthouse (only for 'pointy-headed intellectuals')?

The status of different genres is revealed by the work put into getting *The Silence of the Lambs* (US 1991) considered as a thriller rather than a 'simple' horror film.

Textually it clearly fits, via its narrative, into the cycle of 'slasher' horror films. The figures of psychiatrist and serial killer, separated in the horror genre from *Psycho* onwards, are fused in the 'fascinating' figure of Hannibal Lecter (an 'outcast' figure, familiar from both horror and thriller forms). Jodie Foster plays a version of what the theorist Carol Clover (1992) called 'the final girl' of earlier, much lower-status slasher horror films. Though these were thought to be sexist, woman-hating fantasies, Clover suggests the series of attacks on women in them are avenged, not by a man, but by 'the final girl' to be attacked. Institutionally, the timing of its first release, Valentine's Day 1991, fitted the 'watching horror together' slot sanctioned as an excuse for physical contact for teenage couples. As *Premiere* magazine put it: 'If it is a choice between this and chocolates for Valentine's Day, the bon bons might be a better choice, but then again, *The Silence* promises to be so terrifying, you're bound to end up in your sweetheart's arms.'

But much publicity classified it instead as a 'thriller' or 'psychological thriller', a term which then easily invites the highly prestigious adjective 'Hitchcockian', a mix of authorship and generic status.

Each film genre displays or even showcases different capacities of cinema. 'Thrillers' are said to be broadly distinguished from 'horror' films by displaying:

- less emphasis on gory or 'bodily extreme' special effects
- an overlap with crime films, such as gangster or detective forms, but with more interest in characters who are usually outcast from sympathy
- the 'thrilling' or suspenseful qualities possible in cinema, especially in editing. This often involves a play with knowledge, putting the audience in the (enjoyably) agonising position of knowing what perils and time constraints face the hero. In this sense the thriller is a pleasurably masochistic genre for audiences – see the slogan in the woods which Jodie Foster runs through in the opening scene 'Hurt – Agony – Pain – Love it'.

Charles Derry, in his study of the suspense thriller, argues that this kind of suspense is not necessarily related to the solving of narrative puzzles or the 'vague question of what will happen next' (Derry 1988: 31). It depends on the expectation that a specific action might take place: 'During those moments when suspense is operative, time seems to extend itself, and each second provides a kind of torture for a spectator who is anxious to have his or her anticipation foiled or justified' (Derry 1988: 32). If you like thrillers, you like this agonising torture.

Q   Can you think of any scenes from recent films where this kind of 'torture' of the viewer takes place?

Though *Silence* could be said to fall between the two categories, publicity for it tried to replace associations of 'horror' by adjectives which produced a sense of ambivalence about the film: it is 'terrifying'; 'brutally real'; 'macabre'; 'dark'.

Casting used prestigious actors. Clarice Starling, FBI agent, is arguably an example of the slasher horror cycle's 'final girl'. But she is played by the Oscar-winning actor, Yale graduate, feminist Jodie Foster, in a much praised high-status 'Method' performance, researched via a week at FBI

HQ, cited as an effort towards 'realism'. The film also made *restrained* use of violence and avoided voyeurism and the goriest of special effects (see Jancovich 2000 for more of this argument).

ACTIVITY 3.4

Q *Silence of the Lambs* came out some time ago. Do you think the low status of the horror genre is changing, along with the importance of younger audiences, the popularity of Japanese films, etc.? The BBFC website and its general discussion of horror suggests it now sees the genre as often appealing to very knowledgeable (i.e. unshockable) fan or 'cult' audiences, and therefore as not deserving so many cuts.

Another example of the ways status works with classification of films is shown by reviews of Mel Gibson's film *The Passion of the Christ* (2004). It was taken very seriously by most reviewers, who classified it as a film dealing in a realistic and weighty way with a high-status subject (the last hours of the life of Jesus Christ). The signifiers for this were not only the subject matter but also the use of subtitles for the 'authentic' Roman and Aramaic dialogue (subtitles usually being associated with foreign 'art' cinema), the sonorous music and the film's slow pace.

Only a few critics focused on its emphatic use of hugely gory special effects around the crucifixion (classified by some as 'realism'), and the ways it was discussed as a kind of test of viewing endurance or toughness (as had parts of Gibson's previous film *Braveheart* (US 1995)). All this suggested that it might be considered as a kind of horror film. But this was a scandalous label for others, because of the low or even playful status of the horror genre and its often young, fan audiences.

Fewer critics pointed to ways in which the film stayed within the generic convention of 'biblical epics'. Christ (born in Palestine) and his family are played by fair-skinned actors (as in years of European tradition) rather than more realistic-looking, darker-skinned actors. And only certain parts of his teachings are focused on, certainly not those which would encourage radical social change on behalf of the poor.

Genres, escapism and verisimilitude

Whether horror, thriller, romance or 'reality TV', popular forms have often been seen as 'escapist' and therefore as a lower kind of cultural production than 'true art'. This often turns out to be because they involved industrial production and were aimed at non-elite audiences. Hollywood's products, for example, were initially intended to entertain working-class audiences for an evening between one day's work and the next, rather than to be experienced at elite gatherings, such as in opera houses. In addition, certain snobberies about America as inferior to Europe meant that Hollywood was assumed for years to be incapable of producing anything worthy of serious attention. This low estimate of the audience has until recently been inseparable from contempt for popular or genre forms, though now such objections have far less power.

> 'The so-called "fun" of commercial American cinema . . . would feel less oppressive if it didn't already inform the experience in the US of news, politics, fast food, sports, economics, religion and leisure in general, making it less an escape than the very (enforced) essence of American life' (Rosenbaum 2002).

The 'escape' that entertainment forms are said to provide is often described, contradictorily, as *both*

- carrying various kinds of **propaganda** or ideology (which suggests entertainment is related to 'the real')

and yet

- encouraging audiences to escape from 'real' questions via mere fantasy.

Though all stories and entertainments are imaginary, not 'real life' in one sense, they are a material part of most of our real lives in several others. We pay money to experience them, directly or indirectly; we spend time and imaginative energy 'playing' and trying out roles in their worlds; and genre forms such as soap operas, appearing several times a week, sometimes find themselves entwined with news debates. Moreover, we are never completely 'blissed out' in enjoying entertainment. Even the 'frothiest' or most gory kinds of 'escape' make connections to real-life questions of intimate relations, or anxieties about damage to the body.

In these debates we need to recall that all media forms, from television news to heavy metal music, are constructed through work with codes and conventions: there is no neat division to be made between 'the real' and 'the imagined'. Yet some genres are perceived as having more **verisimilitude**, or connection to the 'real'.

This 'real-seemingness' involves the ways that media forms tend to combine systems of what seems 'real', 'likely' or 'probable'. For example, the gangster film or the 'courtroom drama' (like other 'male' genres) have

Verisimilitude from the Latin for truth (*veritas*) and *similis*, meaning 'like', 'similar'. A term with key connections to '**realism**' gives them (and their audiences) higher cultural status than others.

always had higher status than, say, the musical, because they make a more explicit reference to public or political events from the world outside the film (using newspaper headlines, naming real-life politicians or criminals, and so on). Famous gangster or courtroom films worked in black and white or, later, in the sombre colours of *The Godfather* series or *The Sopranos*. Black and white is often seen as closer to the realist codes of documentary and historical footage. Until relatively recently gangster films made little use of the flamboyant colour, camera angles and movements enjoyed by fans of the musical (and felt to be 'unrealistic' by non-fans). Similarly the happy ending (so 'proper' for a musical) is not considered realistic in Hollywood gangster movies, even though many real-life gangsters are alive and well and living in expectation of a natural death. This was one of the ways that the ending of *Goodfellas* (US 1990) refreshed the conventions of the genre, and *The Sopranos* has taken this further, combining the mundane life of a gangster's family with his murderous 'business'. Then again, Jet Li and others have been argued to bring martial arts grace and almost the lightness of the musical to the gangster-like Hong Kong action movies.

> Marsha Kinder argues that it is the choreography of performers like Jackie Chan, Chow Yun Fat and Jet Li that demonstrates the 'difference' of the Hong Kong action film. She claims the musical as a structuring device, suggesting that Jackie Chan is a physical performer in the mould of Gene Kelly (Kinder 2001: 89).

Here are more examples of different kinds of cultural verisimilitude or 'realistic seeming-ness'. First, two which suggest how oddly mixed are the ways we experience 'appropriate' conduct of genres:

- Dinosaurs seem to exist in *Jurassic Park*: they can eat people, move neatly around a kitchen and even tap their claws in apparent impatience – all of which is highly improbable. But they cannot speak English (is this really all that less likely?) because that would be 'unlikely' according to the rules of how creatures behave in science fiction.
- Yet the sea creatures in the animated film *Finding Nemo* (US 2003) do speak American and Australian English, and most audiences find that no cause for comment.

Second, a suggestion on how an 'escapist' genre has had to 'update' itself to keep its real-seemingness. Romantic Hollywood comedies since around 1984, argues Krutnik (2000), needed to try to revive the potency of romance in an era where monogamy is discredited, along with romantic idealism. He argues that 'new romances' seek to reconcile old-fashioned romance with erotic openness: Meg Ryan's simulated orgasm in *When Harry Met Sally* (US 1998), or romantic comedies which find it very difficult to fully endorse the central character saying 'I love you', or *Four Weddings and a Funeral* (UK 1994) with its final proposal: 'Will you not marry me for the rest of your life?' William Paul (2002) has also argued that contemporary romantic comedy has to take account of women's increasing participation in work and other activities outside the home, of easily available contraception, and of changes in some men's sense of how they want to 'be a man'.

Further, in terms of cultural verisimilitude, such films now have to relate to another group of films aiming at younger audiences: 'gross out' or 'animal' comedies, like the *Animal House*, or *Porky's* series with their raunchiness and 'bad taste'. Such changes have impacted on the language and situations of 'romcom' (see *There's Something About Mary* (US 1998) and its notorious semen hair gel scene) and been woven into the kinds of narrative roles, performances, language and situations that work for this genre.

ACTIVITY 3.5

Make a note of the different kinds of fiction you enter into this week.
- How much time do you spend in each fictional world?
- How 'realistic' would you say it is? Why?
- Which is your favourite genre? Why?

An example of the ways that generic expectations frame news stories

'The arrest of Sir Mark Thatcher . . . reads like a twist in a rather implausible thriller. All the ingredients are there: exotic location; soldiers of fortune; mysterious puppet masters; political intrigue and, naturally, huge sums of cash. But the fabulous nature of this affair should not distract from the seriousness of the charges against Sir Mark and the men already on trial for plotting a coup against the government of Equatorial Guinea' (Editorial, *Independent*, 26 August 2004).

Other kinds of classification

Genre is not the only kind of classifying which positions or 'frames' media products for us, setting up expectations in some ways and not others. A formal classification system is operated in the UK for film, videos and DVDs and some other digital material (e.g. games) by the **BBFC**.

This Board has no regulatory powers but does decide for which audiences a product is presumed to be suitable, and sometimes amends or cuts it to fit the presumed nature of this audience, especially if it believes

BBFC: The British Board of Film Classification, formerly the British Board of Film Censors, is an independent, non-governmental body, which has exercised responsibilities over cinema since 1913, and over video since 1985, including DVDs. See its excellent student website at www.sbbfc.org.uk.

harm to children is at stake. It is charged with checking that material is not in breach of criminal laws (e.g. on cruelty to animals, children; on incitement to racial hatred, blasphemy, etc.). Final powers on film remain with local councils, which can overrule any of the BBFC's decisions, though this rarely happens. In cinema, the categories of those allowed entry include 'Accompanied by a parent' and 'Only when over 18'. For video the advice might be, for example, 'Contains moderate sex references and one hard drug reference'.

For British broadcast television, one key classification has been the timing of the programme ('before or after 10 p.m.' etc.), within what is called the Family Viewing Policy, itself based on, and helping to reinforce, a particular conception of the usual household. Like genre classifications, these processes have material effects. A programme (such as *Buffy*) which falls between 'teen' and older audiences may find itself cut when screened on BBC2 at 6.45 p.m. but uncut for a late evening showing.

Old joke about classification: 'If I like it, it's erotic, if I don't, it's porn'.

While *censorship* in the sense of cuts imposed by the BBFC does take place, it is now quite rare, and small scale. In fact, classification is not simply a post-production decision. Sometimes it involves self-censorship, 'vetting', etc. by the makers of films and TV about what they should and should not include for particular audiences, which genre to tell a story through and so on. Sometimes they will consult the Board at the very beginning of production for advice in these areas (e.g. 'I'm making a serious film about the health advantages of massage. What problems may I run into? Will it be classified as porn?')

Sometimes distributors such as Miramax will reshoot and re-edit many of the independent films it acquires, so that the product is adjusted to meet the demands of an assumed 'typical audience'.

Q   How far could ratings be said to work not as censorship but as advertising?

A   Potential audiences may be attracted, as well as put off, by different ratings labels. Parents want to know which films might frighten their children, and broadly whether they contain images of violence, hard drug use, etc. Equally, teenage audiences might want to seem 'cool' by feeling they are getting to see something which is in the next age range to their actual age. Film-makers will sometimes refuse to take out certain sections in order to get a more adult rating.

Melodrama (from Classical Greek *melos* = 'song', and *drama* = 'drama'): a term often used negatively, or as simply referring to 'women's films'. Historically it refers to a kind of theatre emerging from censored seventeenth-century drama, which was not allowed to use words. It evolved an elaborate language of gesture and spectacle, much of it inherited and reworked by early cinema, and crossing many genres. See Gledhill (1987).

Figure 3.6 A famous moment from a gangster movie shows how generic elements combine with other classifying and censorship pressures on early US gangster films. During the 1930s Depression, years of high unemployment, there was pressure on Hollywood from pro-censorship bodies to 'punish the gangsters', who were popular working-class figures in cinema. Narratively these films would therefore often end with a gangster's public death on the street, as here. The policeman embodies the Law, which calls the gangster to account and punishes him, while the woman, often cradling the gangster's head and weeping for him, perhaps embodies audience affection. The visual setting of the church steps may have, for gangster genre fans, resonances of repentance (from the early years of the genre). They also provide a sumptuous setting for a tableau or frozen expressive moment – very simply often embodying 'rise and fall' as the gangsters staggers down them to his death. Such expressive staging ideas were inherited and reworked from stage melodrama across a range of Hollywood silent and then sound-era films (see Gledhill 1987).

Certain genres are taken as the appropriate place for some but not other closely related kinds of activity. In television, for example, very recent events in the real world are categorised as part of the *news genre*. After a certain time, though, such events are classified as the *history genre* and come under quite different rules, notably involving less need for impartiality. This has been true of treatment in 2004 of the 1984 Miners' Strike and of the death of Dr David Kelly during the period leading up to the 2003 invasion of Iraq. Both of these have recently been given dramatic treatment, presumably because they are now seen as 'history' and therefore open to partisan treatment rather than the impartiality said to be the aim of news.

Q   do you think the distance between what is seen as 'history' and what is seen as 'news' is now shortening?

Conclusion

The bulk of this chapter has tried to argue that cultural forms require and indeed produce a certain amount of innovation, as well as the pleasures of repetition.

- What kinds of innovation are unacceptable or 'off limits' now? In which genres? For which assumed audiences? Why?
- How can we contest the power of statements, often made by Hollywood and other producer institutions, that 'the audience wants a happy ending' or 'you can't have a film dealing with politics like that'?
- How do commercial drives play in all this, such as major blockbusters' habit of building in opportunities for product placement, whether of mobile phones, cars or computer games?

A cultural approach to genres and formats is interested in such questions. It asks whether some of the repetitions within genres, such as the sense of what constitutes a 'happy ending', excludes some identities and imaginings, and might be reinforcing dominant or oppressive sets of values. Equally the pleasures of a particular genre or format, including their reassuring and ritual-like repetitions, can often reveal surprising connections to the structures we all have to make our way through, and the mental play we make with them.

References

Altman, Rick (1999) *Film/Genre*, London: BFI.

Bourdieu, Pierre (1984) *Distinction: A Social Critique of the Judgement of Taste*, London: Routledge.

Branston, Gill (2006) 'Genre', in Marie Gillespie and Jason Toynbee (eds) *Analysing Media Texts*, Buckingham: Open University Press.

Clover, Carol (1992) *Men, Women and Chainsaws: Gender in the Modern Horror Film*, Princeton, NJ: Princeton University Press.

Corrigan, Timothy and White, Patricia (2004) *The Film Experience: An Introduction*, Boston: Bedford/St Martin's.

Derry, Charles (1988) *The Suspense Thriller: Films in the Shadow of Alfred Hitchcock*, Jefferson, NC: McFarland.

Gledhill, Christine (ed.) (1987) *Home Is Where the Heart Is*, London: BFI.

Hill, Annette (2002) 'Big Brother: the real audience', in *Television and New Media*, 3, 3.

Jancovich, Mark (2000) '"A real shocker": authenticity, genre and the struggle for distinction', *Continuum: Journal of Media and Cultural Studies*, 14, 1: 23–35.

Kinder, Marsha (2001) 'Violence American style: the narrative orchestration of violent attractions' in J. David Slocum (ed.) *Violence and American Cinema*, AFI Film Reader, London and New York: Routledge.

Krutnik, Frank (2002) 'Conforming passions?: contemporary romantic comedy' in S. Neale (ed.) *Genre and Contemporary Hollywood*, London: BFI.

La Place, M. (1987) 'Producing and consuming the woman's film', in C. Gledhill (ed.) *Home Is Where the Heart Is*, London and New York: Arnold.

Neale, Steve (2000) *Genre and Hollywood*, London: Routledge.

Neale, Steve (ed.) (2002) *Genre and Contemporary Hollywood*, London: BFI.

Paul, William (2002) 'The impossibility of romance: Hollywood comedy 1978–1999', in S. Neale (ed.) *Genre and Contemporary Hollywood*, London, BFI.

Rosenbaum, Jonathan (2002) *Movie Wars: How Hollywood and the Media Limit What We Can See*, London: Wallflower Press.

Further reading

Buscombe, Ed (ed.) (1988) *The BFI Companion to the Western*, London: André Deutsch/BFI.

Gledhill, Christine (1997) 'Genre and gender: the case of soap opera', in Stuart Hall (ed.) *Representation: Cultural Representations and Signifying Practices*, London, Thousand Oaks, New Delhi: Sage.

Redmond, Sean (ed.) (2004) *Liquid Metal: The Science Fiction Film Reader*, London: Wallflower Press.

CASE STUDY: J-HORROR AND THE *RING* CYCLE

- • **Horror cycles**
- • **The beginnings of the *Ring* cycle**
- • **Replenishing the repertoire through repetition and difference**
- • **Building on the cycle**

- • **Industry exploitation and circulation**
- • **Fandom and the global concept of genre**
- • **Summary: generic elements and classification**
- • **References and further reading**

Horror cycles

Chapter 3 emphasises the fluidity of genre as a concept, the constantly changing repertoires of elements and the possibility of different forms of 'classification' by producers, critics and audiences. Horror is a genre with some special characteristics in cinema:

- • consistently popular since the 1930s in Hollywood and earlier in some other national cinemas
- • attracting predominantly youth audiences
- • until the late 1960s, not given the status of a major studio release
- • 'open' to the influence of changes in society – in both 'metaphorical' (i.e. through 'symbolic themes') and 'realist' (characters and settings) terms
- • repertoire expanded through the development of specific 'cycles' of closely related films
- • specific 'studios' associated in this development (e.g. recently Dimension, a Miramax brand)
- • specific writers/directors/stars have gained a high profile with fans.

In Hollywood, one of the most popular cycles of horror films of the 1990s began with *Scream* (1996) and *I Know What You Did Last Summer* (1997). This cycle involved a clever reworking of earlier films in which young people were terrorised by a 'slasher', eventually cornered by the 'Final Girl' (see the

references to Carol Clover's work in Chapter 3). The 'knowingness' about horror, and cinema generally, in these films was often developed as comedy (e.g. in *Scream 2* (1998), the classroom discussion about film sequels). The success of the cycle was exploited further with a 'spoof' of the 'spoof' in the *Scary Movie* series.

At the end of the decade, a rather different kind of film, a 'ghost story with a twist', *The Sixth Sense* (1999), was a massive worldwide hit. It was followed by the Spanish film *The Others* (2001) and several other ghost stories, some of which looked back to gothic traditions (the isolated country house shrouded in fog in *The Others*), while others were more contemporary in setting and aesthetic. ('Gothic' refers to the popular eighteenth-century novels in which shocking events took place in dark and mysterious castles – see Jones 2002: 2.) In the space of a few years, the focus had shifted to a new cycle (although 'slasher' movies continued to be made). Part of the shift was concerned with re-establishing horror as 'serious'/'chilling' rather than comic/ironic. It also saw horror regaining some status as a relatively big-budget, mainstream genre.

ACTIVITY 3.6

***Scream* and the horror repertoire**

Jot down quickly what you think are the main narrative, thematic and audio-visual stylistic elements in the comedy/horror repertoire of films like *Scream*.

Figure 3.7 The ghost does not appear until late in the *Ringu* narrative but Ryuji, the psychic, has a 'vision' in a crowded public square.

The beginnings of the *Ring* cycle

When DreamWorks released *The Ring* in 2002, they managed both to extend the new ghost cycle and to draw on elements from earlier 'teen horror films'. Other possibilities in terms of identifying elements in *The Ring* include the much earlier cycle of 'demon children' and 'possession', dating from the 1970s (*The Exorcist* etc.). However, the mixture of elements in *The Ring* is more complex than might at first appear, since *The Ring* was a remake of a Japanese film made in 1998 (i.e. before *The Sixth Sense*). To get the full

Ring synopsis

An urban myth begins about a videotape recording which kills anyone who watches it, precisely seven days later. Four teenagers die mysteriously and a reporter becomes involved when she realises that one of the victims is her niece. The reporter tracks down the tape and is cursed herself. Determined to solve the mystery and prevent her own death, she seeks help from her small son's father, her estranged partner. Her anguish increases when she realises her son has watched a copy of the tape. The couple eventually uncover the history of a young woman with psychic powers, seemingly murdered in the 1960s. Somehow, the ghost of this young woman is responsible for the videotape. They find the body of the girl in a well, but the 'ghost' remains active and the videotape remains potent.

benefit from this case study, you need to have seen one or preferably both of the versions of the *Ring* narrative. A very brief outline of the story elements is given in the box below.

The *Ring* cycle began in Japan with a 1991 novel, *Ringu*, by Suzuki Kôji. This was the first of three novels and a book of short stories, each of which deals with different stages in the evolution of the *Ring* phenomenon. Adaptations of novels (or *manga* – graphic novels) are common in Japanese cinema, as in Hollywood, but they do not necessarily confer generic status on the film version. In the case of *Ringu*, the film-makers changed the gender of the lead character and made the 'helper' her ex-husband, in order to meet the expectations of a cinema audience familiar with the Hollywood cycles described above. Director Nakata Hideo and screenwriter Takahashi Hiroshi had experience of low-budget horror films and they brought distinctive ideas to the presentation of the story.

The first *Ringu* film was a big success in Japan and prompted the adaptation of two of the other stories. The first sequel, *Rasen*, was actually released soon after *Ringu*, but failed to make an impact. A new sequel and a prequel were successful and the original film was remade for the first time (as a Japanese co-production) in South Korea. Further remake rights were bought by a Korean-American producer Roy Lee, who has since become the leading industry figure in the development of similar Hollywood remakes of East Asian films (see Heianna 2005). He sold the remake idea to DreamWorks.

By 2005 it was possible to identify a distinct cycle of films which shared a number of elements and which could all in some way be traced back to the success of *Ringu*. The impact of the cycle has been such that other, less closely related, horror films from both Japan and South Korea have received at least a DVD release in the UK and US – leading some critics (and fans) to refer to 'J-horror' and 'K-horror' as new classifications. Because the *Ring* cycle includes adaptations of the same basic story in Japan, South Korea and the US, we can explore the ways in which similar genre elements can be developed differently.

Replenishing the repertoire through repetition and difference

The successful exploitation of the *Ring* cycle can be explained in several ways. Horror's repertoire has expanded as circulation of films within the international market has become easier, especially via DVD distribution and internet retailing, and both film-makers and audiences have become more aware of what is on offer. *Ringu/The Ring* marks a development for both American and East Asian ideas about horror.

Characters

Ringu can be seen as responding to the long cycle of American 'teen' horror with its high school 'victims' and young female 'investigator heroes' (from Jamie Lee Curtis in *Halloween* and Jodie Foster in *The Silence of the Lambs* to Neve Campbell and Courtney Cox in *Scream*). In *Ringu*, the initial victims are high school students and the investigator is Reiko, a single parent desperate to protect her small son. In several of the J-horror stories, there are 'single-parent/child' relationships with children somehow 'caught' between separated parents. Family relationships (including those

between adult children and their ageing parents) are central to *Ringu*.

In the American remake, Reiko becomes Rachel, a protagonist who is at the same time both more assertive and more disorganised than her Japanese equivalent. Similarly the American boy is very different. It may be a function of child acting styles but, as in *The Sixth Sense*, the American boy seems unnaturally self-possessed next to the quieter (and perhaps more mysterious) Japanese child. There are some interesting representation questions here (see Chapter 5) about stereotypes.

If several characters are relatively easily transferred between cultures, the ghost, Sadako, is 'new' to western audiences, both as a visual icon and because of what she represents (see below for discussion on ghosts in Japan). Ghosts and ghost stories have always been important elements in Japanese (and Korean and Chinese) cinemas. Sadako's appearance – the long white dress, the long straight black hair masking the face – can be traced back to traditional Japanese stories from the seventeenth century and earlier. Samara in the American version retains something of the original, but struggles to match the simplicity and power of Sadako.

Figure 3.8 The opening section of *The Ring* follows the Japanese original very closely, with the single mother and her son visiting the funeral reception of their niece/cousin.

Setting

The writer Suzuki Kôji draws on Japanese ideas about water as a suitable 'medium' for ghosts and spirits to inhabit. Sadako has been imprisoned in a well and was seemingly born in a sea cave. The setting, complete with driving rain, islands, ferries, etc. as well as an overall colour scheme which privileges blues, greys and greens, is transferred to the American remake. These elements recur through the three *Ringu* films and are also central to *Dark Water* (from a Suzuki short story collection devoted to 'water horror'). Water as an element in horror is not unknown in American cinema, but the consistency of its use in these films is unusual.

Budget

This becomes an aspect of the repertoire in the sense that the Japanese film must work within the constraints of a low budget whereas the American film with $40 million to spend can afford spectacular effects. This alone may push the American film towards a more 'action-orientated' narrative.

Audio style

Perhaps the most distinctive formal difference between *Ringu* and American horror generally is in the use of sound effects and music. For a low-budget film, *Ringu* had a very sophisticated sound track:

> [Nakata] cites the ability to manipulate the degree of horror simply by changing the length of a sound, even by a mere tenth of a second. The soundtrack is the key. . . . It is a sense of horror driven by calmness that's shattered by a sudden change in tone that shocks the audience. Nakata's soundtracks are described as dynamic and exquisite.
>
> 'I tend to stress long intervals in my tracks,' he says. 'Other people tend to use different

sounds altogether to express horror, but I can increase the perception of it to the maximum by utilising a very quiet sound.'
> (from an interview with Nakata on http://int.kateigaho.com/win05/horror-nakata.html)

Nakata worked closely with composer Kawai Kenji, so: 'Your ear cannot separate the melody from the sound effects because they are all so well integrated in the overall soundtrack' (from an interview with Nakata on http://www.horschamp.qc.ca/new_offscreen/nakata.html).

Some of this survives in the American remake, but inevitably 'extra' music seeps in.

Visual style

The elements of water, rain and darkened rooms produce an overall look which is muted. It is different from the 'gothic' look of European and American horror (with dark shadows and silhouettes). Gabriel Beristain, the cinematographer for *The Ring Two*, sought to replicate this look in some way:

> For *The Ring*, cinematographer Bojan Bazelli had infused every frame with a textured, cyan (blue-green) look that lent the story a unique aura of foreboding. Many of the film's admirers singled out Bazelli for praise, citing his cinematography for a flair and style that transcended the typical approach to a horror picture . . . 'That was my first mandate for the project: blue and muted, with the tonalities of the first film. They wanted to preserve that look.'
> (Gabriel Beristain, quoted in Silberg 2005)

The 'look' was eventually changed for *The Ring Two*, because, as Beristain argued, the location had shifted in terms of place and season, but Nakata who directed the second American film insisted on keeping certain scenes in a 'monochromatic' look that went with the 'video world'.

'Tone'

The American remake came after the enormous success of *The Sixth Sense* which reintroduced the American audience to the ghost story and brought back a 'serious' tone to the horror film after the 'playfulness' of the *Scream*/*Scary Movie* films. Films like *The Others* built on this return to less 'gory', more psychological horror.

Thematic

The new cycle deals with 'ghosts', but not in the way that European and American horror tends to make use of them. Concepts of the 'supernatural' are different in East Asian cultures, partly because the Buddhist/Shintoist religions in Japan do not have such clear concepts of 'good' and 'evil'. In western stories, the narrative often climaxes with evil (i.e. 'diabolic') forces defeated by good ('godly') heroes. In the Japanese stories there is no such expectation. Ghosts in Japanese culture are in one sense much more 'personal'. Dead characters often come back to tell things to their families.

> In America and Europe most horror movies tell the story of the extermination of evil spirits. Japanese horror movies end with a suggestion that the spirit still remains at large. That's because the Japanese don't regard spirits only as enemies, but as beings that co-exist with this world of ours.
>
> (Suzuki Koji interviewed on http://int. kateigaho.com/win05/horror-suzuki.html)

Where there has been violence a ghost may return to the scene of the crime, seeking a means of 'satisfaction' or 'sleeping easy'. This is the basis for the *Ju-on* films (2000–5) in which all the people who enter a house are pursued to their deaths. The American series often have victims who are killed because they have 'sinned' in some way (e.g. teenagers having sex), but in *Ju-on* there is no 'justification' for the deaths.

The 'differences' between the American and Japanese films are not clear-cut. For instance, two teenagers die at the beginning of *Ringu* during sex – a cheeky comment on the American films? Certainly, Nakata and Takahashi are happy to name their American/European influences from *The Haunting* (US 1963) to *The Exorcist* (US 1973) and *Poltergeist* (US 1982). But it is the combination of elements from these films with the Japanese perspective – both in thematic terms and in the visual and aural aesthetics – which makes the films 'different'. Bound up in this 'difference' is a very strong element evident in much Japanese popular culture – the tension between the traditional and the modern. Japan is represented in global culture by both high-quality 'new technology' goods and traditional cultural activities such as *kabuki* theatre and *sumo* wrestling. The *Ringu* narrative takes a traditional ghost and marries it to a history of 'communication technologies' with audio recordings and photography as well as telephone technologies – in fact all forms of 'electro-mechanical' reproduction.

Perhaps the most interesting aspect of the thematic of the Nakata/Takahashi/Suzuki films is the emphasis on the disintegrating Japanese family. Family is just as important in East Asian cultures as it is in the US and the rise in the number of 'broken' marriages and single-parent families is a serious social issue in a society where social conventions still rely on traditional familial roles for men and women.

Tony Williams (1981) identified several 1970s films as 'family horror'. Instead of the threat of a monster coming from 'outside' (i.e. as in the 'European gothic' horror narratives of *Dracula* etc.), the monster was now 'within' that central icon of American society, the family. Horror was being employed to represent metaphors about the revolt against 'American values' that came in the form of Civil Rights, the rise of feminism, resistance to the Vietnam War and the collapse of confidence in American politics leading to Watergate and the impeachment of President Nixon. A similar 'crisis of confidence' has occurred in Japan since the stagnation of the economy in the 1990s.

Perhaps these films with their (single) children and estranged parents (and the disturbing absence or neglect of grandparents) are a metaphor for a society with a lack of vitality? Sadako is also the name of a girl from Nagasaki who became a worldwide symbol of the young lives blighted by the radiation from the atomic bombs dropped on Japan by the Allies in 1945. There is no obvious connection to *Ringu*, but the coincidence reminds us that Japanese genre films have often worked with a conscious subtext – e.g. the *Godzilla* films, starting with *Gojira* (Japan 1954), which reference the apocalypse of nuclear war.

Building on the cycle

After *Ring 0* (2000), the fifth film in the cycle, director Nakata and *Ringu* producer Ichise Takashige adapted a Suzuki short story not directly associated with *Ringu*. Japanese cinema has a strong genre tradition based on studio production procedures. The success of *Ringu* meant that Nakata and Ichise applied some of the same elements that had worked so well in *Ringu* to a slight story which could have been treated differently.

Dark Water appeared in 2002 and again featured a young woman, a single parent with a small daughter, attracting a ghost in a rundown apartment block. Some similar elements (e.g. high school girls terrorised by a ghost, a young female investigator) also featured in *Ju-on* (2003) directed by Shimizu Takashi and again produced by Ichise. This relentless horror film was first produced (by the same team) as a 'direct to video' or 'V-cinema' film in 2000. Following Japanese film industry practice for low-budget genre films, there are now several *Ju-on* films, perhaps as many as five.

With the success of *The Ring* remake, Hollywood producers were quick to exploit the new cycle themselves. Disney (Touchstone) invited Brazilian director Walter Salles to remake *Dark Water* for 2005 release; DreamWorks invited Nakata Hideo to remake his own *Ringu 2*, also for 2005, and Hollywood horror auteur Sam Raimi acted as executive producer for *The Grudge*, a relatively low-budget American

remake of the *Ju-on* story, filmed in Japan by Shimizu himself. Despite poor reviews, *The Grudge*, with Buffy star Sarah Michelle Gellar in the lead, quickly earned over $100 million in late 2004.

By early 2005, the phenomena of 'J-horror' and its Korean equivalent were well established, boosted further by productions elsewhere in East Asia. Korean films have managed to be both 'popular' – competing strongly with Hollywood in the Korean domestic market – and 'artistic' or experimental. According to Grady Hendrix (2004):

> The ghosts of *The Ring* and *The Sixth Sense* hover uneasily over much of 'K-horror' . . . the current cycle begins in 1998 when high-school ghost flick *Whispering Corridors* became a smash hit . . . a ghost story in which a spirit can't move on until the wrongs inflicted on it in life have been avenged.

Director Kim Ji-woon's *A Tale of Two Sisters* (2003) has been widely admired by critics and fans in the UK and is set for yet another American remake. In 2002 Kim joined Peter Chan and Nonzee Nimibutr for a Korean/Hong Kong/Thailand 'compendium' film of three horror shorts, simply titled *Three*. The Thai/Hong Kong connection has also supplied *The Eye* (2002) by Oxide and Danny Pang, Hong Kong brothers resident in Thailand. Several of the genre elements from *Ringu* appear in these films and in *Inner Senses*, the Hong Kong film from 2002 featuring the last role for film and pop star Leslie Cheung.

Industry exploitation and circulation

Altman (1999) suggests that film producers are to some extent responsible for developing genre cycles through their practice of including what are seen as successful elements of current box office hits in their future productions. At the same time, the marketing of current films will develop from currently successful strategies. In the West, horror films are often released

Figure 3.9 In this strange composition from *A Tale of Two Sisters*, a character looks under the kitchen sink for the cause of disturbance. Behind her, a figure with long black hair materialises for a few seconds.

in late October to provide an integral element of the 'Halloween experience'. In Japan they appear around the time of O-bon, the Buddhist 'Festival of the Dead' (13–16 August).

The profile of Japanese and Korean films in the UK has to a considerable degree been created by the independent distributor Metro Tartan and its video label 'Extreme Asia' – a broader classification than genre, simply implying that these films 'go beyond' what might be available from Hollywood. The company has given a limited cinema release to various titles via an arrangement with the UK exhibition chain UGC. Coupled with exposure via film festivals such as Rotterdam and Edinburgh, these releases have generated sufficient press and fan interest to kickstart successful video and DVD releases. The number of people who have seen *Ringu* in the cinema, on Channel 4, or on rented or purchased DVDs is still limited and considerably fewer than for the American remake. Nevertheless it is significant and has encouraged further interest by producers.

Another development in the media marketplace following the success of *Ringu* is the release of translations of Japanese novels in paperback in the US and UK. There is a strong relationship between genre fiction in paperback and on cinema and television – a relationship that media studies sometimes overlooks,

possibly in an attempt to distinguish itself from English literature. Popular Japanese cinema very often draws on novels as source material and the relationships between the films and the original novels of Suzuki Kôji (sometimes referred to as the 'Japanese Stephen King') are well worth pursuing (as are the *manga* versions of the stories with their adaptations to the combined visual/textual conventions of the graphic novel). The original stories prove to be much more 'Japanese' in their detailed descriptions of Tokyo locations and both more 'rationalist' in approach and much more masculine-centred in terms of the central characters, although the focus on Sadako remains.

The 'feminisation' of the stories to appeal more widely to young women in the cinema audience was first deemed a success in Japan, but was equally taken up in Hollywood. *The Ring* and *The Ring 2* both feature Naomi Watts, and Jennifer Connelly leads in *Dark Water*. These are two rising female stars and *The Grudge* helped to consolidate Sarah Michelle Gellar's career. The classification of these films is important if they are to reach the widest audiences. In America they all received PG-13 ratings and in the UK '15'. This opened up a horror market traditionally limited to 'R' or '18' rated films seen as off-putting to some female audiences. *Screen International* noted this trend (Kay 2005), suggesting that it was part of an organised industry move to seek to address the 'four quadrant audience demographic of male/female, young/old'. We might note here that all J-horror titles are written and directed by men. As a contrast, seek out *Ginger Snaps* (Canada 2000), scripted by Karen Walton.

Fandom and the global concept of genre

The *Ringu* 'phenomenon' is best represented by its 'virtual presence' on the internet. This exists in different forms. Several websites provide detailed histories of the development of the different versions of the stories, discussions of characters and storylines and generally answer questions via a FAQ (Frequently Asked Questions) page. The films also figure on various 'bulletin boards', email lists, etc. Contributors may simply want to know where to find films, but often they want to argue for or against the 'original' or 'remake' version of the stories.

These discussions are aided by the various online DVD retailers in South East Asia, since it is now possible to buy good-quality DVDs from Hong Kong, China and South Korea. So, even if a film has not been released in the UK or US, fans may have seen it on an imported DVD. Critics are important too. The chance to send preview DVDs to knowledgeable and influential horror genre critics, such as Mark Kermode in the UK, or to experts on Japanese or Korean cinema, means that distributors feel more confident that they can release a film with the prospect of some media coverage.

It is fans who identify and build an audience for 'cult films'. Matt Hills (2005) points out the way in which interest in *Ringu* also helped other Japanese genre films to gain a reputation in the West, particularly the more visceral horror/fantasy/science fiction films associated with directors such as Miike Takashi (e.g. *Audition*, Japan 1999) and Fukasaku Kinji (e.g. *Battle Royale*, Japan 2000). Hills goes on to observe (through a study of postings to 'The Ring Forum' on the internet) that American fans of the original Japanese films are sometimes surprisingly accepting of the Hollywood

remakes on the grounds that the 'clueless teens' who see these films may eventually find the originals as a result of their exposure. This may then threaten the status of *Ringu* as 'cult', but fans maintain their 'superiority' because they knew about it first and understand it best.

Summary: generic elements and classification

The story which begins in *Ringu* as a 'mystery' becomes a 'horror' story and then in *Ringu 2* turns more towards 'science fiction' with an emphasis on a rational explanation for what has happened. It includes the following elements drawn from the repertoires of the three genres:

- an urban legend among high school students
- a young woman as investigator
- a child in peril
- family conflicts
- science and the paranormal (a scientist with some paranormal powers)
- a classic ghost figure
- a mysterious video recording
- archive materials
- a muted colour palette
- an unsettling musical score and sound effects

- distorted photographic images
- a corpse in a well
- a scientist with a theory
- hospital patients with severe mental health problems
- 'possession' of a child
- an ineffective police investigation.

ACTIVITY 3.8

Working with repertoires

Look through the list of elements above. Which elements would you expect to find in:

- a horror film?
- a mystery film?
- a science fiction film?
- a thriller (see Chapter 3)?

ACTIVITY 3.9

Adaptations and remakes

Take any 'pair' of versions of the same story – either a Japanese film and its American remake or a novel/*manga* and its film version – and compare the use of elements from the various genre repertoires.

- Does the 'mix' of elements suggest a specific genre or a 'hybrid' form?
- How has the narrative changed because of either the cultural change or the change in medium?

References and further reading

Altman, Rick (1999) *Film/Genre*, London: BFI.

Heianna Sumiyo (2005) Interview with Roy Lee in *Kateigaho International Edition* posted on http://int.kateigaho.com/win05/horror-lee.html.

Hendrix, Grady (2004) 'Back with a vengeance: the psychic delirium at the dark heart of K-horror', *Film Comment*, 40, 6, November–December.

Hills, Matt (2005) 'Ringing the changes: cult distinctions and cultural differences in US fans' readings of Japanese horror cinema', in Jay McRoy (ed.) *Japanese Horror Cinema*, Edinburgh: Edinburgh University Press.

Jones, Darryl (2002) *Horror: A Thematic History in Fiction and Film*, London: Hodder Arnold.

Kay, Jeremy (2005) 'To PG or not to PG, that is the question', *Screen International*, 8 April.

Kermode, Mark (2005) 'Spirit levels' in *Sight & Sound*, August.

McRoy, Jay (ed.) (2005) *Japanese Horror Cinema*, Edinburgh: Edinburgh University Press.

Silberg, Jon (2005) 'Back to the well', *American Cinematographer*, April.

Wells, Paul (2000) *The Horror Genre: From Beelzebub to Blair Witch*, London: Wallflower.

Williams, Tony (1981) 'Family horror', *Movie*, 27/28.

Websites

Estigarribia, Diana (2002) 'Reeling: J-horror', posted on www.entertainment-geekly.com/web/general/jun2002/reeling_jhorror.

Gang Gary Xu (2004) 'Remaking East Asia, outsourcing Hollywood', posted on www.sensesofcinema.com/contents/05/34/remaking_east_asia.html.

Two fan sites dealing with the Ringu/Ring cycle

http://ringufan.intelligent-light.com/
www.theringworld.com/

(All web addresses live on 11 July 2005.)

(Note: In this case study, we have followed the Japanese convention for presenting names, giving the family name first and the personal name second.)

4 Institutions

- Defining 'institution'

- An institutional analysis of photography

- Applying ideas about media institutions

- Media institutions and society

- References and further reading

'Why did they do that?' It's a question you have probably asked, coming out of a film or watching a music video for the first time. We are puzzled because we have expectations about an artist – a director, an actor, a musician – or a particular genre. Behind the question is a suspicion that some faceless media corporation has imposed a new ending on the film or persuaded a band to use a new producer. If media studies had adopted the auteur or author principle as a means of understanding texts, the answer to the question would be simple – go and ask the artist. But media studies doesn't do that because it recognises that production is mainly an industrial and commercial process and it takes place in a social, political and cultural context. The shorthand way of describing the impact of the type of production process used, and the context of production, is to refer to it as '**institutional**'.

The concept of *institution* in media studies sometimes gets rolled up with *industry*, but we are keeping them separate. Chapter 7 deals with the economic and financial or business activities of media producers. The concept of institution deals with ideas drawn from sociology, psychology and politics. As such, the institutional aspects of media activities are sometimes difficult to grasp because they refer to less tangible processes and relationships than, say, company balance sheets or employment contracts. This chapter attempts to define what we mean by 'institutional' in media studies by working through examples of specific media institutions and then applying the ideas raised to a series of key debates which can in turn be picked up in several of the other chapters and case studies, allowing you to integrate 'institutional analysis' with such key concepts for our chosen institutions as '**objectivity**' and '**quality**'. Chapter 16 deals with regulation.

Defining 'institution'

> enduring regulatory and organising structures of any society, which
> constrain and control individuals and individuality – the underlying
> principles and values according to which many social and cultural
> practices are organised and co-ordinated – the major social sources of
> codes, rules and relations.
>
> <div align="right">(O'Sullivan <i>et al</i>. 1994)</div>

O'Sullivan here is referring to institutions generally, but let's think about
the different kinds of institutions you may have experienced.

We all grow up within a range of different institutions. Some of these
are 'formal' – education, the health service, the legal system. We are part
of these institutions. We know what to expect of the services they offer;
we know how to behave within them. We share (or perhaps tolerate and
sometimes come actively to oppose) their values. They are formal because
we are often legally 'registered' with them. But we also belong to a
range of social institutions such as 'the family', a religious community
perhaps or a club. Within this group too, our behaviour is controlled or
constrained even as we may share and activate ideas and values. We all
act, to some extent, in institutionalised ways. Everyone working with
or dealing with a sector of the media industries will also be subject to
'institutional constraints' as well as 'institutional opportunities'.

Let's take a simple example, a visit to a local multiplex cinema. The
film we are going to see has been produced in an institutional context,
'Hollywood'. It will be roughly 100–120 minutes long, in colour. It will
probably have stars and feature a music sound track and perhaps have links
to other media products, such as video games. Many of the decisions about
how the film was made are economic, but others are institutional – they
are concerned with how the production team work together, how they
have been trained to think about 'quality', 'professionalism', 'the budget',
'art', 'entertainment' and the audience.

Cinema is also a 'social institution' – as audiences, we share certain
values with the producers and we behave in the auditorium in a particular
way. In the UK we don't talk through the film and we watch it in the dark
– it isn't like this everywhere. The cinema is probably a CEA (Cinema
Exhibitors' Association) member and the adverts we see are subject to the
ASA code and monitored by the CAA (Cinema Advertising Association).
We expect the film to be given a certificate by the BBFC (British Board of
Film Classification).

We don't think too hard about 'cinemagoing' – it seems almost like
a natural process. But it has taken a long time for ideas about cinema to

develop. Why should a film be around 100–120 minutes in length? Why not one hour or four hours? Why only one film in 'the show'?

ACTIVITY 4.1

The culture of cinemagoing

Either

- go and see a Bollywood film in a cinema specialising in such films or try to go to a cinema in another country

or

- ask your grandparents about going to the cinema in the UK in the 1940s and 1950s.

How are these experiences different from Friday night at your local multiplex?

It is unusual now to have breaks in film screenings. But an 'intermission' in long films was common in the 1950s and 1960s and is still common in screenings of **Bollywood** films in the UK. Small cinemas used the break to sell ice creams, but the **multiplexes** prefer us to buy food and drink before the screening.

Classifying media institutions

Work on media institutions is similar to that on **genre** – the two concepts are closely related. Like genre, institution is a fluid term. In our first example above, everyone is part of several different institutions – as a family member, a student, a patient, etc. In the same way anyone working in the media or on any media text needs to relate to more than one institution – more than one set of relationships and processes. We'll explore what this means by working on an extended example.

An institutional analysis of photography

'Photography' is an example of a media *practice* – an organised set of media activities which has developed over a long period and is easily accessible as a means of creating a media text. Photography is also an *institution*, and that means that photographers and photographs are in some way subject to constraints or conventional modes of working. It's an interesting example of a media activity because, although a photograph can exist as a media text itself, most of the time we come across photographs as collections in an album or an exhibition or as photographic images which are used in other media texts such as magazines, newspapers, posters, websites, etc.

This dual role of the photographic image sets up a number of broadly 'institutional' questions, involving both the production and the reading of photographs:

- Is the photograph on its own the same as the photographic image reproduced in a magazine or newspaper?
- Can the meaning of a photographic image change, depending on the type of media text in which it appears?
- Do photographs have a different value or status, depending on the context within which we see them?

An analysis of some specific images will enable us to explore these issues. Figure 4.1 shows three images of people in the UK. In the first image a young man dressed as a boxer leans against a wall, in the second a middle-aged man in a suit is surrounded by young boys dressed for a mosque school and in the third three women are laughing together behind a shop counter, each wearing a striped tabard. This is a description at the **denotative** level.

By analysing the images carefully at the **connotative** level, we can suggest some meanings. Our starting point may well be via a genre of photography. All of the images are in some way **portraits** – concerned to show people rather than landscapes or buildings. The framings are such that the human subject is the focus of the image, rather than the background. Portraiture is a definable genre with conventions, audience expectations, etc. and also an **institutional category**. A portrait photographer will run a particular kind of business with specialist

Figure 4.1b 'Portrait' of the late Robin Cook.

Figure 4.1a 'Portrait' of Amir Khan.

Figure 4.1c 'Portrait' of bakery workers.

equipment and possibly a permanent studio. He or she will have trained specifically for the work and will have developed particular ways of working – ways of putting portrait models at their ease and then lighting them for effect. We could explore this further but if you've studied the images you will have realised that none of them is a straightforward portrait. Each is in fact best defined by a particular mix of genre and institutional category. We could best continue by thinking about these questions:

- Are these portraits of famous people or particular kinds of people?
- How might the images have been 'captured'?
- Have the images been 'manipulated' or 'edited'?
- Where might the images have first appeared – who owns the rights?
- What might be the purpose of each image – how might readers be expected to react?
- Are there any other 'category labels' that might be appropriate?

These are interrelated institutional questions and in answering them we can learn quite a lot about photography as an institution. Figures 4.1a and 4.1b are of well-known people – the boxer Amir Khan who won a silver medal at the 2004 Olympics and the late Labour MP Robin Cook, who resigned from the Blair Cabinet during the build-up to the 2003 Iraq War. Figure 4.1c is of unnamed women working in a Turkish bakery in North London.

Amir Khan is clearly 'posing' for a portrait which was probably composed specifically to be used in future **promotions** – either by his own management or by other agencies seeking an audience interested in one of the brightest new sports stars in the UK. In other words, the photoshoot itself was the event. The pose is familiar – the young man with one foot pressing back against the wall and the wall itself suggesting an urban environment for someone who is 'street smart'. It fits the image of a young and hungry boxer – in the same way that it fits similar images of young music stars acting the 'rebel', posed against a wall. In institutional terms this is a good promotional image, related in some ways to the idea of a 'pin-up' portrait or poster. Check the internet for Amir Khan images, putting 'boxer' with his name to avoid the Indian film star – you may be surprised at what you find (or maybe not).

Robin Cook is also posing but for a different purpose and in a different context. First, the photoshoot isn't the main reason why he is in the situation depicted – although it is certainly related. Cook was undertaking a tour of constituencies in the period before the 2005 General Election was called, focusing on Labour marginals with significant Muslim populations. Cook's action in resigning was thought to make him a more popular figure with Muslim voters. In this image he poses with young boys at the London Muslim Centre in Whitechapel. This could be seen as a **photo opportunity** – an arranged visit by a politician specifically to be photographed, usually for television news or daily newspapers. But this was not a particularly 'newsy' story and the image actually appeared some days after the visit itself. It was used to accompany 'The Robert Chalmers Interview', a feature article in the *Independent on Sunday* magazine.

The 'Robert Chalmers Interview' is the kind of feature article that can be found in any newspaper supplement. Most of these features will include at least one large 'portrait' of the interviewee, with a pose and setting deemed appropriate for the content of the interview. This particular interview (30 January 2005) has the subheading: '[.] Robin Cook talks openly about love, lies and launching a comeback'. The interview is generally supportive, matching an image that spreads over a page and a half and shows Cook to be comfortable among the apparently happy and friendly boys. The article runs to five pages and carries several other (much smaller) images. Interestingly, the photographer, Andy Paradise, does not seem to have been with the interviewer who spoke to Cook in Haworth in West Yorkshire and in Westminster. But we presume that interviewer and photographer discussed how they would like Cook to be presented. Here is the basis for an interesting set of questions about how the shoot and the interview were conducted and how much influence the interviewee had over the portrait. Who decided what would make the best central image for the interview? (We must presume that the picture editor on the *IoS* had the final say.)

The third image (Figure 4.1c) is different again. This time, there is a sense of 'capturing the moment'. The slight blur in the presentation of the woman on the left suggests that, although the three were asked to pose together, the photo was taken as they were still 'joshing' with each other. This is still a 'well-composed' image, but it has an air of informality that isn't found in the other two. In generic terms it would probably be described as a **documentary** image, representing the reaction of the three women to a photographer who came into their place of work one day. Again, this fits a conventional institutional purpose. The image appeared in a special *Guardian* supplement celebrating the diversity of London's population ('The world in one city', 21 January 2005). These three women were working in a Turkish bakery shop in North London and the image helps to represent both a vibrant ethnic community and one which is represented by at least two generations of women.

These three images, though all 'portraits', were created and published in three different, discernible institutional contexts. By placing them together in an academic text, we have changed the institutional context again. Our purpose has been to demonstrate the process of 'institutionalising' portraiture, and in doing so we have also had a secondary objective of displaying images which also help to demonstrate the diversity of Muslim culture in the UK as a whole.

ACTIVITY 4.2

Different institutional categories of photography

Take any two contrasting institutional categories of photography (e.g. fashion photography and sports photojournalism). Check out books and magazines dealing with photography and look at how the two types of work are presented. Try and list the differences between the two types in terms of:

- relationship with a client – who pays the photographer's fee?
- relationship with the subject of the photograph
- the environment in which the photographers work – how much control do they have?
- the equipment the photographers might use
- a description of a typical working day
- what the photographers might consider as a 'good photograph'
- the different markets in which publications carrying the photographs might be sold.

How important are these institutional differences in thinking about the photographs themselves?

The status of the photograph and the photographer

The three images in Figure 4.1 could conceivably have been produced by an 'amateur' photographer, but we presume that because of the commercial uses of the photographs, the photographer was paid an appropriate fee (at least one of the photographers was a freelance with his own web page). These are 'professionally produced' photographs with *commercial* status – but they could also be '*art*' photographs, perhaps included in an exhibition of a single photographer's work or else in a 'themed' display of related photographs. Commercial images may be cropped or manipulated by a designer or picture editor – the photographer gives up 'ownership' in return for a fee or salary. An 'art' image is likely to be published 'as is' or after processing by the photographer alone. Of course, 'amateur' photographs are sometimes published and commercial photographs do appear in galleries, but the original status is maintained

Partly thanks to the ease of digital photography, several images in this book were taken by the authors. Can you identify them?

and the 'crossing over' into a different category is noticeable. The definitions of categories change over time and it is worth noting that a photograph is normally accompanied by 'anchoring text' which makes the category explicit (even if it is only 'Majorca 1996' scribbled on the back of a snapshot).

Every picture tells a story

Figure 4.2 This photograph counts as a 'group portrait'. It is clearly a snapshot with poor composition and lack of definition in the image. The photographer is unknown but the pencilled note on the back of the small photo reads 'Persia 1943'. It sits in a family album, but images like this have another value – as archive material. The British and Russians had invaded Persia (now Iran) to create a safe supply route for arms to the Soviet Union. This was a little-known aspect of the Second World War. Another feature of the photograph is the presence of Signalman George Stafford, the company driver (standing far left), with the Officers' Mess – a good example of the 'mixing' of officers and men. This could be the kind of image used in a television documentary about the period, reclassifying the photo as 'archive material'.

Figure 4.3 The damaged bicycle belongs to yet another institutional category – legal evidence. Stored in the case files of a local solicitor, this represents the work of a high street commercial photographer asked to produce a high-quality image that will demonstrate the extent of the damage done to the bicycle. Like the image in Figure 4.2, it would not be hard to see this photograph in another context – perhaps mounted in an exhibition as a commentary on 'still life'. It has in fact been used in a publication for this purpose.

Figures 4.2 and 4.3 could both be studied in relation to their implied 'narratives' – see Chapter 2. They could also be considered as material for researchers – see Chapter 10.

- Who makes the decisions about which category is appropriate for which kinds of photography?
- Who decides which category has higher or lower status?
- Can anyone become a photographer and contribute work in these particular categories?

These too are institutional questions. Photography is an *organised* activity. No matter that anyone can point a camera and press a button, we all recognise that a more formal media institution called 'photography' exists with its own rules and regulations. At its simplest level, the distinction between amateur and professional is based on the organisation of professionals. You can't become a 'professional' simply by selling a photograph. The definition of professional is based on:

- status as an employed or self-employed person with a reputation for good work
- training and qualifications
- membership of a professional association
- competitions, awards and recognition
- access to 'industry standard' equipment and the skills to use it.

These criteria are important in excluding some people from becoming professional photographers and in 'standardising' expectations about what constitutes a 'professional photograph' or even a 'good photograph'. They are 'institutional constraints' within which photography practice develops.

'Professional' has two rather different meanings in everyday speech. It can refer to adherence to a code of conduct and a high level of skill – 'she is highly professional in her work' or to a rather automatic or 'detached' performance of the expected role – 'don't worry about him, he's a cynical old pro'.

- *Employment status* is important in that it will influence decisions about what will sell or what will meet a set brief. Most professionals are dependent on the work they produce having currency in the contemporary market. Some photographers might be 'grant-aided', enabling them to undertake **'avant-garde'** work, but also constraining them with the funding criteria.
- *Training and qualifications* are important in photography, which, like journalism but unlike the film industry, has had a long history of 'scientific' and 'technical' training provision, as well as more art- and design-orientated education. There are specialist courses at certain colleges which have become associated with certain types of photography, such as the documentary tradition at Newport School of Art and Design (University of Wales). Students are influenced by their tutors and the traditions of the department and carry these into their future practice. Assessment in the form of National Vocational Qualifications is a way of 'proving' professional competence.
- *Professional associations* support members and help to 'maintain standards'. They may operate a code of ethics which modifies behaviour and puts pressure on members to conform. They preserve the status of

See Chapter 14 below for discussion of broad ethical questions, some of which are institutionalised by companies making documentary programmes.

Like many other activities which began in Victorian Britain, photography has a 'Royal Society' which welcomes amateur and professional members. Compare this with the Royal Television Society, which is professional only. Film and radio don't appear to warrant royal patronage in the same way. Excellence in radio work is rewarded by a 'Sony' award.

The British Institute of Professional Photographers has 4,000 members across the world and it exists to 'enable members to gain professional recognition and to continuously improve their skills. The BIPP represents, supports and promotes image making and image makers.'

members by lobbying government in their interest and negotiating better deals and conditions with buyers of photographic services and equipment suppliers. They also publish journals and run conferences which act as forums for discussion as well as the circulation of new ideas. What does the Code of Conduct in the box below tell you about photography as an institution?

The Code of Conduct of the BIPP (British Institute of Professional Photographers)

- A member shall present himself, his work, his services and his premises in such a manner as will uphold and dignify his professional status and the reputation of the Institute.
- A member shall exercise all reasonable skill, care and diligence in the discharge of his duties, and, in so far as any of his duties are discretionary, shall act fairly and in good faith.
- Any confidential information acquired by a member in the course of his professional duties shall not be divulged by him to any third party.
- No member may corruptly offer or accept any gift or inducement.
- A member may use only in conjunction with his own name the Institute designatory letters to which he is entitled and he shall not use any other designatory letters or other description to which he is not entitled.
- A member shall at all times and in all respects conduct his professional and business operations within the law, both criminal and civil.
- A member knowingly condoning a breach of this Code shall be responsible as if he himself had committed such breach.
- A member shall co-operate fully with any investigations into an alleged breach of this Code.

NB Words implying the masculine gender shall also be taken to include the feminine gender.

The code can be found on the website at www.bipp.com.

- *Awards and prizes* are important in confirming which groups of photographers are recognised as being at the forefront of contemporary practice. They will receive publicity which will strengthen moves to change practice.
- *Industry standard equipment* is another barrier to new entrants to the profession, not just because of cost but also because of the training needed to use it – often, the necessary support to learn new techniques

is available only through professional associations. It could be argued that digital technologies have eroded some of the 'mystique' of 'professional equipment' by making advanced features available at lower cost, but the issue of access to training remains important.

'Amateur photography' can also feel like an institution, especially if it excludes 'outsiders': there is little in amateur or popular photography magazines to help us map our course. There, the concept of photography is limited, being addressed mainly to white heterosexual males. Not much is offered to women and the existence of working-class, black or lesbian experience is barely acknowledged. It is orientated, primarily, to 'know-how' and assumes an interest in tourism, the landscape and glamour (Spence and Solomon 1995).

The quotation from Spence and Solomon recognises the force of institutional factors in photography. It also emphasises how much they can be perceived as discriminatory. Refer back to the BIPP Code and note that the reference to gender discrimination has appeared since we first quoted the code in 1999 – do you think the situation has improved in the last ten years? Despite the ease of use of digital cameras, there are still magazines and clubs for amateur photographers which attempt to institutionalise photography as a hobby. Various groups of photographers have recognised the possibility of discrimination and set up organisations or campaigns to promote their own interests, which would otherwise be seen as marginal.

ACTIVITY 4.3

Amateur photography

Check out the website of *Amateur Photographer* magazine (www.amateurphotography.com) or skim through this or similar magazines in a library.

- What impression do you get of 'amateur photography' as an institution?
- Is there much evidence of relatively new forms of photography such as the use of camera phones?
- Do you think it is important to distinguish between photography as a hobby and the social uses of photographs of friends and family?

Awards are often given by the professional bodies and sponsored by major manufacturers – reinforcing the sense of an organised and institutionalised practice. The most famous awards ceremony is Oscars night, shown around the world. How much does this event 'represent' the institution of Hollywood cinema to the world audience?

Photography is very much associated with ideas of 'identity' and the politics of who controls the images which contribute to those ideas. You will find plenty of examples of photographers working against 'institutional' influences on identity.

'Disability imagery' is one example where the 'subjects' of institutional image-making have fought back: 'My personal journey of private crisis, of the slow gaining of understanding of disability as an external oppression, and on into the disability movement, vitally informs my photographs. . . . Charity photography is a form which is at once stubborn and fragile. A photography which . . . is based on a medical view (or model) of disability cannot lead to the empowerment and liberation of disabled people' (Hevey 1992).

The website of the London University of the Arts at http://www.arts.ac.uk/library/479 7.htm provides a good starting point to explore photography organisations.

Applying ideas about media institutions

From the analysis of photography, you should be able to move on to any other media institution, using these points as a guide:

- *Establishment* Established institutions are *enduring* – they are recognised as having been established for some time. They have a history that informs (and perhaps constrains) the present and the future work undertaken by them. At best, because there are no overnight institutions, they have tried out ideas and established 'support systems' for members; at worst a sort of institutional inertia can operate within their norms. At the start of the twenty-first century photography is struggling to come to terms with digital imaging and the challenge to very long-held views about photographs as evidence. Most media institutions feel slightly threatened by ideas such as **convergence** because they appear to undermine long-established identities.

- *Regulation* Institutions *regulate and structure* activities: they make rules and they suggest specific ways of working. In broad terms, institutions provide stability and preserve the status quo and, of course, 'organise change'. The professional associations are important in regulating the behaviour of their members.

- *Collectivism* Institutions are, in one sense, *collectivist*. They organise individuals and individuality in order to achieve a common goal. (This goal may be that chosen by a small group or even an individual at the top of the hierarchy – institutions are not necessarily democratic.) This is particularly important in media institutions in which individual creative ideas are prized but may have to be sacrificed for the good of the group (often the financial security of the organisation).

- *Work* Institutions develop *working practices* that have an underpinning set of assumptions about the aims of the institution and its ethos. They recognise training and qualifications in the specialist skills necessary for the job and will probably have developed specific job titles and descriptions (sometimes recognised by trade unions and staff associations and used as the basis for pay and conditions).

- *Values* All the people associated with the institution – directors, managers, employees – are expected to share the *values* associated with its ethos and to behave accordingly in their relations with others, both inside and outside the institution. It must be staffed by recognised professionals, whose education and training will effectively exclude casual intruders as new staff.

- *Status* The wider public will be aware of the *status* of the institution and of their own expected relationship to it. Again this is particularly important for media institutions, because the audiences for media texts are 'organised' as part of the network of relationships.

The rules of institutions often invite subversion. Tony Garnett, a celebrated BBC producer, is quoted in the first edition of this book: 'I always obey the rules. The BBC rule is that you refer upwards when in doubt. I don't play games. I simply believe management are much too busy with their enormous problems to be concerned with my small preoccupations' (p. 272).

'Popcorn' and 'carrot cake'

Thinking about media operations in terms of 'institution' requires a step back and a concentration on the kinds of issues outlined above. How can we think about cinema in institutional terms beyond those mentioned at the start of this chapter? Paul Brett, head of the British Film Institute's Cinema Services in 1999, used the terms 'popcorn' and 'carrot cake' to distinguish 'mainstream cinema' and arthouse or specialised cinema in a 1999 Strategy Consultation Document. In simple terms, if a multiplex cinema has a large concessions stand and the air is filled with the unmistakable odour of popcorn and cola, it is reasonably safe to assume that the ethos of mainstream cinema prevails. In the arthouse we might expect to find carrot cake and 'real' coffee.

The crucial point here is that the audience and the income for the two types of cinema are different and therefore the exhibitors have to adopt a different mindset in order to attract customers. Most of the successful independent cinemas that show 'specialised cinema' will cater to audiences with a restaurant/bar, possibly a shop selling film magazines, DVDs, film notes and education events. They will screen films in 'seasons', hold festivals and special events, all listed in a detailed brochure each month. The multiplex operation will want an ethos of 'entertainment' and 'fun' to prevail without too much earnest discussion – and they know they will make more profit from concessions than from the films.

Figure 4.4 *Ghost World* (UK/US/Germany 2000) is a 'smart film' that appeals to audiences in the more 'art'-orientated cinemas. In one scene, the Thora Birch character fails to keep a job selling concessions in a multiplex because she blithely tells the customers that the popcorn is coated in 'chemical goo' and doesn't try to persuade them to 'go for the large size'.

Gomery (1992) suggests that American cinemas began to sell concessions in a big way during the Depression in the 1930s. Before then, cheap foods were associated with 'low-class entertainments', but cinema chains soon realised the enormous profits that could be made.

'Munching at the movies': 'Concessions account for a quarter of all revenue in UK cinemas but half the profits, with cardboard cartons full of popcorn and drinks each making up a third of all sales' (*Screen Digest*, Report, April 2005).

Figure 4.5 Cornerhouse Cinema, Manchester, showing the ground floor bar and first floor café.

Art cinema vs. mainstream cinema

We can pursue the popcorn/carrot cake distinction further by looking at other ways in which art films and art cinema differ from mainstream cinema. The following list of oppositions is not meant to suggest a rigid distinction and indeed the UK Film Council is working hard to increase the number of 'carrot cake' films shown in multiplexes (see Chapter 13), but the list does help us to understand the institutional differences between the two types of cinema:

Art/Specialist cinema	*Mainstream*
Independent production/ distribution	Major studio finance/distribution
Low budget	High budget
Director more likely as star	Actor more likely as star
Complex narrative	Easy to follow narrative
'Style' can be more important than story	'Story' usually more important than style
Genre not important or critiqued	Genre appeal
'Alternative' values/morality	'Mainstream' values/morality
First seen at festivals	First seen via commercial previews
Berlin, Venice, Cannes festival prizes	'Top 10 charts', Oscars
Reviewed by specialist media	Reviewed by mainstream media
Advertised only in specialist media	Advertised in popular press, radio and television
Few prints in distribution	Many prints in distribution
Shown only in 'specialist' cinemas	Shown in all cinemas

Sex and violence allowed if for 'art'   Sex and violence restricted
Subtitled films   Mostly films in English, including
     'dubbed'

It could be argued that some of the 'oppositions' on this list refer to 'genre' and some to 'industry' distinctions, but overall they suggest a different set of expectations and, in turn, different behaviours by production crews, cinema staff, critics and audiences. The last two pairs are indicative of institutional constraints. In the last few years, the distinctions have blurred in relation to subtitles, with films like *Amélie* (France 2001) and *Hero* (China/US 2002) playing in multiplexes to large audiences. Even so, there are expectations that films with subtitles are not mainstream (even though they might be accepted as such in their own language markets) and both audiences and exhibitors need a lot of encouragement to accept them as such. These prejudices have a different but related place in the debates about certification of films. Scenes including erect penises, 'real' sexual activity and sexual violence have been passed uncut in films such as *The Idiots* (Denmark 1998), *Irreversible* (France 2002) and *9 Songs* (UK 2005), seemingly on the grounds that audiences of middle-class intellectuals will not be corrupted by 'art films'. Yet similar scenes are refused (or rather 'self-censored' – an important institutional skill for producers) in mainstream cinema. Interestingly, such art films do not usually go on to attract large audiences eager to be depraved. Perhaps audiences are more capable of making up their own minds than the institutional practices of the film industry regulators allow?

ACTIVITY 4.4

Your local cinemas
Discuss your local cinemas with your friends.

- If the same film is playing at very different cinemas (i.e. a small independent cinema and a multiplex), what makes you choose one over the other?
- Try to interview the cinema managers. How do they describe their regular audience members? What do they think audiences want from a visit to their cinema?

ACTIVITY 4.5

Outlining media institutions

Drawing on the analysis of media institutions above and thinking particularly about:

- regulatory bodies (Chapter 16)
- working practices
- training and qualifications
- professional associations and awards

sketch out a description of the institution of 'radio' as understood in the UK.

Can a single organisation be an institution?

When you come to study media institutions, you may be asked to write about institutions using a single media text or company as a starting point. It's important that you recognise that these exist in an institutional framework – a framework within which all the companies producing similar products (or offering similar services) are also working. The *Sunday Times* is constrained in the way it approaches journalism by an understanding of the standards of journalism appropriate for a broadsheet newspaper. Similarly, its parent company, News Corporation, is a major global corporation which is also constrained by the ways in which such corporations are expected to behave. Any particular company may be at the forefront of trying to shift institutional boundaries, but we still want to study them as part of a group.

The BBC is often referred to as an institution, because of its uniquely long-established position in the UK system in terms of funding and self-regulation and its strong ethos that still to a certain extent refers back to its 'founding father', **John Reith**. Some BBC staff (and importantly, some significant audience groups) would argue that there is a distinctive BBC 'way of doing things'. Yet the BBC doesn't operate in a vacuum. There are several ways in which the 'working practices' of the BBC will be affected by what happens elsewhere:

- Professionals at the BBC are likely to be 'members' of other institutional groupings; e.g. 'broadcast journalism' is itself an institution with its own training and qualifications body, BJTC (Broadcast Journalism Training Council – www.bjtc.org.uk) which also includes staff working for ITN, Sky, etc.
- Staff who join the BBC may have been trained elsewhere and got used to different ways of working (see the case of Andrew Gilligan on p. 122).

John Reith (1889–1971) was the first Director-General of the BBC between 1927 and 1938. He expounded firm principles of centralised, all-encompassing radio broadcasting, stressing programming standards and moral tone. To this day, the BBC claims to follow the Reithian directive to 'inform, educate and entertain' (from the entry on **Wikipedia**).

- In any media activity that involves working with technology and within developing broadcast 'formats', working practices will be influenced by the technology suppliers, the format innovators, etc.

For many years the BBC was known by the affectionate, if patronising, term, 'Auntie'. The connotations of this were that the corporation was reliable and family orientated but also perhaps a little stuffy. Attempts to throw off this image have risked something of a backlash, although the growth in the number of BBC television channels means that some, such as BBC3, can cater for a younger audience without alienating older audiences for BBC1. Overall, the BBC needs to cater for everyone, but its radio stations already segment the audience across Radios 1, 2, 3, 4 and 5 with 1 Extra, 6, 7 and Asian Network on 'digital only' services.

The 'staid Auntie' image of the BBC was challenged by the London bureau chief of Fox News, whose attack on the corporation for its 'institutionalised leftism' (after it had reported fans' reactions to the takeover of Manchester United by an American businessman) was headlined 'An aunt with attitude' in the *Wall Street Journal* (reported in the *Guardian*, 31 May 2005).

John Peel and the BBC

When the veteran radio broadcaster John Peel died in 2004, there was an enormous outpouring of affection from radio listeners and music fans of all ages in the UK. This was undoubtedly a tribute to Peel's ability to communicate his basic humanity and love of popular music, but partly it was a function of the strange institutional relationship between the BBC and a very individual broadcaster. The BBC gave Peel a secure base from which to develop a loyal fanbase for a programme of 'alternative' music. It is unlikely that a commercial broadcaster would have allowed someone to continue this work for so long. Because of its dominant position within the national radio marketplace, the BBC could also provide 'universal access' to Peel's show. At the same time, Peel allowed the BBC to appear to be more 'daring' and less 'comfortable' than its reputation might suggest.

Media institutions and society

Human society has always had the means to express ideas and emotions through forms such as storytelling, dance, music and art. Modern media have extended those capacities, in terms of realism, reproduction and distribution to mass audiences. The institutional questions which arise are not necessarily 'new', but they arouse concern and interest because their potential impact is so great. Consider the following issues about the role of the media and the nature of media texts:

- the 'truth' of claims to represent 'reality'
- the hurt and damage to individuals caused by offensive media texts

- the potential damage to society inflicted by stories celebrating and perhaps encouraging corruption and depravity
- the potential loss of national, regional and cultural identity through submission to a dominant culture.

Some of these issues are raised in other chapters and case studies as well, and in some cases they are linked with questions of economics – what kinds of media activity can we afford, what are the implications for employment or balance of trade? Here, we will consider some of the issues relating to 'journalism' as an institution.

The case of journalism

The basic definition of journalism is 'the profession of writing for public journals'. The broad professional category covers all writing in the media concerned with news, current affairs and 'documentary' features.

The cub reporter at the gardening club show, the columnist on a national paper, the sub-editor who writes the captions for paparazzi photos, the film reviewer on a website and the foreign correspondent reporting for the BBC in a war zone are all journalists. They share certain values and are subject to similar institutional constraints, but there are also important differences.

Journalism is one sector of the UK media industries with a history of clearly defined training routes for entry and progression through the profession. In print journalism, the NCTJ (National Council for the Training of Journalists) and the large regional newspaper groups have organised training schemes which allow journalists to start 'at the bottom' and learn their trade 'on the job'. The situation in broadcasting is slightly different (see www.bjtc.org.uk) but many broadcast journalists begin in the print media.

To some extent these schemes are now in competition with degree and postgraduate courses which produce highly qualified entrants with less experience (a development not necessarily welcomed in some parts of the industry). Nevertheless, most journalists receive an introduction to acceptable working practices with a strong institutional sense of what it means to be a journalist. This introduction is not value-free, and discrimination based on gender or race has been identified and challenged by journalists who established new codes of conduct within the profession. Campaigns against racist reporting have been developed (see National Union of Journalists guidelines in the box below) alongside pressure groups designed to promote opportunities for Black media workers or workers with disabilities. The situation regarding gender-based discrimination is more complex. Women are certainly being recruited into all forms of journalism (Skillset Census 2004 suggests 49 per cent of workers in the category 'Journalism and Sport' are women), but there may still be questions about whether or not all kinds of journalism are open to men and women in the same way.

NUJ guidelines on race reporting

- Only mention someone's race if it is strictly relevant. Check to make sure you have it right. Would you mention race if the person was white?
- Do not sensationalise race relations issues, it harms Black people and it could harm you.
- Think carefully about the words you use. Words which were once in common usage are now considered offensive – e.g. half-caste and coloured. Use mixed-race and Black instead. Black can cover people of Arab, Asian, Chinese and African origin. Ask people how they define themselves.
- Immigrant is often used as a term of abuse. Do not use it unless the person really is an immigrant. Most Black people in Britain were born here and most immigrants are white.
- Do not make assumptions about a person's cultural background – whether it is their name or religious detail. Ask them, or where this is not possible check with the local race equality council.
- Investigate the treatment of Black people in education, health, employment and housing. Do not forget travellers and gypsies. Cover their lives and concerns. Seek the views of their representatives.
- Remember that Black communities are culturally diverse. Get a full and correct view from representative organisations.
- Press for equal opportunities for employment of Black staff.
- Be wary of disinformation. Just because a source is traditional does not mean it is accurate.

Downloaded on 6 June 2005 from www.nuj.org.uk/inner.php?docid=78.

In an illuminating study of *Women in Radio* (Mitchell 2000), the gendered nature of radio work was confirmed, women being less likely to present current affairs, but contributors noted a number of changes in the image of the news reporter. The hard-bitten hack in the raincoat found in the pub has given way to the dedicated young professional more likely to be found in the gym when not working late – young women are possibly more likely to fit this ideal. Also, new technology in the news room means that more interviews are conducted over the **ISDN** line than 'foot in door' or 'face to face'. Again, women are thought to be better at this form of work than men (Mitchell 2000: 252).

'In this business, you have to think like a man, act like a woman, and work like a dog' (Martha Jean Steinberg, quoted in Mitchell 2000: 205).

'Women leapt in to fill these [radio] vacancies and they were largely university-educated women who were not there because they had financed their own trip abroad, or because their husbands, fathers or brothers had played any role in their career' (Sebba 1998).

A beginning on a local newspaper is often the first stage on a progression through different media institutions, including local radio, regional television and then national newspapers, radio or television. This has happened for many years but has been further encouraged by the 'convergence' of media forms. Journalists in any medium are expected to share skills, knowledge and understanding about what makes a 'good story' and how to produce accurate and interesting material to deadlines. However, the different media have different institutional constraints. Broadcast journalism has traditionally operated 'impartially', drawing on a sense of 'balanced reporting' as required by the charter of the BBC or by Ofcom in the case of other broadcasters. By contrast, print journalists work in a more politically charged environment where stories clearly have *angles* and columnists in particular are expected to represent the editorial *line*. This isn't expressed as partiality, of course, but as 'comment'.

Andrew Gilligan was the BBC journalist at the centre of the controversy over the death of government weapons expert David Kelly in 2003, which prompted the Hutton inquiry and the subsequent resignation of the BBC Director-General and Chair of Governors. Gilligan was a former *Sunday Telegraph* defence correspondent, recruited in 1999 by the editor of *Today* on Radio 4 to 'sharpen up' reporting on the BBC's 'flagship' current affairs programme. The inquiry decided that Gilligan's claim that government advisers had 'sexed up' a document were unfounded and that his notes of a meeting with David Kelly were 'unreliable'.

The BBC was considerably 'embarrassed' by this finding and we might conclude that had Gilligan had more broadcast experience, he might have handled the situation differently and made his charges stick through better 'fact-checking'. One consequence of this affair was that the BBC decided to set up its own in-house 'College of Journalism'. There are over 7,000 BBC journalists and by April 2005 two interactive computer training modules had been accessed by 6,500 staff, including senior personnel (*BBC Newswatch* on news.bbc.co.uk 11 April 2005).

A 'red-top' tabloid might list 'ten things you never knew about salmonella' – another angle.

An *angle* on a story refers to the direction from which the journalist approaches the material. A news item on the agency wires might refer to an outbreak of food poisoning. One journalist might decide to follow up the story by concentrating on the issue of public health: which shop, factory, etc. might be responsible, how are the local authorities handling the outbreak of infection? Another journalist might approach the same material by linking it to other recent outbreaks and asking questions about central government food policy. These are two angles on the same story.

A *line* is a policy set down by the editor (perhaps at the behest of a proprietor such as Rupert Murdoch) stating what the paper believes in and therefore how stories will be presented. The idea that such a line exists will be denied by many editors and journalists, but it becomes apparent whenever the paper decides to go against its usual line. The most obvious example of a line is the general support for one particular party at election time. In 1997 the *Sun* surprised most readers by switching allegiance from Conservative to Labour. In 2005 it stuck with Labour even though commentators thought it might change.

ACTIVITY 4.6

Editorial policy

Over a couple of weeks try to follow the same few big news stories in two newspapers with strong identities (e.g. the *Sun, Mirror, Daily Mail, Guardian* or *Daily Telegraph*).

- Can you identify an editorial line in any of the papers on a particular story?
- Can you find examples of reporting or comment which appear to contradict the editorial stance of the paper?

Although it is still possible to find writers with different political views working on the same broadsheet paper (especially the *Guardian* or the *Independent*), it is increasingly the case that the press is seen to be 'partisan'. This emphasises the difference between print and broadcast journalism, but also puts pressure on the broadcasters. Newspapers can 'set an agenda' on a particular story which is picked up by radio and television. Viewers and listeners then expect impartiality from broadcasters but, with the context of the story already set, it is difficult to 'reset' it. And, with the increased competition in news presentation, ignoring the story may not be possible. The result is that broadcasters can be sucked in to a style of coverage they may not be trained or professionally inclined to handle.

One of the features of contemporary newspapers is the rise of the 'columnist', which to a certain extent has matched the decline of the 'reporter' and the general move to more 'entertainment' (or 'infotainment') forms. Newspapers have responded to what their proprietors have seen as the market trends by shifting resources away from large numbers of relatively poorly paid reporters 'on the ground' to a smaller number of highly paid commentators based in London (most national daily papers are now entirely London operations, whereas they once operated out of large bases in Manchester, Birmingham and other cities). This change has had an impact on, and has in turn been influenced by, changes in journalism training and the consequent 'institutionalisation' of the new forms. To a certain extent the same process is evident in local newspapers where 'features' have grown at the expense of 'news'.

In the aftermath of 9/11 we can note that there have been significant changes in the way that journalism is presented to us, not least in the rise of internet-based coverage of events (including 'blogs' and the circulation of digital images and video as phone cameras come readily to hand) and the possible intervention of non-journalists, particularly academics, in ongoing debates. 'National' newspapers are now widely available around the world via the internet, as are 'national' radio broadcasts. Email allows responses to be 'posted' to newspapers and television stations almost immediately – and if the originating publication won't take the response, there are numerous other electronic outlets that will.

Ethics and values

One of the main institutional factors in any media practice is a shared sense of values. This often translates into a set of ethics, perhaps inscribed in a code of conduct such as the photographers' code outlined on p. 112. The difficulty with ethical behaviour is that it often runs counter to what might produce a 'good story' (another institutionalised feature of work in many media) which might produce higher circulation or ratings, professional kudos and financial reward. This is the basis for the narratives of much of the literature and film based on journalistic adventures. Few media practitioners set out to behave unethically; most media organisations attempt to deal with such behaviour through some form of redress and also try to prevent it happening again.

The *Guardian* created controversy in 2004 when it invited readers to write to voters in the US with their views on the Presidential Election. It made good copy for the newspaper, with angry responses from some US journalists, but arguably pushed voters towards George W. Bush in protest. How would you react to receiving emails from the US suggesting how you should vote?

In the film *Under Fire* (US 1982) a photojournalist fakes an image persuading revolutionaries that their inspirational leader is still alive – they go on to defeat the evil dictator. Is it ever right to do something 'unethical'? How many times can ethical codes be ignored before they become meaningless? See Chapter 14 on the ethics of documentary and photojournalism.

Responsible DJs?

In January 2002, Radio 4's *Feedback* programme of listeners' comments ran a piece on Radio 1 DJs. Listeners, including a parent of an eighteen-year-old, had complained about references to excessive drinking over the Christmas holiday. One DJ had run a competition for the most 'evil' cocktail made up from left-over Christmas drinks. Another had boasted about how much she had drunk the night before, inviting listeners to phone or email with their own exploits. *Feedback* effectively asked, 'Is this celebrating dangerous drinking?' Or was it just a bit of fun, as the Radio 1 producer concerned suggested?

- What do you think?
- What would be your advice to DJs?

As a public service radio producer, you wouldn't want to encourage dangerous drinking. Equally, you would want a slight edge of danger to a Radio 1 show to keep up the audience's interest.

Reporting the tsunami

When the tsunami struck in the Indian Ocean on 26 December 2004 it presented a challenge to news agencies in how to cover such a major story taking place in several different locations at the same time. In the aftermath of the event several debates began in the trade press about how two particular organisations, BBC News and Sky News, had approached their coverage.

- BBC News was criticised for its slow response in sending senior personnel to the region – an issue of both logistics and management priorities. Head of BBC TV News Roger Mosey defended the management of his news teams and pointed out that despite Sky News' innovations (including the 'personal message' about missing persons presented ticker-tape style), 'multi-channel' viewers chose BBC News 24 ahead of Sky News (*Guardian*, 5 January 2005).
- Sky News was seen by some commentators as 'first with the news' but also criticised for the inappropriate tone of some bulletins:

> Kay Burley wearing lip gloss in Sri Lanka seems desperately inappropriate; Alex Crawford's report at the opening of Sky's first bulletin produced for Five, in which she personally intervened in a mother's search for her child, was terribly misjudged.
>
> (Matt Wells, *Guardian*, 5 January 2005)

Rachel Attwell, head of BBC News 24, in an interview for the *Independent*, pinpointed the institutional differences she saw between the BBC and ITV News/Sky News, 'acknowledging the rival's keen eye for a softer angle that would not suit the BBC'. This is a reference to Sky's focus on Thailand where most British tourists were located, compared to the BBC's focus on Sri Lanka and Indonesia as major disaster areas for local communities. There is also an issue of fact-checking: 'Ninety-five per cent of the time, it pays off for Sky: they put out a story from one source and it turns out to be right and so they are first. We will wait for a second source' (interview by Ian Burrell, *Independent*, 17 January 2005).

Sky News and BBC News both went £1 million 'over budget' during their tsunami coverage (*Guardian*, 25 May 2005). At the peak of the emergency, the BBC had over 90 staff in the region, Sky News 80, ITV News 32 and CNN 80 (*Broadcast*, 14 January 2005).

We've argued that 'journalism' is recognisable as a set of work practices and ethics which runs across different media. The process of convergence of technologies and ownership has been matched by a similar convergence of attitudes towards previously distinct forms of journalism in press and broadcasting. A useful summary of where journalism is heading is provided by Michael Bromley (1997), who argues that debate over the state of journalism and its likely future in the early part of the twenty-first century involves four interrelated areas:

- technological change
- new business structures
- the functions of news
- the coherence of journalism as an occupation.

ACTIVITY 4.7

The state of journalism

Taking these four points, check through the preceding section and the relevant sections of other chapters and case studies in this book to put together a coherent view of the 'state of journalism'. You should look in particular at Chapter 6 and 'Case study: News' and Chapter 8.

References and further reading

Bromley, Michael (1997) 'The end of journalism? Changes in workplace practices in the press and broadcasting in the 1990s', in Michael Bromley and Tom O'Malley (eds) *A Journalism Reader*, London: Routledge.

Carter, Cynthia, Branston, Gill and Allan, Stuart (eds) (1998) *News, Gender and Power*, London: Routledge.

Gomery, Douglas (1992) *Shared Pleasures: A History of Movie Presentation in the US*, London: BFI.

Hevey, David (1992) *The Creatures that Time Forgot: Photography and Disability Imagery*, London: Routledge.

Holland, Patricia (1998) 'The politics of the soft smile: soft news and the sexualisation of the popular press', in Cynthia Carter, Gill Branston and Stuart Allan (eds) *News, Gender and Power*, London: Routledge.

Mitchell, Caroline (ed.) (2000) *Women in Radio*, London: Routledge.

O'Sullivan, Tim, Hartley, John, Saunders, Danny, Montgomery, Martin and Fisk, John (1994) *Key Concepts in Cultural and Communication Studies*, 2nd edition, London: Routledge.

Sebba, Anne M. (1998) 'Women and the fourth estate', in Mike
    Ungersma, *Reporters and the Reported*, Cardiff: Centre for Journalism
    Studies.
Spence, Jo and Solomon, Joan (eds) (1995) *What Can a Woman Do With a
    Camera?*, London: Routledge.

The Media Handbook series from Routledge provides useful material on
institutional issues, especially:
Holland, Pat (2000) *The Television Handbook*, 2nd edition, London:
    Routledge.
Keeble, Richard (2001) *The Newspapers Handbook*, 3rd edition, London:
    Routledge.
McKay, Jenny (2000) *The Magazines Handbook*, London: Routledge.

Free Press, the newsletter of the Campaign for Press and Broadcasting
Freedom, is a good source of information on stories concerning industrial
relations, regulation and other institutional issues. Visit the CPBF website
for updates on Campaign policies. As well as the Michael Bromley article
cited above, there are several other useful articles in *A Journalism Reader*.

Websites

www.cjr.org
www.cpbf.org.uk
www.mediachannel.org
www.nuj.org.uk
www.presswise.org.uk
www.reportingtheworld.org

CASE STUDY: TELEVISION AS INSTITUTION

- An outline history of UK television
- Ownership and control in the television industry
- Financing television
- Public service broadcasting (PSB)

- Audience questions
- The culture of production
- References and further reading

'The UK's media world has changed dramatically and unpredictably since the BBC's last Charter was agreed nine years ago. Digital television, the internet and mobile telephony were hardly mentioned in 1995, yet all three have become part of everyday life for more than half the population of the UK. The broadcasting landscape will change just as dramatically and unpredictably over the course of the next decade. The UK is about to enter the second stage of the digital revolution' (*Building Public Value: Renewing the BBC for a Digital World*, 2004).

Television is the medium that is central to most people's lives in the developed world. Most of us watch television for a minimum of three hours per day and it provides us with information and ideas as well as entertainment. Because of its central position in our lives, we tend to both take it for granted and expect it to develop and grow with us. But television may, in several different ways, be changing more than we think. We need to stand back – to distance ourselves from our everyday experience – and look carefully at how television is changing as a social **institution**. To do this, we will also have to consider how it is changing as an industry, so you should cross-reference the discussion here with the 'Case study: The Media Majors' and discussion of television in Chapter 16.

An outline history of UK television

The early years 1936–55

In the beginning, the new television service was constrained, in terms of both geographical and social 'reach'. Initially a limited service for the metropolitan middle class, it was a long time (including the closedown from 1939 to 1946 because of the disruption of the Second World War) before the single BBC channel was widely available. It was 1952 before the signal could be received by 81 per cent of the population. The television service required a viewing licence on top of the existing radio licence, and by 1955 the number of television licence payers had risen to 4.5 million (out of around 14 million households).

A universal public service 1955–82

The highly controversial introduction of 'commercial' or 'independent' television (ITV) in 1955, in London and then around the country (set up partly with **public service** rather than simply commercial principles), did much to fire up the BBC, which was allowed to introduce a second channel with colour and a higher-resolution picture in 1964. Colour transmissions began in 1967 but the 'switchover' to the new 625 lines of UHF from the original 405 lines of VHF took over twenty years. It was 1985 before the old system was finally switched off – an interesting contrast with the current timetable for switching to digital broadcasting in a very different television environment. In this period, ITV companies were obliged to operate on a purely regional basis, serving a distinctive community and abiding by tight regulatory controls laid down by the franchising authority, the IBA (Independent Broadcasting Authority – at first the ITA). (See 'Case study: Selling audiences' following Chapter 8 and the discussion of 'Wales and West'.) Filmed American series became commonplace on UK television during this period and 'live links' via satellite introduced overseas news and joint broadcasting events.

The beginnings of pluralism 1982–90

Channel 4 went on air in 1982 with a new remit, to widen the range of programming and to serve a diverse range of audiences not served by the BBC and ITV. Channel 4 was innovative in several different ways (see Holland 2000: 17). It was a public sector organisation that was funded via advertising revenue, initially sold by the ITV companies. It didn't make its own programmes, but commissioned independent companies as a **'broadcaster-publisher'** and created a new form of television channel. Channel 4

promised a wider spread of viewpoints and a third source of news and current affairs during a period of great social unrest in the UK.

In Wales, S4C was also set up as a public service broadcaster-publisher. This period saw the UK introduction of satellite broadcasting (two companies, Sky and BSB, began broadcasting, but Sky soon took over BSB to form BSkyB) and the re-emergence of cable television (it had previously been used to relay terrestrial signals and some local services) offering a variety of channels on broadband cable.

The multi-channel environment, 1990 onwards

The Broadcasting Acts of 1990 and 1996 legislated for a new television environment in which regulation of 'independent television' was loosened, Channel 4 gained control over its own advertising revenue from ITV, and digital broadcasting promised to provide even more channels than analogue cable and satellite, as well as 'interactivity' and computer services. Channel Five was launched as a final terrestrial channel (i.e. analogue bandwidth was now used up). Throughout the previous thirty-five years, the BBC and 'independent television' (i.e. ITV and later Channel 4) had shared the audience on a roughly equal basis. From now on, the audience share of 'other broadcasters' would grow steadily, undermining the settled terrestrial broadcasting environment.

ACTIVITY 4.8

Television as social history

Television has become an important part of our experience of national and international events. Why do you think the following events are important in television history (relate them to the periods outlined in the box above)?

1953	Coronation of Elizabeth II
1969	Landing on the moon
1984	The Miners' Strike
1997	The death and funeral of Diana, Princess of Wales

A similar history is observable in most other developed countries, with technology and economic activity being the driving force for change and the US usually (but not always) leading in terms of innovation.

Various commentators have found ways to analyse this history. John Ellis (2000), one of the foremost academic analysts of UK television (who has also worked within the industry), has represented the history like this:

- the era of scarcity
- the era of availability
- the era of plenty.

'Scarcity' refers in most countries to the restricted number of channels available up to the late 1970s (terrestrial broadcasts are limited by the availability of suitable 'bandwidths' of radio waves). New technologies such as broadband cable, DBS (direct broadcasting by satellite) and now digital free-to-air or DTT (digital terrestrial television) have allowed the move to the era of 'availability' by creating space for many extra channels. But in the early years of the twenty-first century, Ellis suggests, television is moving towards a future which is being promoted by producers and distributors, but which audiences are only coming to terms with quite slowly.

In Ellis's terms the producers and audiences are actually 'working through' an 'age of uncertainty' as television begins to redefine itself. We can see this in the refusal by a significant section of the UK audience to 'buy in' to the new world of plenty: after a decade of promotion, '**multi-channel television**' has 'penetrated', to use the market jargon, just over two-thirds of UK households (*TV International Database*, reported in *The Times*, 22 April 2005). To the surprise of many industry pundits, much of the recent growth has been via the Freeview service for terrestrial digital channels. In other words, some of the new audiences for digital television have still to be convinced that they need to pay extra for more channels.

If we recognise that 'uncertainty' is a feature not just of the UK television environment, but indeed of global television, we can explore what is causing these changes and what they might mean with reference to some of the major questions which are raised in Chapters 4 and 8, 'Institutions' and 'Industries':

- What is the pattern of ownership and control in the television industry?
- How is television financed and how are its activities regulated?
- How has technological change affected the 'culture' of both television production and television viewing?

Ownership and control in the television industry

Throughout the history of television, there has been a major difference between the ownership and control of television in the US and that in Europe (and indeed in much of the rest of the world). Television in America grew out of a system of 'commercial broadcasting' set up to exploit the profitability of radio services. In Europe, radio and early television were seen as means for communicating both entertainment and information. In the UK, a licence to broadcast was vested in a public corporation, the BBC, following the General Strike in 1926. The original BBC was a small private company that did not have the power to resist state interference, but the new corporation had a measure of independence from the state. In Germany, broadcasting was used by the Nazi Party as an integral part of their propaganda machine in the 1930s. After the Second World War, in which the BBC had played a crucial 'morale-raising' role, the Allied authorities made sure that complex regulatory controls were in place when new broadcasting licences were granted in Germany to regional public sector broadcasters within a federal structure. ARD, the broadcasting service based on this model, was formed in 1950. A monopoly state broadcaster (RAI) was established in Italy in 1954 and in France in 1945. TVE in Spain was established in 1956.

In most continental European countries, 'commercial' (i.e. profit-making) broadcasting by private sector companies had been introduced by the 1980s, but usually within a regulatory framework that sought to protect the 'public service' ideals vested in the state broadcasters. The balance between private and public sector broadcasting in television began to shift in the 1980s for two reasons:

1 The new technologies of cable and satellite broadcasting offered opportunities to introduce new channels and new services.

2 The general shift towards 'free-market' economics and 'deregulation' of public services and utilities resulted in various forms of 'privatisation' and 'contracting out' to the private sector. In France, the privatisation of the main public broadcasting channel, France 1, in 1987 created the current French market leader TF1 (with 35 per cent of audience share in 2004).

The new opportunities attracted media entrepreneurs from other sectors into the previously stable European television market, including News Corporation (US), Bertelsmann/RTL (Germany), Mediaset (Italy), Vivendi/Canal+ (France), etc., as well as the telecommunications companies Liberty Media (US) (a product of the US telecommunications anti-trust actions) and Telefónica (the privatised Spanish telephone company). These companies have moved into terrestrial and satellite/cable television (including pay-TV). The companies do not stay within national boundaries and they often have 'cross-holdings' of shares within each other's companies.

Network	Channels	Distribution	Owner
BBC	BBC1, 2, 3, 4, CBBC, CBeebies, News 24 etc.	Terrestrial Analogue, Freeview, Cable, Satellite	BBC (Public sector corporation)
ITV	ITV1, 2, 3, 4	Terrestrial Analogue, Freeview, Cable, Satellite	ITV plc, Scottish Media Group, Ulster Television
Channel 4	C4, E4, More4, Film Four	Terrestrial Analogue, Freeview, Cable, Satellite	Channel 4 (Public sector corporation)
Five	Five	Terrestrial Analogue, Freeview, Cable, Satellite	RTL (Bertelsmann)
Sky	Sky One, Sky News, Movies, Sport, Travel etc.	Freeview (News, Travel only) Cable, Satellite	BSkyB (News Corporation)
UKTV	UK Gold, Drama, Style etc.	Cable, Satellite	Flextech/BBC
Flextech	Living, Bravo, Trouble	Cable, Satellite	Telewest, (Liberty Media 25%)
Turner	TCM, Cartoon Network, CNN	Cable, Satellite	Time Warner
Disney	Disney, ABC, Jetix etc.	Cable, Satellite	Disney
Viacom	MTV, VH-1, Paramount Comedy	Cable, Satellite	Viacom
Discovery	Discovery, Animal Planet, Home & Health, Science, Wings etc.	Cable, Satellite	Discovery (Liberty Media 50%)

Figure 4.6 Television holdings in the UK as at August 2005.

The overall success of the privately owned broadcasters (some have failed) has put pressure on public broadcasters and the concept of **'public service broadcasting'** or **PSB**. For the generation born after 1980, into a world that would soon bring the internet and multi-channel television, the concept of public service broadcasting must be difficult to grasp because it seems to go 'against the grain' of everything else that has happened in terms of media development. However, apart from in the US, most young people do have a sense of the importance of a public service, like the UK National Health Service, which is 'universal' and 'free at the point of delivery' – in other words, the system is paid for out of general taxation and is accessible to everyone, irrespective of income or where they live. The same principle lies behind PSB – a publicly financed broadcasting service, available to everyone without any extra charge above the tax contribution. However, other public utilities such as water, gas, electricity and telecommunications have been privatised, so why not television and radio?

A universal service?

BT, the privatised UK telephone company, applied to remove a roadside telephone box from a remote road, even though a mobile telephone signal could not be obtained at that location, meaning that no emergency contact was possible (reported on Radio 5, 2 September 2004).

The regulator Ofcom has decided that there should be investment in the transmitter network to allow the BBC to carry more digital channels (DTT) rather than build new transmitters to allow DTT signals to be received in remote parts of the UK. Should it be satisfied that when the 'digital switchover' is completed in 2012, only 98.5 per cent of the population will be able to receive free DTT services? (*Guardian*, 2 June 2005).

Simple economics suggests that some services will be much more expensive to provide in certain kinds of locations. If 'profit' or 'return on investment' is to be achieved, people in remote rural areas must pay more or do without – that is the logic of the marketplace. Is this fair? The same people in rural areas must pay more petrol tax because there are no public transport services and they must put up with the siting of wind farms and other forms of power stations that people in towns don't want on their doorsteps. In the case of broadcasting, it might mean that 1.5 per cent of the population (900,000 people) are unable to participate in television 'events', unless they subscribe to a satellite service on Sky. (See Chapter 16 for more on 'free markets'.)

We'll return to the concept of PSB, but first we should note that the current pattern of ownership in European television is based on a 'mixed economy' of private and public control and the means of financing this pattern of provision is changing quite dramatically.

Financing television

Finance is obviously an economics and business issue, but it is also an institutional issue in that it affects people's attitudes towards services and their sense of 'ownership' over them. For many years there were just two options for the funding of a television service:
- some form of taxation to fund a public service
- the sale of advertising 'air time' to fund a commercial/privately owned service.

The UK system whereby everyone who owns a television set pays a standard licence fee has several advantages. Because the money is collected by a separate agency and goes directly to the BBC, the service is independent of day-to-day government control (although raising the level of fee income still requires a government decision). It is also an efficient means of generating a secure income (not immediately affected by the current economic climate). (See Chapter 16 for more on financing television.)

Advertising income is less secure and depends on two factors – the popularity of programmes (i.e. the promise to advertisers that their advertisements will be seen by target audiences) and the general economic climate (i.e. advertisers will be reluctant to spend money when consumer spending is depressed). In some countries, advertising is allowed on public service channels to supplement public funding.

The arrival of multi-channel television meant a challenge to the traditional 'binary system' of public funding and advertising. The threat to public funding comes via questions over the 'legitimacy' of charging all viewers for a service they may not wish to receive. Now that the BBC share of the total television audience is below 30 per cent, can the licence fee be justified? BBC1 is now the single most important channel in the UK, so abolition of the BBC would not be popular. However, opponents of the licence fee argue that it is set at too high a level and that the BBC should not be making 'popular' programmes with large budgets. A competitor like BSkyB would prefer to see the BBC making only 'worthy' programmes on arts and current affairs. This would, of course, both boost the ratings of competitors and make the licence fee case even weaker.

Advertising revenue for ITV is even more under threat. In 1985, ITV (which at that time also sold advertising space on Channel 4) had an audience share of over 50 per cent. By 2005 that had fallen to little more than 20 per cent (with Channel 4 now selling its own space for a 10 per cent share). (All figures are from **BARB** – Broacasting Audience Research Board, www.barb.co.uk.) A quick glance at the US points to an even more depressing outlook, as illustrated in the box below.

This is the future for Europe. Subscription fee income from a basic cable or satellite 'package' is beginning to replace advertising revenue as the main source of income for commercial television. On top of this come payments to **PPV (Pay Per View)** operations and a relatively new source of income – the thousands of audience members who phone or text

'Broadcast television is fading into oblivion. Just two web sites, Google and Yahoo!, now account for more advertising revenues than do the prime time schedules of the three traditional television networks – ABC, CBS, and NBC – combined. In contrast to the explosion in e-commerce, broadcast TV viewers are fleeing to cable programming, which now easily beats broadcast TV in the ratings. And those left to watch broadcast programs don't stick around for the commercials. Remote controls, VCRs, and the growing popularity of personal digital recorders are rendering the 60-second TV spot a quaint black and white video clip' (Hazlett 2005).

into programmes. This last is an important process in 'learning' to pay for television by viewers keen to vote on reality TV shows – accepting a cost for participating in a show on 'free' television.

ACTIVITY 4.9

Paying for television

How do you prefer to pay for television? Think about all the ways you could pay at the moment:
- licence
- buying advertised brands
- subscription or PPV
- texting, phoning, interactivity.

Does your mode of payment have any impact on how you enjoy a programme or how you 'value' it? (Some people argue that you only value what you pay for directly. Others value the existence of 'freely available' programmes.)

Soon after this case study was first written, two reports suggested that the threat to advertising-funded television might be exaggerated. In the US the networks announced higher than expected advertising revenues, and in the UK Ofcom reduced the charges it expects ITV to pay to use the analogue TV frequencies. These are indeed uncertain times. The rosier the prospects for ITV plc, the more attractive it will look as a potential purchase for a larger multinational corporation.

The regulation of television will be partly concerned with how these revenues – from public or private sources – are acquired and used in the production or acquisition of a range of programmes. In the US, where public funding is marginal in an almost wholly commercial system, regulation by the Federal Communications Commission (FCC) is limited to the renewal of licences to broadcast. (See Chapter 16 for detailed discussion of regulation of broadcasting.) In the UK, the creation of Ofcom means that a large and potentially powerful independent agency has been created to grapple with the future of broadcasting and telecommunications during this period of change and 'uncertainty'.

Ofcom has direct responsibility to regulate all forms of broadcasting except the BBC, which remains 'self-regulating' under Royal Charter, although with a new BBC Trust to replace the Governors. The Trust will consult Ofcom on 'programme standards and production quotas', but this might change in 2011 with the next BBC Charter renewal (Guardian, 2 March 2005).

Since 1990, the regulation of ITV and Five has been 'light touch' in terms of any public service requirements. Channel 4 has a more clearly defined public service remit which derives from its establishment in 1981 as a publicly owned channel created to broadcast innovatory programmes for a diverse range of audiences. But Channel 4 receives no public funding and must rely on advertising revenue that is now seriously under threat. One of Ofcom's tasks is to help create a television environment in which Channel 4's remit can be fulfilled. When the controller of Channel 4 resigned to join an American broadcaster in 2001, he remarked: 'That ancient phrase, public service broadcasting is a battle standard we no longer need to rally around. It's become a pointless juju stick' (Michael Jackson quoted in the Guardian, 10 December 2001). Ofcom appears to have risen to this challenge.

Public Service Broadcasting (PSB)

The concept of PSB has been argued over for many years, but in 2003 Ofcom began a consultation exercise. If you search on Ofcom's website (www.ofcom.org.uk) you will find numerous mentions of the debate this consultation set up, but a good starting point might be this reference to the Communications Act 2003:

> the purposes of public service broadcasting require the provision of:
> - programmes dealing with a wide range of subject-matters
> - television services that are likely to meet the needs and satisfy the interests of as many different audiences as possible
> - a proper balance of programming
> - services which maintain high general standards of programme-making.

Ofcom went on to identify four 'core components':

- range and balance (range of genres and sub-genres, balance of genres, availability)
- quality (decency, production values, challenging and innovatory programming)
- diversity (of audiences, producers, values and opinions)
- social values (cultural diversity, 'informed democracy' and educated citizenry).

The exercise ended in February 2005 and the findings included some new ideas about how UK television might be conceived. Ofcom had tried to consider the role of PSB in a rapidly changing television environment and had attempted to look ahead to changes yet to come (the Communications Act requires Ofcom to review PSB every five years).

The PSB challenge

Ofcom is working to sustain PSB as an institutional framework within which the 'core components' outlined above can be promoted and embraced by television audiences. But as we have seen so far, various factors, external and internal, are threatening to break up that framework. The loss of advertising revenue means that it is more difficult for ITV to make 'prestigious' programmes, even if the relaxation of ownership rules has created a much larger and potentially stronger ITV plc. However, the relentless march of multi-channel TV is not inevitable. The launch of ITV2 and rebranding of Granada Plus as ITV3 on Freeview have been successful, and in May 2005 ITV2 was the most watched 'digital-only' channel. If ITV can eventually establish itself properly on Freeview, it may be able to rebuild some of its lost audiences and be in a stronger position to negotiate with BSkyB over how its channels are made available to satellite viewers.

Freeview

Created as a joint project between BBC, BSkyB and Crown Castle (the privatised ex-BBC transmitter group), Freeview was set up as a free DTT service when ITV's ONDigital service failed in 2002. In June 2005 it had some 30 per cent of the digital market, growing faster than BSkyB or cable by recruiting the 'refuseniks' who don't want to pay for digital services. ITV has had to 'buy' extra channel space on the platform.

Increased competition to provide digital services pleases Ofcom since it must prepare the audience for the analogue switch-off in 2012. This switch-off carries several implications, some of which are not immediately apparent, but the fundamental point is that in institutional terms, the 'digital world' is a very different place. The analogue system featured 'spectrum scarcity' – meaning that only a limited number of channels were licensed for broadcast by the regulator (ITC, now Ofcom). ITV and Five are privately owned operators that have previously received 'access to broadcast' at relatively low cost. This assumed that:

- potential ad revenues were high
- the broadcasters would fulfil certain PSB requirements.

Ofcom now appears to have accepted that ad revenues on terrestrial television will fall and that the PSB requirements for ITV and Five must be reduced accordingly. In their turn, ITV and Five must think about how they will be able to survive the transition to the digital environment. In July 2005, RTL took complete control of Five and announced its interest in acquiring other UK TV businesses (with the possibility that it would buy Flextech from Telewest, giving access to several digital channels).

In the final consultation document of its PSB Review in 2005, Ofcom stated:

> The overarching theme of this final report is competition for quality. To us, this means three concrete things: a competitive marketplace, plurality of PSB commissioning and production, and enough flexibility in the system for provision (and providers) of PSB to change over time, as the needs and preferences of citizens change.

If we 'unpack' this statement, three separate issues emerge.

'Competition for quality' means that the regulator must ensure that there are enough producers and distributors competing, not just for audiences, but to provide programming of high quality.

'Plurality of PSB' means that the BBC should not be the only PSB commissioner/producer. If Channel 4 cannot afford to carry PSB programming because of falling advertising revenue, it may need other forms of income, possibly from the licence fee. Ofcom may also fund a new PSB provider (see below).

'Flexibility' is a reference to the whole period leading up to and following the switchover when Ofcom may change licensing arrangements to meet changing circumstances – a warning to all sides of the industry?

Whatever Ofcom does decide to do (and whatever the support given by the Department of Culture, Media and Sport), the strategy needs to target those four criteria of range of programmes, quality, diversity and social values. Let's look at one possible innovation and one trend in television culture that will have to be accommodated.

A public service publisher (PSP)

The **PSP** would be a new provider of digital content, commissioning independents to produce programme material that would be electronically published via television, internet, phone technologies, etc. It could also be based outside London to encourage regional production. It would receive public funding, requiring an extra element from the licence fee or a new source. Predictably, while some independents welcomed the new idea, ITV and Channel 4 were less positive, although they might be allowed to bid to run the PSP. The BBC would not be allowed to bid as the purpose of this proposal is to ensure 'plurality' of PSB. (The PSP is also discussed in Chapter 13.)

Audience questions

Who might access the output of a PSP? This is an important question since:

- the television audience is 'fragmenting' and 'segmenting' (see Chapter 8)

- fewer programmes attract a 'national audience'.

Perhaps the biggest single change in television as a *social* institution is the almost complete disappearance of 'event television', when the whole country watches the same event, or even the nightly agreement of a large audience on the most important programmes to watch. Before multi-channel TV, a major 'event' programme might have attracted an audience of 25 million and the Top 10 programmes each week would have attracted 15–20 million. The Top 10 for the week ending 29 May 2005 ranged from 11.6 million to 8.9 million, and comprised four episodes of *Coronation Street*, three of *EastEnders* and two of *Emmerdale*. At No. 3 was Liverpool's win in the Champions League (which with 900,000 from Sky Sports 1 just reached 11 million). The 'population' for television viewing in the UK is 55.47 million (aged 4+), so one of the few 'event' programmes reached just 20 per cent of the population.

It isn't just the fragmenting of the audience, but the observation that the audience frequently fragments along class, gender and especially age divisions. When most of the audience was watching either BBC1 or ITV, both with a clear PSB remit, there was a reasonable certainty that a majority of the population would share the experience of a range of programming, including news, current affairs, drama, etc.

Dr Who and the 'family audience'

In spring 2005, BBC1 took the brave decision to broadcast a new series of *Dr Who* with Russell T. Davies as the main writer with editorial control (making him rather like Joss Whedon as creator of *Buffy the Vampire Slayer*).

The new series was expensive at £10 million (*Guardian*, 31 March 2005) for thirteen 45-minute episodes (average BBC drama cost is £500,000 per hour: see 'BBC Broadcasting Facts and Figures', www.bbcgovernors.co.uk). Saturday night is often considered as something of a 'wasteland' for audiences. The concept of a family watching together on Saturday night belongs to the 1980s when, at the height of ITV's popularity, BBC1 pulled out all the stops to grab the audience. The new *Dr Who* was a resounding success, finishing with an audience of nearly 7 million and peaking at over 10 million. This doesn't seem very large, but it represented 44 per cent of the audience at 7 p.m. ITV's offer of an Eddie Murphy film on 18 June did not even make the Top 75. Many newspaper commentators described watching the programmes with their children and the final episode gained a further 740,000 viewers when it was shown on BBC3 on the Sunday. The relaunch of *Dr Who* was a success and proved that if broadcasters make good 'family' programmes, they will find an audience. Like *Buffy*, *Dr Who* will repay further viewings of episodes with rich subtexts on DVD and repeats. (All figures from *Broadcast* 8 July 2005.)

Figure 4.7 'The Doctor Dances' episode of *Dr Who* proved to be not only 'scary' but to allow Russell T. Davies to celebrate 'single mothers' and the coming of the Welfare State in Britain in the 1940s, among other themes.

ACTIVITY 4.10

'Event' or 'family viewing'

Think about the television events that you have viewed with other people (family or friends).

- What made these broadcasts so important?
- Why did you see them with other people? (Choice or circumstance?)
- Do you think such events are occurring more or less frequently?
- Are there any regular programmes you like to watch with others? If so, which and why?

Channels now have 'identities' or brands that attract specific audiences. The BSkyB audience will be younger and more family orientated, ITV will be older, possibly more female and more working class. Channel 4 will be younger and more middle class. Demographics in the UK point to an ageing population – i.e. the proportion of the population over fifty is increasing (and therefore the proportion under fifty is decreasing). This ought to be of interest to both television service providers and advertisers. The ageing population throws up some interesting possibilities. Older people may:

- have more time to watch television
- be less interested in premium channels/subscription for sport or movies

- be more interested in dramas or documentaries than in reality programming
- vote in local government and general elections

and, importantly, some older people will have more disposable income than young people. (These statements are of course, qualified by class, gender and income, but they are broadly credible.)

Ofcom must ensure that the criteria of range, quality, diversity and social values works for this group as well as for the young families with multi-channel television, broadband computer access, etc. So it must be careful how it awards public funding for PSB and ensures that all audiences benefit.

The programme makers

Television *production* is a relatively 'young' culture. When *Broadcast* (8 July 2005) carried out a survey of its readers working in television and radio, it discovered that they were mainly aged 26–35 and very few had children. The under 25s and over 50s made up only 15 per cent of the total. The survey was based on very small numbers (only 340 out of 3,400 emails were answered) but it is still an interesting indication of who is 'active' in the broadcasting industry. When BBC *Question Time* invited a group of school and college students to produce an edition of the programme in 2005, the students suggested that the studio audience should be made up of only those under 25 and over 50. Do you draw any conclusions from this?

There are signs that broadcasters do understand the demographic changes. In June 2005, BSkyB took over Artsworld, the subscription channel set up by a former Channel 4 boss, Jeremy Isaacs. The highbrow arts channel offering opera, ballet, art cinema, etc. had been faring badly against BBC4 and it seemed a surprising move by Sky under the leadership of James Murdoch, son of Rupert. But BSkyB's steady expansion

could be checked by the 'refuseniks' and their preference for Freeview. Sky Movies and Sport are not appealing to a significant minority of the population – in institutional terms, Sky's ethos, its 'values', are a problem. Brands like Artsworld might be a start in rebranding.

The culture of production

It is worth remembering that people (rather than companies or organisations) make television programmes. If profound changes are taking place in UK television, it is because the attitudes and behaviour of television industry personnel are changing as well. In a lengthy review of Georgina Born's book about the BBC under John Birt and Greg Dyke (Born 2005), the playwright David Edgar, writer of several high-profile television dramas, surveys the whole history of public service broadcasting and suggests that there are three scenarios to describe what has happened to the BBC, and by extension the rest of public service broadcasting, since the 1980s:

1 As in other public services (NHS, education, etc.) the application of market conditions has shaken up complacent hierarchies of white, middle-aged, middle-class men and produced a 'leaner', 'sharper' public corporation more able to respond.

2 New technologies and increased choice have enabled 'ordinary viewers' to find out what it is they like and therefore to resist an elite telling them what's good for them. (Edgar describes this as the view set out by Dawn Airey, one time head of Channel Five.)

3 The **segmentation** of audiences has produced the possibility that specialist channels (BBC3 or BBC4, or in the US HBO) will produce high-quality programming within a specified remit (Edgar 2005).

Whichever of these scenarios is believed by the personnel inside television, they must adapt to a changing environment. Two points about the UK television workforce are important (alongside the age factor mentioned above):

- the process of 'casualisation' – more short-term contracts and less full-time employment – continues
- television is a difficult industry to enter – new entrants need a high level of education and some form of private income to support their work experience (and to live in London with its expensive housing).

In these circumstances, how, for example, do production crews react to a change in management style and to their working environment? We can recast the arguments about the changes in public service broadcasting by focusing on just one type of production which is often the subject of debate in terms of quality – the drama series.

In the so-called 'Golden Age' of television drama, productions took place 'in house' at the BBC or one of the bigger ITV companies such as Granada. The production staff were employed by a drama department and they drew on resources (equipment, props, actors, etc.) that were held centrally by the broadcaster. A certain degree of 'creative freedom' was possible and the drama producer was in a management role within the broadcasting organisation and able to make informed decisions. This was a situation which the reformers of the 1990s saw as 'featherbedding'. If the producers had to go out and buy their resources on the open market, they would become more efficient. This policy was known as 'Producer Choice' in the BBC. Its partner was the **Production Quota** which forced the broadcasters to 'buy in' series created by smaller independent companies – initially 25 per cent of broadcast material.

Red Productions, headed by Nicola Schindler in Manchester, is a good example of an independent production company specialising in drama. Red has been extremely successful with commissions for different broadcasters, including *Queer as Folk* for Channel 4 and *Clocking Off* for BBC1, series which helped promote the careers of their writers Russell T. Davies and Paul Abbott. Further Red Productions have appeared on BBC2, BBC3 and ITV1. The continuity of

a small production group (writer and producer) must give confidence to writers trying something new. On the other hand, Red is not the broadcaster so there is always another tier of management control which could prevent transmission. The lack of a large institutional base also means that the production teams are required to work in different places with different production teams. Red's success means that this could well be in Manchester or Cardiff (for Davies) rather than London. Schindler, Davies and Abbott all worked for broadcasters (all were at one time at Granada) before they became 'independents'. Would they have been as successful if they had stayed as 'staff members' of a larger company?

To a large extent, television has become like the international film business with the large broadcasters (in the UK this means BBC, ITV, Channel 4, Five and BSkyB) as studios buying in programmes from independents. The difference is that at the moment, BBC and ITV still produce the bulk of their peak-time programmes (especially soaps) 'in house'. Even so, the outlook for television industry personnel is laden with 'uncertainty'.

ACTIVITY 4.11

Planning for switchover

Check back over this case study, 'Case study: The media majors' and Chapter 16. Choose one of ITV, Channel 4 or Five, and research what they are saying about the final move to digital television.

Are they moving to or expanding on Freeview?

Are they setting up new channels on BSkyB's Astra satellite service?

Are they trying to change their image (and possibly their audience)?

References and further reading

Bignell, Jonathan (2004) *An Introduction to Television Studies*, London and New York: Routledge.

Born, Georgina (2005) *Uncertain Vision: Birt, Dyke and the Reinvention of the BBC*, London: Vintage.

Building Public Value: Renewing the BBC for a Digital World posted on www.bbc.co.uk/thefuture/pdfs/bbc_bpv.pdf 2004

Creeber, Glen (ed.) (2001) *The Television Genre Book*, London: BFI.

Edgar, David (2005) 'What are we telling the nation?', *London Review of Books*, 7 July.

Ellis, John (2000) *Seeing Things: Television in the Age of Uncertainty*, London: I.B. Tauris.

Hazlett, Thomas W. (2005) 'Broadcast TV on life support', posted on *Financial Times* website, news.ft.com, 2 June 2005.

Holland, Patricia (2000) *The Television Handbook*, London: Routledge.

Miller, Toby (ed.) (2002) *Televsion Studies*, London: BFI.

Websites

www.ofcom.org.uk
www.bbc.co.uk/info
www.itvplc.com
www.mediauk.com/tv

5 Questions of representation

One of the key terms of media studies is 'representation', a rich concept, with several related meanings.

- It emphasises that, however realistic media images seem, they never simply *present* the world direct. They are always a construction, a *re*-presentation, rather than a transparent window onto the real.

- It prompts the question: how do groups, or situations, get routinely represented in the media? This relates to the world of political *representatives*: people who 'stand in' for us – as union or school reps, or our representatives in Parliament, etc.

- It signals the way some media *re*-present certain images, stories, etc. over and over again, making them seem 'natural' and familiar, and thereby often marginalising or even excluding others, making them unfamiliar or even threatening.

The media give us ways of imagining particular groups, identities and situations. When these relate to *people* they are sometimes called stereotypes or types; when they offer images of *situations* or *processes*, the term 'script' is sometimes used, with the implication that we grow familiar with these and often know how to 'perform' them in our own lives, to the exclusion of other ways of being. These imaginings can have material effects on how people expect the world to be, and then experience it, and how they in turn get understood, or legislated for, or called names, or not given employment.

Stereotyping and 'scripts'

Stereotype comes from Greek *stereo* = meaning 'solid'. It is a printer's term for solid blocks of type used to represent something which would otherwise need lots of work with individual pieces of type to show fine detail. Just as electronic publishing has replaced this 'solid' print, so the concept of stereotyping now needs to be rethought.

For example, 'motorists' are not stereotyped as such – though 'boy racers' and increasingly 'SUV' or '4-wheel-drive owners' are. As cycling becomes more environmentally necessary, do you think stereotypes are developing of the 'selfish, aggressive cyclist' and the 'virtuous green cyclist'?

Stereotyping has been a key concept in media studies, and is now perhaps too taken for granted. Many mistakes are made in using the term, which does *not* describe actual people or characters. Brad Pitt is not a stereotype. But the way his image is constructed does carry some and not other stereotypical assumptions about 'masculinity', 'toughness-with-tenderness', etc. Stereotypes are widely circulated *ideas* or *assumptions* about particular groups. They do not exist about all groups. They are often assumed to be 'lies' that need to be 'done away with' so we can all 'get rid of our prejudices' and meet as equals. The term is more derogatory than 'type' or even 'archetype' (which mean very similar things but have higher status as terms).

Stereotypes have the following characteristics:

1 They involve both a categorising and an evaluation of the group being stereotyped.
2 They usually emphasise some easily grasped feature(s) of the group in question and suggest that these are the *cause* of the group's position.
3 The evaluation of the group is often, though not always, a negative one.
4 Stereotypes often try to insist on absolute differences and boundaries where the idea of a spectrum of difference is more appropriate.

Let's explore (1) in a little more detail. Stereotyping is a process of categorisation. This is necessary to make sense of the world, and the flood of information and impressions we receive minute by minute. We all have to be 'prejudiced', in its root sense of 'pre-judging', in order to carve our way through any situation. We make mental maps of our worlds to navigate our way through them, and maps only ever represent parts of the real world, and in particular ways.

- We all employ typifications in certain situations.
- We all belong to groups that can be typified, and stereotyped in this way – as students, lecturers, Londoners, etc. We often make sense of people we meet on the basis of gestures, dress, voice and so on, very much as we construct a sense of characters in the media.

ACTIVITY 5.1

Discuss the points above. When did you last meet a stranger and apply 'typification' to his or her dress, accent, etc.? What were the key signifiers for you? Why did you interpret them as you did? Because of any media images? Were you right in your estimate? Or did your 'snapshot' encourage you not to pursue the conversation?

- And in fictions there is often not enough space to amplify every figure that appears – hence the shorthand use of 'types' as background characters.

ACTIVITY 5.2

Look at any recent film or TV programme where you felt particular groups were 'typed' as background characters.

   Did you feel this was a fair, or a subtle typing?

   If not, how would you have scripted or shot them, given the time, budget and other shapings of the text?

Let's move on to (2). Stereotypes work by taking *some* easily grasped features *presumed* to belong to a group. They put these at the centre of the figure, and then imply that *all* members of the group *always* have those features. They then take the final step of suggesting that these characteristics (often the result of historical processes) are themselves the cause of the group's position. One of the seductions of stereotypes is that they can point to features that apparently have 'a grain of truth'. But they then repeat, across a whole range of media, jokes, etc., that this characteristic is and has always been the central truth about that group.

CASE STUDY 1: RACIAL STEREOTYPING

Let's take an example. For many years, in Hollywood cinema and other discourses, Black slaves working on cotton plantations before the American Civil War of 1861–5 were often stereotyped through such signs as:

- a shuffling walk
- musical rhythm, and a tendency to burst into song and dance readily
- (in characterisations of female house slaves) bodily fatness, uneducated foolishness and childlike qualities – see 'Mammy' and Prissy in *Gone With the Wind* (US 1939).

To say that these demeaning stereotypes embody a grain of truth may seem insulting. But consider the following facts:

- Slaves on the Southern plantations in the nineteenth century had their calf muscles cut if they tried to run away from slavery (the shuffling gait of the stereotype).
- Slaves were given hardly any educational opportunities. The results of this surface in hostile uses of the stereotype, which demean efforts to

Figure 5.1 Hattie McDaniel as 'Mammy' in *Gone With the Wind* (US 1939), playing a character rooted in a familiar oppressive stereotype of the older Black plantation woman. The actor was one of the very few Black performers ever to gain an Oscar, here for her supporting role. See Shohat and Stam (1994) for an excellent discussion of such performances.

make music and dance out of very simple resources to hand. These attribute 'rhythm' to primitive, animal qualities, thus justifying slave owners' prejudices, like 'they couldn't benefit from education anyway'.

- The women were often treated as little more than breeding stock by the slave owners. Once they had given birth to numbers of new slaves, and their bodies were perhaps enlarged by repeated pregnancies and little medical care, they were often moved into the main house and used as nursemaids to the white children. Again, hostile use of the stereotype invites us to account for the Mammy's size in terms of her physical laziness or ignorance rather than her exploitation at the hands of the slave system.

Point (3): though historically oppressed groups have been heavily stereotyped, this usually happens through more than one stereotype. As the title of a famous book on racism and Hollywood (*Toms, Coons, Mulattoes, Mammies and Bucks*, Bogle 2003) suggests there were always several heavily used figures of Black Americans.

Each stereotype itself changes over time, and relates to broader historical discourses, such as those of colonialism or patriarchal values. As Bogle points out, some of the terms in his title were neutral ('coon' referred to rural whites until around 1848) until historical changes turned them into racist slurs. Some are used sympathetically, as in Black Civil Rights reformist propaganda, or the sentimental use of Irishness in *Titanic* (US 1997). Of course they still depend on broadly racist discourses, which bundle people together on the basis of a supposed shared 'racial' unity. But it seems a shame to ignore the work that may have gone into a character or a subversive performance, by simply dismissing it as 'just another

Similarly there is more than one major stereotyped image of Englishness: 'politely reserved', 'stiff upper lipped', 'tea drinking' or 'lager louts'. In response to Bogle, a book on Hollywood Italians by Peter Bondanella was titled *Dagos, Palookas, Romeos, Wise Guys, and Sopranos* (London and New York: Continuum, 2004).

Another power of stereotypes is that they tend to discount those who don't fit the category, e.g. a North American who is shy (not outgoing, 'loud', etc.) will not seem like a typical North American to someone attached to that stereotype.

Mammy/thick Irishman/dumb Welshman'. (See later comments on *Father Ted* as an example.) One of the problems of using the idea of 'stereotypes' is that we may overlook the media's contradictoriness. When the Welsh actor Rhys Ifans in *Notting Hill* (US 1999) performs the stereotypical lustful working-class Welsh dork lost in the sophisticated metropolis, the skill of his performance, as well as the (over-)familiarity of the fictional type as type, works to undercut the role's referential quality, i.e. as referring to and confirming certain images of Welshness.

Racism doesn't necessarily mean a hatred of non-white groups. More accurately it involves *any* account of the world which argues that:

1 people can be divided into 'races', usually via observable differences in appearance. Some accounts are obsessed with 'colour, hair and bone' difference, which are used to argue for an absolute difference between 'black' and 'white'. Some such differences exist, but in far subtler varieties than the relatively few 'races' (Negro, Aryan, etc.) listed by racists.

The next steps of the racist position imply that:

2 these supposed simple groupings (by 'blood') give fundamental explanations for behaviour and character; indeed, that they account for more than any other factor, such as class, upbringing, gender

3 and that some races are inferior to others, and 'innately' prone to certain kinds of behaviour.

Racism resembles stereotyping in the way it takes broadly observable features of a group, puts them at the centre of any account of that group, exaggerates them and (usually) gives them a negative value. Sometimes, as with Nazi ideology, a positive, even superior valuation is given – to the Aryan or 'white' race. Racism has been summarised as 'the stigmatising of difference along the lines of "racial" characteristics in order to justify advantage or abuse of power, whether economic, political, cultural or psychological' (Shohat and Stam 1994).

Finally, (4) stereotypes often seem to insist on absolute boundaries, whereas in reality there exist spectrums of differences and of discourses.

But this idea of spectrums is not usually how arguments against stereotypes are made. More usually, anti-stereotype arguments involve one of the dominant values of western culture: that we are all unique individuals, which stereotypes will not allow for. In some ways this is true

See Chapter 4 'Institutions', for the NUJ (National Union of Journalists) guidelines on race reporting.

Black theorist Paul Gilroy on gun violence being blamed simply on 'blackness': 'They learned their selfishness from Mrs Thatcher, their ruthlessness on the games console, their studied ignorance from the media, and their love of the bling-bling life from the celebrity culture that has debased our civil society' (*Guardian*, 8 January 2003).

See Chapter 6 'Ideologies and power'.

ACTIVITY 5.3

Think of the 'cut-off points' at which age categories or named skin colours shade into their opposite (black/white; childhood/adulthood; old/young).

Say how you have experienced one such important boundary.

(We note later the interesting case of disability. Most of us will experience this temporarily, through injury or illness, but rarely remember 'being disabled for a while'.)

(however much it ignores the social structuring we're all shaped by). Yet it is much more helpful to think of differences as involving *shared* and *changing historical* structures within social orders. We can then understand many of our experiences as being typical, or held in common. Arguably then our differences are due not to 'unique essences' but to the particular ways in which very big, shared social forces (such as class, gender and ethnicity) have intersected and mixed in your or my unique instance (along with some genetic elements and personal histories). Crucially, this broadens the opportunities for understanding both other people's uniqueness and their capacity to act together to challenge unjust social structures.

Another powerful way of approaching the influence of representations, this time of *events* and *situations* rather than constructed characters, is to think of the media as circulating dominant '**scripts**'. These shared expectations get 'performed' with hugely different degrees of commitment, or subversion, by us, the 'actors' (see Durkin; Goffman). They involve important images of how life may be lived; how to behave with others in particular situations, and so on. The very conventionalised ways in which romantic encounters are often portrayed may make you might feel you will know when 'true love' hits you because you've seen its stages 'scripted' so many times. Maybe you have even rehearsed it in private fantasy moments.

Chapter 2 defined scripts as: 'shared expectations about what will happen in certain contexts, and what is desirable and undesirable in terms of outcome' (Durkin 1985: 126).

The power of a repeated 'script', setting up expectations, from cinema? New York, 11 September 2001: a witness, standing near the WTC Twin Towers when they collapsed, who fled only after the first tower went, said: 'I just felt safe. It was a movie set and I was an extra, so nothing could hurt me' (summarised from Hari 2001).

Equally you may have tried to copy the ways that 'being a proper man' is framed and 'scripted' by repeated media imagery, often involving, above all, notions of 'toughness' (see Katz, *Tough Guise* (1999)). These scripts often include a sense of when is the appropriate time to resort to violence, how you do or do not express emotion, etc. Of course they differ depending especially on ethnicity and class. Katz, for example, suggests that the scripts for American Black and Chinese young men, never plentiful, are hugely structured towards violent notions of masculinity since they occur mostly in gangster and kung-fu genres. And, very differently, two theorists noted of the events now called 9/11 that 'news organisations – together with their sources – lacked a readymade "script" to tell their stories, a frame to help them and their audience comprehend the seemingly incomprehensible' (Zelizer and Allan 2002: 1).

ACTIVITY 5.4

Can you think of any 'scripts' that you have learnt from the media? In songs, soap operas, gangster forms? What sorts of situations are most often scripted for you in computer games?

Have you ever been in a situation for which you had not previously come across some kind of media 'script'? What was it? What experience did you draw on to deal with it?

CASE STUDY 2: REPRESENTATIONS AND GENDER

The distinction between sex and gender is a key one, even though the two terms may be used in different ways. Sex, in this context, is not the same as sexuality, which refers to people's sexual orientation, activities and imaginings. *Sex difference* refers here to the classification of people into male and female, depending on physical characteristics: sex organs, hormonal make-up and so on.

Gender differences are culturally formed. Though they exist on the basis of biological classification, 'the body', they build a huge system of differentiation over and above it. So whereas your sex will determine broadly whether or not you can bear a child, for example (though even this

To put it another way, sex says 'It's a boy'; gender says 'Oh, good' and gets out the blue baby clothes, the train set and guns, and a whole set of assumptions (adapted from Branston 1984).

'When I was 3 or 4 my mother was already teaching me to see dust and other people's feelings' (woman interviewed in Hite 1998). The skills produced by such socialisation are then said to be 'natural' and to 'suit' women to certain kinds of employment in a self-fulfilling prophecy. See Chapter 6 'Ideologies and power'.

is not a universal truth), some gendered positions have taken a huge second step. They insist that *because* women bear children, they should be the ones to stay at home and bring them up. 'It's only natural' says a whole social system of laws, tax arrangements, childcare – and media images.

Figure 5.2

ACTIVITY 5.5

- How can you tell which of the very simply drawn characters in Figure 5.2 is male and which female?
- Which lines on the drawing told you?
- Try to find other, similar examples in birthday cards, children's comics and cartoon characters.
- What does this suggest about the ease with which assumptions of gender difference circulate in our culture?

Feminist studies of gender roles seem to show both that there have been huge changes in attitudes to gender difference, and that these coexist alongside long-standing cultural stereotypes. The changes would include the sexual and gender attitudes revealed in vastly popular programmes such as *Big Brother* (Channel 4 2000–), which was won in 2004 by a transsexual called Nadia, of Portuguese origin (the ease with ethnic difference in the programmes was often commented on). But these coexist with, for example, the fact that in the most prestigious levels of news, such as election reporting (see Ross 2004) a woman has not yet 'anchored' the key General Election night coverage on a major UK channel. It is still difficult to imagine a woman commentating live on an important (or, as yet, any) men's TV football or rugby match, even if female sport 'anchors' and interviewers are appearing. Perhaps the authority of the white male voice is hard to hand over to a woman (see Branston 1995). And finally, in 2005 there was controversy over the decision, yet again, to appoint a man to the job of BBC political editor (see Polly Toynbee's 'Another rottweiler joins the macho pack of matadors', *Guardian*, 22 June 2005).

ACTIVITY 5.6

Devise a brief content analysis-based survey of men's and women's roles in TV or magazine adverts to explore how their relationship to domestic labour is represented (use the methods explained in Chapter 1). If men are shown doing this work, is it often in a jokey way? Why?

One fascinating area of representation is: where and when is a category ignored? This can be particularly revealing in the area of gender difference. In *Tough Guise* Katz points to work on newspaper accounts of US school massacres, or road rage incidents. These are overwhelmingly committed by males, but the stories are overwhelmingly ungendered. Often they simply speak of 'the Columbine killers' or 'drivers', thus ignoring discussion of violent masculinities, and thereby naturalising them.

ACTIVITY 5.7

Research the coverage of public exam results this year or last, in local and national press. See how gender differences are reported, or ignored.

In the last few years there has been anxiety about boys' results not matching girls' – but hardly any comment for all the years when the reverse was often the case. Gender therefore not seen as an issue, it went 'unmarked'.

Of course other categories also go unmarked, with oppressive consequences. While 'Black on Black' gun crime is often discussed, 'nobody said the Camden town binbag murders [was] an example of 'white on white' crime' (Paul Gilroy, *Guardian*, 8 January 2003).

'according to usage and conventions which are at last being questioned . . . men act and women appear. Men look at women. Women watch themselves being looked at' (Berger 1972: 45, 47).

Gendered representation also works with taken for granted textual habits. Especially powerful within audio-visual media such as films, TV and music video/DVD is 'the look'. The ground-breaking work of John Berger (1972), Erving Goffman (1976) and, most famously, Laura Mulvey (1975) suggested that women have learned to see themselves as being 'looked at'. This has accrued through countless cultural forms (and outside them), from classical painting to Hollywood cinema. Men, however, have been represented as mostly the ones who do the active looking, along with other kinds of socially valued and purposeful action.

Mulvey's work explored this for Hollywood films of the 1950s and 1960s. She argued that three interlocking system of looks in cinema can be seen as 'male', and as constructing women characters as 'to be looked at' instead of the subject of the action. These looks go from camera to characters; between the characters on screen; and between the audience and the screen. Much has changed since then, including Mulvey's own take on 'the look', but it remains a suggestive way into gender imagery, especially since soft porn forms are becoming increasingly mainstreamed.

Other theorists have since explored the changing relations of men to 'the look', as, from the 1980s, advertisers sought to make men feel they should take an interest in whole areas of appearance-related consumer goods (from stylish clothes to haircare) previously defined as 'feminine'. In order to do this ads needed to display desirable male bodies, an increased display which has arguably legitimised not only women looking with desire, but also male-on-male looking, and same sex desire.

Whatever approach we take to current gender imagery, it appears hugely contradictory. As Ros Gill (2006) writes:

confident expressions of 'girl power' sit alongside reports of 'epidemic' levels of anorexia and body dysmorphia; graphic tabloid reports of rape are placed cheek by jowl with adverts for lapdancing clubs and telephone sex lines; lad magazines declare the 'sex war' over while reinstating demands for beauty contests and championing new, ironic modes of sexism; and there are regular moral panics about the impact on men of the new, idealised male body imagery while the re-sexualisation of women's bodies in public space goes unremarked upon.

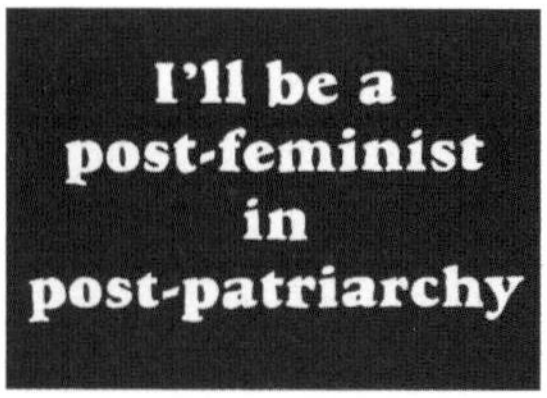

Many women feel that the balance of representation has tilted back towards sexist images and language, updated by the 'alibi' of images of women seeking revenge or, more prevalently, by the use of irony ('I was

I'll be a post-feminist in post-patriarchy

Figure 5.3

only joking. Don't you have a sense of humour?'). The 'laddishness' of breakfast TV or music radio (including female presenters), of magazines like *FHM*, or the use of women in traditionally 'sex object' casting poses (Wonderbra ads, *Playboy* magazine, etc.) with playful captions all point to some of the contradictions that Gill describes, and suggest that a simple use of the idea of 'stereotyping' is no longer adequate for this landscape.

> **Q**   How satisfying do you find 'girl power' media images of female 'empowerment', such as the remake of *Charlie's Angels* (US 2001) or the character Lara Croft?
>
> **Q**   How far do they fit with what's sketched here as 'postfeminist'?
>
> **Q**   How far can such imagery always be read ironically, as 'postmodern play'? Making and circulating it involves real jobs, advertising budgets, space taken up – and also involves other images being thereby excluded?

The term '*post-feminism*' suggests that we are now 'beyond' the need to struggle for gender equality: 'postmodern' playfulness or irony is said to be the proper response to all that. Young women are said to take for granted the equal pay and the freedoms struggled for by earlier feminists.

But freedoms are now defined differently – 'It's OK to love shopping/have plastic surgery/go binge drinking like the men' – while persistent inequalities of pay and job opportunities, as well as women's anxieties about their body shapes, get ignored. Instead, women are said to enjoy 'trying on' identities (even those of pole-dancers) or are satisfied to be able to look at eroticised images of men (see Jeffreys 2005).

> **Q**   How far do these attitudes fit with what's sketched as '*post-feminism*'? Might '*retro-sexism*' be a better term?
>
> **Q**   How far can such imagery be read ironically, as 'just play'?
>
> **Q**   How prevalent do you feel it is? See the idea of a 'spiral of silence' in our case study on news (p. 194). Might this concept apply here?

See During (2005) for an account of feminism's impact on men and women.

'The pink cotton T-shirt's lettering reads: "So many boys, so little time." It's an old line, which usually raises a smile. But . . . this T-shirt is a '5–6 years' size. . . . What about the thong for 7 year olds . . . or the padded bra for a 9-year old?' (Christina Odone, 'Sexy kids', *New Statesman*, 15 July 2002).

Debates on positive and negative images

As you will see in the case of groups such as asylum seekers who often need to hide their identity, sometimes people from outside the group will have to work with and on behalf of those who are overwhelmingly represented in hostile terms or even denied representation. See the US Civil Rights movement in the 1960s for an earlier example.

History suggests that once an oppressed group, such as women or 'Black' people, perceives its political and social oppression, it begins to try to change that oppression. This occurs *at the level of representation as well as at other levels*. Those seeking to change systems of imagery have argued, first, for more images of a particular group. In the early stage of 'getting a voice' there may be few images or stories that centre sympathetically on oppressed groups, as opposed to ones where they feature as villainous or untrustworthy 'types'. This may be the result of violent historical processes, including wars or colonialism, which have left a long legacy of hate-filled, insulting or trivialising images. There are long histories to the stereotyping of ethnic 'others' such as Mexicans or Native Americans in westerns, Arabs and Muslims (not the same) in contemporary Hollywood, or Irish people in British culture.

Once such visibility is achieved, it is often argued that more positive portrayals are needed. What is at stake in trying to replace 'negative' with 'positive' images? It sounds simple, but raises complex issues, involving:

Figure 5.4

- debates around how to define the 'community' being represented
- questions of what are to count as 'positive' representations
- the effect of employment practices and discrimination in media production processes on such images.

Let's take the last point first. Groups that are heavily stereotyped (as 'problems' or even 'potential terrorists') are likely to have less **access** to influential positions in the media or to other kinds of power. This can set up a vicious circle of unemployment, and of lack of pressure on news rooms etc. from inside to represent certain issues. In the case of asylum seekers it may even be the case that they dare not be photographed or quoted by name, for fear of reprisals in their homelands.

When images of the group do begin to be produced, they have to bear what has been called the **burden of representation**. This involves questions such as:

- What is *assumed to be* the reality of the group which is demanding adequate representation? Most groups large enough to make such demands are not homogeneous (think of the differences which are clumped together under the term 'students'). Which group members have the power to define what is positive and what is negative about an image? The success of the BBC television series *Goodness Gracious Me* (you may remember the 'Let's go for an English' sketch) and its spin-offs can be seen as part of a claim of younger British Asians to define their own group(s), sometimes in opposition to the 'better-behaved' images of an older, more threatened generation.
- How to construct characters belonging to the group (particularly visible in the case of skin colour) if they have been relatively absent from media images previously? This can mean that when they do appear they are read as 'representing' the whole community, making it respectable. This is a real burden to those trying to construct the newly visible images.

For many years there were very few images of Black British people on television, and those images which did exist were of Blacks as 'problems' or (more sympathetic, if patronising) as 'victims'. When Black characters *did* appear, they were often felt to need to 'stand in for' or *represent* the whole of their particular 'community'. These 'positive' images often consisted of strict parents, noble teachers, respectable corner shop keepers and so on – clearly a narrowing of the range of representation compared to the roles available to white characters. As a result, some members of such groups felt that being represented in various and ordinary, even 'negative' ways might be a positive step.

EastEnders' variety of Black characters – some involved in petty crime, some parents coping with family difficulties, some in love and so on – was

'Pictures of perfection make me sick and wicked' (Jane Austen, in a letter, 1817).

'There are no such things as negative images. There are just undeveloped stories which give the result, not the process' (Ayoka Chenzira, Edinburgh Film Festival, 1985).

'There is a sense of urgency to say it all, or at least to signal as much as we could in one film. Sometimes we couldn't afford to hold anything back for another time, another conversation or another film. There is the reality of our experience – sometimes we only get the one chance to make ourselves heard' (Pines 1992: 101).

'any negative behavior by any member of the oppressed community is instantly generalized as typical. . . . Representations of dominant groups, on the other hand, are seen not as allegorical but as "naturally" diverse. . . . A corrupt white politician is not seen as an "embarrassment to the race . . ."' (Shohat and Stam 1994: 183).

'I like the sissy [stereotype of gay men]. Is it used in "negative" ways? Yeah. But my view has always been: visibility at any cost. Negative is better than nothing' (Harvey Fierstein in Russo 1981).

argued as a kind of advance. Others, in the mid-1980s, picketed the film *My Beautiful Laundrette* (UK 1985) because of its images of gay and drug-dealing Asian-British characters. 'Negative' images are not always best opposed by (someone's idea of) 'positive', but by the availability of a range of fuller ways of being imagined.

There is another, quite different attitude towards 'positive' and 'negative'. Supposing members of a group with good grounds for surliness, and for lack of cooperation with a social system or situation (slaves in US plantation conditions pre-1870, for example) are represented as always smiling and whistling contentedly at their lot? They may well wonder whether this image is 'positive' only for those who want to be reassured that all is well with an unjust set-up. So sometimes members of heavily stereotyped groups have responded by taking on the denigrated identity that an abusive nickname gives them. Examples would be Black people calling themselves 'niggers', or gays calling themselves 'queens' or 'queers'.

'Taking on a denigrated identity is a way of wrong-footing opponents' (Andy Medhurst, lecture at Cardiff University, 1990). Examples would be gangsta rap's use of 'nigga', or lesbian and gay activists who deliberately call themselves 'dyke' or 'queen'.

Figure 5.5 One representation of cotton picking in the US in the pre-Civil War (1860–5) period. **Q** From whose point of view is this scene constructed? By what means? How else might an encounter between black cotton workers and plantation owners have been represented?

'Sam Jackson uses "nigger" all the time . . . that's just who he is . . . I'm a white guy who's not afraid of that word. I just don't feel that whole white guilt and pussy-footing around race issues. I'm completely above all that' (Tarantino, *Sight and Sound*, March 1989). Discuss?

Q There is heated debate about whether people outside those groups have the right to apply such labels. What do you think?

It seems there is no such thing as the '100 per cent right on text' or 'positive image' which is guaranteed to challenge hostile audiences all on its own. We have to understand images within particular histories, both of the media and more broadly.

A different approach to 'positive' substitutions. There's a lovely moment at the end of the film *Sleep With Me* (US 1995) involving a character who, throughout the film, has been a keen card player. Only in the very last shot do we see him away from the card table, in long shot, and suddenly realise he is in a wheelchair. Without any reference to disability, he has been constructed, through framing, for most of the film as 'just the same as the other characters'.

Genres and realism

The call for 'realism' arises since the media are said to reflect (rather than represent) society, and accuracy is understandably demanded by groups which have previously been invisible. How successful the call for more realism will be depends very much on

- the degree of powerlessness of the group seeking it
- the kinds or genres of media in which they are likely to feature.

It raises questions such as:

- How do different genres affect the demand for 'realism'? What of the needs of exaggerated character types for comedy or fantasy, for example?
- Are stereotypes reworked and used in exaggerated ways as they become familiar, so that they do not necessarily work in hostile ways? How does this process run alongside older, less tolerant ways of imagining the group?

Figure 5.6 The Hollywood production designer Cameron Menzies (1896–1957) sketched this design, probably for *The Thief of Bagdad* (sic) (US 1940). He made full use of orientalist imagery of nomadic tent-dwellers and cunning, evil character types. These have existed since the Crusades, which were military campaigns from the eleventh to the thirteenth century, backed by the Roman Catholic Church. They originally tried to take 'the Holy Land' from Muslims (see www.wikipedia.org). Such imagery has fascinated western storytellers, and has been 'played with' and recirculated over and over in such O.T.T. fictions.

The images continue to circulate, sometimes playfully, as in *The Mummy* films. They embody a very hostile and limited view of 'Arab' groups, which now exist very differently in the real world (and almost exclude women, except as decorative dancers).

The imagery can get called on, or revived, within much more dangerous, less playful political rhetoric, like that of George W. Bush after 9/11, when the 'lairs' and 'cunning' of 'the Orient' were once more evoked to justify military invasions. (See 'Case study: News'.)

If we always simply call for 'realism', we may ignore the fact that media texts do not have a straightforward relationship to the rest of the real.

They may belong to a genre (radio comedy or horror film) which is not experienced by audiences in the same way as, say, the news or current affairs. Audiences' and, especially, fans' degree of familiarity with a genre's conventions will influence its 'reality effect', and what they take for granted in order to get at its pleasures. The idea of images as reflecting reality is far too straightforward and mirror-like, especially for fantasy forms (e.g. horror, comedy, SF or animation). It suggests there is a fairly simple thing called 'reality' to be 'reflected' in a one-to-one, undistorted glass. Yet comedy, for example, seems to *depend* on the exaggerations of stereotyping, which are understood playfully by audiences, not always as a 'reflection' of 'the real'. Dafydd ('I'm the only gay in the village') in *Little Britain* (BBC 2003–), for example, is a complex combination of ludicrous pouting presence and rubber costume, and a failure to realise how acceptable or indeed common it is to be gay, or to imagine it is daring to state that identity. The whole character, like many others in the series, such as the delinquent teenager 'Vicky Pollard' ('No but yeah but yeah but yeah but no . . .') is partly constructed out of an assumption that the audience will feel superior to 'outmoded' prejudice about such figures, though for some it will shade into a less attractive self-congratulation at their own knowingness. Others may feel irritation at the Welsh setting as signifying such backwardness, and yet others that it has no sense of the persistence of attacks on and hostility to gay people.

'Gay characters and references to the existence of homosexuality were routinely laundered off the screen for . . . half a century' (Russo 1981: 63).

One example: genre expectations of 'sophisticated sex comedy' meant that fans of *Sex and the City* (US HBO 1999–2005) focused on expectations of the *next* joke, clever saying, great dress or comic reversal of fortune, rather than on the 'unrealistically' elite lifestyles of the central women characters, or their inability to critically analyse their relationship and work problems. Of course those same audiences might be aware *outside* that series of the need to change sexist employment structures etc., but might 'forget' about it temporarily, if the pleasures of the programme were absorbing enough. (See Bignell 2004: 216–20.)

The *Father Ted* series (Channel 4 1995–8) likewise gave a 'hilariously overblown' version of the 'stupid' Irish stereotype, but it mixed this with satire on the priesthood, so 'stupidity comes to stand in for the inflated status of Catholicism in an increasingly secular Ireland' (McRobbie 2005:

'THE MOTHER IN LAW' JOKE AND FORMAL PLEASURES

When the late Les Dawson said the line: 'I knew it was the mother-in-law 'cause when they heard her coming, the mice started throwing themselves on the traps', there were several pleasures on offer:

- his delivery, gravelly Northern voice and timing, especially as contrasted with –
- the verbal surprise of the comic exaggeration – the image of those mice!
- the economic elegance of a well-crafted joke, well delivered.

However, this joke's economic elegance also works because a quickly recognisable stereotype is in play (the 'mother-in-law'). This offers the pleasures of speedy recognition, but also of 'community', of feeling a 'we'-ness and a 'them'-ness for a moment.

Questions include:

- From whose point of view is it being told? Whose is excluded? Who is the 'them' outside this cosy community?
- How is the group on the receiving end of the joke treated in the rest of the media? Does that change how we might experience the joke?

To make this last point clearer: in the case of mothers-in-law, we may feel OK to laugh, since this is rather an outmoded target. Changes in family structures have eroded the power of mothers-in-law of many working-class couples, who had to live in 'her' home for the first few years of married life. Maybe the degree of exaggeration itself signals the joke's distance from reality. To put it in semiotic language: pleasure is more from the play of the signifiers than from agreement with the way the sign represents its referent.

However, you might feel differently if you were an older woman, and the object of many contemptuous jokes and comedy sketches. (Or you might not, if age were only a relatively unimportant one of your several identities.) And when jokes centre on groups that are being abused on the streets or in the home, for whom there are fewer 'communities of feeling' to enter, it becomes a much less easy thing to laugh at them.

Q Can you think of a recent joke you have heard to which you might apply the same analysis?

Another example: 'Propp's original study worked with fairy tales from hundreds of years ago when many women would die in childbirth, and the role of ('wicked') stepmothers could therefore be a shared reference point for audiences' (from Chapter 2 'Narratives'.

112). Similarly playful and overblown are the Scottish over the top *Rab C. Nesbitt* character (BBC 1988–99) as well as the characters in *Goodness Gracious Me* (BBC 1996–8), and *The Kumars at No. 42* (BBC 2001–3).

Historical and institutional processes

Debates over representation cannot be restricted simply to the level of textual analysis. They need to bear in mind media institutions and their different processes and relationships to the rest of the real world. It matters, for example, that *Father Ted* was written by two Irish writers, or that *Goodness Gracious Me* was authored by members of the groups it was satirising. More broadly it's important to recall the ways that historical changes can widen (or narrow) imaginings and the range of images possible. This is where too much focus on (textual) stereotypes can be limiting.

- One of the achievements of the US Black Civil Rights struggles in the 1950s and 1960s, or the anti-corporate globalisation movements now, is to have put on the agenda different images of ethnicity, and of admirable lifestyle scripts (see www.Adbusters.com).

- The needs of capitalist entertainment industries to make profits in ever more fragmented markets inevitably leads to constant and unpredictable changes in the images offered to groups for self-representation. It remains true though this is usually within the limits of assumed purchasing power. The 'pink pound', for example, was a key factor in persuading advertisers that they could target gay audiences through buying space in certain programmes, magazines, etc. For poorer groups (such as asylum seekers) the prospects for changing representations have to lie elsewhere, often in alliances with sympathetic members of dominant groups.

- Changes to employment patterns in media industries, often named *affirmative action* or *equal opportunities* policies, mean that, wherever possible, people from particular groups (Black Britons, or women, or those with disabilities, for example) are appointed to jobs *if their suitability is more or less equivalent to that of other candidates*. These can

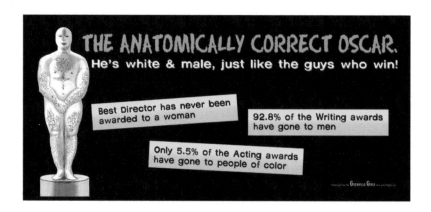

Figure 5.7 Thanks to the US-based group www.guerrilla-girls.com for use of one of their striking campaigning posters.

be 'positive' in helping to produce expectations and role models other than the unspoken conviction that 'women or Blacks or gays can't do that work because I've never seen one doing it'.

A surprise for those who believe that post-feminism has achieved equality for women: Martha Lauzan (2004) discovered that in 2003, women comprised only 17 per cent of the individuals working in key behind-the-scenes roles on the top 250 US domestic grossing films. This is the same percentage of women who worked on the top films of 1998. Approximately one out of five US films released in 2003 employed *no* women directors, executive producers, producers, writers, cinematographers or editors. Men directed more than nine out of ten films.

In addition, affirmative action may also open up a newsroom or a drama unit to workplace discussions and experiences which are far from those of the people usually in charge. If people with disabilities work on a newspaper, it makes it harder to resort to the stereotype that 'disabled people are always helpless victims'. The BBC's Frank Gardner, badly injured in a gun attack in Saudi Arabia in 2004, is now a fine example of that institution's use of an expert correspondent. Cutaway shots to him in his wheelchair, after one of his lucid accounts of the Middle East, often come as a shock to those who first see them.

Another example was Levi's 2005 ad campaign for Red Tab jeans featuring beautiful young people wearing little else but pairs of tight-fitting jeans who are described as 'blind' in a small caption, and who comment on how good the jeans felt, rather than looked (see *Media Guardian*, 1 August 2005, for discussion).

Several Black journalists have commented that racist headlines in **tabloid** (or 'red-top') papers would be harder to justify in the newsroom if there were more non-white British journalists employed there.

Disabled people are the largest 'minority' group in the UK (estimated at 10–12 per cent). 'Most of us will at some point in our lives be disabled – whether congenitally, or through old age, illness, or accident and so on . . . our culture is dangerously close to denying the inevitability and necessity of . . . messy or "negative" feelings, as part of normal life' (Jessica Evans in Briggs and Cobley 1998: 349).

- Broadening of access to dissenting mechanisms like the **right of reply** has also been important. Newspapers have always had massive power to circulate hostile images of groups such as asylum seekers (see 'Case study: Images of migration'), or individuals like George Galloway. Those targeted have had far less power to circulate their replies and are often discredited by unfounded allegations, unless they have access to expensive lawyers. Under pressure these might later be quietly retracted in an obscure part of the newspaper. The right of reply lobby (see the Campaign for Press and Broadcasting Freedom) asks for the reply to such stories to be given equal prominence to the original story. Thus an untrue *front-page* headline would have to be corrected on a later *front page*.

- Activities which broaden audiences' ability to come across, and feel comfortable with a wide range of media forms and imaginings are key. Paradoxically, they may involve challenging the power of certain lobbying groups seeking to close down certain images. For example, abortion now seems to be a particularly sensitive issue, partly as a result of lobbying. Often it is hardly explored, even as an option to be rejected by a character in a soap, where issues can be given fuller airings, over time. This seems to be due not so much to audience hostility as to broadcasters' over-sensitivity to religious and other increasingly vocal pressure groups.

Or it may involve campaigns around the kind of regulating which in fact opens up media forms and encourages audiences to feel at home with 'different' images and works. The public service remit of much of British broadcasting has been crucial here, seeking 'not only to represent a "realistic" cross-section of characters but also to advance public understanding' (Bignell 2004: 220), even where this takes programmes into unfashionable territory.

> Compare a Chicago film critic on US isolationism: 'even bad or mediocre foreign movies have important things to teach us. Consider them . . . precious news bulletins, breaths of air, (fresh or stale) from diverse corners of the globe; however you look at them, they're proof positive that Americans aren't the only human beings' (Rosenbaum 2002: 108).

Conclusion

There are many examples of the media systematically narrowing imagery of particular groups, even of misrepresenting them (see 'Case study: Images of migration'). But we have also tried to argue against the suggestion that the media have huge powers *all on their own*, simply at the level of texts, or stereotypes, to socialise people into beliefs, roles and behaviour. We've also tried to question the most conventional uses of the term 'stereotype', since often this now:

- is used to refer to real people or characters, instead of as a set of images
- is a barrier to proper understanding of how images change and are struggled over through time
- ignores how they are played within different genres

- ignores how they get understood by audiences, or often performed by members of the groups in question
- and finally can ignore how they relate to much more powerful discourses, which get left out in too much attention to 'stereotypes'.

People are not always successfully socialised by media images. Indeed, in the rich media environments which most people inhabit (multi-channel TV, cable, the internet) some would say that instead of 'representing' life, as though quite separate from it, the media now 'fold into' everyday life. This may be true of some sections of the world. But media misrepresentations through powerful channels still undoubtedly take place, with real effects in the rest of the real world – on the street, in the workplace. Many find ways to challenge or subvert these – as well as lazily going along with the easiest blamings or images on offer.

References

Berger, John (1972) *Ways of Seeing*, Harmondsworth: Penguin.

Bignell, Jonathan (2004) *An Introduction to Television Studies*, London: Routledge.

Bogle, Donald (2003, anniversary edition) *Toms, Coons, Mulattoes, Mammies and Bucks: An Interpretative History of Blacks in American Films*, New York: Continuum.

Branston, Gill (1984) *Film and Gender*, London: Film Education.

Branston, Gill (1995) 'Viewer, I listened to him . . . voices, masculinity, in the Line of Fire', in Pat Kirkham and Janet Thumim (eds) *Me Jane: Masculinity, Movies and Women*, London: Lawrence and Wishart.

Briggs, Adam and Cobley, Paul (eds) (1998) *The Media: An Introduction*, Harlow: Longman.

Campbell, Duncan (2001) 'Hollywood still prefers men', *Guardian*, 5 December.

During, Simon (2005) 'Ch. 6: Feminism's aftermath: gender today', in *Cultural Studies: A Critical Introduction*, London: Routledge.

Durkin, Kevin (1985) *Television, Sex Roles and Children*, Milton Keynes: Open University Press.

Gill, Ros (2006) *Gender and the Media*, Cambridge: Polity Press.

Goffman, Erving (1959) *The Presentation of Self in Everyday Life*, Garden City, NY: Doubleday.

Goffman, Erving (1976) *Gender Advertisements*, London: Macmillan.

Hari, Johann (2001) 'Law of the jungle', *New Statesman*, 10 December.

Hite, Shere (1998) *The Hite Report on Women and Love: A Cultural Revolution in Progress*, London: Viking.

Jeffreys, Sheila (2005) *Beauty and Misogyny: Harmful Cultural Practices In The West*, London: Routledge.

Lauzen, Martha (2004) *The Celluloid Ceiling: Behind-the-Scenes Employment of Women in the Top 250 Films of 2003*, www.womenarts.org.

McRobbie, Angela (2005) *The Uses of Cultural Studies*, London: Sage.

Mulvey, Laura (1975) 'Visual pleasure and narrative cinema', *Screen*, reprinted in L. Mulvey *Visual and Other Pleasures*, London: Macmillan.

Pines, Jim (ed.) (1992) *Black and White in Colour: Black People in British Television since 1936*, London: BFI.

Rosenbaum, Jonathan (2002) *Movie Wars: How Hollywood and the Media Conspire to Limit What Films We Can See*, London: Wallflower.

Ross, Karen (2004) *Framed: Women, Politics and News Media*, Coventry: University Research Monograph.

Russo, Vito (1981) *The Celluloid Closet: Homosexuality in the Movies*, New York: Harper & Row.

Shohat, Elaine and Stam, Robert (1994) *Unthinking EuroCentrism: Multiculturalism and the Media*, London and New York: Routledge.

Zelizer, Barbie and Allan, Stuart (eds) (2002) *Journalism After September 11*, London and New York: Routledge.

Further reading

Aintey, Beulah (1998) *Black Journalists, White Media*, London: Trentham Books.

Dyer, Richard (1997) *White: Essays on Race and Culture*, London: Routledge.

Geraghty, Christine (2004) *My Beautiful Laundrette*, London: I.B. Tauris.

Gilroy, Paul (2002) *There Ain't No Black in the Union Jack*, 2nd edition, London: Hutchinson.

Gilroy, Paul (2000) *Between Camps: Nations, Cultures and the Allure of Race*, Harmondsworth: Penguin.

Malik, Sarita (2001) *Representing Black Britain Black and Asian Images on Television*, London: Sage.

Medhurst, Andy and Munt, Sally R. (eds) (1997) *Lesbian and Gay Studies: A Critical Introduction*, London and Herndon: Cassell.

Pointon, Ann with Davies, Chris (eds) (1997) *Framed: Interrogating Disability in the Media*, London: BFI.

Stafford, Roy (2001) *Representation* (Teacher's notes pack on representation and fiction films).

Other resources

Katz, Jay (1999) *Tough Guise: Violence, Media and the Crisis in Masculinity*,
Media Education Foundation.
www.afterellen.com
www.cpbf.org.uk
www.justlabour.yorku.ca/Aguiar.pdf

CASE STUDY: IMAGES OF MIGRATION

Some heated debates, certainly in wealthier parts of the world, concern migration or 'immigration' (sometimes called 'asylum seeking', though it is not the same). Here we will try to apply to migration some ideas from Chapter 5, asking:

- How do different migrating groups, or situations, get represented, or under-represented in the media?
- Do some media *re*-present certain images, stories, 'scripts', etc. over and over again, making them seem 'natural' and familiar? Does that often marginalise or even exclude others?
- What are the varieties of ways in which such representations occur across different media?

'Asylum seekers' (and many other migrants) are largely at the first stage of struggles over representation – the stage where there is a huge need to simply contest very limited and negative images, misinformation and prejudice. Despite the work of a few films (see below) imagery around them is a long way from the confident, O.T.T. play of comic series like *Father Ted* or *Goodness Gracious Me* about other groups. Nevertheless, complex questions still arise. Let's first unpack that term 'migration'.

Thinking about 'migration'

Stereotypes, we argued, involve both a categorising and an evaluation of the group being stereotyped. They give the impression of absolute boundaries where the idea of a spectrum or continuum of difference is more useful. In other words they produce a narrow label for a large and unwieldy reality: 'Southerners', 'Northerners', 'football fans'.

We've used the word 'migration' here because it draws attention to several meanings given to the widespread movements of people, or 'people flow' as some suggest we should call these journeys. These spark very charged debates, given the relatively new phenomenon of globally mobile terrorist networks (see Chapter 15). And they raise difficult questions about hyphenated identities (such as

---

Q How many kinds of sizeable geographical journeys can you think of?

A Tourism and exploration

- Economic migration', i.e. travelling to get work, both inside (internal migration) and outside the borders of a country of origin (arguably, including moving away from home for a job, or even to study or for temporary contract work)
- The moves, of those British people who can afford it, to southern Europe or other warmer places; these are regularly celebrated in 'lifestyle' TV programmes, books and articles
- 'Globe trotting' as part of a 'high-flying' lifestyle or work (stars, sports figures, chief executives, etc.).

Muslim-British) and what demands each of the components of these complex titles are entitled to make on those who choose to name themselves thus.

To explore immigration debates it's well worth thinking first about which journeys are represented positively and made to feel 'natural': tourism, for sure and a historical example, the departure of the persecuted Pilgrim Fathers to North America in the seventeenth century, and then the steady, often violent advance across a land inhabited by Native Americans. Other large-scale journeys, however, are not naturalised, let alone celebrated. Broadly, if the journeys involve the poor they're called 'migration'; if they involve corporate executives, 'homes in the sun', etc., they are called 'relocation' and usually welcomed.

(Both tend to get swallowed up in *some* abstract uses of 'diaspora'; see Chapter 16.)

Q Which of these are viewed sympathetically? By whom? Which are represented in more hostile ways? By whom?

'few . . . in [the] world today do not have a friend, relative, or co-worker who is not on the road to somewhere or already coming back home, bearing stories and possibilities . . . more people than ever before seem to imagine routinely the possibility that they or their children will live and work in places other than where they were born' (Appadurai 1998: 4, 6).

One of the appeals of stereotypes is that they offer entertaining short cuts through huge, complex and often painful sets of knowledge. Journeys labelled 'migration', for example, involve relations of inequality and dependency between the richer and the poorer countries of the world. Many would argue that the conditions of poverty and violence in some poorer countries are partly a result of such factors as trade restrictions by the rich countries (which Oxfam estimates costs developing countries around $100 billion a year) or the support given to violent and repressive regimes by western arms traders.

People do not usually leave their homes on such long and dangerous journeys for trivial reasons. Evidence suggests that many refugees intend only a temporary stay in another country, and hope to return home once savings targets have been reached (see Castles 2003). Other complex issues arise around these moves, which are much more demanding to explore than a few stereotypes. They include the debates as to whether modern states need to have borders. Security in an era of global terrorism and drug trafficking; paying collectively for public services; universal social security: all these depend on agreement about who belongs within a nation's shared community of interest.

Figure 5.8 Catherine Zeta Jones, economic migrant . . . with homes in several continents? Her image is often celebrated for her 'gypsy' look, a description which draws on romantic images of wanderers but ignores the very hostile uses of it for attacks on 'travellers'.

But how to balance that, now, with the cost of anti-terrorist measures, tagging asylum seekers, and patrolling borders? How difficult does it become to point out that migrants, working in low-paid jobs, often contribute *more* to hospitable countries in taxes etc. than they take from them?

'Race hate and race violence does not rise and fall according to the numbers of immigrants coming to Britain. It rises and falls to the extent to which people's prejudices are inflamed and made respectable by politicians and newspapers' (Paul Foot, on ITV's *What the Papers Say*, 1976).

ACTIVITY 5.8

See how well you understand these terms.

Who is an asylum seeker? Anyone who has applied for asylum against persecution under the 1951 UN Convention on Refugees, and is waiting for a decision. It's estimated that there are 13 million worldwide. Developing countries produce 86 per cent of the world's refugees but also provide asylum to more than two-thirds of them. (See www.oxfamgb.org.)

Who is a refugee? Anyone who has been granted asylum under the UN Convention (signed by the UK along with 144 other countries). The legal definition of 'refugee' is someone who

owing to a well-founded fear of being persecuted for reasons of race, religion, nationality, membership of a particular social group, or political opinion, is outside the country of his nationality, and is unable or, owing to such fear, is unwilling to avail himself of the protection of that country.

News media and the right to representation

Let's apply a few of the news case study's concepts to explore how discourses and images of migration represent, and often misrepresent, only a few features of these complex debates, over and over again. One key area is words: the terms used, especially in news headlines, as compared to other possible terms which might have been used.

News, especially print news, also works with a particular sense of 'news values'. Once a story, or theme, or set of 'scripts' is established as controversial or 'newsworthy' it tends to achieve headline status more easily. Keywords such as 'swamping', 'flooding',

Who is an illegal asylum seeker? No one. It cannot be illegal to seek asylum since everyone has the fundamental human right to request asylum under international law. Even the term *'bogus asylum-seeker'* is misleading. It pre-judges the outcome of an asylum application – like describing a defendant as entering a 'bogus plea of innocence' during a trial. (See RAM website.) A more accurate term is *'failed asylum seeker'*.

Who are 'illegals' (the US term is the threatening *'illegal aliens'*)? Those who work without legal permits, for whatever reason. As a direct result they are often paid illegally low wages, and work in illegally poor conditions, sometimes organised by official 'gangmasters'. But employers' actions are not the focus of many hostile uses of this word. Instead:

- it conjures up images of semi-criminal activities, such as prostitution, drug dealing, theft;
- the term *'illegals'* is often used as though it were the same as *asylum seekers*. In fact *'undocumented immigrants'* is probably a better term.

The Office of National Statistics, which records the net annual flows in and out of the UK, uses the terms *'in-migrants'* and *'out-migrants'*. And many prefer the term *'people flows'* for migratory moves.

'wave', 'influx', 'sponging' rule out the possibility that migrants might have anything to offer to the host country (and lock into long-established rhetoric around Britain as an 'island race'). In summer 2005 some tabloid papers irresponsibly confused terrorist stories and prejudices about asylum seekers and Muslims. In such heated moments, other, more sympathetic views, can easily become part of the 'spiral of silence' (see 'Case study: News').

Some news media, especially parts of the ratings-hungry tabloid press, will go further. The item in the box below is an older example of shoddy reporting, which puts together some sensational elements and unspoken assumptions:

- 'foreigners have barbaric food tastes and practices – here's a great example'
- 'asylum seekers are showing disrespect for the royal family'
- talk of 'fears' rather than proof – which means you can allege almost anything
- the visual contrast of the traditionally white and elegant swans with the criminal (dark?) asylum seekers. This was implied in the front page layout, which simply had a large picture of a white swan, but the *Sun* refused us permission to reproduce this.

Misleading headlines in the newsagents' shop are seen by many more people than buy the papers which display them. So a retraction of downright misrepresentation (much later, and much less prominently positioned in the newspaper) is a very poor substitute for thoughtful and accurate journalism.

See RAM (Refugees, Asylum Seekers and the Media) website for more details of this story which became a kind of folk tale for a while. Imagine how it may have affected the lives of asylum seekers, or indeed anyone who seemed 'East European' (for which the 'signs' are usually those of accent only).

On 4 July 2003 a front page 'exclusive' in the *Sun*, which has a circulation of 3.5 million daily, announced:

SWAN BAKE Asylum seekers steal the Queen's birds for barbecues
Callous asylum seekers are barbecuing the Queen's swans. . . . East European poachers lure the protected Royal birds into baited traps, an official Metropolitan Police report says. Steve Knight of the Swan Sanctuary [says]: 'To these people they are a perfectly acceptable delicacy.'

On p. 7 the story was headlined: '**ASYLUM GANG HAD 2 SWANS FOR ROASTING**'. It continued:

Police swooped on a gang of East Europeans and caught them red-handed about to cook a pair of royal swans . . . two dead swans were also found concealed in bags and ready to be roasted. The discovery . . . confirmed fears that immigrants are regularly scoffing the queen's birds.

Other refugees, angry and suspicious about the story, contacted RAM Communications Officer Nick Medic, an exiled journalist from Eastern Europe. They made a collective complaint to the PCC (Press Complaints Commission). Calls to four relevant London police stations revealed no record of the alleged offence.

Steve Knight (see above) told Nick the *Sun* had not been faithful to his words. When the police were asked about the 'official report' they replied:

We never released a report on this subject to the *Sun*. . . . Nobody has been arrested or charged in relation to offences against swans by the Metropolitan Police recently . . . The

Sun . . . referred to asylum seekers being responsible. We have no information at all that supports this contention.

The *Sun* offered to publish this statement:

A report in the *Sun* on the 4th July about the disappearance of swans in southern England stated that asylum seekers were responsible for poaching them. While numerous members of the public alleged that the swans were being killed and eaten by people they believed to be Eastern European, nobody has been arrested in relation to these offences and we accept that it is not therefore possible to conclude yet whether or not the suspects were indeed asylum seekers.

What RAM asked for:

SWAN BAKE: CORRECTION AND APOLOGY

A report in the *Sun* of the 4th July, headlined on the front page SWAN BAKE, stated that gangs of Eastern European asylum-seekers were responsible for the disappearance of swans from southern England.

The story was based on unsubstantiated allegations made by unnamed members of the public who claimed to believe that swans were being killed and eaten by Eastern Europeans. The police have confirmed that nobody has been arrested for such offences, and they have no evidence that asylum-seekers or Eastern Europeans are responsible for reported reductions in the swan population.

The *Sun* accepts that it is not possible to conclude whether the offences described actually occurred. We would like to apologise for any false impression that may have been given.

What the PCC (Press Complaints Commission) ruled:

. . . the newspaper was unable to provide any evidence for the story which, to its readers would appear to be a factual account.

[it] should have ensured that the article was presented as conjecture . . . the Commission noted that the publication had offered to print a clarification . . . to ensure that readers were aware that the statement was based on inconclusive material.

. . . your [RAM's] proposed draft clarification was more comprehensive, but . . . the original proposal constituted sufficient remedial action . . . (and) [we] concluded that no further action was required on the part of the newspaper. . . .

The 'grain of truth' in stereotypes?

We argued that stereotypes take a recognisable feature of a group, put it at the centre of the image, and then go on to suggest that it is always true of the entire group. Asylum seekers, like many powerless groups, are often ridiculed or even attacked because they cannot afford as much, or are not given the same resources, as most of the rest of the host population. Negative images take the *results* of this deprivation, whether that be appearance, or difficulties with language, or desperation for money, or even resort to crime. They put these at the centre of the description, as the cause of the group's situation. Asylum seekers are over and over again implied to be *by their nature* always on the look-out for scams or even criminal possibilities. This 'inherent' nature is blamed for their predicament.

ACTIVITY 5.9

Examine the next article you come across which raises such fears on its front page.

- List the key terms it uses and repeats, especially in the headline. What choices have been made there?
- How is asylum seeking *framed* – i.e. what larger contexts are given, such as the conditions being fled from? How many facts or statistics are used? Which organisations are quoted?
- How are photos used? Is it true that most images of asylum seekers are:
  - absent, replaced by images of government officials?
  - images of men, reinforcing the notion that the majority of asylum seekers are lone males?
- not local to the area of Britain featured in the article? Or are they photographs of refugee camps, people behind fences, etc?
- If the article is in a local paper, has there been any attempt to help local people imagine the plight, appearance, abilities, families of those written about?
- Are there any photos of families, in familiar work or home situations?
- Is there any sign that the reporters are 'on the spot' if the story concerns a British town?

Speers (2001) is a useful example of how to explore such issues.

ACTIVITY 5.10

Q Conduct a survey to discover how much your friends think an asylum seeker receives in state benefits.

A According to a November 2000 Mori Poll most people believe this to be over £110 per week. In fact, their benefits are below the basic level. In 2005 a single adult received £38.96 per week in addition to accommodation and utilities – substantially below what is considered the minimum level of income necessary to maintain an acceptable standard of living. For the twelve months in which their claim for asylum is considered they are not allowed to work, though claims are being processed much faster than in the past.

Historically, groups fleeing persecution or hunger, with different cultures and traditions, have often been negatively imaged by the new cultures they enter as migrants. Terry Eagleton, coming from an Irish family, has written of the kinds of truths put in play in stereotypes of nineteenth-century Irish immigrants. It is not true that 'all Irish are lazy'. But it is true that the Irish immigrants who flooded from their small farms to the industrial cities of Victorian Britain in the wake of the Great Famine were accustomed to a less crippling work discipline than their British counterparts. 'This could look like indolence, since their lives as small tenant farmers involved sporadic bursts of labour, but a fair bit of leisure too, with much enjoyment of fairs and feast-days' (Eagleton 2000). History later produced 'the Paddy' figure out of the men recruited for the backbreaking work of building nineteenth-century roads and railways, and the abiding sense of the verbal abilities and love of sociability which could be said to come from a largely rural society.

ACTIVITY 5.11

Find out if any of your friends have families or connections with 'the Irish diaspora'. Ask them how they feel the media represent 'Irishness' now. Do they feel there have been significant changes to these images?

A drain on resources?

Paying their Way: The Fiscal Contribution of Immigrants in the UK, published by the Institute for Public Policy Research in 2005, shows that immigrants contribute relatively more to the public purse than the UK born. Total revenue from immigrants grew in real terms from £33.8 billion in 1999–2000 to £41.2 billion in 2003–4 – a 22 per cent increase.

On average per annum each immigrant generated £7,203 in government revenue, compared to £6,861 per non-immigrant, with each immigrant accounting for £7,277 of government expenditure on average, compared to £7,753 per non-immigrant.

Nick Pearce, IPPR director, said: 'Our research shows that immigrants make an important fiscal contribution to the UK and pay more than their share. They are not a drain on the UK's resources.'

(See RAM website.)

Varieties of media representations

Different groups view migration differently: some may oppose migration for fear of worsened housing conditions, criminal activity, etc., while some employers may favour or turn a blind eye to the recruitment of illegally low-paid migrant workers. These conflicting pressures on governments make for mixed messages in immigration policies.

Similarly the media offer mixed messages. Not all news forms will take the hostile line cited above. The liberal broadsheet press (*Guardian*, *Independent* etc.) will often follow up such stories in different ways, as will some current affairs programmes on TV.

In Dover Groups of European tourists are routinely mistaken for illegal immigrants, according to the Home Office-funded charity Migrant Helpline (based in Dover). It points out how fantasy thrives in a climate of distrust. One tale involves a resident who reported asylum seekers in Argos buying 'expensive goods'. They turned out to be the crew of a cruise ship. (See Mark Townsend and Gaby Hinsliff, 'Truth about Calais "immigrant menace"', *Observer*, 17 April 2005.)

However, a unique problem faces asylum seekers who might want to change hostile representations: they often dare not be photographed, filmed or even quoted by name, for fear of reprisals in their homelands, or having their application turned down, or causing family friction. This, along with the repetition of stock images of male asylum seekers with their faces partially covered, captioned as 'breaking into Britain', strengthens an image of criminality. And terrorist attacks can easily be used to fuel such fears. Hard to see how a right of reply could operate for them.

ACTIVITY 5.12

See how the news story you selected for Activity 5.9 was followed up or commented on by other media. If it was a local story, contact local refugee organisations to see if they attempted to correct or amend it. Contact national refugee organisations such as RAM, the Refugee Council, Oxfam, Migration Helpline for comment.

Some media, especially film and TV, have offered powerful ways to imagine the situation of asylum seekers, especially post-9/11.

ACTIVITY 5.13

What media forms and genres are best suited for this purpose? Soap operas on both radio and TV have been said to be able to image, over a long period of narrative time, the effects of such situations as those of rape victim, or AIDS patients, or sufferers from traumatic stress.

Can you find any examples of soaps dealing with the situation of an asylum seeker? If so, discuss how it has handled this. If not, say why and how such a storyline might be represented.

Films you might look at include: *Dirty Pretty Things* (UK 2002) which unusually draws attention to a huge and growing group: the migrants employed as cleaners in the metropolitan offices and hotels which service global corporate capitalism; *The Last Resort* (UK 2000); Ken Loach's *Bread and Roses* (UK/US/Germany 2000), also dealing with corporate migrants working as cleaners, this time in Los Angeles; *Maria Full of Grace* (US/Colombia 2004); *Brothers in Trouble* (UK 1995). Slightly different is *Keltoum's Daughter* (France/Tunisia 2004), and from a different era but an astonishing film: *Fear Eats the Soul* (West Germany 1974).

In This World (UK 2002) is a drama-documentary which follows the perilous journey from a huge refugee camp in Pakistan to Britain of two Afghani asylum seekers, Jamal, aged about fourteen, and his older cousin Enayat. The director, Michael Winterbottom, was partly moved to make it by a 2001

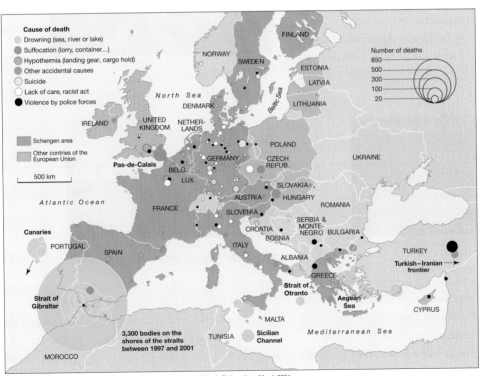

Sources: Olivier Clochard, Migreurop network (pajol.org), Potiers, 2003. *Le Monde Diplomatique,* March 2004.

Figure 5.9 A map showing different kinds of deaths, for thousands of asylum seekers making the journey to Europe. The size of the circles illustrates the numbers of deaths.

news story of fifty-eight Chinese immigrants found suffocated in a container at Dover, and he has described it as a passionate tribute to nearly 1 million refugees a year who take enormous risks to seek a better life. The film uses maps to help viewers locate themselves in the story. Figure 5.10 shows another one, not used in the film, from France, which shows the numbers of deaths of asylum seekers in the borders around Europe.

A film can take our imagination to new places, and it's often a few sequences, as well as the overall narrative, which does this. Here is a brief account of a key sequence in the film. We'll try to describe not just its content, but the way it signifies it, makes it mean. Try to apply this approach to other films that you find striking in their representation of 'scripts' or situations you have not, and are probably not likely to, ever had to act out.

For part of their journey two central characters need to travel to Italy in a container lorry, illegally, even though they have paid scarce money for transport. The journey becomes a nightmare; shortage of air, food and water leads to the death of Enayat and several others.

held, and then more smoothly, placed in front of him (on a lorry?) as he blindly runs and runs away from the ghastly scenes in the container. This burst of energy is a relief for the audience. It takes us out of the terrible claustrophobia of the container's dark interior. And Jamal changes from someone who has had to be watchful (of potential tricksters, of people who despise him) to someone energetically expressing his desperation. For the first time he shows deep emotion, in tears, which the camera skilfully catches. The running goes on and on until we're invited to wonder: where is there for him to run to in this foreign land? And what has he now learnt about the harshness of some lives?

Figure 5.10b *In This World* 2

Figure 5.10a *In This World* 1

Figure 5.10c *In This World* 3

When they arrive in Trieste, Jamal staggers out and then runs away from the container and the dead within it. The sound track holds the baby's shrieks, as the only one left alive; the Italians' voices as they get to the bodies; the sound of traffic; Jamal's feet on the road and coat flapping; and a mourning musical score. He runs, the camera first following him, roughly, hand

There follows a fade to dark, then Jamal appears again, the caption telling us two weeks have passed. He appears in the guise of a familiar figure to tourists and city dwellers: the begging, hassling migrant, involved in petty theft (he steals a woman's purse, after the waiter at her table has offered her the luxury of choosing a kind of water – 'still or sparkling?'). But the film, while

Figure 5.10d   In This World 4

not approving what he is doing, has given us a sense of how he has got there.

This film, and especially these moments from it, powerfully challenge what we suggested was achieved by many hostile images: to blame the stereotyped group for their position, by leaving their fuller histories out of the account. The issues raised by 'people flows' take us into the most crucial challenge of our modern world – the inequalities between rich and poor, both inside and across nations.

We hope you can appreciate that the images and media resources offered us are all too often inadequate to their subjects. Maybe you will want to help change that, for all our sakes.

References and further reading

Appadurai, Arjun (1998) *Modernity at Large*, Minnesota: University of Minnesota Press.

Castles, Stephen with Mark J. Miller (2003) *The Age of Migration: International Population Movements in the Modern World*, 3rd edition, Basingstoke: Palgrave-Macmillan.

Eagleton, Terry (2000) *The Truth about the Irish*, London and New York: St Martin's Press.

Hochschild, Arlie and Ehrenreich, Barbara (eds) (2003) *Global Woman: Nannies, Maids and Sex Workers in the New Economy*, London: Granta.

Poole, Elizabeth (2002) *Reporting Islam: Media Representations of British Muslims*, London: I.B. Tauris.

Refugee Media Group in Wales (2004) *Let's Talk to the Media. Practical Guide for Refugee Community Organisations and Refugee Practitioners on Working with the Media*, Cardiff: JOMEC, Cardiff University.

Speers, Tammy (2001) *Welcome or Over Reaction? Refugees and Asylum Seekers in the Welsh Media*, Cardiff University: Wales Media Forum.

Other resources

http://integration.originationinsite.com/
www.openDemocracy.net
www.ramproject.org.uk

ACTIVITY 5.14

These images are often highly gendered.

- Write a pitch document for a film or TV programme/serial to illustrate one story from the millions available about the girls and women who are 'traded', or who enter the wealthier world as nannies, cleaners or sex workers.

- Try to look at Hochschild and Ehrenreich (2003) who suggest, regarding nannies and sex workers, that there is an unequal trade in 'something that can look very much like love' (p. 4), as well as in oil and minerals, between rich and poorer countries. They draw attention to the painful situation of women who come to 'the West' to work as nannies, for example, while having to leave their own children in their home country.

6 Ideologies and power

- Origins of the term: Marxist approaches
- The persistence of class and its (in)visibility
- Post-Marxism and critical pluralism
- Discourses
- Lived cultures
- References
- Further reading

The concept of **ideology** has been a key one for media studies. It is now often replaced by 'values', so that 'ideologies' gets reserved for 'fringe' or non-mainstream party political positions, or is used to suggest a position is 'extreme'. It is always the other side – never one's own – that has an ideology. Watch for this kind of use of the term. We believe it still has a key role to play in suggesting very ordinary connections between media and different kinds of power. It refers to:

> Check out politics syllabuses and how they define ideologies. One UK A level board, for example, currently lists four belief systems: Socialism, Conservatism, Liberalism, Environmentalism – but not, say, racism or sexism.

- sets of ideas which give some account of the social world, usually a partial and selective one
- the relationship of these ideas or values to the ways in which power is distributed socially
- the way in which such values and meanings are usually posed as 'natural' and 'obvious' rather than socially aligned, in other words, working with or against particular sets of power.

Origins of the term: Marxist approaches

The first time it was argued that ideas are not free-floating but instead systematically linked to social power was in France, in the period leading up to the 1789 Revolution, which replaced feudal relations in France. Most discussion of ideology in media and cultural studies comes out of the later work of **Marx**, who, writing in the nineteenth century, questioned another, supposedly 'natural' but unequal order of things. He analysed the new profit-dominated system – **capitalism** – and the power of two classes within it, the rising industrial manufacturers (or capitalists) and the working class (or proletariat).

Some useful terms

Mercantilism describes a new social class system emerging in the sixteenth and seventeenth centuries, led by merchants who accumulated wealth obtained through colonial exploitation, slavery and war; an especially useful bridging term as it draws attention to the key role of the slave trade and imperial wealth in the development of western capitalism.

Industrial capitalism – in the late eighteenth and early nineteenth centuries a new class of industrial entrepreneurs exploited technological innovation using accumulated capital (from the slave trade, mercantile exploits, etc.). The factory system of production began and political power overall was wrested from landowners by these 'capitalists'.

Socialism arises partly from the experience of workers in this new factory system. It is broadly a belief in collective or public ownership, and the rights of all working people to full representation in political systems (in which they were a majority when socialist ideas first developed in the nineteenth century). It was developed through trade union power, often supported by 'Nonconformist' churches.

Corporate capitalism (sometimes called 'post-industrial') – the contemporary form into which capitalism has developed, attempting to supplant all other forms of economic life. Large corporations are owned by institutional shareholders (pension funds, insurance funds), making many 'stakeholders' in the economy, though the control of corporations remains largely with the managerial class. It is only 'post-industrial' in the sense that much manufacturing gets moved around the globe – often to low-wage economies.

Some ideas, though they form a system and can even be rigid, are not classified as 'ideological'. Someone may have obsessive ideas about personal cleanliness, and relate them systematically to the moon's size. But these are not called ideological since they cannot be shown to relate to the distribution of social power.

Feudalism: a system in which the poor had duties towards the landowners, those of 'noble birth'. Ideologically this was justified by a worldview in which the Earth was made by God, the sun revolved round it, and everything on Earth had a natural place in this divinely designed order.

Capitalism: a competitive social system, emerging in seventeenth-century Europe, involving private ownership of accumulated wealth and the exploitation of labour to produce profit, which creates such wealth.

Class: Marxism understands class as the antagonistic social formations created and perpetuated in the process of production, between owners of and workers within various industries.

Marx (see Chapter 1) argued that **class** difference, or people's relationship to the means of producing goods and wealth, was key to the kinds of values and political ideas that they have. Do they *own* factories, banks, country estates, or do they have to earn their living by *working for* the owners of factories, banks and so on? He was especially interested in capitalists' relationship to their employees, the working class, who, he argued, had the power to change history by their united action and practical experience of working together rather than competitively.

He used (loosely) the concept of ideology to help account for how the capitalist class protected and preserved its economic interests, even during years of unrest and attempted revolutions. Three of his emphases have been particularly important:

A Marxist account of ads, for example, would emphasise how their focus on the product, and the magical powers claimed for it, renders the work of producing it, by workers, invisible, or even 'natural'. The product can seem to appear from nowhere. See Williamson (1985).

- The **dominant** ideas (which become the '**common sense**') of any society are those which work in the interests of the ruling class, to secure its dominance. Marxism sees this as leading to fundamental misrepresentations of the real conditions of life. It is those who *own* the means of production who thereby, also, control the means of producing and circulating the most important ideas in any social order. This is said to be key to why the meaning-making bodies in any society (which now include the media) represent political issues as they do. It implies that the working class needs to develop its own ideas, and struggle for the means of circulating them, if it is to successfully oppose capitalist rule.

A contemporary 'upside down' ideological definition: the label 'Defence' instead of 'Arms' budget, for the US in particular. Bigger than that of NATO, China and Russia combined, it helps conceal the massive vested interests of arms manufacturers. See Campaign Against the Arms Trade at www.caat.org.uk and *Why We Fight* (US 2004).

- Related to this, he posits a **base–superstructure** model of the social role of institutions such as the media. He argues for a relationship between the ways the basic needs of a social order are met (through the factory production of capitalist orders, or rural production within landlord–peasant relations, for example) and its superstructure, i.e. its 'secondary', less basic institutions, such as religion and cultural life. Such a model is also often called **economic determinist**, since the economic 'base', and who owns it, is argued to determine, not just to influence, cultural and political activity, as in the media.

- A final step is the argument that, through these sets of power relationships, the dominant class is able to make workers believe that existing relations of exploitation and oppression are natural and inevitable. This power 'mystifies' the real conditions of existence, and how they might be changed. It conceals the vested interest that dominant groups have in preventing change.

Antonio Gramsci Italian Marxist activist (1891–1937) who took part in political struggles in Italy, involving Church and State, North and South, peasants and modern industrial workers. As a result his theories showed a keen awareness of the need for complex struggles and negotiations.

The Italian Marxist **Gramsci**'s term 'hegemony' became a key way of thinking how dominant value systems change through struggle. Gramsci emphasised their relationship to everyday *lived cultures* and to 'common sense', which he suggests is very mixed, the result of all kinds of historical 'traces'. Instead of an emphasis on the imposed dominance of a ruling class, and the determining power of the economic base, Gramsci argued that particular social groups in modern democracies struggle for control of consensus, or *hegemony*. In this they use persuasion and consent as well as occasional brute force. Because of these struggles, power is never secured once and for all but has to be constantly negotiated in a to-and-fro tussle. The key point from this for media studies is that people are not forced or duped into a false consciousness of the world, but have their consent actively fought for all the time – nowadays, crucially, through the media.

A cartoon shows a man giving a feminist a bouquet of flowers. She says: 'Oh, what a lovely bunch of hegemonies.'

The phrase 'making a difference' is often used now where years ago people might have spoken of 'changing the world'. In many ways it embodies a Gramscian rather than an older Marxist view of what change can achieve. 'The tipping point' is another phrase which suggests how important qualitative moments of change can be.

Spectrums, propaganda, censorship

The two activities of **propaganda** and overt **censorship** often reveal moments and areas where the daily struggle for willing consent (one form of hegemony) has come under intense pressure. A resort is then made to more conscious manipulation of ideological positions (often accompanied by physical force – an invasion, or a banning).

Censorship exists as part of a *spectrum of activities*:

- beginning with the ways we all self-censor what we say or write before committing to it
- ranging through everyday processes of news shaping by 'official sources', self-censorship as a 'good professional' etc.
- through examples of **classification**, which does not ban directly, but might put controversial programmes on at 'post-watershed' times, or strongly suggest that some films or video tapes should be shown to some age groups but not others.

The **BBFC** classifies film, DVD and video, but it also has the power to censor films. This occurs if agreement cannot be reached with a film-maker on where a cut may be made if the film is to be released. Examples of state intervention across this whole spectrum include:

- occasional direct government pressure on news and current affairs (as in several British governments' objections to critical *Newsnight* and Radio 4 *Today* items)
- direct censorship of reports, especially of casualties or enemy successes, or torture by 'your' side
- allowing only a certain 'pool' of approved journalists into a war zone, as in the 1982 Falklands and 1991 Gulf wars, or, arguably, the 'embedded' system of war journalism in the 2003 invasion of Iraq
- the 'classification' of 'sensitive' documents

See Chapter 16 '"Free choices" in a "free market"?'

See Chapter 3 'Genres and other classifications'.

BBFC (British Board of Film Classification) seeks consensus on its age-related classification bands for films and videos by means of regular public consultation exercises. See Chapters 3 and 16 for more discussion.

December 2004: the US Office of Foreign Assets Control (OFAC), under the 1917 Trading with the Enemy Act, criminalised any US publisher who publishes the work of any writer in Iran, Iraq, Sudan, North Korea or Cuba. The penalties: $1 million for the publisher, ten years in prison and a $250,000 fine for individuals.

'The Bush administration is classifying documents at the rate of 125 a minute . . . sparking accusations . . . of excessive government secrecy. . . . According to the security oversight office, federal departments classified 15.6m documents last year, with . . . unclear categories such as "sensitive security information". Meanwhile declassification has slowed' (*Guardian*, 4 July 2004, p. 16).

Propaganda direct manipulation of information for certain purposes, usually by governments or political parties. It is a kind of **discourse**, one which openly presents itself as wanting to persuade its audience. Though it usually urges political positions ('Vote for *x* or *y* party'), it may also be used for non-political messages (e.g. not to drink and drive). Arguably, advertising is also a propaganda system.

- banning fiction and entertainment material which is seen as related to a war or terrorist incident. An episode of *CSI* directed by Tarantino was pulled from the Five schedule on 12 July 2005 because its subject matter was thought too close to the London bombings.

State propaganda usually occurs in times defined as 'national emergency' (e.g. important strikes; the 'war on terror' in 2001) when, with the cooperation of the leading media organisations, the state will try to control and shape public perceptions in particularly direct ways, such as broadcasts by the head of state, adverts, etc.

It is not just states which censor and propagandise. Huge conglomerates (such as Rupert Murdoch's News Corporation) also wield such powers.

- In 1998 Murdoch intervened to prevent publication of former Hong Kong Governor General Chris Patten's memoirs, which were critical of the repressive Chinese regime. He also took the informative and often critical BBC World Service TV off his Star network, whereupon the Chinese government gave him permission to start a cable TV station, and later to show the film *Titanic* in China (see Wheen 2004: 231–2).

- There have also been reports that his friendship with Ariel Sharon, Israel's Prime Minister, and his extensive Israeli investments led executives on his paper *The Times* who were terrified of irritating him to rewrite articles extensively (see 'Case study: News').

- The anti-Europe stance of his British newspapers (*Sun, The Times* and *Sunday Times*) and Sky TV news channels seems connected to European resistance to his attempts to take over sectors of their media (see www.cpbf.org). There is 'suspicion that, in spring 2004 . . . Murdoch made it clear to Blair that unless there was a British referendum on the EU constitution, the *Sun* would switch support to the Conservatives' (*Guardian*, 14 June 2005).

Marx's original emphasis on the determining role of ownership and economic relations is still active in **political-economy** writings such as those of Graham Murdock in the UK, and Robert McChesney, Toby Miller and Janet Wasko in the US. The sense of political struggle is more muted than in Marxist approaches, but this work is a corrective to much of media theory's over-emphasis on textual elements, though at its best it tries to work with such approaches. As Janet Wasko puts it:

Mosco has defined . . . political economy as 'the study of the social relations, particularly power relations, that mutually constitute the production, distribution and consumption of resources' . . . it is an indispensable point of departure (for media analysis) . . . economic factors set limitations and exert pressures on the commodities that are produced (and influence what is not produced), as well as how, where, and to whom those products are (or are not) distributed.

(Wasko 2001: 29)

This improves on Marxist models of ownership as simple control, and is needed in the complex conditions of twenty-first-century global media and ownership patterns. But it does this without sacrificing a sense of the key pressures exerted by ownership. Increasing concentration of power in the hands of a very few enormous media corporations, and of a very few executives within those, leads to

- a decline in the *range* of material available (e.g. in satellite and cable television programming, or cinema) as global conglomerates exclude or swallow up all but the most commercially successful operators (hence the obsession with broadcast ratings) or those remaining few which are state-funded

  Bruce Springsteen's 1992 line '57 channels (and nothin' on)' puts this position concisely.

- a tendency to exclude the voices of those lacking economic power, except via entertainment forms, or in their role as audience 'within' TV via telephone votes, purchases, etc. For obvious reasons this is key in expensive advertising-funded media systems such as TV

- the dominance of corporate advertising and marketing within culture generally. This is especially true of many 'lightly regulated' US television channels, where heavy advertising sometimes seems almost to equal programme time. It is also powerful in 'blockbuster' cinema, with films which are full of product placements, tie-ins, marketing deals, etc., often seeming like adverts for the accompanying DVDs, computer games, fashions, food, drink, etc.

  See Chapter 9 'Advertising and branding' and 'case study: Celebrity, stardom and marketing', and Case study: The media majors'.

- the prevalence of 'easily understood, popular, formulated, undisturbing, assimilable fictional material' (see Wasko's (2001) account of Disney for a fascinating exploration, and also debates around some parts of 'reality TV').

  See Chapter 14 for discussion of 'reality TV' and documentary forms.

The persistence of class and its (in)visibility

1 It used to be easy to signify, through physical appearance, that a figure stood for 'wealth' or 'poverty'. Nineteenth-century charity pioneers like Dr Barnardo used images of thin and raggedly dressed 'street urchins' to appeal to the conscience of the wealthier. 'Third world' charities often still do this. And until relatively recently, artists and cartoonists have often used large body size, as well as dress, as an indicator of wealth: the 'fat capitalist' or greedy lord. Changes to this 'code' help us

Figure 6.1 A nineteenth-century photo of a British street child (c. 1870–77) from the charity Barnardo's (www.barnardos.org.uk), named after the philanthropist Dr John Barnardo.

'Conspicuous consumption': a term coined by the Norwegian-American economist and sociologist Thorstein Veblen (1857–1929) to describe the consumption of goods and commodities for the sake of displaying social status and wealth. Not used to describe eating disorders.

'Greed . . . is good. Greed is right. Greed . . . captures the essence of the evolutionary spirit. Greed has marked the upward surge of mankind' (Michael Douglas as Gekko, based on a real-life US stockbroker, in *Wall Street* (US 1987)). The speech was controversial because it couched an increasingly prevalent commercial attitude in an older, moral language.

glimpse the complex ways in which class divisions are now rendered visible – or often invisible (see Munt 2000). It is now likely that a well-toned, slim or even thin body is the result not of food shortage but of careful diet and affluence (the ability to shop for healthy food, afford regular training at a gym, etc.). However, aspirations to this appearance often produce anorexia or bulimia which further complicates matters – what are *those* slim bodies evidence of? And of course 'traditional' poverty can still produce rickets and thin bodies.

2 It's also possible that expensive-looking clothes, jewellery, even cars, may conceal huge levels of debt. All these changes now make it difficult to 'read off' from physical appearance alone what might be the truth of someone's economic position. Of course this may be one reason for aspiring to such an appearance, given the broader ideological approval of wealth and its display. It is one of many factors making it hard to broach questions of social class, as compared to more visible identities, such as gender, or certain ethnicities and religions.

3 Obesity, which in some cultures is prized as evidence of having plenty to eat, is, in the 'developed world' likely to be the result of both cultural and material deprivation and addictions (though genetics, and even a choice not to be a 'slave to fashion', may also come into play). As part of the complicated attitudes to such bodies, 'greed' (rather than addiction) is often said to be the cause of being over-weight. Ideologically this view shifts blame away from the very addictions which often result from the marketing practices of many major junk food brands.

4 Other contradictory ideological contexts for such blamings include post-1980s celebrations of extreme wealth (see much celebrity coverage) and justifications of corporate greed – which is usually called 'growth' and seen as virtuous. Such wealth is hardly ever represented, as in Marxist theory, as directly related to the labour of those who mostly produce the wealth on display – working people.

5 In 2005 two moral panics surfaced which clearly involved class differences. People known as 'chavs' and 'hoodies' were accused of routine anti-social behaviour. Much of the media attack was conducted through a fascination with dress and other codes of appearance. See www.wikipedia.org for good accounts, and also research its discussion of the website www.popbitch.com, which circulates many of these abusive terms.

Q   Were you or your friends affected by these panics?

ACTIVITY 6.1

Look at media images of stars, royalty, etc. and try to describe how huge wealth is signified visually, in terms of body size and dress. Is it as distinct as the large stomach and 'top hat' attire of the nineteenth-century capitalist?

Moving on from these points to ideological ones, how is extreme wealth discussed? How often, and in which media, is it related to:

- inequality?
- where it comes from? (a Marxist would answer: 'the labour of others')
- kinds of glamour and 'to-be-desired-ness'?

See Chapter 9 'Case study: Celebrity, stardom and marketing'.

Post-Marxism and critical pluralism

Several historical changes have affected the power of 'classic' Marxist theories:

- Ironically, even though Marx emphasised the dynamic nature of capitalism, he thought that its capacity to satisfy basic human needs would lead to an egalitarian society. In fact corporate capitalism has flourished partly on the growth of non-basic desires and distinctions.
- The collapse of eastern bloc state socialism was disturbing for those who thought it had moved Marxist ideas in action.
- The renewed power of 'free market' emphases from the 1980s has permeated most areas of life. These have their media theory equivalent: a tendency to *simply* celebrate audiences' powers in relation to media, rather than, at the same time, weighing corporate media ownership and the limits it sets to audiences' activities or fans' demands.
- Equally influential have been some so-called **postmodern** positions. Despite their emphasis on 'deconstructing' dominant ideologies, they often seem to have constructed their own: an abandonment of any attempt at constructing a better world.
- Part of this has been a growing scepticism about the claims of science or reason to possess either absolute truth, or to involve necessarily benign consequences for the world. (This matters, since Marxism had claimed scientific status for its theories.)

Such changes led to

- the suggestion that to talk of one dominant ideology, directly related to economic power, implies an improbably argument-free ruling class, which is able to smoothly 'make' the rest of us go along with its interests. We're talking of capitalism here, rooted in competition and certain kinds of contradiction. Such analysis often makes very

Postmodernism: a complex term with several meanings, usually involving a sense of contemporary culture as self-reflexive, without the ability to represent, let alone act upon, the world, and as having rejected 'grand meta-narratives' such as Marxism, belief in progress, etc. (see Bennett *et al.* 2005; Wheen 2004).

The recent ideological aggressiveness of the George W. Bush administration has led to renewed interest in the warnings of US President and ex-General Eisenhower (1890–1969) against the growth of a 'military-industrial complex', which some would now call a 'US military-industrial-entertainment complex' (see *Why We Fight* (US 2004) for a good account).

See www.fawcett.org.uk for up-to-date news of campaigns for women's equality with men – especially if you feel equality has been achieved.

Whenever you hear the word 'natural', reach for your knowledge of the power of ideologies.

See Chapter 5 'Questions of representation' for further discussion.

patronising assumptions about anyone other than the person doing the analysing. If the wheels of ideology roll so smoothly to produce conformity, how has the person analysing their workings come to have his or her 'outsider' perceptions?

- the challenge of newer politics has offered new ways of analysing other kinds of inequality. These are based in the ways that gender or ethnicity, for example, crucially affect 'life chances' rather than being absolute determinants, as class was in the Marxist model.

A good example of such **identity politics**, as they are called, is given in some feminists' argument that inequality derives from more than unequal pay in the realm of production or work. It also stems from the realm of *reproduction*, meaning both the reproduction of future generations (the family) and the household work needed to reproduce social orders (caring for the workforce). Men's social position and power can often be shown to exploit women's domestic and even emotional work for them and their children (see Andermahr *et al.* 2000). And because of the assumed 'naturalness' of women's caring role in the home, they tend to be overwhelmingly employed in the 4 Cs: caring, cleaning, catering and cash registers (see www.fawcett.org.uk; and Hochschild 2003). We might add call centres, which involve the kinds of 'emotional labour' skills which many women learn, both in caring for the family and in growing up with the expectation they will have families, and anyway have 'natural' abilities to work/care in this way. Black theorists have likewise explored the ways in which inequalities between races have been constructed and maintained, and how they have often cut across class and gender difference.

Emotional labour: a new view of labour, theorised by Hochschild (2003), which replaces some of the heavy, mostly male, manual labour, in Marxist accounts of class struggle. It refers to the effort expended to manage or regulate one's emotional reactions in certain kinds of work. *Examples* would be the requirement to smile at the checkout or perform 'vocal smiling' in call centres, and to suppress expressions of irritation or anger, despite possibly rude customers or a hectic workplace.

The stereotypical customer service call centre is such a workplace, but much of women's paid work (e.g. nursing, teaching, caring, shop work) involves this previously unseen, or rather untheorised, kind of labour.

Some would argue that too much of Marxism's interest in class differences has been lost in such 'identity' emphases. We do still live in deeply unequal capitalist societies, driven by profit, high consumption and competition. But these now operate on a global scale, with relations of exploitation spread across and between continents.

At the other extreme to Marxism, **pluralist** models have developed, seeing the media as floating free of power, rather as the 'free market' suggests a realm of pure and equal exchange of goods for money. They emphasise the apparent diversity and choice of media forms and products. They argue that, if certain values or fiction forms are dominant, it is because they are 'genuinely popular' and have won out in this 'free market of ideas'. These voices include some of the biggest media corporations, such as Disney or News Corporation, keen to downplay the economic clout and inequalities of their far-flung empires, or their control over copyright enforcement and employment policies. Time and time again, for example, the 'popularity' of US cultural forms is attributed to 'universal' appeal rather than globally orchestrated power.

Of course there is diversity in media, which have to circulate many different ideas and identities to remain fresh and profitable. But we still need an account of power to understand how some ideas and imaginings get to circulate more freely than others. Thus, developing the original Marxist and Gramscian emphases, others (e.g. Thompson 1997) suggest we now live in times of a complex play between several kinds of power:

- economic power
- political power
- coercive, especially military power
- 'symbolic power', i.e. the means of information and communication, including churches, schools and universities, and the images circulated by the media.

Such approaches are sometimes called **critical pluralism**. They acknowledge that there may be a struggle between competing discourses or accounts of the world, but insist that this is not an amicable free-for-all. Some discourses are parts of powerful institutions and have easier access to credibility, material resources, legal power, publicity: access which will be fought for if necessary. An important example would be what has been called 'the commercial speech of the consumer system' (i.e. major marketing and advertising campaigns) and the identities and desires it has vast powers to sustain, and those it marginalises, such as the poor.

The emphasis on a single 'dominant ideology' was challenged by writers such as Abercrombie *et al.* (1980). They argued that, though dominant ideologies do exist, and struggles do take place for hegemony around them, they are not the most important means for making social orders hang together. The fact that huge state bodies for surveillance and armed control exist suggests, in fact, that we do *not* inhabit unified social

President G.W. Bush gave a speech in 2000 at the Alfred Smith dinner for New York's wealthiest socialites during which he remarked, 'This is an impressive crowd – the haves and the have-mores. Some people call you the elite, I call you my base.'

We could say that if there is a dominant ideology at the beginning of the twenty-first century, it is this: 'Everything is relative. As consumers we have many freedoms. There is no such thing as a dominant ideology.'

orders, running contentedly along. The power of state force is always in the wings. And there is the 'dull compulsion of the economic' or the need to earn a living as well as the hugely time- and energy-consuming work of reproduction, in the feminist sense given above, relating to both child rearing and domestic labour. This leaves us little room, time or power to challenge systems of values which most people either disagree with or feel to be irrelevant.

Discourses

This multiple sense of ideas and values running alongside and within bodies of power, often brute power, brings us to 'discourses' and 'lived cultures'. These offer a more dispersed sense of how power structures maintain themselves. Media studies tends now not to use the model of a single dominant versus a single oppositional set of ideas, both of which can be traced to class struggle (the Marxist model). Instead it has turned to ideas of powerful and not so powerful ideolog*ies* and identit*ies* which are often said to operate through *lived cultures* and powerful or marginalised *discourses*. Let's look at the components of this approach.

The term '**discourse**' has a long history. For our purposes we can trace it to the work of the French theorist **Foucault** but it also involves earlier roots in language study which are invaluable for media study. Discourse analysis is interested in exploring what values and identities are contained, prevented or encouraged by the day-in, day-out practices and (often unspoken) rules of a particular *discursive formation*, which involves not just language but other bodies of power: buildings, qualifications, rules for professional accreditation, etc.

'Discourses' (of the law, fashion, politics, etc.) involve regulated systems of statements or language use. Regulated here simply means that the 'appropriate' language for a given area operates with rules, conventions – and therefore assumptions and exclusions. The discourse of medicine constructs some truths as likely to prevail (the role of 'the patient' as deferring to the expert doctor) and others to be without legitimacy (a more patient-centred medicine). This means that hospitals are built which embody these beliefs and hierarchies (see Bennett *et al.* 2005: 93).

Examples

I

If you have studied *science* you may have used 'scientific discourse' to describe experiments. 'Scientific impersonality' will be signified in

Michel Foucault
post-structuralist philosopher, sociologist and historian of knowledge (1926–84). Best known for his work on the relationship of power and knowledge, involving the power of discourses, especially in the areas of madness and sexuality.

Interviews are a good example of the 'discursive formation' of broadcasting, always operating within unspoken 'rules of the game' (including legal ones, as well as time and studio constraints) whether the interviewee is a politician or an entertainer.

The language of TV weather coverage shows tiny but cumulative changes over the years. In the second edition of this book, we quoted a BBC News reporter on floods in Italy, May 1998: 'This was Nature at her most unforgiving . . .'. Today such comment is more likely to involve speculation about global warming.

Figure 6.2 Cartoon by Posy Simmonds published in the 1970s. Taken-for-granted phrases and words form a key part of discourses around social groups.

ACTIVITY 6.2

See if you can devise a similar mountain for any group you are a member of.

---

writing up an experiment. The account will ideally seem to come from nowhere (no mention of the person who conducted it), and therefore to conceal its human fallibility in favour of a kind of remote authority. (British TV news often operates in a similar way.) This rightly is seen as part of the need for science to be as 'impartial' as possible. But it also embodies the power of traditionally remote, usually male, authority figures and 'voices' within such discursive formations. Currently such impartial language can often conceal hugely biased corporate connections, e.g. with drug companies.

Foucault argues that discourses actually create 'regimes of truth' and therefore our perceptions. The term 'child' has not always been used of 'young adults' and is notoriously hard to define in years and between different cultures. But the power to define someone as a 'child' has enormous legal, financial and other implications. (See Holland 2003; Scraton 1997.)

2

The powerful term *'terrorist'* defines certain acts of force in particularly negative ways. It is often used by states which themselves routinely authorise even more violent force: armies, automated weapons, 'shock and awe' bombing, for example. But the term seeks to mark an absolute divide along the spectrum of *which* acts of force are seen as justifiable. Some minority discourses argue that the violent actions of the very powerful (e.g. US armed and covert interventions against many regimes with which it has disagreed) might be labelled 'state terrorism'.

Q   What is the FBI's official definition of terrorism?

A   'There is no single, universally accepted definition of terrorism. Terrorism is defined in the *Code of Federal Regulations* as ". . . the unlawful use of force and violence against persons or property to intimidate or coerce a government, the civilian population, or any segment thereof, in furtherance of political or social objectives" (28 C.F.R. Section 0.85).' (See www.fbi.gov.)

The power to apply or even to 'rumour' this term has real legal and political force. Yet in the aftermath of 9/11 movements which got lumped together under this label, as being 'terrorist', acted from very different political motives, with and without warnings, with very different methods, against many different regimes.

Since the 1970s, media studies has often pointed out that earlier nation-based insurgencies, such as the American Revolution against British rule in the eighteenth century, or Nelson Mandela's ANC fighting the apartheid regime in South Africa, used illegal methods of force which would now be called 'terrorist'. Later the key figures were renamed 'freedom fighters' or 'patriots', or even became official statesmen (in the case of Mandela and the early leaders of the 'United States'). The term 'terrorist' was argued to be one of the ways in which the more powerful delegitimised the struggles of the oppressed, once peaceful channels of protest had been closed to them.

However, now, terrorist attacks like the ones on Madrid and London in 2004 and 2005 are much less easy to slot into the model of a coherent, nation-based resistance movement, linked to more peaceful modes of protest. The global scope of what get labelled as 'acts by Al-Qaeda' is something quite new, as is the way that it arguably operates like a powerful 'brand', with unregulated franchises operating in various countries.

'Suicide bomber' is a term many seek to limit to 'Muslim' extremists. But arguably the earliest of such self-destructive acts of violence would be the blinded Samson's bringing down the temple on his enemies in the Old Testament (and see Pape 2005 for current debates). The question *why* people (usually men) volunteer for such appalling acts is often left out of accounts of them, or is simply attributed to 'fanaticism'. Watch for how often this occurs in news stories.

'History is always written by the victors' (Walter Benjamin, critical theorist, writing in 1940) sums up this kind of knowledge.

Though this commercial metaphor may seem shocking, ideologically it

- embodies the power of commercial discourses in the twenty-first century
- focuses on the ways that global media circulated the ghastly spectacle of '9/11', timed perfectly as 'global spectacle'.

If we add the emphasis on 'unregulated' for the groups now choosing to relate themselves to 'Al-Qaeda' it may explain something of these terrible events.

Try to understand these contexts for the term 'terrorism' the next time you hear it used. This may be difficult since it is so 'taken for granted', especially, and understandably, after an atrocity.

3 'Famine' and 'relief'

The word 'famine' emerges from a biblical discourse, in which mysterious scourges (locusts, plagues) descend upon people from God, and are uncontrollable by human action. Unlike terms such as 'food supply crisis', the term 'famine' obscures financial–political relations between those who trade in food, within long histories of exploitation. Involved in the use of 'famine' is the power to circulate knowledge, or perpetuate ignorance, about:

- western 'food mountains' (to keep prices high) which might be used to relieve shortage, as well as western reliance on 'Third World' food and minerals
- price fixing ('tariffs') and speculation around poorer countries' harvest prices by wealthy 'futures' speculators, who buy up commodities (i.e. crops) in order to gamble on the future prices. This can result in low prices which, overnight, wipe out the profits of a whole year's work for poor farmers
- corruption within 'Third World' countries, often in collaboration with corporate interests, and stashing its proceeds, unchecked, in western banks
- struggles around the policies of the IMF (International Monetary Fund) and the WTO (World Trade Organisation) as well as the global corporations who largely control food supply.

Words and images of 'relief' for such suffering often have their roots in missionary versions of 'saving' and 'civilising' – despite the often barbaric actions of the colonisers who preceded the missions. Thus well-meaning charity appeals still often use:

- the camera placed above the pitiful victim, preferably a child, in its mother's arms, in a position which echoes the Mother and Child of countless Christian paintings

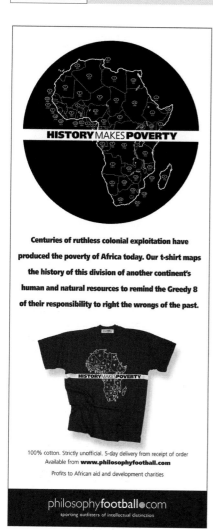

Another example of turning a discourse around: 'When I give food to the poor they call me a saint. When I ask why the poor have no food, they call me a communist': Dom Helder Camara, Archbishop of Recife, Brazil (1909–9), a pioneer of Latin America's liberation theology movement, which argued that the Gospels justified social change, not social acquiescence. Known as the Red Bishop during Brazil's 1964–85 military dictatorship.

Figure 6.3 At the time of the Live8 concerts one group countered the main slogan ('Make Poverty History') by another one, 'History Makes Poverty', suggesting a greater emphasis on the West's role.

● a child and other victims who are given no name, or access to the sound track or translation facilities.
These unwittingly suggest that the child exists in a victim's dependency relationship to the West, and even help perpetuate the situation by excluding a sense of such people as active in their own fates.

'The Third World' is itself a term with huge and rather patronising assumptions. It has been challenged in environmental discourses by terms such as 'the developing world', 'the South' or even 'the Majority World'.

ACTIVITY 6.3

Look at any fundraising effort on behalf of 'the third world', such as the Live8 concerts in July 2005. How did they try to negotiate these issues? What terms do they use (or you prefer) to 'Third World'?

Lived cultures

An interest in 'lived cultures' partly takes us back to the ideas of Gramsci. He argued that 'common sense', an 'obvious' guide to many people's ideas, can be explored as a complex set of traces, rather than a simple class-based ideology. These traces may come from hundreds of years ago and may be somewhat contradictory ('God helps those who help themselves') but they are also constantly changing, and jostle with much more recent beliefs in our minds.

The personality is strangely composite: it contains Stone Age elements and principles of a more advanced science . . . the historical process to date . . . has deposited in you an infinity of traces, without leaving an inventory [list, as in catalogue]. The first thing to do is to make such an inventory' (Gramsci 1971: 324).

He emphasised that hegemony is a lived process, never simply imposed, or floating free in ideas alone. The power of 'common sense' (rather than what he called 'good sense') comes from its relationship to dominant assumptions which have day-to-day material existence – in cultural practices, rituals and activities. (This is one of the points where media studies comes close to cultural studies.)

Examples

I

Billig explores the construction of *national identity*, arguably so useful to those who wield political power, making stirring speeches to persuade young men and women to fight and even die in wars of economic interest. He suggests that such a 'strong' version of national identity is not something that is constantly 'there'. Instead 'one needs to look for the reasons why people in the contemporary world *do not forget* their nationality' (1995: 7; emphasis added), which is always 'there, and can then be called upon in moments of struggle'. He suggests this is achieved in established nations by 'banal nationalism', a set of banal, or everyday, lived practices. These form a continuous 'flagging' via everyday tiny reminders of nationhood; not a flag waved with fervent passion in the sports parade or war, but the 'flag hanging unnoticed on the public building', the daily salute to the Stars and Stripes in US schools, national symbols on coins and stamps, national history memorialised in street names, or the use of words such as 'we', 'us', 'them' 'home', 'foreign' in news reporting.

'The sports pages in newspapers are not optional extras. . . . There are always sports pages, and these are never left empty. Every day, the world over, millions upon millions of men scan these pages, sharing in defeats and victories, feeling at home in this world of waved flags' (Billig 1995: 122).

Marines raise flag on Iwo Jima, Feb. 23, 1945

Figure 6.4 Recall this, from Chapter 1, 'Case study: Ways of interpreting'? The stamp, issued in 1945 and again 50 years later, is an example of the tiny components which together make up a 'lived culture'.

'Since Sept. 11, many newsies have – like many Americans – rallied around the flag. The Stars and Stripes have been conspicuously displayed in the logos of most of the news nets, and some anchors [for] Fox News . . . and NBC . . . for example – have taken to wearing flag pins on their lapels' (*Variety* (US trade journal), 25 September 2001).

2

Other everyday lived cultural practices relate to ideologies of gender and 'the family', whether those be 'happy endings' as meaning 'love and marriage' in countless fairy tales and romance forms, or the ways the 'familiar' photo album reinforces a particular sense of 'family'. These photo collections usually (without anything ever being said) exclude certain kinds of imagery. Family arguments, the unequal sharing of work in the home, boredom, child labour in the paper round (let alone child abuse) are not part of the discourse. Nor is the blurredness of the spectrum of 'single parenting'. Because of overtime patterns, or the need to travel long distances or even abroad for work, much parenting, even within conventional couples, is 'single' for much of the time, certainly in the UK. How to represent this, in images designed to emphasise 'the whole family'?

3

The lived cultures of sport, especially as constructed by corporate media, could also be examined for the ways they reproduce and 'refresh' our sense of such categories as gender and nationality, as well as the desirability of physical and financial power (the 'big hitters', 'size matters') which shares the discourse of big corporations.

> 'There is not much eccentricity on the current men's tour. Modern players are supremely self-interested and well-subsidised vagabonds. . . . To interview one of the . . . star (tennis) players is a bit like meeting a young PR executive for a successful global brand. Speaking a weird, rigid, globalised English, they offer little more than smooth generalisations. . . .
>
> How to make these people interesting? One possible answer is jingoism [as in coverage of Tim Henman: David Lloyd analysed his problem as lying in his serve and forehand but this never emerged on BBC's coverage]. 'Instead there were the old, crossed-fingered expressions of hope and the rhetoric of soft nationalism. When Henman was knocked out . . . the BBC mobilised behind Andrew Murray, from Scotland, but . . . resident in Barcelona.'
>
> (Jason Cowley, Sport column, *New Statesman*, 4 July 2005)

Economic determinants clearly shape some of our sense of the relative importance of men's and women's sports. Overall media coverage of men's sports massively exceeds women's, which is given less than 10 per cent of time available (and usually has smaller prize money) except when the Olympics take place. But linguistic marking and other 'natural-seeming' practices of the media reinforce the ideological differences of gendered sports.

- Women's sports are likely to be subject to gender-marking, e.g. in women's basketball, the images of the players are typically subject to sexualisation (see Brookes 2002). In tennis Anna Kournikova was not a top-ranked tennis player yet attained celebrity status arguably because of her appearance – a lesson not lost on little girls, along with the heavily marketed dolls they encounter. The more successful 2004 Wimbledon champion Maria Sharapova is treated similarly.

- Sportswomen are sometimes still infantilised in television commentary, as 'girls' (it's rare to hear male sports people called 'boys'); by the use of the first name; by repeated reference to their marital or family status (e.g.the tennis achievements of the Williams sisters were often related to their father's coaching in a way not seen with male sports stars).
- Women's achievements are less often held up as representation of the nation (as happens for rugby teams etc.). It is more usually seen as a personal affair, partly perhaps because they are less likely to be competing in the big team sports which depend on institutional support and funding all the way from early schooling.

ACTIVITY 6.4

Explore the ways that everyday sports commentary – the descriptive terms used, interviewing styles, camera angles, etc. – 'carry' these broader values around gender, nationhood and race.

In 2005 UEFA President Lennart Johanssen claimed sponsors of women's football could cash in by making use of a 'sweaty, lovely looking girl playing on the ground, with the rainy weather. It would sell.' Johanssen had condemned his Fifa counterpart Sepp Blatter for comments in 2004 calling for players to wear 'tighter shorts'.

'Women's football is now the fastest growing sport in [the UK], with the number of teams rising tenfold in ten years, to 4,500. The reason it's still regarded as fairly amateur is that it had no formal support or training structure for years. In 1921 the FA in effect banned women's football . . . asking all its clubs to refuse women access to pitches . . . which relegated them to the most basic of sports grounds, with no changing facilities' (Barbieri 2005).

Finally, it's worth emphasising the ideological power of 'common sense' as it relates to the power bodies of 'professionalised practice'. This erupts in news reporting at moments of crisis. Some kinds of speedy assumptions are taken as 'common sense', and others are discouraged. For example, in 1995 a federal US government building in Oklahoma City was bombed, resulting in nearly two hundred deaths. For days there was speculation about who the bombers were, mostly focusing on Islamic extremists. Yet only hours after the bombing a tiny agency, Inter Press, pointed the finger, accurately as it turned out, at the American far-right militia or 'survivalist' movement (Timothy McVeigh was convicted years later). It worked not on inside information but on simple deduction, involving:

- the date (the anniversary of the ending of the Waco siege, highly significant for the survivalist militias)
- the fact that a government building was bombed (given those unofficial militias' hatred of central government)
- the proximity of Oklahoma to Waco.

It was proved correct. The 'rush to judgement', along with the rush to get 'the story' first, was shown to be a very dangerous professional practice.

In summary, the Marxist emphasis on economics and class struggle as the basis of ideology has been replaced by an interest in other kinds of

- inequality
- power formations
- ways of circulating and changing dominant assumptions.

Likewise media studies' early focus was on '**bias**'-centred studies of news processes, with the implication that the media 'conceal' or 'mask' the 'true' processes of class struggle, and that these exist only in binary forms. This has been replaced by an exploration of fiction, entertainment and fantasy forms; an interest in how audiences can be an active rather than duped part of media processes; and a sense that while concentrated levels of power do operate, they are complicated by many confident new identities. This brings us to our case study on news.

Bias originally meant 'oblique line', and by the end of the sixteenth century was applied to the game of bowls. It now signifies ideological 'slant' in debates around factual reporting, though its origins suggest an over-reliance on a binary 'true/false' view of the plural values and identities which may be struggling for dominance in any news story.

References

Abercrombie, Nicholas, Hill, Stephen and Turner, Bryan S. (1980) *The Dominant Ideology Thesis*, London: Allen & Unwin.

Andermahr, Sonya, Lovell, Terry and Wolkowitz, Carol (2000) *A Glossary of Feminist Theory*, London and New York: Hodder Arnold.

Barbieri, Annalisa (2005) 'Sport', *New Statesman*, 20 June.

Bennett, Tony, Grossberg, Lawrence and Morris, Meaghan (eds) (2005) *New Keywords: A Revised Vocabulary of Culture and Society*, London and New York: Blackwell.

Billig, Michael (1995) *Banal Nationalism*, London: Sage.

Brookes, Rod (2002) *Representing Sport*, London and New York: Arnold.

Connell, Robert (2000) *The Men and the Boys*, Cambridge: Polity.

Golding, Peter and Murdock, Graham (1991) 'Culture, communications and political economy', in James Curran and Michael Gurevitch (eds) *Mass Media and Society*, London: Edward Arnold.

Gramsci, Antonio (1971) *Selections from the Prison Notebooks*, London: Lawrence and Wishart.

Hochschild, Arlie (2003) *The Commercial Spirit of Intimate Life and Other Essays*, San Francisco and Los Angeles: University of California Press.

Holland, Patricia (2003) *Picturing Childhood: The Myth of the Child in Popular Imagery*, London: I.B. Tauris.

Munt, Sally (ed.) (2000) *Cultural Studies and the Working Class*, London and New York: Cassell.

Pape, Robert (2005) 'The logic of suicide bombing', interview in *The American Conservative* magazine, available via http://www.amconmag. com/2005_07_18/article.html.

Scraton, Phil (ed.) (1997) *'Childhood' in 'Crisis'?*, London: UCL Press.

Thompson, John B. (1990) 'Ideology and modern culture: critical theory', in *The Age of Mass Communications*, Stanford, Calif.: Stanford University Press, p. 7.

Thompson, John B. (1997) *The Media and Modernity: A Social Theory of the Media*, Cambridge: Polity.

Wasko, Janet (2001) *Understanding Disney: The Manufacture of Fantasy*, Cambridge: Polity.

Wheen, Francis (2004) *How Mumbo Jumbo Conquered the Modern World*, London: Fourth Estate.

Williamson, Judith (1985) *Consuming Passions*, London: Marion Boyars.

Further reading

Eagleton, Terry (1994) 'Ideology', reprinted in Regan, Stephen (ed.) *The Eagleton Reader*, Oxford: Blackwell, 1998.

Foucault, Michel (1988) *Politics, Philosophy, Culture: Interviews and Other Writings 1977–1984*, London: Routledge.

Hall, Stuart (ed.) (1997) *Representation: Cultural Representations and Signifying Practices*, London, Thousand Oaks, New Delhi: Sage.

Marmot, Michael (2005) *Status Syndrome: How Your Social Standing Directly Affects Your Health and Life Expectancy*, London: Bloomsbury.

Marx, Karl and Engels, Frederick (1965; first published 1888) *The German Ideology*, London: Lawrence and Wishart.

Strinati, Dominic (2004) *An Introduction to Theories of Popular Culture*, London: Routledge.

Other resources

Why We Fight (US 2004) DVD.

CASE STUDY: NEWS

News is a globally important media form. It flows at incredible speed, 24/7, across radio, TV, print, mobile phones and the internet, in both local and international contexts, and, increasingly, in ways both formal and informal (such as 'blogs' and the immediate use of mobile phone footage in disasters like the tsunami of 2004 or the London bombs of 2005).

Its audiences are huge, and modern democracies depend on accurate news to give adequate accounts of a complex world, even though this is far from always being the case. It matters greatly that news is understood as being 'made' and not 'natural' or 'given'. It matters what kind of news is made, under what conditions, what spaces and budgets it occupies, and the support or criticism it is given by its audiences.

This case study explores:

- the relationship of news to dominant discourses and values
- how these are negotiated and expressed as parts of news institutions (see also Chapter 4).

News and dominant values

Two points are often made about news within media studies:

- It is not transparent, not unbiased, not the 'window on the world' it often sets itself up to be.
- Its constructed versions of events usually serve dominant interests. This matters particularly with television news, from which most people get their sense of the world's happenings, especially at moments of perceived crisis.

One landmark in British studies of news has been the work, from the 1970s onwards, of the Glasgow University Media Group (GUMG), among the first to argue an ideological influence for how news is constructed. Much has changed in the news landscape since the 1970s, when the BBC and ITN news programmes claimed enormous authority for themselves, since they were flagship programmes for the two main UK broadcasting stations. The strikes and war stories that GUMG investigated were interpreted by them as more polarised (split into only two sides, often around economics or social class) than would now seem to be the case. In a post-Cold War, 'free market' 'multi-channel' world, there is more awareness of issues such as gender, ethnicity, religion, sexuality as they shape our lives and are themselves shaped by new technologies.

Media studies now tends to make more modest claims for the (purely textual) influence of particular news bulletins, given:

- the proliferation of news technologies and forms, leading to '24-hour news' and internet uses in official and unofficial news forms
- lower budgets for many news programmes (except for 'star' presenters' salaries), allowing little time for extended items, meaning less expensive foreign or expertly researched coverage, and a tendency to go with speculation or rumour (e.g. about the MMR

vaccine: see Speers and Lewis 2004) rather than informed debate

- the deployment of huge amounts of PR information and 'spin' both inside and outside news
- the increasing overlap between news and the comment traditionally offered by current affairs.

Nevertheless, though news programmes may not directly affect belief, many would argue that they can hugely *influence* audiences and politicians, if only by their selection of items for inclusion as 'news' or by the ways they set up issues and encourage them to be 'framed', discussed and understood. In other words, they are still able to set the **agenda** of issues which we find ourselves thinking about (sometimes called **gatekeeping**), selecting some information for consideration and leaving some unexplored or unannounced. And news is still often able to set the agenda for giving the 'green light' to current affairs and investigative documentary teams.

> An agenda is a list of items to be discussed at a meeting, usually drawn up by the person chairing the meeting, who has the power to arrange them in order of importance. In relation to news, terms such as 'hidden agenda' or 'agenda-setting' draw attention to the importance of this power to frame and channel audiences' attention and discussions.

All this makes news still hugely powerful, though sometimes in unexpected ways. It may, for example, encourage silence. Those already confident of sharing majority opinion voice their views, while those who do not conform fall silent. Elizabeth Noelle-Neumann (1993), writing of the influence of opinion polls, described this as a 'spiral of silence', with well-reported polls able to solidify the preferred meaning of events by emphasising a supposed 'majority view' of them, or the 'popularity' of a particular figure (see Lewis 2001: 32–34, 35, 121). For example, in 1997 when Diana, Princess of Wales, was killed in a drink-driving accident, it became difficult to describe

the crash in that way, or to say that you were not particularly moved or were even annoyed by the scale of news coverage. Similarly when suicide bombers killed fifty-two people in London in 2005 it became difficult to point to a possible link with outrage at the 2003 invasion of Iraq (see Pilger 2005; Pape 2005) and the estimated 25,000 civilians killed there since then, partly in 'shock and awe' US bombing.

ACTIVITY 6.5

Make a note of a day's major news headlines. Think whether they affect what you and your friends talk about (i.e. have they 'set the agenda' for your talk?). Then note the headlines a few weeks later.

- Do you wonder what happened to stories which, in the first set of headlines, seemed urgent and important?
- When and how did they recede into less important status?

Quote you might discuss: 'I suddenly felt things were "back to normal" when Ground Zero stopped being the only news item' (Anon).

ACTIVITY 6.6

Watch the title sequences of late evening BBC and ITV news programmes. How do they announce the nature (or genre) of the programme to follow? Note:

- the kinds of imagery and music used (futuristic hi-tech studio? an emphasis on speedy news-gathering technology and lots of staff behind the scenes – the trustworthiness of the institution producing the news? or the informal lower budget setting of Channel 5?)
- the dress, demeanour, accent, tones, positioning of the presenter(s).

Q Are such arrangements trying to claim authority for the news? If not, what sort of programme is being announced?

ACTIVITY 6.7

Examine a corporate internet news site such as CNN, BBC, NBC. Can you apply to it any similar questions of how authoritativeness is claimed?

'In depth [news takes] a long time, but we're constantly being told that the attention span of our average viewer is about 20 seconds and if we don't grab people – and we've looked at the figures – the number of people who shift channels around in my programme now at six o'clock, there's a movement of about 3 million people in that first minute, coming in and out' (George Alagiah, BBC newscaster, quoted in Philo and Berry 2004).

News values

However dispersed 'news' is now, it is not as obvious a 'thing' as it may seem to be. News does not exist, free-floating, waiting to be discovered in the world outside the news room, as is suggested in many images of news reporting. **News values** systematically *construct* rather than simply *accompany* the '*gathering*' of news. They are not consciously held values. Indeed, many journalists would say that their main ideal is the achievement of **objectivity** or truth, and this remains an important aspiration, whatever the problems with stating it as an absolute standard. This is especially true in an era where channels such as Fox News are argued to have almost abandoned that ideal (see *Outfoxed* DVD).

'Isn't it amazing that the amount of news that happens in the world every day always just exactly fits the newspaper?' (Guardian Unlimited ad, 2001).

News is the end product of complex processes of evaluation and framing. These begin with a usually speedy sorting and selection of events and topics according to professionalised news values (and lived practices), defined as 'the professional codes used in the selection, construction and presentation of news stories in corporately produced press and broadcasting' (O'Sullivan *et al.* 1994). They end with a particular sense of the audience.

There have been many different definitions of news values since Galtung and Ruge laid out a now famous pioneering list in 1965 (usually dated as 1981 when first published in English). Their argument that news is structured according to unspoken values rather than 'discovered' remains a key one. We will outline (and update) several though not all of their key terms.

- *Frequency* or the time scale of events perceived as 'newsworthy'. Those events which become news stories will be of about the same frequency as many news bulletins, i.e. of about a daily span. An oil spillage will be perceived as a news story; the slow work over time of legislation or protest which makes it less (or more) likely to occur will not feature as news. However, such protest might be treated in current affairs or documentary programmes, especially if Greenpeace, say, staged an effective demonstration which coincided with the frequency of the news bulletins.
- *Threshold* or the 'size' of an event that's needed for it to be considered 'newsworthy'. Commonly occurring events happening to individuals will not usually count (except for local news) unless they involve either a celebrity or an unusually violent or sensational happening.
- *Proximity* or the perceived closeness of an item to the values of the audiences for that news institution. News is circulated, on the whole, by national broadcasting organisations or by regional arms ('CNN Europe') of news conglomerates. Understandably it often consists of items relating to that region. But it's also understandable that

'About 1,000 people were drowned when a ferry sank on Lake Victoria in 1996. There were no pictures because no one has camera crews near Mwanza, Tanzania. No pictures, no TV story – just a mention. But every time there's a brisk breeze in Florida we have a hurricane story because the pictures pour in from all the American networks' (Lindsey Hilsum, 'World view', *New Statesman*, 13 December 2004).

Figure 6.5 An image of sustainable technology, used in the collection of rainwater. Unlikely to be used as 'good news'.

objections arise to such 'First World' stories making up much of the material which the big news agencies sell to 'Third World' broadcasting stations; and to the corresponding way in which western audiences are often given, in return, little of 'Third World news' except through 'coups, crises and famines' or the same official, usually male, figures getting in and out of cars, addressing news conferences, etc.

'If it bleeds, it leads' (journalistic wisdom).

ACTIVITY 6.8

Try turning down the sound on coverage of a 'big' diplomatic story whose content you know already. Assess how informative the visuals are.

ACTIVITY 6.9

Take a big news story and follow it through two or three different media (print, TV, radio, internet). How differently is it developed in each? Why?

This circle of what gets recognised as a 'big story' can be a vicious one. It is reinforced by broader language processes and everyday practices: e.g. the use of 'we', 'us' and 'them' in news language; the sense of where is 'here' and where 'somewhere foreign'.

- Why are countries still referred to as 'the Middle East' or 'the Far East'? Far from where exactly?
- Why are military commanders called 'warlords' in the 'Third World' (including Bosnia) but 'Chiefs of Staff' in the West?
- Why does the US refer to its 'defence budget' when its arms expenditure is usually bigger than those of its nearest 'competitors'? Does this influence the need to construct images of powerful enemies? (See Lewis 2001; *Why We Fight* 2004.)

- *Negativity*: 'If it's news, it's bad news' sums up the feeling that long-term, constructive events are much less likely to feature as news than a catastrophe or images of violence. News does use 'positive' stories, often of medical breakthroughs, and as the 'happy ending' of some bulletins. But generally news tends to take the normal or everyday for granted. It is driven to make stories out of the deviant: crime, dissidence, disaster. In turn, news processes often augment the scapegoating of 'out' groups, because of the ways it feeds on the thrill of their deviancy – all those

- When a little-known (in the West) politician was elected President of Iran in June 2005, he was described as 'hardline' by nearly every news agency. More, he was said to be a 'hardline conservative' who would stand up to the Americans. But US President Bush could also be seen as a 'hardline conservative'. Perhaps they should get on well together? Again, such words actually tell us next to nothing.

Look at how a speech by a foreign leader is contextualised in different news media. If possible explore responses both 'at home' and abroad.

masked or digitally blurred faces, for example. It may shape news coverage of 'Third World' issues in terms of 'coups, crises and famine', now joined by 'terrorism', 'evil', or 'ancient hatreds' as explanation of complex processes such as the Israeli–Arab conflict. These values seem 'obvious' to many hard-pressed reporters, perhaps because they fit neatly into existing understandings in echoing fictional images and discourses. In such an ecology of news, small, hopeful initiatives, such as charities which adapt technology to collect rainwater to help villages, stand little chance of being publicised.

- *Predictability*: though news is taken to consist of random events 'out there', a lot of time is spent (often at 'editorial conferences') trying to anticipate what will be 'newsworthy', deciding where on the planet to employ expensive overseas-based staff, equipment, etc. Or if the media expect a particular turn (say, 'violence') to certain events, the drive will be to report according to those expectations. Examples include large demonstrations, the Notting Hill Carnival until recently, big football matches, G8 and other world trade protests. Even if these turn out to be mostly peaceful, the few skirmishes which

occur are often heavily focused upon (as 'newsworthy'), partly to justify the numbers of reporters assigned to the expected violent event.

Slightly different: events classified as 'news' are often known about weeks and months ahead – especially in the case of the increasing amount of PR-related material – or years in advance for conferences, anniversaries, annual reports, sporting events, book or film launches and so on. 'The news should really be called the olds', as someone once put it. Some newspapers even publish 'diaries' for the week ahead.

ACTIVITY 6.10

Watch the evening news on BBC or ITV.
- Where did reporters seem to be located, ready for stories?
- Which items were predictable (anniversaries, conferences, etc.)?
- List the items (film premieres, awards, new products) which seem to have been offered by PR agencies.
- Is there a difference between the main TV channels and radio news? Especially Radio 5? Or the BBC World Service, if you ever hear it?

Other kinds of events, such as famines, or the long-term effects of pesticides, are also predictable. But they are not usually part of the diary, since they cannot be 'dated' nor are they 'cut and dried' in terms of their beginnings. 'By the time the pictures are horrific enough to move people, it is almost too late', as one journalist put it. Where there are big but steadily present 'domestic' issues, such as unemployment or homelessness, there's a feeling that, though they go on happening, the journalist cannot keep on writing the same story. S/he looks for a 'twist', perhaps a way of personalising or even sensationalising it, or simply leaves it as 'not news'.

- *Continuity*: if an event is defined by the powerful news companies as big enough, resources will be diverted to it for some time, and often even 'non-events' which seem part of that story will be covered. 'The driver of the car in which Diana, Princess of Wales, was killed has still not regained consciousness.' Of course this takes resources away from other areas where crucial events might be happening.

- *Composition*: the 'story' will be selected and arranged according to the editor's sense of the balance of the whole bulletin, or page. If many home stories have been used, even a fairly unimportant 'foreign' story may be included. Or a big story may dominate the schedules, so that the day becomes one in which to 'bury bad news', such as high unemployment statistics.

ACTIVITY 6.11

Look at the balance of items in a radio or television news programme. Again, using broadsheet papers as your source of a fuller news agenda, see whether you feel the composition has been adjusted as suggested above.

- Within the bulletin, do certain items seem ordered so as to be grouped together, either for contrast or to suggest connections?
- List the items in an order that would invite different connections. Using your research, say what conception of their audience each news programme seems to have.
- Who used the words 'a good day to bury bad news' and when?
- Can you find any recent items which seem to have been 'buried' on a day dominated by other news?

- *Personalisation*: wherever possible, events are seen as the actions of people as individuals. This runs all the way from endless shots of politicians getting in and out of cars (respectable 'personalisation') through hospital waiting lists being put on the agenda by 'Baby x' or a pensioner not getting the attention s/he needs, to 'celebrity gossip and scandal' which is a kind of personalisation usually dismissed as 'trivial', part of 'dumbing down' etc. (See 'Case study: Celebrity, stardom and marketing'.)

Thompson (2000) and others have argued that political scandal within a 'culture of visibility' means that, despite the money poured into PR attempts to 'secure consent' to certain versions of events, and the fiercely restrictive UK libel laws, politicians have to take note of the charges. Political scandal can lead to reforms and can rightly highlight questionable activities and hypocrisies. For someone who is legislating strict 'pro-family' policies to be secretly having an affair himself or herself, for example, is arguably a matter of public concern.

To take the argument further, so might be the failure to experience run-down public services by those legislating on their funding from the privilege of private education, health or travel arrangements. Some politicians, such as Ken Livingstone, the Mayor of London, always travel by public transport and make a point of being photographed doing so.

'Travelling with Tony Blair in his car through London is a bizarre experience: does he remember life before outriders stopped every traffic light at every junction so he could speed through in minutes what usually takes an hour?' (Polly Toynbee, 'How could Cherie Blair do this without blushing?', *Guardian*, 8 June 2005).

ACTIVITY 6.12

Watch or listen to a high-profile political interview.

- What seem to be its unspoken 'rules of the game'? What topics are off limits? What questions do not get pursued, and why, do you think? Is it pre-recorded? Why?
- Is the tone deferential, or hostile, or even abusive?
- Is the speaker thanked? In what tone of voice?
- How does all this relate to 'the spiral of silence' suggested above, or the ideological frames through which we're invited to view politicians?

Two other areas of the construction of news deserve mention: narrativisation (which Galton and Ruge list) and visual imperatives.

- *Narrativisation*: items are from the start called 'stories' and they are shaped into narrative form as soon as possible. War and now often 'terrorism' coverage draws on an existing repertoire from Second World War narratives, the last 'virtuous' modern war. Themes such as 'War is hell but it makes heroes', 'The women wait while the men fight', make reference to this last 'good' war. After '11 September', and again in London, post-7 July 2005, the rhetoric of this 'good war' against Hitler was revived via references to the London blitz (which quickly became the narrative of the London 2005 bombings).

  Individual stories which fit these older war discourses can circulate powerfully. The 'rescue' of Private Jessica Lynch was a highly embellished incident but one which audience research (Lewis *et al.* 2004) showed was the second most recalled incident of the 2003 invasion of Iraq.

  The 'rescue' in Iraq of a 'captured young maiden', the fresh faced blonde, white Private from West Virginia offered a feast of orientalist as well as western chivalric and US

frontier echoes, even as the images shown were of her in modern American military uniform. . . . As I write, she has recently challenged the Pentagon version of her rescue, an act which may be her most courageous one.

(Branston 2003: 8; and see www. jessicalynch.com and www.journalism.org)

- *Visual imperatives* are said to be especially important in television news (and of course unimportant in radio, where sound codes are key). These imperatives drive towards stories that have 'strong' pictures, whether of celebrities, 'biblical-looking' famines, or of scenes which resemble a blockbuster film, as in people fleeing from the explosions at the World Trade Center, 2001, or the 2004 tsunami. Increasingly, if wars are heavily censored or inaccessible to picture technology, computer-aided graphics are used to give a sense of what might be happening. Debates on visual imperatives need critical consideration. For example:
  - Radio's agenda is very similar to television's, although it cannot operate 'visual imperatives'. Why is this, if the visual is so important to news?
  - Television or press stories which lack pictures but are deemed important use computer-aided graphics to assist visualisation. Photographs do not always 'lead'.
  - 'Less newsworthy' controversial or speculative stories, or ones involved with long-term processes, are rarely helped in this way, even though they could be. Again, the visual imperatives tend to follow, not lead existing news priorities.
  - 'Soundbites' or vivid short phrases used over and over again in coverage of some stories, could be argued as equally important, and as deriving from verbal, radio and print-related forms. It was a key part of the story that shifts occurred around what to call the attacks on the World Trade Center and the Pentagon: 'Attacks

HOW SPECIAL FORCES COULD SWOOP ON BIN LADEN

Figure 6.6 'Hard news'? 'Visual imperative'? A comfortingly convincing-looking image from the early stages of the 'war on terrorism' in 2001. What does it say of such 'news' practices, given the failure of massive and prolonged bombing of Afghanistan, and then Iraq, to find Osama bin Laden?

on America', 'Ground Zero', '11 September', or '9/11'? Unsurprisingly, this last which is also the US emergency telephone dialling code (like 999), won out.

Yet verbal elements often go unexplored in media study compared to visual determinants.

'News professionals' and news cultures

News values are *professionalised*: a person must acquire them in order

- to become a journalist, either through training on the job, or achieving qualifications (see Chapter 4 'Institutions')
- to function effectively as a journalist (which may involve less formal learning contexts, such as canteen gossip about who's a good 'source' and what is now the 'house style' of your paper or radio station).

They are a good illustration of the 'taken-for-granted discourses' and 'lived cultures' we discussed in Chapter 6, all the more powerful because so taken for granted. For example, it is often argued (e.g. by Schlesinger 1987 from his observations in news rooms) that, like most television professionals, journalists make programmes for other television professionals, partly because their sense of their majority audience is very flimsy. 'They won't understand it', 'We'd love to run the story but the public just don't want to hear about it' are statements often made on the basis of very little systematic attempt to find out exactly what audiences might want. This is despite the fact that simple overnight ratings figures are now supplemented by email and other instant messages from audiences.

Though news is often thought to be about 'reporting the facts', news teams quickly develop a sense of news sources – 'whom to rely on' for 'hard stories', i.e. stories full of facts, statistics and quotations from official sources which won't risk libel action. Studies (see Schlesinger 1987) show that journalists tend to rely on white, middle-class, middle-aged professional males as sources, especially when 'expert' opinion is accessed. These tend to work in either accredited bodies such as a big world news agency – Reuters, Press Association, Associated Press or United Press International, which send stories directly into the computer systems of bodies such as News International – or, increasingly, one of the big PR (public relations) or corporate communications companies. Controversy has raged in recent years over the degree to which government 'spin doctors' or press officers should try to construct news, though this has always happened via the timing and phrasing of press releases. (See Chapter 1 above on 'spin'.)

All these are the *preferred sources* of news for its *primary definers*. They are sorted so that '*copy tasters*' can select items to be used. Most news rooms scan the morning newspapers and listen to the radio from early in the day. This is now more of a two-way street than it once was, as up-to-the-minute television news and its pictures, as well as internet items, often constitute newspaper headlines the next day. But whatever the direction of the flow, such news structures tend to favour those who already have enough power to employ press officers, to distribute press releases and publicity or to hire Reuters to make up a VNR (video news release).

ACTIVITY 6.13

Get hold of a press release. Write a news story out of it. Then compare this with the way the release was handled by different news media.

Frenzied circulation and ratings wars between organisations have accelerated the professionals' emphasis on being 'first with the big story' rather than 'the one that got the story right'. This trend is accentuated by new technology, such as digital cameras, mobile phone cameras, portable computers and satellite phones. These mean that a reporter can input a story with photos into a newsdesk terminal almost as soon as it is written. The internet has become a volatile (and only partly reliable) source of news stories taken up very quickly by mainstream media.

See the film *Shattered Glass* (US/Canada 2003) for a fascinating 'true story' of how easy it is to fabricate sources via the internet.

ACTIVITY 6.14

Listen to the BBC World Service for an hour or so. Make notes on how different its news agenda and the coverage of 'non-domestic' items are to those of
• the tabloid press
• the broadsheet press
• terrestrial television news programmes
• other radio news programmes.

Partly as a result of such pressures, far fewer foreign correspondents are now permanently employed to develop expert, intimate knowledge of a particular country. This tendency may be intensified by the ability of news agencies to arrange speedy satellite or videophone transmission of instant judgements from someone based in a comfortable hotel.

Foreign news also highlights a gendered aspect to news in general (which stories do women get to cover?). It has until recently been seen as a 'hard' form unsuited to women, despite the distinguished careers of women from Martha Gelhorn in the 1930s to Maggie O'Kane, Lindsey Hilsum and Orla Guerin more recently.

'In the 1960s a third of Fleet Street journalists were based outside London, either in the regions or on foreign postings. Now 90% of national newspaper staff work in London' (Nick Cohen, writing on the growth of lifestyle, opinion and 'light' columns as compared to investigative or first-hand reporting, *New Statesman*, 22 May 1998, see also www.reportingtheworld.org).

Gender and news gathering

'In the 1950s, women reporters interviewing people on the streets were assumed to be soliciting. More recently Associated Press reporter and Vietnam correspondent Edie Lederer had to get an "I am not a prostitute" certificate from the authorities before she could travel in Saudi Arabia to report the Gulf War' (Sebba 1994).

On stories which women reporters 'pick up on'

'Kate Adie once told me that a little documented aspect of the Afghan war against the Soviet Union was the high casualty rate of rural women. The men had taken up positions in the surrounding hills. Traditional restrictive laws meant that women were forbidden to leave [their] quarters. Attacks by Russian helicopters bore down on the villages killing thousands of women. It is believed that more women than fighting men died in that war' (Abdela 2001).

Correspondents may also learn a professional, distant, authoritative language with which, for example, to sanitise wars. We now often hear about atrocious modern weapons through a veil of language: 'smart

bombs'; 'daisy cutters'; 'surgical strikes' (implying that this is an operation for 'the patient's own good'); 'carpet bombing' (sounds like vacuuming); 'taking people out' instead of assassinations; and so on. The early stages of the bombing of Afghanistan in 2001–2 produced the statement that this, one of the poorest countries in the world, was 'not a target-rich environment'.

ACTIVITY 6.15

Record the financial section of a major news bulletin. Jot down the specialised phrases and terminology (e.g. NASDAQ) and research their meanings. Try to write the bulletin in accessible language. Does this exercise give you more, or less, sympathy for financial journalists?

'Professional' reporting of financial news also uses obscuring metaphors such as 'the pound had a bad day/bounced back/took a hammering', 'the NASDAQ dived' or 'getting the economy back on the rails'. These both re-mystify and naturalise the already mysterious workings of stock exchanges.

Impartiality and news

Broadcast media in Britain (unlike the press) are legally required to be politically impartial: i.e. broadcasters cannot express a point of view on 'major matters' but have to make 'balanced reports'. We think the attempt to make impartial or balanced news is worth renewed support in the light of:

- increasingly partisan and biased TV (and US right-wing 'shock-jock radio') news channels and other outlets, of which Fox News is the most striking
- tabloid forms which are so heavily reliant on celebrity and PR-led forms as to be operating a kind of commercial bias against fuller news coverage.

The Murdoch media and impartiality

'Fox News . . . endeared itself to the conservative right in its approach to the Middle East. 'It now refers . . . to Palestinian suicide bombers as "homicide-bombers"' (*Guardian*, 1 July 2002). Sam Kiley, a correspondent for *The Times*, resigned in September 2001, blaming its allegedly pro-Israel censorship of his reporting . . . when [he] interviewed the Israeli army unit responsible for killing a twelve year old Palestinian boy, he was asked to file the piece without mentioning the dead child' (*Guardian*, 5 September 2001, quoted in Philo and Berry 2004: 255).

But the question of balance is always a difficult one. 'Balance' tends to be between those points of view that are assumed to reflect existing public opinion. Thirty years ago, this was defended as reflecting the Labour–Conservative axis of parliamentary politics, with a stopwatch eye to how much time each party was given on television. Now, the political spectrum stretches further (though opinion that falls outside 'parliamentary democracy' is still often deemed unacceptable by the BBC and ITV).

Academic studies of news often involve hundreds of hours of recorded news broadcasts. The Glasgow UMG focused initially on industrial items such as strikes. They argued that the news consistently favours the interpretations of the already powerful because journalists share assumptions about the real world which are rarely seriously questioned, such as the view that strikes are harmful and disruptive. Furthermore, journalists rely on official sources to an extent that systematically outlaws different accounts of events.

It is crucial that such critical positions on news continue to be tested. But, especially when dealing with arguments which put all the blame on 'spin' (or attempts to secure hegemony), as though a fully objective account existed somewhere, you should bear in mind that objectivity or impartiality is an impossible goal for any statement or story because:

- To decide to select an item for the news is to make a decision about other items that cannot be told, because of time or space restrictions. Therefore any story has already been prioritised, or had some value set on it.
- Since there are always several positions from which to tell a story, and it is impossible to produce an account from completely 'outside', a position on it will inevitably have been chosen.
- To say that objectivity is possible is to imply that an unarguable interpretation of an event exists prior to the report or story.

Nevertheless, we can reasonably argue that news can and should be as adequate and informative as possible for particular purposes. Revelations in the UK about 'fakery' in television documentaries and the hiring of actors to pose as guests on talk shows rightly produced strong reactions in the late 1990s. An important breach of the ethical standards of those programmes, designed to offer reliable information, had taken place. When audiences ('citizens') need to be informed about the justification for and conduct of, say, a war or major government spending decision, it is right to object to unnecessary censorship or 'spin' or fakery in such stories – epecially if these exclude critical positions from outside the conventional spectrum of opinion.

To return to the beginning of the chapter: the argument that television news is constructed, not transparent, is no longer surprising. 'News' exists now not just as BBC or ITV news. Twenty-four-hour television news services, as well as proliferating radio stations, with their news-related phone-ins and chat shows, inevitably offer different accounts of events, and pose different problems for news managers. The internet, said to be unpoliceable and unregulatable, is a growing source of news, dissent, subversive blogs, and ways of organising. Even the 'rule' that music is never to be used as accompaniment to television news stories is occasionally broken.

A weblog (usually shortened to **blog**) is a web-based publication consisting primarily of periodic articles (normally in reverse chronological order). Easy to set up and maintain, and often functioning in very personal ways, like diaries, they often rely on existing news agendas and items, but arranged with a personal or campaign focus.

Referring to the digital torture images from Abu Ghraib, made by participants, one activist writes: 'Digital and internet based technologies make participants in any event potentially irrefutable witnesses to what really happened . . . these "citizen reporters" now represent a significant challenge to the compromised intermediaries of corporate journalism' (David Edwards, editor of www.medialens.org, 'The rise of the people's news', *New Statesman*, 24 May 2004).

On 20 June 2005 the *Guardian* reported: 'Billed as a leftwing contender to rival the might of CNN and Fox, and weighing in with an annual budget of just $25m, Independent World Television (IWT) plans to create a news network that will counter a corporate media culture . . . IWT plans to start broadcasting to 25m US homes by 2007 . . . the station's advisory board [includes] Naomi Klein, Gore Vidal, Tony Benn and Greg Philo of the Glasgow Media Group.'

See www.iwtnews.com.

What's Wrong with TV News

and how you can help build a global independent alternative

A video featuring interviews with Phyllis Bennis, Salih Booker, Jeff Cohen, Laura Flanders, Linda Foley, Amy Goodman, Naomi Klein, Bob McChesney, Joanne St. Lewis, and IWTnews Chair Paul Jay

Figure 6.7 Excerpt from www.iwtnews.com

Nevertheless it's unlikely that audiences understand the broader processes of news construction as they relate to dominant values. Indeed Philo and Berry (2004) suggest, from focus group work, that people very much appreciate being given a better sense of how news works, as well of the political events it covers. In relating news to ideologies it is clear that:

- 'Dominant values' now go further than stories of strikes and wars. They include the complexities of global capitalism, and involve powerful identities such as ethnicity, religion, age and sexuality.
- News images need to be understood in closer relation to the circulation of entertainment forms and celebrity (see 'Case study: Celebrity, stardom and marketing').
- Audiences' *use* of news needs to be understood when its influence is discussed. There are striking examples of their rejection of certain stories.
  a) During the events which began at the World Trade Center in September 2001 it was notable that critical voices, such as those of the peace movement, or of critics of US policy in the 'Third World', were not given proportional time to those assuming that war was the best response to terrorist attack. Nevertheless in many programmes, where members of the public were invited to express views, such opinions had clearly been seized upon, or even sought out, often via the internet.
  b) Similarly boycotts, such as that of the *Sun* on Merseyside for libelling Liverpool soccer fans after the Hillsborough tragedy (see Scraton 1999), occasionally take place, and are a key site of consumer power in this area.

Media studies usually reserves consideration of fan or consumer power for 'entertainment' forms. Yet growing numbers of people seem to be 'news' or 'politics' fans, and examples of their often resistant understandings of news deserve exploration and even celebration.

References

Abdela, Lesley (2001) 'Diary', *New Statesman*, 24 September.

Branston, Gill (2003) *Out of a Clear Blue Sky: '9/11', Media Study and Memory*, Coventry: Coventry University.

Galtung, J. and Ruge, M. (1981) 'The structure of foreign news: the presentation of the Congo, Cuba and Cyprus crises in four foreign newspapers', in Stan Cohen and Jock Young (eds) *The Manufacture of News*, London: Constable.

Lewis, Justin (2001) *Constructing Public Opinion: How Political Elites Do What They Like and Why We Seem to Go Along with It*, New York: Columbia University Press.

Lewis, J. et al., Cardiff University School of Journalism, Media and Cultural Studies (2004) *Too Close for Comfort? The Role of Embedded Reporting in the Media Coverage of the 2003 Iraq War*, Cardiff: JOMEC.

Noelle-Neumann, Elizabeth (1993) *The Spiral of Silence*, Chicago: University of Chicago Press.

O'Sullivan, Tim, Dutton, Brian and Rayner, Philip (1994) *Studying the Media*, 2nd edition, London: Arnold.

Pape, Robert (2005) 'The logic of suicide bombing', interview in *The American Conservative* magazine, available via http://www.amconmag.com/2005_07_18/article.html.

Philo, Greg and Berry, Mike (2004) *Bad News from Israel*, London: Pluto Press.

Pilger, John (2005) 'Blair's bombs', *New Statesman*, 25 July.

Schlesinger, Philip (1987) *Putting 'Reality' Together*, London: Methuen.

Scraton, Phil (1999) *Hillsborough: The Truth*, Edinburgh: Mainstream.

Sebba, A. (1994) *Battling for News*, London: Sceptre.

Speers, T. and Lewis, J. (2004) 'Jabbing the scientists: media coverage of the MMR vaccine in 2002', *Communication and Medicine*, 1, 2.

Thompson, John T. (2000) *Political Scandal: Power and Visibility in the Media Age*, Cambridge: Polity.

Further reading

Allan, Stuart (2000) *News Culture*, Buckingham: Open University Press.

Carter, Cynthia, Branston, Gill and Allan, Stuart (eds) (1998) *News, Gender and Power*, London and New York: Routledge.

Chambers, Deborah, Steiner, Linda and Fleming, Carole (2004) *Women and Journalism*, London: Routledge.

Philo, Greg (1990) *Seeing and Believing: The Influence of Television*, London and New York: Routledge.

Other resources

Outfoxed: Rupert Murdoch's War on Journalism (US 2004) DVD

Why We Fight (US 2004) DVD

http://english.ohmynews.com

http://en.wikinews.org

www.cjr.org

www.IndyMedia.com

www.medialens.org

www.opendemocracy.net

www.reportingtheworld.org

www.ZNet.org

7 Industries

- Media production as a factory process
- Long-life media – a different process?
- Types of activities
- Six stages of media production
- Organisation of production
- The media business environment
- 'Independence' and 'alternatives' in the media industries
- References and further reading

The common view of 'the media' equates their activities with glamour and excitement, creativity and controversy. There are such moments, of course – more perhaps than in other types of work – but everything that the media do is ultimately concerned with money and commercial activity. In this chapter we explore the industrial and commercial activities of media organisations, using some of the tools of economic analysis.

Since the 'industrial revolutions' of the nineteenth century, different industrial sectors such as oil, motor vehicle manufacture, etc. have become the central focus for economic growth during a specific period, first in the leading national economy and then in other developing economies across the world. Media industries are important in the now dominant economic activities associated with 'communication' and 'information'. Media studies has tended to focus mainly on the production of goods and services destined for the 'mass' consumer audience and concerned mostly with entertainment and information for personal use. But it is difficult to separate this activity from the communication of 'business information' and the technologies and systems that sustain it. For clarity, we will refer to media industries (which would include 'creative industries') and telecommunications industries, which have now become part of the distribution (see Chapter 13) of media goods and services. Within each media industry we will identify sectors, such as production, distribution, exhibition, etc.

Economists usually classify industries in terms of whether they produce 'goods' or 'services'. Media industries are slightly difficult to categorise since they do produce 'goods' – you only have to wander round an HMV

Depending on your course, you may find discussion of media 'industries' is subsumed under the heading of 'Media institutions'. We think these are best kept distinct. Institutions are discussed in Chapter 4.

'Taken as a whole the creative industries make a huge contribution to our economy, as well as to our social and cultural life. They produce a higher proportion of our total wealth – 8% of GDP – than anywhere else in the world. The £11.4 billion they contribute to our balance of trade is well ahead of the construction industry, insurance and pensions, and twice that of the pharmaceutical sector' (UK Secretary of State for Trade and Industry, Patricia Hewitt, 29 April 2005, quoted in *Screen International*).

or Virgin Megastore to realise just how many CDs, DVDs, video games, magazines, etc. are available. But these 'goods' are merely inexpensive platforms which enable us to gain access to the data which provide entertainment or information. Producing media texts and then distributing them widely is more like a 'service' function. Given this ambiguity, different parts of the media industries are organised either like manufacturing plants or like service providers.

Media production as a factory process

Media activity can be related to traditional forms of 'factory production'. This may sound a surprising claim, but we can compare the production of something like a daily newspaper with that of, for example, tinned baked beans. The two production processes share:

- initial investment in plant and machinery – **fixed assets**
- a research and development (**R&D**) department charged with looking to the future and devising new designs, new recipes
- a daily demand for the product, requiring continuous production and a constant supply of raw materials (paper, ink and 'raw news'; beans and cans)
- employment of a workforce with specific skills
- some form of 'quality control' on a production line
- distribution of the product to all parts of the market
- stimulation of demand, including market research to ensure up-to-date information about performance of the product and the satisfaction of customers
- advertising the product to keep it in the public eye and to attract new buyers.

These common features are important – media industries usually make decisions based on standard business principles. Yet media industries are different from most other forms of manufacture, and it is these differences (sometimes called 'specificities') which we want to explore in more detail.

We should also note that most media activity is about producing a single 'original product' which is then duplicated or 'reproduced' – the possibility of different forms of reproduction is one of the interesting features of media activity. For the moment, let's stay with the production of print-based news and think about its specific features:

- The 'raw material' is not homogeneous – skill and cultural, aesthetic and political judgements are necessary in selection of events which will be marketed as 'news'.
- The price of news varies – some is free, some (especially if celebrity-related) may be very expensive to purchase or access or, in the case of foreign news, reporters may have heavy expenses (and need protection).
- The product is not always a necessity and demand can fall if consumers' tastes change (national newspaper sales in the UK are in decline).
- Production and distribution patterns are not fixed – the product can be transmitted electronically and reproduced locally.
- Staff costs will generally be greater than in more basic forms of manufacture because a greater variety of skills are required in the process.
- This particular product has a shelf life of only one day (really, only half a day).
- Revenue from sale of the product is only part of the business – a large proportion comes from the sale of advertising space. Advertisers therefore have a significant influence on the fortunes of the product.

These points suggest that managing this kind of media production process is a particularly complex (and risky) business. The two most important considerations for the newspaper producer are:

- the collection and processing of suitable news material
- the distribution of the finished product.

The actual production (i.e. page make-up and printing) of the newspaper is perhaps not as crucial as you might think in determining the success of the product. Certainly, the quality of the feature material and the 'look' of the paper will contribute greatly to its long-term reputation, but they won't necessarily boost the circulation as dramatically as a sensational story. Nor will they immediately impress the advertisers. Media products such as newspapers depend on a complex mix of factors for their success – it's the same news and similar features most of the time, so why the different circulation figures and different advertising revenue for individual newspaper titles?

Part of what makes commercial media products different (from other goods and services) is the definition of the **target audience**. It doesn't just matter that the product is sold, but that it is sold to a specific readership identifiable by advertisers. *The Times* distributes roughly twice as many

See Chapter 13 for more discussion of the economics of distribution in the newspaper business.

Research the 're-launch' of papers like the *Guardian* and the *Observer* in 2005/6. Did they attract new readers?

copies of each edition as the *Guardian*, but the *Guardian* is able to offer advertisers a more clearly defined readership group with specific interests, so despite a smaller circulation, the *Guardian* is attractive to specific advertisers. 'Case study: Selling audiences' suggests some ways in which audiences can be specified.

If poor distribution means that the product doesn't get to the customer in time, all the production effort will be wasted. All industries depend on good distribution, but there are special considerations for many kinds of media products.

Long-life media – a different process?

In film or music production there is a rather different production process, or at least a different emphasis, from that of the daily newspaper, or even the daily or weekly television programme. Purchase of a CD or a ticket for the cinema has to be a more calculated decision by a consumer (measured against a higher price and a greater commitment of time and effort). The 'product' is not 'consumed' completely – we may return to experience the film again at a later date and we will listen to the CD repeatedly. With a shelf life longer than the single day of the newspaper, there is the possibility of building an audience for a film or a musical performance over several weeks as well as developing a number of associated products.

It is even possible that as a collector's item the product will increase in value over time. Since the product is also reproducible from a 'master copy', it can be 'relaunched' again in the future at minimum cost and attract a new set of buyers. Walt Disney was the first to recognise this phenomenon, and by using it secured the future of his film studio (which began as a small 'independent'). He saw that animated films did not date as quickly as live action features and that, since a large part of his audience was made up of young children, he could rerelease classic films such as *Snow White and the Seven Dwarfs* (US 1937) and *Pinocchio* (US 1939) every seven years to a new audience. This strategy has been altered by the advent of video recording, but it is still relevant and has been applied to other classic films such as *Gone With the Wind* (US 1939) and *Star Wars* (US 1977). A recyclable product is also a recyclable **brand** name, and the modern Disney company has benefited further from **merchandising** spin-offs. Like Warner Bros, Disney has recognised the value of its brand names and has opened retail outlets to maximise profits. Music companies have also realised that 'classic recordings' can be digitally re-mastered and repackaged for collectors and for new audiences.

The *Guardian* sells at a higher price and also takes more advertising, especially specialist classified advertising, in G2 sections such as *Media*, *Education* etc., than some other 'quality' papers.

Gone With the Wind is still the most successful film ever made (adjusting box office for inflation) and has been re-released many times. In 1998 it was released by New Line, the 'independent' arm of Warner Bros. Time Warner acquired the rights when they merged with Ted Turner's company. Turner had bought *Gone With the Wind* as part of the MGM film library and it was the most valuable asset in his portfolio. The new release added twelve minutes of new footage in a digitally re-mastered version. Two hundred prints were released (*Screen International*, 12 June 1998).

Merchandising The marketing of a wide range of consumer goods bearing images from a specific media product has a very long history, but the sheer scale of current merchandising dates from the release of *Star Wars* in 1977.

> Newspapers have a short life as consumer products, but they have always had a long-term value as **archive** material. Possibilities for this were once limited by storage space and difficulty of access (e.g. in libraries) but can now be commercially exploited on CD-ROM and online.

Types of activities

So far we have referred both to 'media industries' and to specific production activities. Until the 1990s, each medium of production was seen to involve distinct industrial processes:

- film
- television
- radio
- newspapers
- magazines
- music recording
- video games.

We should also include book publishing as a media activity. The next Harry Potter film will be a major event in the media industries – and so will the next Harry Potter book launch.

Now, we commonly refer to the **convergence** of different industrial processes so that similar activities are common to more than one media industry. The main technological engine for this development is **digital** media production. Workers in all the seven industries above sit at 'workstations' concentrating on very similar computer screens, manipulating a mouse and 'dragging' files whether they contain sounds, images or text. At the other end of the process, the pattern of ownership and control across media industries means that most of the major companies involved have an interest in at least four out of the six traditional industries as well as in the 'new' industry of electronic media (i.e. internet services, computer games, etc.).

But it is still worth exploring the differences that remain between the two main groups of media activities. There are other differences but the five oppositions shown in Figure 7.1 raise interesting questions. To some extent the technologies that emerged in the 1990s such as DVD and CD-ROM have bridged some of the gaps (e.g. television series on DVD are sold like films) and audiences too are beginning to influence the industry by their willingness to access media products in different ways (e.g. looking at news stories on the internet).

Film companies have exploited their archives of past productions, repackaging them for retail on DVD and selling rights to broadcast to specialist satellite and cable television channels. As films now make as much money (and usually more) from television and video as from

Newspapers and 'live' radio and television broadcasting	Recorded music, film production, recorded television and radio
continuous production and distribution – steady cash flow	sporadic production, regular but not daily distribution, possibility of interrupted revenue flows
high fixed costs (printing plants, studios)	each production has a separate budget (long term fixed costs can be avoided)
high proportion of revenue from advertising	revenue from 'rentals', merchandising, product placement
universal distribution in a restricted area (i.e. national, regional or local)	no limits on potential global distribution
output taken to be entertainment and 'information'.	output taken to be entertainment and 'art'.

Figure 7.1 Comparison of news/broadcasting and recorded music/film production.

theatrical release, the major film companies do in fact achieve a steady flow of income, allowing them to survive a string of box-office failures. Without this 'subsidy' from past successes, more of the major studios would have been sold (e.g. like MGM and United Artists).

At the same time, television companies have moved away from producing their own programmes and have begun to buy in more programmes made by smaller 'independent' production companies. Channel 4 was the first UK television channel to be set up as a 'publisher broadcaster' – making no programmes itself and avoiding the burden of paying for expensive studio facilities. Television companies have also tried to break out of the restrictions of a local market by selling certain prestige programmes abroad. However, only the BBC in the UK is large enough to sustain an international broadcasting presence (through BBC World and overseas channels such as BBC America and the World Service on radio).

UK television broadcasters (including the BBC) were required to commission at least 25 per cent of their broadcast programmes from 'independents' by the Broadcasting Act 1990.

BBC World can be seen in 256 million homes outside Europe and North America (see www.bbcworld.com).

BBC America (see www.bbcamerica.com) announces itself as 'a digital cable and satellite channel dedicated to bringing audiences a new generation of award-winning television featuring razor-sharp comedies, provocative dramas, life changing makeovers and news with a uniquely global perspective'. It shows other non-BBC UK programming as well and is supported by advertising since UK licence-fee income cannot be used overseas.

Newspapers have attempted, with various levels of success, to exploit their brand names and extend their market reach through use of new technologies, making archives available on CD-ROM and setting up electronic titles on the web. The *Guardian* has been particularly successful in attracting a much wider readership for its Guardian Unlimited website than for the paper itself (which also prints in Europe and in its *Guardian Weekly* format for distribution worldwide). These activities definitely help secure the *Guardian*'s reputation with readers and therefore with advertisers.

See Chapter 13 on distribution of Guardian Unlimited.

Magazines have developed brand names that have allowed them to launch both television and radio services (these are known in the UK as 'Masthead' programmes and are regulated by Ofcom as 'sponsored' programming).

ACTIVITY 7.1

Magazine industry

How do you think the magazine industry fits into this analysis? Does its reliance on advertising make it more like newspapers and broadcasting? Or does the relatively high cost of a magazine and its potential status for collectors make the industry more like film and music?

Six stages of media production

No matter which media industry, there tends to be a similar production process in place, and you need to be aware of the stages of production as set out in the box below. The terms used by professionals in each separate industry differ but the most often studied industry is film, and we will use that industry here to explore the questions raised by its specific organisation of the process. There is more detailed discussion of the production process in Chapter 11.

Six stages of media production

- negotiating a deal
- pre-production and preparation
- production
- post-production
- distribution and marketing
- 'exhibition'/retail.

Negotiating a deal in contemporary Hollywood

The international film industry is dominated by a handful of major companies, still referred to as 'studios', even though they do not all own studio facilities as such and the majority of films they handle are actually made by small independent production companies. A film begins as an idea, 'pitched' to a studio. It is conceived as an individual product and put together by a producer as a '**package**' of a story, stars and a director and crew. There are a number of ways in which the package can be financed, but for big-budget films the 'deal' will nearly always involve one of the **major studios**.

The six Hollywood majors have survived seventy years or more. Few other industries have such established brand names and it is the exploitation of these brands via global distribution of films (and videos) that keeps the majors ahead of the pack of smaller companies.

Major studios

- Warner Bros
- Sony Pictures
- Universal
- Disney
- Paramount
- 20th Century Fox.

ACTIVITY 7.2

Major studios

Do some quick internet research into the history of the current major studios. Try to find:

- When their famous logo first appeared – has it altered much since then?
- On what kinds of other products does the studio brand now appear?
- Have you seen any films in which the logo has been altered to match the theme/style of the film?

The six major studios are all part of larger **media conglomerates** and members of the **MPAA** (Motion Pictures Association of America). These studios are powerful not because they make films, but because they dominate distribution and because they still own libraries of past films (many of which they made under the **studio system**, 1930–60). MGM/UA is still listed as a studio, but was acquired by Sony in 2004. DreamWorks, the studio set up by Steven Spielberg, Jeffrey Katzenberg and David Geffen in 1994, is a major film producer, but only distributes films in North America (i.e. not worldwide) and has not yet been listed as a major by the MPAA. New Line, producer of blockbusters such as *The*

Lord of the Rings trilogy, is, like several other listed 'independent' producers, owned by a major (in this case, Time Warner).

In July 2005, NBC-Universal were reported to be preparing a bid for DreamWorks film studio (*Guardian*, 29 July 2005).

> The MPAA and its international presence, the MPA (Motion Pictures Association), act as the 'trade association' for Hollywood, representing the interests of the major studios (especially in relation to piracy) and running the certification scheme for films and DVDs in the US (see www.mpaa.org). MPAA President Dan Glickman is the 'voice' of the major studios. Although some 600 or more films are made in the US each year, only 200–300 are made by MPAA members and most figures referring to 'Hollywood' refer to these films only.

The concept behind a new film could be developed from many sources, but to interest the studios in the relatively 'conservative' atmosphere of Hollywood it will probably need to be supported by evidence of previous success associated with the ingredients of the proposal:

- a sequel to a recent box-office hit (e.g. sequels such as *Spider-Man 2* (US 2004) and the next episodes of 'franchises' such as 'Harry Potter' and 'James Bond')
- a remake of a box-office hit from another film industry (e.g. *Ringu* (Japan 1998) remade as *The Ring* (US 2002))
- an adaptation of a best-selling book (e.g. films based on John Grisham novels)
- an original story by an award winner such as Sofia Coppola (who won a scriptwriting Oscar for *Lost in Translation* (US 2003))
- an original idea from a successful director/star team, e.g. Steven Soderbergh and George Clooney
- a new twist on a story from a currently popular genre cycle (films like *Troy* (US/Malta/UK 2004) which followed *Gladiator* (UK/US 2000)
- any combination of the above.

It isn't always easy to work out why a deal 'seemed like a good idea at the time'. It can take as long as two or three years for a 'deal' to produce a finished film. In that time the 'big star' attracted to the project might have faded from view or public taste might have changed. Film producers have to make educated guesses about what will work with audiences a year or more in the future, and they have to gamble with very large sums of money.

This gamble is taken by a normally conservative financial sector which can take enormous risks in terms of the production budget, when the chances of success at the cinema box office are actually quite small – most

Figure 7.2 An extract from 'The Business: Understanding Filmmaking' on the website www.skillset.org/film/business as presented by Skillset and the UK Film Council's Lottery Fund. Storyboards by David Allcock.

films lose money on theatrical release. (The combined total of expenditure on new films by Hollywood studios is often not much less than the total box-office receipts in the same period.) There are, however, good reasons why Hollywood continues to make profits.

Each of the major Hollywood studios finances a **slate** of seven or eight big films every year with a **production budget** of around $70 million or more each, aiming for a smash hit during the two critical seasons which run in North America from May to August and from Thanksgiving (late November) to Christmas. Some critics refer to these as 'ultra-high-budget films' (see Maltby 1998). The studio will also probably release another dozen or so 'medium-budget' films costing around $20–30 million. The budget for each film will include half as much again to spend on **P&A** (prints and advertising), giving an average spend of $100 million on a big-budget film. With an outlay of over $1 billion on the slate, at least one film must be a big hit (grossing $200 million or more) for the studio to generate some initial income. In many cases, the subsequent DVD release will be the main source of income, but this usually requires at least some success in cinemas to raise the film's profile. If a studio is very lucky and has a record-breaking blockbuster (e.g. *Titanic* with $1.8 billion worldwide box office in 1998), then profits can be substantial (*Titanic* was so expensive to make and market that it took two studios to distribute it). However, many films flop badly at the cinema box office and in 2004 Halle Berry as *Catwoman* attracted only $40 million of ticket money in North America for a film with combined production and marketing costs of over $130 million for Warner Bros.

'Tentpole movie' is another term for the 'ultra-high-budget' film, presumably on the grounds that one big blockbuster provides the support for the whole slate, just as the pole holds up the big top in the circus. This is one of the slang terms used in the famous entertainment industry paper *Variety*.

When the major studios owned their own cinema chains in the 1930s and 1940s, they made most of their profits from their cinemas.

Film rentals

It's common practice for the film industry to publish box-office figures, and they appear in the weekly 'Top 10' as published in newspapers and on the internet (e.g. see www.boxofficeguru.com). However, these figures are misleading as evidence of profitability. The 'rental charge' (what the exhibitor pays to the distributor) starts high in the first week and gradually falls. Around 50 per cent of final box office is retained by the cinema exhibitor, and $100 million at the box office means that only $50 million is returned to the distributor (usually the studio that produced the film). This explains why for most films it takes the international and ancillary markets' revenue to push the final total into profit.

The most dramatic example of box-office failure was the epic western *Heaven's Gate* in 1980. So much was lost that the studio, United Artists, collapsed completely and is now little more than a name. That was at a time when the majors were financially vulnerable. The relative stability of the majors' more recent operations is explained by two developments in the 1990s:

- the increase in the importance of the **international theatrical** (cinema) market, which is now regularly more valuable than the North American (US and Canada) or **'domestic' market**
- the development of **ancillary markets** in video, pay television,

The sorry tale of the decline of United Artists is told in one of the best books about the studios, *Final Cut* by Steven Bach (1985).

Studios are now concerned to sell films in all territories. Casting an actor from a specific territory can sometimes help open a film there. For *Batman Begins* in 2005, Warner Bros used Ken Watanabe as the focus for a marketing campaign in Japan, where previous Batman films had underperformed.

Figure 7.3 Posters for Hollywood films playing in a Croatian holiday resort in summer 2002.

computer games and merchandising, which are now more important than the traditional test of success at the North American box office. (The situation in the UK mirrors the American experience. UK audiences pay most to watch films on satellite and cable. DVD retail comes next. Cinema box-office revenues have been rising and now compete with DVD rentals. See the annual *BFI Handbook* or UK Film Council Statistics for figures.)

Keeping faith in *Alexander*

Early in 2005, Oliver Stone's version of the Alexander the Great story was released in North America to general critical derision. The failure of this costly film (production budget $155 million, US box office $35 million) was a major blow to the relatively small Anglo-German independent company Intermedia that had gambled heavily on its release. But, instead of accepting defeat, Intermedia went ahead with an international release, knowing that historical epics (such as *Troy*) generally perform better outside North America. The eventual worldwide box office was $168 million – not a success, but not the resounding failure it would have been without the international market.

The result of these changes in markets is that a higher proportion of ultra-high-budget features are likely to go into profit eventually. Maltby (1998) suggests that as many as half the blockbusters will turn a profit, compared to one in ten in the pre-video days. The majors can expect very long 'streams' of income from a successful film, so that in any single financial year they are guaranteed some income even if all the current releases are relative flops. It is this guarantee that keeps them in business and allows them to price out competitors by pushing up budgets.

The guarantee is valid only for what have been termed '**high-concept' movies**. Justin Wyatt (1994: 8) suggested that these represent 'a style of film-making modelled by economic and institutional forces'. High concept emphasises:

- successful pitching, especially via market research, and pre-sold marketability
- easily summarised idea (in twenty-five words or less, according to Steven Spielberg)
- successful saturation advertising (see Branston 2000: 48).

The seven bullet points on p. 215 refer to the basis of this pitching process (i.e. by reference to a proven source) and, if you add big stars and spectacle to the mix, you should be able to 'pitch' your own ideas.

ACTIVITY 7.3

Pitching a film

What ideas have you got for a new blockbuster film – one which would definitely interest a Hollywood studio?

- Choose one of the preferred sources and develop your idea.
- Think carefully about whom you would cast and, most important, try to sum up the idea in a single line (e.g. *Alien = Jaws* in space).
- Test out your outline on a friend. How well does it stand up?

The 'pitch' process is brilliantly satirised in Robert Altman's film *The Player* (US 1992).

This strange business, in which producers feel more secure with a large budget, sees investors nervous about 'low-budget' pictures. The budget may be artificially forced up towards the average (a form of 'institutional constraint'?) and star names added at large fees, even when the story doesn't necessarily need stars. What might be a 'big-budget' production in Europe – $10–20 million – is automatically seen as a 'small film' in Hollywood and thereby marginalised for North American distributors.

There are some small independent producers and distributors who succeed outside the orbit of the majors. Sometimes they can spot new markets ahead of the majors, or they are prepared to take on controversial issues or even controversial audiences. It is still possible to make low-budget films on strict production schedules and to sell them to specialist markets without the massive P&A spends of the majors. But it is becoming much more difficult. By the late 1990s nearly all the successful independent distributors had been 'acquired' by the majors, which continue to run them as separate businesses to maintain their image of 'independence' and, arguably, as their 'Research and Development' arm (see Wyatt 1998 on Miramax and New Line).

'There are two kinds of films an indie can make nowadays. There's the big picture if you have a property and a package that the studios want, and the much smaller ones under $20 million' (Moritz Borman of Intermedia, *Screen International*, 8 April 2005).

Given this background, it is not surprising that the setting-up period can be lengthy, and scripts may pass through the hands of many studio executives before they are '**greenlighted**'. The gestation period for some films may be ten years or more. During this time a good deal of **development money** may have been spent by a studio on an option on the rights to the idea (known as the property) without a foot of film ever having been shot. What the owner of the property fears most is it being put into **turnaround** – a limbo-land for script ideas which languish with one studio until another comes along which is prepared to pick up the option (i.e. to pay enough to cover the development money paid out by the first studio). It's a wonder films get made at all.

Pre-production

Once the go-ahead has been given, the production team has a great deal to do before shooting begins. Parts must be cast (the lead players were probably decided as part of the original deal), locations chosen, costumes researched, dialogue coaches and wranglers (animal handlers) hired, hotel rooms booked, etc. All this may take several months, during which time the script will be reworked and the direction of the project may be altered. A starting date is announced and reported in the trade press (*Hollywood Reporter, Variety*, etc.) and eventually the cameras will roll (although it is not unknown for the plug to be pulled on the whole enterprise at this stage).

This preparation period is crucial to Hollywood production, and many commentators have identified the extra work on polishing the script and preparing storyboards for action sequences as the key to the high technical quality of the finished product. But it isn't the only way to make a film – there are several highly regarded European and independent American films which have been made without a finished script.

At this point the producer should have a clear idea of the final budget. This will be used in the monitoring of progress on the shoot. If any costs look like over-running, changes to the script may have to be made. Figure 7.4 shows the outline for a feature film budget. The 'below the line' costs refer to the running costs of production. 'Above the line' costs refer to creative inputs.

Production

This stage is often called **principal photography**, and it is likely to be the shortest period of all. Modern films usually **wrap** in around fifty days of shooting – an average of two to three minutes a day – depending on the demands of the script. The low-budget producer will aim to halve that time by clever use of set-ups and tight scripting. Efficient directors are those who can come in 'on' or even 'under' budget. Keeping a whole crew on location a day longer than the planned schedule can add considerably to the overall cost, and directors and crews who can stick to schedules will be rehired.

Special effects which require shooting with actors can be a major problem and cause some productions to come back to studio lots or specialist facilities (including those in Britain); others go to locations offering cheaper labour or good deals on permissions (using famous buildings or locations), taxation, etc. Hollywood has at various times made films in the south-eastern United States (Florida, Georgia, Alabama) or Canada, Europe and Australasia.

'Shooting' is the most visible aspect of the production process and is frequently itself filmed in order to be used for publicity purposes (e.g. 'making of' documentaries for television that also end up on the DVD release). It therefore generates the most interest from the public. It also involves spending money 'on location', and there is a great deal of competition between locations to attract Hollywood productions.

The producer Andrew Eaton and his director partner Michael Winterbottom have been referred to as 'guerrilla film-makers' because they ignore many of the production conventions of Hollywood film-making, shooting on the street with minimal crews and often improvising on the set – to the reported consternation of Hollywood actors such as Tim Robbins in *Code 46* (UK 2003).

	$ million
Above the line costs (ATL)	
1. Story rights	1.00
2. Writers' fees	1.00
3. Producers' fees	2.50
4. Directors' fees	2.50
5. Actors' fees	26.00
6. Stunts etc.	0.50
7. Subsistence	1.00
Total ATL	**34.50**
Below the line (BTL)	
8. Extras, stand-ins	0.75
9. Wardrobe, make-up, etc.	1.70
10. Camera and film	1.50
11. Building sets	3.00
12. Set operation	1.00
13. Lighting	0.50
14. Sound	0.13
15. Special effects ('physical' – snow etc.)	0.25
16. Locations	0.60
17. Transport	1.75
18. Second Unit	0.90
19. BTL subsistence	1.40
Post-production	
20. Digital effects	0.10
21. Editing	1.50
22. Titles	0.10
23. Music	1.20
24. Sound	0.60
25. Previews	0.10
26. Labs	0.25
Completion and miscellaneous	
27. Insurance, royalties etc.	0.40
28. Publicity	0.10
29. Miscellaneous expenses	0.10
Total BTL	**17.93**
Grand Total	**52.43**

Figure 7.4 Budget outline for a typical Hollywood feature film. This is based on figures published in *Premiere* in July 2000.

Film production services

The film production process depends on access to a wide range of specialist services. Technology for filming (cameras, lenses, lighting, mounts, etc.) and for post-production (editing and film-processing) involves high levels of investment and close cooperation between film-makers and technologists. The major studios have sought to maintain these relationships – even to the extent of buying into the companies involved.

These and other services (e.g. financial, legal and promotional) are concentrated in Los Angeles. 'Professional services' can be distinguished from the 'low wages' production work which moves abroad. Keeping these services together in LA also means a strong sense of 'Hollywood community' (not something all film-makers necessarily welcome).

Post-production

The longest stage in the process may well be post-production. Here the film is edited – some might say this is where the film narrative is actually created. The relationship between the director and the editor (or 'cutter') may be relatively distant or it may be very close, as in the case of Martin Scorsese and Thelma Schoonmaker, who work together for many months to complete a picture.

The increase in the importance of film sound during the last ten years has added to the work in post-production, with more time spent on tidying up dialogue through '**looping**' or Automatic Dialogue Replacement (**ADR**) (actors record their lines again while watching themselves on a loop of film, played through until they can lip-sync perfectly) and adding sound effects using the **Foley** Studio. Special visual effects are also added at this stage. The completed film then goes to the laboratories for **colour grading** and other adjustments required to produce suitable screening prints. More production is now moving to digital formats, which can be less expensive but can also require substantial amounts of 'standardising' for theatrical screenings and DVD release.

Distribution and marketing

Every part of the process is important. The success of a film can depend at least as much on how it is handled by the distributor as on the film itself – indeed many experts call distribution the key to power in the media industries. Distributors promote and market films in particular

territories and negotiate release patterns with exhibitors. The distribution of most big-budget Hollywood films is directly controlled by the majors themselves. In North America each major studio usually distributes its own pictures. In the UK, Paramount and Universal, with MGM/UA, are joint owners of the biggest distributor, UIP. In the other important cinema markets around the world the majors may have an agreement with a local distributor, but as the international market grows they are increasingly opening their own offices in every territory.

MGM/UA was bought by Sony in 2005 – check to see who is now distributing MGM/UA films in the UK.

In 2004 the 'major studios', through their own distribution companies or in partnership, took around 80 per cent of the North American market. A majority share for American films is evident in most territories in the world, with rare exceptions such as India, China (although Hollywood distribution is growing here) and South Korea. The growth of exhibition sites, especially in Europe, South East Asia and South America, has seen the international box office matching the domestic market. (For more on film distribution see Chapter 13.)

In terms of the kinds of economics set out above for films distributed by the majors, it is important to note that a film costing $70 million to make and $30 million to distribute must make money for the exhibitor (the cinema owner) as well as for the distributor (who may also be the rights owner) – see the film rentals box on p. 217. To make a profit from a theatrical release, a 'studio picture' costing $100 million in total needs a gross box office of $200 million or more. In 2004, twenty-three films had a worldwide box office of over $200 million, but some of these films had budgets even larger than $100 million. *Van Helsing* made $300 million, but had estimated production and marketing costs of over $200 million.

The distribution process usually means that major studio films open on a **wide release** in every major city in North America (on average around 3,000 screens) simultaneously. If the film is successful, it may last in cinemas several weeks, but a high percentage of the profits will come in the first weekend when the marketing blitz will propel audiences into cinemas. 'Hit' or 'miss' status is often determined at this time. Traditionally, the North American release of any Hollywood film came first, followed a few weeks and sometimes months later by releases in other territories. However, the problem of piracy has caused some major releases to be launched simultaneously in every territory on virtually the same day. *X2* (US 2003) was the first major film to do this, opening in most territories between 30 April and 3 May. *Screen International* started an 'International Chart' in 2004 in order to log the progress of major openings worldwide. The alternative distribution strategy is the **platform release** in which the film opens in only a few major cities and then gradually moves out to the wider market, helped by 'word of mouth' and critical response. This strategy has proved successful for numerous 'smaller', more art-orientated films such as *The Motorcycle Diaries* (US/Argentina/Chile/Peru/Germany/France/UK 2004), the Spanish language film about Che Guevera which eventually made $16.7 million in the US, partly through a focus on Hispanic audiences in selected US cities.

Figure 7.5 Gael García Bernal as Ernesto ('Che') Guevera in *The Motorcycle Diaries*. Mexican actor Bernal is a recognised star of both international commercial and 'art' cinema.

Hollywood once believed that the VCR could kill the industry (see Gomery 1992). But by the late 1980s, video retail and rental on films had passed cinema box office. It is now recognised that audiences who love movies rent or buy videos (i.e. now DVDs) and go to the cinema most often (*Screen International*, 8 March 2002).

Once a film has finished its first theatrical run, the next window is a DVD release, which now typically means a rental and retail release on the same day. For DVD, the studios have tried to restrict releases to specific 'regions' (e.g. Region 1 North America, Region 2 Europe, etc.) but internet sales (and 'hacked' DVD players) have rendered this rather pointless. Following DVD release, the next window is for pay television and then finally 'free to air' television another year or so later.

Exhibition

In the US the major studios were barred from ownership of significant cinema chains following the anti-trust legislation at the end of the 1940s, which signalled the decline of the studio system – see Maltby (1995) for a detailed account of the way in which Hollywood studios were organised between 1930 and 1950. Overseas there were no such restrictions, and in the last few years Warner Bros and UCI (owned by Paramount and Universal) have built multiplexes in many cinema markets, including the UK, where other US chains such as Showcase (owned by

Viacom/Paramount's parent company, National Amusements) are also receptive to Hollywood films. Warner Bros and UCI have now sold their chains in the UK, having been successful in helping to expand the market for Hollywood films.

Ownership or control of every stage of production is known as **vertical integration**, and it has obvious advantages for the majors in ensuring that they will have a cinema available to take a film when it is ready for release. Independent distributors who are trying to find outlets for their films can face problems. Coupled with the cost of advertising and prints, this lack of access to cinemas is one of the main ways in which new entrants to the film business are kept out. (See Chapter 13 for more on specialised cinema distribution in the UK.)

The distribution patterns of films and the exhibition practices in the UK have changed significantly since the American exhibitors moved in, and now much more resemble what happens elsewhere in Europe and North America. Attendance habits have changed as a result. Although there are more screens, there are fewer cinemas (older cinemas have continued to close as multiplexes open) and virtually none in suburbs or small towns. Even in larger towns there may be only a single cinema. People are prepared to travel further to the cinema and most of us now have a multiplex with ten or more screens within half an hour's drive.

Increasingly, cinema exhibition is being considered as a global business and exhibitors have begun to notice how enthusiasm for cinema is different in different countries. The UK and Ireland are treated as a single territory. Although box-office figures for the two countries are usually just lumped together, closer examination shows that the Irish are much more 'frequent' attenders at cinemas. As a consequence, cinema chains are investing in new Irish multiplexes – and the corollary is that the UK is still 'underscreened' compared to countries such as France (over 5,000 screens compared to the UK's 3,400 with similar population numbers).

The building boom of '**multiplex cinemas**', first in the US in the 1980s and then around the world, helped in the exploitation of blockbuster films and their tie-in merchandising – many multiplexes being built in shopping malls.

American 'out of town' mall culture poses serious planning problems, not least encouragement of car travel. More recent cinema building has seen a move back to city-centre sites in the UK.

Cinema in Ireland

'The population of the Republic of Ireland stands at 3.9m and records about 4.5 visits per person per annum. By contrast Northern Ireland with a population of 1.7 million records 3.2 visits per person per year' (*Screen International* online, 5 February 2004).

'Six new multiplexes will open in Ireland this year, in a construction boom that is tipped to boost Irish cinema admissions by 20%. Ireland has one of the highest rates of cinema-going in Europe . . . and the flagship Irish sites of multinational operators UGC (Cineworld), UCI and Ster Century consistently outperform their sites in the UK' (*Screen International* online, 1 April 2005).

Frequency of attendance is highest in Iceland, North America and Australia at around five cinema visits per year by each person over four years of age. In Europe, Spain and France lead with around three visits but Germany and Italy are often below two visits.

In Italy, the tradition has been that major films are not released in the summer when audiences prefer to be somewhere else. This is slowly changing as new, air-conditioned multiplexes are being built to accommodate new audiences attracted by heavy marketing on the back of international campaigns for big films released as part of Hollywood's summer season (but European holiday traditions still mean that some indoor cinemas close in August).

ACTIVITY 7.4

Cinema attendance

Consider the cinema attendance figures presented in this section.

- If you were a cinema exhibition company, what kinds of factors would you consider to explain the differences, especially between Northern Ireland and the Republic and between England, Wales and Scotland (under three visits) and the island of Ireland?
- What kinds of changes might you make in England?
- Look at a weekly chart in *Screen International* to see what kinds of films are attracting audiences in the UK, France and Spain. Are the same films doing well in each territory? Are there any differences?

The major change for the exhibition sector will come with digital projection systems, which will require all cinemas to invest in new equipment. In the past with CinemaScope (a new screen in the 1950s) and Dolby Sound (new sound systems in the 1980s), this proved to take quite a long time and exhibitors took some convincing to buy the new technology. Digital projection could be a long time arriving, but new cinemas may have the equipment from the start. In March 2005 an American company, Avica, announced plans to set up a digital network in Ireland, with more screens envisaged than in the UK plans from the UK Film Council (*Screen International*, 30 March 2005). The years from 2006 to 2010 are likely to be crucial for the 'digitalisation' of cinema exhibition. (See more on this in Chapter 13.)

Organisation of production

Once we have been able to develop a model to describe the production process, what kinds of issues can we explore? Here are some from an industry approach.

ACTIVITY 7.5

The production process model

To test out your understanding of the six-stage model (p. 213), jot down some notes on what you think would happen in each stage of the production process for

- a new magazine for dance enthusiasts
- the first recordings by a new band.

You might have difficulty in deciding into which stage to put a particular activity – don't worry about this: using the model is not necessarily about getting the 'right answers' but more about helping you to understand the process. This exercise should help in both your industry studies and your production work.

Structure

How significant is the structure of the industry (the **pattern of ownership** of large and small companies in different sectors) in determining how media products are produced and what kinds of products appear? Two important questions centre on integration and regulation.

Forms of business organisation

If you wish to study media industries in detail, you will need some basic understanding of business structures. Media organisations are diverse and can take any of the following forms.

Private sector (organisations owned by individuals or groups of shareholders):

- *Sole traders*: freelances in the media industries are often self-employed, 'one-person' businesses.
- *Partnerships*: ownership by two or more people governed by partnership agreements is common in small production companies.
- *Private company with 'limited liability'*: 'private' companies are owned by shareholders, often from a single family. Such companies do not offer shares for sale to the public via a 'stock exchange'. One major media corporation, Viacom, is owned by a private company.
- *Public limited company*: owned by shareholders and the shares are freely traded – most large media corporations are actually owned by 'institutional shareholders' such as pensions funds or insurance funds.

In this chapter and in the 'Case study: The media majors' we will often refer to companies being 'owned' or 'controlled' by larger companies. In many cases, this simply means that the larger company owns a sufficiently large percentage of the shares of the smaller company to be able to influence its behaviour (usually 30 per cent or more).

- *Holding company*: some business organisations exist only to own (to 'hold') other companies; the UK cinema industry has been characterised in recent years by the buying and selling of cinema chains by companies which exist solely to find a profitable use of their capital (i.e. they weren't set up to offer specific goods or services).
- *Conglomerates*: large corporations which own several subsidiary companies in different sectors – the major media corporations are sometimes referred to as conglomerates.

Public sector:

- *Charity or trust*: 'not-for-profit' organisations, sometimes run by volunteers, with special financial and tax status – local arts organisations are often in this category. The Public Broadcasting System (PBS) in the US receives donations from individuals and charitable foundations (as well as some financial support from the federal government).
- *Government department*: some media activities have been carried out by civil servants (e.g. regulation of telecommunications in the UK), but this is now unlikely.
- *Public corporation*: a body set up by Royal Charter (BBC) or Act of Parliament (Channel 4) which is non-profit making (profits go back into the business since there are no shareholders) – not to be confused with a *public limited company* (see above).

Integration refers to the growth of organisations by means of the acquisition of other organisations in the same industry. **Vertical integration** refers to an organisation established in one part of the production chain gaining control of the other parts of the production and distribution process, e.g. a Hollywood studio being bought by a cinema chain (as when National Amusements bought Paramount as part of Viacom). A fully integrated media organisation would control every aspect of the production process. In the past, this has meant newspapers being produced by companies who even owned the trees from which the paper was made.

Horizontal integration refers to media organisations acquiring control of their competitors within that segment of the production process (it is theoretically possible for an organisation to be both vertically and horizontally integrated, but that would mean that one organisation was effectively the whole industry). Ultimately, one organisation may control a majority share of the market – a **monopoly** position. More usually, there is at least one other competitor – creating a **duopoly**, as in UK cinema exhibition for many years up to the 1990s, or UK television – or a small number of competitors of roughly equal status: an **oligopoly**.

Most media industries – indeed most large-scale industries of any kind – are oligopolies. Economists refer to the relationships between organisations in an oligopoly situation as **imperfect competition**. (See more on ideas about competition and 'free markets' in Chapter 16.) There are likely to be unwritten agreements between the oligopolists as to standards, pricing policies, labour relations, etc. Because governments are likely to be concerned at the political implications of media monopolies, action is likely to be taken against 'too much' integration. This concern has increased as traditionally separate industries such as publishing, broadcasting and film have moved closer together. In the US, monopolies have been broken up in the past by 'anti-Trust' decisions by the Supreme Court or the Department of Justice. Microsoft have been involved in legal action over their monopoly position in computer operating systems since 1994 in both the US and Europe.

ACTIVITY 7.6

Researching ownership

Use the newspaper archives in your library and/or the internet to trace the changes in ownership and control of UK media activities in the last few years involving each of these groups: Granada, Pearson, EMAP. This should give you some idea of the complexity of UK media business.

Control of acquisitions in the media industries and subsequent oligopoly practices can be exercised in two ways:
- Public sector media organisations, financed and controlled by the public purse and public accountability, can be set up. Nearly all countries have some form of public broadcasting (radio and television) and many have set up publicly funded agencies which play an important role in financing and distributing films and other media products.
- The activities of media organisations can be regulated by government or public sector 'watchdogs'. Regulations often cover not only monopoly ownership or control and financial dealings but also the range and 'quality' of products (including technical quality) and sometimes the sensitive content of products. (See Chapter 16.)

Location and local–global relations

The location of media industries is important for two main reasons:

- As a major employment sector (possibly the largest in some parts of Europe), the location of media production facilities is a contentious issue in many countries where the 'spend' of media industries is a major factor in the local economy.
- If the media producers are all located in one area, then their media products are likely to be influenced by the culture of that area, which may or may not align with that of media consumers elsewhere, even within the same 'nation-state'.

The Hollywood studios have always prided themselves on the international appeal of their products. Yet, within the US, studios have traditionally been careful to censor material in order not to offend audiences in more conservative areas. Once, of course, this meant pandering to a form of racial 'apartheid' in the Southern states. Getting the balance right (between culturally conservative and liberal parts of the country) is difficult. Films and television programmes are usually financed in New York and made in Los Angeles, and this twin axis has traditionally controlled the US media. The location of Ted Turner's operation (CNN especially) – a new competitor based in Atlanta – was therefore of some significance. The South (from Florida across to New Mexico) is both the area of economic expansion and the home of 'neo-conservative' political views and a growing Hispanic population. The phenomenon of bigoted talk-radio 'shock jocks' (another Southern strength) is also a symptom of a shift in the geography of the American media.

In the UK the concentration of media production in London and the south-east has led to complaints about metropolitan bias. The growth and spread of a new speech pattern – so-called 'estuary English' – have been blamed on the London base of media commentators, and the restructuring of both ITV and the BBC has been scrutinised in order to guarantee more regional production. Similar arguments could be made about national newspapers, which once had major regional editorial offices – Manchester, for instance was the base for several dailies (including the *Manchester Guardian*, which moved to London).

The *Guardian* responded to some of these criticisms with a rebranding of its masthead in the North of England to 'the Guardian North' in 2000.

Perhaps the major concern over location is the fear that media production in one country may be completely controlled from another country. This fear extends to both the news media and to media seen to be important agents in building a cultural identity. It can be argued that the spread of 'international news services' such as CNN has had a beneficial effect in those parts of the world where repressive governments can muzzle their own media but cannot stop the inflow of satellite images (or indeed BBC World Service radio broadcasts). On the other hand, most western

Figure 7.6 The new digital weather map introduced on BBC television in 2005 was immediately criticised because its 3D rendering of a view from over the English Channel made the north of the British Isles and, especially, Scotland appear to be smaller than in reality.

Figure 7.7 BBC North on Oxford Road in Manchester city centre. BBC reorganisation announced in 2004 is expected to see Children's Programmes, Sport, New Media and Radio 5 Live move to Manchester, where BBC and Granada already share facilities. In September 2005 Lancashire had more Premiership football teams than London – worth remembering when, after the successful 2012 Olympics bid, London journalists complained about BBC Sport moving out.

countries have expressed concern about the ownership of media companies operating within their national boundaries being held by non-nationals (Rupert Murdoch had to take out US citizenship in order to acquire his US television holdings). This fear relates to anxiety over the 'unregulated' international media market outlined in the previous section.

The economic benefits of attracting media business into an area can be considerable. With a weak sterling/dollar exchange rate, the choice of the UK and Ireland as the base for Hollywood feature film production in the early 1990s generated a great deal of local business in some of the more remote parts of Wales, Scotland and especially Ireland (where government policy has been to invite production companies indirectly and to offer a range of incentives) (see Chapter 10). Similarly the weakness of the Canadian dollar saw many US productions heading for Vancouver, Toronto and Montreal at the end of the 1990s. (In 2005 the weakness of the US dollar started to move productions elsewhere.)

See Chapter 15 for interesting developments in 'global television news'.

The emergence of Al Jazeera TV, post-9/11 and the invasion of Iraq in 2003, has provided an interesting case study in the location of an alternative voice to CNN and other western broadcasters inside the Arab world (but one not necessarily supported by all Arab governments).

ACTIVITY 7.7

Media industries in the local economy

Investigate your local authority (at a county or city level) and its attitude to media development.

- Does it operate a film office?
- Does it have a media policy? Or does it refer to 'cultural industries'?
- What kind of economic benefits are expected?

Work patterns and employment

Work in the media is often perceived as glamorous and highly paid. In reality, this description fits only a small percentage of the workforce. We can recognise different groups of workers:

- technical (production, transmission, etc.)
- creative (writers, performers, designers, etc.)
- production organisation and management
- professional services (finance, legal, etc.)
- auxiliary support services (clerical, administrative, catering, etc.).

Technical staff represent a problem for employers in terms of both initial training and reskilling as technologies develop. The move to digital processes has now largely been completed, but technological innovation continues apace. Media corporations in some sectors (film especially) have a poor record on training, expecting staff to 'work up from the bottom' or simply recruiting staff trained by somebody else (the BBC used to train the majority of broadcast technicians in the UK before deregulation). This 'short-termism' (i.e. not worrying about the future) is now being addressed, but it still remains a problem.

Work contracts in media industries

In the UK, one of the distinctive features of employment in the media industries is the use of **freelance** workers. In newspaper and magazine publishing, feature writers are often freelances commissioned to produce individual pieces or given short-term contracts on a particular title. (See Chapter 11.) In film and television production, much of which is carried out by small companies who recruit crews for specific productions, a large number of creative and technical personnel are freelance. The BBC is a rare example of a large employer in the media, but even here freelances will not be unusual.

Freelances need to be distinguished from part-time and temporary staff. In general, freelances will be better-paid with fees based on nationally agreed rates. Some media personnel will be 'unpaid' – such is the clamour, especially in London, to work in some media (e.g. as 'runners' on a film shoot).

A clear picture of the workforce in film, broadcast and audio-visual sectors in the UK can be seen in the 'census reports' produced by Skillset (see the 'Research' section of www.skillset.org).

The annual Skillset census is useful for dispelling the myth that some media industries personnel try to put across – that a media studies degree is not relevant for work in the media industries. The figures show that most people working in the industry in the UK have some form of graduate or postgraduate media qualification.

Differing labour costs for technical staff have led to shifting locations for media work: a common feature of globalisation. Much colour printing is now undertaken in the 'Pacific rim' countries, which have access to both high technology and lower wage costs (and digital material can easily be transmitted from editorial offices in Europe and North America). Hollywood productions are periodically attracted abroad by lower staff costs.

Where was this book printed? Check other recent books in your library.

Creative personnel have usually been considered by media theorists in terms of how personal expression survives within an industrial system. Other issues, however, relate to the ownership of creative ideas and the rights, including **copyright** (see Chapter 11), which ensue. Media corporations attempt to control these as much as possible through contracts. Most of the high-profile cases of disputes over rights have come from the music industry or from cinema – where high-profile stars and directors have learned how to ensure they can maintain control.

The concept of the 'director's cut' is an example of how a 'star author' can assert contractual power. Less obvious is the power of certain stars who take a percentage of box office gross receipts – i.e. before a film officially moves into profit.

Production management staff are those who make sure that the project is completed and that it gets distributed. Media corporations tend to concentrate on ownership of properties and rights rather than direct control over employment. They do of course control what freelance staff and independent production groups do through contracts and financial support. Supporters of the system maintain that the arrangement means that production groups are 'lean and mean' and highly competitive, that they are not hampered by institutional inertia. One disadvantage is that training and retraining and other initiatives which require industry-wide action become much more difficult to organise. (Much of Skillset's work in the UK is concerned with making sure the 'barriers to training' for freelances are not insurmountable.)

The professional services sector in the media industries requires a high degree of specialisation, especially in legal and financial fields, and again tends to favour location in metropolitan centres (where specialist agencies will find sufficient work to support a practice). More general support services such as catering are not so location-conscious.

Technological development

Technological change affects every part of the production process and not just the 'production' stage. As an example, the development of broadband cable and the transmission of digital media products at high speed around the world is primarily about distribution, but there is equal interest in the exhibition of the product in the home via a digital 'set-top box' or in the presentation theatre using digital projection. The 'deal', especially the international deal, will perhaps be aided by video-conferencing and access to internet sites making dissemination of specialist information and research material possible. Post-production may also benefit – digital video can be edited 'on location' and beamed back to the studio.

The media business environment

Ownership and influence on products

The ownership and control of media companies is an issue in media studies because of a belief that the nature of the product, and in particular the content of news and factual material or the ideological limits of a whole range of products, may be influenced by business considerations or the 'proprietorial' whims of chief executives. Conversely, the lack of production opportunities for smaller and non-commercial producers means that only a narrow range of media products are easily available to audiences.

Recognising the possibility of proprietorial control was relatively straightforward when newspapers were run by 'press barons' and Hollywood studios by autocratic moguls. Or at least that is the stereotypical view of these entrepreneurs. Does ownership influence products? Certainly, newspapers sometimes develop a distinctive editorial line that can be traced back to a proprietor or leading executive. There are some specific examples of this, such as the control over the Express Newspapers group exerted by owner Richard Desmond, or the Republican sympathies of top figures in Fox News. But sometimes the editorial line has been developed over many years and may stay much the same even if ownership changes. Much more likely is that management style and management aims will change the broad direction of a media company's activities (e.g. the impact of Rupert Murdoch's takeover of British newspapers such as the *Sun* and *The Times*). There are high-profile personalities behind the 'faceless' media corporations and these 'players' often become the focus for stories about the media – see more in 'Case study: The media majors'.

Ownership and control are primarily about costs and market share and the potential for profit. It is to achieve these two economic aims that companies grow through takeovers and mergers. Vertical integration makes sense if costs are reduced because each process is kept within the company. Horizontal integration should mean more market share and a reduction in average costs. If two music companies merge, they can use one headquarters building, one marketing team, merge some labels, etc. and still sell the same number of records as a joint company as when they were separate companies.

The product will be changed if doing so makes it less costly to produce or more likely to attract an audience/readership. Certain kinds of ownership, such as transferral to the public sector, may mean that 'non-commercial' products, meeting social objectives or regulatory requirements (e.g. education projects), become possible.

Modern media companies are most likely to be part of a **conglomerate**. The parent company is likely to be engaged in several different media sectors and possibly related sectors such as the manufacture of technology or the provision of telecommunications (see 'Case study: The media majors'). The range of activities encompassed by the widest definitions of 'media' is vast and includes some of the fastest-growing industrial sectors. It is inevitable that our representation will need updating by the time you read this, but it should still give you a good grasp of the international market. Note these features:

- The Hollywood studios are often the most familiar names in the group of brands held by media conglomerates – i.e. they are used in television and other media as well.
- The major media corporations span North America, Europe and Japan.
- It still isn't clear whether we should include computer and telecommunications companies as 'media corporations', but companies such as Microsoft are bigger than the purely media companies.

Financial control

Modern media corporations are owned by shareholders. The 'cross-holding' of shares of one media corporation by another is widespread (especially in Europe). The major shareholders are often 'institutional' – insurance companies or pension funds far removed from the production which generates the profit. Thousands of small shareholders are represented by 'fund managers' and have little chance to influence corporate affairs. The future of the corporation lies very much in the hands of accountants and financial advisers who look at the balance sheets rather than the product as an indicator of the health of the company. Ultimately, stock exchanges can determine the fate of corporations.

This observation, which is relevant for all modern corporations, shouldn't be seen as 'proof' that all industrial media production is devoid of creative work or that because it is industrial it will all be the same. It does, however, suggest the kinds of influences which are present when media corporations make decisions to buy or sell subsidiary companies or to cease production (i.e. close down a newspaper title or shelve a feature film). There are a few media industry figures with a personal fortune big enough to enable them to become significant 'players' in the media market, and there are a handful of executives whose reputation is such that their activity (or even their presence) can dramatically affect the financial status of a company, but even so the accountants set the 'bottom line' on most projects.

Media production takes place in what can sometimes seem a quite contradictory business environment. Financial security matters more than individual creativity, yet in the mid-1990s a financially secure company (Sony) made a mess of operating two Hollywood studios, Columbia and Tri-Star, while good creative management turned round a company in difficulty (Disney). Good management can still be undone by events that nobody could foresee – such as the collapse of the so-called 'dotcom economy' which made the alliance between Time Warner and AOL look such a mistake just a few years later in 2004. We might argue that some management strategies are more effective in allowing the development of an environment in which creative decisions can be made. We might also note that the attitude of financial markets towards media industries is important. In the US there is a positive attitude towards investment in the media industries, especially Hollywood, despite the disasters. For good or ill, US investors seem to be attracted by the glamour (see the increasingly high profile of the Oscars ceremonies each year) and will risk their money accordingly. Contrast this with the UK, where it has proved very difficult to persuade financial institutions to finance British films or new media generally.

The contemporary media business environment is in a constant state of turmoil as conglomerates buy and sell companies in an attempt to keep on board the bandwagon – a wagon which is surely rolling, but no one is sure in exactly which direction. The failure of the 'dotcom' revolution to

The announcement in July 2005 of the 'retirement' of Rupert Murdoch's son Laclan from News Corporation was taken by commentators as a sign that News Corporation may be broken up when Murdoch himself leaves the stage. Not even the Murdoch family's 30 per cent of the business is enough to ensure a 'dynastic succession'.

sustain growth has injected some reality into the claims for future growth, but still industry executives speak enthusiastically about 'new products' and 'new opportunities'. We have picked out four trends which do seem to be important and which we think you should study: libraries, brands, distribution and synergy.

Libraries

New distribution systems and the multiplication of channels on digital television have been developing faster than the output of new product. Anyone who controls a library or 'back catalogue' of recognisable media products is now in a good position to exploit these resources. Hollywood film libraries, the rights to well-known popular songs, photographic archives – all these are being snapped up by the large media corporations. They are catalogued and presented online in different collections, generating revenue as immediate product and then again as they are reproduced by their media users.

Libraries are also a form of security for the major corporations in a precarious business such as film distribution. DreamWorks is in a relatively precarious position as a 'new' studio because, if its new releases fail at the box office, it does not have much revenue from library material coming in at a steady trickle – the lifeblood which sustains the established majors.

Brands

As the international media market grows and companies attempt to operate in several different countries, the marketing of new products becomes more problematic. If a company wants to build its presence in Poland, Thailand and South Africa, will it need different logos, a different company image to appeal in different cultural contexts? Brands are expensive to develop (see Chapter 9). The power of the international brand, instantly recognisable everywhere, goes some way to explaining the longevity of the Hollywood studios. There cannot be many parts of the world where Warner's shield, Paramount's mountain and MGM's lion are not familiar to a mass audience. (Many of MGM's famous films are now owned by Time Warner, but the lion stays on them.) The move to merchandising, utilising the studio logo to the full, is evidence of the new importance of the logo.

Conglomerates think carefully about brands and company names. When Canadian drinks company Seagram bought MCA, it changed the film operation back to 'Universal Pictures' – the traditional studio name.

But when Disney bought Miramax, it kept the name alive because it was a strong 'brand' in the 'independent film' market. The brand 'Universal' now belongs to two different companies – General Electric which bought the television and film businesses to merge with NBC and Vivendi which owns the music company MCA/Universal.

New distribution formats

The move to digital media products means that sounds, pictures and text can all move together down broadband cable or digital broadcast technologies. The companies which control the cable systems and telecommunications networks are in a powerful position. Once again, the world market is very much dominated and influenced by the major North American companies which have prospered in the largest telecommunications market.

There are big corporate battles in Europe with the privatised state monopolies competing with new companies such as Vodafone, but it is the American telecommunications market which still holds the key, with the prospect of mergers between the cable companies and telephone companies on the one hand and mergers, or at least close cooperation, between the owners of digital networks and the 'software' providers such as Microsoft and the Hollywood studios on the other.

Synergy

Synergy is media industry jargon for the extra 'energy' produced by linking two complementary companies or products. The marriage of cable television and telephone supply is a good example. Selling telephone services helps reduce the cost of installing cable; installed cable allows attractive pricing of telephone services; and so on.

The attractions of synergy are obvious, but achieving a profitable outcome is not straightforward. Sony has struggled to make ownership of 'hardware' and 'software' companies pay off. Making movies is not necessarily going to make selling DVD players any easier. Matsushita and Philips both tried and gave up, selling their interests in MCA/Universal and Polygram in the 1990s. More recently, Viacom emerged as a conglomerate that encouraged each of its constituent companies to become the source of new creative ideas that could be exploited by other companies in the group. Nickelodeon and MTV gave birth to films which could be exploited by Paramount with book tie-ins through Simon and Schuster. But in 2005 came the first signs that Viacom might be better off concentrating on the activities that earned the most profit for shareholders rather than securing the biggest share of the market. This is a new trend in which some conglomerates have sold subsidiaries in order to become more focused. Synergy may turn out to be a luxury at a time when the media market 'turns down'.

'Independence' and 'alternatives' in the media industries

So far we have discussed media production and consumption in terms of the **mainstream**: large-scale activity, with a clear commercial purpose, driven primarily by a profit motive and representing mainly dominant views in society. This is the province of the major players, but these aren't always the same companies in each media industry. A film and television 'major' such as Disney is known as an 'independent' in the music industry (see 'Case study: The music industry, technology and synergy'). Sometimes, the majors brand some of their output as 'independent' by setting up or acquiring a separate company (e.g. Time Warner acquired the 'independent' film companies Fine Line and New Line and kept their identities separate).

Being 'outside the mainstream' often simply means a more localised form of production, and may include educational and training material, parish newsletters, fanzines, etc. But sometimes 'outside the mainstream' is a more conscious decision by a professional producer – an attempt to distinguish media output or to offer something which is alternative in some way.

Using the term 'independent' and linking it to alternative media production is problematic. Most media productions require collaboration between creative and technical teams, and they need an organisation to distribute the work. All media work is 'dependent' on technology, funding, etc. What we are concerned with here is how producers approach such dependencies. There are a number of options:

- The '*maverick*' (the word means a stray animal without a brand) doesn't want to be part of the mainstream because, for example, s/he feels oppressed by the 'bottom line' structures of profit and the resulting constraints on risk, or perhaps on the ability to make local or topical references which this can involve. Such media-makers often, but not always, find ways to continue working with the minimum of compromise over the content and style of the work. This may mean targeting a niche audience, working for only a select group of funders or making use of the idea of 'art', which can invoke and support different kinds of practice.
- 'The *artist*' wants to maintain control, usually working with a small group of regular collaborators, but will be willing to see her/his work

With the coverage of films and film production on the internet and the extra material on DVDs, it is possible now to discover much of what goes into producing an 'independent' film.

Figure 7.8 The Venice Film Festival is one of the oldest and most prestigious festivals. The 'Golden Lion' is a coveted award and helps to promote films across international markets.

being discussed as 'art' and therefore outside mainstream commercial markets. The art market, in film, video or audio, is just as institutionalised as the mainstream but involves slightly different activities for the media producer (e.g. festivals, exhibitions, different spaces for review and publicity, etc.) as well as different forms of financing (sponsorship, public and other arts funding, etc.). (See Chapter 4 'Institutions'.)

- The *'politically committed'* media producer has the aim of making some kind of statement or working with particular groups of collaborators on social issues, and will look for opportunities to do this, perhaps via forms of distribution not controlled by the majors or by accessing different funds (public funding, arts foundations, etc.).

See Chapter 14 'Documentary and "reality TV"' and 'Case study 2: Michael Moore'.

Big-hitting 'independents'

Next to the *Lord of the Rings* blockbuster films from a 'studio' independent company, New Line, the two biggest independent producers in recent years have been Mel Gibson and Michael Moore. Gibson usually works in the mainstream as a Hollywood star, but his 2004 *The Passion of the Christ* became the biggest independent hit of all time (Gibson owns his own distribution company in the UK, Icon films). Michael Moore has always attempted to be independent. At one time his *Fahrenheit 9/11* was to be distributed by Miramax, but when they withdrew he went ahead with the independent Newmarket Films.

At various times certain media producers (not Mel Gibson, but perhaps Michael Moore in some ways) have been 'ahead of the mainstream', creating media products in new ways or with new forms. This has been called the **avant-garde**. The mainstream takes a little time to catch up, but then often 'incorporates' aspects of such work into mainstream production (see the comments on extending the boundaries of the mainstream above). If there is any form of avant-garde in contemporary media production, it might be expected to be found in the 'new media', utilising digital technology and perhaps drawing on 'high art' modes such as video art.

Alt. culture

Digital media technology has the potential for exploitation in new kinds of media work. Music and video producers have benefited from access to relatively inexpensive but good-quality equipment. If the majors won't distribute the music conventionally or it is too expensive to use them, distribution is possible via the internet. This won't necessarily be a big market, but if costs are kept to a minimum it can be viable. It also offers a chance to producers in different parts of the world to reach new audiences. The changes in political activity, moving away from traditional political parties to so-called 'single-issue' campaigns and new alliances, possibly across national boundaries, have produced a range of websites offering both different ideas and new ways of presenting them. Circulating images, songs, jokes and web-links is an integral part of internet culture. In the early days of the internet one of its most attractive features for many users was the array of news groups, the most popular of which the were the 'alt.' groups in which, possibly, 'alternative' views might be found.

The 'alt.' tag has been taken up in other media so that 'alt. country' emerged as a music genre in the 1990s defined as 'not Nashville'. However, as soon as it produced its own stars such as Ryan Adams, the majors became interested. 'Independence' is often presented as an attractive, rebellious place completely outside the commercial compromises of the mainstream. This is, unfortunately perhaps, a rather romantic notion, but nevertheless one you need to consider.

Mike Figgis is one of a small number of otherwise mainstream film-makers who have experimented with digital technology in films such as *Timecode* (US 2000), featuring four frames of simultaneous action (a continuous ninety minutes), in different locations, on the same screen.

ACTIVITY 7.8

Alt. culture

Survey your recent media activities and purchases.

- How many of them might be described as 'independent' or 'alternative'? Do they fit any of the three categories above (maverick, art or politics)? Do any of them consciously use the 'alt.' or 'indie' tag?
- Was this description part of their appeal to you? Use a search engine such as Google (see Chapter 9) to look for 'Alternative Music' and 'Alternative Politics'.
- What kind of websites do you find? Do your findings suggest that there are forms of 'alternative culture' and potentially alternative production?

References and further reading

Most of these references are also suitable for further reading.

Bach, Steven (1985) *Final Cut*, London: Jonathan Cape.

Balio, Tino (1998) '"A major presence in all of the world's important markets": the globalisation of Hollywood in the 1990s', in Steve Neale and Murray Smith (eds) *Contemporary Hollywood Cinema*, London: Routledge.

Branston, Gill (2000) *Cinema and Cultural Modernity*, Buckingham: Open University Press.

Gomery, Douglas (1986) *The Hollywood Studio System*, London: BFI/Macmillan.

Gomery, Douglas (1992) *Shared Pleasures*, London: BFI.

Gomery, Douglas (1996) 'Toward a new media economics', in David Bordwell and Noel Carroll (eds) *Post-theory: Reconstructing Film Studies*, Madison and London: University of Wisconsin Press.

Lacey, Nick and Stafford, Roy (2000) *Film as Product in Contemporary Hollywood*, London: British Film Institute.

Maltby, Richard (1995) *Hollywood Cinema*, Oxford: Blackwell (2nd edition 2003).

Maltby, Richard (1998) '"Nobody knows everything": post-classical historiographies and consolidated entertainment', in Steve Neale and Murray Smith (eds) *Contemporary Hollywood Cinema*, London: Routledge.

Miller, Toby, Govil, Nitin, McMurria, John and Maxwell, Richard (2001) *Global Hollywood*, London: British Film Institute (2nd edition 2004).

Neale, Steve and Smith, Murray (eds) (1998) *Contemporary Hollywood Cinema*, London: Routledge.

Wasko, Janet (2001) *Understanding Disney*, Cambridge: Polity Press.

Wasko, Janet (2003) *How Hollywood Works*, London: Sage.

Wyatt, Justin (1994) *High Concept: Movies and Marketing in Hollywood*, Austin: University of Texas Press.

Wyatt, Justin (1998) 'The formation of the "major independent": Miramax, New Line and New Hollywood', in Steve Neale and Murray Smith (eds) *Contemporary Hollywood Cinema*, London: Routledge.

Trade press

Broadcast

Press Gazette

Screen International

Websites

uk.imdb.com

www.boxofficemojo.com

www.mpaa.org

www.skillset.org.uk

CASE STUDY: THE MAJOR PLAYERS IN THE MEDIA INDUSTRIES

- • **The majors**
- • **The European majors**
- • **Other American corporations in Europe**
- • **A special case**
- • **Media corporations outside North America and Europe**
- • **Debates about consolidation**
- • **References and further reading**

The majors

In most of the world's major industries, economic activity is dominated by a small group of 'major players'. Since the 1990s with the end of the Cold War and the privatisation of many publicly owned utilities (especially in telecommunications) in Europe, the opportunities for global expansion by the majors have greatly increased. The 'consolidation' of media interests through mergers and acquisitions is often made to seem inevitable, through metaphors like 'the free market'. But markets are volatile and although skewed in favour of larger companies, nothing is guaranteed (see Wheen 2004). We have updated this book every three years since 1996 and something surprising has often happened between editions.

Figure 7.9 gives an overview of the global media conglomerates – the eight corporations which combine media activities in at least three different sectors and across international boundaries. There are several shared features among these corporations:

- • The strongest brands, recognisable across the world are the Hollywood studio logos – only the two European corporations lack access to such brands.
- • In the US, all the main television networks are owned by one of the corporations.
- • Most of the corporations (Sony is the exception) are identified primarily with media and communication systems and content ('software' and distribution) – a significant change from the 1970s and 1980s when more general conglomerates owned media companies.
- • Although the corporations appear to compete fiercely, they also cooperate on joint ventures and may invest in each other's companies through 'cross ownership'.
- • Although they are privately owned corporations, they will be consulted by governments and may benefit from public funding (e.g. from the UK Film Council).

	Ownership (Shares held by other media companies)	Headquarters	Total Assets 2004 ($billion)	Gross Income 2004 ($billion)	Employees
Time Warner	4% Liberty Media	New York, NY	123.34	42.1	84,900
Sony		Tokyo	88.63	66.9 (2005)	162,000
Viacom	71% National Amusements	New York, NY	68.0	22.53	38,350
Disney		Burbank, California	53.9	30.752	129,000
News Corporation	17% Liberty Media	New York, NY	51.24	20.45	38,000
NBC Universal	80% General Electric, 20% Vivendi	New York, NY	n.a.	12.89	16,000 approx.
Vivendi Universal	4% Liberty Media	Paris	58.64	29.03	38,000
Bertelsmann		Gütersloh, Nordrhein-Westfalen	25.82	23.21	76,200

Figure 7.9 The major global media corporations.

But although these features are shared, the corporations also have distinctive features and here we will briefly look at each one. (It is difficult to present financial data for different companies using all of the same criteria. Figures for sales/turnover are used here to give only a rough indication of the size of the company. Most financial data have been taken from www.hoovers.com, which posts a brief company profile for all major corporations. All values are expressed as US dollars to make comparisons easier.)

Time Warner (2004 sales: $42 billion)
www.timewarner.com/corp/
Usually quoted as the world's largest media company, Time Warner was established in its present form by Stephen J. Ross, who bought the ailing Warner Bros film studio in 1969 and over the next twenty years built up a vertically integrated media conglomerate through various acquisitions and new ventures, culminating in the 1990 acquisition of Time Inc., the leading American magazine publisher and cable TV company. Warner Bros was one of the original five 'film studio majors' set up in 1923, but by the late 1960s it had fallen into the hands of Kinney Enterprises, a company which made money from activities as diverse as funeral parlours and car parks. After the death of Ross, the acquisitions continued with the absorption of, first, Ted Turner's media company in 1996 and then the merger with America Online (AOL) in 2000. This merger saw Time Warner as the junior partner with AOL's financial worth vastly overvalued during the period of 'dotcom mania'. Only three years later 'AOL' had disappeared from the new company's name.

Like most of the Hollywood studios, Warner Bros made films in the UK during the 1930s (at its studio at Teddington). In 1945 Warner Bros became the principal shareholder in the vertically integrated UK studio ABPC (Associated British Picture Corporation, running ABC cinemas). This lasted until 1968 and was an early example of what has become commonplace in recent years. Warner Bros returned to the UK as a major exhibitor in the 1990s through a partnership with the Australian cinema chain Village Roadshow. Warner Village Cinemas was eventually sold to the UK chain Vue in 2004. This pattern is set to be repeated in other territories through Warner Bros International Cinemas (WIBC). (China, Japan, Italy and Spain currently have WIBC chains.) Time Warner bought the leading UK consumer magazine group IPC in 2001.

In America, Warner Bros consolidated its strength in television with the establishment of 'the WB' as a national TV network in 1995 (focusing on younger audiences). Warner Bros Television claims to be the biggest provider of 'primetime series' to all six US networks with twenty-two series in 2004–5. The post-AOL merger experience was difficult for the company financially and it sold the Warner Music Group, which is now a 'stand-alone' company (see www.wmg.com), in 2003. Other sales included sports franchises and a half share in the cable TV station Comedy Central.

In 2005 Time Warner has stabilised as a media conglomerate with major strengths in print publishing, film and DVD, television and online services. Major brands include:

- Time Inc., IPC, DC Comics in publishing
- Warner Bros film and television production/distribution
- New Line and Warner Independent – 'independent' film companies
- WB TV Network
- HBO, Time Warner Cable
- Warner Home Video
- CNN, TNT, Cartoon Network, TCM, etc.
- AOL Online services.

Sony (2004 sales: $66.9 billion)
www.sony.com/SCA/index.shtml
Compared to the other media conglomerates, Sony is a relatively young company, set up in 1946. It is unusual in being primarily an electronics manufacturing and systems company including both 'consumer' and

'professional' media equipment in its product range. Sony is a genuine global company with offices and manufacturing or distribution plants in all major countries. Its innovations are well known and the VCR, Walkman, etc. would make it an important corporation in any study of the media industries. But it was Sony's acquisition of CBS Records in 1988 and Columbia Pictures Entertainment in 1989 that announced a new strategy for the company. With the purchase of MCA-Universal in 1986 by Matsushita (Panasonic, JVC, etc.), this move signalled the strength of the fast-growing Japanese economy at a time of American downturn. Libraries of films and recorded music were now available to help Sony exploit its new consumer media technologies. However, the promised **synergy** has proved difficult to exploit, even with the launch of a third synergised technology, the Playstation in the mid-1990s.

Columbia Pictures, with its distinctive logo of a woman in classical garb holding a torch aloft, dates from the 1920s. Throughout the studio period, Columbia was one of the 'little three' studios without the financial support offered by ownership of a cinema chain. Although there is a large library of classic films, it is somewhat less glamorous than that held by Warner Bros. Columbia was, however, the first Hollywood studio to get involved in television production, in 1948, and in 1982 it set up a second producing studio specifically to make films for cable television with HBO and CBS. This became Tri-Star which was then merged with Columbia to form Columbia-TriStar as part of Sony Pictures Entertainment. A significant move for a film company owned by a Japanese conglomerate was the establishment of Sony Pictures operations in Asian markets including India and China, involving major film productions and television networks.

Columbia Records is the oldest surviving brand name in recorded sound going back to 1888. The company helped set up the Columbia Broadcasting System (CBS) in 1927 and was in turn bought by CBS in 1938, before being sold to Sony in 1988. Sony then acquired the rights to the Columbia name outside North America (owned by EMI) and promoted the new worldwide brand. In 2004 Sony merged its music interests with Bertelsmann (see below) to form Sony BMG.

Sony Pictures Entertainment is a much bigger studio than Columbia ever was and has recently had major success with blockbusters such as the *Spider-Man* franchise. If the conglomerate has a weakness, it is that it doesn't have an outlet in North America via television, broadcast or cable/online.

ACTIVITY 7.9

Profiling Sony's media interests
Undertake an internet search to add detail to the brief profile of Sony outlined above. Concentrate on Sony as a media company (i.e. ignore the manufacturing side):

- How are Sony's media interests organised – in which countries, which groups of activities, etc.?
- Which brand names does Sony use?
- How does Sony operate in the UK – how does it originate and distribute media products in the UK?

Time Warner	Film studios, TV production, TV stations/network, comics, magazines, publishing, internet services
Sony	Film studios, TV production, recorded music, video games
Viacom	Film studio, TV production, TV stations/networks, radio stations, publishing, outdoor advertising
Disney	Film studios, TV production, TV stations/networks, radio stations, theme parks
News Corporation	Film studio, TV production, TV stations/network, publishing, newspapers
NBC Universal	Film studio, TV production, TV stations/network, theme parks
Vivendi Universal	Film library, TV network (Europe), recorded music, video games, telephony
Bertelsmann	TV production, TV stations/networks (Europe), radio stations, publishing, recorded music, internet

Figure 7.10 How the majors line up in different media industries.

Viacom (2004 sales: $22.8 billion) www.viacom.com
Unique among media conglomerates, Viacom is a major corporation effectively controlled by a private company, National Amusements Inc. This family firm, headed by Sumner Redstone, runs cinema exhibition chains in various territories, including Showcase in the UK. It is what is known in America as a 'closely held corporation'. Viacom itself was originally a small company set up by CBS, the US television network. Redstone used Viacom as a vehicle to acquire a 'portfolio' of well-known American media brands such as MTV, Blockbuster (sold to shareholders in 2004), Paramount and CBS, as well as major interests in book publishing, other television and radio broadcasting and outdoor advertising.

Paramount Pictures was one of the first of the five major Hollywood studios, founded in 1912 by small distributors and quickly merged with cinema chains Famous Players and Lasky's. It was this market strength that was attacked in 1948 by the US Supreme Court decision to force a de-merger of the studio and its cinemas. Paramount then struggled as a producing studio until the 1970s when under the ownership of Gulf + Western it produced big hits such as *The Godfather* (US 1971). Since Viacom purchased the studio, Paramount has been run as a 'lean and mean' studio looking to profit from synergies with other Viacom companies but not spending as heavily on blockbusters as other studios. A classic Paramount move was to earn $300–400 million as a late partner on the release of *Titanic* when Fox became frightened at the spiralling costs of production. Paramount has tended to make money from small films (i.e. low budgets, relatively big box office) such as *The Rugrats* movies (from Nickelodeon) and *Save the Last Dance* (from MTV).

Viacom's big strength is in television and radio networks with broadcast networks CBS and UPN (United Paramount Networks) and cable channels BET (Black Entertainment Television), MTV, Nickelodeon, etc. Along with Infinity Outdoor Advertising (billboards etc.), Viacom can claim to be the major seller of advertising space in North America (and with significant presence in other territories).

In 2005, with Sumner Redstone (born 1923) expected to relinquish control, reports suggested that Viacom may start a new cycle of 'de-merging' consolidated businesses to produce better returns for shareholders. Two new corporations, Viacom Inc. and CBS Inc., were announced for 2006. Check if this ever happened – analysts did raise some doubts (money.cnn.com in June 2005).

Disney (2004 sales: $30.7 billion)
http://corporate.disney.go.com/index.html
In the late 1990s, Disney grew as a company when it acquired ABC, the third national television network in the US. This was a major boost to Disney's existing television interests and also added the sports cable networks under the ESPN brand. Disney is now organised around four distinct 'activity centres': Studio Entertainment, Parks and Resorts, Consumer Products and Media Networks.

As a film studio Disney has a more humble background than any of the other majors. The animation studio started by Walt Disney in the 1920s was originally a small independent with feature films from 1937 being distributed by the then major studio RKO. It wasn't until 1955 that a new Disney subsidiary, Buena Vista, became the sole distributor of Disney films, which now included live action. In the 1990s, Disney developed two more studio brands, Touchstone and Hollywood Pictures, to make films outside the 'family entertainment' ethos of Walt Disney Pictures. Disney's acquisition of the 'independent' studio Miramax proved controversial when *Pulp Fiction* became a big hit in 1994, calling into question Disney's 'family' focus. The creators of Miramax, the Weinstein brothers, split from Disney in 2005, leaving behind the brand and a 600-film library, but taking the Dimension brand for horror films with them. Disney has also benefited from a long association with the innovatory animation company

Pixar (*Toy Story*, *The Incredibles*, etc.) but in 2005 this too seemed to be ending.

The 'Disneyland' theme parks began life in the 1950s alongside associated television programmes, and the characters from the animated films also became the basis for the Consumer Products division. Disney is very much a global brand with theme parks across the world – the eleventh Disneyland, in Hong Kong, opened in September 2005 (see Chapter 15 'Whose globalisation?'). Global deals also include a distribution agreement with Studio Ghibli in Japan to release films like *Princess Mononoke* and *Spirited Away* in the West.

Disney has been a focus for news stories and analysis by media academics partly because of its strong 'family image' and involvement in several instances of 'self-censorship' and also because of the personality of its chief executive Michael Eisner, who in 2004 announced his retirement after over twenty years as head of the corporation.

ACTIVITY 7.10

Talking about Disney

'Google' for news reports about the Disney Corporation and about Michael Eisner.

- What kinds of stories seem to be associated with Disney?
- What image of 'corporate life' in a media conglomerate emerges from these reports?
- How important is the company's 'Americanness'? (see Chapter 9 'Advertising and branding', and 'COE effect'.)

News Corporation (2004 sales: $20.45 billion)
www.newscorp.com
Perhaps the most discussed media organisation in UK media studies, News Corporation is the result of the Australian-American Rupert Murdoch's attempts to build a global media major. Apart from the music

industry, News Corp. has significant holdings in all the other media industries and it is indeed a global company with strengths in Australia, Asia and the Pacific Rim as well as Europe and North America. The initial power base was in the Australian newspaper business. The focus on Murdoch (rather than on some of the other 'media moguls') has been because of the large share of the UK media market controlled by News International, the confusingly named UK company responsible for the *Sun, News of the World, The Times*, etc. News Corporation also has the biggest share in British Sky Broadcasting (35 per cent) and the potential for Murdoch to exert 'too much' power over UK media has meant that regulatory decisions have often seemed to hinge on preventing him gaining access to a terrestrial television station such as Five.

In the US the purchase of 20th Century Fox film and television interests and the development of Fox TV as the fourth major network have helped Murdoch to gain notoriety, especially for the 'hawkish' (i.e. pro-war) and 'neo-conservative' stance adopted by Fox News. The lack of objectivity of this station is compounded for many critics by the onscreen claim that its news reporting is 'Fair and Balanced'. Fox News (and the whole question of political power wielded by media corporations) is explored in the documentary *Outfoxed* (US 2004) which is subtitled *Rupert Murdoch's War on Journalism*. Details of this film can be found on www.outfoxed.org. Murdoch himself is a combative figure, who frequently criticises regulatory regimes in the UK and elsewhere in Europe, but there is a danger in 'demonising' him as an individual and failing to study how a large corporation like News Corp. actually operates.

20th Century Fox was one of the original five studio majors, famous for the introduction of CinemaScope in 1953. It has often been associated with very large-scale films such as the *Star Wars* series and *The Day After Tomorrow* as well as *Titanic*, but it has also gained a reputation for clever marketing of the smaller films distributed by its classics division, Fox Searchlight (e.g. *The Full Monty* in 1997). News Corp. also has strength in book publishing through HarperCollins.

NBC-Universal (2004 sales: $12.8 billion)

www.nbcuni.com

Universal was one of the first Hollywood studios, founded in 1912. Like Columbia (see above), Universal lacked the cinema chain that would have made it a vertically integrated major studio. As one of the 'little three' (United Artists was the third), Universal became well known for inexpensive genre cycles including the Dracula and Frankenstein films, musicals and comedies. In 1952 the studio was bought by the Decca Record Company and in 1962 Decca was in turn acquired by MCA – the company headed by Lew Wasserman that grew out of a talent booking agency. This was a sign of the changing power base in Hollywood. As a film and television producer/distributor, Universal became more powerful in the 1970s and 1980s but was sold again to Matsushita in 1986 and to the Seagram Drinks Group in 1995. Seagram then acquired another would-be film and music 'major' in the form of Polygram (originally part of Philips) but then sold the whole company to the French conglomerate Vivendi in 2000. Vivendi was soon over-extended and in 2004 it entered a deal with NBC, the US network television broadcasting subsidiary of the giant General Electric Company. This saw Universal split into a film and television operation controlled by NBC with the music interests remaining with Vivendi.

NBC-Universal is owned 80 per cent by General Electric and 20 per cent by Vivendi. It comprises the film and television studios, television network and theme parks in the US and overseas.

Vivendi-Universal (2004 sales: $29 billion)

www.vivendiuniversal.com

The French conglomerate Vivendi appeared on the world stage as a major media player in 2000 with the acquisition of Seagram Universal. Vivendi began life as a water utility company in the nineteenth century,

but in the 1980s and 1990s it took advantage of the 'new technologies and deregulation' environment to move into 'pay-TV' with Canal+ and telecommunications in France and later Morocco. Vivendi's chief executive in this period, Jean-Marie Messier, was aggressive and 'American' in his business dealings and by 2002, with all its acquisitions, Vivendi was indeed a major player. However, the aggression could not be sustained and, with mounting losses, Messier was ousted. Following the deal with NBC and the divestment of the water and waste utilities business to another company, the 'slimmed down' Vivendi remains in control of Universal Music – the leading music major – and Canal+, an important player in European film and television with the third largest film library in the world (including many US and UK titles). The company still has its telecommunications interests and also significant investments in video games through Vivendi Universal Games.

Bertelsmann (2004 sales: $23.2 billion)

www.bertelsmann.com

Bertelsmann has a history as a German family company with its origins in print publishing in the nineteenth century, but its main growth has been since the 1950s, with the transformation to a public limited company in 1971. Printing services, including e-services, remains a strength and the company acquired the world's biggest consumer book publishers, Random House, in 1998 to join one of Europe's biggest magazine and newspaper groups, Gruner + Jahr, acquired in the 1960s.

Bertelsmann Music Group (BMG) has been built up around the acquisition of the American labels RCA and Arista and former independents such as Zomba Music. In 2004 BMG was merged with Sony Music to form a jointly owned company.

Television and radio broadcasting is a major strength – even though RTL (91 per cent owned by Bertelsmann) is primarily concerned with Europe. Through RTL (a company developed from the former Radio Luxemburg) and its international production subsidiary Fremantle (formerly Pearson Television),

Bertelsmann can claim to be the biggest player in European television with interests in channels in many countries, including Five in the UK (now wholly owned by RTL). Fremantle is known the world over for drama series and reality shows made by Grundy and Thames such as *Neighbours, The Bill, Baywatch, Pop Idol, The Price is Right*, etc.

The European majors

Apart from Vivendi and Bertelsmann, there are several other major players in Europe, primarily concerned with broadcasting and print. You can use this section to learn more about the television industry in particular and cross-reference with the 'Case study: Television as institution' and Chapter 16 '"Free choices" in a free market"?'.

BBC (2004 income: $5.1 billion) www.bbc.co.uk
The BBC is an important media brand, recognisable worldwide, but perhaps in danger of being overshadowed by CNN, Fox News and the other brands of the majors outside the UK. The Corporation gains some advantages from its public sector position in the UK – not least the financial security of a guaranteed income via the licence fee. But this status also constrains the BBC's activities since any profit from sales (such as programme rights or advertising on cable channels such as BBC America) must be used to support public service broadcasting. The BBC is not allowed to use its position to compete commercially (as it was deemed to do with some of its digital services, resulting in criticism by the Department for Culture, Media and Sport).

BSkyB (2004 sales: $6.6 billion) www.sky.com
Now, in revenue terms, the No. 1 UK broadcaster, BSkyB is available in over 50 per cent of UK homes and also in Ireland. BSkyB is effectively controlled by its founder and major shareholder, Rupert Murdoch's News Corporation. In 2004 Murdoch's son, James, became the new chief executive. Most of BSkyB's

subscription revenue comes from sport and movies; compared to the BBC and ITV, BSkyB does not produce (or commission) very much original programmimg.

ITV plc (2004 sales: $5.24 billion) www.itvplc.com
Consolidation has in some cases been tacitly supported by governments and regulators. In the UK the longstanding rules on ownership of commercial television licences have been gradually loosened to allow a final merger of the last two ITV companies in England and Wales, Carlton and Granada, which became ITV plc in 2004. The change in the UK government's stance could be seen as a recognition of the vulnerability of the UK's relatively small television companies in the face of the majors' global ambitions. The long merger process saw both Granada and Carlton refocusing on television with the sale of Granada's catering interests and Carlton's other businesses such as Technicolor in 2000. This process has been termed the 'disposal of non-core assets'. ITV (i.e. Granada and Carlton) made a serious mistake with the digital operation ONdigital which collapsed in 2002, but looks to be slowly recovering with the success of ITV2 and ITV3 on Freeview. ITV plc is now the major private sector producer of television programming for UK terrestrial television (making programmes for BBC, Channel 4 and Five as well as ITV) and the largest international supplier of television programming in the US. It also holds the biggest library of television titles in the UK and shares the market for film titles with Canal+.

NTL and Telewest (2004 sales: NTL $3.8 billion, Telewest $1.27 billion) www.ntl.com, www.telewest.co.uk
Much as Granada and Carlton took several years to eventually merge, the UK's two cable operators looked set to finally merge in 2005 after several years of buying up smaller operators. The two companies emerged from the chequered history of cable in the UK, which attracted North American telephone

companies into a deregulated market with the encouragement of the Thatcher government in the 1980s. NTL was originally an American company that bought the privatised UK transmitter network. Telewest emerged after a series of mergers and acquisitions involving several North American interests (including John Malone and Liberty Media – see below – which also has a stake in NTL). Both NTL and Telewest have struggled against BSkyB's satellite operations and have had major financial problems. A merged company might stand a chance of developing cable's potential. Telewest also owns Flextech (though it is expected to sell it) with its cable channel brands such as Bravo and Living TV and the UKTV channels (which have rights to show reruns of BBC programming).

Telefónica (2004 sales: $42.3 billion)
www.telefonica.com/home_eng.shtml
One of the privatised telephone utilities, Telefónica is now the largest telephone company in the Spanish- and Portuguese-speaking markets across the world. In 2000, Telefónica bought the production company Endemol, creators of *Big Brother*. It is also the part owner of the Spanish commercial TV channel, Antena 3.

Fininvest and **Mediaset** (2003 estimated sales: Fininvest $14.7 billion; Mediaset $3.9 billion)
www.fininvest.it/ www.gruppomediaset.it
Silvio Berlusconi has dominated the media in Italy to an even greater extent than Rupert Murdoch in the UK – dominance compounded by his position as Prime Minister and leader of the Forza Italia party. The Berlusconi family are the major shareholders in the Fininvest Group, a holding company which led the commercialisation of Italian television broadcasting through the establishment of Mediaset in 1980. Fininvest has since reduced its stake in Mediaset to 35 per cent, but it has built up a portfolio of interests which includes publishing, film production and distribution, financial services and AC Milan FC.

There are also partnerships and 'cross-holdings' with other European media companies. Analysts have had difficulty keeping track of Berlusconi's interests.

European state broadcasters

Most European countries still have a state broadcaster: ARD and ZDF in Germany, TVE (Spain), France Télévisions, RAI (Italy), etc. ARD is unique in being a consortium of regional broadcasters, ZDF is the 'second German television service'. (See 'Case study: Television as institution'.)

Lagardère (2004 sales: $18.2 billion)
www.lagardere.com
Although the company name may not be well known in the UK or US, Lagardère's brands, including magazines such as *Elle* and *Red* and authors such as Stephen King, published by Hodder Headline, certainly are. Lagardère combines interests in 'high-technology engineering' (a 15 per cent stake in EADS – the world's No. 3 aerospace company) with its strength in magazine publishing (it claims to be the world's leading consumer magazine publisher), newspapers, book publishing, radio/television and new media and retail/distribution.

Pearson (2004 sales: $7 billion) www.pearson.com
Pearson plc represents a good example of a media company which has reversed the trend to 'conglomeration'. The publisher of the *Financial Times* and Penguin Books sold its interests in television to Bertelsmann and its 'leisure parks' (including waxworks Madame Tussaud's and The London Eye) to a venture capital group. Pearson now concentrates on 'information and education publishing' (Pearson Longman Education).

Other American corporations in Europe

Liberty Media (2004 sales: $7.68 billion)
www.libertymedia.com

'Liberty Media is a holding company owning interests in a broad range of electronic retailing, media, communications and entertainment businesses classified in four groups; Interactive, Networks, Tech/Ventures and Corporate.' This statement from the company website gives a capsule description of a media organisation which is not really on the media consumer's radar, apart from, perhaps, its cable shopping channel QVC. But Liberty, headed by 'mogul' John Malone, is seen by industry analysts as an important player, partly because of its history as a product of the business struggles of the American telecommunications industry following the anti-trust actions against AT&T (originally the Bell Telephone Company) in the 1980s. Liberty Media emerged in 2001 with significant interests in cable television (including a 50 per cent stake in the Discovery channels). It is a significant shareholder in News Corporation (18 per cent) and holds smaller stakes in Time Warner and Viacom. In Europe, Liberty has sought relationships with several European television interests.

Gannett (2004 sales: $7.4 billion) www.gannett.com
A 'news and information' company, Gannett is the biggest newspaper publisher in the US with 101 newspaper titles headed by *USA Today* and including

titles published for the US armed forces. Its other interests include a string of TV stations and several specialist advertising and information businesses. In the UK, Gannett purchased Newsquest, the second largest UK regional newspaper group with 300 titles, in 1999. In Bradford, West Yorkshire, as in many UK city regions, all local newspapers are owned by a company with its headquarters in McLean, Virginia.

Clear Channel (2004 sales: $9.4 billion)
www.clearchannel.com
Clear Channel is generally recognised as the major player in US radio, owning, operating or selling airtime for over 1,200 stations and another 220 stations overseas. A similar television operation is smaller with some forty stations. Its other two strengths are in live music promotion and outdoor advertising. In the UK, Clear Channel has three main interests, with the sports agency SFX joining the outdoor and live promotion operations (www.clearchannel.co.uk). If you want to know how 'media and sport' are interrelated in the UK, the SFX website (www.sfxsports.co.uk) may be a good place to start, with its representation of Alan Hansen, Gary Lineker and Gaby Roslin alongside Michael Owen and Steven Gerrard. In the US, Clear Channel has been subject to criticism that its domination of radio and live shows

Figure 7.11 Here is a typical example of modern media corporations at large in our streets. O$_2$, itself a major player in telecommunications after splitting from British Telecom, advertises using one of Clear Channel's 'outdoor' sites in Manchester. (See 'Case study: Researching mobile phone technologies'.)

has meant that some acts have been 'frozen out' of radio because of their refusal to appear on live shows. Other claims include the banning of the Dixie Chicks music after their criticism of George W. Bush. The company website includes a 'Know the facts' section with detailed rebuttals.

A special case

Microsoft (2004 sales: $36.84 billion)
www.microsoft.com
Apple (2004 sales: $8.28 billion) www.apple.com
If we wanted to represent the powerful corporations with interests in the broader telecommunications or 'information industries', we would have to include many more corporations. However, these two computer companies have both got a direct interest in the media industries. Apple is the computer platform of choice for many media professionals in design, music and video production with software such as Final Cut Pro used by video producers. Apple is also attempting to sell hardware and software combinations directly to consumers as a 'one stop' digital hub for images, video and audio with the iLife suite that includes iTunes, iPhoto, iMovie, etc. Microsoft hopes to sell a more limited range of products to a much wider market – the 90 per cent of computer users on Windows. The importance of these two corporations for media students is that they may at any time enter into relationships with media majors, which could significantly alter the balance of power in an oligopolistic market.

Media corporations outside North America and Europe

The majors are generally concerned with English-language media. The exceptions are those European companies with strengths in local print and broadcasting markets. In other parts of the world, there are dominant local players in print media and broadcasting, but film, video and music tend to be dominated by subsidiaries of the global majors. The size of some of the markets suggests that eventually significant media corporations will emerge onto the world stage from India (with a new 'middle-class audience' estimated at 300 million) and China (with film production already seeing cooperation between Hong Kong, Taiwan and Mainland Chinese interests). The *Independent* newspaper group in the UK has invested in an Indian Hindi language newspaper and Associated Newspapers (*Daily Mail* etc.) is considering an Indian newspaper launch (*Guardian*, 6 April 2005).

Japanese media corporations

East Asia is an obvious focus for future developments in the media industries, with a strong film industry in South Korea and mature media industries of all kinds in Japan. Surprisingly, perhaps, Japanese media corporations have not had a great deal of impact in Europe and North America (apart from Nintendo and Sony in video gaming). There are reasons for this. Japan has twice been the leading film producer in the world, in the 1930s and again in the 1960s, and has a studio tradition not unlike Hollywood. However, the studios have not evolved into conglomerates on the American model.

In television, the Japanese system has followed European models with a public broadcaster, NHK, alongside private sector broadcasters, often linked to major newspaper groups (Japanese newspapers have the largest circulations in the world – over 10 million for *Yomiuri Shimbun*). The newspapers and television stations are generally recognised to have specific political perspectives (see Wikipedia entries on Japanese media). Cable and satellite television have not developed as widely in Japan as in the West and in print publishing there are distinct local preferences (*manga* – graphic novels – are the most popular form of reading material for all age groups). One media company that does seem to be following a more European model is Kadokawa Shoten, the print publisher, film/video producer and electronic media producer behind the *Ringu* films (see 'Case study: J-horror and the *Ring* cycle').

The other way in which media producers outside Europe and North America can have a global presence is through local-language productions, which also appeal to diaspora populations overseas and can be exported to similar media markets across the world. The two main examples of this are:

- so-called 'Bollywood' films which are increasingly being produced, at the 'top end' of the market, for NRIs (non-resident Indians) in the UK and North America. The Hollywood studios are clearly interested in this development and the Indian studios/distributors may find themselves vulnerable to Hollywood competition. (The Oscar-nominated *Lagaan* (India 2002) was distributed by Sony in many territories.)

- In Latin America, the most popular form of television drama is the *telenovela*, a form of television serial, similar, but not the same as, the soap opera format. These are made in many countries, in Spanish, and exported throughout the Hispanic world, including the US, and to many other markets across the world, dubbed into local languages. The same format also exists in Brazil, where the biggest producer is TV Globo. With the large Brazilian market and other Lusophone (Portuguese-speaking) markets, as well as dubbing into Spanish, there is a wide distribution of these products. Silvio Waisbord in an article entitled 'Grandes gigantes: media concentration in Latin America' (2002) on www.opendemocracy.net, suggests that though there are no global majors based in Latin America, companies such as Globo have been able to acquire interests in other media

and are becoming local monopolists. They also offer the possibility of partnerships with American or European majors (Telefónica (see above) is now an important player in Argentina) to exploit the local market further. Waisbord points out that **'public service broadcasting'** as seen in Europe is not present in Latin America. (See Chapter 15 on the launch of Telesur.)

Debates about consolidation

Does this 'consolidation' of corporate power in a handful of companies matter? The debate between media academics on www.opendemocracy.net from 2001–3 suggested that it does (access the list of articles by searching for 'Global media ownership', or any of the named contributors below, on the website). James Curran (2002) summarised some of the main points in the debate:

- Is media concentration increasing?
- Does the development of private media concentration matter?

Taking the first question, Curran refers to Benjamin Compaine who sees little change in the market share of the top fifty US media corporations during the 1990s: some declined in importance; others, like Amazon, were new. But many others supported Bob McChesney in arguing that 'media concentration is advancing on a global scale'. Curran argues that both are to a certain extent correct. The changes in media ownership in the 1990s were sometimes defensive as new competitors emerged and some attempts at expansion have failed. Yet Curran concludes that the move towards consolidation on a global scale will continue.

On the second question, Curran suggests four reasons why private media concentration does matter:

- The private concentration of symbolic power potentially distorts the democratic process.
- The power potentially at the disposal of media moguls tends to be exerted in a one-sided way.

- The concentration of market power can stifle competition.
- There is a one-sided protection of our freedoms: a state of constant alert against the abuse of state power over the media, reflected in the development of numerous safeguards, not matched by an equivalent vigilance and set of safeguards directed against the abuse of shareholder power over the media.

Here Curran is arguing against what seems to be a majority opinion in support of a free market position (see Chapter 16 for more on this). Several academics, such as David Hesmondhalgh writing on music, argue that despite the consolidation of ownership, there is still a 'diversity of content' in media products and a number of 'alternative voices'. But as Curran argues, for every *Simpsons* series made by Fox, there is pressure on News Corporation journalists in the press and broadcasting to support conservative and consumerist ideologies. Oligopolies exist to defend the interests of their constituent members – they do not invite new entrants to their industries and they do not tolerate alternative ideologies for long. Instead they 'absorb' and re-present alternative ideas as part of the mainstream. Those who support the diversity of the marketplace are likely to cry 'foul!' at state intervention in the media, though they rarely object to the many areas where big corporations are supported by state regulation and subsidy (see Wheen 2004). They rarely campaign against the power of private media organisations.

Conclusion

The debate on opendemocracy.net is worth exploring in detail. Since 2003, several events, including the coverage of the Iraq War and the UK debate about BBC reporting, have moved the debate on, but the central question about the concentration of ownership remains. In 2005, Viacom looked as if it might start a process of de-merging its interests and NBC was considering attempting to buy DreamWorks –

seemingly opposite movements. The computer company Google, only four years old as a public company, was valued on the New York Stock Exchange at more than the value of Time Warner and several other media corporations combined. But so was AOL when it merged with Time Warner before the first dotcom bubble burst. The 'majors' stay 'major' by surviving over a long period of time. How many company logos like those of Warner Bros, Paramount and Universal are still recognised around the world after eighty years or more?

ACTIVITY 7.11

The consolidation debate

Decide what your own take on the 'consolidation debate' might be by rereading this case study and Chapter 16 '"Free choices" in a free market"?'.

- Research one or two of the major corporations in terms of their global market share.
- Prepare a short presentation entitled: 'Does the market power of the major media corporations matter?'

References and further reading

Curran, James (2002) http://www.opendemocracy.net/content/articles/PDF/37.pdf.

Gomery, Douglas (1998) 'Hollywood corporate business practice and periodizing contemporary film history', in Steve Neale and Murray Smith (eds) *Contemporary Hollywood Cinema*, London: Routledge.

Hesmondhalgh, David (2001) http://www.opendemocracy.net/debates/article.jsp?id=8&debateId=24&article=46.

McChesney, Robert W. and Herman, Edward S. (1997) *The Global Media – The New Missionaries of Corporate Capitalism*, London and New York: Continuum.

Wheen, Francis (2004) *How Mumbo-Jumbo Conquered the World*, London: Fourth Estate.

Websites

en.wikipedia.org

www.hoovers.com

www.ketupa.net

www.opendemocracy.net

www.peakpeak.com/~jking/media/main_players.html
(accessed 11 June 2005)

DVD

Outfoxed (2004)

The business operations of the media corporations are best followed in the trade publications for each industry. *Screen International, Variety* and *Billboard* are particularly useful in that they cover a wide range of 'entertainment media'. For a more defined UK perspective look at *Broadcast, Media Week, UK Press Gazette*. Many of these publications operate a website – it will probably require a subscription to get at detailed information, but there are 'free' headline news stories as well.

CASE STUDY: THE MUSIC INDUSTRY, TECHNOLOGY AND SYNERGY

- An outline history of the music industry
- The structure of the industry
- Synergy, convergence and the contemporary music industry

- References
- Further reading

The 'music industry' is integrated with other media industries, but also has its own unique features. In this case study we look at those unique features and focus on the way in which music products have been so important in the introduction of all kinds of other media technologies. Musical performances and recordings have always offered the potential for **synergy** and **convergence** – helping the development of other media industries through sales of related music products and incorporation of music in other products.

An outline history of the music industry

Beginnings

The gramophone was invented at roughly the same time as film projection, and together the new technologies spread around the world at the start of the twentieth century. The first companies to exploit the possibilities of the gramophone produced both the machines themselves and the 'software' – cylinders at first, but then discs. Some familiar names were involved from the beginning, HMV (His Master's Voice), Columbia, Victor, etc. Recorded music was one of the first forms of mass-produced 'home entertainment'. Previously, music-making in the home had required both the musical skill and the resources to purchase instruments and learn to play them.

Some of the first companies involved in the new industry were already involved in publishing sheet music or manufacturing musical instruments. One company made billiard tables for wealthy homes, but another produced gramophones alongside typewriters – another key technology of the period. This link between business and media technologies was revived in the 1990s when music moved to computers that were first developed as business tools. The early growth was not confined to America. Companies developed quickly in Europe and around the world – HMV India was founded in 1901.

> 'Music companies' earned a great deal of revenue at this time from the sale of 'sheet music'. The publishing rights to popular songs meant that even though the mass audience couldn't afford to buy a gramophone and records, they could buy the music and play/sing the songs themselves.

1920s – radio

The gramophone industry was boosted in the 1920s by the arrival of commercial radio services. Not only did the new services (primarily in America) offer the opportunity for recorded music to be played to a mass audience, but the manufacturers of gramophones found themselves well placed to become involved in the production of radio sets. This period saw the foundation of RCA-Victor (the Radio Corporation of America joined with the Victor Record Company in 1929).

The rapid development of radio had helped to create the economic 'boom' that eventually ended with the Wall Street Crash of 1929 and the start of the Great Depression. But this was also a period in which sound was developed in the cinema – first on disc and later on film. RCA became part of one of the first modern media corporations when in conjunction with theatre chain Keith-Albee-Orpheum, it formed RKO Radio Pictures, partly to promote its own 'sound on film' system. RKO was one of the 'Big Five' major studios that established the Hollywood studio system in the 1920s. It was also one of the first **media conglomerates** encompassing radio, recorded music, vaudeville ('live' light entertainment) and cinema with its showcase at the 6,000 seat Radio City Music Hall in New York. (An outline of RCA history is available on the website at www.rca.com.)

The early record companies established themselves overseas in all the principal markets. The Victor Company of Japan was bought by the Matsushita Electronics Company in 1954 and as JVC introduced the VHS cassette in 1977.

1930s and 1940s: jukebox and Hollywood

Record sales plummeted at the start of the 1930s with the impact of the Depression. But still the influence of recorded music spread. The jukebox, a striking example of 'new technology', playing sixteen or twenty-four different records, became an alternative to radio as a means of both providing entertainment in bars and clubs and creating interest in particular performers (providing record labels with a means of assessing popularity). Music was an important element

of films in the 1930s and 1940s with musicals and music performances featured in other genres. There were also 'musical shorts' featuring popular music stars. 'Soundies' were short films that could be seen and heard on special jukeboxes.

One important development in this period was the 'institutionalising' of different genres of popular music, particularly black music (known at the time as 'race music') and 'hillbilly' or country music. Supported by a distinctive culture and a chain of dedicated radio stations and record labels, these were the first indications of both 'market segmentation' and 'roots

Figure 7.12 *Caldonia* (US 1945), an eighteen-minute 'extended short' featuring one of the top black stars of the 1940s, Louis Jordan, who wears a 'zoot suit' with a 'reet pleat and a drape shape'. The tagline refers to a popular Hollywood film called *Here Comes Mr. Jordan* (1941) (John Kish and Edward Mapp, (1992), *A Separate Cinema*, Noonday Press: New York).

culture' in the commercial media environment. Both black music and country music found their way into Hollywood, although the films that featured the music were usually B pictures or independent productions (black cinema existed to a certain extent outside the mainstream at this time, with segregated audiences in the southern states). Mainstream popular music was dominated by 'big bands'.

1950–60s: Hollywood and rock 'n' roll

The music industry expanded in the 1950s with the explosion of rock 'n' roll (a fusion of the black music and country music which had been 'marginal' in the 1930s) and the growing affluence of young record buyers. It was also encouraged by:

- the introduction of vinyl 'singles' and 'albums' to replace the brittle shellac records with limited playing time
- the increasing focus on the youth audience by Hollywood studios
- the development of television as home entertainment with its own need to attract younger viewers (a need further promoted by advertisers).

The links between music, radio, film and television grew strong in the 1950s and 1960s. For example, the pop singer Ricky Nelson first appeared as a child in a television sitcom, the *Ozzie and Harriet Show*, featuring his real-life family, headed by bandleader Ozzie Nelson. As a teenager he became a 'teen idol', combining good looks with country-tinged rock 'n' roll and in 1959 he appeared in a major Hollywood western with John Wayne (*Rio Bravo*). This period also saw the first chart-rigging and 'payola' scandals, in which radio DJs were accused of artificially creating hit records, and the establishment of television variety shows.

Television 'specials' hosted by leading mainstream singers such as Nat King Cole and Perry Como were ratings winners, but the most important shows were those like *The Ed Sullivan Show* that introduced new 'stars'. Until this point, popular music, apart from

the biggest mainstream acts whose national profile was reflected through Hollywood, was primarily a regional affair. Records were promoted by local radio stations and often by local record labels. These would be picked up and distributed by bigger labels, but often an artist would remain a 'regional star', especially if the music genre was not nationally popular (i.e. blues, country, soul, etc.). But when early rock 'n' roll performers like Elvis Presley appeared on *The Ed Sullivan Show* (shown only from the waist up – conservative American television decreed his act was 'lewd'), they were immediately seen across America on networked television. In the UK in the 1950s, with only limited access to American records on BBC radio programmes, Hollywood films were crucial in introducing the new music and films such as *Blackboard Jungle* (1955) and *The Girl Can't Help It* (1956) paved the way for live shows from touring American stars. UK television responded with shows such as *Oh Boy!* (ITV 1958–9), with British acts often 'covering' American hits.

1970s Hollywood and the soundtrack album

Hollywood embraced pop stars in the 1950s and 1960s, mainly because they attracted a youth audience. But they put the stars into conventional genre vehicles (see any of the Elvis Presley films, most of which stripped the star of any musical excitement) and made little attempt to use the music itself as an important ingredient. This was despite the takeover of Universal Pictures in 1952 by Decca Records and the establishment of music labels by other studios. It was not until the post-Beatles period in the late 1960s that the studios began to recognise that the performers and their audiences were far more sophisticated than they had imagined and that successful films would be those that were sensitive to the new pop culture.

Significant films were *The Graduate* (1967), which featured new songs by Simon and Garfunkel and saw both single and album success working to help the film, and *Easy Rider* (1969), a low-budget success that put the 'counterculture' of sex, drugs and anti-war protest onscreen and produced one of the first hit 'soundtrack albums'. Sound tracks had sold before, but usually they were based on previous stage musicals etc. The early 1970s was a very bad time for Hollywood in terms of box-office revenues (i.e. before the arrival of *Jaws* and *Star Wars*). Rock music looked like the future.

There are various 1970s films which have been cited as 'turning points' in the relation between Hollywood and the music industry. *American Graffiti* (1973), *Saturday Night Fever* (1977) and *Grease* (1978) in their different ways all suggested that synergy could work (*American Graffiti* was a nostalgia film using 1950s music, the other two were more traditional in genre terms). Sell the film, sell the album – the two could not be separated. Where previously the studio had commissioned a songwriter, there was now a prolonged negotiation over music rights to existing titles. Music companies were talking to studios. Sometimes they were part of the same company (e.g. Warner Bros) – but sometimes the cost of rights proved too high.

At the end of the 1970s, music on film also benefited from the introduction of Dolby Stereo in cinemas. After nearly fifty years without any major developments in cinema sound, the success of films like *Star Wars* in 1977 convinced cinema owners that they should invest in the new system. It is significant that *Star Wars* produced a successful soundtrack album of 'theme music' and that composer John Williams became a new 'star' name.

1980s: MTV

During the 1980s, music companies benefited from three separate technological innovations:

- the CD
- the videocassette
- cable and satellite broadcasting.

The CD represented a major opportunity to persuade customers to re-equip with new audio technology and to buy new versions of old favourites in the new format. At the same time, the videocassette increased interest in the possibility of collecting video recordings of music stars and helped to launch the new format (Hollywood was initially reluctant to release films on cassette, so 'music videos' were needed to drive the new market). The new format also encouraged the concept of 'music television' with an increase in the demand for film and video recordings to be made. The music companies wanted such recordings to help market the performers and their new material; the fans wanted the recordings to keep. In retrospect, the potential for 'music television' was there for all to see, but when MTV was launched it took some time to become a success. The music television concept needed a dedicated channel and this was provided by the developments in satellite broadcasting and cable television.

A further innovation in this period was the portability of recording and playback devices, especially the Sony Walkman. The Walkman allowed music fans to change the way they listened to music – in effect to consume more music, because they were not restricted by location. Initially a cassette technology, Walkmans moved to CD and then to MiniDisc. This last was not ultimately successful, partly because the smaller size did not offer a major benefit to compensate for the loss of compatibility with other systems. That would come with computer files.

1990s: music goes digital

Compact disc technology offered a means of storing music in a digital format. Digital recording techniques were also developing in the 1980s. However, the innovation that would revolutionise 'digital music' was the development of suitable hardware and software for *distribution* of digital files over computer networks. This was achieved largely through compression techniques that eventually produced the MP3 standard. Everybody could use MP3s whereas other compression software only worked on particular computer platforms. MP3 meant the development of a means of:

- converting existing digital music tracks to computer files that can be played on any computer
- 'burning' a new CD of collected files (or 'copying' an existing CD)
- transferring files to a portable MP3 player (lighter and holding more tracks than a Walkman)
- 'swapping' MP3s with other users over the internet
- downloading legitimate (i.e. purchased) MP3s to a home computer.

What we should note here is that technologies such as MP3 have been used, much as earlier technologies (i.e. cassette technology), to copy existing material, but also to change the ways in which both producers and consumers think about music products. We will return to this second point once we have looked at the contemporary industry.

The structure of the industry

Given this history of development, closely tied in with other media, how is the music industry organised today? Not surprisingly, some of the same handful of large media conglomerates discussed in Chapter 7 and 'Case study: The media majors' are also the 'majors' in the music industry worldwide:

ACTIVITY 7.12

UK music history

The outline history above refers to the biggest music market, in North America. In the UK, the history is similar, but often with events lagging a few years behind. Use the internet and reference books to find out about the following and try to outline some of the important events in the history of the music industry in the UK:

- Radio Luxemburg (1930s–60s)
- *NME* and *Melody Maker* – first charts (1950s)
- Radio Caroline and Radio 1 (1960s)
- Rough Trade and Beggars' Banquet (1970s record labels)
- *The Tube* (Channel 4 in the 1980s).

	Groups: Labels	Other Music Interests
Universal Music Group (Vivendi) (www.umusic.com) Headquarters: Santa Monica, CA, New York, NY	Island Def Jam Music Group, Interscope A&M, Geffen, Lost Highway, MCA Nashville, Mercury Nashville, DreamWorks Nashville, Mercury, Polydor, Universal Motown Records Group, Decca, Deutsche Grammophon, Philips, Verve Music Group, etc.	Music publishing, distribution and sale of music products for telephony and download.
Sony/BMG (50:50 partnership) (www.sonybmg.com) Headquarters: New York, NY	Labels in 30 countries including Arista, BMG, Columbia, Epic, J Records, Jive, LaFace, Legacy Recordings, Provident Music Group, RCA Records, RCA Victor Group, RLG – Nashville, Sony Music Nashville, Sony Urban Music, Sony Wonder, So So Def, Verity, etc.	(Music publishing and manufacturing are not included in the joint operation, remaining with the parent companies.)
EMI Group (www.emigroup.com) Headquarters: London	Labels in 27 countries, including Astralwerks, Blue Note Jazz, Capitol, EMI Records, Mute, Parlophone, Virgin, etc.	EMI Music Publishing, Control over Screen Gems, Virgin Publishing etc. New Media, Studios, Manufacturing, Distribution
Warner Music Group (www.wmg.com) Headquarters: New York	Asylum, Atlantic (Bad Boy, Lava, Elektra), East West, Warner Bros. (Reprise, Warner Nashville, Sire, Nonesuch, Maverick, Warner Jazz), Warner Music International, Rhino Entertainment, Word Entertainment	Warner/Chappell Music Publishing, WEA music distribution

Figure 7.13 Major music companies and labels.

- Sony and Bertelsmann as Sony/BMG
- Vivendi-Universal

In addition, Warner Bros Music has recently separated from its parent in a 'buy-out' and there is a fourth major company in the form of EMI (sales 2004: $3.9 billion). The existence of a British company which concentrates solely on music in the ranks of the majors is an indication of the importance of the UK music industry – the UK has the highest per capita sales of recorded music and overall counts as the third biggest market. EMI is the third-ranked music company worldwide and the No. 1 in music publishing with rights to a million songs. Attempts by EMI to merge with Warner Bros and Bertelsmann were rejected by the EU – but BMG was allowed to merge with Sony. UK government statistics suggest that 41,000 musicians, performers and composers work in the UK industry. (See DCMS website at http://www.culture.gov.uk/creative_industries/music/.)

Two 'major' Hollywood-based groups, Disney and Viacom/Paramount, are classed as 'independents' in the music industry. News Corporation is the only media conglomerate without significant music industry activities.

The music industry is not 'integrated' in quite the same way as cinema. The 'majors' are primarily distributors, but not so much 'exhibitors' – in the case of the music industry, the exhibitors are effectively the radio and television stations and the retail outlets. Note here that Disney (owner of American broadcaster ABC) and Viacom (owner of CBS, MTV and VH-1) have a major presence as exhibitors/broadcasters.

The importance of 'independents'

In one sense the music industry is still a 'cottage industry' since the vast majority of the 41,000 'creative talents' in the UK work alone or for small companies. Ninety per cent of the UK industry is classed as 'SME' (Small or Medium Enterprises). It is these SMEs which produce the music, eventually distributed by the majors, organise local gigs and manage new acts. One of the features of the industry over the past twenty years has been the career path of performers who begin with a small independent record label and gradually move to a contract with one of the majors. (As popular music stars age, they tend to go back to the independents as their market importance declines.) The majors have also created their own small specialist labels in the hope of finding new talent.

In Chapter 7 we discuss the concept of 'independence' in the media industries. Here, we want to note that in the music industry, small independent companies have been able to develop new record labels very quickly. The Zomba company, founded in 1975 in the UK, saw spectacular growth in 2000 with its Jive Records label – home to Britney Spears and the Backstreet Boys. Even though Zomba became a 'global' label while still independent, Bertelsmann bought a 20 per cent stake in the company in 1996 and finally acquired control in late 2002. In 2004, as part of the newly formed Sony–BMG partnership, the 'Zomba Label Group' (including LaFace stars Usher and OutKast) was recognised as the major presence in the American music market, dominating both the *Billboard* and *Radio and Records* charts. While BMG certainly provided Zomba with a sound basis for expansion, Zomba in turn allowed BMG to become a stronger presence in the music market.

A global industry

It is in the global market that the music majors differ from the usual approach of the multinational conglomerates. The Hollywood studios rarely attempt to make films directly (i.e. to finance a local operation) in overseas territories (apart from the UK and now China). Infrequently, they pick up local films for possible international distribution, but mostly they deal in American films. By contrast, the music companies tend to buy local record labels and to acquire a 'roster' of local artists in addition to their marketing of global acts.

Historically, the music industry has been able to develop in all parts of the world, partly because, unlike film and television, audio recording is a relatively simple and inexpensive process with minimum requirements for technology. It also requires far less organisation of talent and can draw upon deep reservoirs of local performance skills and musical knowledge.

Hollywood became dominant in international cinema by the late 1920s in most territories, taking a significant share of every market, usually through dubbing. But although the large American and European music companies set up operations in most territories worldwide, 'domestic' artists and repertoire have managed to remain important, especially in Asia, the Middle East and Latin America. Nevertheless, the top artists worldwide remain English-speaking. The following music albums sold more than 5 million copies in 2004 (source: International Federation of Phonogram and Videogram Producers, IFPI 2005, www.ifpi.org/):

- *Confessions*, Usher
- *Feels Like Home*, Norah Jones
- *Encore*, Eminem
- *How to Dismantle an Atomic Bomb*, U2
- *Under My Skin*, Avril Lavigne
- *Greatest Hits*, Robbie Williams
- *Greatest Hits*, Shania Twain
- *Destiny Fulfilled*, Destiny's Child.

Significant profits are made around the world, but as in most media markets, performance varies between territories. Overall, 2004 saw the market stabilise after several years of decline with total sales of around $34 billion. For the industry there were encouraging signs:

- The US and UK markets were strong (47 per cent of the world market is represented by the US/UK).
- Digital sales in the US and UK grew quickly.
- Music DVD sales are also growing and replacing lost revenues from older technologies (i.e. tapes).
- Latin America saw a 12.6 per cent increase in sales, partly owing to economic recovery in the continent.

But major problems still remained:

- 'physical' piracy – illegal CDs in many territories, especially Asia, Eastern Europe, Latin America

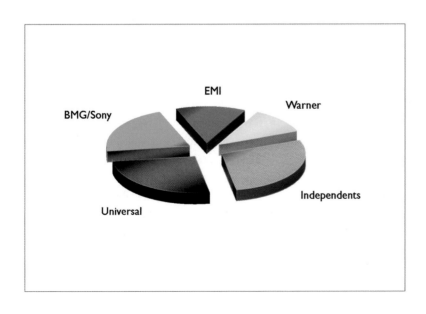

Figure 7.14 The international music market.

- 'virtual piracy' – illegal downloads, especially in Sweden, Finland, France, Spain and South Korea.

Piracy in all its forms remains the major problem for the industry. 'Convergence' means that piracy is now common in both music and cinema/television – both in downloading and 'printing' CDs/DVDs. This means that the majors have even more of an incentive to tackle the pirates. However, the IFPI Report also focuses on the growth of legal downloads and this trend points us towards several interesting questions. (All figures from IFPI Reports 2005.)

Synergy, convergence and the contemporary music industry

The music industry has been uniquely placed to help each of the other media industries at crucial stages of their development. It has provided opportunities for **synergy** that have been exploited by radio, television and cinema and now by 'new media'. In 2002 the excitement in the UK over the voting for ITV's *Pop Idol* and the subsequent release of the winner's first single showed benefits for television, phone companies and the music industry. In 2005 the UK music industry decided to combine the traditional 'Pop singles chart' with the 'Downloads chart' established only in 2004. Early expectations were that this might see significant changes in the types of music represented in the chart, based on the assumption that sales of CD singles had

'Music and the internet are both natural and unnatural bedfellows. The creation and consumption of music is a personal, cultural experience, and the technology of the internet changes the mode of consumption in a way that is both appealing and threatening – and certainly disruptive' (Martin Mills of Beggars' Banquet Records Group, in the Introduction to *Consumers Call the Tune*, Department of Culture Media and Sport, April 2000).

been driven by young (i.e. 12–13) girls, whereas 'downloaders' were assumed to be largely male and over 15. How do you think the charts have changed – if at all – since the merger of charts?

The boxed quote from 2000 is underpinned by a real concern that the music industry is 'threatened' by new media. This belief was shared by many when 'file-sharing' (i.e. illegal downloading) first began via Napster and other technologies. But since the launch of Apple's iTunes in the US in 2003 and the UK in 2004, and the swift rise to 'must have' accessory status for the iPod, views have begun to change. Now, downloading is big business, with the participation of major players from both the music industry (e.g. Sony/BMG) and the computer industry (Microsoft, Roxio and Real Player as well as Apple).

Compare the 2000 quote above with this extract from a presentation by Alain Levy, chairman and CEO of EMI Music in 2004:

What does our digital strategy include?
- We want to enable consumers to find and consume any music . . .
   . . . in any form . . .
   . . . at any time . . .
   . . . in any place . . .
- No longer only about the number of discs sold
Where will we be in 3–5 years time?
- Composition of the 'music pie' is changing – from 100% CD to 75% CD, 25% digital distribution of some form
- It is becoming a much bigger 'pie' overall – new products: e.g. downloads, ring tunes, ring backs, dedications
   – new platforms: e.g. mobile, digital radio
   – new channels: e.g. Starbucks, airlines, mobile superdistribution
- EMI Music will no longer be a physical record company, but a digital music business at large
(Downloaded from http://www. emigroup.com/financial.html, 4 June 2005)

EMI have clearly taken on board everything that has happened since 2000. Like much of the industry, they have taken the view that while it is important to fight organised piracy, there is much to be gained by embracing the new digital market. Another report on the same website suggests that research has shown that customers who buy music online buy more 'units' than those who make only traditional music shop purchases. In 2005 EMI started to sell CDs which included computer software and effectively 'sanctioned' the purchaser to make a digital copy for home use.

Hardware and software lessons

The presence of Microsoft and the other computer players in the music market is significant in that they are concerned to make profits via the software coding that controls the downloading, transfer, storage and playback of digital files. At the time of writing, iTunes and the iPod are at the centre of the battle between Apple and Microsoft over computer operating systems. The link between the iTunes Music Store and the iPod player is an important 'proprietary' link via which Apple sells more iPods and more downloads since one requires the other. (In 2004, 1 million tracks were available for download and 200 million downloads were made. iPods accounted for 20 per cent of all MP3 players sold worldwide (source www.pro-music.org).)

It is generally agreed that although Apple has regularly produced the best-designed hardware and software, Microsoft 'stole' the market by separating the software from the hardware and allowing Windows to spread to machines from different manufacturers. In 2005 when Apple released its new operating system 'Tiger', it again moved far ahead of Microsoft and began to attract more 'converts' to its products. But still the doubts remain about Apple's refusal to allow its products to be fully exploited by other hardware producers. Many of the people who have bought iPods have followed fashion rather than chosen a hardware/software combination and Apple will be vulnerable when the price and 'compatiblity' of other manufacturers' MP3 players prove more attractive than the iPod's design.

Apple do not control music libraries – they are dependent on deals with music companies. At the time of writing, significant recording artists are still not available via iTunes (e.g. no Beatles, since the two 'Apple' brands are still in legal dispute). Where an artist has had a long career, it is likely that recordings on major labels will be available, but not all those on smaller labels. The music industry is indeed in parts a cottage industry and for the less mainstream acts, fans may need to go direct to the artists themselves to purchase recordings – something else helped by websites.

A further complicating factor will be the development of further 'synergies' between mobile phone technologies and digital music software/online music stores. This has already introduced companies such as Nokia and Motorola into the music industry equation. In June 2005, 'Crazy Frog', a 'ringtone', became the No. 1 'single' in the UK.

These digital music developments were first introduced in North America and Western Europe,

Figure 7.15 Heavy promotion of the iPod as a 'must have accessory' has helped Apple's brand recognition. Even in silhouette, these characters display the connections between music and fashion – compare with Figure 7.12 Poster for Louis Jordan on p. 258.

where customers have clearly been prepared to pay for downloads (as is often the case with Apple, UK customers paying much more than in the US). Elsewhere, the industry is still struggling with pirate CDs etc.

Listening to and 'owning' music

In the early 1970s, when the music industry first began to make large profits from albums or 'LPs', considerable effort was put into designing the packaging – the 'album cover' or 'sleeve'. Albums became complex art objects – sometimes opening out into two or three sections (the 'gatefold') – with extensive 'sleeve notes' about the performers and the music, as well as photographs, graphics and original artwork. An album cover was something to be coveted – protected by a plastic sleeve and carefully studied when the album was played.

CDs were disappointing replacements for vinyl for 'collectors' since everything became miniaturised – but in other ways they saw a development in the amount of text that could be crammed into booklets placed inside the jewel case. Digital downloads offer only a small digital image to accompany a track. The concept of ownership of an 'art object' has gone.

'Everyone's a winner'

The internet may be good for the music business because it makes a 'miss' profitable. In a traditional record shop, most business was concerned with either the current 'Top 100' artists or music from a limited range of specialist genres. As a consequence, shelf space was taken up by a limited number of titles, the most popular of which had to be stocked in multiple copies to meet demand.

By contrast, an internet 'download store' does not have any shelf space to worry about and can stock a million titles. Many of the songs will have only one or two buyers, but virtually every title will find someone willing to try it. The profit to the online seller is the same for each one – popularity is meaningless and a 'miss' is as good as a 'hit'. (Look back to the quote from Alain Levy at EMI on p. 264.) 'Hits' still have an extra value in advertising terms – they bring customers to the website, but once they are attracted, online sellers have developed new ways to coax buyers into trying something new, such as recommendations ('other purchasers of "x" also bought . . .') or lists compiled by other users of the website. The databases used on these sites can easily display everything produced by a specific music performer, often ranked according to popularity and complete with reviews.

(Based on Jack Schofield, 'A miss hit', *Guardian*, 25 March 2005)

The 'culture' of owning and listening to music has changed alongside the economics of distributing and retailing the products. It is still an open question whether these changes have increased the range of music available to anyone who wants to listen or whether they have created a new marketplace from which some consumers and some recording artists are excluded. There is no doubt that if you are prepared to use the internet to search for music, virtually everything is available somewhere – as a download or purchasable via mail order. But there are still many people without internet access and others who won't risk electronic payments – and globally there are millions without even mains electricity. In some ways, new technologies have allowed the cottage industry to become viable again locally. You can get CDs from friends who burn them on their computers, from local bands who distribute them at gigs and from local labels who supply the few remaining speciality shops.

ACTIVITY 7.13

How do you buy music?

Do your own research into music use and purchase.
Ask a cross-section of people of different ages some
simple questions:

- What kinds of music do they listen to?
- Do they buy music or swap with friends?
- How do they buy/obtain music (shop/mail
  order/download/from the artist)?
- What do they think of the range of music available
  to them?

What conclusions do you draw from your findings?
Now check your conclusions against the arguments
about 'free markets' in Chapter 16.

References

This case study was researched solely on the internet.
The following websites proved useful:

www.bl.uk/collections/sound-archive/record.html
  (See p. 335 on research at the National Sound
  Archive.)
www.culture.gov.uk/creative_industries/music/
www.ifpi.org
www.pro-music.org
www.rca.com
www.riaa.com

Further reading

Dickinson, Kay (ed.) (2003) *Movie Music: The Film
  Reader*, London: Routledge. (This useful collection
  has several articles directly relevant to the
  arguments here.)
Negus, Keith (1999) *Music Genres and Popular Cultures*,
  London: Routledge.
Shuker, Roy (2001) *Understanding Popular Music*,
  London: Routledge.

8 Audiences

- **Media representations of audiences**
- **Academic representations of audiences**
- **The effects model**
- **Media influence**

- **The uses and gratifications model**
- **'Encoding/decoding'**
- **Cultural approaches**
- **References**
- **Further reading**

Media representations of audiences

Many would say that 'the audience' is not simply those who have media 'delivered' to them, but is a group now often present in the media, especially in phone-ins, confession shows or TV's 'reality television' such as *Big Brother*, *Wife Swap* and make-over programmes. There's more discussion of 'reality TV' in the third section of the book, including the terms on which this (tiny) part of the audience gets 'cast' and therefore enters into visibility. This chapter explores how else the media, and also academic theories, have represented audiences.

Audience members have often tried to be represented in the media, voicing their concerns or pleasures. **Access** has traditionally meant programme-making (such as the *Open Space* slot on BBC TV) where power, including editorial control, was handed over to a group or individual outside the broadcasting institutions. There are a few examples left: video diaries, for tiny amounts of time, and five-minute slots such as those at the end of Channel 4's news bulletin. BBC's *Feedback* (Radio 4) slot is a chance for listeners to do just that, though within broadcasting the assumption often seems to be that audience members will interact with programme-makers on the channel's website. Relatively few programmes emerge from outside TV's world, where professionals are often said to make programmes partly for each other's approval, and often with a very London-centred slant and view of 'the audience'. This is ignoring the audience-in-the-media which is present in the expansion of (cheap) daytime television talk shows, 'reality TV', interactive computer

Feedback is the BBC Network Radio listeners' feedback programme, produced for Radio 4 by an independent production company. *Feedback*'s content is entirely directed by the letters, emails and faxes it receives from listeners. See BBC website.

technologies, and the merging of the two in digital television. Radio and television phone-ins, 'letters to the editor' slots in newspapers and magazines, and chat shows routinely allow parts of the audience 'into' the media, though on rather special terms.

ACTIVITY 8.1

Take your favourite radio phone-in, feedback programme or television chat show and examine on what terms members of the audience manage to get a hearing. Look at the following:

- What does the title sequence promise?
- How is the studio set up, visually and aurally? How does the show seem to have been 'cast' via choice of audience members?
- If a feedback programme, what voices have been chosen for particular letters? Why?
- How does the host organise or 'frame' interruptions, noise levels, 'expert' contributions, escalation of conflict?
- What seem to have been the criteria for choosing any experts used in it?
- How is the show concluded or summed up? Did you feel this was adequate?

Opinion polls are another form through which an often skewed 'snapshot' of a sample of the audience is given media space (see Lewis 2001). These are highly constructed:

- The pollsters construct the questions.
- Key phrases, designed to trigger certain responses, are often used to structure the direction and limits of discussion (such as 'illegal asylum seekers', which is actually a nonsense term: to apply for asylum is to go through legal channels).
- The work of questioning (on the street or door to door) is poorly paid and hard to check.

Then, the print and television media select which parts of the results to emphasise, amplify or ignore. There is repeated evidence, in both the UK and the US, that people polled want good health, education and public services and would consider higher taxes to pay for them (Lewis 2001). Yet this gets far less coverage in elections than the 'horse race' aspect of politics: simply, who's ahead? There is some pressure to ban such 'betting' polls during UK elections, given their potential influence on the perceived result.

See the DVD *Outfoxed* for arguments about the effects of early declarations of results on the first election of George W. Bush.

The last ten years have also seen a surge in representations of fandom, especially internet fandom for entertainment forms. Fans have produced

Jane Feuer, speaking in the 1997 conference 'Console-ing Passions', suggested that for some lesbian fans of the sitcom *Ellen*, the 'coming out' of the main character, while politically admirable, deprived them of the pleasures of making their own secret reading of phrases etc., assumed to be 'not seen' by the rest of the audience.

alternative versions of their favourite shows or films, and the entry of fans into higher education has also led, via writings on fandom, to greater visibility for such audience creativity and pressure on media-makers. New television formats such as *Big Brother* have not only put (highly selected) sections of 'the audience' literally on stage, in broadcast auditions for example, but has also allowed viewers/fans to vote on which contestants should be eliminated from the shows, and to have their own discussion area, e.g. in *Big Brother's Little Brother*.

Though fans love the characters and 'spaces for play' made available by their favourite media products, they also often resent the huge powers of copyright, cost, censorship, scheduling and publicity decisions which the producing corporations maintain and patrol. However, it is hard to see how activity simply at the level of lobbying for plot changes will affect such power structures.

Academic representations of audiences

Media studies also produces images or models of audiences. There have been some very abstract speculations made about audiences, such as the psychoanalytic models deployed by writers like Laura Mulvey. Here we will mostly focus on empirical research methods, though we'll look at a very influential piece of textual work on news which began the move from a tendency to assume things about audiences from 'the text', towards closer investigation of actual 'readers'. A useful way of thinking of audience(s) is as *the groups and individuals addressed and often partly 'constructed' by media industries.*

Remember from Chapter 1 that 'empirical' means relying on observed experience as evidence for positions taken in debate.

Kitzinger (2004a: 168–9) helpfully suggests that the impetus for empirical research (both academic and non-academic) into audiences can be grouped into four areas:

- *'market' driven*: seeking to track audiences as consumers, and monitoring such issues as attention flow, or the numbers of 'eyeballs' which your product is attracting. Corporate responsiveness to fans' comments might be seen in this context
- *concerns about morality and 'sex 'n' violence'*: focusing on the supposed corrupting power of media and often deploying laboratory-based evidence
- *responses to technological developments*: such as TV in the 1950s when it was a new medium, to children's and other groups' use of the internet today
- *questions about culture, politics and identity*: concerned with the media's role in framing public understandings and also the ways that we use media texts and objects in relation to identities, pleasures and fantasies, as well as within relationships.

These broad areas sometimes overlap. They are also very differently funded, with big media corporations being notably well equipped to run focus groups etc. to develop their marketing. Across this broad spectrum of research, major assumptions tend to cluster around either one or the other end of the scale: the **effects model** and the **uses and gratifications model**. Let's broadly outline these.

The effects model

The effects model (also called the **hypodermic model**) is the name given to approaches that emphasise what the media do *to* their audiences. Power is assumed to lie with the 'message'. The media are often called 'the mass media' or 'mass communications' as though to emphasise the size and scale of their operations. The language used in this model often implies that meanings are 'injected' into a single mass audience by powerful, syringe-like media. The next step is often to describe the media as working like a drug, and then to suggest that the audience is drugged, addicted, doped or duped. This model often uses what are called **quantitative** research methods: counting items (for example in answers to questionnaires) and drawing conclusions. But it's also used by more abstract theorists.

'There are in fact no "masses" but only ways of seeing people as masses' (Raymond Williams, 'Culture is ordinary', 1958).

- The **Frankfurt School**, for example, theorised at a very early stage the possible effects of modern media, especially in response to German fascism's use of radio and film for **propaganda** purposes in the 1920s and 1930s. Later, in exile from Nazi Germany, the major Frankfurt theorists explored the early power of US media, including advertising and entertainment forms. Its members developed a variant of Marxism known as *critical theory*. They emphasised the power of corporate capitalism, owning and controlling new media, to restrict and control cultural life in unprecedented ways, creating what they called a 'mass culture' of stupefying conformity, with no space for innovation or originality. Despite the abstract power of some of their writings, the group hardly produced ideas of active and lively audiences who might oppose such control. Nevertheless as control of the media has become ever more corporate and concentrated, their writings are often worth rereading.

- A slightly different emphasis on effects was developed by researchers into what was, then, the new phenomenon of television in the US in the 1950s and 1960s. They were alarmed by a perceived increase in violent acts and their possible relationship to violence-as-represented-on-television. But unlike the Frankfurt School, they were not interested in linking these to a critical analysis of late capitalist society. They

'It is the height of hypocrisy for Senator Dole [powerful US Republican politician], who wants to repeal the assault weapons ban, to blame Hollywood for the violence in our society' (Oliver Stone, June 1995).

See Michael Stephens in
www.Popmatters.com, 17 June
2005, arguing that the demand for
shows providing a window into
the ghetto – from *COPS* to *The
Wire* and even the *Grand Theft
Auto* games – has expanded in
direct proportion to the
increasing safety of US
middle-class life. The US middle
class is encouraged to eliminate,
not just danger, but the slightest
inconvenience from their world.
Hence the desire for 'ghetto
tourism'. How might we relate
this speculation to (a) 'effects'
debates on 'violent media' and
(b) UK uses of such imagery?

On the Bobo doll work Jane Root
quoted the following: 'As she
entered a laboratory, one small
four-year-old girl was heard to
say "Look, Mummy, there's the
doll we have to hit"' (*Open the
Box*, London: Comedia, 1986).

focused on the power of television to do things *to* people – or rather,
to *other* people. Contemporary organisations such as Media Watch UK
(formerly the NVLA or National Viewers' and Listeners' Association)
or parental movements in the US try to have television and other media
more closely censored and classified, based on this model, arguing that
they are the most important causes of 'violence', and of the decay of
standards of 'taste and decency'.

- Another term you will come across is *behaviourism*, which influenced
  some researchers studying the effects of media on children. *Behavioural*
  scientists tried to understand human *social* behaviour by modifying the
  laboratory behaviour of animals. B.F. Skinner is one of the most famous.
  You may have heard of Pavlov's dogs, laboratory animals whose feeding
  times were accompanied by a bell ringing, until eventually they would
  salivate whenever the bell rang, with or without the food. Clearly their
  laboratory behaviour had been violently modified. Scientists working
  on such experiments hoped that control by reinforcement could also
  be applied to human behaviour – though in different ways. American
  advertisers were interested, and some media researchers felt that there
  might be similarities in the 'repeated messages' or 'reinforcement' of
  television and their effects on audiences.

  A now notorious piece of research was called the 'Bobo doll
  experiment' (Bandura and Walters 1963). It showed children some
  film of adults acting aggressively towards a 'Bobo doll', then recorded
  children acting in a similar way later when left alone with it. The
  implication (that children copy violent behaviour) was then extended
  to violent media content, which was asserted to have similar effects.
  This research method ignores several basic problems:

- Findings cannot necessarily be neatly transferred from laboratory
  animals to human beings.
- If people are likened to laboratory animals, they will be assumed
  to be empty vessels, passively absorbing simple messages.
  Cognitive psychologists have argued instead that children actively
  construct, rather than passively receive, meanings from the media,
  and that these interpretations are affected by prior knowledge and
  experience.
- People (a group which includes children!) are often very willing to
  please those conducting experiments, with a shrewd sense of what
  responses are the favoured ones. They also know quite well how to
  mess things up entertainingly.
- A simple, controlled laboratory experiment has very limited
  application to the complicated conditions under which we interact
  with various media in our social lives outside the lab.

- Outside the laboratory, the 'effect' of media may not be shown in our measurable *outward* behaviour, such as voting or shopping – or violent acts. Broadly cultural effects (on attitudes etc.) are harder to measure.

Media influence

Within the effects model the power of the media, especially television, is usually assumed to be negative, never positive. If you look closely at the kinds of writing that urge censorship (which ironically include tabloid editorials), they often fall into one of two contradictory positions, sometimes contributing to **moral panics**:

- 'The media produce inactivity, make us into students who won't pass their exams or "couch potatoes" who make no effort to get a job.'
- 'The media *do* produce activity, but of a bad kind, such as violent "copycat" behaviour, or mindless shopping in response to advertisements.'

Of course media messages can have 'effects' of a quite simple, though immediate kind: a weather forecast may encourage you to put a coat on; the flashings of strobe lighting effects can be dangerous for epileptics. But usually a broader, more ideological *influence* is being claimed for the media.

'In 1976, a group of friends from Los Angeles who often gathered together . . . to indulge in hours long sessions of television viewing, decided to call themselves "couch potatoes". With tongue in cheek publications such as *The Official Couch Potato Handbook* . . . they started a mock-serious grassroots viewers' movement' (Ien Ang (1991), *Desperately Seeking the Audience*, London: Routledge).

ACTIVITY 8.2

Take any recent panic over media effects – perhaps involving the internet. Make notes on the language of the pro-censorship writers, including:

- the tell-tale use of 'them' rather than any admission of the 'we' of researchers' or campaigners' own involvement in viewing
- implications that 'things were all right' in some earlier age, often thirty years or so ago
- visual and verbal stereotyping or 'other-ing' of the group or person being panicked over.

'The mass audience' here is usually assumed to consist of the 'weaker' members of society, especially the 'lower orders'. In the nineteenth century, novels were thought to be potentially harmful for working-class women; more recently there have been similar fears that romantic novels, and then soaps, then TV render people (especially women) passive, helpless, drugged with trivia. Children, too, feature in such discourses:

Figure 8.1 An image of the bored TV consumer, reduced to his and her zapping fingers.

worried over in the 1950s because of the supposed harm done by American comics; then from the 1980s to the present in relation to horror films, computer games, gangsta rap; mobile phones, text messaging . . .

Important concerns can get raised in such panics (such as the radiation effects of intensive mobile phone use on still-developing brain cells). But the debates are often strikingly isolated from other factors affecting children's use of media, such as:

- under-funded or unstimulating childcare, school and leisure activities
- children's awareness, their 'play' with fictional conventions, in particular in parts of the horror genre
- children's awareness that the computer skills acquired (e.g. through playing games) allow entry to adult status, and are highly job-marketable, as well as exciting
- the pleasure of 'escaping' into the text messaging, games, or the 'community' of mobile phone messages, as well as the safety and convenience they offer.

Thinking about the models which underlie different approaches makes it easier to see when the logic of a particular model has led researchers to 'throw out the baby with the bathwater', as has happened with some effects work.

More sophisticated research into broader *influences* of the media or 'the new effects work' (Kitzinger (2004a)) emphasise subtler, less direct capacities of the media to influence our perceptions, agendas, etc.

In a classic study, Lazarsfeld *et al.* (1944) explored, over six months, the influence exerted on voters by the media during an American presidential campaign. They concluded that voters were resistant to media influence, since individual predispositions or political preference influenced which media they consulted. The term *two-step flow* was coined to describe the important influence not of 'the media' but of local networks and opinion leaders, whose views often mediated those offered by the media. Media effect began to be seen as one of reinforcement via such *intervening variables*.

Gerbner and Gross (1976) produced work in the US which suggested that the more television you watch, the more likely you are to have a fearful attitude to the world outside the home. Such questions have been revived recently around British television programmes such as *Crimewatch*, and the suggestions of Michael Moore, or of Adam Curtis in *The Power of Nightmares* (BBC 2004) that we are living in a culture of fear, now deliberately stoked by politicians grossly exaggerating legitimate fears of 'terrorists' and the media glad to have such 'sexy' headlines with which to sell their products.

Greg Philo's work over the years, with different members of the Glasgow University Media Group, has suggested another form of broad influence or effect. Long after the end of the British coal miners' strike of 1984–5 the group discovered that audiences had tended to forget important details of news reporting, but did remember key themes and phrases, such as 'picket line violence'. These, through repetition, became part of popular consciousness, and then memory about the strike, even if it could be shown at the time that they were mythical or greatly exaggerated.

When the 1984–5 coal miners' strike was over, the National Council for Civil Liberties reported that 'contrary to the impression created by the media, most of the picketing during the strike has been orderly and on a modest scale'.

A related piece of work, in 2004, strongly suggested that perceptions of the Israel–Palestine conflict were skewed partly by the failure of news organisations to explain key terms, or to give historical background to images of violent conflict. In one group, for example, 'it was apparent that a relatively straightforward piece of information, such as that the Israelis controlled water supplies and how this affected Palestinian agriculture, had a strong effect on how a [focus group] participant understood the intractability of the conflict' (pp. 241–2). Further, 'a clear majority in the groups as a whole stated that their interest increased when they knew more . . . the relationship between understanding and interest in news was very marked.'

'Every time it comes on [the Israeli–Palestinian conflict] it never actually explains it so I don't see the point of watching it. . . . It's like the Kosovo conflict. I don't want to watch it, I don't understand it – I switch it off' (comments from two members of the GUMG focus groups in Philo and Berry 2004: 240).

The uses and gratifications model

At the other extreme of academic images of the media, the uses and gratifications model emphasises what the audiences and readerships of media products do *with* them. Power is argued to lie with the individual **consumer** of media, who is argued to consciously use TV, the internet,

Figure 8.2 Using the media for particular kinds of gratification.

etc. to gratify certain needs and interests. Far from being duped by the media, 'the audience' is represented as made up of individuals free to reject, use or play with media meanings as they choose. The needs to be gratified would include those for diversion and escapism, for information, for comparing relationships and lifestyle of characters with one's own, or for sexual stimulation. This model first found expression in the US in the 1940s and has been associated with television, and with socio-psychological approaches to media.

In the 1950s this approach seemed like a breath of fresh air, resisting the easy pessimism and crudely behaviourist emphases of early effects work. Researchers (often well funded and sometimes working with advertisers) questioned people as to why they watched television, and concluded that 'personality types' in the audience gave rise 'to certain needs, some of which are directed to the mass media for satisfaction' (Morley 1991). These needs were grouped in such categories as cognitive (learning); affective (emotional satisfaction); tension release (relaxation); personal integrative (help with issues of personal identity); social integrative (help with issues of social identity).

Unlike the Frankfurt School's position, this model was clearly not interested in critiquing capitalist mass culture. Indeed some of its extreme adherents came close to denying *any* influence for the media, and never explored critically such concepts as 'social integration' – integrated into what, exactly? Just as metaphors of drugs, addiction, passivity characterise the 'effects' tradition, so the 'uses' approaches positively buzz with words like 'choice', 'consuming', 'freedom' and 'users'. This has one big attraction: we're much more likely to *want* to identify ourselves as active readers, zap-happy operators of the TV or computer remote control, than as the passive dupes of some brainwashing media corporation. There are fascinating comparisons with 'free-market' imagery in general here, which have seen a huge revival in the last twenty years.

More recently there have been two developments. Some writers (see Jenkins 2000; Barker and Brooks 1998; Hills 2002) have explored the activity of **fans** and 'cult' viewers, whose pleasure in certain texts might be miles away from either the meaning intended by their makers or the meaning produced by most other viewers. This work has done much to rescue the image of fans as 'lonely obsessives' or unbalanced potential stalkers. With the development of the internet, these fans were able, in a limited way, to become 'producers' of their own episodes of favourite shows (such as *Buffy*) as well as consumer activists, lobbying television companies who wrote out favourite characters, for example.

Others, interested in globalisation, have explored the very different uses to which people in different cultures put media products which we in the West assume can only be used in particular ways. Of course it is significant that this research is often funded by the corporations who stand to profit from sensitivity to global tastes.

'Encoding/decoding'

During the 1970s, the Centre for Contemporary Cultural Studies (**CCCS**) at Birmingham University, under Stuart Hall, worked with a combination of semiotic, structuralist and more sociological approaches (see Gray 1999 for fuller account) to texts. Though this is not strictly speaking audience work, it did open up the possibility of more integration of textual speculations about the audience and research into actual audience members. Hall's paper 'The television discourse – encoding and decoding' (1974) opposed or 'refreshed' several key approaches. It opposed 'content analysis' (see Chapter 1) and other approaches assuming an easily measurable relation between text and audience. It was also a move within Marxist debates, away from the 'single' idea of a dominant ideology towards Gramsci's more complex model of hegemonic dominance, one which has to be constantly struggled for and negotiated (see Chapter 6 'Ideologies and power').

Hall's position also went beyond then current uses and gratifications approaches, insisting instead that, far from being autonomous and utterly individualised, audience members share certain frameworks of interpretation and that they work at **decoding** media texts rather than being 'affected' in a passive way. David Morley's (1980) (again very under-funded) work, some with Charlotte Brunsdon, on the *Nationwide* early evening magazine programme, took this further and tried to focus on:

- power structures *outside* the text which often shape audience members' responses: class, gender, ethnicity, age, etc.
- power structures *within* texts which are part of media institutions. These mean that programmes are often under pressure or try to promote a 'preferred reading' which is argued to be in line with dominant values, but which struggles with other possible meanings in a text.

This broadly Gramscian model of hegemonic power in the media (i.e. power which is constantly having to work to win consent, rather than just being imposed from above) went along with Hall's three types of audience readings:

- **dominant**, or *dominant hegemonic*, where the reader recognises what a programme's 'preferred' or offered meaning is and broadly agrees with it (updated example: the flag-waving patriot who responds enthusiastically to President George W. Bush's latest speech)

An example from the *Financial Times* magazine, 21 May 2005: 'Intel (corporation) anthropologists . . . [made] a 3 year study of how technology is used by Asia's fast growing middle class. [They] found Chinese families who take their mobile phones to temples to be blessed or burn paper cell-phones in funeral rites, and Muslim devotees who use the GPS on their phones to locate Mecca for prayers . . .'

- **oppositional**, where the dominant meaning is recognised but rejected for cultural, political or ideological reasons (the pacifist who understands the speech but rejects it)
- **negotiated**, where the reader accepts, rejects or refines elements of the programme in the light of previously held views (the viewer who agrees with the need for some response to the attacks of 11 September 2001 but does not agree with the military means which Bush announces).

One of the questions raised about this work can take us into our next section:

- It's fine to question a few people about videotaped programmes in a college setting. But to extend this to 'the audience' more generally, we need to know, among other things, how likely they would be to watch those kinds of programmes outside that setting. This led to considerations of **genres**, **discourses** and *domestic contexts for viewing* (see below).

'Cultural' approaches

More recently there has been a turn to audience **ethnographies**, or fieldwork research, largely derived from **anthropology**, where a researcher attempts to enter intensively into the culture of a particular group and provide an account of its meanings and activities 'from the inside'. He/she often employs *participant observation* methods, participating in the lives of the groups to be studied for an extended period of time, asking questions and observing what goes on. When the research is written up, it often tries to show a respect for the group studied by providing life histories, case studies and verbatim quotes from them. Problems remain:

- How can the observer ever know the extent to which his or her questions, presence even, have affected the group 'under observation'?
- Have questions, and what the researcher hears in the answers to them, been selected to fit his or her pre-existing agenda or theory?
- There is usually an imbalance in power between researcher and researched. How might this affect the findings? See the Intel Corporation example above: how does corporate funding of such research affect its uses?
- Often media research which is given this name relies on a much smaller sample, and shorter time span, than classic 'ethnography' or anthropological work.

Nevertheless, it seems likely that more can be learnt from careful, small ethnographic accounts than from the assertions of theory on its own, or from simple, number-crunched questionnaires alone. The key areas which recent media ethnographic work has investigated include

- the domestic contexts of media reception
- genre and cultural competences
- media technologies and consumption.

Morley (1986) and others (see Geraghty 1998) explored ways in which the home – the 'domestic context' for most viewing – structures TV viewing. Such research suggested that home, far from being simply 'the private sphere', our 'retreat from the world', is as cross-cut by kinds of social power as anywhere else. In particular, television viewing is often structured by gender and age power relations:

- For men, often coming home after work or a day spent outside it, viewing can be an experience very different from what it is for women, who, whether or not they work outside the home, are likely to see it as a place of (house)work. It's much easier for men to watch in an uninterrupted way than it is for women, who are often expected to manage the interruptions and disputes that break out among children, as well as get on with 'housework'.
- Because women's (house)work is always there, in the home, women have spoken of their special pleasure in carving out time for themselves to refuse their domestic duties for a while and enjoy a video or a novel.
- The remote control, and who wields it, has long been a key symbol of power within families (and other groups). Even when many children have a TV or computer screen in their own room, it remains significant.

All this has powerful implications for theories which imply a very concentrated relationship of viewer or text. Television viewing has never felt like that a lot of the time. This is partly because of the **flow** which Raymond Williams (1974) and others have suggested is the characteristic experience of television, especially in commercially funded systems, keen to keep fingers off channel buttons, keep 'eyeballs' on their channel so as to have evidence whereby to sell more audience attention to advertisers. This is possibly the best funded of all audience research.

Television is now not the only media technology in the home. Research has suggested for some time that computer games, CD-ROMs, the internet and mobile phones have created a new world of 'living together separately' in the home. Two out of three children now have their own television set in their bedroom. Even more working-class children (71 per cent) than middle-class children (54 per cent) had their own sets in 1999. Yet, asked what their definition of a good time was, young people opted for 'going out with my friends'. Watching television was frequently mentioned as involved in a boring day (see *Guardian* editorial 'Bedroom culture: children want more than television', 20 March 1999, reporting research from the London School of Economics).

Figure 8.3 An ad which tries to visualise the huge and usually invisible 'audience' for the internet. It also tries to shift gendered ideas of the typical user.

ACTIVITY 8.3

Interview your friends and other students to find out:

- How many computers, televisions or mobile phones do you have in your household? Where are they? Are they all of the same quality and size? Who uses which? For what?
- Have you ever successfully waged, or needed to wage, a struggle for the TV remote control? For a mobile phone?
- If you have a computer in your bedroom do you remember having any rules around using it?
- Do you watch any programmes because you *know* you'll disagree with them, or enjoy ridiculing them?
- Do you have 'special occasion' viewing? If so, what arrangements do you make? Does this make television (or DVD) viewing more like cinema going?

The cultural contexts for media use have been explored by the French academic **Pierre Bourdieu**. One of his starting points was that in capitalist societies, access to capital (economic power) is distributed differently to different groups. In a similar way, he researched whether access to '**cultural competences**' is unevenly shared. By cultural competences he meant shared knowledge, and perspectives which are taken for granted within different social groups.

Some of these have higher status than others, such as knowledge of Shakespearean quotations or, perhaps now, of computer terminology. His concept of cultural competence is useful in understanding the cultural contexts of media use, and the pleasures which particular audiences or readerships might take in different media forms.

This theory was later applied to TV. It was assumed, for example, until the 1970s that women's soaps and magazines were an inferior media form, which anyone could understand but which would only interest a rather stupid or trivial-minded audience. But feminist work such as Charlotte Brunsdon's (1981) suggested that the pleasures offered to women by soap opera required particular 'feminine' learnt skills and competencies from outside the text, such as reading 'emotional turmoil, understanding the complexities of familiar relationships' (Gray 1999: 28). Women were more likely to realise the significance of certain kinds of looks between characters, small-scale gestures, silences and so on, or to feel easy with a lot of 'relationship talk' ('yakkety yak' to those hostile to soaps). Their involvement in the skills of domestic labour meant that they were competent to pick up on key parts of soaps' narratives, carried by such intimate gesture and talk.

Women are argued to have access to such competences through years of informal training for their presumed future role as nurturing mothers; or as carers in jobs such as nursing or teaching; or through their confinement to the home, except in periods of high male unemployment. We're certainly not arguing that no male viewers ever come upon, or develop, the competences to enjoy romances or soaps, or that some women may not be irritated by those forms. But informal gender training from early on

Pierre Bourdieu
French cultural sociologist and later anti-globalisation activist (1930–2002). Began ethnographic work after being conscripted into the French army during the Algerian War of 1958. *Distinction: A Social Critique of the Judgement of Taste* (1984) explored how the supposedly natural, universal quality of 'taste' is actually formed along class, cultural and educational lines.

'I realized very quickly at my posh school that . . . you didn't say that person is really awful because they are working-class, you said "Oh my God, that person doesn't appreciate a certain piece of literature, or, that person is wearing a really awful sweater". Twenty years later when I discovered the work of Pierre Bourdieu, I . . . realized he was talking exactly about this' (Judith Williamson, cultural critic, accessed on www.dot-dot-dot.nl/issue4).

'So what was the significance of that little look then?' (much-used male query on soaps and everyday interactions within them).

ACTIVITY 8.4

A little survey. Ask as many boys and men as you can for adjectives which define what a 'real man' is like. List or record them. Many researchers have found that the word 'tough' is the one most often used.

means that certain responses to some genres (like the sad-ending romance) are made unacceptable for some groups ('big boys don't cry') and natural seeming for others.

From the male side of *gendered competences* it's been argued that boys are socialised into acting tough in the face of eighteen-rated videos, computer games and horror films, which in fact they sometimes find hard to 'stomach'. Our culture still expects men, in the end, to differentiate themselves from women along the lines of 'toughness'. Young men are encouraged not to cry, not to explore feelings and to try to appear as decisive and hard as the heroes of action adventures. (The swift decisions necessitated in computer gaming often seem to embody these qualities.) Fortunately they do not all follow this encouragement.

ACTIVITY 8.5

To explore the relative status of cultural competences in your household:

- Jot down whether certain people seem to find some genres difficult to follow and need to have help in finding out 'what's going on'. Does this relate to what might be called 'cultural competences' in some genres and not others?
- Are any of your viewing choices ever ridiculed by other members of your household?
- If so, in what terms, and about what kinds of programmes?
- How insistent or lighthearted or serious is the ridiculing?
- Does it ever prevent you from watching the programme?

The Simpsons often operates a 'double mode of address', using 'adult' allusions and jokes, which may fly 'over the head' of the assumed child audience. *Xena: Warrior Princess* has likewise been said to produce the possibility of a 'parallel' lesbian reading alongside the 'children's adventure story' of its main marketing.

Some theorists of **cult** forms (such as 'trash television') have suggested that some fans have the privilege of 'double access' to both 'naive' enjoyment of the form 'for itself' (a low-status competence) and a knowing humour at its codes (higher-status). Further, they suggest that this, rather than older familiarities with 'high' cultural forms such as Shakespeare or opera, is the form which cultural privilege or 'capital' now takes. Such knowingness seems particularly marked in some fan cultures.

ACTIVITY 8.6

- Do you ever describe yourself as an 'addict' of a media form (TV programme, magazine, novel)?
- Do you think this is a way of apologising for your interest in it?

Other 'cultural competence'-related work has suggested the reasons for young women's reluctance to use computers. This work suggests *not* that young women are incapable of using machines or technology but that they resist, or feel ill at ease in, the world of the 'computer virtuosos', the 'techno-heads'. These are often young men who seem to be involved in an intimate relationship with their machines, one which is often strongly competitive and macho – 'mine's bigger and faster than yours' – centred on very masculine games genres, such as the action adventure and science fiction, and valuing the skill of swift, automatic decisiveness. Attempts are being made to counter such perceptions, both in television programmes and in schools, since a very real fear is that the predicted 'information-rich' and 'information-poor' distinction will work along the lines not simply of class, and the world's North–South divide, but also of gender.

ACTIVITY 8.7

Do you experience such gender contrasts? Collect some recent images of scientists and computers in PC magazine advertising and television programmes such as *Tomorrow's World*.

- How far do they conform to the suggestions above? How do they represent machines? What efforts seem to be being made to change the gender balance of such images?

We are all members of different media audiences, though we're not all 'the audience'. The term is one of a relationship – between those using or enjoying or cursing particular media, and those 'texts' which they relate to. When you read about 'audiences' it's worth bearing this in mind, as well as who is representing them in particular ways, and why that might be.

References

Bandura, Albert and Walters, R. (1963) *Social Learning and Personality Development*, New York: Holt, Rinehart & Winston.

Barker, Martin and Brookes, Kate (1998) *Knowing Audiences: 'Judge Dredd': Its Friends, Fans and Foes*, Luton: University of Luton Press.

Barker, Martin and Petley, Julian (eds) (2001) *Ill Effects: The Media/Violence Debate*, 2nd edition, London and New York: Routledge.

Bourdieu, Pierre (1984) *Distinction: A Social Critique of the Judgement of Taste*, London: Routledge.

Brunsdon, Charlotte (1981) '*Crossroads*: notes on soap opera', *Screen*, 22, 4: 52–7.

Geraghty, Christine (1998) 'Audiences and "ethnography": questions of practice', in Christine Geraghty and David Lusted (eds) *The Television Studies Book*, London and New York: Arnold.

Gerbner, G. and Gross, L. (1976) 'Living with television: the violence profile', *Journal of Communication*, 28.

Gray, Ann (1999) 'Audience and reception research in retrospective: the trouble with audiences', in Pertti Alasuutari (ed.) *Rethinking the Media Audience*, London: Sage.

Hall, Stuart (1974) 'The television discourse – encoding and decoding', *Education and Culture* 25 (UNESCO), reprinted in Ann Gray and Jim McGuigan (eds) (1997) *Studying Culture*, London: Arnold.

Hills, Matt (2002) *Fan Cultures*, London and New York: Routledge.

Hite, Shere (1988) *The Hite Report on Women and Love: A Cultural Revolution in Progress*, London: Viking.

Jenkins, Henry (2000) 'Reception theory and audience research: the mystery of the vampire's kiss', in Christine Gledhill and Linda Williams (eds) *Reinventing Film Studies*, London and New York: Arnold.

Kitzinger, Jenny (2004a) 'Audience and readership research', in *The Sage Handbook of Media Studies*, London: Sage, pp. 167–81.

Kitzinger, Jenny (2004b) *Framing Abuse: Media Influence and Public Understandings of Sexual Violence against Children*, London: Pluto.

Lazarsfeld, P., Berelson, B. and Gaudet, H. (1944) *The People's Choice*, New York: Duell, Sloan and Pearce.

Lewis, Justin (2001) *Constructing Public Opinion: How Political Elites Do What They Like and Why We Seem to Go Along With It*, New York: Columbia University Press.

Lewis, Lisa (ed.) (1992) *The Adoring Audience: Fan Culture and Popular Media*, London: Routledge.

Morley, David (1980) *The Nationwide Audience*, London: BFI.

Morley, David (1986) *Family Television: Cultural Power and Domestic Leisure*, London: Comedia.

Morley, David (1991) 'Changing paradigms in audience studies', in E. Seiter, H. Borchers, G. Krentzner and E. Warth (eds) *Remote Control Television: Audiences and Cultural Power*, London and New York: Routledge.

Philo, Greg (1990) *Seeing and Believing: The Influence of Television*, London and New York: Routledge.

Philo, Greg and Berry, Mike with Gilmour, Alison, Gilmour, Maureen, Rust, Suzanna and West, Lucy (2004) *Bad News From Israel*, London: Pluto.

Rose, Gillian (2001) *Visual Methodologies*, London: Sage.

Stephens, Michael (2005) 'Safe danger & virtual slumming: gangsta rap, *Grand Theft Auto* & ghetto tourism' www.Popmatters.com 17 June.

Williams, Raymond [1958] (1988) 'Culture is ordinary', in *Resources of Hope: Culture, Democracy, Socialism*, London and New York: Verso.

Williams, Raymond (1974) (2nd edition 1990) *Television: Technology and Cultural Form*, London: Fontana.

Further reading

Bignell, Jonathan (2004) *An Introduction to Television Studies*, London and New York: Routledge.

Billig, Michael (1993) *Speaking of the Royal Family*, London: Sage.

Stafford, Roy (2003) *Audiences – An Introduction*, London: BFI.

www.mediawatch-uk.org

CASE STUDY: SELLING AUDIENCES

Academic research is a tiny body of work compared to advertising and marketing research. Remember, as you study contemporary advertising and its relation to audiences:

- The effects model of readers' engagement with the media is alive and well here. Whatever the playfulness and irony within the ads, advertising agencies try to persuade companies using them that they affect customers' buying habits. In an important sense they set out to *sell* audiences (sometimes called 'eyeballs') or at least 'audience attention'.

You, dear reader, are a target: most readers of this book probably fall into the 'young millennials demographic' (13–24 age bracket in 2005).

- Yet contemporary marketing talk sounds innocent of any desire to affect people. Terms such as 'level playing field', 'the market', 'the discriminating consumer' all attribute power to the picking and choosing customer (as theorised in the uses and gratifications model). This is surprising, given the time spent on researching the audiences to be 'targeted' in different national 'territories'.
- Whatever the arguments about the effects on our buying habits, the very act of targeting particular groups helps to create and consolidate them.

For example, the previously unknown concept of 'the teenager', for example, was, by the late 1950s, an accepted part of advertising (and political) rhetoric. It helped to create a new identity for people in a certain age range with growing spending powers.

It has also been argued that 'the New Man' of the 1980s was largely a creation of advertisers, eager to persuade men to buy a range of new consumer goods in areas such as body care which had traditionally been seen as women's concerns.

And it is now said that children are a group invited to feel increasingly assertive about their 'pester power' over parents, who technically have money power. (See Schor 2004 on the spending power of the 4–12 age group, risen in the US from $6.1 billion in 1989 to $30 billion in 2002 – a 400 per cent increase. Children are also calculated to influence $330 billion of adult purchasing).

ACTIVITY 8.8

- How would you define when your 'childhood' began and ended?
- Was it partly related to your power to buy things?
- Were you aware of the term 'pester power' when younger?
- How did the media that you used construct 'childhood' for you and your friends?

Advertising agencies and their sources

Ad agencies exist to devise, produce and place ads and other marketing activities for their clients, the manufacturers of (often branded) products. They are usually divided into departments specialising in ad/brand design (the 'creative' team); those buying 'suitable' spaces on television etc. (media buyers); and those who oversee the operation (account managers).

Advertisers in newspapers and magazines still use scales culled from the NRS or National Readership Surveys, originally designed to investigate magazine and newspaper sales distribution. The NRS scale currently divides audiences according to the 'Chief Income Earner' (CIE) in a household (see Figure 8.4).

Though such indicators of social class are important, several objections have been made to the occupation-based surveys of readerships:

- The NRS questions rely on the occupation of the 'CIE'. But in many households the income is made up of part-time work by both partners.
- They see the family as a single consuming unit, without generational or life-stage distinctions and conflicts.

NRS Population Estimates by Social Grade
January–December 2004

Grade	Adults 000's	%
A	1,594	3
B	10,188	22
C1	13,757	29
C2	9,923	21
D	7,636	16
E	4,165	9
	47,263	100

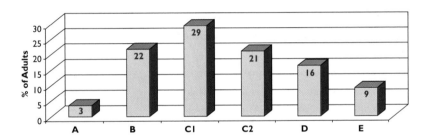

Definitions

Adults
For the purposes of the Survey, 'Adults' are defined as all individuals aged 15 or more living on mainland Great Britain. The Survey does not cover N. Ireland. Over the period January–December 2004, the estimates published by the Survey relate to a total adult population of 47,263,000 individuals.

Social Grade
Social Grade as defined by the Survey is determined by the occupation of the Chief Income Earner (CIE) in each household. A brief description of the grades used in the Survey is as follows:

Grade	Social Status	CIE's Occupation
A	Upper Middle Class	Higher managerial, administrative or professional
B	Middle Class	Intermediate managerial, administrative or professional
C1	Lower Middle Class	Supervisory or clerical and junior managerial, administrative or professional
C2	Skilled Working Class	Skilled manual workers
D	Working Class	Semi and unskilled manual workers
E	Those at the lowest levels of subsistence	State pensioners or widows (no other earner), casual or lowest grade workers

Figure 8.4 Summary of the NRS or National Readership Surveys. You can explore them further on http://www.nmauk.co.uk/nma/do/live/factsAndFiguresNRSFAQ#m5.

- They underestimate the ways in which a 'flexible labour market' has brought about rapid changes of occupation, and kinds of work that no longer smoothly fit the groups used.
- A rarely made objection is that the chart leaves out big landowners, aristocrats and others of the top 1 per cent of the population (which owned 23 per cent of Britain's wealth in 2002). See www.statistics.gov.uk for the latest figures.

> '40% of the population no longer has a job that fits the system at all' (*Guardian*, 17 July 1995, report on the government's decision to change the way class is measured by the Office of Population Censuses and Surveys).

From the 1970s onwards agencies also began to use new categories, aimed at specific audience groups, by means of demographics which 'measured the population in terms of occupational class, age, sex and region to read off certain values and assumptions about spending' (Brierley 2002). These often divide potential buyers by geographical location, using postcodes or national census returns (as with ACORN or A Classification of Residential Neighbourhoods).

> 'Billy Piper's Rose initially mistook their first assault as part of a rag-week stunt: "To get that many people dressed up and being silly, they must be students," she said, a nice nudge to the programme's core demographic' (Thomas Sutcliffe, *The Independent*, 28 March 2005, reviewing *Dr Who*).

Psychographic profiles are another, very different approach to occupational and geographical models.

They use questionnaires mailed to members of a panel who are invited to respond to statements such as: 'A woman's place is in the home' or 'The use of cannabis should be made legal'. On the basis of such exchanges consumers have been classified as belonging to a number of lifestyle categories – a typical model for these would be the American VALS (Values and Lifestyles) system which classifies people into: needs-driven, outer-directed, inner-directed and integrated.

Agencies may also research consumers' feelings about a product by using **focus groups** comprising a few selected consumers who are presented with an issue to work on by loosely ranging talk, or asked about the image a particular product has for them, again in a freely associational way.

Nevertheless, the fragmentation of most media forms and therefore advertising outlets, as well as audiences' use of remote controls, video, the internet, mean that audiences' habits have become much less easy to predict. This is regardless of how skilled an agency's media buyers are about the most effective medium, and the best vehicle in that medium, for a specific campaign.

> The **internet** is being used by advertisers, and not only via the ads and spam on many websites and links.
> 1 'Cookies', or small files which collect information about what users do when they visit websites, can give some picture of that user – as a potential consumer. They are valuable not simply for market research purposes but also for targeting users with ads and offers (see www.cookiecentral.com).
> 2 Bloggers and fans are targeted by all the major cinema studios. These have departments devoted to this sector, which are especially interested in 'bloggers' who are also 'young millennials' aged 13–24, said to be tuning out

of traditional media and into iPods, smart phones, etc.

According to Intelliseek's data, more than 5 per cent of all blog conversations discuss or reference movies. A lone blogger shares his admiration for Orlando Bloom and posts his thoughts. Others, searching for Orlando Bloom references, are sent a link to the blog, which links to the film site. In essence, the fan can be doing the marketing for Fox. However, this is not without problems: millions of blogs, in hundreds of languages, means the company can't always understand what is going on.

(summarised from *Screen International*, 13 May 2005, p. 12)

Television and advertising

Most commercial or 'independent' television has been traditionally funded through the sale of advertising space by the television companies. This is often described as 'selling audiences to advertisers'. Actually it is audiences' attention that advertisers hope to purchase, and British regulations permit on average only seven minutes of advertising per hour, so the commodity is a limited one.

A major funding system for television is still that of buying and selling ad time, the opposite of the notion of non-commercial public service still at work, though not exclusively, within the BBC. It began in the US during the 1930s Depression, with radio the perfect medium for advertisers wanting access to audiences confined to the home. The huge success of soap company-funded serials (soaps) soon went along with a construction (and simultaneous selling) of housewives' attention during the day and in the evening of men still in employment and some children.

Scheduling took off, closely related to the ratings or estimated audience numbers for programmes. John Corner defines scheduling as a strategy within television institutions which tries to 'identify particular

Ratings-consciousness does not apply only to commercial broadcasting. The BBC needs to justify the licence fee, and an important marker of such success is judged to be how many people are watching or listening to its programmes. Hence ratings and scheduling battles exist even where actual sales of audiences' attention are not involved.

times of the day and particular sequences of programming in order to obtain either specific kinds of audiences or the broadest possible audience, and to obtain the best audience responses' (Corner 1991: 13). The choice of where and when to place a programme on radio or television is usually made with a competitor's programming in mind. The classic, most notorious example was the death of Grace Archer in the then phenomenally popular radio soap *The Archers*, timed to coincide with, and draw publicity away from, the 1955 launch of ITV in London. But broadcasters have traditionally worked with ideas such as prime time, the period from around 7.30 p.m. to 10.30 p.m., when large audiences are watching (though more recently the younger, hipper audiences presumed to be available after pub closing times have accounted for the later placement of *Big Brother* or *The Mark Thomas Comedy Hour*).

Commercial television and radio programmes are now routinely made to attract audiences in order that advertisers can buy time or 'slots' (and more recently sponsorship deals) to catch their attention. Sometimes a guaranteed-numbers audience will be 'purchased' (measured in CPTs or Cost Per Thousand), spread across a number of slots. Cost depends on the time of day, year (Easter and November/first two weeks of December are especially expensive), the number of other products in the same field, and the TVR, which signifies the TV rating, or percentage of a particular audience that has seen a commercial break. Costs are further refined by region and target audience (housewives, men, children, etc.).

Price differences

Below are example costs for advertising on the ITV1 Network and the ITV1 regions. All costs are based on 30" commercials.[22]

Region	11.00 2.5 TVR's e.g. Trisha	18.15 7 TVR's e.g. Local News	Centre break 26 TVR's Coronation St	21.20 14 TVR's e.g. ITV Drama	300 TVR campaign based on average delivery
Anglia	£697	£1,952	£7,251	£3,904	£83,666
Border	£50	£140	£519	£279	£5,985
Central	£1,342	£3,758	£13,959	£7,516	£161,067
Granada	£664	£1,860	£6,907	£3,719	£79,700
London (LWT and Weekday London)	£2,844	£7,962	£29,575	£15,925	£341,247
Meridian	£1,054	£2,951	£10,961	£5,902	£126,471
Scottish and Grampian	£438	£1,227	£4,557	£2,454	£52,584
Tyne Tees	£266	£745	£2,766	£1,490	£31,920
Ulster	£190	£533	£1,979	£1,066	£22,833
Wales and West	£459	£1,284	£4,771	£2,569	£55,045
Westcountry	£178	£497	£1,846	£994	£21,306
Yorkshire	£506	£1,417	£5,262	£2,833	£60,714
Total ITV1	**£7,974**	**£22,328**	**£82,932**	**£44,656**	**£956,912**

22 Source: BARB DDS, ITV Estimates, average spot costs.

Figure 8.5 ITV plc chart of average costs. See www.itvplc.com.

Schedulers have traditionally used the following terms:

- pre-scheduling Starting a programme just before its rival programme on the other channel.
- inheritance factor Some audiences seem to 'trust' and watch one channel for most of the evening, so programmes of lesser appeal are put on after popular ones, in the hope that the audience will continue watching . . .
- pre-echo Audiences watch part of the programme before the one they want so as not to miss the beginning. This is used to try to build up an audience for the less popular programmes, and a voice-over advertising upcoming programmes on the same channel now regularly accompanies end credits.
- common junction points Where two programmes start at the same time on BBC1 and 2, for example, the chance for cross-trailing arises: 'And now a choice of viewing on BBC.'

ACTIVITY 8.9

Watch a few hours of television on BBC or ITV at the weekend.

- What scheduling decisions seem to have been made?
- Which programmes are pitched 'against' each other within terrestrial broadcasting?
- How do the programmes connect to the ads being shown during them?
- About how much time is spent per hour on advertising forthcoming programmes on the channel you are watching?
- How soon into the credits of programmes is the voice 'trailing' the next few items? Do you find this annoying?

Huge amounts of money, time and energy are invested in audience measurement, as competition for audiences intensifies between the television networks, the cable companies and indeed other media. This emphasis began in 1955 with the advent of

ITV. 'Advertisers were terrified that people would not stay with the commercial break . . . the frequent, nervy measurement of audience totals began at this moment' (Beckett 2001). Now the main audience assessment for BBC and ITV is conducted by BARB (British Audience Research Bureau, www.BARB.co.uk), set up in 1981 to clarify the competing claims of BBC and ITV for the biggest audiences. Until then the BBC had also used an 'Appreciation Index' (AI) of comments on programmes, sent in periodically by selected viewers, which were then circulated privately. (A version of this process continues today for radio and TV – see BBC Press Releases.)

BARB is a limited company, jointly owned by the BBC, ITV, Channel 4, Channel Five, BSkyB and the IPA (Institute of Practitioners in Advertising). It operates a helpful website, but its full data are available only to BARB subscribers, who pay a £3,850 (2005) annual registration fee and an annual subscription which depends on the subscriber's business. The company subcontracts every stage of the ratings-gathering process to other companies (see Beckett 2001). It compiles 'ratings' of programmes, suggesting how many, and what kinds of, viewers are watching them from a sample taken in 5,100 homes which they calculate to involve 11,500 viewers. These crude but 'fast' numbers are the main way in which audience appreciation of programmes is measured. They can be measured on a minute-by-minute basis, collected and digested overnight, and distributed at TV company meetings the next morning to allow easy comparisons to be made with rivals' ratings.

These ratings are made by recording the viewing habits of a sample of viewers from the 11,500 maximum available. (The size varies depending on how much the television company will spend.) Machines called People Meters (or 'black boxes') are attached to these viewers' television sets, and record, every five seconds, which channel the set is tuned to and which members of the household are watching. In addition the amount of VCR recording is measured and incorporated within seven days, as is the playback of broadcast programmes which carry an electronic code, and of 'non-coded', bought or hired videos, in an attempt to chart audiences who are now partly freed from the schedules.

'last week . . . the advertising agency Lowe Howard-Spink Lowe . . . found that at least one third of the audience "vigorously and continuously" tries to escape television commercials . . . the most zealous practitioners of this "ad avoidance" are that most desirable group, "young and early middle-aged fully employed males"' (*Observer*, 21 May 1995).

This is now routinely enabled, e.g. with Sky channel digibox technology which can 'cut out' the ad breaks.

Recent changes

However, British broadcasting has been fragmented, first by video (allowing viewers to 'reschedule' programmes), then by the arrival of Channel 4, and later by cable, satellite, digital and broadband forms of broadcasting and 'rescheduled' recordings. In fact it has become increasingly difficult to register the small numbers of viewers for some channels.

In August 2004 Ofcom identified 2003 as a crossover year when, for the first time, subscription (dominated by BSkyB) pulled in more money for TV than advertising. But 'ancillary' was said to be the fastest-growing source of funding – meaning sponsorship, and premium rate phone calls such as those to *Big Brother* or tele-shopping channels. In prime time 70 per cent of ITV's output will be sponsored, said its head of sponsorship and branded content in 2004 (*Guardian*, August 16 2004). In summer 2005 Channel 4 was said to be considering a quiz programme based entirely on phone-ins.

Sponsorship has only occurred in British TV since the 1990 Broadcasting Act. It was deliberately not chosen as the main funding mechanism in the

Television Act (1954), which established commercial television. It is seen as a way of catching the zapping viewer with a sponsor's credit rather than (or as well as) ads during programmes, as in Vizzavi mobile phone company's sponsorship of *Pop Idol* (2002): 'Your brand is closer to the programme . . . a message before other advertising cuts in . . . It . . . allows the advertiser to build a closer relationship with a consumer . . . it's like saying "We know what you're into and we support it too"' (*Observer*, 8 January 1995).

It is not the case, if it ever was, that advertising simply seeks to reach the largest possible audience. At both national and global level, regional differences are carefully studied and 'pitched' to. Products are test-marketed in particular areas, for example, and some magazines produce London supplements to try to catch the attention of a concentrated and relatively affluent young audience.

However, among all this 'diversity' and current uncertainties, some assumptions remain in place. Because all British broadcasting is partly public service-regulated, both ITV and BBC have worked with the regulated Family Viewing Policy (FVP) which, drawing on effects approaches, has responded to lobbying groups such as the NVLA (National Viewers' and Listeners' Association). The FVP constructs profiles of audience availability and type, and then an image of family life from which it prescribes what should be viewable at particular times:

- 16.15 to 17.15 on weekdays is 'children's hour'.
- 17.15 to 19.30 is presumed to be family viewing time, but with all material broadcast suitable for children to view alone.
- 19.30 to 21.00 is when no material unsuitable for children viewing with the family is broadcast.
- 21.00 onwards: it is assumed that parents are responsible for any children who may still be watching.

This relates to the so-called 'nine o'clock watershed', a barrier to certain kinds of language and violent or sexual imagery. Interestingly, it does not exist for radio broadcasting. (Currently the audience survey board

for radio is called RAJAR (Radio Joint Audience Research, www.rajar.co.uk, owned jointly by the BBC and commercial radio stations.) Nor does it yet apply to junk food and other kinds of arguably unsafe advertising.

ACTIVITY 8.10

Keep a week's diary of your family's viewing policy and see how it corresponds to the official one. How are such practices affected by:

- TV in children's bedrooms?
- mobile phone technology, time spent texting, etc.?

Summary

There is now much emphasis on the difficulty of scheduling – indeed some are using the term 'crisis' of the funding of TV. Video, cable, digital, internet and other multi-channel developments, as well as 'zapping' and the fragmentation of older 'certainties' such as family structure, all make it seem a more volatile process than previously. At the same time huge amounts of money hang on somehow getting a sense of what audiences are up to.

Huge gambles are still taken, such as spending £1 million per episode on the 'new' *Dr Who* series in 2005 and releasing it on a Saturday evening. The success of this attempt to recreate the 'family viewing experience' surprised everyone. (See pp. 136–7.)

Our two main approaches – 'effects' and 'uses and gratifications' – can be seen at work in debates around this new 'ecology of broadcasting'. It's often said that viewers are completely unpredictable, too busy 'surfing' the networks, 'grazing' across channels to be drawn in by ads or measured by ratings. The active consumer is alive and well in this discourse. Yet huge amounts of advertising and sponsorship money are still spent trying to attract the attention of various audience segments, and, also, simply to establish 'brand' credibility through sheer frequency of mention (see Chapter 9). This has several results:

- Programme-makers and advertisers still battle for 'good' slots, i.e. regular ones and ones within prime time. Programmes (such as the controversial US sitcom *Ellen*) can be effectively stopped, not at the production level but by constantly moving them around the schedules so that viewers can't find them. This acts as a kind of censoring activity.

- Effective schedulers are still highly sought after within television and radio. Witness the careers and salaries of people such as Michael Grade, renowned for his scheduling skills.

- In both Britain and the US key episodes of hit dramas and comedies are not videotaped but watched as they go out. It seems that the idea of a communal viewing experience is not completely dead, though audiences for these rare moments are smaller than for similar events in the past.

- Some audiences do 'graze', at certain times of the day, but most need to have fixed viewing or listening slots in their routines which schedulers are keen to discover and to target.

Q Do you have any such slots?

In such a volatile TV ad-funding situation the reliance on simple 'blackbox' methods for measuring ratings such as BARB's is understandable. Yet the problems of such reliance on these methods remain:

- Ratings figures are not transparent in their meanings. High ratings for various programmes may be due to curiosity, the weather, the fact that there was little on other channels. As audiences get smaller these inconsistencies become more apparent, though hard to track.

- Like the use of 'testcards' for panels viewing new

Hollywood releases, the emphasis on ratings often means that the unfamiliar, the new, is not given time to take root but too quickly shifted from that prime 9 p.m. or 10 p.m. slot. Yet the success of a channel depends on innovation as well as stabilities.

- Ratings-derived advertising funding also plays havoc with one of the original arguments for the British adaptation of US commercial television: that the ITV system would be made up of regionally based companies serving and sustaining local identities. In fact only rarely does a 'regional' programme get on to prime-time commercial television.

Moreover, the regional nature of commercial television allows additional advertising pressure to

Regions

Regional overlap area

Figure 8.6 Geographical identities in relation to consumer power for advertisers in the 'regions' of commercially funded television. Check the borders of your own *geographical* region (e.g. 'Wales', 'Midlands') against where it figures in *this* map. Parts of the wealthier South West, for example, are included in 'Wales and the West' in order to attract advertisers.

be applied in any region where sales are slumping. Overall, advertisers have disturbing amounts of power to shape broadcasting by niche marketing, encouraging the making of certain television genres and constructing others as unprofitable or even undesirable. Worryingly, it has been suggested that advertisers sometimes prefer programmes that are not too involving and so do not detract from attention to the ads (Curran and Seaton 1997: 223).

Finally, it is worth remembering, in debates led by the press about deregulation or the selling off of the BBC etc., that the press also lives largely by advertising revenue. The position taken by particular newspapers on television controversies exists in relation to contradictory drives, as well as to the political sympathies of those who own and control those industries:

- Deregulation: How far would the extension of television advertising (for example, if the BBC were to be completely commercialised) undercut newspaper advertising revenues by bringing down costs and widening the pool of media available to advertisers?
- Ownership: Who owns the paper which is arguing against the BBC? Is it Rupert Murdoch's News Corporation, which owns a large share of the British press and broadcasting and has a particular interest in acquiring more?

The regional or 'local' press is the largest print advertising medium in the UK, taking nearly £3 billion a year. According to the Advertising Association, in 2004 'adspend' in the regional press grew by 6.0 per cent to £3.165 billion, in line with UK 'adspend' which also grew by 6.0 per cent. Regional press is the only medium to have increased advertising expenditure every year for the last thirteen years.

(*Advertising Association Advance Yearbook Data 2005* on www.newspapersoc.org.uk)

How appropriate/representative is it that newspapers with circulation of a few hundred thousand accuse television programmes of attracting 'only' four or five million viewers?

the rightwing press that prepared the way for Thatcher's deregulation of television in the '80s [argued] that one of the objections to the licence fee was its expense. Yet people are now paying around £1,000 a season (nine or more licence fees) . . . to see all the football matches they want from various non-terrestrial channels.

(Lawson 2001)

ACTIVITY 8.11

Research the comparative costs of the licence fee and TV sports channel subscriptions now.

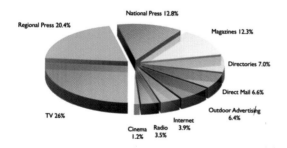

Figure 8.7 A pie chart showing the share which different media took in advertising spending in 2004.

References

Beckett, Andy (2001) 'Numbers game', *Guardian*, 20 November.

Brierley, Sean (2002) 'Advertising and marketing: advertising and the new media environment', in

Adam Briggs and Paul Cobley (eds) *The Media: An Introduction*, 2nd edition, Harlow: Longman.

Corner, John (1991) *Popular Television in Britain: Studies in Cultural History*, London: BFI.

Curran, James and Seaton, Jean (1997) *Power without Responsibility: The Press and Broadcasting in Britain*, London: Routledge.

Lawson, Mark (2001) 'What's on?', *Guardian*, 19 November.

Schor, Juliet (2004) *Born to Buy: The Commercialised Child and the New Consumer Culture*, New York: Scribner.

Further reading

Brierley, Sean (2002) *The Advertising Handbook*, 2nd edition, London and New York: Routledge.

National Consumer Council (2005) *The Shopping Generation*, comments on www.ncc.org.uk.

Names of useful journals are given in the Useful Information section. You might also try approaching an ad agency and asking for a back copy of *BRAD* (*British Rates and Data*), which will give you the current rate in every UK publication, including broadcasting. Maybe your school or college has a staff member responsible for publicity who can lend you one.

Websites

For next day ratings see MediaGuardian.co.uk/overnights.

9 Advertising and branding

- **Advertising: debates and histories**
- **Marketing and branding: histories and debates**
- **The influence of 'commercial culture'**

- **References**
- **Further reading**

To advertise originally meant 'to draw attention to something', often by word of mouth. It is now the media form we most often encounter, most of the time. It seeks to stimulate demand for products in an often hugely crowded 'marketplace', and to appeal to those who, globally speaking, already have lots of possessions. It funds most of the world's media, directly or indirectly; it's glimpsed on billboards, on the sides of buses, on internet and mobile phone screens, as 'spam' email and so on. We, the consumers, through the cost of the goods we buy, fund all this, of course.

Advertising is arguably the most powerful and pervasive form of propaganda in the history of the planet. Try to avoid all advertising for a single day and you will probably have stayed in bed with all screens and radios turned off.

Figure 9.1 Sponsorship deals now often demand a huge, unavoidable slice of all the images of some great achievements.

Advertising: debates and histories

Don Slater has defined advertising's function, along with marketing (which tries to identify the market for a product), as 'the cultural redefinition of goods'. Along with capacities to distribute and price goods (an area where big corporations clearly have advantage) it is a key means of shaping markets and competitive relations between companies (Slater 1997: 45).

Yet advertisers are aware of audiences' knowledge of their tricks and strategies, and they now make endless, self-reflexive play with them, with amusing, enjoyable and often stunning-looking results. Some media theorists emphasise the 'freedom' of readers of ads to interpret them as they choose or to simply ignore them. Other approaches stress the broader power of brand advertising, the corporate distribution and pricing power that makes brands globally prevalent, helping to shape our deepest imaginings, anxieties and appetites.

The South African company De Beers sought in 1947 to redefine diamonds, saying they would 'make diamonds a cultural imperative in a woman's life'. Their advertising continues to try to redefine these small rocks in this way.

Figure 9.2 Even the grand Venice Film Festival, 2004, had to discreetly acknowledge its commercial sponsors.

ACTIVITY 9.1

- How many forms of advertising have you encountered this week?
- Jot down where you encountered them.
- Have you ever advertised? Where: 'free', student or other local paper? The internet? Postcards in a shop window?

By contrast to branded advertising:

- What is the smallest ad you've ever seen? What was it trying to communicate, and to whom?

Advertising has drawn the attention of generations of analysts. Often students are fascinated by tales of '**subliminal ads**' as evidence of the sheer power of this media form. But the major objections to advertising have included the following:

> **Subliminal**: imperceptible but powerful. Used (of) messages inserted into advertising and other media messages. Said to have measurable effects on behaviour in 'bypassing' the 'conscious' brain. The theory is now discredited, though still circulates among conspiracy theorists, and stories of 'backward messages' in rock and roll songs, or frames included in ads and political broadcasts, have persisted. See www.wikipedia.org.

- It brainwashes its audience, not with subliminal ads but with base, deceptive promises and appeals, designed to promote consumerist materialism, waste, hedonism (pleasure seeking) and envy.
- It defends itself by arguing that it helps us to be 'rational consumers'. Yet even if this meant assessing all the claims of all the kinds of any one product, say shampoo, that are available – with over four hundred kinds of shampoo at the last count, it would take more time than most people ever have.
- Related to such over-production of certain goods, advertising is part of the built-in drive to '**planned obsolescence**' and high consumption on which modern capitalism depends and which, in the fairly near future, may have catastrophic environmental results.
- It acts as an unnecessary business expense, which adds significantly to the costs of goods for customers. Large monopolies such as Procter & Gamble spend millions advertising products (such as soap powders) that compete with those of their own subsidiaries.
- For all its 'free market' claims, it in fact produces barriers to competition. Young companies cannot afford the expenditure needed to break into markets via the costly work of creating 'brands'. These allow big corporations to 'shout louder' and go along with their goods being highly distributed in crowded markets. (This argument is applied to Hollywood films in the case study.)
- Its use of glamorous body images, 'scripts', etc. leads to huge degrees of conformity, especially around already powerful identities involving the 'approved versions' of appearance, gendered behaviour, and how differences of class, ethnicity, disability and age are imagined.

Advertising can arguably be found as far back as Greek and Roman public criers, shouting the wares of local traders. But its recognisable

The Man in the White Suit (UK 1951) centres on a character who invents a cloth that never gets dirty and won't wear out. Laundry workers and textile workers attack him as anti-social. The comic structure of the film 'saves' him when the cloth disintegrates after only a few days – but not before further social and economic upheavals. Worth a look for comparisons with current debates.

A market, in business terms, is the total of all the potential sellers and buyers for a particular product (and the number of products likely to be exchanged).

modern form appears with the nineteenth-century industrial revolution, the over-production of goods for existing western markets through new manufacturing techniques, and then the drive to expand markets as part of global imperialist conquest. In the 1850s in Britain, the Prime Minister Gladstone removed regulations and taxes on advertising. Manufacturers were soon able to appeal to consumers over the heads of retailers, through the young media industries. In the US, potential customers began to be educated (informally, by advertising) into the possibilities and attractions of consumption.

For many years ads were described as though they operated in trivial and irrational ways, and as though that was why they had a 'brainwashing' effect – on females. 'Femininity' is often constructed as being irrational and bound up with consumption (shopping, fashion and the domestic sphere), not production or 'serious', i.e. paid, work outside the home. But the influence of advertising cannot be understood outside other powerful contexts'.

> The year 1916 saw the launch of the automatic washing machine and the opening of Clarence Saunders Piggly Wiggly store in Memphis, the first grocery outlet to allow shoppers to browse the shelves themselves rather than have a clerk make up their order. A new imaginative landscape was being assembled in which domestic drudgery would be abolished and personal choice extended. The home would cease to be the focus of continual worry about making ends meet and become an arena of self expression and social display. The labour of maintaining basic living standards would give way to the pleasures of constructing lifestyles. The task of selling this vision of personal liberation was delegated to the emerging advertising industry. The swelling ranks of copywriters and image engineers were changed with maintaining the mass demand needed to keep the new system of mass production running at full tilt.
>
> (Murdock 2004)

Real gains and freedoms for women were represented by many new products. These saved hard, repetitive labour in the home, and also offered the pleasures of the new shops where they were sold – safe and pleasant public spaces for women who were otherwise often largely confined to the home. In cities, goods were displayed, usually at fixed prices, in large, attractively laid-out department stores in safe shopping districts ('factories for selling' in Rachel Bowlby's (2000) words; see also Pumphrey 1984). The attractions were like those of early picture palaces: attention paid to opulent visual display and comfort, with rest rooms, restaurants and polite service – a rare treat for many working-class people.

> Campaigning politics have also been conducted within 'consumption'.
> The suffrage movement (for votes for women) as well as the anti-slavery
> movement sometimes organised consumer boycotts and made their own
> plates, mugs, etc. with appropriate colours (green, purple and white for
> suffrage) or slogans. Selfridges decorated its shop window in these colours
> for a time.

ACTIVITY 9.2

Q Are there any parallels between these nineteenth-century attractions of
shopping and modern malls?

Q Do malls work as 'safe' public spaces? Did your local mall experience the panic
around 'hoodies' of 2005?

Most cinemas are now placed in malls, rather than being 'stand-alone' as previously.

Q How does this affect your experience of film going? Does it make it a more
'special' occasion?

    Where is your nearest shopping mall/cinema? Does it contain outlets for
goods connected with films?

Q Does the mall cinema work as a little 'Utopian' space – the colours, the
abundance of sweets, huge packets of popcorn, cleanliness, polite service, etc.?

(Generally most multiplex cinema income is generated by confectionery sales
rather than tickets for films.)

In step with these developments, by the end of the 1920s US
advertisers, consciously or unconsciously, began to try to transform the
buying habits of shoppers or consumers (largely women). The success of
the US government's **propaganda** during the First World War convinced
advertisers that they too could use social psychology or **behaviourism,**
the name given to research into human motivation and ways of associating
(see Packard 1979 and also Adam Curtis's 2002 BBC TV series, exploring
the connections to the Freud dynasty in the roots of advertising's emphasis
on self-gratification).

Lifestyle advertising developed. This went beyond a simple outline of a
product's uses towards encouraging potential buyers to associate it with
a whole desirable style of life, and to feel that not owning the product

might lead to personal failure, unpopularity, etc. Along with this, fashion and the need to keep up with fashion through consuming goods was newly emphasised. This was done partly through the glamour of Hollywood movies, their stars and their product placements (see below). But also key was the manufacturers' adoption of planned obsolescence for certain products, such as cars (see Packard 1979) which could otherwise easily be made to last a consumer's lifetime.

In the 1920s the positive connotations which fashion gave to change, novelty and youthfulness undermined traditional attitudes, which endorsed 'thrift, self-sufficiency, home cooking, family entertainment, hand-made and hand-me-down clothes' (Pumphrey 1984). These older attitudes were often oppressive for women, generally the ones expected to do the 'making' and the 'handing down'. The liberating roles of both advertising and the mass consumption of labour-saving goods and ready-made food have been hailed by theorists of consumption.

Advertising in the 1920s (and since) has used *two* major figures for women. The first is that of the independent, unmarried woman (called a '*flapper*' in the 1920s) which offered a challenge to nineteenth-century constructions of femininity on the level of style, image and consumption (rather than in other areas such as political struggles for the vote or equal pay). The second model is the more traditional, though equally constructed, figure of 'the housewife', invited to feel she had sole responsibility for keeping the home and its inhabitants clean and the meals on the table at the right times. Interestingly, this figure too was (and continues to be) set up as 'modern'. Ads, even those encouraging the most paranoid levels of anxiety about 'germs' and 'dirt' in the home, in many ways did not seem to treat their addressees patronisingly. 'The Housewife' was constructed as having a *serious* responsibility (keeping the home clean and safe) and as *democratically* joining 'hundreds of thousands of American women' said to have benefited from this or that product. She was encouraged to think of herself as both a private *and* a public figure, one who was being offered the opportunity to take advantage of modern devices – in other words to be connected with technological and social advances.

Some computer inkjet printers will now stop working after printing a set number of pages – even if they could potentially print many more. Does this 'forced obsolescence' feature in their advertising? (*Guardian*, 19 May 2005).

'Dirt is matter out of place' (Mary Douglas (1996), *Purity and Danger: An Analysis of the Concepts of Pollution and Taboo*, London: Ark).

Other products are also sold via democratic claims. The website www.shootingindustry.com claims that 'America's fascination with handguns began a few hundred years ago . . . when Sam Colt [inventor of the Colt 45 handgun] truly "made all men equal".'

'The irony is that, as technology has improved, so that it is easier to wash, we insist on washing everything far too often. The increasing number of cases of asthma, allergic reactions . . . may be one side effect of removing all "dirt" from our lives' (Suzanne Moore, *New Statesman*, 13 August 2001, p. 28).

Figure 9.3 Parodying brand advertising: from the Adbusters website www.adbusters.org.

See both versions of *The Stepford Wives* (US 2004) (US 1975) or the series *Desperate Housewives* (US 2004–) for contemporary ways of handling the questions raised by the still powerful image of 'the perfect housewife'. Do some adverts also play with this ideal?

But it is important to hang on to a more critical view of the role of advertising even as we register the reasonable grounds for the appeal of many products. As with the 'flapper', there are gaps in this image. Why should such labour-saving devices actually mean more work for women, via the much higher standards of cleanliness expected of them? If women's work in the home was so important, why was it not counted or paid as work? Why could not men, or older children, share involvement with this work in the family?

For both these mythical figures, advertisers constructed a kind of *self-surveillance* in which women were repeatedly invited to take part, asking questions about how clean, how safe was their bathroom, kitchen, cutlery or toilet, and how appealing was their hair, skin, figure or personal aroma.

ACTIVITY 9.3

Look through television ads during programmes which seem scheduled to attract female audiences (e.g. morning or afternoon television).
- Do you think self-surveillance is still invited? How can you tell?
- How does the camera position viewers in relation to the women in the ads?
- Are there any ads addressing men in ways that encourage self-surveillance?
- How are they similar to or different from those addressing women?
- What kinds of questions are women shown putting to themselves in ads for: cosmetics, clothes, household cleaners?

Spam and internet advertising

*Spam** is the practice of sending the same message (usually commercial) to thousands or even millions of people, electronically. By definition it is sent without the permission of the recipient. Though this lack of permission in fact applies to most advertising, the sending of spam is particularly intrusive (as you'll know if a message has ever stubbornly stayed on your screen when you're trying to work on something else). The cost of delivery, storage and processing is borne directly by the recipient, rather like junk mail with postage to be paid by the receiver. And message boxes easily overflow and become unusable.

Link spam is a specialised form which targets all the hyperlinks or other details of visitors to a site. Adding links that point to the spammer's website increases the page rankings for the site in the biggest search engine, Google. This works rather like **agenda** setting for news (see 'Case study: News', p. 194) and means the spammer's commercial site would be listed ahead of other sites for some Google searches, increasing the number of potential paying customers and visitors.

*The term 'spam' was derived from a 1970 *Monty Python* sketch, in which all conversation in a café is drowned out by a group of Vikings chanting the word 'spam' over and over. In May 2004, it was reported more than 80 per cent of all emails in the US were spam. See wikipedia for more.

Advertising is often represented as being incredibly smart, up to date, and savvy about the questions raised in the past by its critics. Yet older practices persist, and not only in the area of gender representations. Despite the ironic self-awareness and regulation of western advertising, many dangerous ads and marketing ploys are still used in the 'Third World' and Eastern Europe, as well as in poorer areas of the 'First World'.

Figure 9.4 Old-style, macho, no-health-warning cigarette ad, Mauritius, 1997. In the UK manufacturers are obliged to give considerable space on the packet to health warnings. But in addition to using unsafe advertising like this, BAT (British American Tobacco) is accused of smuggling cigarettes to poorer countries such as Vietnam. Kenneth Clarke, MP, is BAT deputy chairman and former Tory Health Secretary. He is paid £170,000 fee as a part-time director and head of Corporate Social Responsibility for BAT: an insight into the global power of tobacco money (see *Guardian*, 29 April 2005).

'Tobacco claims 4.9 million lives a year, and if the present consumption patterns continue, the number of deaths will increase to 10 million by the year 2020, 70% of which will occur in developing countries' (http://www.mb.com.ph/MAIN20 05053035828.html). Some protest groups refer to 'tobacco poisoning'.

Tobacco and alcohol companies, for example, are rushing to ensure that their brands are known in Eastern Europe and China before more regulated health restrictions are imposed. New mothers in 'developing'

'[In India] . . . television has brought the lifestyle of the urban middle class . . . to villages where women still collect cow dung to fuel their cooking fires. . . . Though [washing machines and fridges] have little practical use in a farm hamlet with no running water and only a few hours of electricity each night, they have become status symbols in one of the world's fastest growing consumer markets' (*Guardian*, 4 January 1995).

countries are often encouraged in hospital to begin the habit of buying expensive packeted baby food milk instead of learning, like some western women, the advantages of breast feeding as a cheaper and healthier practice – if the mother is well fed herself of course.

'With total [Eastern European] sales of 700 billion cigarettes a year . . . [many East European governments] following the entry of Western firms . . . weakened or revoked their tobacco-advertising laws. Consequently, cigarette marketing is aggressive and widespread. Once again, ads often portray a successful Western lifestyle. . . . The fact that the tobacco is "American blend" is often featured prominently on . . . packets' (Rob Cunningham (1996), 'Smoke and mirrors: the Canadian tobacco war' available on the IDRC website).

Marketing and branding: histories and debates

'McDonald's recently announced it would spend the summer of 2006 paying hip hop artists $5 each time they mentioned a Big Mac. . . . On an urban music chatroom . . . one fan wrote "Big Mc rhymes with heart attack, do you think they'd give me money for that?"' (Stephen Armstrong, 'I'm drinkin' it – they're payin' me for it', *Guardian*, 11 July 2005).

Marketing can be defined as the sum of the ways in which a product is positioned in its particular market. This includes areas related to distribution (many marketing courses start with the 'Four Ps: Product, Placement, Promotion and Price: see Myers 1999) and often, now, to the 'brand' image of the product or its owners.

Advertising or marketing agencies coordinate different kinds of activities, in competition with each other. **Public relations** or **PR** is a set of activities, involving the selling of persons or companies, using many of the same techniques as advertising – competitions, free offers – but also arranging incidents, 'spontaneous' happenings, the setting up of fan clubs, dates, even staged relationships to be reported by the media as news (see the career of publicist Max Clifford). All of these activities can overlap with those of the **advertising agencies** who make ads and manage campaigns, 'placing' or buying space for ads in particular media.

Branding associates certain meanings with products, which usually seek to establish something called a USP or Unique Selling Proposition. The economics of branding brings whole new dimensions to advertising. At the simplest level branding involves trying to persuade customers of a product's quality prior to purchase or experience by means of the reputation or image of the producing company. Coca-Cola, for example, the top global brand, worth nearly $70 billion in 2004, cites '400 brands in over 200 countries' on its website, and seeks to bind them together by the one trade-marked name, colour, font and shape.

USP: Unique Selling Proposition: the supposedly unique quality of products which advertisers seek to communicate to potential buyers. Their attempts occur in a world with many possible substitute products for big brands (e.g. the huge numbers of more or less equally efficient detergents, toilet rolls, razor blades, etc. – make your own list).

ACTIVITY 9.4

Global companies such as Coca-Cola and Pepsi have their own in-house divisions dedicated to product placement, including the influencing of scripts (see Wasko 2003). US television shows such as *Sex and the City* use blatant showcasing and naming of expensive shoes, clothes and other fashion items.

● Watch for product placement in the next movie or television programme you see. The link to http://www.brandchannel.com/brandcameo_films.asp may be useful.

● What do you think the product owners hoped to get from the placements?

By contrast, for the raunchy teenage comedy *American Pie 2* Universal had sensibly entered into a product placement deal for condoms. But they pulled out of an agreement to have TV commercials linking the film and condoms because at the last minute the MPAA [Motion Picture Association of America] would not allow condoms to feature in any ad that may be seen by general audiences (reported in *Guardian*, 1 August 2001).

Brand recognition: all you need to know about marketing in a few steps

You see a gorgeous guy at a party. You go up to him and say, 'I'm fantastic.' *That's direct marketing.*

You're at a party with a bunch of friends and see a gorgeous guy. One of your friends goes up to him and pointing at you says, 'She's fantastic.' *That's advertising.*

You see a gorgeous guy at a party. You go up to him and get his telephone number. The next day you call and say, 'Hi, I'm fantastic.' *That's telemarketing.*

You see a gorgeous guy. You get up and straighten your skirt; you walk up to him and hand him his drink. You offer him a lift, remind him of your name when he forgets it, tell him he's gorgeous and then say, 'By the way, I'm fantastic.' *That's public relations.*

You see a gorgeous guy. He walks up to you and says, 'I hear you're fantastic.' *That's brand recognition.*

It is now often argued that the versatility of modern capitalism means that individual products (e.g. a bar of chocolate or a pair of trainers) are not unique for very long: product specifications can easily be copied by rivals in a few days, and the difference between products anyway is often minimal. How many kinds of shampoo can there be? Brands, however

Interbrand is a company which annually ranks companies for their 'brand value', based on the percentage of their revenues that can be credited to their brand. This includes assessment of market leadership, stability and global reach. To qualify for the list the brand must have a value greater than £1 billion and derive a third of its earnings outside its home country. This excludes huge brands such as Visa, Wal-mart, CNN and Mars. See www.interbrand.com.

(e.g. Cadbury's, McDonald's), making a range of products, can be made to seem stable guarantees of 'quality' and sometimes indeed do provide that, though at some expense. The matter of reputation and perceived quality is crucial. Some firms have 'reputation management' sections, and there are a growing number of 'corporate social responsibility' experts, some of whom try to ensure that the rhetoric of the company's annual report is made to mean something.

Equally, though, 'anti-globalisation' protesters have sometimes shrewdly targeted such activities. The promises of brands like McDonald's in particular have been brilliantly explored by the film *Supersize Me* (US 2004) and the book *Fast Food Nation* (2001), as well as taken to court in the 'McLibel affair', brilliantly supported by internet campaigning: see http://www.spannerfilms.net/?lid=1316 and http://www.mcspotlight.org/.

Naomi Klein (2000) suggests that the current importance of brands goes back to the mid-1980s when management theorists began to argue that successful corporations must primarily produce brands, associated with a range of products, as opposed to pushing their actual, different products. The partial recession in the US in that decade went hand in hand with the startling success of new kinds of corporation: Microsoft and Nike, and later Tommy Hilfiger and Intel.

> These . . . made the bold claim that producing goods was only an incidental part of their operations, and that thanks to recent victories in trade liberalization and labor-law reform, they were able to have their products made for them by contractors, many of them overseas. What these [parent] companies produced primarily were not things, they said, but *images* of their products. Their real work lay not in manufacturing but in marketing.
>
> (Klein 2000: 4)

Others have summarised this as 'not value for money but values for money'. Klein points out that

> creating a brand calls for a completely different set of tools and materials [from creating products]. It requires an endless parade of brand extensions, continually renewed imagery for marketing, and most of all, fresh new spaces to disseminate the brand's idea of itself.
>
> (Klein 2000: 5)

A key moment came in 1988 when Philip Morris, the tobacco company, purchased Kraft for $12.6 billion – six times the valuation of the company. Philip Morris were willing to pay for the word/brand 'Kraft'. Great news for the ad world, which could now claim that advertising expenditure was a 'real' investment rather than an unnecessary 'frill' (see Klein 2000: 7–8).

Another key moment, however, has been '9/11' or more precisely, the massive military responses which the US government chose to make to it (since 9/11 itself provoked worldwide demonstrations of sympathy for the US, and many relatives of the dead asked for a legal, peaceful response to what was a criminal act). The US response to 9/11 involves what is called **COE** or **Country of Origin Effect**: consumers' awareness of the place of manufacture or ownership of a branded product, and purchases or boycotts related to that. It works both ways: slave-like conditions in the factories of suppliers in some countries have sparked huge protest campaigns, like the one against Nike. And the 2003 'shock and awe' attacks on Iraq seem to have damaged the shiny US-owned image of some top brands. Products such as Mecca Cola, Muslim Up and Qibla Cola, for example, were produced, trading directly in opposition to the US values which Coke was said to enshrine (see websites: www.qibla-cola.com, www.mecca-cola.com).

Joke circulating later, in 2002, when Philip Morris (a $15 billion tobacco giant) changed the name of Marlboro cigarettes to Altria: 'We've shortened the name so it doesn't make you cough when you ask for a packet.'

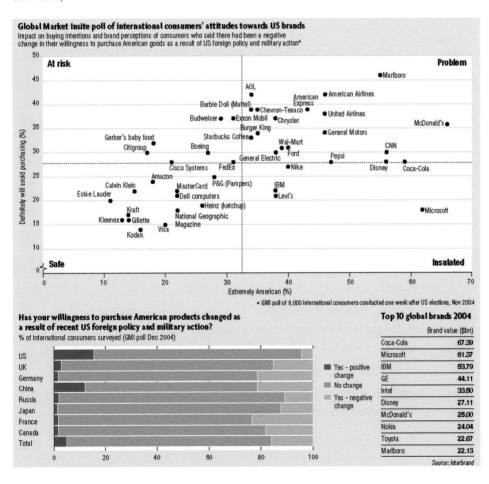

Figure 9.5

'Tarnished image: is the world falling out of love with US brands?' (*Financial Times*, 30 December 2004).

307

Coca-Cola returned to Iraq after an absence of nearly forty years in July 2005, triggering a Cola war in a lucrative but potentially hostile market, battling with Pepsi for 26 million customers.

The upsides for Coke include a thirst-inducing climate and burgeoning Islamic conservatism which has banned beer and other alcoholic drinks in much of the country. The downsides, besides Pepsi's head start, are a raging insurgency and banditry which threatens supply routes, and a perception that Coca-Cola is linked to Israel and 'American Zionists'. . . . The response in Baghdad was mixed . . . Abu Ream, a shop owner . . . repeated a widespread urban myth: 'If you hold up a Coke can to the mirror the writing says "No Allah", . . . or maybe "No Mohammad". I can't remember which. . . . Coca-Cola denies any political or religious bias. '. . . We are a local business that employs local people. . . . Our Palestinian bottler employs 250 Palestinian bottlers.'

('Cola wars as Coke moves on Baghdad', *Guardian*, 5 July 2005)

One final area of branding: the concept of synergy. This refers to:

- the combined marketing
- of 'products' or commodities (this includes people such as 'Britney Spears', or *The Lord of the Rings* DVD)
- across different media and other products (in music, toys, internet and television programmes, T-shirts, theme park rides and so on)
- which are often owned by the same corporation (such as Time Warner or Disney)
- such that the total effect is greater than the sum of the different parts.

Synergy has been around for some time. The 'escapism' of entertainment forms is often into worlds which turn out to have very recognisable products in them. Even fantasy forms, such as the James Bond films, have always blended conspicuous consumption, brand-name snobbery and product placement for certain luxury cars, champagnes and watches. But the strategy now is crucially linked to branding.

Virgin is a British example of 'brand extension': from stores to air travel to finance and railways – as well as of the dangers that one part of the brand's operations (railways, say) can affect the rest of its reputation.

Gary Lineker 'extended his brand' advertising crisps. See www.walkers.co.uk. How much fatty fast food like crisps did he eat in the training which produced his 'brand'?

See also the film *Supersize Me* (2003), *Jamie Oliver's School Dinners* (Channel 4 2005), website www.channel4.com and discussion in Chapter 14 below.

The influence of 'commercial culture'

Branding and marketing 'talk' are now regular parts of the ways in which organisations previously thought of as non-commercial describe

Figure 9.6 An example of synergy: a New Zealand Tourist Board image advertising not only a hugely successful film and its locations, but also, through the 'Pure New Zealand' wording, the farm produce exported from that country.

themselves – such as schools, towns, universities. Some people even speak of having 'rebranded' themselves. The supposedly non-commercial BBC spends huge amounts of money on studio sets and logos for its main news programmes: a kind of 'branding as quality'. Just as news or serious current affairs programmes like *Panorama* used to act as 'flagship' programmes, now prestigious soaps or series like *CSI* can be understood partly as competitive 'branding' initiatives by the main British television channels.

Some media studies accounts of advertising analyse particular ads *outside* these full marketing, branding, distribution and pricing contexts, at first for understandable reasons (see Williamson 1978). But in this process huge powers are attributed to the ads themselves as texts. Even later, in the 1980s, when study of the media included broader histories of advertising, there was still a tendency to assume the *effects of individual ads*. To some extent such work was swayed by the well-established hype of advertising itself, crucial to maintain itself, and ironically selling manufacturers the promise of increased sales. In the 1950s, for example, advertising often succeeded in taking credit for stimulating British consumer demand after the Second World War, whereas it's arguable that the Welfare State was at least as crucial in this change, giving millions of ordinary people proper health care, pensions and secondary education for the first time (see Brierley in Briggs and Cobley 1998).

Such improvements accompanied the rise of supermarkets and then hypermarkets (tending to privilege consumers with cars by inviting even larger amounts of shopping). These are now key to understanding distribution as it relates to advertising. Supermarkets pile the goods high. Their initial novelty in the 1950s was to suggest by their very layout, as well as by accompanying advertising, that shoppers could choose for themselves the nature and number of items they would buy. This replaced being advised by the corner shopkeeper or even the polite assistant in the department store, and then constrained by having to carry the goods home by hand.

ACTIVITY 9.5

Find some writings on advertising which put a heavy emphasis *on its power alone* to influence people into buying certain goods.

- How would you want to qualify them?

Note when you next visit your local supermarket what we might call its careful *mise en scène*. (Slightly pink lighting over the meats? Smell of bread enticing you through the store towards the bakery? 'Dump bins' full of goodies, like a kids' party? Sweets to prompt tired children to exert their 'pester power' over parents at the check out? Muzak pacing your visit, its rhythm depending on the time of day – slow to encourage you to shop, fast to encourage customers out?)

- How do its attractions, and the way it invites you to buy certain goods at certain points in your trip, relate to the power of ads and the products you in fact purchased?

'Market research suggests that children often recognise a brand logo before they can recognise their own name. Much child-directed advertising aims to turn kids into fifth columnists within their families, nagging their parents to the checkout. . . . In the US a typical child will watch more than 30,000 TV ads . . . every year, many made by the fast food industry which has an annual American TV advertising budget of about $3 billion. About a quarter of children in the US aged between two and five have televisions in their bedrooms' (Meek 2001: 4).

ACTIVITY 9.6

Some have argued that the saturation advertising aimed at young children should be legally defined as a corporate crime. What are the issues at stake in such a position? Do you agree? What has been your experience of such advertising and your own 'pester power'?

ACTIVITY 9.7

After the huge success of *Jamie Oliver's School Dinners* programmes (Channel 4 2005) with their focus on children's addiction to harmful junk foods, the government announced that it will ban the advertising of junk food during the times that children watch TV, if a voluntary code fails.

   Research how this ban is progressing. (See Chapter 10 'Research'.)

Big brands have the power to distribute their products in this way, and now control, for example, much of agricultural production via their deals with supermarkets, insisting on the prized best positions on supermarket shelves, or succeeding with the nimblest of pricing policies across the globe (see Lang and Heasman 2001). Indeed, supermarkets themselves are huge brands, controlling thousands of farmers (or 'suppliers') through their pricing policies.

When you encounter discussions of the 'popularity' of particular products, remember that the influence of advertising, important as it is, must always be seen in the context of other kinds of capitalist power. It is never simply a matter of 'the power of the text', the advertisement itself, let alone the consumer's rather limited power to make smart fun with, or

Tesco's became the first British supermarket to make £2 billion profit in 2005. ActionAid's web bulletin on 11 April 2005 pointed out that

> when you pick up that perfect apple from the supermarket shelf you do not see its rotten core. To make the biggest profits possible, retailers force farm owners to accept less and less for their crops. The farmers cut costs by lowering their workers' wages and working conditions

including spraying pesticides while women are working in the orchards. ActionAid 'wants . . . companies like Tesco to pay as much attention to people's rights as to the appearance of their apples'. Or their prices on the shelf, as we in the 'West' encounter them.

Figure 9.7 Millet's *The Gleaners*

See, if you can, the French director Agnes Varda's documentary *The Gleaners and I* (France 2000) which looks at gleaning – the ancient French legal right to follow the harvest for bits of the crop not gathered. Varda notes the contemporary practice of supermarket suppliers dumping tons of perfectly edible potatoes, often simply because they are the wrong shape. This is done at short notice, and in different fields, so that the gleaners (often the rural poor and unemployed) won't know where they are dumped, and the potatoes will therefore go green and become inedible in a few days – a hugely wasteful and even cruel practice.

Figure 9.8   Urban gleaners picking cherries in a site awaiting 'development', Cardiff June 2005 (taken with permission).

ignore, such messages. Distribution, marketing synergies, trade-marking and pricing are among the other crucial aspects of 'popularity'. What else is available, at what price, with what reliability attached to its name? (This applies to media products too, of course.)

ACTIVITY 9.8

Have you ever seen a major ad (with prime-time placement on TV, for example) for a product which it has been difficult to obtain? Choose a prime-time TV ad and research in your local supermarket:

- How easy is it to find the product?
- How does its pricing relate to its marketing, its position in the store, etc.? Is it on special offer while it is being intensively advertised?
- How many other similar products could you count on display?

Focus groups: small groups of consumers of a product, usually representative in terms of age, class, etc., which take part in guided but free-wheeling discussion of the product and its associations. These are taped for later close analysis, to help producers assess the likely success of changes to the product's image. See Stoessl in Briggs and Cobley (1998) and also Kitzinger (2004) summarised in Chapter 8 'Audiences'.

Finally, advertising has always been keen to locate, augment and profit from the cutting edge of cultural fashions and change. In the last twenty years this has been researched via processes such as **focus groups** and more recently 'viral' or 'peer to peer' advertising. Viral advertising is said to work like a virus in the community or in a computer – 'infect' one consumer who spreads it to others. This also uses the idea (see Gladwell 2001) that there is a 'tipping point' in any process, including successful marketing, but especially in the spread of good 'word of mouth' which successful ad campaigns try to build. It is all a long way from simple psychological or 'effects' models.

Advertisers have also learnt from developing knowledge about the media. Media studies started some fifty years ago, and many of its assumptions are embedded in journalistic and other media discourses, and have usually been encountered by the graduates who work in PR. The processes of advertising's necessary attempts to keep up to the minute means that it has to take risks, such as pursuit of the so-called 'pink pound' of gay consumers via attractive images of gay people. Many would applaud this as giving visibility to identities whose very existence has previously been censored.

Ads, however, inevitably address us as shoppers, as consumers, promising to solve all the cutting-edge dilemmas they evoke simply by separate acts of purchase. In the process some rich contradictions are thrown up:

'. . . alcohol companies have, as a gesture of goodwill, started putting "please drink responsibly" on billboards, which is a bit like showing a Land Rover coursing through a snowy landscape chasing a spy and saying "please cycle more" at the end.' Zoe Williams, 'Morals go to the market', *The Guardian*, 25 October 2005).

'A woman . . . is almost continually accompanied by her own image of herself. . . . She has to survey everything she is and everything she does because how she appears to others, and ultimately how she appears to men, is of crucial importance for what is . . . thought of as the success of her life' (John Berger (1972), *Ways of Seeing*, Harmondsworth: Penguin).

- Television car ads often show speeding cars in pristine natural landscape – pristine because devoid of other cars and their polluting results.
- Women's magazines often produce challenging articles and even campaigns around topics such as date rape; women's guilt at their supposed inadequacy as mothers, wives, home-makers; child abuse; the dangers of sexualising very young children in advertising imagery. It's precisely on such topicality that they sell their space to advertisers.

  But the bulk of the ads that fund the magazines appeal to readers on the basis of feelings such as anxiety about weight or housework and images of sexualised toddlers, 'perfect' skin, hair, kitchens, relationships – even if many of these are dealt with ironically and with a sense of humour.

- Research into anorexia suggests that young women's (understandable) absorption in fashion can very easily lead to dissatisfaction with, and an inability to imagine as desirable, any but the most conventional (usually thin or at least adolescent) body. There are signs that this is also becoming a problem with young men. Ros Gill (2006) argues that 'the body has become a new (identity) project . . . [one] fraught with difficulties . . . for young men who must simultaneously work on and discipline their bodies while disavowing any (inappropriate) interest in their own appearance'. Discuss?

References

Bowlby, Rachel (2000) *Carried Away: The Invention of Modern Shopping*, London: Faber.

Branston, Gill (2000) *Cinema and Cultural Modernity*, Buckingham: Open University Press, especially Chapters 1–3.

Brierley, Sean (1995) *The Advertising Handbook*, London and New York: Routledge.

Briggs, Adam and Cobley, Paul (eds) (1998) *The Media: An Introduction*, Harlow: Longman.

Dibb, Sue (1993) *Children: Advertisers' Dream. Nutrition Nightmare? The Case for More Responsibility in Food Advertising*, London: National Food Alliance.

Gill, Ros (2006) *Gender and the Media*, Cambridge: Polity.

Gladwell, Michael (2001) *The Tipping Point: How Little Things Can Make a Big Difference*, London: Bantam.

Kitzinger, Jenny (2004) 'Audience and readership research', in *The Sage Handbook of Media Studies*, London: Sage, pp. 167–86.

Klein, N. (2000) *No Logo*, London: Flamingo.

Lang, Tim and Heasman, Michael (eds) (2001) *Food Wars: The Global Battle for Mouths, Minds and Markets*, London: Earthscan.

Meek, James (2001) 'We do ron ron ron, we do ron ron', review of Eric Schlosser (2001) *Fast-Food Nation*, London: Allen Lane, *London Review of Books*, 24 May.

Murdock, Graham (2004) 'Building the digital commons; public broadcasting in the age of the internet', http://www.com.umontreal.ca/spry/spry-gm-lec.htm.

Myers, Greg (1999) *AdWorlds: Brands, Media, Audiences*, London: Edward Arnold.

Packard, Vance (1979) *The Hidden Persuaders*, London: Penguin.

Pumphrey, Martin (1984) 'The flapper, the housewife and the making of modernity', *Cultural Studies*, 1, 2: 179–94.

Slater, Don (1997) *Consumer Culture and Modernity*, Cambridge: Polity.

Wasko, Janet (2003) *How Hollywood Works*, London: Sage.

Williamson, Judith (1978) *Decoding Advertisements: Ideology and Meaning in Advertising*, London: Marion Boyars.

Further reading

Coward, Ros (1984) *Female Desire: Women's Sexuality Today*, London: Paladin.

Curtis, Adam (dir.) *The Century of the Self* (BBCTV 2002) (some copies available on internet).

Goffman, Erving (1976) *Gender Advertisements*, London: Macmillan.

Marcuse, Herbert (1964) *One Dimensional Man*, London: Routledge & Kegan Paul.

Schlosser, Eric (2001) *Fast Food Nation*, Boston, MA Houghton Mifflin.

Williamson, Judith (1985) *Consuming Passions*, London: Marion Boyars.

Wilson, Elizabeth (2003) *Adorned in Dreams Fashion and Modernity*, London: I.B. Tauris.

Other resources

Nader, Ralph, website www.nader.org

www.grumbletext.co.uk

www.interbrand.com

www.treehugger.com

CASE STUDY: CELEBRITY, STARDOM AND MARKETING

- From stars to celebrities
- Stars, celebrities and advertising
- Dumbing down?
- References
- Further reading

'**Celebrity** items' are now more widespread and commonly encountered than ever before. They blend into news and current affairs, especially in the UK and US where huge amounts of apparently 'straight' news coverage is skewed towards them, often in an attempt to boost ratings via 'human interest' and glamour; often because of the ease with which PR firms offer links to them.

Commercial advertisers are keen that we associate these figures with their products and brands. But equally, health bodies used the 2005 news that Kylie Minogue had breast cancer to publicise awareness of both the disease and improvements in dealing with it. It's a contradictory phenomenon, like much of the media.

Here we will consider:

- how celebrity coverage relates to some crucial areas of modern media: stardom, marketing, and news
- and the ways that these are involved with branding and advertising.

From stars to celebrities

Film and media studies have long explored cinematic forms of stardom, and the approaches developed in that work is useful for understanding how 'celebrities' are produced. Economically stardom has been defined as 'a patent on a unique set of human characteristics . . . [which] include purely physical aspects' (Wyatt 1994).

ACTIVITY 9.9

Q   We've linked celebrity to stardom, though some would say the two categories are very different, and that 'celebrities' by definition lack the talent of 'stars'. Do you feel that admitting to a passion for celebrity, e.g. by reading *Hello!* magazine, is like flaunting a shameful secret? Why is this? In that sense is it very *unlike* a passion for certain stars?

The work of Dyer, Stacey, Ellis and others has opened up:

- the 'doubleness' of stars' images: they fascinate on the basis of on-screen and off-screen narratives and performances
- the possible cultural-ideological effects of this.

Film stars and celebrities, it is argued, fascinate us partly through the ways that *parallel narratives* of their lives are constructed, in addition to performances of one kind or another. In 'classic' Hollywood these

'a **star** is
a performer in a particular medium
whose figure enters into subsidiary forms of circulation
and then feeds back into future performances.'

(Ellis 1992: 91)

narratives were partly constructed and circulated by the studios. These publicised the stars as though they were identical to their roles on screen, as well as emphasising a tantalising mixture of 'ordinary' and 'extra-ordinary' in their lives – very much like celebrities now.

Q Can you think of a current celebrity or star who is discussed as a mixture of 'extraordinary'– 'ordinary'?

Today's cinema stars are no longer always seen as identical with the roles they play – partly due to the sheer amount of coverage of stars and celebrities, which reveals far too many aspects of their activities to be 'anchored' in one firm interpretation. Instead the *effort* involved in a performance is often emphasised, sometimes via stories, inside and outside films, of bodily transformation, whether in a gym, or in on-screen unflattering make up for a 'serious' role (see Geraghty 2000).

ACTIVITY 9.10

Q Can you think of recent roles which have referred to the 'off-screen' narrative of the star's life? Is this reference made explicitly (e.g. speculation about Brad Pitt's relationship with Angelina Jolie when *Mr and Mrs Smith* (US 2005) was released)? Or is it carried in the narrative role chosen for the star (e.g. Hilary Swank as poor but gutsy girl in *Million Dollar Baby* (US 2004)?

(Note: When film and media studies try to analyse stars, they often keep separate the star actor/image and the role they are playing through the naming convention 'Bridget Jones/Renee Zellweger' etc.)

The 'star phenomenon' began in theatrical advertising of certain actors' names in the 1820s. It was not immediately transferred to Hollywood,

which at first (from about 1909 to 1914) ignored 'stars' (or actors in whom audiences demonstrated a particular interest). This was partly because of the costs involved in 'manufacturing stardom' on a scale which the studios could translate into measurable box-office revenue; and also for fear of the power which stars might then wield.

Stars (and some celebrities) need all kinds of resources lavished on this ongoing 'manufacture of stardom', both on screen and off. On screen, in films or TV they usually need privileged access to screen space (framing, many moments when they are the centre of attention) and narrative space (via good scripts if possible); lighting and good cinematography; the care of costumers, make-up workers, voice coaches, hairdressers, personal trainers, etc. Skilful casting is also important, though rarely discussed in work on stars, perhaps because it is seen to detract from the star's own intentions in a performance (see Lovell and Kramer 1999; Lovell and Sergi 2005). Off screen a supply of photos, interviews, rumours, preview and publicity materials, etc. is needed to stimulate and satisfy audience interest.

Though perhaps the least of the discriminations against African-Americans during the studio years, the priorities of film technology simply ignored and thereby marginalised them. Skin colour, and the lag in film stock technologies for the expressive lighting and filming of black skins, shored up the unequal allocation of star roles, which were often dependent on close-up and clearly perceptible facial gesture (see Dyer 1998).

'a good director . . . doesn't direct you, he casts you properly in a film. If he casts you right in the part, then you're going to be great in the part' (Tony Curtis in Branston 2000: 119).

Once established during 'the studio years' from about 1920 to 1950, the star system worked lucratively for the studios, the stars and the products they were used to advertise. For the studios, stars were a key part of 'branding' or the promise of certain kinds of narrative and production values. Their large salaries (justified by nebulous qualities such as 'talent' or 'charisma') worked to marginalise the powers of actors' unions, which might otherwise have been able to calculate the costs of acting labour, and then ask for more equal distribution of studio profits. Stars were also literally part of the studios' capital, like plant and equipment, and could be traded as such. James Stewart, making an interesting comparison with sports celebrities, said once: 'Your studio could trade you around like ball players. I was traded once to Universal for the use of their back lot for three weeks' (quoted in Bordwell *et al.* 1985).

Ironically this is still the case. The *Guardian* reported on 9 April 2005 that

> Corbis, the digital image company set up by Bill Gates . . . has bought a company which owns the image rights to more than 50 deceased celebrities . . . from the Marx Brothers to Steve McQueen . . . Sigmund Freud. . . . They are likely to end up endorsing a product they would never have imagined in their lifetime . . . their faces plastered over everything from credit cards to mouse pads . . . their earnings outstripping their mortal returns.

And the *Times Higher Educational Supplement* on 25 March 2005 reported that 'Disney last week clinched a $2.7m deal (£1.4m) with the Hebrew University for the rights to use the image of Albert Einstein in its "Baby Einstein" range of toys.'

ACTIVITY 9.11

Q Have you seen any such copyrighted use of deceased celebrities, such as Marilyn Monroe, James Dean, Humphrey Bogart, Audrey Hepburn, etc.? On what kinds of products? Why do you think they were chosen rather than living celebrities/stars?

Stars, celebrities and advertising

A major area of interest in stars and celebrities is the broadly cultural-ideological influence of such 'double' presences, both on and off screen. Not only does this relate to narrative roles and what gets endorsed and marginalised in their values, but also to the advertising tie-ins of stars and celebrities, and the ways these cement cultures of hyper-consumption.

Stars have *always* functioned as a key part of Hollywood's relationship to broader capitalist structures, especially advertising and marketing. There was alarm in England and Germany as early as 1912 about the ways that American movies were

Figure 9.9 Bette Davis as Charlotte Vale in *Now, Voyager* (US 1942) is transformed from 'plain spinster' to 'fashionable woman' and finally a woman confident in her own identity. Her clothes embody this transformation. Advertising around the film told cinema owners and retailers how to encourage customers to buy them. See La Place (1987) for an excellent account.

functioning as an arm of American exports and marketing. Fashions, up-to-the-minute kitchen technology and furnishings were showcased in 'women's films', establishing tie-ins with manufacturers. In the mid-1930s sketches of styles to be worn by specific actresses in films were sent to merchandising bureaux, which produced them in time for the film's release, then sold them in Macy's Cinema Fashions Shops, among others (see Branston 2000; Eckert 1990; La Place 1987).

The cigarette industry regularly lobbied performers to smoke on screen. These tie-in products were controversial as early as the 1920s. By the late 1930s Hollywood occupied a privileged position in the advertising industry. As Tom Dewe Matthews (1998) points out, drawing on the work of Peter Kramer:

Figure 9.10 Ronald Reagan (B movie actor, later US President, then 'celebrity') illustrating the overlap of discourses of advertising, stardom/celebrity, politics and commercial sponsorship.

Warners had million dollar contracts with General Electric and General Motors, MGM had a tie-in to Bell telephones as well as to Coca-Cola, Paramount was with Westinghouse and all the studios had links to radio networks like CBS and NBC . . . directors in the twenties and thirties were encouraged to junk historical costume dramas and instead . . . [make films] which could show off the latest Bell telephone, General Electric oven or Westinghouse refrigerator.

The context for this was that in the 1930s over-production of manufactured goods had reached crisis point in North America. The large banks funding Hollywood sought its help in shifting goods from warehouses to consumers.

Two adjacent changes occurred throughout the mid-1930s: Hollywood stars showcasing make-up, clothing and other items of dress-up sensibility; and direct tie-ins between screen texts and particular products. . . . By the Depression, Hollywood stars were the third biggest source of news in the United States.

(Miller 2000: 599)

The break-up of the studio system (1940s to 1950s) saw the rise of 'package unit' production and promotion: films treated on a one-by-one basis. Film stars, no longer under seven-year contracts, became increasingly responsible for their own images. Since the biggest stars were crucial to the studios' hugely risky projects, their costs rose. Contracts now also often included large proportions of box-office take – stars began to have more power in saying what they would or would not take part in.

One result was that salaries escalated to their present grotesque levels, which relate to the stars' 'branded' powers. Though the term 'bankable' is often used now as a shorthand for stars' success, they (and some directors and producers) are also defined

Figure 9.11 US politics and celebrity 2: Arnold Schwarzenegger, another figure bringing his star image to Republican politics, driving his Humvee to launch a campaign (for cuts in pension provision etc.) at a fast food restaurant, 2005. The 'Governator' of California (popularity ratings slumping at the time) stated on 1 June 2005, about global warming: 'I say the debate is over. We know the science, we see the threat, and we know the time for action is now.' Will this affect his enthusiastic endorsement of huge, gas-guzzling military-style SUVs (Sports Utility Vehicles), so close to his star image, for civilian use? See Bradher (2002).

as being like a 'brand' (as *an image which persuades consumers of quality prior to purchase or experience*). This translates literally for cinema into 'a performer who can open a film on the strength of their name alone'.

Struggles over control of 'the star's own image' or 'brand' (i.e. the revenues from it) had always taken place, for example over the studio system's seven-year

contracts tying a star to a particular studio (before stars like Bette Davis, Olivia de Havilland and James Cagney challenged those contracts in the 1940s). They take different forms today, though contracts and their clauses are still one of the most closely guarded secrets in the field of entertainment. How many interviews contracted on a publicity tour? Is attendance at premieres mandatory? What percentage share of the box office does the star have? Is there use of body doubles or not?

More straightforward links to advertising continued to exist way beyond the end of the studio system. *Lost in Translation* (US 2003) centred on a fading star, played by Bill Murray, who advertises whisky for large sums of money in Japan, just as has really happened to existing bigger US stars, such as Schwarzenegger, Diaz, DiCaprio. Such ads often coincide with the release of their films in Asia, and equally often with agreements that these ads won't be shown outside Japan. See www.forbes.com.

Sometimes the tension between the star's bankability for the studio and the role s/he is playing becomes pronounced. See Brad Pitt in *Fight Club* (US 1999), looking at a Gucci underpants ad featuring a male body beautiful and speaking the line 'Is that what they think a real man looks like?' Much of the publicity for the movie concerned his enviably transformed body, pecs, etc. – exactly what many real men *do* long to look like.

Again, in an age when commodities are so intensely advertised and branded, companies have been keen to re-exploit films as relatively fresh spaces which are not already cluttered with messages. Of course it's reasonable to feel that products may have to be shown in films about modern life. But the deliberate placing of a product so that its label can be seen, often for some time, is rather different. Some argue that advertisers were re-alerted to the power of movie product

Leonardo DiCaprio refused to allow a doll in his likeness to be made as a *Titanic* tie-in product, and later trade-marked his name.

Tom Hanks's voice (only) was used for Woody's character in *Toy Story 2*. He refused to let the toy be made in his visual likeness (not used in the film) but gave interviews, for press as well as radio, letting his whole star image as well as his voice be *associated* with the film.

See www.cmgww.com for details of one of the world's largest star and celebrity licensing agencies.

See if you can find any stars who seem not to engage in these practices. It is rumoured that Tom Waits and Bruce Springsteen have always rejected approaches to endorse or allow their music to be used as background to ads – unlike Bob Dylan, whose 2005 association with Starbucks, and 2004 appearance in an ad for the lingerie company Victoria's Secrets caused some controversy.

placement by Harry Callahan/Clint Eastwood's famous line 'Go ahead, punk, make my day' and his naming of a .44 Colt Magnum gun in *Dirty Harry* (US 1971). This was said to have done 'more to promote big-boomer handguns than any promotion, before or since' (www.shootingindustry.com).

Another tactic was exemplified when Columbia studios were taken over for some years by Coca-Cola. The film *Missing* (US 1982), about the Chilean coup of 1973, has Pepsi products regularly associated with the 'bad guys'. Guess what the 'good guys' drink? Likewise 20th Century-Fox films, owned by Ruper Murdoch's News Corporation, regularly advertise Fox News Channel. In *The Day After Tomorrow* (US 2004) when most of civilisation is iced over, it seems that Fox will deliver the news. Even the apparently anti-marketing film *The Truman Show* (US 1998) has a clear placement of the Ford Taurus car. And *Castaway* (US 2000) has been called a prolonged ad for FedEx mail delivery – equally amazing, considering its desert island subject matter. One fan wrote 'I will never again be able to look at a purple and orange FedEx logo and not think about Tom Hanks and *CAST AWAY*' (on www.flickfilosopher.com). However much FedEx paid, it was probably worth it.

Some of the most profitable products advertised by films are of course tie-in or spin-off goods. Characters are sometimes said to be 'toyetic', in other words, such that toys could be made of them. So lucrative is

the whole process that many movies (such as the *Star Wars* franchise) are made by corporations which see movies as a fringe benefit rather than the core point of the business. See *Behind the Screens: Hollywood Goes Hyper-commercial* (US 2000) for more detail on the above.

Nielsen Media Research, the leading provider of US TV ratings and 'competitive advertising intelligence', offers a service tracking product placement on the top US networks, including whether the ad is placed in the foreground or background, its time on screen, integration into the storyline, etc. This 'intelligence' comes at a time when products such as Tivo allow some viewers to skip commercials altogether.

Go to www.nielsenmedia.com and www.ACNielsen.com for details of fascinating (and very expensive) ad research. And see http://www.brandchannel.com/brandcameo_films.asp for the product links to recent films.

Celebrity and news

The term 'stardom' is now spread wide, to cover sport, TV and popular music, for example. It overlaps with the term 'celebrities'. These are understood as having the same access to fame as stars, but they are not always as closely associated with specific areas of achievement. Indeed they are sometimes seen as having no major talent apart from an appetite for celebrity and an ability to make fools of themselves, or to appear dressed spectacularly at hugely publicised premieres.

Chris Rojek (2003) attempts to subdivide 'celebrity' into:

- **ascribed** (monarchs, Kennedy family members, etc.)
- **achieved** (those with perceived accomplishments in open competition: sporting, artistic)
- **attributed** (individuals who are represented as noteworthy or exceptional, e.g. by PR processes)
- **celetoid**: a media-generated, compressed, form of media celebrity, e.g. lottery winners, stalkers, whistleblowers, objects of sexual scandal.

ACTIVITY 9.12

If you saw Ricky Gervais's series *Extras* (BBC2 2005) how would you characterise its representation of celebrity, and those who hunger after it? How would you justify your interpretation?

The range of cultural forms available for the construction of fame and therefore celebrity now include popular music, TV (including weather forecasters, children's presenters, survivors of *Big Brother* . . .), sport, politics, cookery, fashion and even accidents which create sudden celebrity for a person.

ACTIVITY 9.13

Arguably, because of the level of achievement needed to become a sports star/celebrity, these figures are different from many other celebrities. Argue whether your favourite sporting figure is a star or a celebrity. Survey media coverage to see which of these terms is used of him/her, and with what implications.

Sport and, in the UK especially football, is a rich source of celebrity/stardom. Not only is it a key part of many people's leisure time, whether participating, betting, playing fantasy forms or spectating. It also forms a sizeable proportion of news coverage – a key site for airing questions around national identity (see Chapter 6 'Ideologies and power'), racism, 'appropriate bodies' and behaviours for men and women, or the limits of competitiveness (as figured in performance drug debates and how far human bodies should be pushed).

It produces celebrities/stars who seem both ordinary (often with 'humble' origins emphasised) and extraordinary (their sporting achievements, wealth, 'fabulous' lifestyle). Like Hollywood stars in the studio period, though much more openly, they are commodities, and capital assets for the clubs and advertisers who sponsor them, traded by their owners, as well as hugely wealthy while their commodity value lasts. This is usually their skills (which usually only last a few years) and, in the case of Beckham, their special appeal in places like Japan. Managers, such as José Mourinho and Sven-Goran Eriksson, are now also part of this coverage, though their skills are not as evident as those on display in the 'stars'.

Occasionally celebrities are seen as having done good with their image – Channel 4's *Jamie Oliver's School Dinners* series in 2005 is such a case. From being someone who was seen as a commercially savvy 'Essex boy' chef (making money from his branding of

Consider the star/celebrity image of the Beckhams and their sons Brooklyn, Romeo and Cruz (at the time of writing). They form an example of how 'parallel narratives' still matter for the production of celebrity/stardom and the possibilities this raises for advertisers.

However gifted a footballer David Beckham has been, and however important his control over his image via his contracts, it was his marriage to 'Posh Spice' which made him a major star. They were called the pop king and queen of England; their lavish wedding played with this idea as did tales of their life at 'Beckingham Palace'. All of this was then recycled in *Footballers' Wives*, which now seems to act as a parallel parody of footballers' celebrity status (except for the absence of any discussion of actual advertising links).

Beckham, simply by virtue of being part of two 'high-profile' people's stories, is much more available for tabloid narrativisation than, say, Michael Owen. Such themes can be broached as work vs. family, the ordinary domestic lives of the extraordinarily wealthy, affairs within a marriage involving two star images (at least in the beginning) crossing over into speculation about Victoria's anorexia, plastic surgery, jealousy, etc.

A repeat of this lucrative set of narrative possibilities, with a different class angle, seems to be building with Wayne Rooney ('Roonaldo'): 'rags to riches' success at a very young age; his treatment of his 'childhood sweetheart' fiancée Coleen; the multimillion pound house and debates on whether it and his cars, her clothes, etc. are in 'good taste'; the allegations of slapping Coleen as well as sex with 'escorts' etc.

Other stars with less high-profile marriages seem to have more limited narrative functions: Michael Owen has replaced 'Saint Lineker' as 'Mr Nice Guy'; 'the dope' is currently played by Rio Ferdinand, 'the thug' by Ian Bowyer.

products, from Sainsbury's supermarket food to a Royal Worcester china range), he became something like a national hero for a short time. It's worth thinking how gender works here.

ACTIVITY 9.14

Q Can you imagine a female cookery celebrity (Delia Smith, Nigella Lawson) having the same impact? If not, why not? Might it be the case that Jamie Oliver's celebrity image, being so 'new masculine', was able to avoid the (feminine) connotations of 'nanny state'? Might appeals for proper regulation of school meals have had this resonance if they'd come from a woman chef, with a female voice-over?

Q Do you think that 'good' celebrity rock stars, doing work for Third World debt, perhaps, like Bono and Bob Geldof, also tend to be male figures?

Dumbing down?

The role of celebrities, along with scandal or gossip in news media generally, is often described as 'dumbing down', 'trivialisation' or 'tabloidisation'. This ignores the fact that all media need a certain amount of 'personalisation' – news as much as popular fictions. Even though the ideology of news announces that it is 'serious', 'objective' and 'factual', it proceeds by endless interviews, stories and photos of individuals – even if simply politicians getting in and out of cars.

Audiences' appetite for celebrity stories (and the resulting boost both to the products they advertise and the advertising revenue of the TV and print news they appear in) can be understood more sympathetically.

Hermes (1999) suggests that the pleasures of celebrity news operate via two approaches:

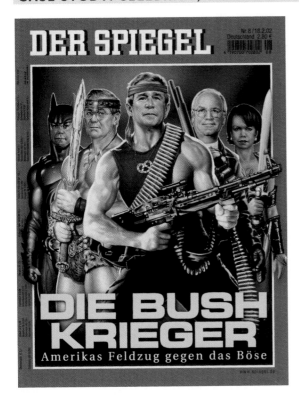

a deep sense that the world is unjust, which points to a more collective sense of social inequality. To enjoy it when things go badly for 'rich and famous people' is a way of imagining cosmic (rather than political) justice taking its toll. Commiseration and indignation are equal ingredients of the pleasure of [such] . . . gossip.

(Hermes 1999: 81)

'I watched an entire hour of news on Fox last week and, except for a minute's worth of news on the half hour, every second was devoted to Michael Jackson and the child molestation charges against him . . . the news channels have discovered that celebrity crime – or, rather, accusing a celebrity of committing a crime – boosts the ratings like nothing else, even war' (Andrew Billen, *New Statesman*, 1 December 2003).

Figure 9.12 US politics and celebrity 3: Because they're so high profile, celebrity images are wide open to parody – all the more effective if distributed widely. This is located in a leading journal in Germany, which opposed the 2003 invasion of Iraq.

- 'the extended family repertoire'. This describes the sense that news gossip brings the powerful down to the level of ordinary human beings, imagined as part of the family, and a place where readers/viewers can test scenarios (divorce, parenthood or the desire for it, ambition, etc.) in case they occur in their own lives (Hermes 1999: 80, 81). It may be especially true of coverage of 'the Royals' in the UK, who have since the nineteenth century been called 'the Royal family'.
- 'the repertoire of **melodrama**'. This refers to a form stretching from nineteenth-century theatre and involving highly polarised struggles between Vice and Virtue: the wicked lord and the innocent maiden etc. (see Gledhill 1987). It seems still to be at play in the pleasures of much celebrity coverage, involving:

ACTIVITY 9.15

Think of the most memorable recent news story involving celebrities which you've come across.

Q   Can you trace the two approaches which Hermes outlines in it?
Q   Or in the way you, or your friends, seemed to engage with it?
Q   Which were the 'melodramatic' elements of response, and which the 'extended family' ones?

Panics about 'dumbing down' often suggest that fans lose their own identities in favour of their admired (or reviled) favourite celebrities or celebrity stories. Hermes suggests that the engagement with the celebrity takes place in a kind of 'playground of identity construction'. She quotes a study of 1960s 'Beatlemania': 'The appeal of the male star was that you would never marry him; the romance would never end in the tedium of marriage. . . . The star could be loved non-instrumentally, for his own sake, and with complete abandon' (Hermes 1999: 80).

In the last few years, however, another, less sympathetic account of 'celebrity news' could be made. At the core of it would be the use of paparazzi photos, along with the less often discussed hypocrisy of tabloid newspapers and the boost to their sales and advertising given by 'kiss and tell' contracts.

ACTIVITY 9.16

Take a recent tabloid or red-top scandalous story. Analyse it to trace the different attitudes (some would say hypocrisy) around such areas as:

- the sexual occurrences which it is dealing with
- the wealth or greed of the participants.

Are photos and verbal text, for example, offering different views of such aspects of the story?

The paparazzi have gone far beyond catching stars in compromising or simply private moments. Magazines such as *Heat* and *Closer* patrol the borders of bodies and behaviour to produce salacious coverage of good-looking celebrities who are drunk or violent, or getting out of a car and revealing some cellulite (only female celebs these, of course, and in shots often grotesquely magnified), or simply looking tired

Paparazzi: photographers who take 'candid' photos of celebrities, usually by assiduously shadowing them in public and, especially, private activities. Technological developments, e.g. longer lenses and higher-speed film, enable paparazzi to shoot their prey from afar, and digital cameras and transmission methods allow for rapid distribution of the resulting photos.

and ordinary . . . and so on. This accompanies the marketing and publicity given to plastic surgery in countless 'reality TV' shows, interviews and documentaries as well as in the prestige US series *Nip/Tuck*. It suggests that female celebrities are used in highly gendered ways to sustain one of the central planks of advertising in the twenty-first century: an anxiety about bodies, especially women's bodies, which 'fail' to conform to very narrow and often near-anorexic standards of 'perfection' (though see Gill (2006) from Chapter 5 on the encouragement to boys to feel these anxieties about their bodies).

'*Heat, Closer, Wow, Reveal, New, Star*. . . . The magazines with the uniform format, hazy celebrity photographs, scandalous straplines and brightly coloured panels. The ones our eyes are drawn to. . . .

'Pretty faces (and bodies) sell magazines. And it's a trait peculiar to the female gender (and understood by the editors of a largely female readership) that they enjoy scrutinising other women. Partly as a result of this, the average head count comes in at a third higher than in the *Daily Mirror* and more than twice that of *Marie Claire*.

'Ten years ago, photos of celebrities with closed eyes, twisted expressions, visible G-strings or half-obscured faces would have been disregarded. Now, photographers and their agents increase their profits – remarkably – by finding a market for their wastage.'

(from Nat Pettinger, 'How bad design gets the best results', *The Independent Media Weekly*, 28 February 2005)

There's a further twist to this use of 'paparazzi'-style photos. In 2005 the *Sun* published photos of a dishevelled, jailed Saddam Hussein in his underpants, and also sleeping under a rough blanket, which it seems were taken by one of his captors. Is this the best way for the press to invite thinking and feeling about this criminal and his crimes? Like the pictures of him being medically examined just after capture in 2004, might such shots, advertising evidence of his 'brokenness', act out those very bullying values which the West had proclaimed itself to be against?

These feelings seem oddly close to the heart of some of the more sadistic forms of mainstream paparazzi/celebrity coverage. The linkage of celebrities with advertising, and the consequent emphasis on their 'perfect' bodies (whether or not entirely made of real flesh and blood), along with their stupendously wasteful lifestyles produces its flipside. Audiences are invited to watch out for and to revel in the 'failure' of those bodies and of celebrity in general: a strange and sadistic structure of feeling for any culture.

References

Bordwell, David, Staiger, Janet and Thompson, Kirsten (1985) *Film History: An Introduction*, New York: McGraw Hill.

Bradher, Keith (2002) *High and Mighty: SUVs: The World's Most Dangerous Vehicles and How They Got That Way*, New York: Public Affairs.

Branston, Gill (2000) 'Stars, bodies, galaxies', in *Cinema and Cultural Modernity*, Buckingham: Open University Press.

Campbell, D. (2000) 'Trouble in Tinseltown', *Guardian*, 20 January.

Dyer, Richard (1987) *Heavenly Bodies*, London: Macmillan/BFI.

Dyer, Richard (1998) *Stars*, 2nd edition, London: BFI.

Eckert, Charles (1990) 'The Carole Lombard in Macy's window', in J. Gaines and C. Herzog (eds) *Fabrications: Costume and the Female Body*, London: Routledge.

Ellis, John (1992) *Visible Fictions*, 2nd edition, London: Routledge.

Evans, Jessica and Hesmondhalgh, David (eds) (2006) *Understanding Media: Inside Celebrity*, Milton Keynes: The Open University Press in association with the Open University.

Geraghty, Christine (2000) 'Re-examining stardom: questions of texts, bodies and performance', in Ros Gill (2006) *Gender and the Media*, Cambridge: Polity Press.

Christine Gledhill and Linda Williams (eds) *Re-Inventing Film Studies*, London: Arnold.

Gledhill, Christine (ed.) (1987) *Home Is Where the Heart Is*, London: BFI.

Hermes, Joke (1999) 'Media figures in identity construction', in Pertti Alasuutari (ed.) *Rethinking the Media Audience*, London: Sage.

La Place, Maria (1987) 'Producing and consuming the woman's film', Christine Gledhill (ed.) *Home Is Where the Heart Is*, London: BFI.

Lovell, Alan, and Kramer, Peter (1999) *Screen Acting*, London: Routledge.

Lovell, Alan and Sergi, Gianluca (2005) *Making Films in Contemporary Hollywood*, London: Hodder Arnold.

Matthews, Tom D. (1998) 'See the movie, ogle the star', *Guardian*, 27 November.

Miller, Toby (1998) 'Hollywood and the world', in John Hill and Pamela Church Gibson (eds) *The Oxford Guide to Film Studies*, Oxford: Oxford University Press.

Miller, Toby (2000) 'Class and the culture industries', in Robert Stam and Toby Miller (eds) *Film and Theory: An Introduction*, Oxford and Cambridge, Mass.: Blackwell.

Rojek, Chris (2003) *Celebrity*, London: Reaktion Books.

Stacey, Jackie (1994) *Star Gazing: Hollywood Cinema and Female Spectatorship*, London: Routledge.

Wyatt, Justin (1994) *High Concept: Movies and Marketing in Hollywood*, Austin: University of Texas Press.

Further reading

Corner, John (2003) *Media and the Re-Styling of Politics: Consumerism, Celebrity and Cynicism*, London: Sage.

Other resources

Behind the Screens: Hollywood Goes Hyper-commercial
(US 2000) Video, available from Media Education
Foundation, Amherst, Mass., US.

Part II
Media Practices

The director (centre) and his producers reviewing footage on the set of *Bullet Boy* (UK 2005). Verve Pictures

10 Research

In Part II we are concerned with 'media practices' – considering both how media organisations go about their business and also how you will be expected to approach your own media productions and academic studies. We have organised the chapters to follow the production process roughly, and we begin with the essential preparatory work of research.

Research is crucial to every form of media production, and the role of researcher is clearly identified in some media industries (e.g. television). In other industries research is perhaps less visible, but think of the work that goes into art direction and costume design on a feature film or the hours of listening that inform the decisions of a record producer. In this chapter we will refer to:

- content research
- production research
- audience research
- academic research.

These definitions refer to the purpose of research, and you need to make sure that you can distinguish between them. There is also an important distinction between *primary* and *secondary* research and between different research methodologies.

Primary or secondary research

Since this distinction applies to any form of research, let's clarify it first. **Primary research** implies that the researcher is the first agent to collect and collate the material. An interview is the clearest possible example of primary research – asking questions and obtaining responses which are 'original'. Interviews may be used to form the background material from

The distinction between primary and secondary research is not always clear-cut. Is a photograph in a newspaper archive secondary or primary? Once it has been 'collected' with other similar photographs in a book, it definitely becomes secondary. The distinction is really about whose interpretation of the material comes first.

which a script or an article is written. Alternatively, the interviews may appear in the finished text, as in the traditional Sunday magazine profile of a prominent figure. A genre of film documentary has also developed where eye-witnesses describe what happened at the time of a particular event. Such interviews are usually rerecorded for the production itself.

Other primary sources may be government records, such as the register of births and deaths or the correspondence and personal papers of individuals or organisations. These are sometimes formally organised into 'archives' (see below). Other forms of primary research can include taking photographs or making sound recordings (of folk songs or birdsong perhaps).

Figure 10.1 An online specialist archive accessible to researchers in educational institutions, Screenonline from the British Film Institute (www.screenonline.org.uk) provides material, including video clips and stills, covering British film and television.

'Deep' research, rather like the ethnographic studies carried out by academic ethnographers, may begin by the researcher living in a community for some time and recording aspects of daily life (see Chapter 8 above). This is the kind of research novelists might undertake to 'get the feel' of a location.

Secondary research implies that someone other than the researcher has collected and organised material and made it available for research, usually in a library or archive. It often means using compiled records such as reference books. Sources need not be reference books as such – you could look at the novels and magazines written in a particular period, or at films or television advertisements.

Secondary research material has connotations of being somehow less authentic because it has already been mediated in some way. So if you look up the letters of a famous novelist, published in book form, they will have already been selected and edited and introduced by someone else – you won't be responding to them directly. In some ways this is a specious argument since every 'record' is a mediated account of something that has happened, but it is still a useful distinction since a reliance on secondary material alone is unlikely to provide as much sense of personal involvement in a story as research that includes some first-hand experience and contains the possibility of finding something which perhaps didn't 'fit' previous researchers' expectations.

Content or background research

Some research is likely to take place even before a programme is **commissioned** or a film **'greenlighted'**. This is background research that helps to set up the proposal – to find out if there really is an interesting story to back up that good idea in the pub. Sometimes the background research has been carried out for another purpose and then used to inform a new proposal. A university dissertation might become the basis for a book and then a television programme.

Once the proposal has been accepted, further research will be needed, not only to inform the script but also possibly to provide sounds and images that might appear in a film or radio or television programme. Content research of this kind may require access to specialist archives.

Picture libraries

Many newspapers and magazines as well as television companies have an in-house picture library where they keep carefully filed copies of images they own (or where they have acquired reproduction rights), covering

Some of the major commercial picture libraries have developed out of newspaper collections, like the Hulton Archive which derived originally from the *Picture Post* and *Daily Herald* archives from the 1930s–50s. These images are now 'rights-managed' by Getty Images which also controls the archives of *Time* and *Life* magazines. See http://corporate.gettyimages.com to get a full picture of what this company offers.

Corbis is a name attached to many of the images you will see on the internet. The company is owned by Bill Gates (www.corbis.com).

topics such as famous personalities, important buildings, locations, etc. Most of these libraries have now been digitised so that images can be traced through multiple searches, e.g. all images of women in uniform in the Second World War. These are then instantaneously available if a news story breaks. All photographs taken by staff reporters on a newspaper are automatically filed for possible future use. These libraries represent important assets for the media corporations and can be sold or leased for considerable sums. In some cases libraries have survived the deaths of the publications which created them and have become profit-earners in their own right.

The market for images is such that photographers have built up their own archives of standard shots (sunsets, cute babies, etc.) which they offer as commercial library pictures. With the growth of CD technology and online services via the internet, there are now many ways in which media producers can acquire high-quality images for advertising or promotion at a relatively low cost. The 'international image market' is such that a small group of companies have carefully bought up the rights to an enormous range of images, all available in digital form – credit card account permitting. In all these cases, users of images have to pay for different services (see the section on copyright in Chapter 11).

Sound libraries

The National Sound Archive is part of the British Library (www.bl.uk), which also includes the Newspaper Library in Colindale (featured in numerous detective novels). You can also use the newspaper archive in your local library.

'Library sounds' – collections of mood music and sound effects at relatively low cost – are available on CD to be used by corporate producers via various licence agreements. Other audio recordings are owned by the broadcasters or the large recording companies. The BBC has extensive archives of past recordings, and these sometimes form the basis of entire radio programmes. There is also the National Sound Archive in the UK which holds a collection of historic and representative recordings.

Regional film archives
Your region may have established a film archive, possibly associated with a university or a library. Films made in the region by professionals and amateurs may be held, along with stills and production materials. Archives are exploring ways of making parts of their collections more accessible to the public and to education. Find members of the Film Archive Forum on www. bufvc.ac.uk/faf/archivesmap.html.

Film and video libraries

Until the 1940s film companies often threw their products away once their initial release to cinemas was completed. Early television recordings often went the same way. Now the companies have recognised the value of their products and have begun to archive them carefully and in some cases have bought other collections as well.

Film archives have the advantage over video in that the basic technology has not changed over a hundred years and, provided that the film has survived physically, it is usually possible to make a viewing copy of any footage. Video formats change frequently and it is already proving

THE BRITISH LIBRARY   The world's knowledge

About us | Collections | Catalogues | Services | What's on | News | Contact us

Home > Collections > Sound Archive

Collections   Sound Archive

print

home

search

back

site map

- Sound Archive Home
- About Us
- News
- Research
- Collections
- Services
- Catalogue
- Links
- Listen

The British Library Sound Archive

Pop Music

Paul Weller © Go! Discs

The Pop music section of the British Library Sound Archive holds one of the most wide-ranging collections of popular music in the world. We do not believe in any simple definition of what constitutes "Pop" music and our collection reflects the diversity of styles that have been popular over the years, from early 20th Century music hall to the latest rock and dance music.

We try to collect and preserve copies of every recording commercially issued in the UK. We also acquire pop videos, radio and television programmes and make our own recordings at festivals, conferences and seminars. All of these, together with our extensive reference library and on-line services combine to provide the premier public research facility for pop music in the UK

Listen to the sound samples on this page with the Real Audio player

All recordings copyright © British Library Board. The recordings on this site are for private listening only; copying, broadcasting or reproduction is prohibited.

Lets have a song upon the gramophone   Catalogue details

Billy Williams recorded in 1913.

Contents:

Commercial recordings
Non-commercial recordings
Library materials
Using the collections
Pop Collection links
Further information

Figure 10.2   The British Library website at www.bl.uk/collections/sound-archive/pop.html. The whole of the British Library website is worth exploring to find out what it offers for researchers.

difficult to replay material on some of the older formats because the relevant video players are no longer in working order.

The National Film and Television Archive (www.bfi.org.uk/nftva) provides a service for film students and researchers, and other national and regional organisations have now begun to market their materials for educational and commercial use. Film research is a highly specialised business, and the British Universities Film and Video Council publishes a guide for researchers. Archiving has a recognisable career structure and the University of East Anglia, for example, now offers a postgraduate course.

The British Universities Film and Video Council (BUFVC) offers a portal for searching various archives at www.bufvc.ac.uk/databases/index.htm.

Other specialist sources

Some forms of research also require knowledge of specific procedures. Political commentators know to go to *Hansard* for a record of parliamentary business and to look up the decisions of parliamentary special committees as well as debates on the floor of the House of

Figure 10.3 Researchers wearing gloves study primary documents in the Insight Collections and Research Centre at the National Museum of Photography, Film & Television.

Insight: The Collections and Research Centre

Insight at the National Museum of Photography, Film & Television in Bradford is a resource centre which allows public access to collections in the museum's archives. There are guided tours of the research facilities and events held on a regular basis. Individuals and groups can view materials by appointment (not strictly necessary, but recommended if there is something you specifically want to see). Make contact via the website at www.nmpft.org.uk/insight. This also provides online galleries with selections from collections and also useful free materials to download.

ACTIVITY 10.1

Research project

Set yourself a research project aimed at collecting material for a magazine article. Choose something general such as 'medical stories' or 'global warming'.

- Compile a cuttings library over a couple of weeks, looking through newspapers and magazines for text and photographs (look at a good spread of papers). Alternatively, download stories from internet sites and store them on disk.
- Tape television or radio programmes or use a notebook to jot down programme details. Make sure you always record your source reference, including the names of photographers or the rights holders for images.
- At the end of your allotted time, review your material. Do you have enough material to help you generate ideas for an article?

- Have you found good images or quotations?
- Have you got all the references?

This is a good practice exercise for all media students – at some stage in your course you will probably have to do this as an assignment.

ACTIVITY 10.2

Research sources

Next time there is a television broadcast of a documentary series covering a historical period, check the credits for details of the research sources (if you have satellite or cable, try the Discovery Channel).

- How many different film archives have been used?
- Are there individuals who have contributed material?
- How many researchers are named?

Watch any major political interview on television (e.g. with a government minister).

- What kinds of questions does the interviewer ask?
- Which questions would have needed some form of research – is there a named researcher for the programme?

Commons. Similarly a great deal of useful information can be found in government statistical reports, court proceedings, etc.

Using a reference library

It is tempting now to do most of your research on the internet, partly because of the sheer speed with which you can collect references and cross-reference or list sources. However, paper documents and printed publications still have an important role as source material and you should make good use of your college or university library. You may also be able to get access to specialist libraries such as that of the British Film Institute, which is part of the National Library (see Figure 10.4).

It helps if you know your way round the **Dewey decimal system** of classification and how to use the catalogue indexes. An important part of the library is the reference section in which you can find yearbooks, trade catalogues and other forms of specialist reference material. Equally important is the Journals section where you can find bound copies of academic journals.

Melvil Dewey (1851–1931) created the library system which has been updated many times. It classifies library material in ten broad groupings. This book is likely to be included in the Social Sciences 300 group – '301 Mass Media'. Specific media such as radio, television and film will be in different groupings.

HOME > FILM & TV INFO > BFI NATIONAL LIBRARY

bfi National Library

"An invaluable tool for anyone who wants to get a handle on the movies"
- Mark Kermode

We provide access to a major national research collection of documentation and information on film and television. Our priority is comprehensive coverage of British film and television, but the collection itself is international in scope.

Catalogue

Search our book catalogue online, your gateway to accessing one of the world's largest collection of books on cinema and television. Plus information on our SIFT periodicals database.

Collections

Includes books, periodicals, audio tapes, cuttings and festival materials and special collections.

Publications

Investigate our wide range of publications about film and television

Events and exhibitions

Events and exhibitions taking place in the *bfi* National Library, with information and reading lists.

Visiting the library

The Library Collections can be consulted in the Reading Room, where you can also access our SIFT Database. Users need to buy day, annual or the new weekly passes.

Information services

We provide information and research services to a wide range of users nationally and internationally, from production companies and broadcasters, to students and members of the public.

About the Library

The history of the *bfi* National Library, with information about our preservation, acquisition and disposal policy.

Film & TV Information

For the answers to questions about film and television.

Moving Image Research Registry

Searchable database of researchers and research projects in the UK.

Last Updated: 22 Jul 2005

Figure 10.4 www.bfi.org.uk/filmtvinfo/library/. Anyone can use the BFI Library in London, but visits should be booked and there is a small fee. Details on the website.

Using the internet for research

The internet is a valuable source of material for research exercises – much of the information in this book has been discovered on, or checked against, a wide range of internet sites.

If you are going to find useful material, you need to learn to search effectively. There are dozens of search engines and reference tools to choose from and they aren't all equally useful. So don't expect that the network you use in college will necessarily be set up for the kind of research you want to do (i.e. don't just use the default search engine). There are several different starting points for internet research and you will gradually find the method which suits you, and your particular research task, best.

We have been reluctant to give too many web addresses simply because they do change over two or three years. A quick search is often more rewarding than typing in a 'known' address.

Internet details

In the material that follows, to avoid confusion, everything that you need to type into a search engine dialogue box is shown between these signs: < >. Most of the time, you don't need to use upper-case letters in your search, so <titanic> should find exactly the same material as <Titanic>. When we refer to a website or webpage we will often only give the main part of the address, e.g. www.google.co.uk – you still need the first part of the address as well, e.g. http://www.google.co.uk. In most cases, we list only the homepage of the website and you may need to search through the site to find what you want.

Using a search engine

If you are stuck as to how to start and want to collect some basic information, a search engine is very useful. There are three types of search engine:

- *simple word search or crawler* You type in a keyword and the software looks for that word across millions of pages on the internet. It will return to you all the 'hits'. They may be in order of the most relevant sites where the word appears in a page title or name – or sites may have paid a fee to be 'placed with' the search engine. The likelihood is that you will receive far more hits than you need and you will need to try to refine the search. Google at www.google.co.uk (the UK 'mirror') is the most efficient general search tool – fast and comprehensive. (See the case study following this chapter for more on using Google.)
- *metasearch engine* In this case the software sends your keyword to several different search engines at the same time and sorts the results for you. This will also return many hits and because it uses several different

engines, you may pick up webpages missed by the single engine. But it may also be more cumbersome to use; www.dogpile.com is an example of a metasearch engine.

- *'directory' search engines* These offer you a presorted catalogue of websites. The search engine's human staff have set up the categories or directories. This allows you to narrow your search and to avoid a great deal of irrelevant material. However, it may be a less productive search and also less up to date. It may also suggest a simple search if it can't find something to match your query. Yahoo (www.yahoo.com) is the best-known search site that offers directories, although it has now mainly shifted to a simple crawler. Yahoo also acts as a **portal** – a gateway to a range of information services.

Using Wikipedia

In the last few years, a new resource has appeared in the form of an encyclopedia, designed and compiled online by its users. 'Wiki' is from the Hawaiian word 'wiki wiki' meaning 'quick' or 'informal'. Although the website has editors overseeing what happens (rather like 'moderators' in chatrooms), anyone who uses the site can start a new page or edit an existing page. This could mean that the site is chaotic and unreliable but mostly that isn't what has happened so far. We have found the English language site at http://en.wikipedia.org/wiki/Main_Page to be useful for writing some parts of this book. (There are other 'wikipedias' in different languages.) The wikipedia page includes a search engine for key words and page links from each major article to smaller 'stubs'. You might find a page on which you know something that could be added – here is your chance to make a contribution.

You should be cautious about any web resource, including Wikipedia. As with other similar sites, you will get most out of it by 'registering' as a user. This will give you slightly more access and control over how you view things – but may not be possible from your college network.

Using a specialist portal

If you are simply looking for a precise item of information, such as when was the film *Saving Private Ryan* released or which company makes *The OC*, you are probably best advised to go to a specialist portal such as the Internet Movie Database (http://uk.imdb.com). IMDB is a database that offers a great deal if you learn how to use it efficiently. It is a portal in that it offers extensive links to material on other sites. Other useful portals are two of the biggest UK-based sites, at www.bbc.co.uk and www.guardian.co.uk. Both of these are very good for general news and media industries material. For something specifically concerned with media studies, you might start with Daniel Chandler's site at the University of Wales Aberystwyth, www.aber.ac.uk/media/.

Main Page
From Wikipedia, the free encyclopedia.

Welcome to Wikipedia, the free-content encyclopedia that anyone can edit.

Other languages
FAQs | Table free

In this English version, started in 2001, we are currently working on 658,047 articles.

CULTURE | GEOGRAPHY | HISTORY | LIFE | MATHEMATICS | SCIENCE | SOCIETY | TECHNOLOGY
Browse Wikipedia · Article overviews · Alphabetical index · Other schemes

Today's featured article

An **open cluster** is a group of up to a few thousand stars that were formed from the same giant molecular cloud, and are still gravitationally bound to each other. Open clusters are found only in spiral and irregular galaxies, in which active star formation is occurring. They are usually less than a few hundred million years old: they become disrupted by close encounters with other clusters and clouds of gas as they orbit the galactic centre, as well as losing cluster members through internal close encounters. Young open clusters may still be contained within the molecular cloud from which they formed, illuminating it to create an H II region. Over time, radiation pressure from the cluster will disperse the molecular cloud. Typically, about 10% of the mass of a gas cloud will coalesce into stars before radiation pressure drives the rest away. Open clusters are very important objects in the study of stellar evolution. Because the stars are all of very similar age and chemical composition, the effects of other more subtle variables on the properties of stars are much more easily studied than they are for isolated stars.

Recently featured: Tony Blair – Norman Borlaug – Blackface

Archive – By email – More featured articles...

Selected anniversaries

29 July: Ólavsøka in the Faroe Islands

- 1030 – King Olaf II fought and died in the **Battle of Stiklestad**, trying to regain his Norwegian throne from the Danes.
- 1907 – The **Scouting** movement began with the first scout camp at Brownsea

In the news

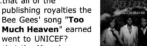

- The **Provisional Irish Republican Army** announces the end of its armed campaign in Northern Ireland and commits itself to use political means only to achieve a united Ireland.
- **Mission STS-114**: NASA grounds the Space Shuttle fleet until problems with foam insulation on the external tank are resolved.
- Unprecedented monsoon rains cause **massive floods** in Maharashtra, India, leaving at least 750 people dead.
- Attempted suicide bombing suspect **Yasin Hassan Omar** is arrested in connection with the **21 July 2005 London bombings** in London.
- **Lance Armstrong** wins his seventh consecutive Tour de France and confirms his retirement from bicycle racing.

Wikinews · Recent deaths · More current events...

Did you know...

From Wikipedia's newest articles:

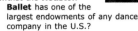

- ...that all of the publishing royalties the Bee Gees' song "**Too Much Heaven**" earned went to UNICEF?
- ...that the **Houston Ballet** has one of the largest endowments of any dance company in the U.S.?

Figure 10.5 The 'home page' of Wikipedia at http://en.wikipedia.org. The appearance of the site is governed by the choice of 'skin' accessible to registered users.

As you visit sites, you can make a note of them and store the addresses as 'bookmarks' or 'favourites', but, if you are working on a network, it may be easier to keep a paper record. As a shortcut, all you need to do is to keep the keyword in the address or URL ('unique resource locator'). Then you can use that word in Google to get to the site you want quickly. For example <'guardian unlimited'> should immediately produce www.guardian.co.uk. You may even find that simply typing <guardian> into Google brings up the Guardian site immediately as the first hit.

In many cases, the quickest and most effective way to find anything is to type it in Google. You are almost guaranteed to find something useful in a matter of seconds. But if your research is going to be successful, you need to develop some strategies for refining your search. In 'Case study: Researching mobile phone technologies' we explore ways to do this in more detail.

How useful is the information you find?

If you have a hundred hits to plough through even after you have refined your search, it is likely that the most useful material will be in the first few that the search engine lists. But how reliable is the information? Anyone can put a website up on the net, so you will need to verify every statement. Check the following:

- Who is responsible for the site? It should tell you on the home page.
- Does the URL give a clue? The last part of the address should tell you: 'edu' or 'ac' is an educational institution (but it could be a student page), 'org' is a 'not for profit' organisation, 'gov' is government, 'com' or 'co' is a commercial site, 'net' is a network provider and 'mil' is military.
- Does the site have a specific viewpoint?
- How up to date is the page? 'Dead pages' can linger on otherwise live sites for a long time and may now be factually incorrect or misleading.

Finding material on the web is sometimes exciting – there is enormous satisfaction in finding something after a long search. But you need to step back. Would it have been easier to look it up in a reference book in the library? How time-consuming is it, if you feel that you have to verify what you find? What you need is experience of using the web to conduct meaningful research and practice at refining searches. There is one area in which the web excels, and that is up-to-date figures. Often these are online before they are published in hard copy. Look for sites involved in media business dealings. Often the trade association for that sector or companies offering market research or industry analyses are most useful. We've put a list of suggested websites in the 'Useful information' section of this book.

Using your web findings

You may be using a network or your own computer, Explorer or Firefox as a browser on a PC or Safari on a Mac, so we can't advise you on how to store your material. But the main point to remember is to keep track of the sites you have visited. It's so easy to use links from one site to another that you can soon lose track of where you have been. You need the URL of each site you have visited for the references listed in your work. You could print out the relevant pages (checking that you have the URL printed on them). But if there is material that you want to quote, this means rekeying it later on. If you can 'cut and paste' from the web page into an open file in a wordprocessor (with the URL pasted in as well) you may save yourself time. You can also save the file direct from the web, but you need to check how the software you are using does this – saving a file as HTML will save all the codings among the text that you want (look for 'print-friendly' versions of files). If you have an email address, you can email yourself the URL to check later on your own machine.

What is worth downloading is any material offered as a 'pdf'. This is a computer file which works on any computer with Acrobat Reader (freely downloadable from www.adobe.com). If your browser has Reader installed, the file will open on your computer and you can save it to disk as well (some pdfs are too big for a floppy disk). You can then read the publication later, exactly as it appeared on screen. Pdfs are increasingly being used for company statements, reports, statistics, etc. and we have used many of them in preparing this book.

Referencing and bibliographies

Research is an essential academic skill, and you will no doubt be expected to provide full references for any sources you have consulted in preparing essays or reports. There are three reasons for doing this:

- References allow anyone reading your work to refer to your original sources, perhaps to find out more background.
- The references you provide are essential in order to avoid any charges of plagiarism – passing off someone else's work as your own.
- A good range of references demonstrates your wide background reading – often part of the assessment criteria for courses.

There are several different methods for referencing academic sources. It doesn't necessarily matter which one you use, although some academic institutions specify a preferred option. It is important to be consistent and thorough. We have used the 'Harvard' system. You'll see the name of an author next to a quotation, followed by a year and sometimes a page number. We like giving the full first name of authors, though often only initials are used. You can then go to the references at the end of a chapter and look up the full entry which will give you the author, year of publication, title, place of publication and publisher. Magazine articles are also listed with the magazine issue number and date. You should give the full URL of any web page you quote, and it may also be useful to give the date on which you visited the site (it may disappear in the meantime).

Production research

This refers to a whole range of logistical issues, some of which, concerning information needed by a production crew, are discussed in Chapter 11 under the heading of 'Recce' and Location. But there are also research tasks concerned with the 'talent' on a programme – finding contestants for a quiz show, compiling possible interview questions or a dossier on a studio guest. Here, background research will be worked on to produce something usable in a live show.

Other forms of production research may refer to props, costumes, etc. and how these are to be used in the final programme. You may have to find not only authentic swords and armour but also trainers to show actors how to use them. The various guides to career opportunities stress that production research in television especially requires a high level of interpersonal skills and that much of the working day is spent on the phone persuading people to do things for the programme. The researcher may also be responsible for checking out all the potential legal, ethical and regulatory issues that may arise if research material is used.

As a student on a production course you might be asked to sign an 'ethics agreement'.

ACTIVITY 10.3

Production research

Record five minutes from two different television programmes – a consumer affairs or 'lifestyle' programme and a 'costume drama' (anything not set in the present day).

Make a note of all the different production research activities that each programme may have involved, including:

- props, clothes, vehicles, etc.
- personality backgrounds
- experts needed
- permissions, copyright
- legal, ethical, regulatory issues, etc.

Does one type of programme require more research?

Audience research

Constructing an audience profile for a particular product or investigating a specific target audience is a specialised area of work. Some media producers employ market research companies to analyse markets and specific audiences for their products. You may be required to do this before undertaking a production – finding out what your target audience wants. You may also conduct some audience research after your production has been presented to an audience in an attempt to find out how it has been received.

Although they have different purposes, audience research may share a number of features with academic research (see below). Both distinguish between quantitative and qualitative research. Production companies want to know about a specific target audience, so they will want to be assured about the sample selected by the research company. It needs to include sufficient people to be representative of different age, class and gender divisions across the different regions where the media product may be experienced. **Quantitative audience research** for producers is a number-crunching exercise and aims to produce audience figures for cinema and broadcasting, and readership figures for print products. Each industry follows different conventions: cinema is usually interested in 'frequency of visits to a cinema'; television looks at 'shares' of a potential audience achieved by a programme, and newspapers are interested in both circulation and readership.

See Chapter 8 for more on this.

In your own quantitative research you will necessarily lack the resources of a research company, but you can carry out worthwhile research if you remember these points:

See Chapter 1 and case study on 'content analysis'.

- Think about your target audience and what you want to know. The better your sample reflects the composition of the audience, the more useful the results.
- The bigger the sample, the more likely the results will be credible;
- Ask 'closed' questions that will produce numerical data that can easily be input into a spreadsheet to produce analyses.

'Closed' questions invite a simple 'yes' or 'no' or a definable number, e.g. 'How many CDs did you buy last month?' None, one, two to five, more than five?

From these points it is clear that your research needs careful planning. If your target audience comprises shoppers or consumers it may be useful to ask simple questions in the shopping centre during the day. But this will not necessarily produce a useful sample if you need to include people in work. As you collect responses you need to note gender, age, etc. if this is relevant.

Research organisations employ a range of methods to collect data. You may have been approached on the street by a researcher with a clip board or you may have been 'doorstepped' at home. Another possibility is a 'cold call' on the telephone (unless you have taken steps to block such calls). In all these circumstances, there must be some doubt as to the usefulness of the data since only those willing to spend time with the researcher will answer questions – many people will refuse to stop or decline to answer at the door or on the telephone. To get round these problems, 'consumer surveys' sometimes offer an inducement – shopping vouchers or free entry into a prize draw. One form of consumer survey is the 'reader survey' that you may have come across in specialist magazines. Here your tastes will be explored in terms not just of what else you read, but also of what other kinds of goods you buy. Research data can be sold to other companies or jointly sponsored by companies with interests in the same audience but in relation to different products.

One reason why you may be asked to take part in research is because research bureaux sometimes target communities by postcode. The ACORN system, used by the marketing data firm CACI, groups consumers by postcode. A postcode usually covers around fifteen households, who may be expected to share certain characteristics. A similar form of audience research is conducted via some film previews where audiences are offered a free screening in return for completion of 'scorecards' about a new film.

ACORN   A Classification Of Residential Neighbourhoods – you can look up your own street classification using www.upmystreet.com.

You can get a good idea of media industry research from the website of BMRB International (British Market Research Bureau): www.bmrb.co.uk offers a wealth of information and will help you see what market research can offer media producers. One of BMRB's strategies has been to develop a TGI (Target Group Index) for various groups including children and young people (partly because most media industry readership surveys ignore readers under the age of fifteen). The following box gives a good example of a new area of research.

Young Chelsea fans

In May 2005, BMRB produced a report on the increasing numbers of young Chelsea fans aged 11–19. This was tied to the success of Chelsea during the 2004–5 season under José Mourinho. Here are some of the 'headline findings':

- More than 280,000 11–19 year-olds support Chelsea.
- The group grew by over 30 per cent in 2004–5 (the number of similar Manchester United fans fell by 6 per cent in the same period).
- The Chelsea supporters are concentrated in London and are 30 per cent more likely to live in the South East than Arsenal fans.
- They are more likely to go to the cinema and to use the internet than fans of Newcastle United or Manchester United.
- They are 50 per cent more likely than the average 11–19 year-old to agree with the statement that they are 'more trendy than [their] friends'.

(Report by Russell Budden for *Media Week*, news item downloaded from www.bmrb.co.uk, 5 June 2005)

As well as confirming what many fans of other football teams might suspect, this research gives us clues as to how the marketing industry works and who might benefit from the collection of such data. It should help the publishers of Chelsea's football programme, website and television service to target parts of their audience and to sell advertising space to agencies. It may interest the agents of stars like Frank Lampard and Joe Cole as well as a much wider constituency of media producers, marketeers and agencies concerned with this age group.

ACTIVITY 10.4

Selling a football brand

Look at the research in the box above and then check the websites of a selection of Premiership clubs (and perhaps other big clubs in Europe).

- Could they benefit from this kind of research?
- Do they all target the same kinds of fans?

Ranking If you want to ask audiences to rank their feelings about a media product, it's a good idea to offer four options rather than three – otherwise many will opt for a non-committal 'answer in the middle'. With four options, they are forced to move towards 'liked' or 'disliked'.

Qualitative research suggests that it is not the number of responses that is important, but the opinions or ideas that respondents express. A questionnaire may still be useful if you offer multiple choice-type questions (possibly a ranking of responses) and also allow some 'open' questions. Other possibilities are interviews or discussions ('focus groups' – see Chapter 8 – are observed discussions) or diaries written by audiences over a short period. Your aim here is to find out what the audience thinks about a media product. How you interpret your findings will depend on your objectives. If you want to use audience responses to help you with your next production, the most useful responses are those that tell you something that you don't already know.

If your only audience is other students on your course, you may face the problem that they are far too polite about your work. Anonymous response forms, direct questions ('What didn't you like about . . .?') or observation may be needed. You can tell a lot by watching and listening to different audiences viewing your work – when do they laugh or groan, when do they fidget, when do they appear rapt? But you may well be better off with a different audience altogether.

'Open' questions usually begin with words such as 'how' or 'why' and invite a response that explores an issue.

Academic research

There is discussion of the most high-profile academic research concerning 'audience effects' in Chapter 6. Academic research uses both quantitative methods (in studying representation issues, for instance – 'content analysis') and qualitative methods, and similar issues arise as to those discussed above in relation to audience research. What distinguishes academic research (most of the time, at least) is the purpose of the exercise. Most commercially funded audience research is designed to produce data to help media producers target audiences more effectively and for advertisers to identify products with advertising opportunities that can demonstrate their efficiency in 'delivering audiences'. Academic research is interested in how media communication works, how producers and audiences behave, how media products change over time and in different social, political and economic contexts, etc.

Academic research begins with a hypothesis – 'a proposition or a question assumed for the sake of argument'. Material is then gathered in an attempt to demonstrate that the hypothesis can be proved. Research findings are collated and analysed and conclusions formed which are then published. Such work is essential to higher education and in recent years has become even more important as funding of universities depends to some extent on the research output of staff. You may well select a university on the basis of its specialisms in media research.

The likelihood is that you will be required to carry out a research project as part of the assessment of your course. An assignment may require you to carry out some form of primary and secondary research. Again, much of the discussion above is relevant in how you organise your work. You will probably be advised to discuss the title of your project with your tutor or supervisor. It is a good idea to have a clear argument in mind, a definite initial question, in such projects and not just to collect as much information as you can. There are two good reasons for sorting this out at an early stage:

- Many students select very broad areas of research, possibly because they think it will be easy to find material (e.g. 'the representation of young men on British television') and they won't need to do that tricky thing: formulate a good research question to which they're looking for the answer. The difficulty with broad areas of research is that it is difficult to produce worthwhile conclusions because it is too difficult to analyse all the available material and to make interesting comparisons. Cutting down the area to include one television genre in one time period might be a better bet.

- Some media texts are difficult to find. This is particularly true of films and television programmes, which are often inexplicably out of print.

On the other hand, certain texts are not only widely available but have also been discussed in academic journals and on internet mailing lists. Although you may want to find an obscure text, and can try advertising in internet chatrooms or other locations, good advice can point you to research topics that will enable you more easily to undertake effective primary and secondary research.

The case study which follows looks at how you might research material on a popular debate in contemporary media studies.

References and further reading

Chater, Kathy (2001) *Research for Media Production*, Oxford: Focal Press.

Clare, Vanessa (2005) *Researching Film and Media Studies: A Teacher's Guide*, Leighton Buzzard: Auteur Publishing.

O'Sullivan, Tim, Dutton, Brian and Rayner, Philip (2003) 'Media research and investigation', in *Studying the Media*, 3rd edition, London: Hodder Arnold.

Skinner, Megan (not dated) *Research: The Essential Guide*, London: BFI (available for free download from www.bfi.org.uk/education/teaching/researchguide/pdf/bfi-edu-resources_research-the-essential-guide.pdf, as at July 2005).

Websites

www.bfi.org.uk (a useful source of information about film and television, it includes pages for the National Film and Television Archive, the BFI Library (the National Library for Film) and a Researcher's Guide. A good 'portal' for all searches on film and television).

www.skillset.org (the Film and Broadcast Industry National Training Organisation with good links and offering access to career advice).

See Chapter 13 for industry audience research links.

CASE STUDY: RESEARCHING MOBILE PHONE TECHNOLOGIES

- **Getting started**
- **Using Wikipedia**
- **Company websites**
- **Keeping your eyes and ears open**
- **Academic research into phone use**
- **Googling**
- **References and further reading**

A common media debate concerns the impact of new media technologies. In this case study we will consider ways of accessing and using research material for such a debate. Depending on your course, you may be asked to give a short written answer to a relatively simple question or to explore a more complex set of questions in a longer essay in which you discuss your research methodologies. In both cases you will need to prepare by undertaking background research.

Let's begin by considering a relatively straightforward question:

Q How has the development of 'text and image messaging' on mobile phones affected the media industries and the media consumer?

You may feel that you can get straight to grips with this question because you are probably one of those consumers who have enjoyed using your mobile phone and have upgraded to get new features. However, if you want to answer the question effectively, you will need to stand back and 'distance' yourself from your own experience to make sure you take account of the wider question. You can then use what you know in conjunction with what you find.

Getting started

There are many ways to approach this kind of question (including using proprietary software packages to help you order your ideas) and you should use the way that suits you best. Here we will use a 'spidogram'. The question is about 'text and image messaging', so we'll put that in the centre. We want to know about its impact on two separate entities, industries/producers and consumers/users. In effect, the three are linked together in a kind of triangular relationship. Now we can see a dynamic relationship between the three, what will we need to do to explore how it works?

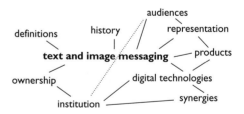

Figure 10.6 Spidergram of producers, consumers and texting.

A definition of each of the three would be useful as well as some further understanding of media industries (ownership) and media consumers (how do we describe/classify them?). The relationship will have developed over time so we need to consider its 'history'. We would expect all our key concepts to be important in some way so it would be good to check through 'representation', 'audience', 'institution', etc. Our final spidogram (Figure 10.6) will give us a sense of the possible ground to cover. Some concepts may be less important than others, but it is useful to have a checklist to make sure we don't miss any obvious points.

Let's look at how we might pursue one or two of these. We might be texting every day, but do we know what kind of technology it is, when it started and how it developed? We will need a workable definition of terms.

Using Wikipedia

Wikipedia is a good starting point for definitions. Type <text messaging> into the search box on Wikipedia's front page (i.e. the words inside the <> symbols). You should be taken to the page shown in Figure 10.7. It won't necessarily look the same on your computer because we have selected a 'skin' – a page design – that we find easier to read, but it should contain the same information. You could also get there by typing <texting>. Of course, Wikipedia is always being updated, so the page might change over time. Even so, we can be confident it will give us some starting points.

The page tells us that the official term for texting is **SMS** (short message service) and it offers links to 'mobile phones' and to 'GSM' (global system for mobile communications) and '3G' (third generation mobile phone technology) – we'll decide if we want to pursue these a little later. It also suggests that the first text message was sent in 1992 to a phone on a Vodafone network. The rest of the Wikipedia entry tells us something about which country has the most frequent 'texters' (Singapore) and about the swift growth of a valuable business. In 2004, there were 500 billion texts sent worldwide, a business worth around $50 billion. Several other related technologies are mentioned as well as some indication of news stories involving text messages. At the bottom of the page we find references and links, to both other Wikipedia pages and to external sites. It might be useful at this point to follow the link for **MMS** (multimedia messaging system). This reveals that there is a second set of technologies associated with sending images and video via mobile phones. We need at this stage to summarise some of our findings:

- 'Text messaging' and 'image messaging' are two separate technologies known as SMS and MMS.
- They work on widely available mobile phone systems such as GSM (Global System for Mobile

Short message service
(Redirected from Texting)

Short message service (**SMS**) is a service available on most digital mobile phones that permits the sending of short messages (also known as **SMSes**, **text messages**, **messages**, or more colloquially **texts** or even **txts**) between mobile phones, other handheld devices and even landline telephones. SMS was originally designed as part of the GSM digital mobile phone standard, but is now available on a wide range of networks, including 3G networks.

The first SMS is believed to have been sent in December 1992 by Neil Papworth of Sema Group from a personal computer (PC) to a mobile phone on the Vodafone GSM network in the United Kingdom.

Contents
1 Technical details
2 Popularity
3 Txt speak
4 Innovations
5 See also
6 References
7 External links

A received SMS being announced on a Nokia phone.

Figure 10.7 Wikipedia page (en.wikipedia.org/wiki/Texting).

351

Communications) – digital telephony systems available worldwide.

- The idea of 'messaging' dates back to at least 1992.
- It involves telephone companies such as Vodafone.
- Messaging is a very widespread activity that has had impact on public and private life.

These are all important areas of research which refer to our original question. We haven't yet looked at the history of the technology (i.e. from 2G to 3G) and we could make a decision at this point as to how much detail we need on both the history and the nature of the technology and its protocols (how it is to be used). You will often have to make a decision like this since you could spend all your time reading background material and amassing more and more detail, without actually developing an argument and answering the question. Here, we will simply note that 2G technologies operating in GSM systems enabled the spread of the practices of texting and image messaging that the question requires us to discuss. We'll now focus on:

- the telephone companies ('**telcos**') – which companies, how do they hope to make profits, how are their activities regulated?

We could continue to explore Wikipedia, but a better bet may be to use selected specialist websites associated with the telcos and the news organisations which report on consumer behaviour. We also need to bear in mind that we are interested in 'messaging' as a media form. This means that we are thinking about mobile phones as a new form of distributing and displaying both traditional media texts and 'new media' ('texting' could itself be described as new media).

Company websites

UK readers will know about most local phone service providers and it shouldn't take long to find two of the biggest, O_2 and Vodafone.

Vodafone's website is at www.vodafone.co.uk and O_2's at www.o2.com (but don't forget they may change website details). Just type <Vodafone> or

<O_2> into any search engine and the company website should come up in the first few hits. Both websites have a similar design and the first question is where to look to find some useful material. The sites most likely to appear on search lists are 'consumer sites', designed to give information and persuade potential customers to sign up with the provider. A good start for us might be to look at the menu for an 'About us' or 'About this site' entry. This will often lead to a corporate site where you can find details of the ownership of the company, the size of its operation and possibly a 'Media Centre' with press releases announcing new products or services or changes in the business operation. On these two websites there is a great deal of information. The Vodafone site tells us that in 2005 there are nearly 50 million mobile phones in the UK and that Vodafone has 14.6 million customers. O_2 claims 14.38 million so we know that we have found two of the biggest companies. What else do we learn about the mobile telephony business?

- Both companies list their operations in other countries – Vodafone has operations in '27 countries, across five continents', making it a global player (see comments on other similar companies such as Telefónica in 'Case study: The media majors').
- The major announcement about technology involves the move to '**3G**' and the new media services this will make available.

Vodafone's site provides a very sophisticated 'flash' presentation which creates a future world of science fiction-like communication. This will give us plenty of ideas that we could follow up. Let's stick with just two aspects of this for a moment:

- How do the telcos relate to the media industries?
- Why are they discussing 3G?

If we go back to Wikipedia, we can find out pretty quickly that O_2 began life as part of BT, once British Telecom, a public sector corporation that was 'privatised' in 1984. O_2 is part of the much wider process described in Chapter 7 and 'Case study: The media majors', in which the newly privatised **telcos** started to look for investment opportunities in new goods and services. Vodafone, on the other hand, was created by an electronics group which applied for the first licences to operate mobile phones in the UK in 1985 (along with British Telecom). The company became independent in 1991 and has grown very quickly through mergers and acquisitions. The 'application for licences' refers to the UK situation where a government regulator grants access to radio frequencies used for all kinds of services. You could follow this line of enquiry through Wikipedia, but it's easier just to 'Google' for <UK telephone regulator>. This produces thousands of 'hits' but the first few are likely to show in the brief description that Ofcom is the UK regulator.

You might just be able to see from Figure 10.8 that it is helpful if your browser has a 'tab' facility. In this exercise we have used a new tab for Wikipedia, O_2, Vodafone and Google, so we can easily select the site we need without having to trawl back through past pages.

We can follow the Google link to Ofcom's website where there is a host of information about regulation of telecommunications, as well as radio, television, etc., since Ofcom is now the UK's 'super regulator'

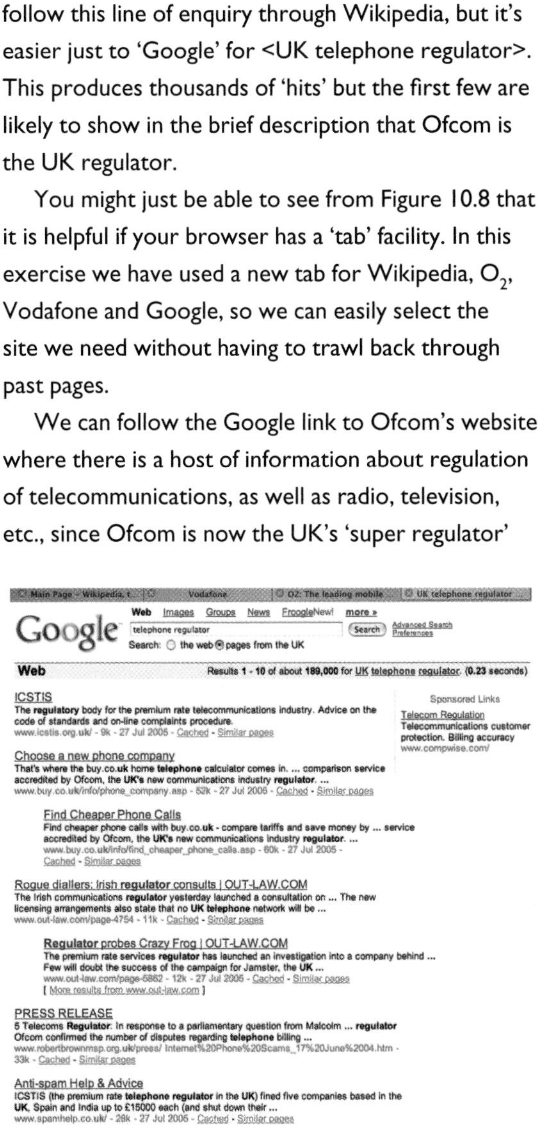

Figure 10.8 Google search results for UK telephone regulator.

looking after media as well as telephone services. Of course we don't need to use the internet to make the connection between media and telephony via Ofcom. The index in a book like this one will take us to appropriate chapters and case studies.

So what is the important connection? Presumably it concerns G3, since G3 licences were the last to be awarded. If we return to O_2's site, we can find a press release announcing a trial in which sixteen television channels will provide material to download to O_2 customers in Oxford. The companies' websites will always want to promote their new services, but you should cross-reference what the companies say with Google searches for comments by industry analysts (and possibly 'users') to get a more distanced view on the claims being made.

Progress review

It is good practice to stop your research at regular intervals and review what you have discovered. So far, we have a rough outline of the development of the technology for texting and image messaging. We know that the companies involved were formed as part of the 'deregulation and privatisation' of utilities in the 1980s and that they grew rapidly with the take-up of these new technologies. They are now hoping to capitalise on the next generation of phone technologies by selling media services such as video, digital music, etc. We seem to have established a basic argument around one side of the original question, but what do we know about phone users? This might be more difficult to research since material is unlikely to be collected on just one or two websites.

Keeping your eyes and ears open

You can find a great deal of information by intelligent internet searching, but you should use other starting points as well. In terms of the use of mobile phones, we might want to address questions of representation. Who uses phones and for what purposes? How can we tie this to media use? Here are two examples of interesting observations that appeared in UK media in 2005.

- Mobile phones save lives and promote small businesses in Africa.
- 'Texting' is the most popular phone service for 'teens' – to the dismay of service providers who hope to sell much more lucrative services.

The first of these stories was broadcast on Radio 4's *In Business* programme (9 June 2005) – not perhaps the station most listened to by readers of this book, but it is important to note relevant stories whenever you hear them and try to check back to sources. (In fact, the importance of texting in Africa came through strongly on Radio 4's 'Africa Day' in May 2005 when people from all over Africa were contacting the BBC.) BBC broadcasts can often be tracked down via the BBC website on www.bbc.co.uk, where you can find a programme home page. The programme in this case was actually 'podcast' and downloadable as an MP3 file. Searching for the programme via Google also turned up this page: www.textually.org/textually/archives/cat_mobile_phone_projects_third_world.htm.

There are links to similar stories around the world that all refer to the same basic point. People in many parts of Africa, where there is a limited electricity supply, a lack of 'landlines' for telecommunications, etc., have been excluded from the supposed 'global village' and all that means in terms of telecomms and media (the 'digital divide' between rich and poor – see Chapter 15). To put landlines or any other physical infrastructure in place would be very expensive, but a wireless mobile phone system means much easier access. In Kenya the number of telephone users has increased dramatically since a mobile company started a network in 2001. Safari.com is a Kenyan company owned by Vodafone (40 per cent) and Kenya's state-owned Telcom Kenya (60 per cent). Mobile users far outnumber those with landlines. The image of African street markets in which traders and customers are exchanging information about prices by mobile phone is not one we think of in the West. Growth is now actually faster in the rural areas than in the cities, since people really need communication technology to live – it isn't a luxury related to extra consumer spending. This is an interesting story, but is it relevant to media use? We might need to think about it as an example of the ways in which 'users' can change the perceptions of industry planners. It could also be important for broadcasters and other media producers trying to reach audiences scattered across large countries with a poor communications infrastructure. Let's consider the second story and see if there is a link.

A report on texting by teens worldwide was used as the basis for an article in the *Guardian* by Natalie Hanman (9 June 2005). The original report, the Youth Report, came from: www.w2forum.com/view/mobileyouth_2005_report and included some interesting facts and figures:

Much to the chagrin of operators keen to see early adopters of mobile technology hooked on more lucrative functions, such as picture messaging (MMS), mobile music and mobile internet, teenagers are keeping things simple – and cheap. . . . Among those teens who text the most, boys outnumber girls by 3:1.

. . . After texting, the next most popular mobile tool for teenagers – particularly girls in their mid-teens – is taking photographs. But instead of sharing these photos by sending a picture message (MMS), young girls prefer the cheaper option of comparing them in person.

These findings question some of the stereotypes that might exist (i.e. that girls text most) and they point to a crucial problem for the telcos who have paid very dearly for 3G licences (Chancellor Gordon Brown auctioned these licences in 2003 and made a considerable sum for HM Treasury). They hoped to target the traditional 'early adopters' of new technologies (usually older males with high incomes) but instead are servicing younger consumers who won't pay for the expensive aspects of the service.

ACTIVITY 10.5

Survey phone users

- Find out which of your friends have 3G phones and what they are prepared to pay for.
- Try and ask the same question of people in different age/gender groups.
- What conclusions do you draw from your findings?

Academic research into phone use

These two stories throw up leads which could be followed up by reference to other chapters in this book and other books and journals. Phone use has clearly changed dramatically since the mid-1990s. The new services and the new ways 'consumers' have discovered to use their phones have created new 'media forms'. We can demonstrate:

- the convergence of technologies and organisations which exploit them in combined telecommunications and media industries
- phone use as an integral part of certain media texts – reality TV, gameshows, etc.
- new media products – streaming video, ringtones, etc.

We can safely assume that market research (e.g. the Youth Report discussed above) and academic research is being undertaken into these developments. How do we access this? Unfortunately, much of the research may be out of our reach because as valuable market data it is expensive to purchase directly or as part of a subscription. We might only be able to read headlines or summaries. But these will still be useful as starting points or guides. Academic research is more accessible, but even here there will be restrictions as to what is available to all users over the internet.

Your college library should provide you with a selection of books and journals. Where will you look for recent publications which might provide source material? You could search through subject catalogues looking for telephone technologies, telephone usage, etc. You could browse library shelves covering 'communications industries', 'sociology of mass communications', etc. (Check the Dewey Classification System to find where these might be.) And you could look to see which academic journals and trade publications your reference library stocks. In university libraries these holdings should be extensive and you may also be able to use research databases which give you access to journal articles online. Access to these services is restricted so we can't expect all readers to be able to use them. Instead, we'll look at more limited searches freely available via the internet.

FindArticles is an American web portal at www.findarticles.com. Its 'front page' offers the possibility of searching for 'free articles' in various categories or from a general search box. The articles in question come from general interest magazines, academic journals and trade publications – all with some kind of reputation as credible sources. When we searched on the site we found these articles quite quickly using search terms such as <text message> and <new media phone>:

'Newspapers See Danger in Text Messaging'
eWEEK, May 2004, BAGNAIA, Italy (AP)

International editors and publishers warned Friday that nontraditional communications – such as cell phone text messages – are rapidly outflanking radio, television, and print media because of their immediacy and proximity to the public.

(www.findarticles.com/p/articles/
mi_zdewk/is_200405/ai_n9519940)

'Media: the rise of the people's news'
David Edwards, *New Statesman*, 24 May 2004

Digital and internet-based technologies make participants in any event potentially irrefutable witnesses to what really happened. Backed up by websites and bloggers around the world, these 'citizen reporters' now represent a significant challenge to the compromised intermediaries of corporate journalism.'

(www.findarticles.com/p/articles/ mi_m0FQP/is_4689_133/ai_n6156736)

Both these articles refer directly to the new role of phone technologies in relation to news – in the first case, gaining access to news and in the second to the possibility that images taken on mobile phones by members of the public could challenge traditional reporting (the article deals with stories about the torture of Iraqi suspects by US military personnel). This raises the question of whether we should be searching more widely for material on the internet – even if we must expect to question the authenticity of our findings. We'll conclude our research by thinking a little more about using a search engine such as Google.

Googling

Google is a general search engine or 'crawler'. Rather a speedy crawler, it finds keywords on millions of pages in a few seconds. Enter <new media phone> in Google's search box and it will produce more than 65 million 'hits'. Likewise, <media studies phone> is not very useful with 21 million hits, most of which are irrelevant for our purposes. We can narrow the focus of the search with some simple techniques. Putting double quote marks around a phrase will search for the specific phrase, so <"media studies" "mobile phone"> produces a slightly more manageable list as we can see in Figure 10.9. The first few hits all look as if they could be helpful and in fact the second entry on the list is written by a UK media teacher specifically for AS/A2 media studies students. (You might wonder why, given the dominance of American websites, there are no US hits here. The reasons are straightforward – American usage is 'cell phone' rather than 'mobile phone'. Also, use of cell phones is less than in Europe

Figure 10.9 Page of Google hits for 'media studies' 'mobile phone'.

or Asia, partly because many 'landline' calls are free.) We can also limit searches to 'UK sites only'.

It looks as if our decision to use these phrases in quotes will prove productive. But although the web pages look useful at first glance, we still have plenty of work to do and we won't always be so lucky. Depending on the keywords entered, you could be faced with sites in other languages and also commercial sites selling phones or media studies textbooks. You can avoid some of this by using Google's advanced search facilities. Figure 10.10 shows how to limit the search to English-language sites, specifically university or college sites within the past year – effectively filtering out many irrelevant hits and reducing the results to 244, as shown in Figure 10.11.

You should be able to find something useful in these results – the listing from Swansea University actually takes you to a page advising you how to carry out research, just as this case study does. The danger of getting too wrapped up in your research is that you

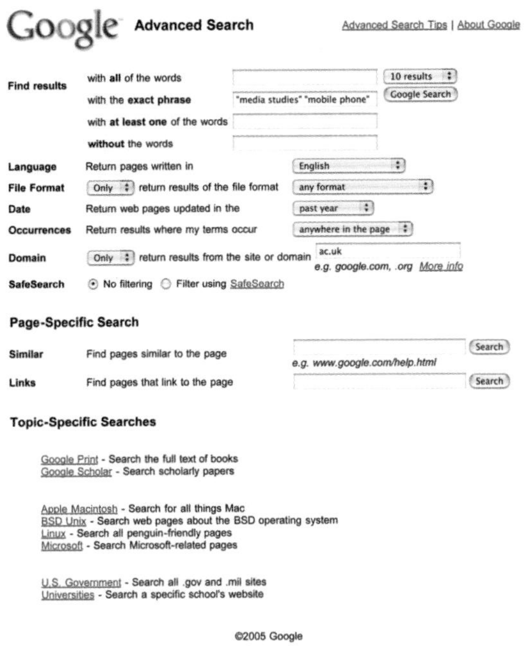

Figure 10.10   Google Advanced Search facilities.

Figure 10.11   Revised page of Google hits.

will go off into interesting tangents, spending time exploring all the fascinating things that people do with mobile phones. Don't forget your original research question. Focus on what the question asks for and then find one or two good examples (mini case studies?) you can explore in more detail, using Google's Advanced Search facilities and seeking out library resources to complement what you find on the internet. Make sure you keep track of all your references and you should have enough material to write your essay.

References and further reading

For this case study, you should simply explore the various research resources cited and make sure that you know how to make the best use of them.

ACTIVITY 10.6

Essay planning

Outline an essay plan for the initial question given at the beginning of this case study.

Use the research materials referenced here and decide which lines of research you would follow.

11 Production organisation

• **The production process in outline**	• **Production**
• **Setting out**	• **Post-production**
• **Negotiating a brief**	• **References and further reading**
• **Pre-production**	

In this chapter we deal with the organisation and management of media production tasks. Along with Chapter 12, the information and advice here will enable you to understand the production process and to approach your own productions with confidence.

The production process in outline

If you discuss the concept of the production process with professionals who work in different media (e.g. magazine publishing, television, etc.), they will probably stress the differences – the specificities – of their own particular work practices. In Chapter 7 we outline a six-stage production process which, while primarily concerned with film, will serve equally well for other types of media production, even if the professionals concerned would not necessarily recognise the terms used:

- development or negotiating a brief
- pre-production
- production
- post-production
- distribution
- exhibition.

These stages represent the production process for a single, coherent product. An established, daily, media product like a newspaper won't need to involve endless negotiation and pre-production (although the inclusion of some material will still need to be negotiated), but when the product was first devised the production team will have gone through these stages. A television or radio series is commissioned as a block – a set number of episodes – and each commission can be treated as a single production.

'Development' is the term used in the film industry. A 'brief' is a design industry term, also used in video production. In many industries a freelance producer, writer or director hopes to be 'commissioned' by a 'publisher' of some kind.

Setting out

Whatever the production task, there are several important questions which need to be asked at the outset.

Purpose

Why are you producing a media text? Most likely it will be to 'educate, inform or entertain'. If it isn't one of these, then it is probably intended to persuade. All production must be entertaining to a certain extent or else readers won't persevere with the text. Your production will be assessed according to the extent to which it 'fits its purpose', and you should bear this in mind throughout each stage of the process.

A criticism of some recent British films is that they were made just because the resources existed to make them – not because the producers had something they wanted to say or because they wanted a big hit. Media products need a clear purpose and a recognised audience.

Target audience

The meaning produced by a text depends to a large extent on the intended reader, and it's futile to try to construct a text if you don't know who that reader is. The audience profile will include the standard age, gender and class information as well as more culturally based distinctions which might include religion, sexual orientation, marital or family status, etc., and environmental factors such as geographical location (see Chapter 8 for further discussion of the descriptions used by media industries).

ACTIVITY 11.1

Thinking about audiences

If you are given a relatively 'open brief' on your course, it's tempting to choose something with a target audience made up of your own peers. It seems easier because you understand the audience. But that can mean that you don't really do the work of thinking about the audience. It can be more useful to try to think about a very different target audience. Imagine you are asked to produce a television magazine format show (twenty minutes of different studio items and filmed inserts). Brainstorm some ideas for a show to appeal to:

- a 'daytime' audience of parents with young children
- a Sunday morning audience of men aged 55+

(Check the BBC website at www.bbc.co.uk/commissioning/marketresearch for ideas about television audiences.)

Budget and funding

Media production requires money – large amounts in many cases. Where does it come from?

Direct sales

This is a typical 'cash flow' problem. The business may be financially viable, but the money coming in isn't always at the right time to cover the necessary expenditure. Smaller companies are often forced to pay bills on time, whereas larger companies can make their smaller suppliers wait.

Not many producers can be self-funding – generating enough income from sales to fund the next production. In most cases, the preparation costs and the delay in receiving income mean that the outlay is too big for a small company to cover.

There are then a limited number of options available. Borrowing the money from a bank will mean high interest payments, putting more pressure on the 'need to succeed'. Selling an interest in your production to a backer is perhaps a less risky venture, but of course it means that, if you do well, a share of the profits goes to your backers.

Pre-sales

Continuing production can be guaranteed if you can 'pre-sell' your products at a fixed price. This way you may cover the whole of your budget with a guaranteed sale. The disadvantage is that if your product is very successful and could command a higher price, you will have forgone potential profits.

Selling rights to a distributor

This saves you the trouble and the risk of selling your product in territories (or to other media) which you don't know much about. A distributor pays you a fixed sum. Once again, you lose profits if the product is successful.

Selling ideas

If you can sell your production idea, you can save yourself the bother of producing at all. You can also negotiate to make your product as a commission for a major producer, leaving someone else to worry about budgets while you just take a fee.

Sponsorship or advertising

You may get someone else to pay for the production (or part of it) as part of a sponsorship deal. Companies may be interested in being associated with a 'quality' product, especially if it addresses a specific target audience that they want to reach. A specialised form of sponsorship involves **product placement**. Print products and possibly radio broadcasts may be funded by the direct sale of advertising space. The danger of sponsorship is that the sponsors' views on the production may compromise your own aims.

Grant-aid

If you have no money and little experience, you may actually be better placed to get started on a project than if you have a track record. Many arts agencies offer grants to new producers. These may be quite small – a few hundred pounds up to a few thousand – but enough to get started. Look in the reference section below for details of the UK Film Council, Arts Council, etc. Be warned: grant applications have strict schedules tied to annual budgets and quite detailed application forms. Make sure you have enough time to get advice and fill in the forms properly. You will also need to evaluate your work – you will probably find that your media studies work is useful in explaining what you want to do. Many grants are aimed at giving help to particular groups of new producers or new forms of production.

For many producers, 'independence' from control or 'interference' by funders is a big issue. On the other hand, some funders can be helpful in budgeting for you (and also giving you 'backing' which will allow you entry into other negotiations with potential buyers etc.).

Style

What style or genre will you use? No matter how 'original' you attempt to be, you will be making references to media conventions. If you don't make these references your readers may have difficulty following the text. You will perhaps be warned not to imitate professional work slavishly, but, at least when you first start out, it is difficult not to draw on work you enjoy or admire. The best advice is to make open your intention to work 'in the style of' an existing producer and to begin by trying to understand all the conventions of a particular genre or style. If you want to go on and break with convention, it is useful to know which 'rules' need to be broken. If you are clear about the generic or stylistic approach which you wish to adopt, you will find it much easier to explain what you want to do, both to the commissioner of the work and to the rest of your production team.

Product placement This refers to the prominent position of consumer items in the decor of films and television programmes and crucially the use of such products by stars. Coca-Cola and Pepsi are reputed to have spent millions on getting their products used by stars in Hollywood features (see Chapter 9 and its case study).

Grant aid has enabled many currently successful film-makers to make a start. Lottery funding is an important source of support, mainly for organisations but also for smaller ventures. Check with your local arts board or screen agency.

Working in a familiar genre can mean greater 'freedom' because the conventions are so well known that audiences can be introduced to new ideas on the back of more familiar ones, e.g. a story about a stranger coming to town could use the conventions of a western.

Schedule

How long have you got to complete the production process? Planning and preparation are essential for a successful production, but even the best plans come to nothing if the overall task is impossible. Calculate the time each part of the process will take and ensure that you know everything about the schedule from the outset. For instance, you may be required to show the unfinished work to your commissioner in order to confirm the inclusion of contentious material, but will that person be available when you reach the crucial decision-making stage? Can your **schedule** be adapted to cope with these problems?

Your schedule will distinguish different parts of the process and you will be able to plan when and where each can take place. Be careful, because some aspects of production are more time-dependent than others, e.g. video post-production always takes longer than you imagine. Some parts of the production process are dependent on other parts having been completed first, so, for instance, if you are producing a print magazine, you must make sure that any work on producing graphics takes place before you start to lay out pages. 'Managing the schedule' is one of the most important aspects of production and perhaps the least appreciated by beginners. Check that you know, at the outset, all the stages your production needs to go through and include sufficient 'recovery time' for each stage in case things go wrong.

'Schedule management' is a key part of all your work in further and higher education.

A schedule for magazine production

Imagine you are setting out to produce a fanzine or a small specialist magazine, say a sixteen-page, 'single colour' (the cheapest form of printing in which you choose just one ink colour) A4-size magazine. You have a number of friends who are going to contribute articles and you hope to distribute five hundred copies. All the desktop publishing (DTP) will be done by you and you will then take a computer file to a printing company. How do you organise the schedule?

The first decision will be the date of publication. This is the date when you want readers to have the magazine in their hands – you need to set a date well before the first date for any events or 'forthcoming attractions' you might list. You can then work backwards to set deadlines for each stage of the production process. You might come up with something like the schedule in Figure 11.1.

This might seem like a long production schedule for a small magazine and you might well be able to shorten some stages – but, even so, it will take you a couple of months to complete the process (in the professional magazine industry, each monthly magazine can take up to three months to produce, so that staff are working on two or three magazines at any one time, with issues being planned while one is being copy-edited and another is being printed). Notice the constraints. You can't be sure about commissioning pieces if you don't know the editorial policy or how much space you will have to fill given the budget. If you want to sell advertising, you must first give the advertiser a sense of what the publication will look like. Once the artwork (i.e. your designed pages) has gone to the printer, there isn't a lot you can do to affect the timing, so Week 8, 'going to print' day, is very important.

If you do send your computer file to a printing company, you must go through a final phase known as '**pre-press**'. This means checking that you are sending all the necessary fonts and images with your file. The magazine may look great on your computer screen, but has the print company got all your fonts?

If you publish a magazine during your course it will need a schedule like this and you will probably need a whole term to do the job properly.

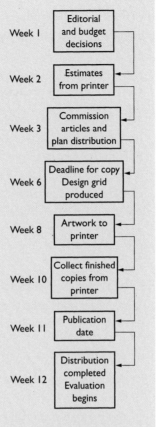

Figure 11.1 A magazine production schedule.

Pre-press A DTP program like InDesign will include a menu item that performs a checking routine on your files before you prepare them for printing. A similar process will be activated if you 'export' files to **pdf**. If you don't respond to a 'missing fonts' or 'missing image links' message, the print driver might substitute a default font or a low-resolution image.

Constraints

Time and money are both constraints, but there are several others. Availability of appropriate technology is an obvious constraint and so is the availability of talent (actors or presenters in an audio-visual production) or creative people on the production team. There may be constraints on the availability of inanimate resources as well – locations, props or archive materials.

Less obvious, but equally important, are constraints on permissions – the rights to use a piece of music, a photograph, a poem, etc. – and restraints created by law: slander, libel, obscenity, the Official Secrets Act, etc.

Your ability to develop a production in relation to the imposed constraints is a major factor in demonstrating creativity in a vocational

If you want to stage an armed robbery on the street as part of your crime thriller video, best tell the police first. One group of university students was arrested and questioned about why they were wasting police time. (The security team on your college campus would also like to know when you are staging a kidnap or an assault.)

context. 'Problem-solving' or 'working within constraints' is what defines the effective media producer. Sometimes, working within constraints produces the most interesting work.

Constraints and creativity in film production

In the early days of the Soviet Union in 1919, when the new state was being blockaded by the West, a shortage of film stock prompted experiments by Kuleshov in which he spliced together 'offcuts' of exposed film and discovered novel effects of juxtaposing images. This was later developed into the celebrated Soviet 'montage' style. A more recent echo of this 'discovery' was the early 1980s 'scratch videos' produced by young and poorly funded video editors who 'stole' clips from broadcast television in order to produce satirical comments on contemporary society. Montage sequences are now routine in music videos.

More recently, the director and cinematographer of *Se7en* (US 1995), David Fincher and Darius Khondji, produced an original 'look' for their film, partly as a result of various constraints.

> The reason it rains all of the time is that we only had Brad Pitt for 55 days, with no contingency. So we did it to stay on schedule, because we knew that if it ever really rained we would have been fucked . . . We decided we wouldn't build any flyaway walls. If the kitchen is only 12 feet, then hem him in. We live in an age when anything is possible, so it's always important to limit yourself. It's important the blinders you put on, what you won't say. I wanted to take an adult approach – not, 'Oh wow, a Luma crane'.
>
> (David Fincher interviewed in *Sight and Sound*, January 1996, p. 24)

Important health and safety issues

You may not think of media production work as being particularly dangerous, but it can be in certain circumstances and, like every other 'public' activity, it is covered by a legal obligation on you to protect both yourself and others from injury.

The best way to learn about specific media production hazards is to address them 'on the job'. Your lecturer should always make clear the fire exits from any accommodation you use and should outline the particular safety requirements when dealing with equipment. These include electrical

Some media jobs are very dangerous – journalists and photographers in war zones are particularly vulnerable.

Figure 11.2   *Welcome to Sarajevo* (UK/US 1997) shows reporters working under threat of snipers during the siege of the city.

connections, trailing cables, very hot and fragile lights, noxious chemicals in photography, etc. If you aren't told about these things – ask. Remember that the legal obligation can fall on you – you have a right to be told, but you also have a responsibility to act safely so that you don't injure anyone else. A good source of advice and information is often the appropriate union (e.g. BECTU for video), which may well have health and safety advisers. The technicians in your college should be well aware of potential hazards.

As a producer, you should be aware of some of the less obvious health and safety issues:

- *Stress* is a potential hazard for production personnel, who are often under pressure to make decisions or to operate equipment quickly and efficiently. You will notice this in 'live' television or radio productions. Stress can build up and affect performance (which in turn could lead to 'unsafe' decisions).
- *Public liability* requires you to be very careful when out on location, where you might cause an obstruction with cameras, cables, lights, etc. As well as seeking permission, you need to warn passers-by of the hazards.
- *Special effects* and stunts can add a great deal to video productions but should only be performed by professionals. You may be able to arrange a demonstration of how they can be performed safely. Even if you think a particular stunt is not actually dangerous, be careful that your enthusiasm does not lead you to neglect basic safety measures (e.g. in throwing water around).
- *Lifting and moving* In the frenzy of getting equipment to where you want it and then arranging it how you want, it is all too easy to strain your

muscles with heavy or awkward objects (and sometimes to damage expensive equipment). Learn how to handle equipment properly and find the crew and the time to move it safely.

Negotiating a brief

Once you have prepared your ideas by considering the issues above, you are ready to try them out and 'pitch' them to a potential funder or a commissioner for a publisher (e.g. a broadcast television or radio company or a print publisher), perhaps in response to some form of 'tender document'. To do this effectively you will need to encapsulate the main points of what you want to do in an **outline**, preferably no more than a couple of sides of A4 paper.

An alternative, when you have an idea but there is no specific tender document, is to send in a **proposal** suggesting something you could do. A proposal will include an outline and an argument as to why it would be successful with a specific target audience or readership. You should address the proposal to the relevant commissioner or editor, and it is sensible to study carefully which market a particular publisher targets. A proposal may also include a 'sample' of writing or script and will therefore be more substantial than a simple outline.

A term often used in television is '**treatment**'. The meaning of this term varies. Sometimes it refers to the style or approach which will be taken to a particular programme idea, and sometimes it is a full working through of ideas or a 'filling in' of the outline, describing what will happen. The production process may require an outline, which is developed into a treatment and finally into a production script.

The process of 'negotiating a brief' will lead to a point where you will be offered a deal with a set of conditions on cost, schedule, etc. Be careful not to accept unrealistic deadlines – remember, it always takes longer than you think. Note also that the commissioner will probably specify points at which you will need to report progress. You have a deal and a brief, but unless you are publishing the work yourself, the commissioner can always decide to shelve your work rather than publish it, so you will need to argue your case carefully throughout production.

Many proposals to write articles or stories are rejected by magazines because they are clearly unsuitable for the readership in terms of either content or style.

For more ideas about proposals for television see Holland (2000).

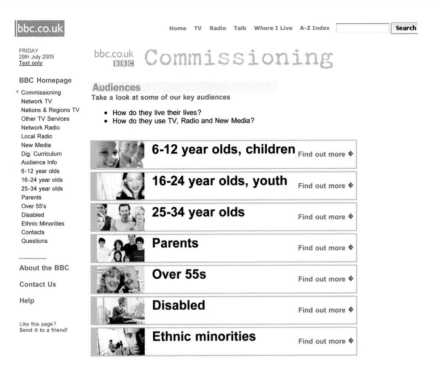

Figure 11.3 The BBC website provides information for would-be writers in its commissioning section. This page at www.bbc.co.uk/commissioning/marketresearch/index.shtml leads to information on audiences.

Pre-production

Research

Sometimes a proposal will have come out of research – perhaps for another purpose. In this sense, research comes before the brief is agreed. Usually, research is a major component of 'pre-production'. Because research is such an important part of academic media work, as well as production, we have devoted Chapter 10 to all issues related to research. Please refer to that chapter now.

Recce

Good preparation is essential for effective media production, and before any audio or video or photography work takes place on location a production company will undertake a series of '**recces**' (reconnaissance). These include checks on electrical power sources (often broadcasters' needs are so great that they bring their own generators), on access for people and equipment and on health and safety generally. At all stages of the production process, you should be aware of the need for *risk assessment*. Facilities such as changing rooms, refreshments and possibly press and public relations spaces are important too. These are the producer's main concerns. The director, camera and sound crews will also want to select locations for aesthetic reasons and to begin to build the constraints created by the location into the production schedule.

Risk assessment

You should draw up a detailed assessment of all the health and safety considerations at this stage. Don't proceed with production if the risks cannot be covered. Here is a short extract from the BBC's strategy:

> Consider each stage of the work. For example for a production there may be significant risks at: the recce, the **rigging**, the rehearsal, the **de-rig** as well as the actual production recording. When all the hazards have been identified their significance can be evaluated and precautions taken to eliminate or control them. Remember, it is always better to eliminate a risk than to attempt to control it.

Check the full documents on http://www.bbc.org.uk/ohss/health~4.htm.

Rigging is the process of setting up the shoot and may involve building sets, scaffolding, etc. and moving equipment. It is recognised as the main focus of risk assessment. See www.skillset.org/standards/article _2786_1.asp for details on all the different job roles in film and television.

ACTIVITY 11.2

Locations

Take a close look at any film or television series (record it so you can study it in detail) and carry out an analysis of the locations used.

- How much of it is shot in a studio, how much on location?
- List all the separate locations. Could you find substitute locations in your locality?
- Now consider the task of the producer. Think of your substitute locations: how would you organise the shooting so that you cut down travelling between locations?
- What kind of permissions do you think you would need for the locations you have chosen?

Many UK cities and regions have recognised the economic benefits that film and television productions can bring to the local economy and have set up offices to help producers find locations, crews and facilities and to sort out permissions. Check with your local Screen Agency to find out which Film Commissions operate in your area.

Figure 11.4 On location you need a recce to work out how you will shoot the scene and what equipment you will need. Here it is a tight squeeze to fit in the crew and extra lights to complement the sun through the window in a three light set-up (see Figure 12.6 on p. 397).

Design

Every media product is 'designed'. Think of a couple of very different products – a magazine and a feature film. In both cases, an important member of the production team is the art editor or art director. They are responsible for the obvious art and design elements in the products – whether the dramatic layout of pages and the use of illustrations, especially on the cover of a newsstand magazine, or the stupendous sets of a Hollywood musical and the credit sequence of the film. But they also contribute to a much broader concept of design – the overall fitness of purpose and coherence of the media product. The opening credit sequence of a film, the choice of typeface in a magazine, are not just attractive and appropriate in themselves. They are designed to announce and complement the other features of the product.

You might want to think about a media product in the same way as one of those exquisitely crafted Japanese lacquered boxes or a designer suit – whichever way you look at them as you turn them over, they present a beautifully finished surface. And when you use them for their intended purpose, they do the job effortlessly. Good design doesn't have to cost a fortune, though. A zippo lighter or a box of matches can be designed well,

Similarly design-intensive are the animated idents used on television such as the long-running series of '2s' on BBC2. You can see a collection of these on http://thetvroom.com/p-bbc-two-2001-a.shtml.

Figure 11.5 One of the animated '2' idents used on BBC2.

and so can the supposedly insignificant media products such as the continuity announcements and **idents** on television or the local football fanzine. And it isn't just in visual terms that we can detect design features. Radio programmes are designed as well and it will be quite apparent if the sound text is not coherent in its style and 'feel'. Good design means that products work well with users, and that must be the first priority for media production.

See Chapter 12 for more on design ideas. Note here that design issues need to be addressed at the preparation stage. Design needs to inform other aspects of production and to develop from the initial ideas about the product.

Production

This is the stage when the main work is done on the material which will appear in the finished product – see Chapter 12 for details. It is useful at this point to discuss who does what and how the roles are defined and integrated as a part of a production team.

The production unit and production roles

The units which you form to undertake production tasks in education or training are not so different from their industrial counterparts. Even in very large media corporations, creative staff work in relatively small teams and in some sectors a production company may be just a couple of people, who hire freelances to work on specific jobs. In every case we can identify a close-knit production team, who work together over a period of time. They may be augmented at particular stages in production by larger groups of people who perform relatively routine tasks in an industrial process.

Let's take our previous example of a small specialist magazine and look at its production in more detail. This could be one of many titles produced by a large international publishing group such as IPC (owned by Time Warner) or perhaps a private venture. Either way, the 'production team' may comprise only a few full-time people such as the editor and an assistant, a couple of 'staff writers' and perhaps an art editor. Outside this circle will be others who, while committed to the magazine, may also be involved in other titles. The same commitment (i.e. to the individual title) will not be found in the printers and distributors, who deal with many different titles over the year. Each production unit is likely to include the following job roles.

Producer

Somebody must take charge of the production as the 'organiser of scarce resources' and the financial controller. This role will also usually require an overview of the purpose of the production and the creative intent. The term is used in film, television, radio and sound recording, but there are differences. In film production, the producer is very much the provider of the budget and the organiser of resources – in most cases the creative control of the project lies with the director, although there are some very 'hands-on' producers (including well-known directors who retain the producer role themselves, delegating some tasks to assistants). In radio and television, the producer is also usually the creative force behind a series. In sound recording too, the producer might be seen as a creative force. In publishing, the same role is likely to be shared by an editor and a production manager.

Director or editor

This role is about creative control – making decisions during the course of the production and maintaining a clear idea of the form and style of the product. In **time-based media** such as film, television or radio, the director is the coordinator of the creative process, literally directing the crew and the talent. In broadcasting, the creative controller tends to be termed an **editor** when the programme material is news or current affairs. The editor of a newspaper or magazine tends to oversee creative and production manager roles. The role of the director raises interesting questions about the managerial style of the decision-taker. The director or editor has to take decisions – 'the buck stops here'.

Television is a producer-led medium according to Jeremy Tunstall in Holland (2000). This book has several accounts of what being a producer means, written by well-known figures. A good example of the creative power of the producer in television is the rise of Phil Redmond, who gained a profile first as the writer who developed *Grange Hill* in the 1970s, but then consolidated his position by forming Mersey Television and producing *Brookside* and *Hollyoaks* for Channel 4 (see www.merseytv.com).

'Each picture has some sort of rhythm which only the director can give it. He has to be like the captain of a ship' (Fritz Lang from Halliwell's *Filmgoer's Book of Quotes* (London: Mayflower/ Granada, 1978)).

Time-based media is a term used mainly by practitioners with art and design backgrounds to distinguish film, television and radio from photography. You may also hear 'lens-based media' used to group film, television and photography.

Researcher

Refer back to Activity 11.2 and compare a low-budget and a prestige documentary in terms of the amount of research required to mount the programme successfully.

See Chapter 10 for more on production research.

Ad seen in the *Metro* free paper: 'Wanted – your stories of weddings that have gone wrong. ITV1 is looking for material for a new programme.' Sifting through the responses is clearly a job for a production assistant.

Investigative newspaper reporters may also be seen as researchers. They may also write up their own reports – something denied to most broadcast researchers.

Several writers have commented on the difference between television and film in terms of 'freedoms and opportunities'. Television drama can give writers time to develop characters and to hone dialogue, but the dramatic possibilities in visual terms are limited and the format length and structure of series or soaps are restricting. On a film there is more creative freedom to tell a story in visual terms but less time to develop characters. A bigger budget is also likely to mean that the script will be revised many times, perhaps against the writer's wishes.

(See Chapter 10.) Every production needs some research, but not always a separate researcher. Most research is 'background' – the checking of information or the compilation of information and ideas on a specific topic. Some production research requires special skills and knowledge, first the general academic skills of using and checking sources, second in relation to a specialist subject (such as military history).

Archives can be very specialised, and film, picture or sound researchers may be seen as specialised roles, perhaps undertaken by freelances or small research companies.

Finding contestants for a gameshow or guests for a talk show could also be seen as 'research', but here the skills are rather different. They may involve developing a 'feel' for what will be televisual, what will be popular, what will be a ratings winner. They may also include the ability to charm or cajole reluctant performers into appearing (for the smallest fee). This aspect of research may be performed by a production assistant – someone much closer to the producer role than the autonomous researcher.

Creative personnel

This is a loose term and may include everybody involved in the production, but here we are referring to those members of the team who are charged with making specific contributions based on specialist skills such as writing, camerawork, design, etc. The task for creative personnel is to carry out the wishes of the producer or director in a professional manner, contributing to the overall production as effectively as possible. Conflicts are possible if the individual contributors wish to 'do their own thing'. There are interesting questions about authorship here – once a scriptwriter has completed work on a film, does she or he have the right to be consulted if the producer or director then decides to cut, add to or alter the finished script?

The director or producer will work hard to maintain a good working relationship with all the creative staff, consulting them (which means explaining *and* listening) on particular aspects of their work and perhaps incorporating their suggestions into the overall production. The director's role requires her or him to maintain the coherence of the whole media text, so if a particular contribution is threatening to upset the balance it needs to be corrected, even if, on its own, it represents a very effective and entertaining element. Here are the seeds of conflict, especially in the supercharged atmosphere of most production processes.

The success of a creative team will depend on good working relationships. This doesn't necessarily mean that everyone in the team

likes each other, but they must respect each other's work and be prepared
to submit to the 'general will' of the team and the ultimate decision of the
acknowledged leader. The most successful producers tend to be those who
have built up and maintained a creative team which has lasted several
years.

Technical personnel

Somebody must be responsible for the operation of equipment and for its
efficient performance (i.e. they must maintain and set up equipment so
that it performs to manufacturers' specifications). Variously described as
'technicians' or 'engineers', these people ensure that creative ideas can
be realised within the constraints which the technology demands. Some
technical operations such as maintenance and servicing may be required
even when no productions are scheduled.

It is a fine line which separates the 'creative' from the 'technical', and
many media practitioners combine both roles. For example, a *director of
photography* (**DP**) on a feature film is very much part of the creative team,
responsible for the overall 'look' of the film and the supervision of camera
and lighting operations. Operation of the equipment will be handled
by the **camera crew**, but the DP, who will have begun a career as part of
the technical crew, will select lenses and perhaps even override equipment
specifications and solve technical problems, based on long experience.
Some media practitioners are seen as possessing 'craft' rather than
technical skills – implying a more personal, 'creative' skill with
technology, beyond that of 'operation'.

In an ideal situation, creative staff have sufficient knowledge
of technical operations to be able to communicate effectively with the
technical team. In turn, technical staff are able to recognise the creative
opportunities which their equipment makes possible and to advise
accordingly. In the production unit, an integrated creative and technical
team generally produces the best results. Often, however, the technical
team is made up of freelances or in-house staff who are allocated to
production units on a rota basis. The ability to communicate effectively
and to develop working relationships quickly then becomes even more
important.

The need for close communication between creative and technical
teams raises two issues about media production training which are
important for all media students:

- It helps if all production staff know something about each
  aspect of production. Too much specialisation means that effective
  communication becomes more difficult.

Camera crews on a film set
normally comprise an operator
and assistants to look after
loading, focus pulling and camera
movements (the job of the
'**grip**'), etc. An electrical crew led
by a '**gaffer**' with a '**best boy**'
will set up lighting under the DP's
supervision.

- It isn't necessarily those with the most creative ideas or the best technical prowess who make the best production team members. Good working relationships are also important, and training should be geared towards development of the appropriate personal and organisational skills.

Freelances

Freelance The term goes back to the period when medieval knights returning from the Crusades would roam Europe offering their services to different rulers.

The **freelance** is a longstanding figure in many parts of the media industries. At one time the term referred to relatively well-known figures such as high-profile writers or journalists who were in such demand that they could afford to offer their services to whoever would pay, rather than relying on the security of permanent employment. This usage continues and now includes television personalities as well as film directors. However, the big growth is in the number of rather less well-known media workers who would probably prefer to be 'employed' as they were in the past by broadcast television companies or daily newspapers, but who now find themselves made redundant and perhaps offered work on a short-term contract basis – often for a series of articles or work on a television series. Whether this should be called 'freelance work' in the strict sense is debatable (they may in some cases be little better off than the notoriously badly treated 'homeworkers'), but in the film, video and broadcast industry freelances now constitute more than half the total workforce.

Freelances pose problems for the continuity of the production team, and they are less likely to be followers of a 'house style'. On the other hand, they may bring new ideas and ways of working to a team. In practice, freelances may end up working for a particular production unit on a fairly regular basis, so this may not be a great change. What is likely, however, is a gradual breakdown of the 'institutional' ethos of some of the large media corporations such as the BBC and a reliance on more generic output (i.e. an industry 'standard') from the host of smaller independent companies (see Chapter 4).

As a 'student producer' you could 'buy in' some freelance help from students on another course who may have specific expertise (especially in areas such as design). If you are looking for employment in the media industries, you should prepare yourself for possible freelance status. A good start is to begin preparing your portfolio of completed production work as soon as possible, keeping your CV up to date and looking for opportunities to gain experience and to acquire a wide range of skills. Freelances have to manage their own financial affairs and actively seek work. It is a very different life from that of a paid employee whose main concern is fulfilling a job description to the satisfaction of an employer. Many higher education courses now include units on business studies, personal finance, portfolio management and CV-writing which are designed to help the potential freelance to survive.

Administrative personnel

Media students are often told about the difficulty of obtaining employment in 'the industry' and the example of starting 'at the bottom'. Making the tea and being a 'runner' are quoted as the lowest entry points. At the other end of the scale, the accountant is sometimes seen as the villain, not only for curtailing creativity through budgetary control but for being 'boring' as well. Making tea and doing the books are of course essential elements in any enterprise, and media production is no exception.

A large-scale production such as a feature film involves hundreds of personnel with an enormous variety of skills and qualifications (see Figure 7.2). Even a small production needs an 'office'. For convenience we have termed these 'administrative' in that they are primarily concerned with making sure that production can go ahead with all the needs of the creative and technical teams catered for. Again, we can distinguish between administrative personnel who are integral to the production team – very often in roles as the extra arms and legs of producers – and those who are brought in as needed, either as freelances or from some central, in-house, agency.

Some roles may be termed 'organisational' rather than administrative in that they are directly concerned with the operation of the production process. The floor manager in a television studio or the continuity role in feature film production are good examples of such important roles where an understanding of the production process is central. It is also worth pointing out that, while the skills necessary for the other administrative roles are generalised rather than specific, the roles do allow new personnel to pick up a great deal of knowledge about the production process.

Presenters

One aspect of production work that many of us fear is presenting – speaking on radio or television (especially direct to camera) or introducing events at screenings or exhibitions. No matter how embarrassed you feel, you should try it a couple of times for the experience and so that you have some idea of what presenters feel in the situations which you might create for them as writer or director. If you are going to become a presenter, then

Figure 11.6 Preparing to speak to camera on location.

you will need to seek out specialist advice on how to train your voice, how to breathe, how to use a microphone and how to read a script. You will also want to study a range of professionals (not just one, or you might end up a mimic).

If you are a writer, the most important thing to remember is to provide the presenter with 'spoken language'. A speech may look great on paper, but it may sound laboured when read aloud. If you can't find a presenter among the other media students, look elsewhere, just as you would for actors. Because you study the media, it doesn't necessarily mean you want to appear as the 'talent'.

Production roles in education and training

So what should you take from these role descriptions in terms of your own education and training? First, wide experience of different production contexts will help to develop your theoretical understanding and your preparation for 'post-entry' training in any specific production role. Try as many roles as possible. You may have thought that being a writer was your dream, only to discover that you have a real flair for sound recording and that the radio studio gives you a buzz.

Copyright and permissions

Media products are often referential or intertextual, making use of previously recorded material. In a highly commercial industry, almost anything that has any kind of commercial potential – i.e. that could be used in another publication – will be 'owned' in terms of the rights for reproduction.

If the reproduction rights on a work have lapsed (which in Europe means seventy years after the author's death) and have not been renewed, the work passes into the **public domain** and anyone can reproduce it without charge. There is a difference, however, between the work of art and the physical media product. For instance, most nineteenth-century novels are now in the public domain, and this means that any publisher can sell a new edition of Dickens etc. But the 'Penguin edition' will remain in copyright as a printed text – you cannot simply photocopy it. If you want to use a 'found' image in a magazine article, you will need to do three things: get a copy of the original photograph (you may need to pay a fee for a high-resolution digital image); obtain permission from the rights holder; and probably pay a further reproduction fee based on the nature of your publication, the size of the image on the page and the position of that page in the publication (you pay most for the front cover).

Audio-visual recordings can involve you in several different sets of 'permissions' and rights issues. Say you want to use a recording of a popular song in a video programme. There are three potential rights holders here. First, the person who wrote the song will want a 'reproduction fee'; next, the singer will need payment for reproduction of the performance; and finally the record label will want a fee for reproduction of their specific recording. In practice two of these may be dealt with by the same agency.

> A conversation about permissions for material in an earlier edition of this book: 'I'm trying to get permission to use a few stills from the Creek ad for Levi's jeans . . . $5,000 each for the last educational publisher in the US? We need to ask everyone involved in the ad? Does that include the horse? He has an agent?' (This last bit is a joke – but only just.)

The industry has developed specific paperwork for media producers to use to request permissions – usually producers don't buy a whole song but only a few seconds. One solution for small producers is to use 'library music', specifically written and recorded for audio-visual productions and catalogued on CDs according to themes. A producer buys the CD and then pays a set fee for a track. This is usually cheaper and less administratively complex than using well-known pieces. Use this resource carefully, though, as overfamiliar library music can sound bland.

Post-production

Once the main material has been produced, or 'found' and collated, it must be shaped into the final product. This involves several different activities.

Public domain and digital technology Digital versions of images and text (and software) are easy to distribute and copy. Public domain (PD) material is distributed free of charge as long as the distributor does not attempt to make a profit. 'Shareware' allows products to be used free, but business users are expected to pay a small fee.

Music rights Performers' rights are handled by the Performing Rights Society (PRS). Recordings are handled by the Mechanical Copyright Protection Society (MCPS). PPL handles Phonographic Performance Licences for use by broadcasters etc.

Music rights are a major headache for producers of low-budget films. *The Killer of Sheep* (US 1977) received high praise from film critics as an important film by an African-American film-maker, but its producers could not afford to clear the music rights. This prevented a proper release until restoration and clearance of rights (anticipated in 2006).

Rewriting and editing

It's very unlikely that you will get your production right first time. Sections in this book have gone through several versions – sometimes with radical alterations, sometimes just a tweak. During your academic career you have probably suffered from constant pressure from teachers to check your work and, even when you think you've finished, to go back and rewrite parts or even the whole of it. If you took that advice and got into good habits, you are now going to reap your reward.

Authors' rights are negotiated by the Society of Authors and the Publishers' Association, and copying fees are collected by the Author Licensing and Collecting Society.

Figure 11.7 Rushes can be reviewed and a short narrative edited on a standard laptop computer such as this Apple iBook.

A good slogan for you: 'Writing is rewriting' – whether for academic essays or 'creative writing'.

Rewriting   This shouldn't be seen as simply a process of spotting mistakes and correcting them. It should also be a creative process – material is 'shaped' during production. Both the original writer and the editor will be involved in trying to work on the script or text. It is worth reminding yourself here that editing is a constructive process, not just a 'cutting out' of the bad bits. It is also time consuming, and a sensible schedule will take rewrites into account. Do be careful about labelling each version of your text, especially when working on a computer which allows you to create several versions of the same picture or text extract in a few minutes. There is nothing more frustrating than finding that when you want to go back to a previous version, you can't easily distinguish which is which.

Editing   is usually carried out by someone other than the writer or director. This means that it is important to establish good communication within the team. There has been a tendency to think of print editing and audio-visual editing as rather different activities. The move to digital production, using a computer interface, means that such differences are disappearing and all forms of editing now involve structuring the text and selecting the most appropriate material to be juxtaposed.

Copy-editing is a specialist editing role in print production. It ensures that the raw text is checked for spelling mistakes, inaccurate information and adherence to house style. A similar aspect of video editing might be a check to ensure that colour grading was matched on separate video sources or that sound levels are consistent throughout. **Sub-editing** is a specific newspaper production activity in which experienced staff cut stories to fit the space available and write headlines and captions.

Special effects and graphics are prepared and added to programmes at the editing stage. In print production, the typesetter attempts to combine text and graphics according to the laid-down design grid.

Proofing

When you get very wrapped up in a production project it is sometimes difficult to be objective about your own work. Sometimes it is even difficult to see what is there at all, and this is where a 'proof reader' comes in. Their job is simply to spot unintentional errors. Ideally, someone who proofs not only has a sharp eye (or ear) but knows something about the subject as well. Authors of printed material are usually supplied with proof copies of their work to check.

'**Proofing**' refers also to checking the correct colours to be printed in a magazine etc. Designers use a carefully calibrated printer to produce a proof for a client before releasing the work for publishing. (Colours look different on a computer screen.)

> *Now, Voyager* is a famous 1940s Hollywood melodrama, starring Bette Davis. The title refers to a line of poetry. In an American film magazine, an advertisement for film sound tracks listed two separate films, '*Now*' and '*Voyager*', under a 'classics' heading.

Test marketing or previewing

If you are unsure about your product in some way (perhaps the design features are not quite right or you simply panic about your great idea), it may be possible to test a draft version of it on a small selected group of readers and see what kind of a response you get. This isn't foolproof, and you could select the wrong test group. Some may argue as well that you

Sunset Boulevard (US 1950) is narrated by a corpse floating in a swimming pool. Director Billy Wilder originally opened with two corpses discussing the story in a morgue, but the Illinois preview audience thought that was too much (according to Otto Friedrich in *City of Nets* (London: Harper Collins, 1987)).

shouldn't be frightened of making mistakes and that the previewing policy leads to very bland products.

Finishing

The most successful media products offer the audience a special pleasure which derives from a quality 'finish'. This means that presentation is as good as it can be within the constraints of the format and the medium. Good finish means that your video begins from black with music and titles fading up smoothly 'in **sync**'. Titles are accurate and carefully designed to complement the visuals. If you have a great set of photographic prints, it does matter how you present them. A good display with thought given to lighting and carefully printed captions or catalogue will enhance the experience for your audience. This should be the final production stage before the product is distributed for the eager public.

Distribution

If you don't present your product to your audience directly, you will need some form of distribution. Other chapters stress that in the media industries this can be the most important part of the production process. You don't want to produce a magazine only to discover that nobody gets to read it or to broadcast a radio programme which nobody hears.

Student productions can get a wide audience if distribution is organised in good time. Check back on the magazine schedule at the start of the chapter, which suggests organising the distribution at an early stage – perhaps finding shops, pubs, cinemas, etc. who would be willing to display free copies of your magazine to be picked up by their patrons (you can afford to distribute free copies in this way if you sell advertising to cover your production costs). Several schools and colleges have taken the opportunity to apply for a Restricted Service Licence (RSL), which allows them to broadcast for a couple of days in a local area. Video productions can be timed to be ready for the various festivals of student work. If you have any ambitions to become a media producer, here is your starting point to get your work recognised. (See Chapter 13 for more on distribution.)

Exhibition

This stage is relevant only for film and video or photography, but it is very important to present your work to an audience in the best possible conditions – it is the equivalent of 'finishing' in print production. For a video screening you will want to make sure that your audience are comfortable and have good 'sight-lines' to see the screen. The sound and picture quality must be as good as possible, with the monitor or video projector set properly and sound levels appropriate for the acoustics in the room. You will want the programme to start at exactly the right place, so set it up carefully beforehand. Would the audience benefit from some screening notes?

Video projection is now widely available. Do leave yourself time to organise projection on a big screen and see whether any adjustments need to be made. (And make sure the equipment and the software work.)

Think about your own experience of going to the cinema. What do you expect in terms of the best viewing environment?

Audience feedback

At the beginning of this chapter we made the point that media production is meaningful only if you know the audience to whom you hope to present your work. It follows that your production isn't finished until it has reached the intended audience and you have gained some feedback. Only then will you be able to evaluate the production decisions you have made. You will also be able to use the feedback material to inform your next production – audience feedback supplies the link which helps to make production a cyclical process.

There are numerous ways in which you can gauge audience reactions to your work. Sitting in with an audience can be useful. When do they go quiet and concentrate? When do they fidget and yawn? What kind of comments do they make to each other? You can formalise this by organising some form of discussion after a screening, or when everyone has read through your magazine. Get someone else to chair the session and be prepared to be open with your audience about what you were trying to do.

If all of this sounds a little daunting, you can always devise a simple audience feedback questionnaire which can be given to everyone when they first come into contact with the product. Audiences will be happy to fill in questionnaires if the questions are appropriate and if the spaces for answers are inviting. If you are lucky, the questionnaire will produce a greater number of responses and perhaps a wider range of respondents than the face-to-face discussion. (See Chapter 10 on questionnaires.)

What will you expect from your audience feedback? We all like praise and like to know that what we have produced has given people pleasure, but, more important, we want confirmation of what has worked and what has caused confusion or even misunderstanding. You should not be dismayed if audiences have read your work in very different ways (see Chapter 8 for discussion about the different readings audiences may make). Every response is useful and will make you more aware of the range of possibilities.

After studying the audience feedback, the final task is to undertake your own evaluation of your production experience. In order to help you do this, your tutor will probably want to organise a formal 'debriefing'.

Debriefing

Most media production courses operate a procedure whereby you are briefed before an activity on what you are required to do and what constraints you face. You are then debriefed at the end of the activity. This is an important part of the process – perhaps the most important part, because it is here that you work out what you have learnt and identify your strengths and weaknesses. Most debriefings are group discussions – either everyone has worked individually on the same activity or work has been organised in groups.

Debriefings work best when everyone is committed to the activity and is supportive of each other. This means accepting criticism from the other group members and in turn making positive, constructive comments about their performance. This isn't easy. If the production has not gone well you might be sorely tempted to 'get your blame in first' or to defend your own actions. If it has gone well you might be tempted simply to tell each other 'you were great'. Neither of these approaches is particularly helpful. If it worked well, why was that? If it didn't, can you work out why, without apportioning blame? The likelihood is that you will have to follow up the debriefing with an **evaluation**, so you need answers to these questions.

It's more than likely that your evaluation of your own production work will form part of your assessment for the course. Examiners often comment that evaluations are the weak point in otherwise good production work. They want you to demonstrate that you are able to 'reflect' on the process you have gone through and that you have recognised what you have achieved and what you can learn from.

Learning from production

We hope these notes will be helpful, but there is no substitute for production work itself. Get involved as much as you can. Make things with a view to finding out about the production process as well as reaching an audience. Listen and learn from other producers. Above all, reflect on what you have done and try to do better next time. And have fun.

References and further reading

Accessible books with plenty of good ideas on relatively low-budget video production are:
Harding, Thomas (2001) *The Video Activist Handbook*, London: Pluto Press.
Watts, Harris (2004) *Instant on Camera*, London: Aavo

For background on production organisation in different media sectors see
the Routledge Handbook Series:

Brierley, Sean (2001) *The Advertising Handbook*.

Fleming, Carole (2002, 2nd edition) *The Radio Handbook*.

Holland, Patricia (2000, 2nd edition) *The Television Handbook*.

Keeble, Richard (2001, 3rd edition) *The Newspapers Handbook*.

McKay, Jenny (2000) *The Magazines Handbook*.

Wright, Terence (2004) *The Photography Handbook*.

Useful reference sources, published annually:

The Guardian Media Guide.

The Writers' and Artists' Year Book, London: A.C. Black.

The Writer's Handbook, Basingstoke: Macmillan.

Technical manuals, dealing with different aspects of production and
different technologies, are published by:

BBC Enterprises (The full range of material can be seen in the BBC
shop opposite Broadcasting House on Portland Place, London W1.
Publications include guides to scriptwriting and training manuals which
are listed in a catalogue obtainable from BBC Television Training, BBC
Elstree Centre, Clarendon Road, Borehamwood, Herts WD6 1TF.)

Focal Press (This imprint specialises in media technical handbooks and
manuals, in particular the Media Manuals series. Most of these manuals
are written for professional or semi-professional media users. Check the
catalogue for Focal Press on books.elsevier.com.)

Peachpit Press (Publishes guides to using software such as Photoshop,
InDesign, etc. UK sales organised by Pearson Education:
www.pearsoned.co.uk/Imprints/PeachpitPress.)

Websites

www.bbc.co.uk/commissioning/
www.bbc.org.uk/ohss/
www.mcps-prs-alliance.co.uk

The two UK agencies dealing with copyright issues for music and sound
performance and recording:

www.itrainonline.org/itrainonline/mmtk/index.shtml
Multimedia Training Kit

12 Production techniques

- **Technical codes in print products**
- **Technical codes in video production**
- **'Narrative' codes in film and video production**
- **Technical codes in audio production**
- **References and further reading**

This chapter is intended both as an extension of Chapter 11 'Production organisation' and as a complement to Chapter 1 'Interpreting media texts' and case study and Chapter 2 'Narratives'.

This chapter will help you to make informed choices when you select and use materials and equipment for media projects. It should also help you to read other media texts in terms of their technical codes.

Technical codes

In Chapter 1 codes are defined as systems of signs. Here technical codes are the choices that can be made in selecting or using materials and equipment on the basis of the technical qualities of the **format** or the technical qualities of the sound image or visual image created. For example you can select paper for printing a magazine on the basis of its colour, weight (thickness) and porosity (the extent to which the ink is absorbed). The quality of presentation of the text or photograph printed on the page will depend on the settings of the printer in terms of resolution, number of colours, etc.

There are several meanings of 'format'. Here it means a different size of paper or type of recording medium, e.g. CD or DVD. But see also Chapter 3.

You won't make your production choices in isolation, but in the context of a specific brief and mindful of the cultural codes of the content of your programme. Sometimes, the association of specific technical decisions with particular subjects has become conventionalised so that stylistic or aesthetic decisions have come to signify a certain mood or atmosphere (the low-key lighting of a film noir, the jaunty music of a television quiz show); a particular format or shape may have been adopted for a specific function (the small portrait photo for a passport). The strength of the technical or cultural connection is revealed when conventions are broken – in comedy texts, for example. Technical codes are helpful in providing a convenient shortcut for presenting conventional texts, but they can also provide an excuse for not thinking about how to represent something, so that the technology is allowed to dictate the creative decision and effectively restricts choice.

We've also decided to include a section on narrative codes in film and television in this chapter, linked with the discussion in Chapter 2. Although these are not strictly technical codes, such has been the power and global spread of narrative cinema that they have developed into a series of conventions related to shot sizes and camera movements that have become formalised as part of 'film language', and it makes sense to deal with them here. Such narrative codes are more difficult to distinguish in print and audio texts, but where possible we have included these in the general discussion.

This chapter concentrates on the technical decisions which you as producer are going to make, mindful that in your proposal you have identified a purpose, a target audience and a genre or style.

A good example of restrictive technology is the development of film and video cameras and lighting techniques which suit northern European skin tones and which are therefore not ideal for showing darker skin. (See Chapter 5.)

Look at some of the issues in Chapter 4 'Institutions'. Technology may be 'value-free' but it is used in value-laden institutional contexts, e.g. there are relatively few women cinematographers or sound editors.

Technical codes in print products

A print product requires ink and paper. There are many different kinds of paper and several different ways of getting ink on to them. Try to begin a print production with a sort through paper samples and possibly a discussion with a print professional about what kinds of paper are available.

Paper

The paper used in this book is 90 gsm, 'coated'. This was changed from the first edition, in an attempt to make the book lighter and easier to handle.

Paper is usually purchased by the **ream** – 500 sheets.

Weight

Paper is classified in 'grams per square metre' or 'gsm'. Standard photocopying paper is 80 gsm. Glossy brochures may use 120 gsm. Above about 150 gsm, paper becomes more like thin card. Weight is important for a number of reasons. At a very practical level, heavier paper means a heavier product and, if it is going to be mailed out, this could mean greater postal costs (heavier paper is already more expensive to buy). However, heavier paper can feel more luxurious. Thinner paper can suffer from 'see-through' or 'bleed' – if it is printed on both sides, heavy black text or illustrations will be visible through the paper and perhaps spoil the visual appeal of the page. This is also affected by coatings (see below).

Coated or uncoated?

The cheapest paper (e.g. newsprint) is 'uncoated' and porous. This means that it feels a little rough between the fingers (ask a printer about paper and she or he will perhaps rub it between the thumb and first finger). It also means that, when ink is applied, it will tend to spread, because it is absorbed by the fibres. You will see this if you use cheap paper on an inkjet printer – the problem is exacerbated because the ink is very wet. Better-quality papers are coated with a layer of non-porous material (or are treated to have the same qualities). Ink is far less likely to spread and coated papers give much better reproductions of photographs as well as feeling smoother. You can choose between 'glossy' or 'shiny' and 'matt' or 'velvet', according to taste (and what you think your readers will like).

Texture, colour and other qualities

Some expensive papers have a textured feel, like old parchment or cloth-based paper. These can be absorbent, but can also look stylish. Paper doesn't have to be white. Different colour ranges are possible, including pastel shades, strong colours and fluorescent colours. If you are a real print fanatic, you may even consider the smell of the paper – it could signify luxury or suggest that it is only a 'throwaway' product. Another technical consideration is the form of binding. If pages are glued together along one edge and the publication has a flat spine, it is known as 'perfect-bound'. Other methods 'stitch' or staple groups of double-page spreads along the central fold, and another option is to 'spiral bind' with a strip of flexible plastic or coated wire.

Size and shape

Half A4 is A5. Twice A4 is A3. Using A4 sheets you can work up or down to see what A1, A2, A6 and A7 might look like.

UK paper sizes are now standardised into the 'A' and 'B' series. You will be familiar with the A4 standard for most academic puposes and A5 for leaflets. The equivalents in the 'B' series are slightly larger. Books and magazines may use older sizes such as 'quarto' or 'royal'. Newspapers are usually tabloid (slightly smaller than A3) or broadsheet (slightly smaller than A2). Depending on your computer software, you may be offered templates for American paper sizes, which are noticeably different.

Often you will make a decision about size and shape on the basis of purely functional criteria – A5 for a booklet, A4 for a magazine. If you are printing on your school or college inkjet or laser printer, a sheet of A4, or possibly A3, paper can be folded to give four pages of A5 or A4. If you go to a professional printer who uses rolls of paper, there are fewer restrictions, and you can use an 'odd' size or shape. This could mean that your product stands out. A4 magazines tend to signify an educational or 'amateur' product – a good example of an institutional sign. Most print products are '**portrait**' (height greater than width), but some are '**landscape**' (width greater than height). Some are square and others tall and narrow. They don't have to open as double pages – they can have two or more folds. All of these considerations affect the way the product is 'read'.

ACTIVITY 12.1

Decisions on paper types

Collect a wide variety of magazines and books and try to distinguish between them in terms of paper size, shape, colour, weight, etc. What conclusions do you come to about the institutional conventions – the 'rules' which enable a product to address a particular audience? Are there examples of products you immediately like or dislike because of the paper choices? If you can find examples, try to compare the same advertisement on different paper stock (e.g. in the matt format of weekend magazines such as the *Independent* and in a shiny, glossy style magazine).

Text and images

It helps to think about the printed page as a single image. Forget about what the words say for a moment: think about text in terms of shapes on the page. This will lead you into consideration of typography and typesetting, as well as grids and white space.

Look at the information at the front of any book, to see if there is an indication as to how the typesetting has been organised.

Typography

As a 'print designer' you have the choice of hundreds of different fonts. A computer font comprises up to 256 alphabetic, numerical and punctuation characters plus various symbols and accented characters. Fonts come in 'families' of different weights and styles, such as bold, light, roman ('upright'), italic, etc. A typeface is another name for a font family.

There are four main categories of typefaces. The main two, used for body text, to be read in small sizes, are known as **serif** and **sans-serif**. The serif is the bar across the ends of the 'arms and legs' of the character. Typefaces used primarily for posters and signs are known as **display** and

Fonts were originally 'founts' – from the foundry, where they were cast in metal type. Germany and North America were the main producers of metal type – e.g. Agfa, Monotype, Linotype, etc.

Times is a **serif** typeface.

Helvetica is a **sans-serif** typeface.

Technical is a **display** typeface.

Zapf Chancery is a **script** typeface.

may be ornate and therefore unsuitable for sustained reading. Typefaces classified as **script** are based on styles of handwriting.

Some typefaces are very old, dating back centuries. Others were designed last week. Classic faces such as Gill, designed by Eric Gill in the 1920s, have moved in and out of fashion. If you are interested, there are several good catalogues or dictionaries of typography in reference libraries. You will find your own favourite faces, but you need to be aware of some typography conventions before you start to experiment, even if you want to break with them. Most typefaces are available in standard formats that can be used on different computer platforms. If you are a Windows user you should note that the print publishing industry is largely Macintosh based and although your fonts will work, they may have different names, and this can sometimes cause difficulties (see below).

- Serif faces are said to be best for long runs of body text, because the serif helps to distinguish the characters in a block of text and makes sustained reading easier.
- Sans-serif faces are commonly used for headings where immediacy and clarity are important. But they are now often used for body text as well. Sans-serif has tended to mean a more 'modern' look in recent years.
- In any single document, you should not use more than two typefaces (i.e. two 'font families') for body text and headings. (You can use display fonts in adverts and you can make use of different styles and weights within the two font families you select.)

Typesetting

With a desktop publishing programme such as Adobe InDesign or Quark Xpress, you can manipulate text with great precision and create exactly the look you want. You can choose the size of the type in points and the space between each line of text (known as the **leading**). A common choice for a book would be 10 point type with 2 points of leading, known as '10 on 12'. Type size does matter: if you make it too large, your product may suggest that its readership is young children. If it is very small, it may be difficult for older people to read (your eyes start to weaken in your forties!). Type can be squeezed up or strung out along a line, either by selecting a specially designed 'extended' or 'compressed' typeface or by manipulating the space between characters (sometimes known as 'tracking').

The look of a column of text is also affected by the alignment or justification (also referred to as 'ranging'). If you justify the text to both the left and right side (sometimes known as 'flush') the result will be a smooth edge, but on each line the space between words will be adjusted, and between some lines it will be noticeably different. The alternative is standard spacing between words, but a ragged right edge to the column of text. There are conventions for some types of publication, so newspapers usually select 'flush'. We like ragged text, which we think is easier to read.

Grids and white space

Before you start designing a page or a poster, it is worth thinking about a **grid** – a basic structure of columns and rows. This will determine the shape and feel of the page, with the body of text sharing space with drawings, photographs, etc. and balanced with open spaces – so-called white space.

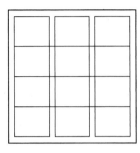

Again there are some basic conventions. If a column is too wide, the scanning-eye can lose the position of the start of the next line. A single column of small type across an A4 page is not advisable. On the other hand, a very narrow column may not work if you get only two or three words per line. Horizontal grid divisions will produce a page with a series of boxes which can be used for text and illustrations. Three columns and three horizontal grid divisions on an A4 page give a range of options with plenty of flexibility.

Figure 12.1 A simple layout grid.

ACTIVITY 12.2

Grids

Devise a selection of grids on a desktop publishing program (usually under 'document preferences'). Create or find some text and **clipart** and try laying out the same page using different grids. Which do you find easiest to work with? Which gives the most attractive result? Compare your own efforts with the layouts in the publications you selected for Activity 12.1.

Refer to Figure 12.2 as an example of a page layout. In DTP terminology the space between columns is the **gutter**. Note the margins. This particular design uses a thin line to mark the margin on three sides. You can probably guess that the side without the margin is where the fold comes. This means that it is a **verso** or left-hand page. The right-hand or **recto** page will have the left margin 'open'. The design here is for an eight-page leaflet, but if it was for more pages, the designer would need to think about making the inside margins slightly bigger to compensate for the part of the page we can't easily see as it disappears into the fold (see what happens yourself if you take several sheets of A4 paper and fold them to make an A5 booklet). Desktop publishing software allows the designer to set up 'master pages' for these left and right pages, so that each page can be set automatically. A separate design can be used for the centre pages, because here it may be possible to run text or images across two pages, making a double-page spread. This term applies to any two facing pages which have material designed across the fold; however, it works best in the middle pages of a folded or stapled publication because these will be printed as a single sheet. Elsewhere in the publication facing pages will be the right- or left-hand sides of different sheets that require careful alignment of page elements and accurate assembly by the printer. Again, it is best to look at a range of print products to see how page designs work – take an old magazine apart to see how the pages fit together.

The text in Figure 12.2 is attempting to persuade readers to think about buying 'e-books', downloaded from the internet. The design must therefore suggest the modernity of the subject. The designer has made a number of decisions. First, the thin line for the margins has also been used to divide up the page into a series of rectangles, including two photographs, one small and landscape and one larger and portrait. There are also three rectangles holding 'headline' text in larger sizes. The grid is not conventional, but it does present the body text in two columns. These are pushed to the right to allow space for the main figure in the photograph.

The type size for the body text is quite small at 8.5 but it is set on 12 points, giving plenty of space between the lines and a general sense of 'openness' (the page reproduction in this book is not full-size – you can use any DTP software to reproduce the type size and leading yourself for comparison). The 'auto leading' for 8.5 would be 10.2. The headlines are similarly set with plenty of leading. The body text and all but the top heading are set in 'Neue Helvetica', a more modern and lighter version of the most common sans-serif type family. There are three different weights of this face in use on the page. The top heading '. . . reading' also looks stretched out, but this is a property of the typeface, OCR-A BT. The 'BT' refers to the foundry, Bitstream, and the name OCR indicates that this was a face designed for Optical Character Readers – i.e. for computers to read automatically. It works well in this mode because it is a 'proportional' font – each character takes up the same amount of space. This means there is as much space for an 'i' as for a 'w'. Because of this, such fonts are not good for body text as they take up more space overall, but they do suggest 'computer' very well. (The 'tracking' here is minus 11 – in other words, text is 'squashed' compared to its default setting.)

Leading is usually expressed as a percentage with the default as 120 per cent (thus 10 on 12 or 100:120).

...reading will never be the same again

eBooks are, quite simply, one of the most exciting innovations in the history of publishing. They extend and enlarge the reading experience, and they improve the accessibility of information.

No one seriously suggests that eBooks will take the place of printed versions, but they do have a number of advantages for students, academics, researchers and others who need rapid access to a wide variety of published – copyright – information.

The eBook, for example, can be searched in a similar way to an encyclopaedia on CD-ROM, so you can quickly locate a reference such as a date, place name or event – and you can easily bookmark related information.

For frequent travellers, eBooks are a tremendous asset: they enable you to carry a basic reference library with you that weighs next to nothing. If you normally travel with a laptop or similar device, you can take as many books with you as will fit on your hard disc. What does this mean in practice? Well, on average, a megabyte of storage will hold two books – and most laptops now come with thousands of megabytes of disk space.

Total commitment

At Taylor & Francis we are totally committed to the eBooks concept. We have over 200 years of publishing experience and we're convinced that eBooks will be an extremely popular innovation. In fact we are currently producing electronic versions of several thousand books on our backlist. Over 1,500 titles are already available.

Storage and display technology will clearly change in the future but you can rest assured that we will support all major eBook Reader formats.

Instead of having a paper volume, bound into a cover, you have an electronic copy that's filed on your computer like any other document. To read it you use a special 'reader' application that displays the text, page by page – without scrolling – on the screen of your PC, laptop or handheld device.

eBooks are one of the most
exciting innovations
in the history of publishing.

Figure 12.2 Sample page from a leaflet about e-books.

The page also uses colour in both the photograph and the text boxes. You will want to think about the choice of photographs in relation to the overall meaning of the page (see Chapter 1), but here you should also note the use of a shallow field of focus to distinguish the young woman from both background and foreground.

ACTIVITY 12.3

Design update

Our example here was designed in 2002. Have design ideas changed since then? Look carefully at a favourite magazine that you consider to be 'contemporary'. Are there any changes you would make to the e-book example?

Images

There are two kinds of images which you can use in a dtp program. The first is called a **bitmap**. This is an image made up of an arrangement of pixels of different colours or shades of grey – a 'map' of '**bits**' of information. Bitmaps usually start life as images from a digital camera or a computer scanner, but you can create them yourself using a 'paint' package. The quality of the bitmap as a printed image depends on two factors – the number of colours and the size of the individual **pixels**. A very high-quality image in a fashion magazine will have 'millions of colours' and a massive bitmap of very small pixels. The result is that you cannot see the individual pixels in the image on the page, and the vast range of colours means that the reproduction will be as close as possible to the original colours of the photograph. This is a high-resolution image. At the other end of the scale is an image with a limited number of colours and a relatively small bitmap. When a bitmap is enlarged or reduced (scaled up or down) the individual pixels are each enlarged or reduced, so that, if the printed image is larger than the original, it is possible to see the individual pixels in a very 'blocky' presentation. This is a low-resolution image, which you will sometimes see in newspapers when the content is so important that the picture editor is prepared to accept the low quality.

A **high-res** image like those in this book is usually 300 **dpi**. An ordinary inkjet or laser printer can't print all the detail, so unless you are sending work to a print bureau, select 150 dpi in your scanner program. Images on the internet are usually 72 dpi – so don't try to enlarge them.

Figure 12.3 Examples of 'pixellation' when a **low-res** image is enlarged too much.

Scanning and printing photographs is a tricky business, and there is not enough space here to go into detail. As a producer, you will usually want to get the best-quality image into your publication. Unfortunately, high-resolution files are very large (several megabytes) and can be difficult to move around. Go for the best quality you can handle and scale down, never up.

The second type of image is known as a **vector** drawing or 'structured' or 'outline' drawing. Instead of the fixed bitmap, a vector drawing is made up of a set of points which are joined by curves. These are stored in the computer file as a formula. When the vector drawing is used in a dtp program, it can be scaled up or down and the computer recalculates the formula for the curve. This way, the image will always be high quality. This is the basis for much of the clipart you will find on your computer. The image is high quality but often has few colours and does not attempt to replicate a photograph. You can draw such images yourself, but you need great skill and knowledge of the drawing software. The industry standard drawing programs are Illustrator and Freehand.

Postscript is a print description language used extensively in publishing in which a whole page – text and images – can be 'described' accurately for perfect printing on a Postscript printer. Most professional printing now avoids direct contact with Postscript through use of pdf (Portable Document Format). If you would like your work to be professionally printed (or sent to someone else to print on any machine), try to produce a pdf.

Clipart is commercially produced artwork – drawings of a wide range of objects and people, available copyright-free as part of software purchases.

Figure 12.4 Clipart example.

Text as image

Fonts for dtp should always be 'outline' fonts which can be scaled like the vector drawings or Postscript files described above. Beware of bitmap fonts which work only at a set size – if you enlarge them they become blocky. You can use certain fonts in a drawing program and then manipulate characters or whole words as if they were images.

Manipulation of images

One of the great benefits of computerised page layout is the range of possibilities for manipulating text and images – changing colour, shape, texture, etc. in a seemingly unlimited number of ways. This boon is also a curse if you let it run away with you. Just as in video production (which includes many of the same effects), it is important to have a purpose rather than just to create an effect for the sake of it. Why might you want to manipulate or distort images and/or text?

First, you may simply want to 'enhance' or improve the image. There are many tools available to do this, including colour controls and balance of light and dark in an image ('equalisation'). Often enhancements may not be obvious at all and so may not act as a code (except in coding 'perfection' or 'high standard of finish'). You may wish to use effects to emphasise text, such as shadow or outline, or a 'fill' pattern instead of solid black or colour.

Figures 12.5a and 12.5b   Examples of a digital effect in Photoshop.

You may also wish to distort the shape of images or construct new images by putting together a collage of some kind. Many of these effects are already programmed for the industry standard image manipulation package, Adobe **Photoshop**. New effects are known as 'plug-ins' for the program. These effects are noticeable, and you might need to be careful not to follow trends just because there is a new plug-in. You can see these trends developing in the magazines – for example, the use of soft grey shadows for headline text a few years ago. Ideally, you want to appear contemporary – clearly up with trends – but also distinctive.

Electronic publishing

It is increasingly likely that you will be undertaking projects that end with a digital file rather than a print product. You may be asked to create a series of pages for a website, a slide presentation or an 'e-booklet', all designed to be 'read' online. Apart from being interesting examples of 'new media', these are also formats that can potentially be emailed to other parties or made available via websites.

There are various software packages available to create these products, but you need to be aware of the professional packages if you want to go further with your practical work.

Web pages

The industry standard software package is Macromedia's Dreamweaver which will allow you to compile text in HTML format and combine it with graphics, animation, etc. It will also allow you to manage your pages (keeping links up to date, etc.) and upload them to a website.

All of the conventions that apply to DTP apply to web pages as well, although you can use colour without worrying about who is paying the print costs. Think about the following points:

- The software will probably offer you 'default' type sizes and faces. Don't get too adventurous, because what you select may not appear on someone else's computer in the same way (they may not have your fonts).
- The computer screen shape is 'landscape' rather than portrait – don't make your reader scroll down a long page.
- Don't make your page too 'busy' and beware of large animations etc. – many readers will just go somewhere else if your page takes a long time to load.
- The only image formats you can use are GIFs or PNGs (for colour line art) or JPEGs (for photographs).
- All images on the Web are 'low-resolution' (72 dpi), so you may need to 'optimise' them in Photoshop – a 150 dpi image will appear over twice the size of a 72 dpi image.

The drawback to working in HTML on a web page is that you cannot control how your page will be seen on another computer. Depending on the browser (Explorer, Firefox, etc.), the platform (Windows or MacOS) and the screen resolution of the monitor (1024 × 768 is a common standard, but many users will have something smaller), your page can look very different. Try viewing it on a range of browser/platform combinations. The best advice is to keep it simple. If you really want a particular typeface for a logo, save it as an image rather than text.

A common print format

There is a solution if you want what you produce to be seen by everyone in the same way – use a pdf as outlined above. If you have software that can produce a pdf (such as InDesign or Quark XPress), it can be read on any computer by Acrobat Reader (free from Adobe). You will notice that quite a few web pages include pdfs to download. Once downloaded, the file can be read on screen or printed out (as long as it has been prepared for 'print'). A pdf can include text, photographs, tables, etc. (If you have a Macintosh, pdf is built in to MacOS X as the default printing/viewing format.)

Presentation

Acrobat Reader is also an excellent package for presenting slides, but most people in business choose Microsoft Powerpoint. Again the usual DTP conventions hold good, but if you are going to project slides onto a big screen as part of your presentation, here are a few tips:

- Think about type size and face – on a big screen you don't want too much text and a sans-serif face at a large size (16 points or more depending on how far away the viewer is sitting) is best.
- White or yellow on a black background works well on a big screen.
- Avoid red (it 'bleeds' badly on a video projector).
- Go easy with the animated transitions between slides – they can get boring.

In all electronic publishing work, remember that it is the quality of the text and images that matters, so design your page to show them off. The best way to learn is to visit different kinds of website and make a note of what you like about a particular page design.

Technical codes in video production

PAL video has a bitmap of 768 × 576 pixels for a standard 4:3 television screen. The US analogue video system NTSC has a 30 frames per second cycle and a bitmap of 640 × 480. Most computer monitors in 2006 will display a minimum of 1024 × 768.

A video image is a matrix – a set of rows and columns – of pixels that can be individually charged to show a particular colour. Your computer screen offers a video image of a specific resolution – in effect a bitmap (which is why you can 'grab' your computer screen as an image and use it in a print product, as we have done in this book). 'Full motion video' changes or 'refreshes' the image twenty-five times per second (on PAL equipment) to give the impression of continuous movement. Each frame of video corresponds to a single frame on a strip of film, which passes through a projector at the slightly slower speed of twenty-four frames per second. (Which is why video versions of films are always a few minutes shorter than the cinema version.)

High definition television (**HDTV**) broadcasts a signal with twice the resolution of standard video. Digital video is used by independent film-makers for convenience and sometimes cost reasons. Digital film produces a very high-resolution image when the celluloid image is scanned. Digital cinema cameras are designed to capture as much detail on a video censor chip as a traditional film camera – look for details of the 'Origin' camera from Dalsa.

The two main differences between analogue video and film are that the video image is relatively low-resolution (i.e. a small bitmap – see 'Technical codes in print products', p. 385 above) and exists only when a timing signal can stabilise the image (i.e. it is difficult to distinguish the single frames easily). Film is high-resolution and stable. You will probably shoot your projects on digital video which is much more like film with higher resolution and a more stable still image. (Much of this section is also relevant for still photography.)

The single most important element in the film or video image is light, or more specifically, light captured by a lens. Technical codes can therefore be classified as follows:

- light
  - sources (positions)
  - type of lamp (colour of light, area covered)
  - brightness, intensity
- lens or aperture
  - focal length
  - size
- sensitivity of film or light sensor
- shutter speed
- special effects.

The term **lamp** describes the physical device which provides the 'light' and is used to avoid confusion.

These are all codes relating to the contrast between light and shade and the effect of light in 'modelling' or shaping figures in an environment. There are some basic rules for a lighting **set-up** as shown in Figure 12.6. Traditionally, film and television use a set-up with three kinds of lamps, placed in specific positions. The **key light** is a bright, powerful light which illuminates a person or object and throws a deep shadow. It usually comes from a lamp above and at an angle to the subject. **Fill light** comes from smaller lamps placed at complementary angles to 'fill' the shadows created by the key light with a softer light. Finally **back light**, from a lamp above and behind the figure, helps to bring it forward from the background and create some depth in the image.

In mainstream film and television, most comedies, musicals, talk shows and light entertainment are presented in high-key lighting. This means

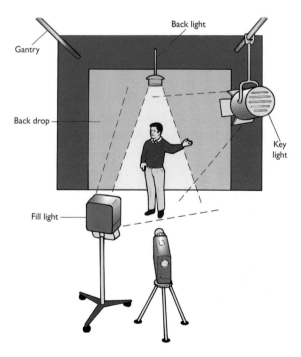

Figure 12.6 Three-point lighting set-up.

Figure 12.7 This crowded shoot on location shows a white reflector and a 2,500-watt key light with 'barn doors'. The umbrella is for the rain, but white umbrellas can be used as reflectors.

The origins of *film noir* lighting are argued to be in German cinema of the 1920s and 1930s during the period of expressionist cinema. **Expressionism** is an aesthetic approach in which the exaggerated outward appearance of things (in this case dark shadows) 'expresses' the inner emotions of the characters.

that the ratio of fill to key is high – most of the shadows are filled in. Light has a texture which is either 'hard' – producing deep and sharp shadows – or 'soft', creating only slight shadows. The texture depends both on the intensity of the lighting element (brightness) and the extent to which the light is 'direct' or diffused in some way with a 'scrim' (a fine mesh) or gauze. Light is brighter when it is concentrated on a 'spot'. This can be achieved with lenses in the lamp or with 'barn doors' (metal hinged flaps). Softer light can be achieved by 'bouncing' or reflecting light off the ceiling or a white sheet.

Light is angled on to its subject, and the texture can be controlled. A third factor is 'colour' – depending on the power of the lamp, light has a **colour temperature**. The most powerful light is bright daylight, which is 'hot' and produces a blue sky. Artificial lights are by comparison 'cold' and tend towards reddish yellow. (You'll notice that this is the opposite of what you would expect, since we tend to equate blue with cold and red with heat.) If you shoot in colour, you must ensure that either the film stock or the video camera is adjusted for indoor or outdoor lighting. The video camera adjustment is known as **white balance**. If these adjustments are not made, the image will have a blue or yellow cast.

Fine gradations of light are difficult to distinguish on a video screen, but are revealed in all their glory in the classic black and white cinematography of 1940s cinema. It is worth trying to see reissued 1940s films on a large cinema screen to get the full effect. *Film noir* lighting was '**low-key**' – so-called because of a low 'fill' to 'key' ratio – often dispensing with fill and back lights altogether to produce stark images with single, hard key lights.

Many different kinds of lamps were used in classical cinema, and you may find references to some exotic names, such as 'pups' or 'babies', 'inkies', 'scoops', 'juniors' and 'seniors'. These refer to lights of different power and purpose. During your course, if you do get access to lighting equipment it is likely to be a kit of '**redheads**', so named because of the reddish colour achieved at relatively low power. You will see these in use by some news crews in an interview set-up on location. The more powerful portable light is a '**blonde**' (again because of the colour of the brighter light).

Natural light also varies in power and texture and film-makers often choose to shoot at only certain times of day to capture a particular lighting effect. Natural light can be used indoors (i.e. through windows, doorways) and can be manipulated via reflectors (and suitable adjustment for colour temperature).

Figure 12.8 *Out of the Past* (US 1947) is a classic *film noir*. In this shot, a table lamp is off screen to the right, throwing a bright light up on to Robert Mitchum.

Figure 12.9 *Chinatown* (US 1974) is a colour film that has a *noir* theme and attempts to find a suitable lighting style.

ACTIVITY 12.4

Experiment with lighting

The best way to learn about lighting and lenses is to experiment. Unfortunately, many inexpensive video cameras are designed to prevent you doing just that. Equipment for 'home' use has automatic controls which try to standardise the image. Look for a video camera with 'manual' iris or aperture control, or at least some means of altering the aperture setting.

- Try to create a *film noir* image, applying some of the lighting techniques described above. Start with a set as dark as possible – a studio or a room with blackout – gradually adding 'lamps' to achieve effects of light and shadow typical of the *noir* image.

Any video camera will be worth using for the next task:

- Try to manipulate natural light by shooting in a room where you can control sunlight through a window to act as a key light. Use a reflector to act as a fill source.

- What happens to the lighting on your subject if you are pointing the camera towards the window or at a white wall? You should be able to work out what is happening (and learn to avoid it – unless you want to create an effect).

Lens and aperture

You will probably have noticed the very long lenses used by sports photographers or wildlife photographers (and some paparazzi) to take close-ups from a long distance away. Sometimes the lenses are so big they need a separate support to keep the camera steady.

Light is captured by the camera via the lens and passes through the aperture to reach the film or video light sensor. The lens and aperture function just like your eye in focusing on the subject and controlling the amount of light. When you are faced with a bright light your iris contracts. In the same way the camera aperture can be made smaller. The smaller the aperture, the longer the focal length achieved by the lens. A longer focal length means a greater depth of focus in the image. Conversely, a shorter focal length means only a limited field of focus.

It's easy to be confused by the terms photographers use. 'Depth of field' is also a function of the type of lens. A 'standard' lens for a film or still camera is given as 50 mm focal length – the distance between the lens and the film on which a sharp image is focused. This lens produces an image with roughly the same perspective as your own view of a scene. A shorter or **wide-angle** lens of 25 mm produces a scene which seems further away, but which 'crams more in'. A long lens, often called a **telephoto** lens, of 80 mm or more will compress the distance between you and the scene. The confusion comes when you realise that the long lens means a shallow field of focus while a short lens means very deep focus. You don't need to know all the details about lenses (unless you want to be a director of photography), but you should be able to distinguish between the use of a wide-angle and telephoto lens as shown in the examples here.

You can check out some of these ideas about lenses with a video camera. Modern video cameras use a **zoom** lens to simulate shorter and longer lenses, so a typical small video camcorder will have a zoom lens offering 'lengths' from, say, 10 mm to 120 mm (these are the equivalent of 20 mm to 240 mm on a 35 mm film camera), with controls often marked 'W' and 'T' for wide-angle and telephoto. If you want to create great depth of field in a scene, use a relatively short lens with characters relatively close to the camera and plenty of action in the background.

In the *film noir*, *Crossfire* (US 1947), the 'villain' is photographed with different lenses as the film progresses. Each time, the lens is slightly shorter, so at the climax of the film his appearance is distorted by a wide-angle lens, creating a very disturbing effect.

One of the disadvantages of a wide-angle lens is that objects very close to the camera can become distorted, even when still in focus. This can work well in a horror film or *film noir* where the face looming into the

Figure 12.10 Wide-angle distortion in *La Haine* (France 1995) as the gun is swung towards the camera.

camera with bulging eyes etc. can be quite shocking. Other distorting lenses can be used to create more obvious effects, such as the circular or 'goldfish bowl' effect.

Our striking still from *The Good, the Bad and the Ugly* (Figure 12.11) shows the dramatic effects of a wide-angle lens and a small aperture. The foreground and the deep background are both in sharp focus. This is an extraordinary shot and was achievable only with the bright desert sunlight and a particular widescreen film format called Techniscope (see Salt 1992) which used a half-size film frame, effectively doubling the focal length.

The widescreen formats introduced in the 1950s all required more light through the lens to capture and project a bigger image. At first it was thought that 'epic' pictures would all be set outdoors or on sets with very shallow fields of focus. The lens manufacturers improved their products dramatically, and improvements in the other parts of the system meant that, eventually, everything that studio cinematographers of the 1940s had achieved could be replicated in widescreen and **Technicolor**.

The history of technical codes in cinema and television has been largely concerned, in terms of the image, with the problem of light. There are three aspects of the problem:
- getting enough light, of the appropriate intensity, tone and texture, onto the scene where it is required
- developing a lens to capture the light
- developing the 'light-sensing' device in the camera.

'Film' is a photochemical technology. An emulsion of chemicals on a celluloid base reacts to exposure to light and changes colour. Throughout the history of the cinema, the basic technology has remained the same, but improvements have been made to the emulsion to make it more sensitive and responsive to a wider range of lighting possibilities. Video cameras have light-sensitive chips which transmit information to be stored on tape

Figure 12.12 *Bloody Sunday*
(UK/Ireland 2002) is a 'dramatic
reconstruction' of events in 1972.
The colour palette and 'hard'
image quality are important in
the attempt to suggest 'realism'.
(See Chapter 14 below.)

or disk. Again their development involves increasing the data flow – the
lighting information to be recorded. Film or video sensing devices can be
ranged from 'fast' to 'slow' in terms of how quickly they can capture light.
A fast film can operate in relatively poor lighting conditions, but the
resulting image is quite 'grainy' – a feature you might notice in newsreel
footage from the 1940s or 1950s. Slow film needs plenty of light to
produce very smooth and glossy images.

Colour film depends on chemical processes which can produce different
palettes. If you read what successful cinematographers and directors
say about their films, you will sometimes find references to a choice
of Eastmancolor or Fujicolor because they favour one group of colours
rather than another. It is also possible to alter the way the colour is to be
recorded, by use of filters on the camera or lamps, or the way it is 'printed'
on the final film, by adjusting the developing time or temperature.

Cinematography

You can find out a great deal about the work of the cinematographer from
websites such as those of the American Society of Cinematographers
(www.cinematographer.com) or the International Cinematographers Guild
(www.cameraguild.com). Roger Deakins, the British cinematographer who
shot *The Shawshank Redemption* and many of the Coen brothers' films, has
been interviewed on both sites. He explains how in *O Brother, Where Art Thou?*
(US 2000) the Coens wanted a dry, dusty look, but the location was lush
and green. The film was first printed to a digital format. All the greens were
manipulated using the computer and the result then transferred to the final
film print.

Speed of shooting and projecting

A film camera has a shutter which closes the aperture and allows the film to be fed through the gate at a rate of twenty-four frames per second. This speed is matched by the cinema projector. But speeds can be manipulated in a number of ways to speed up or slow down the action. Some cameras allow the film to be 'overcranked' so that thirty or even forty frames are recorded each second. When this footage is played at 24 fps, it produces 'slow motion', used to great effect by action director Sam Peckinpah for scenes of violence, such as the climax of *The Wild Bunch* (US 1969) (Figure 12.13). The opposite effect is achieved by undercranking the camera or speeding up the projector. Such techniques can now also be imitated in digital editing.

Figure 12.13   Slow motion during the final shoot-out in *The Wild Bunch.*

Special effects

Some of the digital effects used in photographic images for print are also relevant for video and film, and, when edit suites moved from analogue to digital **nonlinear**, more and more effects became available. **CGI** (computer generated imagery) is now expected in most mainstream films. Special effects using double exposures, glass **matte** screens and front or back projection have been common in cinema since 1896 – modern effects are often based on the same ideas.

Most effects are not meant to be noticed (e.g. the cathedral in *Elizabeth* (UK 1998) is not full of expensive extras dressed in costume – most of those in the background have been digitally generated as copies of those in front). But Spider-Man leaping between buildings is meant to be seen – the 'wow' factor is important in creating the character.

Matte an opaque shape that masks off part of the image captured by the camera lens. Used from early cinema onwards in creating effects by combining images (i.e. partial images combined to make one complete image). Glass mattes, on which elaborate sets can be painted, were still in use on *Star Wars* (US 1977), having been introduced early in the century. 'Digital mattes' are an important part of modern special effects.

ACTIVITY 12.5

Lenses, shutters and film stock

It is difficult to experiment with these codes (although some of you may be lucky and have access to video cameras with a range of controls). It is also quite difficult to recognise some of the subtleties of film stock and colour palettes when watching films on video. But you can learn something by watching a variety of films from different periods.

Watch the openings of three or four films from the history of cinema, ideally one from silent cinema, one from the 1940s, one from the 1970s and one from recent cinema. Note the differences in

- depth of field
- use of wide-angle or telephoto lenses
- quality of the image – colour, grain, etc.
- use of special effects.

What conclusions do you draw about changing techniques?

'Narrative' codes in film and video production

Some decisions about the images which appear in print or in a film or television programme depend not on technical issues but on selection of framings, angles, shot 'size', etc. for the sake of narrative flow. They have become closely bound up with the routines of 'technical' film knowledge and because all of them are concerned with manipulating narrative 'space', we've included them under the heading of narrative codes.

When moving images were first presented as 'films' in the nineteenth century, action unrolled in front of a stationary camera. The action recorded was continuous and lasted for as long as the roll of film in the camera. Even when the idea of filming a series of actions developed, the camera was at first simply placed where the audience might be – in the front row of the theatre stalls. Very quickly, however, film crews learnt how to make the story much more interesting to watch by:

- changing the framing and composition (moving the camera and the actors)
- changing the angle of view
- shooting while the camera is moving.

Framings and composition

These early innovations in camerawork became 'codified' into a 'film language' with precise terms for different **framings**. The basis for the system is the framing of the human body as shown in Figure 12.14. Terms also developed for groupings of people and angles on the action. Although these are 'narrative codes', they are also related to technical codes. A framing of a face in 'big close-up' can be achieved either by moving the camera close to the subject with a standard lens or by using a telephoto lens from some distance away. The effect won't be exactly the same. Using a wide-angle lens close to the face may produce distortion.

Composition refers more to the shape of the subject within the frame or where objects are placed in relation to each other. Ideas for composition (e.g. the use of lighting and colour) have developed from concepts of beauty developed in fine art (see Rose 2001). Figure 12.14 shows how different camera positions and movements are achieved. Again, some of

Figure 12.14 Shot sizes and framings.

these seem to refer to more or less the same effect, but the differences can be important. *La Haine* (France 1995) is distinctive because of its long travelling (or 'tracking') shots. These could have been attempted with a **Steadicam**, but the director wanted the extra control that genuine tracking would give him. (See Stafford 2000 for discussion of camera techniques in this film.)

Mise en scène still appears on many A Level specifications, but its use has been heavily criticised. See Lovell and Sergi (2005: 115), who argue that a *mise en scène* approach emphasises the role of the director over other creative inputs in film-making.

> **Mise en scène**, or the 'setting up of a scene', is a term from 1950s French film criticism, originally borrowed from theatre, which is sometimes used to refer to the way in which the visual image has been organised in a film. Its original use was confined to production design, decor, costume, colour, lighting, etc. (i.e. theatrical elements). Later commentators included all the elements of camerawork mentioned above. In practice it is difficult to distinguish 'camera effects' from the organisation of the scene in front of the camera. When we discuss the 'disturbed *mise en scène* of *film noir*', we mean both the dark shadows and bright pools of light and the tilted frame, high angles, distortions, etc. found in a film such as *Crossfire*.

Editing transitions

Changing camera set-ups means that editing is required. This is also an issue about manipulating 'narrative time'. There are two aspects to consider:

- the nature of the 'transition' between shots
- the relationship between different scenes.

The most common transition is the simple cut – one image replaces another immediately. Careful framing (which means shifting the angle or changing the shot size) can disguise a cut's abruptness and aid the audience's absorption into the narrative, especially when the sound track of music and dialogue is continuous. The cut has no special meaning except to 'move the narrative forward'. In modern cinema and television, 'fast-cutting' at the rate of every five or six seconds also has the effect of generating a fast pace to the narrative (which in turn can make a **'long-take'** style of shooting feel leisurely).

In *Bloody Sunday* (Figure 12.12) 'fades to black' are used frequently between short scenes. The conventional edit would be a straight 'cut' with fades used to signify significant passage of time. The fades here 'foreground' the construction of the narrative (which takes place over one day) but might also be an attempt to persuade us that we are seeing 'real events'. (See Chapter 14.)

Every other form of transition is more noticeable and tends to have a more specialised meaning. Sometimes one image slowly **fades** away at the same time as another fades up, allowing a short period when the images overlap. This is a **'mix'** in television and a **'dissolve'** in the cinema. Traditionally, a dissolve has been a softer kind of transition, often within a sequence signifying time passing. It may also be the signal for a flashback or a dream sequence, usually with some other visual clue. A more marked

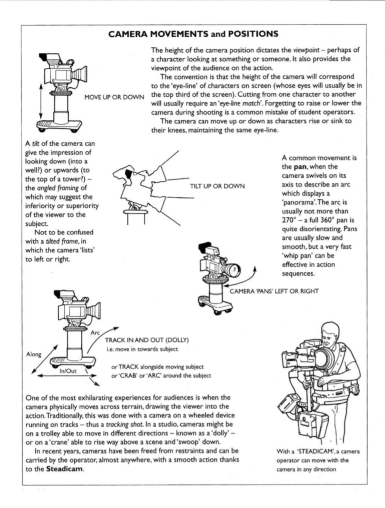

CAMERA MOVEMENTS and POSITIONS

The height of the camera position dictates the *viewpoint* – perhaps of a character looking at something or someone. It also provides the viewpoint of the audience on the action.

The convention is that the height of the camera will correspond to the 'eye-line' of characters on screen (whose eyes will usually be in the top third of the screen). Cutting from one character to another will usually require an 'eye-line match'. Forgetting to raise or lower the camera during shooting is a common mistake of student operators.

The camera can move up or down as characters rise or sink to their knees, maintaining the same eye-line.

MOVE UP OR DOWN

A *tilt* of the camera can give the impression of looking down (into a well?) or upwards (to the top of a tower?) – the *angled framing* of which may suggest the inferiority or superiority of the viewer to the subject.

Not to be confused with a *tilted frame*, in which the camera 'lists' to left or right.

TILT UP OR DOWN

A common movement is the **pan**, when the camera swivels on its axis to describe an arc which displays a 'panorama'. The arc is usually not more than 270° – a full 360° pan is quite disorientating. Pans are usually slow and smooth, but a very fast 'whip pan' can be effective in action sequences.

CAMERA 'PANS' LEFT OR RIGHT

Arc

TRACK IN AND OUT (DOLLY)
i.e. move in towards subject

Along

In/Out

or TRACK alongside moving subject
or 'CRAB' or 'ARC' around the subject

One of the most exhilarating experiences for audiences is when the camera physically moves across terrain, drawing the viewer into the action. Traditionally, this was done with a camera on a wheeled device running on tracks – thus a *tracking shot*. In a studio, cameras might be on a trolley able to move in different directions – known as a 'dolly' – or on a 'crane' able to rise way above a scene and 'swoop' down.

In recent years, cameras have been freed from restraints and can be carried by the operator, almost anywhere, with a smooth action thanks to the **Steadicam**.

With a 'STEADICAM', a camera operator can move with the camera in any direction

Figure 12.15 Camera movements.

signal of time passing, and possibly location change, comes with the fade to black and then the slow fade up to a new scene. The **wipe** was popular in cinema during the studio era (some of the most effective wipes are in the films of Akira Kurosawa, such as *Seven Samurai* (Japan 1954)). It involves pulling or pushing an image out of the way to reveal another beneath, rather as the windscreen wiper on a car reveals the road ahead. Digital editing software offers numerous different kinds of wipes, and used with care they can be very effective.

New forms of transition and new ideas about editing are emerging in contemporary cinema and television. Most of these, like the freeze frames in Steven Soderbergh films (e.g. *Out of Sight*, US 1998) or the speeded-up sequences in Wong Kar-Wai's *Chungking Express* (Hong Kong 1994), are variations on older ideas. Others are developing in music television. One way of avoiding camera movement or doing away with the need for a transition is the use of the zoom lens. In several science fiction films this has now produced the effect of a zoom across space (see the ending of *Men in Black* (US 1999)).

Parallel editing

Very early in cinema, the idea developed of showing two strands of a story happening at the same time. This allows the parallel development of stories and builds up the excitement of suspense stories or chase sequences. Sometimes this is called 'cross-cutting' as attention crosses from one location to another where linked events are being played out. Another possibility, briefly popular in the late 1960s, is the split screen, with different stories occupying different parts of the screen. This technique was successfully revived in *Lola rennt* (*Run Lola Run*) (Germany 1998).

Continuity 'rules'

Some film theorists (especially Bordwell *et al.* 1988) have argued that 'Studio Hollywood' used various rules for framing and combining shots. These combined to form a 'continuity system' or an 'Institutional Mode of Representation'. Some of these unspoken rules are still largely in place because they help audiences make sense of what is going on – thus the '**180-degree**' or '**crossing the line**' **rule**. This is illustrated in Figure 12.16 and demonstrates how camera set-ups must be organised to avoid confusion over narrative space.

Other conventions such as avoiding the '**jump cut**' (caused by cutting together shots that are only slightly different in content and shot size so that the image appears to jump across the edit) are gradually falling away as they become accepted in a range of films. The best advice is to try to develop a consistent style – if you decide to make unusual transitions or to use different compositions, do it for a reason and think about what you are doing. If the images themselves and the story you are telling are interesting, 'breaking the rules' may enhance the audience's enjoyment.

Technical codes in audio production

Ray Dolby (born 1933) An American working in the UK in the 1960s, Dolby pioneered work on noise reduction and his company revolutionised the quality of sound from cassette recorders and, later, cinema projection.

It is possible to think about sound in much the same way as light. The cinematographer 'models with light'. The sound designer models with sound. It isn't very likely that you will have access to full Dolby Stereo sound recording for your productions, but it is important that you should know something about the principles of sound design in film and television and the work of the recording engineer in the music or radio studio.

| Camera A | Camera B |

When Cameras A and B are kept on the same side of an
imaginary 180° line, the two actors walk towards each other.

| Camera A | Camera B |

When the 'line' is crossed, both actors appear to be moving in
the same direction and the audience is in danger of misreading
the scene.

Figure 12.16 The 180-degree rule
is designed to prevent confusing
transitions by not allowing the
camera to 'cross the line'.

It may be helpful to begin by thinking of a radio broadcast or a film
sound track as representing a 'soundscape' (like a visual landscape) or
a 'sound stage' (like a theatrical stage). On this stage will be a number
of performers, a certain distance apart, with background sounds such as

---

ACTIVITY 12.6

Analysing a scene

Take any short scene (two or three minutes) from a recent film or television fiction; or look at a television ad. Take notes on:

- camerawork
- how it has been edited
- how lighting, costume, set design, etc. contribute to the narrative.

Now examine the sound track:

- What are the components of this track: music? voices? sound effects including distortion? How have they been chosen and arranged? Are some louder than others? Why do you think each has been included? Do any seem accidental?
- How have they been shaped around the action or talk in that scene? How close do the voices seem? How have they been chosen, or constructed? How does all this help construct the narrative?

---

traffic, birdsong, etc. How can this mix of sounds be represented to an audience? The secrets are in the capture of particular sounds via microphones and then the mixing and editing process.

Recording sounds

See Chapter 1 for further discussion of the sound image.

Microphone types
'Omni-directional': for vox pops – interviews in the street. Directional 'shotgun'-style microphone: on a 'boom' (pole) or with a pistol-grip, pointed at the action in a drama or interview. Tie-clip: used in a studio. Radio microphone: used by a performer on stage.

The nature of recorded sound is a function of the microphone, the **acoustic** qualities of the location and the sensitivity of the recording medium. There are several different kinds of microphones, categorised by different mechanisms for capturing sound and by different pick-up or response patterns (see Figure 12.17). A directional microphone with a very tightly defined response captures dialogue without background sound. This 'cardioid response pattern' indicates sound picked up from immediately in front of the microphone with limited responses to each side. The same effect can be achieved with a microphone positioned close to the speaker's lips like a 'tie-clip' microphone. By contrast, an omni-directional microphone picks up dialogue plus all the background noise. Some microphones can be 'switched' between different responses.

The sound that is 'picked up' has various qualities determined by the frequency range of the microphone – its capacity to pick up high- and low-frequency sounds such as a whistle and a bass drum. Other qualities are more difficult to describe, but sound engineers refer to the texture of sound – 'hard' or 'soft', 'fat' or 'thin' – or the 'colour' of sound – 'warm', 'bright', 'round', etc. Some of these qualities are emphasised by particular types of microphone. For example, the large microphones which you might see in newsreels from the 1940s are renowned for giving a rich fruity sound. If you are interested in developing audio production ideas, you should investigate the different kinds of microphone available for your practical work, but note that professional microphones are expensive and you may find only a limited choice.

More controllable, and equally important in terms of the quality of sound, are the acoustic qualities of the recording location. Sound is carried in waves created by pressing air. When the sound waves meet a soft absorbent surface they are effectively 'soaked up'. You've probably been at a party where, as more and more people arrive, the music has to be turned up louder – almost as if the bodies soak up the music. Conversely, when sound waves meet hard, shiny surfaces, they bounce back and in some cases produce echoes. If you set out to record a conversation in a student canteen with vinyl floors, formica tables and large glass windows, you will probably get a terrible clattering noise, even with a reasonable-quality microphone. But the same conversation in a room with carpeting and curtains may be perfectly acceptable. Just as a television director or film-maker may elect to shoot in a studio, where the lighting can be set up very precisely, sound recordists may use a studio space which is designed to be acoustically 'dead' – i.e. there is no background 'noise' or atmosphere. Suitable sounds can then be added to create the finished product.

The recording format is important because it too has a frequency response and may alter the quality of the sound. You may have several options on your course including digital audiotape (**DAT**) or **MiniDisc** as well as direct to an **MP3** device or hard-disk recording on the computer. Formats tend to be chosen for specific purposes and the current situation is very flexible. You will find professionals who favour one format over another.

Editing and mixing

Until quite recently it was standard practice for all radio interviews and features to be physically edited by 'cutting and splicing'. Disk-based editing has taken over almost completely, but you may come across both. As well as assembling the audio material you want, the editing stage also allows you to 'process' the sound and to add sound effects.

One practice used to achieve the effect of a 'location' is to record the dialogue in a studio and add the atmosphere as a sound effect. This involves using an audio mixer, which allows different sound sources on separate 'tracks' to be mixed together. The 'level' and frequency ranges of sounds can also be manipulated to produce a fluid 'soundscape', analogous to an edited visual sequence.

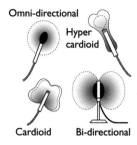

Figure 12.17 Microphone response patterns (cardioid = 'heart-shaped').

Noise in sound recording is a term used to describe any unwanted sound.

Audio mixers range from simple 4 track machines to much larger 8, 16 or 32 track machines.

Stereo means 'solid' – i.e. sound with width and depth or seeming to be 'all around'.

ACTIVITY 12.7

Compiling a radio sequence

Record two or three short interviews (a couple of questions only) with a range of people. If possible, conduct one interview in a location with 'atmosphere' and one in a 'dead' acoustic space.

- Try to add some atmosphere to the 'studio' interview.
- Edit the interviews together and add an introduction and a link.
- Listen to your edit. Are the 'levels' (the loudness) consistent throughout?
- Are the joins noticeable? How could you make them less obvious? (This will depend on your equipment.)

Stereo and the sound stage

All of the comments above apply to 'mono' recordings, where the sound has been recorded at a single point via the microphone. It is also possible to use a stereo microphone to record sound 'in depth' – not only to record the sounds but to place them in position on the sound stage. A mono recording can be placed within a stereo sound stage set-up using an audio mixer. The creation of the stereo sound stage is at the creative heart of modern stereo radio, television and cinema sound. The sound designer attempts to create a 'sound image', which means that every person who speaks and every significant sound (a footstep, a phone ringing, etc.) is heard clearly, but also in the context of a believable background – a city street, a busy office, etc. This is all possible with modern technology, which has allowed a greater frequency range and less noise through the use of noise-reduction systems such as Dolby.

Modern film sound is highly sophisticated and usually is carefully rerecorded after shooting using 'looping studios' or **ADR**, where actors repeat under studio conditions their lines spoken on location. Foley technology is then used to add the sound effects (Figure 12.18). Typical effects produced by Foley artists are footsteps, the rustle of clothing, etc., which are difficult to record with a microphone and a character in action.

In terms of 'technical audio codes', it is useful to have a set of terms to describe sounds used in a mix, based on a combination of the technology used to create or capture them and their narrative function. In a mix for narratives (in drama or advertising) in radio, film or television, we can distinguish

- dialogue spoken by the important characters in a scene
- sound effects – the specific sounds which carry narrative information, such as a knock on the door

ADR = Automated (or Automatic) Dialogue Replacement.

Jack Foley was a Universal Studios engineer who developed techniques for recording sound effects. See www.filmsound.org.

Figure 12.18 A Foley studio.

- background or ambient sound which gives the scene atmosphere – the general hubbub in a bar
- 'non-diegetic' sound – sound which doesn't come from the fictional world of the narrative. The clearest example is theme music. Music playing on a jukebox in the scene is diegetic.

Sound has received less attention in film studies than it deserves. Since the success of *Star Wars* and Dolby Stereo in 1977, film producers and cinema managers have recognised its importance (see Murch 1995). The later introduction of digital sound systems such as DTS enhanced its importance, and, with DVDs and digital broadcasting, television sound is also improving. Next time you go to the cinema, especially to a Hollywood blockbuster, try to listen carefully to the sound track, along the lines suggested in Activity 12.8. You will notice how the opening music tries both to wake you up – pay attention, back there! – and to pin you to your seat with sheer volume. But in the main narrative it is the range of sound frequencies which is important. Watch out for moments when the movement of the narrative hangs on a sound. Walter Murch describes his work on the opening of *Apocalypse Now* (US 1979):

> You are looking at Saigon, you are in a hotel room, but you begin to hear the sounds of the jungle. One by one the elements of the street turn into jungle sounds: a policeman's whistle turns into a bird, the two-stroke motorcycles turn into insects, and item by item each thread of one reality is pulled out of the tapestry and replaced by another one. You are looking at something very improbable, which is a man sitting in an hotel room. . . . Although his body is in Saigon, his mind is somewhere else.
>
> (Murch 1996: 161)

The classic 'sound recording' film is *The Conversation* (US 1974), with Gene Hackman as the surveillance agent who becomes obsessed with a recording.

Traditional dialogue recording in film or television allows each character to talk in turn. More 'realistic' is the technique which 'overlaps' lines by different characters. This can be achieved by miking each character in a scene and allowing each a track on a mixing desk. An appropriate balance can be achieved later. This multitrack technique was pioneered by director Robert Altman.

Wonderland (UK 1999) is an innovative film in terms of sound. Much of the action is set in London bars and *cafés*. Instead of taking over a bar and using 'extras', the director shot scenes in which the actors mingled with the usual bar patrons and the sound crew captured the dialogue (and some of the ambient sound) via radio microphones.

ACTIVITY 12.8

Sound and vision

Take a short sequence (two or three minutes) of video, either something you have shot yourself or a sequence copied from a film or television programme. Play the sequence without sound and concentrate on the meaning suggested by the images alone.

- Take two or three very different music tracks (or sound effects) and play them in conjunction with the visuals.
- How much difference does the sound make?

(See more intriguing exercises in Chion (1994).)

Skills development

The only way to develop your skills in using sound (and print and video) is to practise and to explore new techniques and approaches. Don't be afraid to fail – if it doesn't work, try something else. Even if you don't intend to become a media practitioner, the more you know about production techniques, the easier you will find it to understand how media texts produce their meanings.

References and further reading

Barwell, Jane (2004) *Production Design: Architects of the Screen*, London and New York: Wallflower Press.

Bordwell, David, Staiger, Janet and Thompson, Kristin (1988) *The Classical Hollywood Cinema*, London: Routledge.

Bruzzi, Stella (1997) *Undressing Cinema*, London: Routledge.

Lovell, Alan and Sergi, Gianluca (2005) *Making Films in Contemporary Hollywood*, London: Hodder Arnold.

Chion, Michel (1994) *Audio-vision: Sound on Screen*, Chichester: Columbia University Press.

Murch, Walter (1995) 'Sound design: the dancing shadow', *Projections*, 4.

Murch, Walter (1996) 'Scene by scene', *Projections*, 6.

Rose, Gillian (2001) *Visual Methodologies*, London: Sage.

Salt, Barry (1992) *Film Style & Technology: History & Analysis*, London: Starword.

Stafford, Roy (2000) *La Haine*, York Film Note, Harlow: Pearson Education.

Street, Sarah (2001) *Costume and Cinema*, London and New York: Wallflower Press.

Books by practitioners or interviews with them are sometimes useful in revealing how they work. The Projections Series edited by John Boorman and Walter Donohue for Faber & Faber carries excellent materials on film production techniques.

The film *Visions of Light: The Art of Cinematography* (US/Japan 1992) is available on video and demonstrates techniques from the history of Hollywood cinema.

DVDs offering director or cinematographer commentaries can be useful (but many of them are not). The DVD for *Far From Heaven* (US 2002), Todd Haynes's remake of Douglas Sirk's *All That Heaven Allows* (US 1955), is particularly interesting in showing how a 1950s scene has been reimagined in 2002.

Websites

desktoppub.about.com

homerecording.about.com

mediastorm.org/AudioPT2.html

www.bbc.co.uk/learning/subjects/media_studies.shtml

www.bbctraining.com/onlineCourses.asp (useful, free online
   advice/training)

www.filmsound.org

www.howstuffworks.com

www.planet-typography.com

See also references for Chapter 11.

13 Distribution

The last stage of the media production process involves getting the product to the target audiences. Often, this is the least studied part of the process and also the one which media practice courses are least likely to feature in detail. Neglect of distribution practice is a weakness that needs putting right and we've decided to make it the focus of this chapter.

Chapter 7 and 'Case study: Selling audiences' following Chapter 8 address related issues.

There are two main problems. First, the distribution practices of media industries are very specialised, so we need to look in detail at specific sectors. Second, most media production in television, radio and the press is concerned with selling advertising space as well as selling the product. Even when advertising is not carried, as on BBC channels, distribution (including scheduling) is influenced by the rest of the market which is advertising-led.

Distribution structures in media industries

In most media industries, the 'majors' are concerned to control distribution of their own product – either directly or through some form of partnership. They know that success depends on getting the right product to the target audience at the right time. Mainstream media products in all media industries are delivered to audiences along well-organised distribution channels.

National newspapers and magazines

Distribution in the print publishing industry involves a three-stage process, from publisher to wholesaler to retailer. As outlined in Chapter 7, newspapers have a shelf life of less than a day, so efficient distribution is important. The UK wholesale market is dominated by just three companies (W.H. Smith, Menzies Distribution and Dawson News) which between them control over 75 per cent of the market. The remainder is shared by smaller independents. The big three also join forces to distribute specialist magazines to niche retailers via Worldwide Magazine Distribution Ltd (WWMD). This domination means that the market is subject to periodic reviews by the UK regulator, the Office of Fair Trading (OFT).

The established system has been deemed to serve the public interest, since the wholesalers work on a regional basis. All retailers (mostly newsagents) in a particular area get their newspapers from a single wholesaler at agreed rates. The publishers organise getting each edition to the wholesalers as quickly as possible. This means finding a printer in each major region so that transport time is reduced to a minimum. Sometimes a newspaper title is printed by a rival group if that means more efficient distribution.

In May 2005, following a change in UK law related to the European Union, the OFT announced that although newspaper distribution could continue under the present system (because of the requirements for rapid distribution), it had decided that magazine distribution under the same system could be seen as 'anti-competitive'. It suggested that some retailers might wish to negotiate different deals (i.e. from a different distributor outside their region). The OFT recommendation has to take account of the competition laws, but the magazine industry was dismayed by the announcement and immediately began a campaign to maintain the traditional system. It may seem odd, but in this case they argued that price-fixing by an **oligopoly** guarantees delivery of all magazine titles to all retailers in any region. In an 'open' market, the magazine publishers argued that the only beneficiaries would be the big supermarket chains, which would be able to force distribution charges down by special deals. The wholesalers would have to compensate by charging more to small retailers. This has echoes of several other retail battles involving the supermarkets (i.e. cutting prices paid to farmers and other suppliers and driving out small retailers).

Newspaper distribution has not, as yet, been significantly affected by **digital** transmission. This has been important in the production process (news arrives on journalists' desks as digital data) and newspapers have electronic versions on the internet, but these are not as convenient to read as the printed version. Would you be willing to download a daily paper, rather than buy one from the newsagent? Certain specific newspaper functions have already been usurped by other media. Once, sports fans

A monopoly will be investigated by the Competion Commission at the request of an industry regulator if any company holds a 25 per cent share by value of a specific market – which is the case here.

Supermarkets are very powerful retailers. In the US in 2004, Time Inc. announced a new women's magazine to be distributed only by the giant Wal-Mart chain, whose 2,950 discount and Supercenter stores account for 15 per cent of all US newsstand space (from www.usatoday.com, dated 23 September 2004). This follows action by Wal-Mart to remove or cover up titles such as *Maxim*, *FHM* and *Glamour* – under pressure from religious lobby groups (from www.bettydodson.com, accessed 13 June 2005). Similar actions in 'covering up' titles have been taken by Tesco in the UK.

ACTIVITY 13.1

Magazine distribution

- 'Google search' for an update on magazine distribution in the UK. Use keywords such as 'Office of Fair Trading' (or OFT) + 'magazine distribution'. Also search on the website for the Periodicals Publishers Association (PPA) at www.ppa.com.
- Interview your local newsagent on this issue. How is the system working for them – can they compete against the supermarkets?

In June 2005, you could subscribe to a full digital download of the *Guardian* and *Observer* for a combined price of £10.79 per month (see www.guardian.co.uk/digitaledition/subscribe). A similar fee purchased a more limited range of material from the *Independent*.

bought Saturday evening newspapers to find out the results of the day's sports events – now they listen to the radio or access the internet.

Radio and television

'Broadcasting' is a form of distribution which is subject to **statutory regulation** (see Chapter 16) and the introduction of new technologies for getting the signal to the viewer/listener. The 'deregulation' and 'liberalisation' of broadcasting in the 1990s (see 'Case study: Television as institution') completely changed the broadcasting environment in the UK. We can think about distribution in the following terms.

Figure 13.1 Audiences can now watch certain forms of television on large screens in public places, including this giant outdoor screen in Manchester, which also shows student films and other digital material.

- *Analogue versus digital* Broadcasting is shifting from **analogue** to **digital** with 'analogue switch-off' announced in 2005 to take place in stages, by region, between 2008 and 2012. Digital means a better-quality signal and more channels in the same bandwidth.

- *Delivery 'platforms'* In many parts of the country, viewers and listeners have the option to choose from 'terrestrial' (i.e. received via an aerial), satellite or cable. All require some form of 'tuner' or 'decoder' and all are currently available as analogue or digital. When ITV's ONDigital collapsed in 2002, it was replaced by the Freeview service which surprised the industry by its rapid recruitment of customers. In 2005, Freeview emerged as a serious competitor for the hitherto unchallenged BSkyB.

- *Content and carriers* Few television broadcasters have direct control over the carrier of their signal. The cable companies are involved in only a small selection of the many channels they carry. Regulation means that most carriers must offer viewers all the main BBC channels plus Channels 4, Five and ITV1. Otherwise 'content' owners or channels must negotiate distribution deals with carriers.

The situation in the radio industry is more straightforward, with 'free-to-air' radio transmissions under the control of the broadcasting station and further distribution negotiated with satellite and cable. Regulation of broadcasting means that although there are disputes between content provider and carrier, most can be resolved by the regulator.

Television transmitters in the UK are operated by either Castle Communications (purchasers of the BBC's transmitters) or NTL (purchasers of ITV transmitters).

BSkyB broadcasts from the Astra satellite, owned by SES-Astra, a Luxemburg company with satellites over Western Europe and North America.

New media 'broadcasting'

Since 2004 there have been several significant innovations which could dramatically change broadcasting in the UK – initially only on the margins, but eventually, perhaps, across the board:

- Ofcom, in its review of Public Service Broadcasting (see 'Case study: Television as institution') in 2004, proposed a new type of broadcasting agency – a **public service publisher** (PSP) that would commission programming content for distribution via broadband internet connections and mobile phone technologies as well as existing broadcasting modes (some commentators believe that future broadcast services will be 'received' mainly via broadband internet connections).

- A PSP may be able to take advantage of television services for 3G mobile phones, as announced by Virgin Mobile and BT Livetime in June 2005 (http://about.virginmobile.com)

- The possibility of video on demand (VOD) delivered through telephone 'landlines' is technically feasible, but still requires the right economic conditions (*Guardian Media*, 13 June 2005).

Ofcom: The Office of Communications, established in December 2003, the statutory regulator for radio, television and telecommunications.

Podcasting grew very quickly in 2005 with major players such as the BBC and Apple as well as many smaller producers making music and speech programmes available. A crucial aspect of the new medium is the subscription facility which allows material to be downloaded automatically to computers registered with the podcaster.

- The spread of 'flash drive'-based MP3 players such as the iPod has encouraged the development of **podcasting** – recordings of radio programmes posted on websites (e.g. by the BBC) to be downloaded and replayed at the listener's discretion (this could be compared with the impact of Personal Video Recorders such as the Sky Box which record programmes automatically for later viewing).

Recorded music

'Case study: The music industry' (following Chapter 7) explores the issue of distribution of MP3s in the media industry which has been most affected by internet usage. As well as 'digital downloads', **CDs** are among the main commodities purchased online. This is partly because an online retailer can carry a much greater range of product than a traditional retailer.

Record stores have perhaps been most affected by general conditions in retailing. This means fewer but bigger stores, with pressure on small independents. In addition, a small range of 'chart music' is increasingly available in supermarkets, petrol stations, etc. All of this means that, if your tastes go beyond chart music and you have lost the services of a knowledgeable local dealer, the chances are that you will be better off buying online or through conventional mail order. In the sense of finding specialist material, these comments about music recording also apply to video (VHS/DVD) and specialist magazines.

As an example of the changes in retail outlets, the small town of Keighley with its typical shopping centre, boasted two dedicated record stores in the early 1990s and three music departments in more general stores. By 2004 this had been reduced to just two small sections in W.H. Smith and F.W. Woolworth. In place of the lost record stores are two videogame shops and four dedicated mobile phone stores.

Digital media products

Digital transmission has had an impact on all the traditional media industries, but it also offers the possibility of new media products. Making a distinction between what is a 'new product' and what is simply an electronic version of an existing product is not straightforward. For instance, in the case of electronic versions of existing print publications, if this means that the publication is distributed over the internet, but the reader then prints out the publication and reads it as hard copy, all that has happened is that the mode of distribution has changed (presenting a print publication, the equivalent of exhibiting a film, has stayed the same). If, however, the reader 'uses' the publication 'on screen', then a new exhibition practice is developing. So-called 'e-zines' or 'e-books' hold the promise of further developments in handheld readers (with mobile phone technologies?).

Digital transmission and digital distribution systems have undoubtedly changed the media environment significantly in music and broadcasting, and the next area for possible change is in film distribution. (See Chapter 7 for comments on digital projection.) Digital distribution is likely to mean that films can be 'downloaded' to cinemas direct from the distributor (with in-built codes which render the film unviewable after the rental expires, or if the film is copied). If you visit your local cinema and speak to the projectionists, you'll discover that cinema operation hasn't changed significantly over a hundred years. Films still arrive in several reels in large metal cans. The reels have to be spliced together ('made up') before projection and the whole operation reversed before the reels are packaged up and sent to the next cinema. Digital distribution could mean:

- cost savings on transporting cans of film
- no physical damage to delicate prints (they wear out after a limited number of screenings)
- different security issues (i.e. protection against copying, no physical print to steal).

This is a big and expensive change to implement, even if the long-term benefits could be great. Cinema history and the recent history of technological innovation suggest that this move (and the take-up of new media products) may take longer than predicted. In 2004, the UK Film Council announced a scheme which would provide support for cinemas to equip with digital projectors, as long as applicants for funding were prepared to show a certain quota of 'specialised films'. The Digital Screen Network was being put together as this book was being written. However, there were still sceptical voices in the exhibition industry (partly because it was felt that the equipment to be installed would soon become obsolescent).

Cinema prints Each time a traditional celluloid film print is run through a projector it is subject to some damage. Most film prints are destroyed after the initial release in cinemas. A few that have the least damage are stored for occasional 'repertory' screenings. A later 'rerelease' will mean striking new prints.

Beware any media commentator who makes emphatic statements about which technologies will be successful and which will fail. They are often wrong.

CASE STUDY 1: FILM DISTRIBUTION AND EXHIBITION IN THE UK

Film distribution (i.e. 'renting' films out to exhibitors and encouraging audiences to seek out screenings during a specified 'release period', when the distributor controls the rights) has its own unique procedures. The success or failure of a cinema release determines how the DVD and television releases will be handled subsequently. In the international film business, the rights to screen a film are sold in respect of distinct 'territories' such as the UK (which includes Ireland in this context). Most major Hollywood films are distributed directly by the studio which financed the film. In the UK this means that the cinema box office is dominated by a handful of major distributors, as shown in Figure 13.2.

Any mainstream film not taken up by these five majors (e.g. some of the other studio brands such as New Line etc.) will probably go to Entertainment, a UK independent specialising in Hollywood films. In 2004 only two films in the UK box-office Top 20 were not distributed by these companies. *The Passion of the Christ* at No. 16, starring Mel Gibson, was distributed by Gibson's own company, Icon, and *Lost in Translation* at No. 19 was released by the independent, Momentum. In any year, the five major distributors will account for around 90 per cent of the box-office rentals.

UIP (Paramount/ Universal/UA/MGM)	7	*Shrek, Bridget Jones: The Edge of Reason, Shark Tale, Van Helsing, Lemony Snicket, Bourne Supremacy, School of Rock*
Warner Bros	4	*Harry Potter, Troy, Scooby Doo Too, The Last Samurai*
Buena Vista (Disney)	3	*The Incredibles, Starsky & Hutch, The Village*
20th Century Fox	3	*The Day After Tomorrow, I, Robot, Dodge-Ball*
Sony Pictures	1	*Spider-Man 2*
Independents	2	*The Passion of the Christ* (Icon), *Lost in Translation* (Momentum)

Figure 13.2 Distributors and the Top 20 box office films, 2004.
Source: UK Film Council *Research and Statistics Bulletin,* March 2005

Exhibition

The distributors have to place films with cinema chains – the exhibitors. The exhibition sector was shaken up in the late 1990s and again in 2004 by both new multiplex building and changing ownership. The distribution of cinema screens at the end of 2004 is shown in Figure 13.3. The Hollywood studios have effectively dominated the UK film industry for so long that they no longer need to own the cinemas. By 2005 most of the cinema chains in the UK were owned by companies financed by entrepreneurs or general business groups (albeit managed by experienced cinema staff). These entrepreneurs see cinemas as good sources of 'cash flow' (much of which comes from popcorn and soft drinks – see Chapter 4 'Institutions'). Odeon/UCI, Cineworld/UGC and Vue/Ster Century dominate the business. Only Showcase (the cinema brand of National Amusements, owners of media giant Viacom) remains in American hands, but the other chains are deeply committed to distributing Hollywood films.

The first operator of a UK multiplex was AMC (American Multi-Cinema) which opened a ten-screen cinema in The Point, Milton Keynes, in 1985. This was eventually sold to Stelios Haji-Ioannou to become the first 'easyCinema' in 2003. Stelios at first struggled to overcome the distributors' opposition to his pricing policies, but in 2005 he was rumoured to be looking for a West End cinema.

AMC built new multiplexes in Manchester and Birmingham in 2001 and 2003.

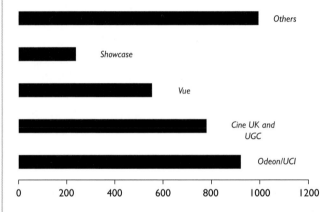

Figure 13.3 Chart of number of screens per cinema chain.

A Hollywood blockbuster is released 'wide' with one or more prints being sent to each multiplex. The Harry Potter films tend to go out on over a thousand prints in the UK (i.e. two or three prints per multiplex). A more usual figure would be four to five hundred. Each print costs over £1,000 so this is a significant investment. The **wide release** depends on blanket promotional and advertising coverage for the first weekend, and produces a 'buzz' or 'word of mouth', which means you may find yourself seeing a film you'd not initially have chosen to see, in order to discuss it with friends. Free trailer packages and electronic press kits are sent to radio and television stations and newspapers. Preview screenings for journalists are arranged. Stars give interviews, and newspaper and television advertising guarantees exposure. This package of measures will cost the distributor over £1 million, but if it ensures an opening of £2 million or more the spend will be justified and the impetus will have been given to a final box-office

A different tactic for certain major releases is to create a **platform** – releasing the film on a limited number of sites in key cities (major cities plus student centres) in order to create a buzz, and then widening with further promotion. This worked well famously with *Trainspotting* in 1996, but in recent years has been more successful in North America.

total of £5 million to £10 million at least (considerably more for the 'biggest' films).

'Specialised cinema'

The distributors of non-Hollywood product cannot afford to adopt this policy. They must work under very different conditions. The term 'specialised cinema' was coined by the UK Film Council in 2001 to describe what is sometimes called 'arthouse cinema' and includes European and 'world cinema' alongside low-budget British films and so-called 'American Independents'.

Most of the time, specialised film titles are handled by independent distributors. Some of these, such as Pathé, may handle as many films as the 'majors' – twenty or more per year, earning perhaps £1 million per picture on average. But these are exceptions. Forty or more small distributors share a few percentage points of the box office – sometimes earning only a few thousands per film.

All the independents face two problems:

- They can't afford to send out more than a handful of prints at any one time.
- They are often dealing with many smaller independent cinemas rather than a handful of big chains.

The strategy adopted is therefore to open a small number of prints in London and selected cities and let them run for a few weeks before sending the prints out on a long tour around the other specialist cinemas in different parts of the country.

This strategy is very difficult to support with promotional activities. Specialised films rely heavily not only on festivals and awards but also on reviews, yet these appear in the first week of release and probably only in the London broadsheets. Their impact will have lessened when the film reaches cinemas in some parts of the country several weeks later. Similarly, advertisements in specialist magazines are timed for the London release. Local media give little space to specialist films (which often require a specialist reviewer to cover them adequately). Local newspapers are the main source of film reviews for cinemagoers in the UK (source: Newspaper Society Market Research).

The Digital Screen Network, with its requirements that cinemas which receive support must offer a quota of 'specialist film screenings', is one part of the UK Film Council's strategy to increase access to specialist films. It has also helped distributors by funding (more like a special kind of loan)

See Chapter 4 for discussion of 'art' and 'mainstream' as institutional definitions.

A different strategy, now used by some distributors, is to identify a specialised cinema audience in certain cities and then put out 40–80 prints, hoping to capture the whole audience in a few weeks. This was the strategy for films like *Virgin Suicides* (US 1999) and *Ghost World* (US/UK/Ger 2001).

extra prints of selected specialist titles that have been identified as potential box-office attractions. These extra prints help to maximise audiences when/if the films prove popular. In 2005, a further fund was announced with £1 million per year for a national 'audience development programme'. You can find out more details about all these schemes on www.ukfilmcouncil.org.uk.

The Film Council measures are an attempt to address the question so many people ask: 'I heard about this really interesting film on *Jonathan Ross*, but it never seems to come to my local cinema. Why not?' Around four hundred films are released in the UK each year, but only about half of them reach most parts of the country. A large percentage of British films never get released at all. Film distribution is certainly a good example of the 'free market' not delivering diversity of product, or at least not to all potential audiences. (See Chapter 16 on 'free markets'.)

ACTIVITY 13.2

Specialist film titles

Log the new film releases in any single month. (There will probably be thirty or so.) The broadsheet newspapers should review each release (or look at the releases in a magazine such as *Uncut* or on websites such as www.launchingfilms.com).

- How many of the titles appear at your local cinemas?
- Are they shown at the multiplex or a specialist cinema? How many screenings do they get in total?
- Which films aren't shown in your locality? Would you like to see any of them?
- How did Jonathan Ross (or similar pundits) review them? How much time were they given, and in which part of his programme, compared to the time given to major releases in any given week?
- How much time did Ross give to the week's major release? Did he then (wittily) dismiss it as a waste of time?

Sight & Sound is the UK 'journal of record' which should review every film released in the country.

Distributing 'advertising-led' products

Film exhibition, like other public events, offers advertisers a 'captive audience'. Unlike television ads that can be ignored, ads shown on the big screen before the feature can have considerable impact. The companies

See Chapter 8 and its case study for more on the use of product placement, tie-ins, etc. inside movies, as well as in the official 'ad break'.

that sell this screen space are aware that particular cinemas attract certain kinds of audiences, but they have no input into film production in order to persuade producers to make particular types of films – Hollywood producers are not concerned to tailor their product to the needs of British advertisers. However, '**product placement**' in films, of internationally known brands such as Apple and Coca-Cola, is an important consideration for film-makers.

The total UK spend on advertising in cinemas was £159 million in 2004, representing just 1.8 per cent of total annual advertising expenditure in the UK (source: Cinema Advertising Association). Cinema is a market for advertisers to exploit but not to 'lead' in terms of influencing production. Advertisers will, however, have a general impact on film production in welcoming the distribution of family-orientated films with merchandising that enables tie-ins with fast food outlets, breakfast foods, etc.

The committed fans (e.g. of comic-book heroes such as Spider-Man) are often the most difficult audience to please. Most producers will aim to attract the mainstream audience first – unless they are producing a 'specialised' product for a niche audience.

In other media, especially commercial television and radio, the content of the programming is much more closely related to the needs of advertisers to reach specific audiences. A good example of this is the scheduling of programmes on Channel 4 to deliver a youth audience or an ABC1 young adult audience. Where film has been termed a 'producer-led' medium, television has now become 'advertiser-led'. A third possibility is 'audience-led' media – where audience demand leads producers to make particular kinds of products. 'Give the people what they want' is a phrase some producers use, but do you think this is actually what happens in practice?

In an advertising-led medium, the person in charge of production or publication has a difficult series of questions to answer:

- What is the source of revenue? Is it purely advertising revenue from selling space or sponsorship, or is there the chance of selling the media product as well? Will pursuing one source of revenue damage the chances of increasing the other?
- How will advertising revenues be maximised – by increasing sales as much as possible or by targeting particular audiences (i.e. those most prized by advertisers)?
- How important is the overall 'quality' of the media product in retaining viewers, readers, etc.? Is there a regulator to be satisfied?
- How important are distribution and promotion issues in maximising revenues?

These points all come together when we consider what has been happening in the national newspaper industry over the last few years. The UK is a unique market for national newspapers with a large population concentrated in a relatively small geographical area. London-based 'nationals' penetrate to all parts of the British Isles (i.e. including the Republic of Ireland), although they may take second place to Scots, Irish and Welsh 'nationals' in those countries. Few other countries (apart from Japan) have such a range of national, as distinct from regional or local, newspapers.

The main newspaper groups (News International, Associated Newspapers, Trinity Mirror, Express Newspapers, Barclay Brothers, Guardian Trust, Independent News and Media) are important media players in the UK. However, sales are declining in all sectors and national newspapers are facing increasing competition for advertising revenue from the regional press, radio, cinema, internet, etc. They clearly have to do something. Pricing is one weapon. Lowering the price – a price war – has already been tried, but the 'victims' such as the *Independent*, *Daily Telegraph*, *Daily Express*, etc. refused to die and the aggressors (usually News International) lost significant amounts of revenue. Putting up the price can offset lost sales, but only for so long. In 2003, the *Independent* introduced a new strategy – 'going tabloid'. What has happened since offers an interesting case study on the distribution and 'presentation' of the product.

'Giveaways' – CDs and DVDs – are another aspect of the circulation war. They provide a boost to sales, but are expensive.

Some newspapers boost figures with 'bulks' – newspapers provided for airlines, railway companies, hotels, etc. which customers can pick up without payment – and discounted sales.

CASE STUDY 2: TABLOIDS AND 'COMPACTS'

The UK newspaper industry has changed the size and shape of newspapers many times over 125 or so years of mass circulation. After the *Daily Mail* and *Daily Express* 'downsized' from broadsheet to tabloid in the 1970s, the UK market divided into three distinct sectors. At the 'top' were the 'serious', 'quality' **broadsheets** offering large pages with long stories and a balance between image and text. In the middle were the **'mid-market' tabloids** and at the 'bottom' of the market were the **'red-top' tabloids**. The tabloid format, roughly the size and shape of a broadsheet page folded in half, means that stories must be shorter to fit on a single page and that images may often dominate the page at the expense of text. On the other hand, tabloids can present very effective front pages with big headlines and a single strong image, and the format offers good opportunities for centre-page double-spreads. Advertisers, however, may feel limited by the page size.

The sector divisions in the UK are not just about size and shape. There is an assumption that broadsheet = serious, intelligent, up-market, etc. (and possibly for older, more 'conservative' readers) and tabloid implies frivolous, 'dumbed-down', etc. These conventions don't necessarily carry over into the regional press and they are not consistently applied in other countries either. There are plenty of 'quality tabloids' in Europe and at least one downmarket broadsheet (*Bild* in Germany).

The first UK broadsheet to challenge the convention was the *Guardian* when it introduced its range of tabloid supplements in the 1990s. These now run at two supplements per day, inserted into the folded main broadsheet. At first, *Guardian* readers were sceptical, some referring to the supplements as 'comics'. But the idea caught on and spread to the *Independent* and *The Times*.

The *Independent*, facing a severe decline in sales, decided to launch a tabloid edition of the whole paper in 2003, at first only in the London commuting region. This decision was interesting because it raised questions about both the readership and how people literally 'handled' their newspaper. Some assumptions might be:

- London commuters are younger and better educated than groups of readers elsewhere and possibly more amenable to change.
- Reading a broadsheet on the tube or train is more difficult than reading a tabloid because of the lack of room to fold the paper.
- Women are not so used to folding broadsheets as men. (You can decide whether this was a sexist assumption or something observable by researchers.)

Whatever the assumptions were, they proved to be good for business – sales went up. The industry was impressed and *The Times* followed the *Independent*'s lead. For both, this was an expensive gamble since the papers had to be designed twice for different shapes and page sizes and two editions of each paper had to be printed. Slowly, the tabloid formats became available elsewhere in the country and then both papers moved towards the equivalent of the television analogue switch-off – complete change to a tabloid for all editions. *The Times*, perhaps because it is more fearful of being placed next to the existing tabloid *Daily Mail*, has tried to define itself as a 'quality **compact**'.

Such a nice word, 'compact', redolent of 'small but perfectly formed' and somehow 'powerful' – on the other hand, Americans use it to describe small, cheap cars.

Tabloid and broadsheet tackle the same issue

The two front pages shown in Figure 13.4 are from the same week in January 2005 during the period when many world leaders travelled to Auschwitz in Poland to join death camp survivors commemorating sixty years since they were liberated by Allied troops in the closing months of the Second World War. The *Independent*'s editor chose to devote the whole tabloid front page to the Auschwitz story. This was Thursday, 27 January, and the main event of the commemoration had not yet happened. The lead story was in effect a 'feature piece' rather than 'news' and the presentation is more akin to what might be found in a magazine or a magazine supplement in a newspaper. Nothing else is allowed on the front page, which is carefully designed to include a single image, headline and byline and a strip along the foot of the page referring to further coverage of the Holocaust Memorial events inside the paper. It is worth also noting that the headline is more like a caption to the photograph and that it is presented in italic type – almost unprecedented in newspaper practice. The text – the opening paragraphs of the feature – are also presented in an unusual manner, in large (18pt) bold type. Again this looks like a typography convention taken from magazines. Finally, the text and photograph have been centred on the page – there are no conventional columns – and there is good use of white space.

There is no doubt that this is a striking cover, which has an emotional impact as well as simply being 'different' because of its unconventional approach. It could be argued that this is a good example of effective use of the tabloid shape, but it does prompt questions about how it might confuse the reader in an **institutional** sense. Was the event so important (as news) that it needed to drive other stories off the front page?

Figure 13.4 (a) *Independent* and (b) *Guardian* front covers, 27 and 28 January 2005.

The *Guardian* on the same day ran three stories on its broadsheet front page: the lead story with a large image presented a disastrous day for the Americans in Iraq, with thirty-seven killed in a helicopter crash. The joint lead story concerned British prisoners freed in Guantanamo and the Home Office announcement of plans to enable 'house arrest' of terrorist suspects. The third front page story dealt with climate change and oil company lobbying.

The *Guardian* coverage of the Holocaust commemoration led the news on the following day, 28 January, after the main event. Overall, this is a much more conventional broadsheet presentation in that it includes all the other features we expect from a daily newspaper front page. There is a large 'menu' strip across the top of the page, a 'quick index', a front-page advertisement and a topical cartoon. There are also two other front-page stories – another Iraq story and a less urgent story that acts as a lead-in to a feature in the *G2* supplement. However, there is also evidence that the *Guardian* editor considered the Auschwitz story to be sufficiently important to change some conventional aspects. First, the reporter has a picture byline – unusual for a front page – and second, the large image from Auschwitz (which might be described as more 'symbolic' than 'representational' with its barbed wire and blurred background) is enhanced by two further features. One is the small image (a 'symbolic fire on the rail tracks') printed below and the other is the column of quotes presented 'white on black' in large type (14–16 pt) from Tony Blair and others.

Placing the two front pages together allows us to consider some of the pros and cons of selecting the tabloid or broadsheet shape and size. This was an unusual news story/feature and we can ask a number of questions, such as:

- Is it more important to produce a striking front-page layout or one which carries all the important news?
- Does it matter if a newspaper sometimes becomes more like a magazine?
- Do conventional features (advertisements, cartoons, etc.) detract from our appreciation of an emotional story – or do they place the story in its proper, 'real-world' context?

The *Independent* and the *Guardian* target many of the same readers so these are potentially important questions. On most news days, the front pages will not be as distinctively different in appearance as in this example. Nevertheless, issues about typography and layout versus space

> for a range of content will always be part of the tabloid/broadsheet decision. As a final point on this, we should note that on the newsagent's shelves, the *Guardian* would have been folded so that only the top half of the front page would be seen immediately, whereas the *Independent* may have been available from special 'point of sale' display boxes showing the whole front page.

By the time you read this, the *Guardian* and possibly the *Daily Telegraph* will also have changed their shape. The action of the *Independent* and *The Times* in moving to tabloid is part of an international trend and change is almost inevitable for most broadsheets. However, the *Guardian* has decided to move to a third format, known as **Berliner** or 'midi', which is somewhere between broadsheet and tabloid. What is the rationale for this move?

- A response is needed to the new 'compacts'.
- A slightly larger size than tabloid will please advertisers looking for a more striking page image.
- There will still be a difference compared to the tabloid/compact and this will enhance the 'seriousness' and 'quality' of the *Guardian*.
- It will link the *Guardian* more clearly to elements of the European 'quality' press.

But

- The change will cost money.
- With no other UK papers using this size, the *Guardian* will have to build a new printing plant.
- The *Guardian* will have to find ways to help newsagents display an odd shape that is not compatible with either tabloid or broadsheet.
- The paper is contracted to use existing printing resources and will have to pay to break the contracts.
- Some readers will not like the change and they may be lost (although there is not likely to be another broadsheet to go to).

In August 2005, the cost of relaunching the *Guardian* and *Observer* in the new format was estimated as £100 million (*Guardian* 5 August 2005).

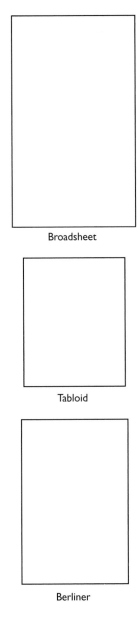

Broadsheet

Tabloid

Berliner

Figure 13.5 The Berliner size and shape compared with tabloid and broadsheet.

ACTIVITY 13.3

Point of sale

Visit a large newsagent and check the display of national newspapers.

- Are any of the papers in their own point of sale display boxes?
- Are any of the papers offering free gifts (especially on a Saturday)?
- Are all the papers displayed together or are they in different locations?
- How are the *Guardian* and the *Daily Telegraph* displayed in comparison with the tabloid/compacts?
- Do you think the newsagent's display has any bearing on which paper customers select?

An advantage of a new printing plant is the chance to put 'full colour' on every page, something which all newspapers are attempting to introduce.

Free papers delivered to homes are often used to 'wrap' direct sales leaflets or 'inserts'. Despised as 'junk' by some readers, this is nevertheless a very important advertising medium.

'Paid for' newspaper circulation is monitored by ABC (Audit Bureau of Circulation). ABC figures for 'free' papers are given under the heading of VFD (Verified Free Distribution). Advertisers need to know these figures.

The rise of the 'national freesheet' or 'lite newspaper'

Another significant aspect of newspaper distribution is the growing impact of free newspapers. In most parts of the UK there are local 'freesheets', often carrying very little editorial content among the masses of **display** and **classified advertising**. These papers are often produced by the same regional press publisher which puts out a paid newspaper. Where the paid newspaper is published on Friday, a free paper, containing nothing 'new' apart from next week's television listings, is distributed to households on a Tuesday or Wednesday. It isn't difficult to see the potential economic benefits of this operation.

The economics of newspaper operation

Like most businesses, newspapers have to consider **fixed** and **variable costs**. **Fixed costs** refers to costs that can't be easily changed as circulation goes up or down. To guarantee production of a paper every day, or even once a week, the publisher must have a printing plant which they own or have use of on a long lease. They must place orders for large shipments of paper and they must have at least some staff on long-term permanent contracts. These costs are there even if they decide to produce no newspapers for a short period. Other costs can be varied, so staff on short-term contracts might not be needed in a slack period.

Income (revenue) comes from the cover price of the paper and from the sale of advertising space. Revenue will be reduced by distribution costs (payments to distribution companies, discounts to newsagents, transport costs, etc.) and the two forms of revenue are linked, so that as circulation goes down, advertising space will have to be priced much lower to attract advertisers.

A free newspaper is possible if the publisher has excess capacity – in other words they could print more newspapers on the same presses without incurring much extra cost (the plant is already there). At the same time, they may be able to use much more 'bought in' agency material and less expensive reporters' time to create material. The marginal cost (the extra cost) of the free paper should be low and if advertisers will pay reasonable rates, the proposition is viable. The big question is: how to distribute? When people want to buy a paper, they seek out a newsagent. Would you go out to a shop to pick up a free paper? Most of us wouldn't (probably because we don't expect something that is free to have much 'value'). The local free newspaper is usually distributed by a company that specialises in door-to-door delivery of 'direct mail advertising'. But how do 'national' free newspapers approach distribution?

The concept of excess or 'spare' capacity can also be applied to satellite and cable television where the extra cost of establishing another channel (with limited content being repeated) is low.

Where is the largest single group of people, all looking for a newspaper, each day? If you have to travel into any major UK city by train each day, you will know that the answer is 'on railway stations'. The first national free newspaper in the UK was *Metro* ('the commuter's favourite') from Associated Newspapers (publishers of the *Daily Mail* and the *Evening Standard*), launched in 1999. *Metro* is distributed as if it were a 'regional' newspaper and there are editions in London, East Midlands, North West, North East, Scotland, West Country, West Midlands and Yorkshire. The only major difference between these editions will be the sports pages and the 'what's on' listings. The Associated Newspapers website (www.associatednewspapers.com) tells us:

It isn't a coincidence that the major distributors, W.H. Smith and John Menzies, have long histories of newspaper kiosks on railway stations.

Metro is read by a young, urbanite audience who are reached as they commute to work in the morning. 64% of readers are ABC1, 74% are aged 15–44. *Metro* readers are time-starved individuals who are increasingly difficult to reach using traditional media. Research shows that *Metro* readers enjoy active social lives, including visiting pubs, restaurants and the cinema. Many of *Metro*'s valued audience never read or were lapsed readers of national newspapers, making them highly sought after by advertisers.

Here, the argument for the free paper is clear. In an advertising-led medium, the holy grail is a new media product that attracts the consumers the advertisers most want to reach. If these consumers don't read

Figure 13.6 *Metro* is distributed or available for free pick-up at railway stations.

traditional media, then give them something new, for free. *Metro* is well thought out – tabloid format, colour and stapled. This last means that when you are standing in a crowded train, the paper will be easier to handle. In the same way, the newspaper stories are short and not too intellectually demanding – 'bitesize' chunks for easy reading between stops.

The material in *Metro* will already have been collected by Associated staff or will be available from the agencies. Associated already prints newspapers across the country and is promoting *Metro* as a national brand via its own website (www.metro.co.uk) and advertising is sold via a central site (advertising.metro.co.uk). This site suggests that over 1 million copies are distributed each day in twelve major cities. The advertising appeal stresses that the readers are 'urbanites' in cities with a combined population of 27 million. Advertising is sold nationally, but also locally (i.e. for local companies) through franchise arrangements with regional partners. These partners include the *Manchester Evening News* and the *Daily Record* in Glasgow, titles owned by *Daily Mail* rivals the Guardian Media Group (GMG) and Trinity Mirror.

In Manchester, where the *Manchester Evening News* (*MEN*) is seen as an important revenue source for GMG, there was an initial competition to provide a free paper for commuters, but in 2001 GMG and Associated came to an agreement to jointly publish *Metro North West* (editorial from Associated, but published, printed and distributed by *MEN*). In March 2005, GMG again followed Associated's lead and brought out an afternoon 'lite' version of *MEN* to be given away from newsstands. The *Evening Standard Lite* was first published by Associated in London in 2004 and so far has not seriously damaged the sales of the 'paid-for' paper (which are in long-term decline). Again the aim is to reach younger readers who would not normally buy a paper.

The GMG–Associated link may be tested by the latest stage in the development of free papers. The London Mayor, Ken Livingstone, is well known for his antipathy to Associated Newspapers and in 2005 he announced that Transport for London would offer a chance for another newspaper group to launch a free afternoon newspaper to compete with the *Evening Standard*, using distribution points in the Underground system. This announcement pre-empted the report from the Office of Fair Trading into the exclusive contract negotiated by Associated Newspapers to distribute *Metro* in Underground and rail stations in London. Transport for London currently receives more than £1 million per year for distribution rights. GMG was reported to be one of the national groups considering a bid to distribute a London afternoon paper.

Free papers are not, of course, a UK-only phenomenon. The website 'Free Daily Newspapers' (http://users.fmg.uva.nl/pbakker/freedailies/index.html) shows what is happening across the world, and in particular traces the progress of the international *Metro* title, which is not linked to the Associated Newspapers title in the UK. The international *Metro* began in Sweden in 1995 as a free paper distributed across transport networks. Although it failed in the UK, Metro International has its HQ in London and publishes different editions in seventeen countries, distributing over 6 million copies daily. There are a further 11 million free newspapers distributed by other publishers across the world, but the 1 million plus copies of *Metro* in the UK is the biggest single circulation. Register on the website at www.metropoint.com to download pdf copies of *Metro* newspapers from around the world.

In Spain and France, a Norwegian company publishes a free paper called *20 minutes* – the time it takes to read on a typical journey.

ACTIVITY 13.4

Reading the *Metro*

Compare *Metro* (or one of the downloaded newspapers from the US or Canada) with a UK national daily 'compact' and 'red-top tabloid'.

- Look at advertising: is the proportion of classified advertising , display advertising and editorial the same in each paper?
- Look at the length and complexity of stories: are there marked differences?
- Is twenty minutes about right for reading the free paper?
- What do you think readers are prepared to pay for?

References and further reading

Little is written about distribution as such. Most of the material in this chapter was researched on websites or in the trade press.

Trade press

Broadcast
Campaign
Press Gazette
Screen International

Websites

www.abc.org.uk

www.launchingfilms.com/uk_film_distribution_guide/index.html
(the website of the UK Film Distributors' Association – offering an industry guide to the whole distribution process).

www.newspapersoc.org.uk (The Newspaper Society, the trade association of regional newspapers).

www.oft.gov.uk

www.ukfilmcouncil.org.uk

CASE STUDY: CONTEMPORARY BRITISH CINEMA

This case study allows us to apply some of the ideas explored in a wide range of chapters to a definable media operation – making 'British films'. It appears here following 'Production organisation', 'Production techniques' and 'Distribution', but it could also have been a case study for 'Institutions', 'Industries' or 'Whose globalisation?'.

The British film industry is widely discussed in the UK press, often in terms of 'boom' or 'bust', characterised by the success of a single film on Oscar night or the revelation that so many 'publicly funded' British films have never even been released to cinemas. More intriguing are these two comments:

- French New Wave director François Truffaut claimed that the terms 'British' and 'cinema' just didn't go together – film is not treated seriously as an art form in the UK's impoverished cultural life.
- Many British film-makers have complained that there is no UK 'industry' as such (i.e. compared to Hollywood). Film-making is a 'practice' with very little structure and no sense of continuity – it is more like a series of 'cottage industries'.

And yet the British film industry retains an importance in the global media economy. In terms of the number of films produced and the size of the cinema audience, Britain may lag behind India and France, but London is in many ways the capital of the 'international film industry' ('international' = outside North America), and successful British films sell very well around the world. These contradictions (i.e. neither a big industry or a successful art cinema, but significant nonetheless) stem for the most part from the relationship between British film production and the Hollywood studio majors. Sharing a language with Hollywood is both a blessing and a curse.

Since the 1920s, when the Hollywood studios became established as the dominant force in cinema across the world, they have been active in the UK, making films in their own or rented studio facilities, distributing American (and some British) films and sometimes building cinemas to ensure that the films are shown. At the same time, the studios have lured British talent – actors, writers, directors, cinematographers, etc. – across the Atlantic to Hollywood itself. By the 1930s it was obvious that British working-class audiences, in particular, preferred American to British films. There have been periods when 'home-grown' British films have done particularly well at the box office, but the long-term bias is firmly in favour of Hollywood. In recent years the domination has been almost total. In 2003, 61.7 per cent of all UK admissions were to purely American films, 19.9 per cent to American co-productions with other countries and a further 13.2 per cent were for joint US/UK productions. That left just 2.5 per cent for UK films (including co-productions with non-US partners) and 2.7 per cent for the rest of the world's producers.

In England, making a film was seen like an indulgence – something you should be punished for, but in America it was more like a way of life.

> (John Boorman speaking about going to America in the 1960s in *British Cinema – the End of the Affair?* (BBC4 2002)).

ACTIVITY 13.5

John Boorman

Find out what kinds of films John Boorman made in the 1960s, 1970s and 1980s. What does his choice of films, and where he made them, suggest about the British film industry?

In practice, it is difficult to distinguish between 'British' and 'American' film-making. Consider the Top 20 'UK' films of 2003 as listed by the UK Film Council. The top four films, which took the bulk of the box office, were all American co-productions. Of the four, two were examples of the most successful form of 'international' film production, as practised by the UK company Working Title. *Love Actually* and *Johnny English* both had budgets far larger than any UK producer could afford without the support of a Hollywood distributor. Although made with British crews and British talent, the films offer an internationally recognisable set of characters and comedy conventions. *Calendar Girls*, by contrast, is a uniquely British story which could, arguably, have been made as a purely UK film. The possibility of repeating the success of *The Full Monty* (UK 1997) (which scriptwriter Simon Beaufoy has referred to as setting up impossible expectations for subsequent British productions) meant that the idea behind the film was pitched to a Hollywood distributor and ended up including a disposable American sequence. Finally, *Cold Mountain* was based on a story about the American Civil War, shot largely in Romania for a Hollywood company. It had a British

director and some British actors, but was primarily an American film.

Institution: what is a British film?

It seems reasonable then to ask the question, 'What is a British film?' It is an important question because the UK government, like many others, is aware of the need to support 'indigenous film production' for economic, social and cultural reasons and they may subsidise 'British' productions. The total 'spend' on films by consumers in the UK is over £3 billion. (Most is spent on satellite and cable film channels, followed by video/DVD retail, cinema tickets and finally video/DVD rental.) Much of that money will end up in Hollywood but it may well come back to the UK if a Hollywood studio then invests in a new blockbuster to be made at Pinewood or Shepperton Studios. Overall, the British film industry does not have such a disastrous effect upon the balance of payments as those in some other European countries and, with the television industry as a 'net earner', film and television production roughly break even in the UK (i.e. imports balance exports).

The money

One way to distinguish what is a 'British' film is to track the money involved in any production back to its 'owners'. This may sound quite straightforward, but the financing of films is often complex and the tax considerations in particular mean that productions may seek to move physical operations between countries in order to satisfy tax regulations and to benefit from various allowances. Film producers distinguish between **'hard' money** (usually a direct investment in a film production) and **'soft' money** (forms of public subsidy via grants or tax concessions). There is a somewhat macho culture involved when American producers claim to prefer 'hard' money, seeing the Europeans as 'soft' in their dependency on 'handouts'. In practice, of course, all film producers will consider soft money options if they mean that films can be made. (But the corollary of this is that soft money may cause some films to be made just because it is possible and not because the film-makers have anything worthwhile to say.)

In the UK, the majority of films are made by production companies set up specifically to make a particular film. These are known as SPVs or **single-purpose vehicles**. (The SPV will be a trading name for one or two individuals with some kind of industry track record who come together to produce a specific film.) In 2003 there were 181 production companies active in the UK (UK Film Council, 2004), but 166 of these were either SPVs or small companies that were involved in only one film in that year. Only four companies were involved in making more than three films in 2003. (In 2005, a new UK tax policy proposal suggested support for film productions across a **slate** of films.) The SPVs will not be able to find all the production budget themselves and will seek partners and access to various soft money schemes. Potential partners might be:

- a UK film or television company with a production budget, such as BBC Films
- a Hollywood studio
- a European co-production partner (possibly a French, German or Spanish TV company).

Other funding sources could include:

- the UK Film Council
- Regional Screen Agencies (RSAs) in England or Scottish Screen, Sgrin or Northern Ireland Film and Television Commission.

If you look carefully at the credits on any British film or check the companies involved (use IMDB or the British Council's film site at www.britfilms.com), you will find that most films show this mixture of partners and funds. Here are a few examples.

Yasmin (UK 2004)

A small production company, Parallax Independent, made this low-budget film about a young British Muslim woman whose Pakistani husband is arrested as a terrorist suspect after 9/11. Scottish Screen provided research funds for its Scottish director and Screen Yorkshire supported the shoot in West Yorkshire. Post-production was funded by a German organisation, Euro-Arts Medien AG. Channel 4 also supported the film and screened it early in 2005 before its DVD release (the film was not released in cinemas).

My Summer of Love (UK 2004)

Again a relatively low-budget film (under £2 million), *My Summer of Love* was originated by its director Pawel Pawlikowski who 'optioned' the original novel about two girls by Helen Cross and developed the project with his partner Tanya Seghatchian for their own company, Apocalypso Pictures. Pawlikowski's long association as a director with the BBC helped bring BBC Films on board to fund the development until the bulk of the money was provided by The Film Consortium (which ran one of the franchises for film investment set up by the UK Film Council). The Film Consortium also had deals with tax partners Baker Street and sales agency The Works. (Source: www.skillset.org/film/stories/my_summer_of_love/article_3636_1.asp.)

The Phantom of the Opera (US/UK 2004)

The screen version of Andrew Lloyd Webber's stage production was produced by Lloyd Webber himself for his own company, Really Useful Group, and director Joel Schumacher's company, with Warner Bros as US distributors for the $60 million budget film. The UK company Scion Films helped organise financing and tax deals and Odyssey Entertainment acted as international sales agents. The film was made at Pinewood and was extremely successful in the international market, achieving the majority of its $150 million box office outside the UK and the US.

Figure 13.7 Roisin (Eva Birthistle) and Casim (Atta Yaqub) in *Ae Fond Kiss* (UK/Italy/Ger/Bel/Spain 2004).

Ae Fond Kiss *(UK/Italy/Germany/Belgium/Spain 2004)*

Ken Loach has been making films in the UK since the 1960s. Since 1996 he has been working mostly in Glasgow with the writer Paul Laverty. Loach has developed specific ways of working with a long-term group of collaborators and he favours projects which attract money from small European companies. *Ae Fond Kiss* depicts the affair between a young Muslim man in Glasgow and an Irish music teacher at his sister's school. It was produced by Sixteen Films, the company set up by Loach and producer Rebecca

O'Brien initially to make *Sweet Sixteen* in 2002 after Loach's previous relationship with Parallax Pictures broke up (see *Yasmin* in this case study).

Bridget Jones: The Edge of Reason *(UK/France/Germany/Ireland/US 2004)*

Like *The Phantom of the Opera*, this film recouped its large ($70 million) budget by performing spectacularly around the world ($251 million), with the majority box office again coming from outside the UK and US. The difference is that the main 'players' in the production were the established UK company Working Title (see below) and their Hollywood partners at Universal Pictures. Miramax, French company Studio Canal and Irish company Little Bird were also involved. The film was shot in the UK, Thailand, Italy and Austria.

Talent and location

Is a film 'British' if it is made by UK technical crews in the UK and employs UK 'talent' (actors, writers, composers as well as director)? The references to *Cold Mountain*, *Phantom of the Opera* and *Bridget Jones: The Edge of Reason* all point to the difficulty of using nationality of personnel and geography as criteria.

Funding *for Ae Fond Kiss*

'The film was pre-sold to "our usual partners", namely EMC in Germany, Diaphana in France, Bianca and BIM in Italy, Tomasol in Spain, Cineart in Belgium and Holland and Film Coopi in Switzerland, who function as distributors and as co-producers. As long as we can raise the money, it makes sense to make the film with our regular European partners. The relationships go back over a number of films so there's a great deal of trust. We describe the film and how we'll do it and that's enough, which is a real luxury.'

The £3 million production was assisted by a British tax scheme, allowing investors to offset tax by investing in the film, through Azure Films, who provided 30 per cent of the total investment needed. Scottish Screen contributed vital investment finance alongside a grant from the Glasgow Film Fund, completing the funding structure.

'The film will also benefit from a sale and lease back arrangement, which is a British tax incentive in addition to the tax back scheme. We simply sell the film to a financial partnership and they lease it back to us' (Rebecca O'Brien from the Production Notes for *Ae Fond Kiss*).

UK film-makers, both in front of and behind the camera, do not face language barriers working in America, or indeed anywhere in the world where 'international' films (i.e. films in English, usually distributed by Hollywood studios) are made.

British cultural identity

It is important to distinguish between 'the British film industry' and the concept of 'British cinema'. The first describes the business of film production in the UK. The second refers to the concept of 'national cinema' that has developed within academic film studies. British cultural content is not necessarily a prerequisite for a 'British film', as *Cold Mountain* illustrates. On the other hand, *Cold Mountain* is not part of 'British cinema' just as Hollywood productions of Shakespeare plays are not usually accepted as part of British cinema, even though Shakespeare is the most produced British writer. 'British cinema' is concerned largely with issues of representations of British culture and the **aesthetics** adopted by British filmmakers. Again, this is not clear-cut. Anthony Minghella, in 2005 the chair of the British Film Institute as well as the director of *Cold Mountain*, might not figure on many British cinema courses, but Michael Winterbottom, director of films like *Code 46* set in Shanghai and *The Claim* set in the Californian Rockies, probably will. (The reasons for this are complex, but Minghella's flirtation with big-budget features made for Miramax and Winterbottom's interest in the aesthetics of his films, which do often feature distinctively British culture, e.g. in *Twenty-Four Hour Party People* about the 1980s Manchester music scene, would be among them.)

The UK Film Council

In 2003 the UK Film Council published its first set of detailed statistics about the UK film industry (offered as a free download on the website at www.ukfilmcouncil.org.uk). In doing so, the UK Film Council to some extent usurped the function of the British Film Institute which had previously taken the lead in defining what was a British film in its annual *BFI Film and Television Handbook*. The BFI is now effectively the agency responsible for film *culture* and is funded via the UK Film Council. The UK Film Council's definition of a British film is based on concepts of 'domestic' and 'inward' investment and different forms of co-production. The statistics group 'British films' into four categories:

- **'Inward feature films'** (single country) The majority of these films will be American-financed films (over 50 per cent of total funding) attracted to the UK by its film industry infrastructure (studios/facilities, crews, locations, etc.). These are what might be termed 'Hollywood British' films (seventeen films, £410 million investment in 2003).
- **'Inward feature films'** (co-productions) This category refers again mainly to American films, but the co-production deal implies a UK company has a significant stake in the film (thirteen films, £320 million).
- **'Domestic UK feature films'** Films made wholly or partly in the UK, by UK production companies (forty-four films, £270 million).
- **'UK co-productions'** (other than inward) Films made in co-production deals with partners from countries with which the UK has formal co-production arrangements (not American – mostly European, but also Canada) (ninety-nine films, £158 million).

These are useful categories, but it is important to note that the statistics do not cover the following film production activities:

- any productions with budgets below £500,000
- work on Indian films, not classified as 'British', using the UK as a location
- work on filmed series destined for television broadcast
- any other services (e.g. effects work) by UK companies offered to the international film industry for work on films not classified as 'British'.

In addition, they refer only to the money spent by UK companies or by foreign companies in the UK (i.e. 'inward investment') and not the total budget for films made as co-productions.

Budgets

A clear distinction emerges from the figures between 'Hollywood' and 'domestic' films. The average production budget for American films made in the UK is £24 million, whereas the average for domestic films is £6.11 million. Perhaps more useful, the 'median' figure (the best statistical representation of the group of differently sized budgets) is £47 million for Hollywood and £3 million for domestic (the 'average' is skewed by a handful of low and high figures in the group). Put simply, a domestic feature cannot compete with a Hollywood film in terms of budget. A 'large-budget' UK film costing £15 million ($27 million) is still only a medium budget film in Hollywood terms. US blockbusters cost $70 million and upwards.

How much does the disparity in budgets matter? In itself, a low budget is not necessarily a 'bad thing'. Some 'domestic' UK films have been highly praised and have had relatively successful international distribution. But this is likely to happen only if they are picked up by a Hollywood distributor. Many UK films fail to find a release at all. Of those that do, many will have only a limited release on twenty screens or less in the UK. Even within the UK, British films tend to need a Hollywood distributor to get them to every cinema. (See Chapter 13.)

The financial dilemma

British film-makers face a number of problems in deciding what kinds of films to make. Most of these are problems associated with the size of the UK market compared to the American market. Should film-makers aim to produce films for the UK market alone, or should they go for America and the international market? This question, which has faced

---

ACTIVITY 13.6

Reading the credits

The next time you have the chance to watch a British film in the cinema, read the credits carefully at the beginning and at the end of the film.

- What was the name of the production company? Was it obviously an SPV?
- Were there any public funds invested (UK Film Council, Arts Council of England, etc.)?
- Was there television money in the film?
- Where was the film made (locations, studios)?
- Could you place the film in one of the four categories used by UK Film Council?

---

the British industry since the 1920s, is extremely difficult to answer. The success of occasional British films abroad has always tempted producers to go for the big market. Invariably, they have been unable to sustain this policy for long, and many production companies have overreached themselves and collapsed. This is as true now as for previous decades. Only Working Title of the current producers looks like answering the question positively (and even so, *Thunderbirds* (2004) was a box-office disaster).

Why is the decision so difficult?

The UK film market is not large enough on its own to sustain a company making films costing more than £5 million. A quick glance at the box-office chart shows that in 2003, only five 'UK' films made more than £5 million at the box office and all of these were essentially 'Hollywood British' films. A 'domestic feature' is usually judged a success if it makes over £1 million. Clearly, international success is essential for profitability. (See Chapter 7 on box-office 'rentals' for more on the economics of the industry.)

The North American market is roughly ten times bigger than in the UK (five times the population and twice as many cinema visits per head) and the potential international market is also around ten times bigger. The 10:1 ratio works out fairly regularly for American films ($100 million box office in North America and $10 million in the UK), but almost never the other way round. Take a very successful film like *28 Days Later*, made for around £5 million and grossing just over £6 million in the UK (approximately $10 million at 2002 exchange rates). Its North American take of over $45 million makes it one of the most succesful UK films ever in that territory – but it still falls way behind the 10:1 ratio. UK films are still 'foreign' in the US, unless they have a major US star. *28 Days Later* also did well in the international market – a further $25 million. Needless to say, much of this success was due to the support of the Hollywood studio 20th Century Fox, which distributed the film through its Fox Searchlight brand.

What films like *28 Days Later*, *Bend It Like Beckham*, etc. have in common is relatively low budgets, clear genre appeal and confidence in their 'Britishness', which doesn't need to be 'toned down'. There is a sufficiently large market abroad to sustain these relatively modest but distinctive films. Bigger-budget films that must seek a mainstream audience often fail because they lose that distinctive edge, ending up as 'mid-Atlantic' – neither British nor American. The same criticism has been made of international co-productions. Earlier in the case study we referred to *Ae Fond Kiss*, a film which performed better in France than in the UK and will have covered its costs without compromising on its content. For British film-makers the lesson seems to be to keep budgets down and preserve identity – or pitch your idea to a Hollywood studio.

The importance of television

The UK cinema industry certainly suffered its biggest decline in audiences when ITV spread around the country in the late 1950s. Later, a common observation by social commentators was that British films suffered because UK television was of such 'high quality'. The truth is that without support from television, 'British cinema' might have disappeared altogether in the 1980s. Channel 4 saved the industry in its darkest days and in the 1990s Film Four, BBC Films and to a lesser extent Granada and Sky helped to expand the industry. Now Channel 4 and ITV plc are themselves under pressure and have had to cut back their operations. The BBC continues to be the source of at least some of the funding for British film production – linked to broadcast opportunities. The UK Film Council statistics show that although 22 per cent of all films shown on UK terrestrial television in 2003 were 'British', only 2.8 per cent were less than eight years old. Many British films are older and shown outside peak viewing, which is dominated by Hollywood (ironic, then, that *Billy Elliot*, a film that had BBC involvement, gained the biggest film audience on television in 2003 – 12 million viewers or the equivalent of £56 million at the UK box office). Television is equally important in other European countries, both as a funder and as an exhibitor. In countries such as France, there are quotas which require television channels to show French films. In the UK, BSkyB is the organisation that makes most money from cinema via its subscription channels, yet its support of the British film industry is not commensurate either in funding production or in showing recent British films.

British film culture

British audiences love films and in the 1940s British cinemas had some of the largest audiences ever seen anywhere. With 1.6 billion admissions for a population of around 40 million in 1946, each person in the country went to the cinema on average forty times a year. The figure is now less than three visits, but add together DVD sales, rental and pay-TV and most of us are still willing to pay to watch a large number of films each year. There is a film-watching habit in the UK, but not a vibrant film culture. The idea of film as an 'art form' is not widely endorsed and the films actually seen by large groups of people do not represent a diversity of ideas and representations. This may seem a surprising statement in a country where film and media studies are rapidly growing academic disciplines, but there are several important indicators:

- It is more difficult to persuade funders of the importance of 'cultural film' rather than straight 'commercial film' in the UK. (The Film Council is responsible for both 'industry' and 'film culture'.)
- The range of different kinds of films given a wide release is narrow by international standards.
- There are proportionately fewer 'independent cinemas' showing non-Hollywood films in the UK compared to other European countries.
- Foreign-language films perform less well at the UK box office than elsewhere in Europe, where both dubbing and subtitling are more readily accepted.
- Certain internationally respected British film-makers (e.g. Ken Loach, Mike Leigh) often earn more from overseas box office than from the UK.
- Most television coverage of cinema concentrates on Hollywood and rarely goes beyond uncritical promotion.

If there's one thing to fight against it's being bland and homogenous. They call films 'products'. I think a film can be commercial *and* interesting.

(Lynne Ramsay, director of *Ratcatcher* (UK 1999) and *Morvern Callar* (UK 2002) speaking in *British Cinema – the End of the Affair?* (BBC4, 2002))

In this climate, it is perhaps not surprising that many UK film-makers either attempt to make Hollywood-style films in the UK or move to Hollywood themselves. Unless the British film audience becomes more aware of a wider film culture, it will remain difficult for British film-makers to get innovative films into cinemas. 'Film education' is crucial to the future of the British film industry.

The current UK audience figures are rising, but this is mostly benefiting multiplexes showing Hollywood products. Overall, people in the UK still go to the cinema less frequently than in many other countries, on average under three visits per year (see Chapter 7 on Irish audiences).

ACTIVITY 13.7

Your views

Do you have your own concept of what is a British film? List the reasons why you do or don't think it is important to be able to distinguish a British film.

British film-makers and film-making traditions

The creative talent employed by the British film industry faces a number of constraints and 'institutional factors' that influence how films are made. For example, theatre and television are relatively highly regarded in the UK compared to film. British actors are far more likely to be trained for the theatre than for film, and British writers are likely to gain more prestige from writing a successful television drama series than from scripting a successful film. As a consequence, it might be argued that it is more difficult to produce the kinds of film stars who grace Hollywood films or to develop a professional film scriptwriting industry along Hollywood lines. Familiar arguments about British cinema that might arise from the theatre background are:

- British films are more 'talky' and less at ease with dynamic movement.
- The acting is less fluid and spontaneous than in Hollywood.

These are quite old arguments and may be out of date in the twenty-first century. What do you think? Is it still the case that there is much more encouragement for drama education that leads to stage productions rather than screen productions?

Having theatre and television as cultural resources for film production is not necessarily a bad thing. UK theatre directors Sam Mendes and Stephen Daldry were responsible for the very successful *American Beauty* (US 1999) and *Billy Elliot* (UK 2000) respectively, but veteran cinematographers Conrad Hall and Brian Tufano must have had a great deal to do with the look of the films. The theatrical background obviously helped with the excellent performances given by the actors, but it would be possible to mount an argument about how other aspects of the film narrative were handled. (*Billy Elliot* also had a first-time scriptwriter, the award-winning radio writer Lee Hall.)

British films are perhaps more likely to be produced with this kind of 'imported' talent because of the relatively small number of graduates from the National Film School and the difficulties they face in getting a first job. Again, by comparison, American and French film schools produce more graduates who appear to get more opportunities. 'Training' for the film industry was almost non-existent (crafts were learnt 'on the job' – a job obtained often through nepotism or working up from being a 'runner') before the establishment of the Industry Training Body, Skillset, in the early 1990s. In July 2005, Skillset announced that seven newly designated 'Film Academies' had been accredited as part of a new network of FHE centres of excellence for vocational education and training in film production (see www.skillset.org/film/training_and_events/screen_academies/).

The career route for aspiring film-makers is likely to take them through television or advertising before an opening in film production becomes available. It is also likely that many British films will be made with funding from television companies with a view to a television screening soon after the theatrical release. This strong television and advertising link has led to two charges about the effects on British film:

- The scale and 'look' of British films is often 'televisual' rather than cinematic.
- Directors trained in advertising are more likely to produce 'glossy' and stylish films, possibly devoid of substance.

You will notice that these charges are to some extent contradictory – are British films visually dull or too frenetically busy? And what does 'televisual' actually mean? The charges are certainly worth investigating – might it be true that Ridley Scott's art school and advertising background is evident in his films? Tony Scott, Hugh Hudson, Adrian Lyne and Alan Parker all emerged from UK advertising in the 1970s and gravitated towards Hollywood. In the 1990s, Danny Boyle and Michael Winterbottom began their careers in television and in the last few years Jonathan Glazer has emerged from advertising and music video (a promising source of directorial talent, given the strength of the UK music industry). Perhaps the most critically lauded of recent directors is Pawel Pawlikowski (*Last Resort* and *My Summer of Love*) who spent spent several years working on documentaries, mostly for the BBC. Paul Greengrass is another documentarist who made the 'drama-documentary' *Bloody Sunday* (2002) and then the Hollywood action film *The Bourne Supremacy* (US 2004).

Realism

One of the major factors in both the production of British films and their reception by audiences and critics is the legacy of 'realism'. (See Chapter 14.) The 'British documentary movement' of the 1930s and 1940s was the first significant British film movement to be recognised by critics outside Britain. Documentary gave the British film industry prestige, and this was further boosted during and just after the Second World War when British feature films learnt from the documentarists how to shoot on location, how to use 'authentic' props and costumes, etc. In the late 1950s the industry went further and used more realistic dialogue (and a wider range of actors). Since then 'British realism' has become associated with two types of films:

- 'Costume' or 'period' films displaying a very high level of 'authentic detail' – e.g. films based on nineteenth-century 'classic novels' or more modern novels about the 1930s and 1940s. This is an issue of 'surface realism', recreating period detail, and is recognised by some audiences as a mark of 'quality'.
- 'Social realist' films dealing with recognisable social problems, filmed in 'real' locations, often using some form of 'documentary style' camerawork and an avoidance of any notions of 'glamour' or false 'prettiness'.

To many older and more middle-class audiences, and certainly for many audiences overseas, these two types of films are what British cinema is all about. The approaches are epitomised for these audiences by the period adaptations of Merchant–Ivory productions and films such as *Vera Drake* (2004) or *Billy Elliot* which use social realism as part of a mix of elements.

Such recognition perhaps works in the opposite way for UK working-class audiences (who usually prefer Hollywood films). They may well steer clear of both period films and social realism. Nevertheless, 'popular British films' such as gangster and comedy films may still be influenced by a general British feeling for realist detail, and it is certainly true that determinedly 'fantastic' or expressionist film-makers in the UK, such as Terry Gilliam or Sally Potter, have had to work harder to gain critical acclaim. In one sense, the critical support for realism over 'fantasy' could be seen as a reflection of a narrow film culture.

British film scholarship has attempted to counter the critics' reliance on realism. Work on *Carry On* films and Hammer horror from the 1950s and 1960s is evidence of a recognition of the commercial success of these series and the ways in which they utilised traditional British genre forms on low budgets. Scholarship has perhaps been less successful in increasing the profile of contemporary British directors who take risks in developing new aesthetics for British films. Let's try to draw together some of

these points in a brief look at three types of British film-making.

1 Mainstream UK film-making

The most commercially successful British films have Hollywood studio support and a much higher budget than is usual for a UK film. Many of the biggest domestic and international successes for the British film industry share similar production backgrounds. In 1993 *Four Weddings and a Funeral* was produced by Polygram (the film division of then Dutch media conglomerate Philips) with Channel 4 and Working Title, the UK production company headed by Tim Bevan and Eric Fellner. Working with only the average UK budget of the time of £2 million, the creative team produced a film that made over £200 million worldwide. In 1996 Working Title and Polygram, this time with UK independent Tiger Aspect, spent considerably more money (£16.2 million) on sending Rowan Atkinson to America in *Bean*. Again worldwide box office topped £200 million. The trick was repeated with *Notting Hill* in 1999 and *Bridget Jones' Diary* in 2001, but by this time Polygram had been bought by Universal.

Bevan and Fellner are two of the most powerful men in the British film industry, but they are also Hollywood 'players' since Working Title is closely

Figure 13.8 *Notting Hill* opened in the summer of 1999 with a premiere run at the Odeon Leicester Square, the launching pad for prestigious British films since the 1940s.

tied in to Universal. The films listed above are just the highest-profile titles in their portfolio (the 'low-budget' brand WT2 produced *Billy Elliot*). They have worked consistently with a group of creative talents – the four films above were all scripted by Richard Curtis – but it is noticeable that they aim for the international rather than UK (or, indeed, American) market. In terms of British film culture, it is their smaller titles, including those from director Stephen Frears, that are perhaps more significant. Their most adventurous partnerships tend to be with the Coen brothers on resolutely American projects.

Working Title have succeeded in maintaining output where other UK production companies have failed. Arguably, this is because they have sheltered within the embrace of a major studio and applied Hollywood production methods: 'It's extraordinary to walk into a British film company on Oxford Street . . . and it's run with complete L.A. efficiency, instead of it being a bunch of ex-BBC, very nice amateurs' (Hugh Grant quoted in *Premiere* magazine, March 2001). Not all their films have been hits, but so far they have been able to 'cross-subsidise' hits and misses.

ACTIVITY 13.8

Working Title

Research Working Title and the careers of Tim Bevan and Eric Fellner. Use the Internet Movie Database to list all their productions and find out about their films. Check the company website at www.workingtitlefilms. com to see what is coming soon.

To what extent does the list suggest that they have been crucial to a sense of the British film industry and British film culture since the late 1980s – or are they more like an international film company that just happens to be based in London?

The British genre tradition

During its genuine 'studio period' from the 1930s to the 1970s, the British film industry managed to produce a steady stream of genre films with carefully managed production budgets – comedies, crime thrillers, horror, etc. This tradition survives in the form of occasional 'one-offs' drawing on genre traditions. Good examples of this practice include successful films such as *28 Days Later* and *Shaun of the Dead* (UK 2004), with their different takes on British horror/science fiction and comedy.

The Hole (UK 2001) is a good example of this practice and helps us confirm many of the points made in this case study. It is clearly a 'genre' film, combining the teen film and psychological horror/thriller. Made with a production budget of £4.16 million (i.e. slightly above the average for a 'domestic feature'), *The Hole* achieved a UK box office of £2.2 million – better than most UK productions. This was achieved from an unusual 'wide' release on 322 prints. Abroad, *The Hole* did well in Europe with 2.8 million Euros in Spain and perhaps half that amount in France and Italy (European releases over 2002 and 2003). These strong European returns mean that the film will have been close to covering costs on a theatrical release – a major achievement. The most surprising aspect of its release is that it didn't get into US cinemas at all – despite the presence of American stars (see below). The eventual DVD release in North America wasn't until 2004. Ancillary markets in the UK had the film in the usual way, a few months after the theatrical release.

Here is a brief summary of some of the aspects of British film that *The Hole* highlights.

Setting, thematic

The story is set in an English public school – a mixed residential school. The British film industry has always had problems producing American style 'high school pictures'. Partly this is because of the lack of uniformity in UK secondary schools (i.e. comprehensives, grammar schools, public schools, etc.), and partly because of the strong tradition of youth pictures associated with 'social realism' or the 'social problem' genre (i.e. links to delinquency). *The Hole* is a rare attempt to make a UK school-based film with genre elements easily recognised in the international market.

Casting

Three of the leads are American (Thora Birch, Desmond Harrington and Embeth Davidtz), although only Harrington is actually playing an American character. Americans (often cast as 'Canadian') were a common feature of British films in the studio period. They lent lower-budget British films a sense of 'glamour' and sometimes American actors with their different backgrounds and approaches to film acting gave producers something different to use in certain types of genre films. In this instance, the casting of Thora Birch was something of a coup since she had recently starred in the surprise success of *American Beauty* (US 1999) and the less mainstream but critically acclaimed *Ghost World* (US/UK/Germany 2001).

Production

Another connection between *Ghost World* and *The Hole* was Granada Films, the vehicle whereby the UK television company invests in features. However, the main source of funding (and the rights holder) was Pathé Pictures, the UK distributor/production company. Pathé was awarded one of the 'franchises' through which the Film Council distributed National Lottery funding and £1.5 million of Lottery money was spent on *The Hole*. The other partners in the production were two small British production companies, Cowboy Films and Impact Pictures. Both these companies had experience and contacts in the international film business, Cowboy Films in advertising and music video, Impact Pictures in features, often drawn from video games, made by Paul W.S. Anderson (e.g. *Event Horizon*, UK/US 1997).

These two companies with Granada provided the three producers on the film, with Pathé's Andrea Calderwood as executive producer. The final contribution came from French pay-TV company Canal+.

Director Nick Hamm had already succeeded as a theatre director and had made a well-received short film. *The Hole* was his third feature film. He read the novel (by the seventeen-year-old Guy Burt) on which the film was based in 1993 and persuaded several production companies to take an option on the rights. When this finally led to a production, the scriptwriters were two recent graduates of the National Film School, Ben Court and Caroline Ip. They have not had another script produced yet, but Hamm went on to make *Godsend* (2004) in America.

Black British film

One of the challenges for the British film industry is to make films that are in some way representative of life in a modern multiracial and multicultural society, both because they want to sell films to every audience and also because 'diversity' is a priority for the agency responsible for film culture, the UK Film Council.

Black and Asian British writers and directors face all the problems outlined above in producing films, plus the extra challenge of making films that run the risk of only appealing to a minority of the UK audience. One feature of UK film distribution since the 1980s has been that even Hollywood films that focus specifically on African-American culture, such as Denzel Washington's directorial debut *Antwone Fisher* (US 2002), are likely to receive only a limited distribution (forty-six prints for *Antwone Fisher*), opening in cities with significant Black populations.

In very broad terms, the history of African-Caribbean film in the UK can be traced back to British Film Institute Production Board funded films such as Horace Ové's *Pressure* (1975) and Menelik Shabazz's *Burning an Illusion* (1981). These films were accompanied by more commercial films, set in Black

communities but made by white film-makers, such as
Black Joy (1977) and *Babylon* (1980). In the 1980s more
avant-garde Black film-makers in collectives such as
Black Audio (*Handsworth Songs* (1986) etc.) and
Sankofa (*Territories* (1984) etc.) made films directly
about the political struggles of Black people in the UK
which were supported and screened by Channel 4 as
part of its remit to broadcast new forms of television
and cater to more diverse audience groups.

However, there was nothing in mainstream film
culture to match the emergence of Black British
popular music, and in the 1990s, without the
support of the BFI and Channel 4, even the more
avant-garde film-making fell away. Instead, the 1990s
saw the gradual rise of British Asian film-making, with
the career of Gurinder Chadha in particular. *Bhaji on
the Beach* in 1993 was co-written with Meera Syal and
achieved something of a cult status as well as critical
acclaim. After working in America, Chadha returned
to UK production in 2002 with the highly successful
Bend It Like Beckham, in many ways a 'feelgood' film
with a Hollywood-style narrative. Meanwhile, Meera
Syal has become a powerful figure in UK television
through shows such as *Goodness Gracious Me* and *The
Kumars at No. 42*. Syal's semi-autobiographical novel
Anita and Me became a feature film in 2002, directed
by Metin Hüseyin. There have been several other
important films from British Asians since the 1980s
and a wider perspective on the history of both Black
British and British Asian film can be gained by visiting
www.screenonline.org.uk, the resource on British film
culture produced by the British Film Institute.

The year 2004 was significant for the diversity of
UK film culture, with two films by white film-makers
that focus on Muslim communities in the UK (*Yasmin*
and *Ae Fond Kiss*, see above). These were followed
in 2005 by two films that in their different ways
signal a revival in Black British film. *A Way of Life* is a
remarkable film written and directed by Amma Asante.
Starting out as an actor in *Grange Hill*, Amma Asante
has developed into a writer, producer and director of
television and now cinema features. *A Way of Life* is an

attempt to address issues about racial violence
by viewing events from the perspective of the
perpetrators of that violence. Asante's central
character is Leigh-Anne a seventeen-year-old white
single mother living 'on benefit' in a South Wales
community and the effective driving force behind a
trio of young men who make a violent attack on one
of her neighbours.

> Wales has a history of some of the oldest Black
> communities in Europe. It's very different to
> London, a lot of the diversity began to grow
> around Cardiff and the docks areas in South
> Wales about a hundred years ago. I wanted to
> explain how that history might impact on us
> today. There is this idea that if you're talking
> about modern UK, a film should be set in
> London, but these are Valleys kids. They don't
> know a lot of black people and that to me
> represents the majority of the UK.
>
> (Amma Asante, from the
> production notes for the film)

The ugliness of the poverty and the violence is
contrasted with the beauty of some of the scenes
shot in natural light. The characters are poor –
and ignorant. The damage they do is despite the
mixed-race backgrounds of both attackers and victims,
which are not properly understood by either side
(and which Asante emphasised by her casting
choices).

A Way of Life was made by Rampart Films, Asante's
partnership with TV producer Charlie Hanson (one of
the producers of *Desmond's*, the Channel 4 sitcom on
which Asante worked in the 1980s) and AWOL Films,
an SPV set up for the production. Support came from
the UK Film Council, Arts Council Wales and ITV
Wales. Although Amma Asante won several prizes at
film festivals such as London, Miami and San Sebastian,
A Way of Life received only a limited theatrical
distribution by Verve Pictures, a new distributor
focusing on less mainstream British titles. *A Way of Life*

Figure 13.9 The gang at the centre of *A Way of Life* are shown in, literally, a 'good light' in this still. Their brutal actions are linked directly to a sense of exclusion, exacerbated by a confusion over their own sense of 'identity'.

Figure 13.10 Ricky (Ashley Walters) and Wisdom (Leon Black) in *Bullet Boy*.

may have more impact than some of the earlier Black British films because of DVD distribution.

Verve also distributed *Bullet Boy* (2005) in cinemas and this film had a relatively 'wide' release for what was still seen as a 'specialised film' (seventy-three prints, concentrated in areas with significant African-Caribbean communities). The release was characterised by an extensive programme of preview screenings and strong interest from the press.

The white director Saul Dibb comes from a documentary background and clearly has an affinity for the street culture of Hackney where the story is set and where co-writer Catherine Johnson lives. Very much a Black film in its thematic, *Bullet Boy* looks at questions of masculinity and 'boys without fathers'. It's family melodrama in which street violence becomes the disruptive agent.

Starring the former child actor and music star 'Asher D' (Ashley Walters), *Bullet Boy* has been favourably compared with celebrated films focusing on similar themes, such as *La Haine* (France 1995) and *Boyz n the Hood* (US 1991). This suggests a film with 'universal appeal', but one which also links to other developments in UK culture, such as the vibrant Black theatre movement which has produced the similarly themed *Elmina's Kitchen* written by Kwame Kwei-Armah. Aesthetically, *Bullet Boy* is also linked to

the work of other British film-makers through the camerawork of Marcel Zyskind (the young Danish cinematographer on Michael Winterbottom's *In This World* (see 'Case study: Images of migration') and *Code 46*) and Danny Boyle's editor on several of his films, Masahiro Hirakubo.

At the time of writing, *Bullet Boy* had not yet been released in North America or Europe. It will be interesting to see what kind of response the film generates and whether it will prove to be 'distinctively British', while still appealing to audiences who don't know the specific community.

ACTIVITY 13.9

Bullet Boy

Look up the film on the Internet Movie Database or any other website with audience responses.

- What do audiences think about this film? That it is distinctively British?
- Or do they complain about what they see as an American formula applied to a British cultural context?
- Look back through this case study. How would you approach an analysis of *Bullet Boy* as a 'contemporary British film'?

References and further reading

'Contemporary British Cinema' (2002) *The Journal of Popular British Cinema*, 5.

Hill, John (ed.) (2001) Supplement on 'Contemporary British Cinema', *Cineaste*, XXVI, 4.

British Cinema – the End of the Affair?, (2002). tx BBC4.

Kirkup, Mike (2004) *Contemporary British Cinema*, Leighton Buzzard: Auteur.

Murphy, Robert (ed.) (2000) *British Cinema of the 90s*, London: British Film Institute.

Murphy, Robert (ed.) (2001) *The British Cinema Book*, London: British Film Institute.

Websites

www.bfi.org.uk/filmtvinfo/library/publications/16+/britishcontemp.html

www.launchingfilms.com

www.screenonline.org.uk

www.ukfilmcouncil.org.uk

Part III
Media Debates

Production still from *Moolaadé* (2005) showing director Ousmane Sembene

14 Documentary and 'reality TV'

- **Documentary and assumptions about 'realism' and truth**
- **Case study 1: 'Direct Cinema'**
- **Performance and documentary**
- **Ethics and documentary**
- **Case study 2: Michael Moore**
- **'Reality TV'**
- **Case study 3: *Jamie Oliver's School Dinners* (Channel 4 2005)**
- **Case study 4: *Big Brother***
- **References and further reading**

The idea of documentary, and its relation to the rest of the real, has changed in many ways in the last few years.

- The massive commercial success of *Bowling for Columbine* (US 2002) and then *Fahrenheit 9/11* (US 2004) (henceforth *F9/11*) in cinemas, mobilising US public political feeling, was a revelation for many. And this happened in an era where it was argued documentary was outmoded; that we are in 'postdocumentary times' (Corner 2002).
- Prior to these successes for cinema documentary, the TV ratings phenomenon of 'reality TV' was one reason why documentary's irrelevance had been proclaimed. Though they are arguably hybrids of documentaries, reality TV shows were seen by many as a corruption of documentary, indeed as the kind of cheap programming which drives serious, expensively well-researched programmes off TV screens.
- Less often discussed, partly because it seems to involve older audiences, is the growing success of 'nature' or 'wildlife' documentary, and the spectacular cinematic equivalent in the success of the drama-documentary *Touching the Void* (UK 2003) or BBC series such as *The Blue Planet* (2001).

This chapter explores:

1. recent debates around documentary, including notions of 'performance'
2. 'reality TV' forms, such as *Big Brother*
3. assumptions about what makes a media text 'realistic'.

More than in most other chapters, we're working by means of big case studies, and the histories, definitions and debates which help make sense of them.

Often cited definitions of documentary: 'The use of the film medium to interpret creatively and in social terms the life of the people as it exists in reality' (Paul Rotha (1939) *Documentary Film* (London: Faber & Faber)); 'The creative treatment of actuality' (John Grierson (1926), in a review of Robert Flaherty's film *Moana*).

THE MEDIA STUDENT'S BOOK

Documentary and assumptions about 'realism' and truth

Let's start with a simple point. 'Documentary' is often set up in opposition to 'fiction', and it tends to circulate and be labelled and reviewed as such within the powerful binary:

Michael Moore drew on this
binary in 2003 when accepting
his documentary Oscar, in the
name of truth, versus a 'fictitious'
regime: 'we live in fictitious times
. . . fictitious election results that
elect a fictitious President . . .
a man sending us to war for
fictitious reasons. We are against
this war, Mr Bush.'

the fictional = lies   *the factual = truth*
entertainment films   *documentary and 'realist' films*

This is partly why the form **'drama-documentary'** causes problems for some viewers: it confuses these apparently neat and powerful boundaries.

Actually such a sharp contrast does justice to neither side of the equation. Fiction is assumed to present utterly imaginary beings, places or events. But it is not necessarily unrelated to actuality, not even in its Hollywood forms (although Hollywood's representations of issues such as working conditions are often there mainly to provide a convincing milieu for individualised stories about triumph over adversity). Documentary is also assumed to be a simple matter, almost as simple as just pointing a camera at 'the truth'. This is hugely bound up with how 'realism' gets thought of.

See Chapter 3 'Genres and
other classifications' for more
discussion on the relationship of
entertainment 'genre' forms and
the rest of the real world.

ACTIVITY 14.1

Think of the last time you called a TV programme or film 'very realistic'. Jot down what was it about that text which made you call it realistic. Was it the subject matter? The way it was shot, lit, acted? Did it seem 'rough'? Did the mascara run? Was the ending not a happy one in a genre where that is expected? Take notes on how and why friends, or reviewers seem to use the term.

The term 'documentary' is left
out of most accounts of genre
cinema (e.g. Neale 2000, 2002)
even though it can be identified
by genre-like aspects. Discuss.

Bordwell and Thompson usefully define documentary as a form which 'purports to present factual information about the world outside the film' (2004: 128). Documentaries are labelled and, by implication, circulate as such. Like news, they are commonly *seen as* particularly truthful, as being a kind of trace of reality, dealing with the factual or unconstructed as far as possible.

It's interesting to note *when* people describe Hollywood films as 'realistic'. It's a term often used about films like those of Oliver Stone which feature:

- controversial subject matter, such as the assassination of President J.F. Kennedy, which is often left out of Hollywood treatment. This attempt

'Nature' documentaries

This chapter mostly concerns documentaries about people. But the documenting of 'wildlife' or 'nature' is an increasingly important part of British TV. This makes use of advanced technology (e.g. the tiny cameras placed on the heads of birds, so we can literally have a 'bird's eye view' of their flight) but often in the interests of the pleasure of seeming to 'eavesdrop' on animal life.

A lower-tech example is *Springwatch* (BBC2) focusing on British wildlife, urban and rural, with average 2.9 million and 3.5 million audiences in 2004 and 2005, outstripping *Big Brother* and *Celebrity Love Island* on several evenings. There seem to be several pleasures involved.

- It has always been argued that the place where the most graphic sex and violence hang out is in 'nature' programmes.
- Now, too, perhaps they relate to increasing awareness of global warming and the environment more generally.
- Within a Britain which has often seen itself through rural imagery, they may also embody nostalgia for a mythic rural existence, as cities become more and more pressured.

'30% of London is green space and water, and unusual sightings occur more and more often . . . British nature means the city as well as the country these days. And its absorption of exotic migrants makes it more interesting to look at than ever before' (Blake Morrison, 'Wild at heart', *Guardian*, 16 June 2005).

ACTIVITY 14.2

Choose a 'nature' programme and explore what assumptions about the 'wild' it embodies, through commentary, choice of clips, scheduling and marketing.

Who has been cast as presenter? Male? Female? A reassuring presence? A 'modern' one? Is the programme's technology discussed? What pleasures do you, or regular viewers, take in it?

TV has also developed its own use of special effects and spectacular takes on the natural. *The Blue Planet* (BBC 2001) was described as 'the definitive exploration of the Earth's final frontier', the depths of the sea, and revealed 'life and behaviour that had never before been filmed'. *Walking with Dinosaurs* (BBC 2000) rivalled *Jurassic Park* in its spectacular effects.

But cinema also has recent spectacular capacities here. The huge success of the drama-documentary *Touching the Void* (UK 2003), which imaged a terrifying and sublime nature in an astonishing mountaineering story, suggests that rather different aspects of 'nature' can be enjoyed in cinema. Spectacle, suspense, even terror were evoked, in ways uniquely offered by the single uninterrupted viewing, on a bigger screen, in the context of a medium usually devoted to fiction (see Austin 2007).

Interestingly, audience members found ways into this extreme story through their own experiences of recovery from apparently devastating disaster (see Austin 2007). Audience responses are hugely under-researched in relation to documentary – a deficiency which you could begin to remedy.

to represent that which is rarely represented is often identified as 'realist'.

- a documentary-like shooting style, often simulating the hand-held shakiness which used to be a guarantee of the authenticity of news or documentary footage. The camera operator had to 'snatch' it, sometimes in the face of armed official hostility.

The less polished a fiction film looks, the more credible or 'realistic' it is found to be: the films of Oliver Stone and *The Blair Witch Project* (US 1999) are examples. A classic example of the 'roughness' that's taken for 'truth' is the accidental footage of US President J.F. Kennedy's assassination, taken by a bystander in 1963 and known by his name: the Zapruder footage. Bruzzi (2005) uses this footage to emphasise how powerful is our sense that 'the truth' about the assassination can be found in these images. She contrasts it with the factual accuracy of the film, which is not the same thing, since a truth often seeks to go beyond 'the facts' to an interpretation. The Zapruder footage does give us a genuine 'trace' of a historic event, a fact if you like. But it's a step too far to assume that the film's roughness or accidentalness is a guarantee of 'truth' – i.e. that it will show you who killed Kennedy and why, questions which it is often used to raise.

Sure, its rawness, date of making, and preserved status guarantee it has not been constructed – in the edit suite, digitally, by special lighting, etc. But to show us more of the key truths about this assassination a camera would have had to be pointing the other way, towards the gunman or gunmen. As Bruzzi writes, using a contrast between fact and 'truth', 'the Zapruder film is factually accurate, it is not a fake, but it cannot reveal the motive or cause for the action it shows' (2005: 430). The same could be said of Figure 14.1, a CCTV image of the four young men who suicide-bombed London in July 2005.

So although rough and indeed authentic footage retains a huge fascination, and is often taken to be 'real', we should not mistake that for the conviction that it can unlock the door to 'the truth' about what it represents. Indeed, there is much more scepticism now about whether a

Figure 14.1 A CCTV image of the four young men who suicide bombed London in July 2005. Now an example of the 'documents' which can now be used as legal evidence and as media image. The roughness and 'snatched' quality of such images, as well as their source, function as presumed guarantee of their truthfulness.

single truth or explanation of *any* complex event can be enough for understanding. If the leap from 'this looks real' to 'this shows the truth' is impossible to make in the case of the Zapruder film, how much more careful should we be when presented with fiction footage which has been constructed to look rough and real.

As the famous French critic André Bazin (1919–58) once wrote, 'Realism in art can only be achieved in one way – through artifice' ("An aesthetic of realism: neo-realism" [1948] (1967/71)).

Q What do you think he means? Apply this to the most realistic text you know.

Another form of realism

The films of Ken Loach (1936–) though scripted fictions (or 'artifices' in Bazin's sense) are often called realist, and aspire to give a more adequate or 'real' account of the world of his characters, a world often neglected by mainstream images and stories.

Loach's films are part of the **social realist** traditions of cinema and television, a different way of relating fiction to factual forms than the 'rough' shooting style which prompt many to call films 'realistic'. Very briefly, the tradition has the following features:

- films shot in recognisable, authentic locations, usually industrial cities, rather than using sets
- authentic regional dialects and cultural references
- non-professional actors (although Loach often uses other kinds of performers, such as comedians) or actors who are associated primarily with this kind of work

Figure 14.2 A key earlier film movement here was **Italian neo-realism**. Try to see *The Bicycle Thieves* (Italy 1948) as an example of this approach, which flourished in a defeated country in the immediate aftermath of the Second World War (1939–45) and was characterised by very low budgets, location shooting, non-professional actors and 'real' stories – though in this case, one adapted from a novel.

- narratives based on the hardships of social disadvantage
- lead characters who are 'ordinary' and working class
- occasional 'observational', 'documentary' style of camerawork and sometimes sound/image combination. For example, he will use a technique which makes a sequence seem spontaneous. A character is spoken to by someone off camera; the camera then pans, as though searching for the speaker, though of course the scene has been set up for that dialogue
- 'spontaneous' naturalistic acting style (Loach shoots scenes in chronological order and actors are unaware of the outcome of their character's actions)
- characters walk in and out of frame, dialogue overlaps.

Let's look at a case study which explores the relationship of technology to documentary form, as well as one origin of the style of shaky hand-held film-making which is most often called realist.

Performance and documentary

We hope to have shown that even the most 'realistic' documentaries, aspiring to give ordinary people their voices, very close to them in intimate filming, nevertheless have to be constructed. Like news programmes, documentaries are necessarily shaped by

- the initial selection of what to film
- the conditions on which consent is given or withheld
- how the event is framed, staged, the 'angle' in both senses

CASE STUDY 1: 'DIRECT CINEMA'

In the early 1960s a new form of documentary developed in the US, known as **Direct Cinema**. This is sometimes seen as similar to *cinéma vérité* (French for 'cinema truth', and developing around the same time) though in fact it is more observational. The modern term is 'fly on the wall' and now describes fairly standard TV documentary techniques. It's now possible for those with digital and mobile phone technologies to eavesdrop or easily record 'real events' (i.e. ones not specially staged for the camera).

In the 1960s, however, the premise of this approach to filming was that new techniques were needed in order to 'tell it like it is' about institutions that were less accessible than is often the case now. These techniques were: the camera and microphone should be as close to events as possible, with the film or tape running continuously. Everything that happens is recorded, nothing is rehearsed or scripted, there is no use of voice-over narration or music – all this in order to try to give the subjects of the documentaries their own voice.

Certain technological advances were key for making this possible. The early 1960s saw the first

- lightweight 16 mm film cameras linked to audio recorders for synchronised sound
- film stocks sensitive enough to provide reasonable monochrome picture quality under most lighting conditions, including small hand-held lights.

In old thatched houses the 'eavesdrip' or 'eavesdrop' was the area of ground on which fell the rainwater thrown off by the eaves (or edge) of the roofs. Someone who stood in this area, with their ear to the door or window, trying to listen to private conversations, became known as an eavesdropper.

ACTIVITY 14.3

Where would you like to be a fly on the wall?

Select a subject you think would interest an audience that you could cover with a small camera. Ask yourself:

- Where would you place yourself to capture sound and image effectively?
- Could you capture all the material you would need to represent your subject to your satisfaction?
- What strategies would you use to try to ensure that your subjects did not 'perform' for the camera?
- Do you think your subject would automatically produce a story, or would you have to restructure the events during the editing process?

Unencumbered by large heavy equipment, the documentary crews were ready to go almost anywhere – and they did, covering rock concerts, high

Key Direct Cinema makers whose films you might look at include Robert Drew, Richard Leacock, the Maysles brothers, D.A. Pennebaker and Frederick Wiseman. There seem to be very few women directing, or used as the subject of these films.

Frederick Wiseman (1930–)
US documentary maker and
trained lawyer who began making
films about the workings and
practices of US institutions in
1967 while working as a law
professor. Other works include
High School, *Hospital*, *Meat*, *Missile*
and *Public Housing*.

'Shooting ratio' is the term for
the ratio of footage shot to
footage actually included in
the final edited product. So
a shooting ratio of 30:1 (not
uncommon for this type of film)
would mean that thirty hours
were shot for a one hour of
finished film, indicating a high
degree of editorial shaping.

schools, presidential primaries and even a Massachusetts state asylum in
Frederick Wiseman's film *Titicut Follies* (US 1967) which, however, was
banned from being shown until 1992, partly because of the ethical issues of
personal privacy which it did indeed raise, but partly because of its stark
portrayal of the appalling 'treatment' of the inmates.

The pioneers of such work had three main problems:

- getting access both to unobtrusive equipment and to permission to
  enter the institutions (schools, hospitals, etc.) they wanted to explore
- avoiding causing their subjects to 'play to the cameras' or perform
- deciding how to reduce the hours of footage to a reasonable length for
  audiences while avoiding a particular editorial position.

The problem of subjects who 'played to the camera' and therefore
behaved 'unnaturally' was partly avoided by selecting subjects for whom
'playing to an audience' was simply part of their usual behaviour. Politicians
such as the Kennedys were followed by performers of various kinds,
including Bob Dylan and the Rolling Stones. But the issues of performance
more broadly continued to be important for documentary.

A major problem, especially for Wiseman's documentaries from inside
institutions, was that the crew needed to spend long enough with the
subjects, filming all the while, for them to begin to feel that they were 'part
of the furniture' (an issue affecting 'performances'). When it came to the
editing stage, though, there were miles of film to sift through and the
question of how to edit those, and how that then shaped what had been
filmed, became crucial. It is often said that they were not conventionally
scripted, but were scripted in the editing suite.

- editing decisions, including simple decisions to abbreviate routine
  happenings.

Bruzzi (2000: 6,7) sums up the points so far thus:

> [we need to] simply accept that a documentary can never be the
> real world, that the camera can never capture life as it would have
> unravelled had it [the camera] not interfered, and the results of
> this collision between apparatus and subject are what constitutes a
> documentary . . . documentaries are performative acts whose truth
> comes into being only at the moment of filming.

ACTIVITY 14.4

Unpack these very condensed points one by one. Try to apply them to any documentary recently viewed.

We need to understand Bruzzi's use of the term 'performative' and 'performance', which are both now important terms in many areas of media (and life more generally). Let's first put them into context. Bill Nichols, in his influential writings on documentary during the 1980s and 1990s, developed a classification of what he called 'documentary modes' (Nichols 1991):

- *expository* – characterised by the sound track's 'voice of authority' and a general attempt to present a fixed meaning about the 'reality' that is represented (still present in some wildlife programmes and current affairs documentaries such as *Panorama*)
- *observational* – the 'fly on the wall' approach, as in Direct Cinema
- *interactive* – the presence of the documentarist is represented in the film, 'selection' of material is foregrounded
- *reflexive* – the process of film-making is not only represented but 'interrogated' so that the reflexive documentary is as much about 'making a documentary' as about the ostensible subject material.

Stella Bruzzi (2000: 2) criticises this classification, seeing it as suggesting documentary practice is a simple linear progression, from the 'primitive' expository documentaries of the 1930s to a supposedly more modern 'reflexive' mode. Bruzzi, by contrast, identifies early 'reflexive' practice in the films of Dziga Vertov in the 1920s and points to the continued use of 'voice-over' and other forms of controlled narration. She also identifies a major problem with the polarisation of much of the discussion about documentary, between those who believe that technology will one day allow the 'perfect' representation of reality and those who believe that reality can never be represented in an objective way (and that, therefore, all documentaries 'fail'): 'the spectator is not in need of signposts and inverted commas to understand that a documentary is a negotiation between reality on the one hand and image, interpretation and bias on the other' (Bruzzi 2000: 4).

Part of this 'reflexivity' is a fifth 'mode' that Nichols introduced in 1994 – the *'performative'*. Bruzzi sees Nichols as viewing 'performance' negatively within an expository or observational documentary (e.g. in Direct Cinema) because it reduces objectivity. She looks at performance more positively, in the work of documentarists who themselves become

Dziga Vertov (1896–1954) Documentary maker, linked with social activism in the decades after the Russian revolution of 1917. Notable for the formal reflexivity and innovation of films like *Man with a Movie Camera* (1929).

Nick Broomfield (1948–)
British documentarist who
becomes a performer in his own
films, especially in the process
of setting up interviews. See
www.nickbroomfield.com.

See also www.errolmorris.com.

performers in their films (e.g. Nick Broomfield, and we could add Michael Moore, and Erroll Morris if you have seen any of his films). In performing their role, she suggests, the documentarist does not *disguise* the process of selecting from reality, but instead '*performs it*' for the camera. It is as if the film-maker says to the audience: 'Look, I'm trying to make an objective statement, but this is what happens when I do' rather than pretending the film could 'eavesdrop' on the real, which could be utterly unaffected by the process of 'documenting'. Even earlier documentaries, which might not seem to reveal the process of construction, were not necessarily taken as 'unconstructed' by their audiences, she suggests.

ACTIVITY 14.5

Research the methods of Moore or Broomfield and say how you think they are 'performative'.

Q How might it *add* to the credibility of a programme or film that we know how it was made, and that the central players knew they were 'playing' in a documentary?

A related aspect of performance is the more specialised notion of 'performativity'. This is related to a sense of 'performance' as having its own surprises.

ACTIVITY 14.6

Q Have you ever had to perform a role – perhaps for work? Has this produced surprises, or meant you did things you did not imagine possible?
Q Or have you ever worn clothes (costume as part of performance) which have made you feel and act differently to usual?

This is a way of emphasising that documentaries don't simply document a 'real' which stays still while it is documented. They are '*performative acts whose truth comes into being only at the moment of filming*' (Bruzzi 2000: 6). Let's try one more activity to explore this tricky but rewarding concept.

ACTIVITY 14.7

Q Can you think of a documentary that records a happening which is a surprise to its makers?

A In *Bowling for Columbine* K-Mart's announcement that it had decided to stop selling ammunition as a result of Moore's campaign was unscripted and unexpected.

Q Can you think of any other such 'performative' moments in documentaries?
One example might be the discovery of how dinosaurs' joints must have worked, made by the animators of the models used for *Walking with Dinosaurs* (BBC 2000).

Two important conclusions from all of this that you can apply in your own analysis and even making of documentary texts:

- Over the whole history of documentary practice, film-makers have mixed documentary modes. Hybridity is not new in this context or, arguably, in any others. Nor are performances by central 'characters' or even directors.

- There is a real world with social issues that can be represented, as long as audiences recognise that such representations are negotiated by film-makers.

Ethics and documentary

Questions of ethics and documentary, which we mentioned in the reception of *Titicut Follies*, have existed throughout the history of documentary. Ethics is the study and practice of morality or behaviour which is 'good' or 'right'.

There are two main ethical concerns for documentary practice:

1 film's capacity, from the beginning, to 'fake' material. A famous early example was Robert Flaherty's *Nanook of the North* (1922) which involved: staging a walrus hunt even though the Inuit had long since stopped walrus-hunting; constructing a special igloo with one wall removed so that an Inuit family could be filmed, in daylight, pretending to go to bed; and so on. The possibilities of faking material, both still and moving, with digital technologies are now very real, and of course raise ethical issues of truthfulness.

2 broader questions, of how the subjects are being represented, are also at stake:

- Is the documentary as fair and accurate as it can reasonably be in relation to its subject or argument?

For every Lumière 'actuality' film (such as *Workers Leaving the Factory* (1895)) there is a Méliès fantasy (such as *A Trip to the Moon* (1902)) with special effects and trick photography.

Figure 14.3 Tom Hanks in *Forrest Gump* (US 1994) apparently meets President Kennedy (d. 1963) in a film using digital special effects.

- What are the implications of the degrees of closeness it achieves?
  Do they disrupt the privacy of the powerless, perhaps without them
  realising? Is there a right to anonymity? To a say in the final edit?
Considerable debate exists around what constitutes 'informed consent'
and who is competent to give it (see Pryluck 2005 and the *Titicut Follies*
comments above).

Être et Avoir (*To Be and To Have* (France 2002)) a documentary about a year in
the life of schoolteacher and his tiny one-class school, unexpectedly made over
£1.3 million. The teacher at the centre of it claimed a share of the proceeds.
The director disagreed, triggering an acrimonious lawsuit, which raised
uncomfortable ethical questions about the exploitative nature of fly-on-the-
wall film-making.

A Paris court ruled that the schoolteacher had no grounds to demand
a €250,000 (£170,000) payment. Had he won, French film unions warned,
the case would 'spell the death of the documentary, undermining the crucial
principle that subjects should not be paid to participate'.

ACTIVITY 14.8

Look at any recent documentary and see how the ethical issues listed above
surface in it. Michael Moore's work has been very controversial in this area. Why?
Read on.

CASE STUDY 2: MICHAEL MOORE

Michael Moore (1954–) film and TV maker, activist, author. Born in a
suburb of Flint, Michigan, where his father and grandfather had worked
in the General Motors plant. Dropped out of university to become a
journalist and political activist, first in Flint, then San Francisco where
he was fired and used his settlement money, as well as selling his house,
to finance his first film *Roger and Me* (1989) a major success, leading to
more films, a career in comic exposé TV documentaries, and his two
greatest documentary successes *Bowling for Columbine* (2002) and

Fahrenheit 9/11 (2004). See www.movies.yahoo.com and his website www.michaelmoore.com.

Michael Moore's hugely controversial film *F9/11* (US 2004) was a documentary, shown in cinemas, and explicitly intended to defeat George W. Bush's attempt to gain the US presidency for a second time by exploring his role in events around '9/11'. To date it has made more money than any other documentary film ever.

Moore makes openly rhetorical documentaries, i.e. films which are up-front about wanting to persuade their audiences of a particular position. This has always been a legitimate role for some documentaries. His films also use the full range of methods open to documentarists:

- recording of events
- interviews
- other materials (e.g. charts, maps, cartoons, archive footage)
- staged events (confrontations, stunts)
- voice-overs and music
- (more controversially) a performance of documenting by the film-maker.

His work, even before 2004, raises key questions:

1 How are we to assess his presence and performance in these films?
2 How fair and accurate are the arguments he puts together, both explicitly and by means of music, cartoons, etc.?

Moore's performances

His presence and performance are key components of his popularity. In his earlier TV series, *TV Nation 1994/5* etc., and in his films, he embodies and performs the role of an 'ordinary Joe' who, with his scruffy appearance, baseball cap, shuffling walk and commonsense questions, cues us for laughter more often than not. This has been important for the marketing of his films, DVDs and books, often sold partly on their comic appeal.

His presence is striking since politically radical figures in the US are usually constructed (by an often anti-intellectual US media) as wealthy East Coast, *West Wing*-type figures. It has also been effective at a time when the multimillionaire George W. Bush was presenting himself as an 'ordinary Joe' to many voters (see Frank 2004).

John Corner (2002) discusses the complex situation of TV documentary but adds 'Documentary within cinema . . . still has the strong contrast with its dominant Other – feature film – against which it can be simply defined as "nonfiction".'

'Music has been essential to [my documentaries]. I can't imagine them without [Glass's] music. Recently, someone asked me why I used Philip Glass for *The Fog of War* and I said . . . "He does existential dread better than anybody"' (Errol Morris, www.errolmorris.com).

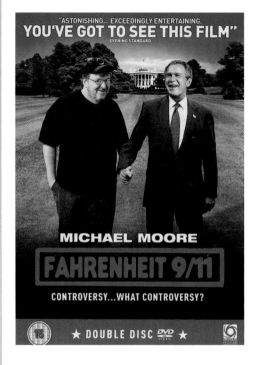

"ASTONISHING... EXCEEDINGLY ENTERTAINING.
YOU'VE GOT TO SEE THIS FILM"
EVENING STANDARD

MICHAEL MOORE

FAHRENHEIT 9/11

CONTROVERSY...WHAT CONTROVERSY?

★ DOUBLE DISC DVD ★

Figure 14.4
Q What kinds of pleasures are being promised here?
A Comic enjoyment of Moore's presence ('Laugh-out-loud funny'); a bold play with political imagery; and openly faked images (clearly he and Bush have never actually strolled like lovers on the White House lawns).

The objections to Moore as a performer are:

- that he hogs the limelight. *F9/11* seemed aware of this criticism, and featured Moore in fewer scenes (and an astonishingly restrained blank screen with only the sound track to signify '9/11' itself).
- that he 'stages' encounters, such as the one with Charlton Heston in *Bowling for Columbine*. These easily become confrontations since Moore is both a large man (physical presence) and also willing to say anything to anyone (performance). This further involves the area of the 'performative', meaning the documentarist openly showing how his film has been constructed and has changed in the making.

Slightly different are objections that his blue-collar, comic style brings limits to his arguments. These occur on several levels.

- There is an attempt to cram too much into the films. As a result, many issues are dealt with superficially – see the cartoon history of US race issues in *F9/11* or the much criticised use of statistics as though they summed up complex issues such as the difference in gun crime between the US and Canada in *Bowling for Columbine*.
- His search for gags and smart comment often raises ethical issues in 'setting people up' as the butt of his humour, knowing they will look ridiculous on screen.

'Blue-collar worker': working class employee who performs manual or technical labour, e.g. in a factory, as compared to a white-collar worker working at a desk. The term originates in work dress codes, with durable shirts of navy blue, which may get soiled at work. 'Blue-collar' is sometimes used for something crude, simple, lacking sophistication.

- This can also stop discussion of more complex debate. Key issues are left out – the role of Israel, for example, in *F9/11*, or the systematic gendering of violence in *Bowling for Columbine* (see Katz 1999).

All of these relate to how far Moore can be said to present fair and accurate arguments.

However, that is not the same as his right to argue, to present a position as a documentarist. Watch for this distinction: some still assume that documentaries should have the same aspirations to objectivity as news, which is not the same genre. However, there is an obligation to be as fair and accurate as possible, even when arguing passionately.

ACTIVITY 14.9

List the number of issues that Moore deals with in either *F9/11* or *Bowling for Columbine*. List and explore the statistics he cites in support of any one of these (e.g. gun crime in Canada and the US), using the well-funded anti-Moore websites which have sprung up, such as www.bowlingfortruth.com as well as Moore's rebuttals on his website.

How adequate do you find the attacks on Moore's performance and methods?

Wider contexts

Like other documentaries, Moore's need to be assessed in broader contexts than the simply textual. His achievements exist both textually and in the areas of distribution and exhibition.

- At both textual and exhibition levels, Moore has achieved, and remained in touch with, a fan base, which means he often speaks for and to an unusually large and involved group. They come partly from his 1990s TV programmes, partly from his excellent website (www.michaelmoore.com) and they have ensured refreshingly activist publicity for his films. They have also provided material within them. The extraordinary footage in *F9/11* of US soldiers in Iraq came from his 'embeds' there – soldiers who trusted him from his previous documentary work, and contacted him about the abuses and sights they saw.
- *F9/11* could never have been made by a US TV station. It was begun in 1999, and cost $3.3 million – a lot of time and money for a risky

See the moving collection edited by Moore, *Will They Ever Trust Us Again?*, letters from soldiers and their families to Moore, often about the efforts they made to see *F9/11* and the impact it had on them.

The website www.MoveAmerica Forward.org, backed by the PR firm Russo Marsh & Rogers, began a campaign intended to pressure cinemas not to book the film, as a way of 'supporting America's war on terrorism'.

documentary on TV. Institutional approaches to documentary need to understand the importance of the body which circulates them. Much legal research, not to mention courage and commitment, is needed to risk a politically controversial documentary on TV. Indeed *F9/11* caused problems for Disney, the initial distributors, which eventually sold it back to Miramax, which had smaller distributors lined up and nevertheless were able to release it on 868 US screens. It was awarded an R-rating, which meant people under seventeen were not allowed into the cinema without a parent or guardian. There was also an unusually high security presence – armed or uniformed guards or local police, with handcuffs showing – at screenings.

Nevertheless it achieved all-time-record takings for a documentary. This is partly because of Moore's staged stunts and ability to showcase even difficulties such as those with Disney. His films and their distribution shrewdly

> create controversy, so mainstream papers and news programmes do a lot of his work for him. Then the web picks it all up and develops it further. Moore uses every multiplication system the modern media world offers. . . . Mainstream politicians wouldn't get away with his aggression and swagger. Moore is unaccountable and can take risks professional politicians never could.
>
> (Jackie Ashley, *Guardian*, 20 May 2004)

- A further context: the weaknesses of his sometimes 'scattergun' approach to issues can be related to the state of news, current affairs and documentaries on advertising-funded, ratings-driven US TV. Commentators have suggested that if the US media were covering politics more adequately there would not be the appetite for the airing of such issues in cinema documentaries. But hence, too, the temptation to attempt too much, too quickly, in a two-hour film; and perhaps too the temptation to go for conspiracy theories rather than the hard slog of exploring, say, the idea of the 'military industrial complex' as the excellent *Why We Fight* (US 2004) does.

Try to get hold of Eugene Jarecki's *Why We Fight* and compare it to *F9/11* in style and subject matter.

'Reality TV'

We now need to consider a key context for Moore and many other recent TV documentaries. This is the term 'reality TV' and the group of programmes which get grouped together under it. Allegedly, the huge success of this cheap programming is driving serious, well-researched programmes off TV screens and is generally contributing to 'dumbing down'. Anxiety is focused on this, rather than the overall privatising of increasingly ratings-driven TV, or the drive towards advertising-funded forms, and PR-related news.

Q   Might this be partly because a panic about the latest low-cost sex documentary on Five is good headline fodder in a ratings- and ad-driven newspaper market?

Many strategies keep programme budgets low. The Gordon Ramsey second 'make-over' series (2005) revisited restaurants that he had helped 'turn around'. The first half hour of the programmes therefore consisted of edited extracts from the first series, as 'context'.

See www.realityTVlinks.com for a list of links to many 'reality TV' shows on US TV.

John Corner, an academic expert on documentary, argues we are now in a 'postdocumentary culture of television' and also refers to a 'new ecology of the factual' (2002: 263, 265). Documentary in its traditional, serious mode is now said to be weakened by:

- extensive borrowing of its realistic 'look' by other programmes
- the strengthening of a performative, playful element within factual programmes, as well as in series such as *Big Brother*, where contestants seem partly driven by the desire to become a celebrity
- a shift in the broader culture, for example a crisis in the very idea of 'the public'; changing forms of citizenship; and a move away from forms of solidarity towards an emphasis on individual consumers.

A striking example of this borrowing was the sitcom-drama-documentary-style series *The Office* (BBC 2001–3), 95 per cent scripted but making unsettling use of awkward, reality TV-style camera work, pauses and silences, as well as 'the furtive, meaningful and unmet glances across the emotional gulf of the open-plan office' (see amazon.co.uk).

ACTIVITY 14.10

The box presents a highly summarised version of Corner's argument. See if you can get hold of the article (2002). Alternatively, try to unpack and test for yourself some of the phrases and positions above.

'Reality television' is now used to describe forms of factual television which increased hugely on British television between 1989 and 1999, often in prime-time pre- and post-watershed slots. The first 'dramatic reality show' in the US was MTV's *Real World* (1992) based on 'fly on the wall' documentaries such as *American Family* (PBS 1973) a twelve-hour eavesdrop on the life of an unhappy American family. But it took the success of the European *Big Brother* and then *Survivor* for the format to become a dominant one.

In Britain the term was first applied to magazine-format programmes based on crime, accident and health stories or 'trauma television'

Gravitas conveys a sense of substance or depth to an individual's personality. It was one of the many virtues that, in Roman times, men were expected to possess, and that conveyed a sense of seriousness and duty.

(*Crimewatch UK, Lifesavers, America's Most Wanted* . . .). 'It often blends apparently "raw" authentic material with the gravitas of a news magazine, combining the commercial success of tabloid content with a public service mode of address' (Dovey 2000: 135).

ACTIVITY 14.11

See if you can identify these elements within a 'reality TV' programme blending these two kinds of material. Jot down: (1) those elements you would call 'tabloid' and (2) those which make up a 'public service mode of address'.

See beginning of chapter. 'Infotainment' was another term which signalled an unwelcome blending of two 'opposite' kinds.

Docusoap: another term which is contentious because it seems to confuse the boundaries of documentary (serious, high status) and soap (trivial, lower status).

The term often now means any programmes which make substantial use of 'ordinary people', blending information and entertainment. It includes '**docusoap**': a hybrid, blending elements of soap (its serial nature with character-driven narratives and a focus on emotional or 'gossipy' aspects of everyday life) with the codes and conventions of one kind of documentary (*vérité* camerawork, which looks hand-held or to be moving spontaneously in response to events; real people not actors; real places not locations). John Corner suggests that the combination presents 'documentary as diversion' and produces 'nosy sociability', positioning the viewer as 'an amused bystander in the mixture and mess and routine in other people's working lives' (Corner 2001).

ACTIVITY 14.12

Look at your favourite make-over programme or other kind of 'reality TV'. What codes, conventions and ways of addressing the audience does it employ? What is absent from it? For example, why do house make-over programmes never take on people's offices, classrooms or other workplaces?

Why does it seem so necessary for male chefs to have X-rateable macho language? How would this work for female chefs?

ACTIVITY 14.13

Q If you saw *Jamie Oliver's School Dinners*, say how it addresses viewers.

CASE STUDY 3: *Jamie Oliver's School Dinners* (Channel 4 2005)

Figure 14.5 The homepage of the Jamie Oliver website. Explore it.

In 2005 Jamie Oliver, a celebrity TV chef, made a series of programmes about state school meals, on which an average 37p a day was spent. The programmes faced the challenge of children's ad-fuelled addiction to junk food and its various effects on health. The series was a huge success,

More than a hundred swear words were bleeped out for the DVD version of *Jamie Oliver's School Dinners*, intended for use in schools. "'Scrotum' [as in 'scrotum-burgers'] . . . was decided at the last minute to be unsuitable for younger viewers: '. . . we felt that 'scrotum' should be bleeped, because if this word was watched on TV in a classroom setting, it would just result in sniggering and the key learnings from the programme being lost'" (*Independent*, 17 June 2005).

prompting government response. Like Moore's *F9/11* it was attached to a campaign, an imaginative website, and already existing public concern about an issue. It also succeeded partly because of

- the maker's physical presence (young, 'ordinary' image, accent, swearing, slightly urchin like, the very opposite of normal public service address, and certainly not the voice of a 'nanny state')
- his performance (willing to take risks, perform stunts, use his celebrity image in revealing how the making of the documentary affected his family life, confront a government minister and a food manufacturer, etc).

It also used two main narrative lures:

1 Will he manage to train the dinner ladies to cook differently, within the training and budget constraints set elsewhere?
2 Will he persuade school students to give up the junk food and begin to enjoy food that is provably better for them?

It was not greeted primarily as 'reality TV', nor even discussed as documentary. Yet as a documentary series it could be said to combine:

- public service broadcasting principles (in the issues it sought to publicise and change, and the amount of behind-the-scenes research which went into it)
- more 'tabloid' Michael Moore-like aspects of performance, physical presence, use of celebrity image, stunts, fun, the 'make-over' of some of the dinner ladies and children, confrontation of key figures.

If you consider it 'reality TV' it might be worth thinking how it stretches the assumptions in that term. It's certainly rare to see such a transformation of workplaces and their practices.

It's maybe surprising how many different kinds of programmes, with very different budgets, we've already mentioned under the heading 'Reality TV': make-over programmes (including dating, homes, gardens, bodies, sex lives . . .); docusoaps (such as *Wife Swap* or *Airport*); the Jamie Oliver series; *Crimewatch* and less expensive 'cops' style programmes.

Annette Hill (2002) suggests that as well as news and current affairs (obvious kinds of TV related to reality) 'reality TV' falls into three main groups:

- observation programmes (often about watching people in everyday places, such as *Airport*)
- information programmes, using true stories to tell us about something, like driving, first aid or pets (e.g. *999*)

- created for TV programmes, putting 'real people' (and increasingly, minor celebrities) into a manufactured situation, like a house or an island, and filming what happens.

Let's finally consider the series most often identified with 'reality TV': *Big Brother*.

CASE STUDY 4: *Big Brother*

Big Brother clearly falls into the last group. Re-read the section on 'format' in Chapter 3 'Genres and other classifications' to understand its commercial roots.

Big Brother is a hybrid form, flexibly mixing game show, talk show, even elements of *The Jerry Springer Show*; but importantly it relates to documentary, in its observation of 'real behaviour', even though 'the conditions for that behaviour have been entirely constructed by television itself' (Corner 2002: 256) and the real people are highly selected, and usually performing, from public audition (2005) onwards, in an attempt to become a celebrity.

In some ways it resembles 'Direct Cinema', not in using shaky hand-held camera work, since the cameras are fixed and hidden in the house and garden, but in its 'eavesdropping' style. Yet it is much more 'scripted' than traditional documentary filming. It drives towards narrative speculation on the part of the audience via:

- the casting process (now partly visible through the screening of one-minute audition tapes for the 2005 series). 45,000 people applied to appear in the first series.
- the editing suite. Decisions on which shots to include were key (9,000 hours were recorded for the first series by twenty-six cameras and fifty-five microphones), so was the choice of potential 'characters' to 'cast' in the first place. Together they invite powerful narrative interest in this kind of 'documentary'.
- the choice of set (rather like the decisions of which institutions Wiseman and others would explore). Here the half hi-tech prison, half trendy designer 'pad' look promises slightly different possibilities for each series, and the jacuzzi has become a routine feature.

It raises the questions we've already explored, but in hybrid and very entertainment-driven conditions:

- Under what terms do people take part in the programme?
- Without wishing to patronise the participants, what ethical guidelines are in place, given that part of the programme's pleasure is watching people make fools of themselves, even if this is part of a performance?

Figure 14.6 The surveillance eye of the UK *Big Brother* logo, reminding some of the term's origins in Orwell's powerful dystopian vision of a future of ubiquitous surveillance, *1984*.

The US hit show *The Apprentice* (2004) had 250,000 applications, whittled down to sixteen by a casting agency after a demanding vetting process involving full-scale rehearsals in mock shows – i.e. contestants were not only being selected, they were being trained to perform.

Ethics: the winner of the first Portuguese edition of *Big Brother* '"threatened to throw himself from a bridge over the weekend", Agence France-Presse reports. Despite initial fame and fortune, he blew his money and is no longer popular . . . a local newspaper . . . said he had been "abandoned by the machines which produced him"' (17 August 2004, www.realityblurred.com).

'Channel 4 yesterday admitted the success of *Big Brother* is tarnishing its image as a public service broadcaster and hindering its attempts to plug a projected £100m funding shortfall with public money' (*Guardian*, 7 January 2005).

As with any such big event, once it's 'on the agenda' it becomes the starting point for otherwise awkward conversations, allows people to talk about other things through it, and even provides holiday games (try using the *Big Brother* voice to ask your companion(s) to 'go to the diary room' etc.).

It is regularly attacked and there have been demonstrations against its introduction in countries as diverse as France and Bahrain. Yet the reasons for its success are more diverse than the simplest moral panics around it suggest.

1 The huge audience figures for the first British *Big Brother* series (2000) – 7.5 million voted on the final eviction – suggest that scheduling it as a summer event (when surrounding programmes are usually made at lower cost), available for showing in pubs, and then as an end of evening event for a 'youth' audience, were all key to its success. So were flexible scheduling moves when its success was established.

2 Viewers' ability to vote on who should leave the house (and, subsequently, on an increasing number of other opinions), via mobile phones, made it interactive, up to a point, as well as hugely lucrative for its owners.

3 There is huge press, internet and mobile phone coverage of the series.

4 More specifically, Annette Hill's research (2002) suggests that the three most interesting aspects for British audiences were:

   - to watch contestants live without modern comforts like TV, mobile phone, radio, reading matter
   - to watch conflict among the contestants
   - to watch them in the confession room.

   Overall, watching people do private things was least liked by British audiences. She also found that young and educated viewers were more likely to watch *Big Brother*, with more women than men, and 16–24-year-olds twice as likely as older viewers.

5 John Ellis related it to widely experienced work values and structures:

   the participants face a very modern dilemma. Thrown together by circumstances, they are mutually dependent but in order to survive have to stab each other in the back by making their nominations for eviction. The experience is akin to a modern workplace with its project-based impermanence, appraisal processes and often ruthless corporate management.

   (Ellis 2001)

It's worth finally hanging on to a sense of the limits of *Big Brother*, given the ways it has been celebrated by some critics, and seen as part of 'audience power'. Yes, the show enabled its audiences to vote and thereby change the outcomes of the ongoing 'narrative', via mobile phones, the internet and tabloid forms. But 'the actual range of opportunities available to the audience . . . was . . . confined to removing or holding on to one or two of the nominated contestants' (Tincknell and Raghuram 2002: 211). The votes were highly conditioned by the repeated offering (by that 'down-to-earth' northern male voice-over as well as the presenters) of a 'preferred' version of events which 'centred on the sexual behaviour of the contestants' (Tincknell and Raghuram 2002: 210). In these processes, like the daytime talk shows on which it drew, the programme tended to support a particular definition of 'ordinary people': as those who are not experts, not even fans with expert knowledge, not people greatly interested in the outside world, let alone politics.

It's a skilful and highly successful example of 'documentary hybrid as diversion', which is reshaping many TV systems. But alongside it run other documentary hybrids: the huge cinematic success of Michael Moore, and a British TV parallel, Jamie Oliver, both using forms which enact a more political sense of the private and public worlds we inhabit.

And also, alongside these, are 'nature' TV programmes and films. These relate to a different sense of the 'planet' rather than 'the world', and also allow us to see (always in mediated ways of course) places most of us could never visit. These, too, may fuel political passions: about the future of the globe we inhabit.

References and further reading

Austin, Thomas (2007 forthcoming) *Watching the World: Screen Documentary and Audiences*, Manchester: Manchester University Press.

Bazin, André (1967/71) *What is Cinema?*, 2 vols London: University of California Press.

Bordwell, David and Thompson, Kirsten (2004) *Film Art: An Introduction*, 7th edition, New York: McGraw Hill.

Bruzzi, Stella (2000) *New Documentary: A Critical Introduction*, London: Routledge.

Bruzzi, Stella (2005) 'The event: archive and imagination', in Alan Rosenthal and John Corner (eds) *New Challenges for Documentary*, Manchester: Manchester University Press, pp. 419–31.

Corner, John (2001) 'Form and content in documentary study' and 'Documentary realism (documentary fakes)', in Glen Creeber (ed.) *The Television Genre Book*, London: British Film Institute.

Corner, John (2002) 'Performing the real', in *Television and New Media*, 3, 3.

Dovey, Jon (2000) *Freakshow: First Person Media and Factual Television*, London: Pluto Press.

Dovey, Jon (2001) 'Reality TV', in Glen Creeber (ed.) *The Television Genre Book*, London: British Film Institute.

Ellis, Jon (2001) 'Mirror, mirror', *Sight and Sound*, August.

Frank, Thomas (2004) 'Bush, the working class hero', *New Statesman*, 30 August.

Hill, Annette (2002) '*Big Brother*: the real audience', in *Television and New Media*' 3, 3.

Mathijs, Ernest, and Jones, Janet (2004) (eds) *Big Brother International: Formats, Critics and Publics*, London: Wallflower.

Moore, Michael (2004) *Will They Ever Trust Us Again: Letters from the War Zone*, New York: Simon and Schuster.

Neale, Steve (2000) *Genre and Hollywood*, London: Routledge.

Neale, Steve (ed.) (2002) *Genre and Contemporary Hollywood*, London: British Film Institute.

Nichols, Bill (1991) *Representing Reality: Issues and Concepts of Documentary*, Bloomington and Indianapolis: Indiana University Press.

Pryluck, Calvin (2005) 'Ultimately we are all outsiders: the ethics of documentary filming' in Alan Rosenthal and John Corner (eds) *New Challenges for Documentary*, Manchester: Manchester University Press.

Rosenthal, Alan and Corner, John (eds) (2005) *New Challenges for Documentary*, 2nd edition, Manchester: Manchester University Press.

Tincknell, Estella, and Raghuram, Parvati (2002) '*Big Brother*: reconfiguring the "active" audience of cultural studies?', *European Journal of Cultural Studies*, 5, 2: 199–215.

Wood, Jason (2005) *Nick Broomfield: Documenting Icons*, London: Faber and Faber.

Other resources

Katz, Jay (1999) *Tough Guise: Violence, Media and the Crisis in Masculinity*, Media Education Foundation.

Salford University has an archive of modern British TV documentary. Go to www.smmp.salford.ac.uk/research/media/cda/index.html.

15 Whose globalisation?

- **A global village?**
- **Globalisation: histories and technologies**
- **Case study: Divine advertising: an exercise in global awareness**
- **Debates: cultural imperialism?**
- **A closer look at US cultural power**
- **Regions, flows, networks**
- **Corporate domination?**
- **References**
- **Further reading**

This chapter explores debates around:

- what is meant by **globalisation**
- how to grasp the structures and consequences of 'globalisation' as they involve media studies.

Globalisation, like all important concepts, currently has many meanings and connotations. But broadly it seems to refer to two related but separate processes that have implications for media:

- the ways in which technologies can overcome global distances, so that some people live in a world which seems borderless, and where images of events can be relayed instantaneously
- the ways that one particular economic system – 'the free market' or global capitalism – now permeates most of the globe.

A related controversy is:

- How far does 'globalisation' in fact mean simply 'global US dominance'?

'Television . . . now escorts children across the globe even before they have permission to cross the street' (Meyrowitz 1985: 238).

The Lone Ranger and his trusty sidekick Tonto face an overwhelmingly large posse of hostile Apache. 'We're in real trouble Tonto,' says the Ranger. Asks Tonto: 'Who's this "we", Paleface?'

The power of dominant 'globalised' imagery

Since the 1970s, hugely increased advertising and PR budgets have gone along with newly globalising images and appetites. These imply that one version of globalisation – 'free market', corporate, capitalist, expansionist – is inevitable.

Coca-Cola was one of the first to launch a TV commercial aiming at a single global brand image – the globe itself – in its 1971 'I'd like to teach the world to sing in perfect harmony' ad (see Myers 1999: 55). Several others have followed suit and the combination of an image of a globe in space, a montage of people of different races in diverse clothing, is now a familiar part of 'commercial speech' or advertising. McDonald's, Fuji Film, British Airways, the Halifax Bank and the Norwich Union insurance company are examples. HSBC's 2005 adverts took further the claims for global sensitivity to local differences which are often made by the biggest brands. Indeed the HSBC ads were said to have hugely aded to its 'brand value': see www.interbrand.com.

ACTIVITY 15.1
Can you find any other examples of globalised images? Does advertising seem to have changed its images of the global since the advent of global terrorism?

A global village?

'Electric circuitry has overthrown the regime of "time" and "space". . . . Ours is a brand new world of "allatonceness". . . . We now live in a global village' (M. McLuhan, and Fiore (1967), *War and Peace in the Global Village*, New York: Bantam).

Q: Key question: who is the 'we'? Exactly how like a village is the planet now?

Visual images can give a misleading sense of these relations. A photo of a woman using a mobile phone in Bangladesh might suggest 'western' privilege in the midst of poverty. Yet she might be using it to save time and energy by avoiding or shortening journeys in areas without transportation. (See case study on mobile phone technology.)

See Chapter 8 'Case study: selling audiences'.

Another much used image for a globalised world is that of a 'global village', a term coined by the 1960s theorist Marshall McLuhan. Like Spielberg's talk of Hollywood's tales being just like those of an ancient storyteller by the fireside, it attractively suggests that 'global' is the same as 'universal', that all of 'us' are cosily sharing the same imagery and products, warming our hands by the flicker of our democratic screens. Yet the next step – talk of the 'freedoms' of the internet, and the 'free market' of global 'networked democracy' – often works at the expense of understanding key inequalities in media power relations.

First, who is the 'we' that has access to literacy and telephones, let alone the computers and modems needed to 'surf' the global internet (a very US image)? Inequality of access applies to parts of the 'First World' as well as the 'majority world'. Where most European teenagers freely roam around using mobiles, in the US, because landline calls are free, the medium has not taken off in the same way (Watt 2004). A global village?

Second, in whose interests is the internet, for example, being shaped? It originated in the Pentagon's military research as well as the 'alternative' enthusiasms of people like Bill Gates. But who now controls which entries pop up first when you type a particular category into a search engine, for example? How is surveillance built in, via cookies etc? Who benefits from the information they collect?

Third, there are risks in *uncritical* celebrations of active audiences across the world, argued to be able to construct resistant meanings and uses for products no matter what is on their screens or who is profiting from their purchases. It is one thing to point out what audiences seem able to do with the most unexpected news images, or how creatively fans can work with their favourite fictions. It is quite another to argue that 'the global market' will do it all for us, that there is no need also to have high-quality national investigative journalisms or inexpensively available, well-researched and regulated media.

'Globalisation': histories and technologies

Power structures and activities on a larger than national scale have existed for many centuries, for example the Chinese, Persian and Roman Empires and the Roman Catholic Church across medieval Europe and beyond.

'Burma's military regime has reluctantly dipped a toe in the cyber sea, but for most of the country's population owning a modem without permission means 15 years in jail. . . . About one in 5,000 people has internet access, and even that is restricted by firewalls and other government-imposed limitations . . . visiting anti-government websites . . . can land a person in jail' (*Guardian*, 22 July 2003).

'The sun never sets on the British Empire.' 'Because God doesn't trust the British in the dark.' Joke circulating in Hong Kong, 1997, as the handover to the Chinese state was negotiated.

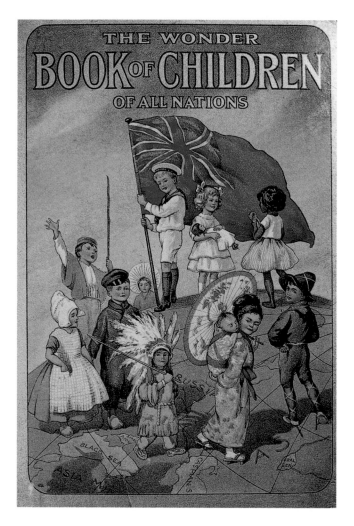

Figure 15.1 Cover of a 1917 British book which assumes 'global' hierarchies of 'race' and gender.

Globalisation is something rather different, and distinctively modern. It grew from the expansion of trade in the sixteenth century, which itself was accompanied and followed by the speed of western imperialist and then post-imperialist power and languages over much of the world. A recent watershed moment was US President Nixon's 1973 cancellation of an agreement (called Bretton Woods) signed in 1944 as the Second World War raged towards its end. This had established stable systems of monetary exchange and international trade regulation. Along with developments in computer technology and electronic communication, Nixon's cancellation opened up hugely speculative financial markets, and accelerated the discourses and powers of 'free trade', 'deregulation' and a corporate capitalism, newly able to chase markets, 'downsizing' and cheap labour across the world (see Grossberg in Bennett *et al.* 2005: 146–50).

Globalisation has been said to occur when activities:

- take place in a global (not simply national or regional) arena
- are deliberately organised on a global scale
- involve some interdependency, so that activities in different parts of the world are shaped by each other
- often involve technologies which make possible instantaneous, as opposed to simply *fast*, communications.

Global interdependency

- The purchases of supermarket shoppers are scanned instantaneously at checkouts and relayed electronically to the shop's storerooms. This has abolished dependence on local growth and harvesting cycles – for some people. For others 'agribusiness' means near-constant labour, oppressive contracts with supermarket chains, and wasteful use of water. Salads picked and washed in Kenya, on estates using huge amounts of precious water, are air-freighted in forty-eight hours to 'save the time' of British consumers. For future generations it's important to estimate, and avoid, the global warming costs of flying such luxury goods across the globe.
- The growth of tourism, fuelled by low carbon taxes, is also involved in such imbalances, as well as having been a huge factor in opening many people's eyes to conditions in parts of the world other than their own.

In many countries, the 'agribusiness market' and tourism mean that local environments are being seriously damaged in order to feed westernised tastes – but at the same time, local people need employment and their governments need foreign exchange. This is an acute dilemma – see 'Case study: Divine advertising' below.

Communications technologies have been crucial to globalising developments of this 'international' economy, beginning with the invention of paper and printing in China, which were traded with Europe, and allowed books and pamphlets to circulate well beyond the places where they were produced. Crucial for later expansion were the development of underwater cable systems by the European imperial powers and companies such as Cable and Wireless and the establishment of international news agencies (see Thompson 1997: 152–9).

It may come as a surprise to learn that underwater cables were so important, yet, until the 1850s, telegraph systems were land-based and thus quite restricted. As Wheen points out, 'The laying of the first transatlantic cable in 1866, which allowed real-time information to be exchanged between markets in New York and London, was at least as significant in the history of global finance as the creation of online share-trading' (2004: 255).

By the 1870s submarine cables had been laid throughout South East Asia and along the coast of Africa. Europe was soon linked to China, Australia and South America. It was the first global system of communication which separated the sending of messages from the need to transport them physically. **News agencies** likewise gathered and disseminated news over huge areas, and eventually, in 1869, agreed to divide up the world into mutually exclusive spheres of operation. Such impressive technological developments are often celebrated via the assumptions of technological determinism, as though they came from thin air rather than corporate drives and shapings. It's worth remembering that such drives more or less corresponded, like the reach of the underwater cable systems, to the spheres of influence of the major European imperial powers (Wheen 2004: 255).

This process has continued, now also around US power. The internet is often enjoyed for its global reach, and is the source of metaphors of a democratising 'networked' world. Some argue that, along with new channels such as CNN, it could be a new 'global public sphere' where opinions could be exchanged outside national communities. But the internet is heavily US dominated, not least by Bill Gates's Microsoft Corporation, and physical access to it is restricted by lack of electricity, computers and telecommunications services. Global news and information, a key part of dreams of 'global citizenship', are also shaped by often US profitabilities. CNN's global coverage often seems aimed at a relatively small group of predominantly male, well-educated and wealthy hotel users. Technologies never develop in a void, especially when they seem to have magically spread over the globe and to offer amazing possibilities.

Figure 15.2 Another surprising reminder of how differently the globe was experienced a hundred years ago. Fishguard, on the far west coast of Wales, is here advertised as the start of the quickest route to New York, London and 'the Continent'.

'In 1924, at the British Empire Exhibition, King George V sent himself a telegram which circled the globe on all British lines in 80 seconds' (Thompson 1997: 154).

Technological determinism: the belief that technology has a logic of its own which determines economic and other social changes. It is often fuelled by science fiction forms which suggest technologies can act 'on their own', often malevolently, and often for the sake of the plot. *The Terminator* series are a classic example.

483

Figure 15.3 An image from the tsunami of December 2004.

The 2004 tsunami highlighted several of the meanings of 'globalisation':

- the instantaneous speed of global communication of a disaster. It was reported by professional and also 'amateur' media forms and technologies, such as mobile phones, camera phones and blogs. Controversy arose over the failure of US surveillance to give warning of it in time to the Thai authorities
- how (often movingly generous) responses to such a disaster can be globally evoked and coordinated
- the global 'free market' inequalities which partly accounted for some of the devastation. This occurs within as well as across countries.

'Some months before the tsunami struck, Oxfam interviewed a woman called Nong, who was stitching underwear for Victoria's Secrets in Thailand. She explained she was afraid of having children because she feared she could not feed them. 'We have to do overtime until midnight to earn a decent income,' she said . . . EU citizens spend $11bn a year on ice-cream alone, while the joint pet-food bill for the EU and the US is £17bn, against the UN budget of $1.25bn, excluding peacekeeping.'

(Mary Riddell, 'Towards a Moral Universe', *Observer*, 9 January 2005)

ACTIVITY 15.2

Take the news coverage of the summer 2005 hurricanes in the region of the US South Eastern Coast. Compare the impact on the well-constructed homes of the wealthier with the devastation of the trailer parks of the poor, in Florida. Is any comment offered on this? How does the disaster compare to hurricanes and tsunamis in other parts of the world? Is this commented on or built into the reports?

CASE STUDY: DIVINE ADVERTISING: AN EXERCISE IN GLOBAL AWARENESS

Contexts for such advertising

The ad in Figure 15.4 offers a very good representation of many of the issues concerned with one aspect of globalisation, 'free trade', which, along with the concept of a 'free' market, is explored here and in Chapter 16. Both concepts depend heavily on the word 'free' and the suggestion that everyone is equally able to enter into buying and selling, importing and exporting, etc. Crucially, the theoretical models that underpin these concepts assume an equal access to knowledge about prices, costs, rates of interest, etc.

Figure 15.4

But some groups always have more knowledge or buying power than the rest of the market. Both trade and markets are often 'fixed' or at least 'controlled' by the most powerful players. The US government supports 'free trade' in principle usually only when its own interests are thereby advanced. A few days after the ad in Figure 15.5 appeared, the *Guardian* published a report from Ghana which explained why poor Ghanaian farmers were unable to sell the rice they had grown locally under difficult conditions. The markets in Ghana were full of high-quality, 'branded' American rice. Although more expensive, the American rice was perceived as 'better value', being clean and white (and heavily advertised). How could American producers afford to produce rice at such low cost (i.e. by American standards) that they could afford to 'dump' it in African markets (i.e. paying for the transport costs on top of the fertilisers, pesticides and other technologies at home)? Simple really: the US government subsidised it to the extent of 72 per cent of the value of the rice crop in 2003 ($1.3 billion subsidy for a crop worth $1.7 billion). Japan and the EU are equally guilty of 'fixing' the rice market (*Guardian*, 11 April 2005).

Global trade, often including trade in media, is distorted by major players such as large multinational food companies, supported by governments or trading blocs. Poorer countries have economies based on producing primary goods (e.g. food, minerals) which are then exported to richer countries in exchange for 'high-technology goods'. But because of the distortions outlined above, producers in Africa and Central America are being forced to suffer worsening labour conditions, over-use of dangerous chemical fertilisers, etc. just to stay in business. Sugar and bananas are the most affected crops alongside rice.

One response to all of this is the Fairtrade movement. Sponsored by a consortium of NGOs (non-government organisations) in Europe and North America, including Oxfam in the UK, Fairtrade schemes focus on 'high-value' products such as chocolate, tea and coffee (see http://www.fairtrade.net. for a list of the participating agencies). They aim to support local farmers in Africa and Central America, in particular by guaranteeing prices and helping to process the crops locally (i.e. turning coffee beans into ground coffee), so that as much profit as possible stays in the country. They then promote the products to supermarkets in Europe as high-quality, 'fairly traded' goods which can command a premium price from 'ethically minded' consumers. And the scheme works. Fairtrade coffee 'brands' such as Cafédirect are growing faster than traditional brands such as Nescafé and Maxwell House (from Nestlé and General Foods, the multinationals which generally control coffee prices).

Divine chocolate is one of the Fairtrade products sold in the UK. You can read about the history of the brand and the context of its development on http://www.divinechocolate.com. The Ghanaian cooperative of cocoa farmers, Kuaka Kopoo, created the Day Company with the UK company Twin Trading and support from The Body Shop, Christian Aid and Comic Relief. The Day Company offers a range of chocolate products which are sold in UK supermarkets.

Interestingly, the products include 'milk chocolate' as well as the dark chocolate from upmarket brands such as Green & Black (now part of Cadbury Schweppes). This suggests that Divine seeks a younger and more 'mainstream' consumers. Although Fairtrade is succeeding, one of the concerns for the Fairtrade groups must be that their products are in danger of being 'typed' as only for middle-class 'consumers with a conscience' who are attracted to 'speciality' brands.

ACTIVITY 15.3

An image of Fairtrade

Q1 How do you think the ad in Figure 15.4 represents Divine chocolate?

Look at the 'Case study: Ways of interpreting' and apply the techniques to this image of a young woman and the chosen background. Don't forget to consider both the anchoring text and the use of typography.

Q2 Who do you think the ad is addressing as a potential consumer?

Q3 Check out the Fairtrade and Divine Chocolate websites. How do you think the ad works in relation to what you understand about the aims of Fairtrade organisations?

Other Fairtrade products include bananas, mangoes, fruit juices and footballs. Choose one of these products and brainstorm some ideas about how you would advertise them in magazines.

Debates: cultural imperialism?

'It is not "domination" by American cinema. It's just the magic of story-telling, and it unites the world' Steven Spielberg quoted in Branston (2000: 61).

The difference between 'universal' and 'global' is crucial. 'What is universal is true everywhere and forever whereas what is global is merely a feature of the planet here and now' (During 2005: 87).

Powerful US media figures such as Steven Spielberg and Jack Valenti (when he headed Hollywood's export organisation the MPA) often talk as though US products themselves simply and effortlessly win global assent and popularity, that they have 'universal appeal'.

Herbert Schiller (1919–2000) was one of the best-known writers to argue a very different position, calling such power 'cultural imperialism'. He suggested that traditional, local cultures are destroyed by the external pressure of more powerful countries and their exports, so that new forms of cultural dependency are shaped, mirroring older imperialist relations of power. Two key points which he made:

- The dominance of US advertising-driven commercial media forces a costly US model of broadcasting, print, radio, and associated technologies on the rest of the world, including non-commercial cultures. This very specific US commercial culture thus becomes normalised.

- This also inculcates desires for US-style consumerism in societies which can ill afford it, and which some would say have better models of how to live anyway, especially now, with the planet imperilled by the over-consumption of its 'developed' parts.

Several criticisms have been since made of such a position.

First, he developed his case in the 1950s and 1960s when US economic dominance of the global system seemed secure and unchallengeable, the very 'heart of the beast' that was also fighting a brutal war in Vietnam. It does not adequately describe all the shifts of the post-1945 period. It has arguably become even more difficult, as Schiller recognised, to apply the theory to the 1990s and after. Global restructuring has now to *some* extent eroded the economic pre-eminence of the US. There are huge debates, for example, as to who actually owns 'the US economy'. Some major US media have been bought by foreign companies: Japanese Sony bought Columbia and TriStar pictures in 1989, to add to CBS records; Bertelsmann bought RCA and Random House publishers; the then Australian Rupert Murdoch bought 20th Century-Fox in 1986; and the French company Vivendi bought the (Canadian Seagram-owned) Universal Studios in 2000.

See Chapter 7 'Case study: The media majors' for up-to-date developments.

Second, globalisation can never be a simple process of homogenisation, or rendering the world all the same. Schiller later argued that the idea of American cultural imperialism should be replaced by the (unwieldy) term 'transnational corporate cultural domination'. Critics argue that even this is an inadequate term for the complex flows, networks and uses of media products in the contemporary world. Globalisation is not simply the West

TNC as abbreviation for trans-national corporations is often used in parts of media studies and other subject areas.

expanding into the rest of the world, but also other countries and their media forms having exchanges with, and even flowing into and out of, the West.

Though globalisation is often characterised as a homogenising process, leading to 'McWorld' (see Herman and McChesney 1997), and this term makes a vivid point, it is a very 'metropolitan' and exaggerated one. For example, much production in sub-Saharan Africa is not capitalist, let alone corporate-homogenised. About 4.5 billion people worldwide do not have access to telecommunications: so much for the image of 'us all' on the internet.

Third, others object that the cultural imperialism thesis implies, in almost romantic fashion, that before the arrival of US media, 'Third World' countries were enjoying a cosy golden age of indigenous, authentic traditions and cultural heritage, untainted by values imposed from outside. Critics argue that this attitude risks patronising what are seen as weaker nations, and romanticising their pre-colonial cultures. Sometimes cultures called 'indigenous' have sophisticated traditions and 'ancient heritages', shaped by long and brutal processes of cultural conflict and indeed exchange. These extend from well before the years of US intervention, often including hundreds of years of European colonial 'enterprise'.

> McWorld and associated terms such as McJob (for low-wage, non-unionised repetitive work): coined from the global spread of McDonald's food chain. Because of the standardisation of a narrow range of product in the 20,000+ McDonald's outlets, and its identification with US capitalism, the term often signifies a completely standardised, Americanised world.

> Bodily adornment and cover are called 'fashion' (and linked to modernity) in the West, but 'tradition' (and linked to the past and to tourism) in the 'developing world'.

Cultural imperialism, indigeneity and Wales

Two tourists were driving through Wales. As they were approaching Llanfairpwllgwngyllgogerychwyrndrobwllllantysiliogogogoch they started arguing about the pronunciation of the name and this went on until they stopped for lunch. As they stood at the counter, one tourist asked the girl who was serving food, 'Before we order, would you settle an argument for us? Would you please pronounce where we are . . . very slowly?'

She leaned over the counter and said, 'Burrrrrrrr, gerrrrrrr, Kiiiiing.'

Footnote: 'Llanfairpwllgwngyllgogerychwyrndrobwllllantysiliogogogoch', the longest place name in the world, the longest valid domain name, and the password to Dildano's HQ in *Barbarella* (US 1968), is played in this joke as an indigenous sign of Welshness. In fact it is said to have been specially concocted as a publicity gimmick in the mid-nineteenth century, when the railway was built between Chester and Holyhead, to try and encourage trains, travellers and tourists to stop at the village.

Figure 15.5 One of the Baka people, in Sudan, who in his handling of technology seems to refute the idea of 'primitive tribes'.

Figure 15.6 COE – country of origin effect? See Chapter 9.

Fourth, the emphasis on US ownership alone (complex though that now is) can ignore contradictions within the 'product'. Not all US television, for example, expresses *only* consumerist values, either in the programmes or even the advertising which finances them. There is some diversity of images, themes and information that can, and indeed has to, appear on commercially funded television. The media's insatiable need for *repetition and difference*, including material which is occasionally critical, up to a point, of dominant interests, is important. Nor do audiences inevitably become, or want to become, consumers *simply as a result of watching ads or programmes*. Audience research suggests a metaphor of *translation* would be a better way to understand what goes on in these global flows, and products, and the local sense and uses which people make of them.

Fifth and finally: how might the interplay work between US cultural or media power – globally popular US imagery of beauty, of power, of excitement – and the recent US use of military and diplomatic force? US brands are currently often associated with the Bush administration, in the so-called COE (Country of Origin Effect). This worked to their advantage in times when to buy a Coke was to buy in to dreams of far-off US glamour, ease and modernity, as displayed in Hollywood films. Now it seems the association often works to the detriment of such brands.

A closer look at US cultural power

Worth remembering that the continent of America (north and south) is named after Amerigo Vespucci (1454–1512) a fifteenth-century Italian merchant and cartographer, and the first European voyager to what is now called Brazil. By contrast, 'Canada' is said to derive from a French interpretation of a native word *kanata*, thus embodying the idea of a hybrid community.

Let's look in a little more detail at the specific factors which both make for US cultural power yet can also complicate our sense of it. The US entertainment giants operate out of huge accumulated experience in making successful products, and from the start these had an international aspect. North America is a continent of immigrants, with ties to other continents and, of course, a history of brutal conquest of other groups, such as the Native Americans. Hollywood cinema is an example of the hybridising as well as the homogenising drives within the growing dominance of US forms. The early 'American' makers and exhibitors in the 1890s were often first- or second-generation migrants to the US, and thus in very close contact with the European popular taste to which they were exporting. Canny textual strategies developed:

- adaptations to titles for different markets
- casting and even shaping different versions of films for global appeal to different audiences
- plots chosen for cultural 'vagueness' or openness, so as to appeal to as broad a market as possible.

The decision to use English as the main language of the US meant that these early US products could ride on the back of the spread of that imperial language. For British cinema ever since it has been double edged: it allows easy passage to some English-language films into the US, but also means that they will compete for English-language markets with US 'product'.

US exporters soon began to use differential pricing strategies for different parts of the globe. This still means that once a US television series, for example, has been distributed in the North American continent (which is usually large enough to allow it to recoup its production costs), it will be offered to every broadcaster in the world, but at different rates. The money made thus is often clear profit. In the 'developed' countries charges are based on audience size (e.g. on the relatively affluent and concentrated audiences who can be contacted by media in big cities). But in Africa the rates may be lowered dramatically, so programmes can be virtually given away for relatively little cost. This process both ensures *overall* profitability and also consolidates habits of enjoying US-style entertainment forms, usually advertising related. Rates are so low that they impact on local production. African or West Indian broadcasters, for example, cannot hope to produce programming of a similar technical quality at a lower price, and their station managers cannot afford *not* to buy in. Sometimes this now involves buying in to a global format or franchise, such as *Big Brother* (see entry in www.wikipedia.org) and then translating it for local tastes.

However, even this kind of successful export operation means that big US corporations need to take some account of local sensibilities. The encounter with different local perceptions, along with global political movements, can lead to unforeseen problems. Disney, for example, when it opened a new theme park in Hong Kong in 2005, got feng-shui agreement for the location, and planned to operate in English, Mandarin and Cantonese. But uproar erupted when they unveiled plans to serve shark's fin soup at weddings and other prestige occasions. Environmental campaigners objected to the slaughter of millions of sharks each year for their fins; Disney claimed it was being respectful of local Chinese culture, which views the soup as a delicacy. It is a classic example of the complexity and financial risks of 'going global' in the twenty-first-century world.

Let's look at the film industry as another example of these interplays. To get a big co-production financed, there will usually need to be complex pre-production negotiations with television, video, cable, etc. funders, sometimes based in those overseas markets where the film will have to sell to recoup its profits. This means that the resulting film may contain unexpected elements that are far from being 'local', even 'local to the US'.

See Chapter 13 'Case study: Contemporary British cinema'.

For global television documentaries as much as for 'global' feature films the motto is often: 'let's make it "language neutral" i.e. with as little sync [sound] as possible and no talking heads. They can add those later for different national markets' (discussion at Sheffield International Documentary Film Festival 2001).

'Tarnished image: is the world falling out of love with US brands? Concern that opposition to Washington's policy in Iraq could harm American businesses abroad is leading some companies to downplay their heritage' (*Financial Times*, 30 December 2004).

Figure 15.7 'McWorld'? Or a major US corporation accommodating to local customs?

ACTIVITY 15.4

Sponsoring sport

Budweiser, as well as Coca-Cola, now sponsors football (or 'soccer') in the UK. But what of that other un-American sport, cricket? Possibly the largest middle-class audience in the world (always welcomed by advertisers) watches cricket in India, Sri Lanka and Pakistan.

● Research the internet to discover which firms sponsor cricket in South Asia.
● What might be the issues facing global corporations who would like to sponsor cricket in that region?

However this limited degree of diversity will tend to go along with the need for at least one 'US' star or director, though, again, this may be someone originally from outside the US, like Catherine Zeta Jones or Ewan McGregor, or Gong Li.

'The rest of the world is judging American values, they say, and one of the criteria is whether Americans can see foreign cultures as something more than a pretty backdrop, more than an exotic stereotype to be appropriated and marketed' (www.modelminority.com). This sort of controversy can be explored as:

● an inevitable part of 'globalisation' under corporate, US-dominated conditions
● part of the very publicity which any high-budget film needs in order to make its returns.

The case of *Memoirs of a Geisha*

In 2005 Rob Marshall directed this big budget ($85 million) film, produced by Spielberg's company Amblin and distributed worldwide by Sony Pictures (Sony is now a big player in Hollywood: see p. 245), based on a best-selling novel by a male westerner and focusing on an iconic part of Japanese culture. It seemed the perfect 'pan-Asian' or even 'global' product. It has no 'white' stars, and was shot in the US. There was huge controversy at the casting of two Chinese actors, Zihi Zhang and Gong Li, a Malaysian-born star of Hong Kong cinema, Michelle Yeoh, and other nationalities in this Japanese story. Marshall argued that he was simply hiring the best talent available. Others argued it showed typical lack of concern by big US money for local traditions and cultures, which could cause huge offence to knowledgeable audience members, and circulate misleading ideas about that culture to others.

Internet message board comment:

And why am I interested in a movie about a Japanese woman written by a white man directed by a white man? Imagine if a Japanese woman wrote a book called *Memoirs of a Cowboy* and it was directed by a Chinese woman. And they decided to cast a Russian guy cos all whites look alike. What a joke.

(www.modelminority.com)

Figure 15.8 Posters for *Drunken Master* (Hong Kong 1994) and *Dil to Pagal Hai* (India 1997) on a wall in Morocco in 1999. Stars Jackie Chan and Shahrukh Khan are as well known across the world as American stars.

Regions, flows, networks

Telenovela: a form of melodramatic serialised fiction produced and aired in most Latin American countries. While resembling a soap opera, the *telenovela* has its own unique characteristics, airing in prime time six days a week, attracting a broad audience across age and gender lines, and commanding the highest advertising rates. *Telenovelas* last about six months and come to a climactic close.

2005: the founding of a Latin American news channel, Telesur, is announced, supported by Argentina, Venezuela and Cuba and attacked by the Bush administration.

June 2005: it's announced that it will soon be acceptable, in the UK, to register website addresses with non-Roman alphabets or with accents on letters. The English-language domination of the internet begins to slip? A further acknowledgement that people in the UK are conscious of their several ethnic identities? And that roughly three hundred languages are spoken here?

Diaspora: dispersal across the globe of peoples who originated in a single geographical location, e.g. the dispersed community formed from the black diaspora of the African–American slave trade. The reasons for such travel (often in a 'to and fro' pattern) range from unemployment, political repression, famine, etc. but also, more recently, education, to join family already abroad, etc.

1

One of the challenges to US media power comes from the 'regional' flows which exist within media. These are often dependent on the historic global spread of imperial languages such as Spanish, English, French and Arabic. Mexico and Brazil are key producers and exporters of *telenovelas* to the rest of Latin America and parts of Europe.

Hindi has replaced French as the 'second language' of films screened in the UK. In Africa and the 'Middle East', Indian and Hong Kong films circulate where Hollywood does not venture. An interesting contemporary instance of these language flows is the popularity of the 'spelling bee' (spelling contest), especially among the children of immigrants to the US. They can be seen as about both the dominance of English and also the ways that the words of that very language embody rich patterns of migration (see the film *Spellbound* (US 2002)).

2

Rather than a 'homogenised' global culture, we might see the centres of traditional cultural power as having been **hybridised**, their 'normal' cultures and languages enriched and complicated, as populations flow this way and that across the globe. A too-US-focused model underplays the pleasures (and pains) of the rich hybridities formed, even within the US, as a result of **diasporas** and migrations. The growing consumer power of diasporic groups, such as the NRIs or Non-Resident Indians, both Hindi- and Tamil-speaking, and Cantonese- and Mandarin-speaking Chinese, is also a key factor complicating ideas that 'globalisation' means 'sameness'.

ACTIVITY 15.5

Look at www.nriol.com and www.nri-worldwide.com. What kind of an image of the group known as NRIs (Non-Resident Indians) does it give?

However, too uncritical an adoption of such perspectives can ignore the inequalities and histories of such exchanges. The brutal slave trade, from the seventeenth to nineteenth centuries, had an enormous cultural side impact: the export of African music to the West Indies, Cuba and Brazil, and then back again. It remains a brutal trade, needing historical understanding, as well as celebration. And it's one thing for high-paid executives to lead nomadic existences between different airports, but quite another for women from poorer countries to have to abandon their families to work as nannies, sex workers or cleaners for wealthier families in rich countries or in other parts of their own country. See Hochschild and Ehrenreich (2003: 4) for an account of this relatively undocumented global flow, a trade in what they call 'something that can look very much like love'.

'Hybridity' and 'diaspora' are often used in very abstract ways. These can flatten out or ignore historical injustices and contemporary tensions in favour of simply relishing the cultural richness which often results from global displacements.

A still controversial instance is '**hyphenated identities**' (whether or not the labels literally use hyphens). These refer to the names chosen to express the complexity of global attachments and histories: 'British Muslim' or 'Anglo-Welsh' (in relation to language use), for example. Neither half of such terms is itself simple, and most people would describe themselves through many more than two, often overlapping, labels.

But such globally related identities often become controversial when the media use the component parts to suggest they tug in opposite directions. One example is found in 2003 debates on the hijab or headscarf worn in French schools by some Muslim girls, especially since the schools are often proud of their secular or non-religious nature.

See Chapter 5 'Case study: Images of migration'.

3

The image of globalisation as a single, simple entity downplays the importance of nation-states and their media to merely 'local' status. It's worth remembering, first, that nation-states and their legislation are bodies which are needed precisely to help manage global capitalism, even if corporations often over-ride their national powers, for example by relocating production to low-paid economies. Far from being truly 'free' or 'deregulated', the free trade treaties of the most powerful, for example, depend on thousands of pages of regulations, and the cooperation of nation-states to implement them. This is especially true as the US, for example, seeks to counter the threat to its huge copyright powers posed by internet forms.

'The North American Free Trade Agreement . . . needs a . . . thousand pages of protocols, weighing 850 kilogrammes! . . . this is an international not a global age – and governments continue to matter' (Miller *et al.* 2001: 41).

See www.nollywood.com which includes links to diasporic groups such as 'Nigerians in America'. The term, like Bollywood, perhaps humorously, suggests a pale imitation of Hollywood, but the industry itself is much more distinctive, though not without problems in a state such as Nigeria. ('Valleywood', used for a proposed big studio facility in Wales, seems a slightly different term.)

Second, there remains a huge appetite for local imagery of our worlds, even in the most difficult conditions. African films will circulate to small, remote villages by mobile cinemas, where audiences often watch them several times. Nigerian cinema ('Nollywood') is the fastest-growing film industry in Africa with several low-budget video films relating to soap forms appearing each month (see http://www.filmmakermagazine.com/fall2002/features/no_budget_nigeria.php). And the tiny Pan African Film Festival in Burkina Faso has been operating successfully since 1969, though some films are cut or not shown in their home producer's nation, such as Morocco, and rely on success at other festivals to get known.

Figure 15.9 The comparatively small cinema where the Fespaco Film Festival, Burkina Faso, was held in 2003. No need to suggest the many ways in which this differs from the Oscars settings, or that of other big global film festivals such as Cannes, London or Venice.

Sinclair *et al.* (1999) argue: 'Although US programmes might lead the world in their transportability across cultural boundaries, and even manage to dominate the schedules on some channels in particular countries, they are rarely the most popular programmes where viewers have a reasonable menu of locally produced programmes to choose from.'

ACTIVITY 15.6

List the number of ways in which your own experiences of the media over the last week have been affected by:

- living in a *global* media economy
- living in a *national* media economy
- living with media which *mix global and national* characteristics
- living with media which cross huge spaces instantaneously.

Try to apply these to your use of TV, mobile phone technology and cinema.

- How many local images of your world have you seen this week? Where?

4

The 'footprints' of different media, in whatever languages, also form key regional 'networks'. BBC World Service, Star TV channels, MTV Europe, Al Jazeera, pirate radio stations – these are all key in shaping understandings of the world wherever they can be picked up. They criss-cross national and religious belief systems as well as the areas of US media corporate power.

Al Jazeera is an interesting example of global mixes. This TV news channel was founded in 1996, partly by staff trained in BBC World principles of attempted impartiality – see the home page. It is located in, and subsidised by, an oil-rich monarchy, Qatar, and has given voice to previously marginalised Arab viewpoints on the world. During the US bombing of Afghanistan it was the source of messages from Osama Bin Laden which the US and British administrations tried to stop being broadcast. Later the station's building in Kabul was 'accidentally' bombed. It now has thirty bureaux, or offices, and launched the first mainstream Arabic news site website in 2001.

Figure 15.10 A channel such as Al Jazeera handles a very different network of views and assumptions some of them troubling to 'western' states. It launches a new English-speaking global news channel, Al Jazeera International, early in 2006 and will also relaunch the English website.

Al Jazeera claims to be free of censorship, though like every news organisation, especially ones with state subsidies, its agenda, wording, etc. are always the product of particular choices. See *The Control Room* (US/Egypt 2003) for a sense of the pressures on such a news channel during recent invasions of Iraq and Afghanistan.

To add to the global mix: sometimes these satellite channels fuel vigorous underground trade in TV equipment – with global brand manufacturers based in Japan.

5

Other powerful networks also exist and complicate global media. The flows and demands of fan cultures deserve mention. And we need to note that the fans are those of Michael Moore's website and internet political humour and protest as well as sport, music, cult films.

More sinister networks also exist, often named in association with 'Al-Qaeda'. These have flourished partly on the ways that 'Middle Eastern' satellite channels, understandably, provide detailed coverage, almost by the hour, of the horrific number of deaths in Iraq, focusing on US as well as insurgent actions. Western media, for example in the aftermath of the 2005 London bombs, have often overlooked this coverage, and the scale of the devastation in Iraq, especially as foreign news budgets get trimmed. As Paul Rogers points out, Iraq is potent because of the ways that the awful facts

> can be expanded, manipulated and developed into much wider conspiratorial frameworks. The reality of Iraq is devastating enough – perhaps 25,000 civilians killed and 70,000 injured in a little over two years – but its dissemination, interpretation and exaggeration on militant websites can add greatly to its power to move.
>
> (Paul Rogers on www.opendemocracy.net, 14 July 2005; see also www.iraqbodycount.org)

No Hollywood films will be released in China for the next five weeks in what seems to be turning into a regular blackout on foreign films over the summer holiday box-office season (*Screen International*, 21 July 2005).

In conclusion, it seems useful then to think of several kinds of regions or networks, different kinds of flow, which are mapped within the term 'globalisation', rather than seeing it all, rather depressingly, as a block domination by the US, important though US power is, and violently enforced as it sometimes has been within media industries (see Miller *et al*. 2005).

Corporate domination?

One strength of the media imperialism argument is its emphasis on the ways that it is not just 'texts' but also the system of capitalist media organisation, especially in television, which has been exported so successfully. Examples: it is almost taken for granted now

- that the financing of many media is by advertising, over-ruling principles of a public right to quality media; viewing uninterrupted by ads, non-copyrighted circulation of publicly important texts, etc.
- that media are in competition for profits, like other capitalist firms
- that 'free trade' imperatives should apply to cultural goods such as films and TV
- that 'development' means developing towards this (now intensely US-driven) capitalist model, with its attendant over-consumption and minimum possible employment levels ('downsizing')
- that this is what modernity has to mean.

All these shape the media in some ways, and deny other ways of developing the media. When other ideas of how to organise our planet are voiced, they are represented in striking ways. Much news coverage of so-called 'anti-globalisation' demonstrations emphasises that the protesters wear trainers manufactured in the very sweatshops they so object to, or that they travel many miles by polluting air transport. These are shrewd points about the extent of dissidents' reliance on the products of advanced global capitalism. But they also embody the way the media insist on using 'globalisation' rather than 'corporate globalisation' as the key term for such protest.

ACTIVITY 15.7

Look at coverage of the next such demonstration for how words and images are used. How differently could it be represented?

Wheen makes a good point about the phrase 'anti-globalisation': 'the problem is not globalisation per se, but the fact that the rules of the game have been set by the winning side – which, while enforcing them elsewhere, feels no obligation to apply them to its own conduct' (Wheen 2004: 245).

Media conglomerates of whatever country operate like other capitalist **oligopolies** – a few large organisations together dominating the market, and often buying up successful smaller companies. They often work together (like **cartels**) to cooperate on perpetuating 'free trade' treaties which will further their interests (see Klein 2001). It is true that the biggest media corporations are often based in the US and, importantly, tend to use either US stars and high-paid personnel, or 'talent' which generally has to move to the US to remain globally 'major'. (Even the Australian Rupert Murdoch has had to take on US citizenship in order to acquire more US interests.)

Employment operates with an eye to costs: jobs perceived as less crucial (such as call centres) will go wherever the corporations (US but also European, Japanese, perhaps Chinese by the time you read this book) can get to pay the lowest wages (see Miller *et al.* 2005). This impacts on US workers too, as corporate employers chase the cheapest, least unionised labour forces across the world, or try to second-guess currency shifts as they budget for locations.

Local producers in Africa have other problems too, such as training and equipment. Training needs to be 'on the job' for at least part of the time

The Take (Canada 2004), a film by Naomi Klein and Avi Lewis, is worth tracking down for its refusal to peddle 'protest porn'. It tries for a gentler approach to radical change within global capitalism.

Q How successful is this compared to 'blockbuster' forms such as the Live8 concerts in 2005 or the eco-blockbuster *The Day After Tomorrow* (US 2004)?

Fifty-seven of the hundred most valuable global brands, as measured by Interbrand, are owned by US companies (July 2005; see www.interbrand.com).

on (expensive) broadcast-quality equipment and with reliable electricity supplies. Most readers of this book will take for granted access to video tapes, batteries, cables, etc. But broadcasters in some parts of the world may be hundreds of miles from mains electricity and water, let alone such equipment. And equipment designed for broadcast use in North America, Western Europe and Japan will not necessarily perform efficiently in tropical conditions.

In addition, in many African countries film distribution is almost entirely in the hands of overseas companies which are unwilling to distribute African films, even though local producers are not lacking in creative ideas or production skills. Several theorists argue that this distribution imbalance could be tackled, especially with government support for organised resistance to international trade agreements, which usually favour US interests (especially since the presidency of G.W. Bush). Alliances to build satellite and digital transmission and distribution systems are important here. Others urge western educationalists, in media studies for example, to teach about cinemas other than Hollywood entertainment forms. This might help develop an understanding and appetite for films that are trying not to copy that model, but to do something different.

Complex alliances already exist around production of African films. See the production credits for Ousmane Sembene's extraordinary 2004 film about female circumcision, globalisation and Islam in Africa: *Moolaadé*. They read: 2004 Senegal/France/ Burkina Faso/Cameroon/ Morocco/Tunisia.

ACTIVITY 15.8

Global cinema

Get hold of cinema listings for your region, either from a newspaper or the internet. Choose a major city with multiplexes and ideally an independent cinema. Using the capsule reviews available, count the number of screens in the city which are running Hollywood as opposed to non-US films. Calculate what proportion of the total these make up.

Spectacle in global media

It often seems that circulating hugely expensive spectacle is one of the 'unifying'(?) forces of global media, seeking to draw global audiences not only into blockbuster films, but also into sports events, national ceremonials or even protests such as the Live8 concerts. Let's examine the dynamics of one such spectacular global event.

Global branding of sporting spectacles means wonderful publicity for Nike and other firms whose logos are emblazoned on the bodies of

NORTH AMERICA Three-day weekend August 12-14 — TOP 10

Rank	Film (Origin) Distributor	Week	3-day gross $	Sites	Site avg $	% change	Total gross $
1	(-) Four Brothers (US) Paramount	NEW	$21,176,925	2,533	$8,360	-	$21,176,925
2	(-) The Skeleton Key (US) Universal	NEW	$16,057,945	2,771	$5,795	-	$16,057,945
3	(1) The Dukes Of Hazzard (US) Warner Bros	2	$13,011,202	3,785	$3,438	-58	$57,459,025
4	(2) Wedding Crashers (US) New Line	5	$11,834,614	3,131	$3,780	-26	$163,860,740
5	(-) Deuce Bigalow: European Gigolo (US) Sony Pictures	NEW	$9,626,287	3,127	$3,078	-	$9,626,287
6	(3) Charlie And The Chocolate Factory (US) Warner Bros	5	$7,412,391	3,304	$2,243	-32	$183,940,297
7	(6) March Of The Penguins (Fr-US) Warner Independent Pictures	8	$6,848,205	2,063	$3,320	-4	$37,723,310
8	(4) Sky High (Jap) Buena Vista	3	$6,309,670	2,807	$2,248	-30	$43,499,197
9	(5) Must Love Dogs (US) Warner Bros	3	$4,575,046	2,420	$1,891	-38	$34,604,972
10	(-) The Great Raid (US) Miramax	NEW	$3,376,009	819	$4,122	-	$3,376,009

UK/IRELAND Three-day weekend August 12-14 — TOP 10

Rank	Film (Origin) Distributor	Week	3-day gross £	3-day gross $	Sites	Site avg $	% change	Total gross $
1	(1) Charlie And The Chocolate Factory (US) Warner Bros	3	£2,886,352	$5,238,768	523	$10,017	-35	$47,296,905
2	(-) The Island (US) Warner Bros †	NEW	£1,481,647	$2,689,210	404	$6,656	-	$2,689,210
3	(-) Crash (US) Pathe	NEW	£818,604	$1,485,778	276	$5,383	-	$1,485,778
4	(5) Herbie: Fully Loaded (US) BVI	2	£672,674	$1,220,912	442	$2,762	-13	$4,654,501
5	(2) Madagascar (US) UIP	5	£648,653	$1,177,314	454	$2,593	-24	$36,567,515
6	(4) Fantastic Four (US) 20th Fox	4	£566,573	$1,028,337	386	$2,664	-31	$19,925,962
7	(3) Wedding Crashers (US) Entertainment Film Distributors	5	£558,492	$1,013,670	337	$3,008	-34	$20,769,564
8	(6) War Of The Worlds (US) UIP	7	£339,078	$615,431	277	$2,222	-41	$53,862,329
9	(-) Fever Pitch (US) 20th Fox	NEW	£272,285	$494,201	255	$1,938	-	$494,201
10	(-) The Rising (India) Yash Raj Films	NEW	£217,321	$394,440	73	$5,403	-	$394,441

$1 = £0.55096 † Figures include previews $383,329 (£211,199) from 336 sites. Screen International

HONG KONG Week ending August 10 — TOP 10

Rank	Film (Origin) Distributor	Week	7-day gross HK$	7-day gross $	Screens	Screen avg $	% change	Total gross $
1	(-) Ah Sou (HK) Filmko Entertainment	NEW	HK$3,941,628	$505,337	31	$16,301	-	$505,337
2	(-) Stealth (US) Columbia Pictures Film Production Asia	NEW	HK$2,864,378	$367,228	31	$11,846	-	$367,228
3	(2) Seven Swords (HK) Mandarin Films Distribution	2	HK$2,725,242	$349,390	39	$8,959	-30	$848,285
4	(1) The Island (US) Warner Bros	2	HK$2,666,679	$341,881	40	$8,547	-49	$1,035,910
5	(-) Doraemon – Nobita And The Wind Wizard (Jap) UFD	NEW	HK$1,998,703	$256,243	26	$9,856	-	$256,244
6	(-) Herbie: Fully Loaded (US) Intercontinental Film Distribution	NEW	HK$1,961,372	$251,458	26	$9,671	-	$251,458
7	(2) The Amityville Horror (US) Panasia Films	2	HK$1,176,653	$150,852	17	$8,874	-55	$496,390
8	(3) Robots (US) 20th Fox	2	HK$948,160	$121,558	39	$3,117	-65	$502,495
9	(5) Madagascar (US) Panasia Films	4	HK$621,223	$79,643	22	$3,620	-75	$2,783,912
10	(8) Marathon (S Korea) Golden Scene	3	HK$173,550	$22,250	5	$4,450	-58	$181,818

$1 = HK$7.8 MPA

RUSSIA & CIS Three-day weekend August 12-14 — TOP 10

Rank	Film (Origin) Distributor	Week	3-day gross RUB	3-day gross $	Screens	Screen avg $	% change	Total gross $
1	(-) The Island (US) Karo Premier †	NEW	RUB27,740,006	$979,865	241	$4,066	-	$1,223,761
2	(1) The Adventures Of Shark Boy And Lava Girl 3-D (US) Cascade Film	2	RUB10,902,889	$385,125	243	$1,585	-32	$1,574,120
3	(-) Going The Distance (Can) Lizard †	NEW	RUB6,064,965	$214,234	76	$2,819	-	$324,017
4	(2) Stealth (US) Cascade Film	3	RUB5,578,486	$197,050	183	$1,077	-47	$1,564,457
5	(3) Land Of The Dead (US-Fr) UIP	2	RUB5,029,724	$177,665	90	$1,974	-46	$843,800
6	(4) House Of Wax (US) Karo Premier	3	RUB3,024,301	$106,828	111	$962	-60	$1,429,954
7	(6) The Longest Yard (US) Cascade Film	4	RUB2,271,368	$80,232	109	$736	-36	$1,077,698
8	(7) Don't Cry Mummy 2 (Rus) Nashe Kino	3	RUB2,234,140	$78,916	116	$680	-23	$734,890
9	(8) Mr & Mrs Smith (US) Central Partnership	9	RUB1,655,088	$58,463	60	$974	-40	$8,637,197
10	(5) Empire Of The Wolves (Fr) Central Partnership	3	RUB1,389,908	$49,096	64	$767	-77	$732,346

$1 = RUB28.31 † Total gross includes previews. Russian Film Business Today

Figure 15.11 A vivid example of the dominance of US-distributed and advertised films globally. How many non-US products can you make out? What proportion of the whole are they? (See website www.globalfilm.org.) Does Bollywood have a presence in the list?

Figure 15.12 The 2004 Olympics, held in Athens.

Hosting the 2004 Olympics is estimated to have cost the Greek economy $10–12 billion (in US dollars), over 5 per cent of the country's annual gross domestic product. When Athens bid for the games, it was before security was being beefed up around the world as a direct result of the US response to '9/11'.

'Last ditch efforts to "clean up" Athens before the Olympics . . . included removing thousands of immigrants, beggars, drug addicts and homeless people from the . . . streets . . . about 70,000 police and military . . . have been drafted in to patrol the capital. "There is a climate of absolute terror on the streets," said a member of a charity working with the homeless and underprivileged youth' (*Guardian*, 11 August 2004).

The golfer Tiger Woods describes himself as 'Cablinasian' (a mix of Caucasian, Black, Indian, Asian) or one quarter Thai, one quarter Chinese, one eighth Native American, one eighth white European (see Coakley 1998: 251). Clearly this multiple ethnic identity has been a crucial part of his global marketability for sponsor Nike.

ACTIVITY 15.9

Use a recording or photos of the opening ceremony of the last Olympic Games. Research the following:

- What were the ratings figures for the ceremony?
- How were rich and poorer nations represented or orchestrated in the ceremony?
- How was the 'local' place of the ceremony represented? How might this differ from the sense which 'locals' had of it? (see http://www.nolondon2012.org if it is still operating).
- How much did it cost 'the locals' to put on?
- How, if at all, are differences or disputes between nations represented?
- How is the spectacle 'gendered'?
- Did the event enable any global justice protesters to highlight issues of exploitation etc. around it?

winning athletes, on stadiums, etc. Simultaneously, this same 'high news profile' makes it possible for movements critical of some exploitative characteristics of these same corporations to publicise those issues. Protesters may be able to build on:

- the claims of some corporations to be operating policies of 'corporate social responsibility'
- the desires of many shareholders, as well as of those working within them, to be involved in a properly respected brand, and to make that 'corporate social responsibility' mean what it says, especially in such high-profile moments.

ACTIVITY 15.10

What differences do you think it makes to choose to use one of the following words when writing: globe, planet, world, the Earth? Write a definition of each word which will suggest their different connotations.

Figure 15.13 'Green' ideas emphasise that we all share this one planet. They often circulate in the small-scale medium of the postcard, the campaign poster, an email group or the internet. This banner was part of a campaign to save a green space in Cardiff. The modern font and scientific message were a surprise to some passers-by, since the image of rural or 'green' places is often a nostalgic, backward-looking one. Such imagery exists in a global context where major car ads, with huge prime-time audiences and press coverage, show cars driving fast and elegantly through pristine, deserted or sometimes green landscapes – which those very oil-burning cars are guaranteed to pollute, if not destroy. The link to small, tree-saving campaigns seems a remote one, but global capitalist forces could soon bring it very close.

References

Appadurai, Arjun (1996) *Modernity at Large: Cultural Dimensions of Globalization*, Minneapolis: University of Minnesota Press.

Bennett, Tony, Grossberg, Lawrence and Morris, Meaghan (2005) *New Keywords: A Revised Vocabulary of Culture and Society*, Malden and Oxford: Blackwell.

Branston, Gill (2000) *Cinema and Cultural Modernity*, Buckingham: Open University Press.

Coakley, J. (1998) *Sport in Society: Issues and Controversies*, 6th edition, New York: McGraw Hill.

During, Simon (2005) *Cultural Studies: A Critical Introduction*, London: Routledge.

Herman, Ed and McChesney, Robert (1997) *The Global Media: The New Visionaries of Corporate Capitalism*, London: Cassell.

Hochschild, Arlie and Ehrenreich, Barbara (eds) (2003) *Global Woman: Nannies, Maids and Sex Workers in the New Economy*, London: Granta.

Klein, Naomi (2001) *No Logo*, 2nd edition, London: Flamingo.

McLuhan, Marshall (1964) *Understanding Media: The Extensions of Man*, London: Routledge and Kegan Paul.

McRobbie, Angela (2005) *The Uses of Cultural Studies*, London: Sage.

Meyrowitz, Joshua (1985) *No Sense of Place: The Impact of Electronic Media on Social Behaviour*, New York: Oxford University Press.

Miller, Toby, Govil, Nitin, McMurria, John and Maxwell, Richard (2005) *Global Hollywood 2*, revised edition, London: British Film Institute.

Myers, Greg (1999) *Ad Worlds: Brands, Media Audiences*, London and New York: Arnold.

Schiller, Herbert I. (1996) *Information Inequality*, London and New York: Routledge.

Schiller, Herbert I. (1997) 'Not yet the post-imperialist era', in Tim O'Sullivan and Yvonne Jewkes (eds) *The Media Studies Reader*, London: Routledge.

Sinclair, John, Jacka, Elizabeth and Cunningham, Stuart (1996) *New Patterns in Global Television: Peripheral Vision*, Oxford: Oxford University Press.

Thompson, John B. (1997) *The Media and Modernity: A Social Theory of the Media*, Cambridge: Polity.

Watt, Nicholas (2005) 'Mobiles split Britain into calls-conscious society', *Guardian*, 5 July.

Wheen, Francis (2004) *How Mumbo-Jumbo Conquered the World*, London: Fourth Estate.

Further reading

O'Sullivan, Tim and Jewkes, Yvonne (eds) (1997) *The Media Studies Reader*, London and New York: Arnold (esp. Section 5).

Other resources

www.dfid.gov.uk

www.opendemocracy.net

The Brand (Canada 2004) DVD

Why We Fight (US 2004) DVD

16 'Free choices' in a 'free market'?

- Politics and economics

- Regulation or 'freedom'?

- Historical background

- Deregulation, liberalisation and media institutions

- The contemporary regulatory environment

- What might a 'free market' mean for the UK?

- References and further reading

Whenever 'the media' are discussed as an important feature of contemporary society, a whole range of assumptions come into play. As we might expect from reading Chapter 6, different ideologies suggest different ways in which media institutions might function socially/politically and how we might understand their activities. In this chapter we want to investigate questions such as:

- Should society expect media institutions to perform certain actions and desist from others?

- Who should decide this and the kinds of controls there might be?

To give some concrete examples of what might be at stake:

- 'It's the *Sun* Wot Won It!' was that paper's proud boast about the General Election result in 1992. Is it a concern if a newspaper plays a decisive role in deciding who governs the UK? (See Chapter 4 on journalism.)

- 'Effects debates' focus on issues such as 'copycat behaviour' linked to the distribution of 'violent' films and television programmes. (See Chapter 8.)

- Broadcasters don't make enough 'quality programmes' for older viewers.

- Right-wing radio 'shock jocks' and Fox News in the US deny 'liberal' views any validity. (See Chapter 6.)

- Large retailers like Tesco or Asda could prevent the distribution of certain magazine titles. (See Chapter 13.)

- Book publishers don't circulate enough work by new writers.

Each of these examples refers to the power of media producers or distributors to do things that others would like to prevent or not do things others want them to do. In Chapter 4 we suggest that 'constraining' the power of organisations and the individuals within them is one of the main functions of the process of institutionalising them.

At the same time the prevailing ideologies of contemporary capitalism emphasise 'economic growth' and 'more choice for consumers'. Can we, should we, attempt to both constrain or direct media institutions in certain ways *and* encourage them to produce more, advertise vigorously and constantly strain to become more powerful? As we will see, this basic contradiction underpins many media debates.

Politics and economics

Some media debates are concerned with political issues – the relationship between media institutions and government or with public debates more generally. Others are primarily questions of economics – how to make the most efficient use of 'scarce' resources (i.e. labour and capital) to produce goods and services. For example:

- Trying to maintain the availability of certain radio frequencies for emergency services or military use might be deemed a political issue.
- Whether Apple should manufacture iPods itself or license other companies to make them instead is primarily a question of business economics.

But the separation of what is 'politics' and what is 'economics' is not clear-cut – in fact it is a function of ideology. If we believe an action is 'purely a question of economics', we are less likely to think of its political consequences. So, in the example above, Apple's decision might mean less work in its factories and more work elsewhere – with social costs and benefits to different groups of people.

After the industrial revolution in Western Europe began in the eighteenth century, the scholars who studied these momentous changes (**Adam Smith, Karl Marx**, etc.) were described as political economists. They made direct links between the growth in production and the development of new nation-states in a capitalist system. It wasn't until the late nineteenth century that 'economics' emerged as a separate discipline, concentrating in a more 'scientific', 'mathematical' way on changes in prices for 'inputs' and 'outputs' without the impediment of political questions. This form of economics has remained dominant, but some media studies theorists have returned to the original formulation and adopted a **political economy** approach to their work.

This isn't an economics textbook, but we do need to note how, in the twentieth century, economic theory developed and changed over time. Despite the supposed separation of politics and economics, governments changed their policies and worked with economic models created

Adam Smith (1723–90) is associated with ideas about 'free trade'. Like Marx, he has often been misrepresented by various political groups.

'the difference between political economy and economics is that, in economics, war is a temporary alteration in price variation, the old joke being that "World War III, should it come, will be noted in two sentences in the *Wall Street Journal*, with an article inside on its effect on soybean futures"' (from the 'political economy' entry on Wikipedia).

Political economy has an affinity with media studies, referring as it does to academic work that draws on different subject disciplines.

according to the prevailing ideologies within the economics communities of academics and advisers.

A model in social sciences is a theoretical construction which in this case enables policy-makers to predict what might happen in the future – e.g. how the population might grow, whether the price of oil will go up, or, in media industries terms, what will happen to UK television when the analogue service is 'switched off'. We will concentrate on two such models and the arguments that surround them. But first we need a clearer idea of what is at stake in terms of controlling or 'freeing' media activities. The arguments focus on ideas of **regulation** and personal freedom.

Models are an important means of exploring theoretical issues. See Chapter 1 and Chapter 6.

Regulation or 'freedom'?

Media activity has an impact on society in two ways.
- As a *social* activity, it can bring benefits associated with better information, insights, understanding and, of course, pleasure in our enjoyment of interaction with media products. At the same time, media activity could be harmful if it led to increased ignorance, encouraged violent and anti-social behaviour or interfered in some way with other forms of social activity.
- As an *economic* activity, it can provide employment and a return on capital, creating wealth for individuals, companies and regions/nations. In a capitalist system based on the concept of risk, it can also be associated with business failure and the social dis-benefits that can bring.

How do we as a society maximise the benefits – social and material – and minimise the dis-benefits? The answer lies in the institutionalisation of media activities and the creation of some form of regulatory framework in which the media institutions are required to operate. What is problematic is that there are also broad issues about how far we as individuals are prepared to allow other people to have a say in how we conduct our media activities as 'producers' or 'consumers'. How do we resolve the conflict between the public and private aspects of our media use? Is the best form of regulation organised by:
- governments?
- the media institutions themselves?
- the operations of the market?

Before we try to explore these questions, we need to sketch in the historical background to the regulation of media industries and how it is aligned to economic models, since without it you will find it difficult to understand contemporary debates fully.

One of the first modern thinkers to address the idea of personal freedom was Jean-Jacques Rousseau (1712–68) in *The Social Contract* (1762). He argued that individuals could only gain freedom by submitting to the 'General Will' of the society embodied in the democratic state – but the state must also act in a moral fashion and preserve the freedom of its citizens.

Historical background

Knowledge is power and has been recognised as such throughout history. Rulers and powerful classes have always tried to keep the mass of the population away from 'dangerous knowledge'. In Europe in the Middle Ages this meant a Christian Church which attempted to maintain a 'priestly language', Latin, as the basis for theological and academic texts. The church had control over education, which was restricted to those who could learn Latin. The invention of the printing press promised to introduce the first 'mass medium', circulating ideas to everyone who could learn to read in their own local or 'vernacular' language. It is no surprise that governments of every kind immediately saw the importance of exerting some form of control over what was printed. Sometimes they banned titles; sometimes they altered them and sometimes they taxed them – raising revenue as well as limiting their availability by artificially raising prices.

The 'mass media' developed as industrial activities from the end of the nineteenth century onwards. Until 1945, political events and associated economic policies produced a turbulent social and business world with revolutions, world war, economic prosperity (in the US in the early 1920s) and then worldwide economic depression. In this context, a difference between US and European ideas about media institutions began to emerge. In Europe there was a tendency towards forms of government intervention in the new industry of radio and television broadcasting, largely for political reasons. (See 'Case study: Television as institution'.) **Public service broadcasting** is also evident in other developed countries such as Canada, Australia and Japan and is generally regulated by a set of requirements laid down in a founding charter or licence and then monitored for performance. But this was also linked to other forms of publicly funded activity in countries with ideologies developed to support collective or cooperative, 'social' ownership. By contrast, US ideas about the new industries stressed 'unfettered' capitalist enterprise and only a very limited role for state intervention.

In the US, political events did give rise to some public sector media activities, such as the theatre programme devised as a means of entertaining and educating the poor as part of Roosevelt's New Deal during the 1930s Depression. This movement promoted the careers of many writers and directors, including Orson Welles, but was viciously attacked by some Hollywood executives. Many of those who took part in the programme were later attacked as dangerous radicals during the anti-communist 'witch hunts' of the late 1940s and early 1950s. In the US, publicly funded media activities have remained marginal: media

Perhaps the first important 'media product' was the Bible printed in 1455 by Johann Gutenberg and celebrated by the media academic Marshall McLuhan in the title of his 1962 book *The Gutenberg Galaxy*. That Bible was in Latin, but the new printing technology was used for William Tyndale's 'Common English' translation in 1525 – he was burnt at the stake in 1536 for heresy.

Stamp duty is still levied on certain legal documents in the UK, but in the early nineteenth century it was used as a means of suppressing radical newspapers. The Newspaper Stamp Duties Act of 1819 was an effective means of 'regulating' newspapers by making them too expensive for working people to purchase. After newspaper and advertising duties were removed in 1855, the popular press began to grow.

Cradle Will Rock (US 1999), directed by Tim Robbins, depicts the true story of a leftist musical drama production in New York in the 1930s and the attempts to prevent its staging.

activity is essentially a business enterprise or the product of an endowment by philanthropists (who have often made large profits from business enterprise). From the development of radio stations in the 1920s onwards, US broadcasting has been dominated by networks selling advertising. Public service broadcasting on European lines has been limited. This means that regulation of broadcasting in the US has been conducted by a federal agency more concerned with maintaining competition than with laying down requirements about programming.

Outside broadcasting, the other media such as cinema, press and advertising developed systems of self-regulation as part of their institutionalisation in the twentieth century. **Self-regulation** means that institutions appoint committees or panels of individuals drawn from within the industry (and sometimes 'independents' from outside) who are charged with enforcing a code of behaviour.

The tradition of certificating films for cinema release dates back to 1912 in the UK. Hollywood introduced a restrictive Production Code in 1930, designed to head off criticism and potential boycotts from religious groups. The press and advertising industries have also developed 'codes' of behaviour as a defence against critics, and like cinema they have been subject to forms of censorship. However, they have not been subjected to the same regulatory environment that has faced broadcasters. (See the list of self-regulating institutions and their codes below.)

The centrality of broadcasting

Broadcasting has usually required some form of **statutory regulation**. Jostein Gripsrud (2002: 260) suggests several reasons why broadcasting is often seen to be the most important medium and therefore the one that gives the most concern to governments (this would have applied to radio in the 1930s–50s, but is now more a feature of television):

- Broadcasting has enormous 'reach', being accessible to almost everybody.
- People spend more time with radio and television than with any other medium.
- Television is located centrally in every country (despite local services, it is the medium which represents a national focus on events).
- Television dominates the agenda of the **public sphere**.
- Television is the most important medium for culture, both in the sense of a 'way of life' and in the sense of art – we get our sense of who we are and how we live primarily from television.

The House Committee on Un-American Activities (HUAC) began investigating Hollywood in 1947 and nine screenwriters and a director were eventually sent to prison for 'contempt' – refusing to 'name names' and to say whether they were members of the Communist Party. Karl Francis's film *One of the Hollywood Ten* (Spain/UK 2000) deals with this period and with the struggles to make *The Salt of the Earth* (US 1954) about a Mexican silver miners' strike.

See Chapter 7 on 'locations' and the handling of media products for a large and diverse market like the United States with its radical and conservative communities.

'In US movies before the 1960s, [the] Production Code dictated that characters got shot without bleeding, argued without swearing, and had babies without copulating' (Linda Williams in Nowell-Smith 1996: 490).

Statutory regulation means that the powers of the regulator are provided by Act of Parliament and are therefore enforceable by law. The BBC has traditionally been allowed to self-regulate, that status having been conferred by Royal Charter.

Public sphere a concept associated with the work of Jürgen Habermas, who used the term to refer to a social space in which everyone should be able to communicate their ideas about the state and the economy. In practice, the opportunities to do so are limited. The concept may always have been idealised. Nevertheless it is a powerful ideal used by many media theorists in opposition to the brute force of 'the marketplace'.

John Maynard Keynes (1883–1946) was a very influential figure, often credited with founding the discipline of macroeconomics, the study of the workings of the whole economy, rather than those of individual producers, consumers, etc. (microeconomics).

For all these reasons, television and, to a lesser extent, radio are considered too important to 'leave to the market', and governments have decided they should be regulated. We should also note the public safety issue of the control over radio frequencies (i.e. interference with communications for vital services).

Changes in the 'orthodoxy' of economic policy and new models

From the end of the Second World War (1945) until the early 1980s, the prevailing economic ideology in the developed world was 'Keynesianism' (named after the British economist **John Maynard Keynes**). This set of ideas saw government intervention in the economy as an essential tool for controlling inflation and unemployment across all the major capitalist economies. Keynesian policies saw governments 'regulating' their own spending so that, if a depression in the economy threatened, spending on public sector goods and services would be increased. The aim of government policy was to maintain economic prosperity and the general economic welfare of all aspects of society (i.e. 'full employment' and low inflation).

These policies provided relative economic stability and were accepted by all political parties in the UK and elsewhere. In Europe this allowed governments to fund public service broadcasters adequately so that programming could be 'producer-led'. Producers had budgets that allowed them to make a full range of programmes. The UK stood out in Europe as having a 'mixed economy' in television with a strong commercial sector in ITV, but one which was regulated alongside the BBC and had certain public service broadcasting obligations.

In the US, television broadcasting was a relatively stable market up to the 1970s, with two, and later three, big commercial networks competing with each other across the country and an array of local channels in each major city. The different approach to regulation in the US did not directly affect Europe at this time. In the era before full globalisation of media activity, the main issue for Europeans was the import of Hollywood films and filmed TV series (westerns, police series, etc.). At various times imports were restricted in an attempt to protect local markets.

In the late 1970s, the economic orthodoxy began to shift for a number of reasons:

- The 1973–4 'oil crisis' raised the price of oil dramatically and caused energy shortages in the West.
- Social unrest at home and military disaster in Vietnam hit US confidence.

The economist J.K. Galbraith (born in Canada in 1908) was a staunch supporter of Keynesian policies and of the welfare programme 'The Civil Society', introduced by the Democrats in the US in the 1960s. This was a hugely controversial government intervention in US life along European lines, tackling poverty, housing, etc. Galbraith's 1958 book *The Affluent Society* predicted what he saw as the future problems of any society which ignored the 'public good' in favour of 'private pleasure'. He coined the term 'private affluence/public squalor'.

Nearly fifty years later this comment seems remarkably prescient in relation to the US and the UK. A revealing insight into debates about government intervention in the US economy can be found in readers' comments on the republication of Galbraith's book in 1998 (look up the book on www.amazon.com). From a European perspective, the fierce attacks on government intervention of any kind, as delivered by some readers in America, seem extreme.

Galbraith's later book, *The New Industrial State* (1967), introduced ideas about the importance of 'corporate power' in the workings of the modern economy. Galbraith became a Harvard professor in 1948 and his ideas are now being discussed, by contemporary commentators such as Naomi Klein or George Monbiot, as if they were 'newly formed'. (See 'J K Galbraith goes mainstream' by Daniel Ben-Ami, www.spiked-online.com, 5 August 2004).

- Worn-out industries in the UK were suffering from chronic under investment etc.
- The whole post-war system of international trade and monetary exchange was collapsing.

Governments began to abandon Keynesianism, partly because what had previously seemed 'impossible' – unemployment and inflation rising together – was now happening. They began to turn towards 'monetarism' and later the promotion of so-called 'free market capitalism'. In its extreme form, as formulated by the US economist Milton Friedman, monetarism meant that governments intervened only in the flow of money in the economy: money was all that mattered, and investment decisions were made only by referring to the prevailing money market conditions (the 'interest rate') and the potential profit from investment (i.e. rather than by whether investment would produce a social benefit). It is important to note here that governments didn't all embrace the new orthodoxy with the same fervour and their actions generally followed the previous distinctions between Europe and the US. Generally, France and Germany were most reluctant to change, the US was most eager and the UK was somewhere in the middle.

'Free market' economics

Before we go much further, it is important to think through how an economic model works. In simple terms, economists study the actions of buyers and sellers in markets and the cost of factors of production such as labour, capital, raw materials, etc. in order to try to predict what will happen. To do this, they use hypothetical constructs. One of these is the 'perfect market' in which everyone has 'perfect knowledge' and buyers and sellers make rational decisions. These decisions act on the levers of the **price mechanism** and the market controls itself with an 'invisible hand'. When the supply of something goes down, the price goes up and more suppliers join the market until the price falls again, and so on.

But this is a theoretical market. In the 'real world', markets are 'imperfect' as knowledge is not equally accessible to all buyers and sellers. Because of social and political considerations, governments, businesses and other organisations and groups of individuals deliberately 'distort' markets, usually, but not always, for good reasons. In the discussion that follows, we are concerned with different emphases on the importance of 'markets' and 'competition' on the one hand and 'intervention' and price control on the other. At one end of the spectrum there are free marketeers who perhaps believe that a free market is possible and that it equates to personal liberty. At the other are societies that accept markets only within a general framework governed by other social priorities (universal access, 'quality' of products, etc.). If we accept that 'globalisation' (Chapter 15) has created a 'global market', we might expect a whole series of disputes between governments whose 'take' on markets is different. We'll look next at what happened in the 1980s and how it has affected the media environment (in particular the broadcasting environment) we now live in.

ACTIVITY 16.1

Study a market

The street market is the closest we get in the real world to the idealised 'perfect market'. Find a local street market:

- Check the prices of the same goods on different stalls – are they all the same?
- How much do the same goods cost in a local supermarket or high street store?
- Are they actually the same goods – or a different variety/from a different supplier?

- How do you think the local market compares to the global market in these goods? Is it helpful to use the street market as a model for the market in films, CDs or television programmes?

Figure 16.1 A typical street market in Italy. Is this a good 'model' for the media industries?

Deregulation, liberalisation and media institutions

Starting in the 1980s:

- The new economic orthodoxy saw a move away from government funding of public sector organisations towards support for more 'open', 'competitive' markets. This meant outlawing what were called 'restrictive practices', selling state-controlled enterprises to new shareholders ('privatisation'), contracting out public services to private companies and encouraging the formation of new markets.

- New technologies – cable, satellite and cheaper broadcasting technologies – offered a sudden increase in the possibilities for new broadcast channels, more choice, but fragmentation of the market. (See Chapter 7 and the case study following Chapter 4.)

New technologies were also important in other media industries such as newspapers and magazines. Newspaper owners, led by Rupert Murdoch, took advantage of new labour laws to break trade union power in order to exploit these new technologies. They were not constrained by public service requirements. Ironically, the *Sun*, Murdoch's best-selling title, had once belonged to the Trade Union Congress as the *Daily Herald*.

Utilities refers to water, gas, electricity, telephone systems etc.

- New global media players emerged, some the result of privatisation of publicly owned 'utilities', capable of moving across national boundaries. In some cases they were welcomed by national governments and sometimes accepted reluctantly.

These changes destabilised the existing broadcasting environment, with public service broadcasters having to react to the presence of US companies or new European private sector companies working to the US model.

In economic terms the introduction of new channels and new services meant that television was no longer something that governments saw as a 'public good', to be treated as a special form of media activity in which everyone shares. Instead, it became a 'private good' just like any other media product such as a newspaper or magazine. (See Küng-Shankleman 2000: 29.)

In 1984 in the new 'free market', the UK government decided that so-called 'video nasties' should be censored by law – some markets are obviously more 'free' than others.

The UK Thatcher government (1979–90) supported this general trend and, with other parts of Europe following, the media market across the world moved into a phase of what some commentators called 'deregulation and liberalisation'. Linked government policies saw:

- the privatisation of what had been public sector monopolies in broadcasting and telecommunications. In the UK, the two best examples of this were the sale of the telecommunications business developed by the Post Office to form British Telecom and the sale of the national network of television transmitters that eventually produced NTL. These new private sector companies were free to attract investment into new media products and services

As we've suggested elsewhere, the language of 'free markets' often employs attractive metaphors, from the cosy image of a market square itself, through phrases such as 'flexible', 'slimmed down', 'downsizing', 'trimming' (these last most often used of 'waste' workers). In Britain regulation is often imaged as 'the nanny state'. Can you think of a more attractive metaphor?

- the 'loosening' of regulatory controls, especially in broadcasting, which allowed previously tightly regulated ITV to lose some of its public service obligations
- the 'opening up' of UK media markets with new licences for broadcasting services, particularly in radio, satellite and cable. Restrictions on 'cross-media ownership' were also gradually lifted. This was the **liberalisation** of the market.

Ironically, this period actually saw an increase in the number of regulators, with the creation of Oftel to look after the new telecommunications industry and of new regulatory responsibilities for the certification of video releases. Nevertheless, the effect was 'less restriction' of certain kinds of media activity, and this was the purpose of deregulation.

Oftel The Office of Telecommunications started a trend for regulators to be called 'Of . . .', e.g. the later establishment of Ofcom or Office of Communications (which absorbed Oftel). Bureaucracies, necessary or not, are often the butt of jokes. When 'road-pricing' was mooted as government policy in 2005, 'Ofroad' was one suggestion for a name for the agency which would oversee it.

The contemporary regulatory environment

Since the 1990s there have been changes in government and therefore some changes in the approach to the surviving public sector in the UK.

However, the media environment created by the arrival of new technologies and new broadcasters is here to stay for the foreseeable future. If the UK government decides to regulate, it must take account of European Union policy (see the discussion of magazine distribution in Chapter 13) and the implications of the global media market. We can identify six different types of regulation, distinguished by how the power to regulate is located.

Labour, in power since 1997, has had an ambivalent attitude towards the 'public sector' and the concept of regulation. It has been happy to raise more money for public expenditure, but often spent it in partnership with private sector businesses.

1 Direct control by government

Some countries are controlled by authoritarian regimes which intervene directly in the activities of the media industries (Myanmar (still known as 'Burma'), North Korea etc.). But such intervention isn't unknown in democracies. It isn't so long ago that the UK government prevented the voices of IRA spokespersons being heard on radio or television, or issued 'D' notices warning that news stories were covered by the Official Secrets Act and should not be published. In this respect the UK has a relatively 'closed' form of government, which is often revealed as such in comparison with the 'open' US system. Aspects of telecommunications activity were regulated by a UK government department until the creation of Ofcom in 2003.

ACTIVITY 16.2

'Closed government' and the individual

Find out what you can about the Official Secrets Act 1989 and the Freedom of Information Act 2000.

- Is there an obvious contradiction in the titles of these two pieces of legislation?
- What kinds of issues do the Acts suggest could be problematic for journalists and media institutions in the UK?
- How does anti-terrorist legislation affect the situation?

2 Delegation by government to an independent statutory regulator

This is the current system used in the UK for commercial radio, television and telecommunications with Ofcom as the regulator, established by statute or Act of Parliament – in this case the Communications Act 2003.

3 Self-regulation by media producers

This has two meanings. In a formal sense the media institution itself appoints a panel to oversee regulation. But it also works 'informally' through individual producers constraining themselves to avoid any chance of later demands for changes or cuts. The BBC is 'self-regulating', although it is being put under more pressure by Ofcom as the nature of 'broadcasting' changes.

4 The general legal framework as a restraint

This is still the case in the UK in relation to obscenity and blasphemy. If legal charges are made against media producers, the results are often not satisfactory for either side. In 2005, proposed new legislation seeking to extend protection from 'race and religious hatred' was attacked by critics as potentially restricting writers and comedians (even though, in case law, protection for Sikhs and Jews already exists). Laws on blasphemy are problematic in secular societies – as atheists ask 'Who protects *us* from offensive remarks?'

5 'Market forces' regulate

If you want to get a sense of how the most vocal 'free marketeers' argue their case, go to the website of Tech Central Station (TCS) at www.techcentralstation.com, 'Where free markets meet technology'.

Audiences are said to use their own judgement over purchases which affects future industry activities through the **price mechanism**. This is the view of the free market model which assumes that it is possible and desirable to allow the market to 'look after itself'.

6 Audience pressure regulates

There is a long history of action by religious and 'culturally conservative' groups in the US which have at different times identified various media products as 'morally dangerous' – cinema, rock music, television, video games. In the UK, there have been similar but less powerful groups, as well as others more concerned with ideas about the 'quality' of programming. In 2004 there were signs that US-style aggressive action by religious groups was starting in the UK with the campaign to stop the BBC broadcast of *Jerry Springer the Opera* and, more locally, (successful) pressure on a theatre in Birmingham to take off a play set in a Sikh temple.

UK regulators

In the UK, as in most other countries, regulation currently represents a rag-bag of different strategies. All six types of regulation operate in some way.

UK regulators

Self-regulation

ASA The **Advertising Standards Authority** is an example of self-regulation by the advertising industry. An independent panel drawn mainly from outside the industry uses an agreed Code to monitor advertisements and sales promotions placed in the press, on posters, internet sites and other electronic media and cinema screens. In November 2004, Ofcom 'contracted out' the regulation of all broadcast advertising (i.e. radio and television) to the ASA. Website: www.asa.org.uk.

BBFC The **British Board of Film Classification** was set up as a self-regulating agency by the UK film industry in 1912. (It was first titled the British Board of Film Censors.) Under the Video Recordings Act of 1984, the BBFC also became the agency for the compulsory certification of all video (and now DVD) titles in distribution. In this sense, the BBFC has a statutory role. Website: www.bbfc.org.uk.

PCC The Press Complaints Commission represents self-regulation for the newspaper and magazine industries. It undertakes to investigate complaints about editorial material in all UK national and regional newspapers and magazines, through application of a Code drawn up by editors. Website: www.pcc.org.uk.

Statutory regulators

Ofcom The Communications Act of 2003 established a new UK regulator vested with powers formerly held by a range of different regulatory bodies as well as some new concerns. Ofcom replaced the ITC (Independent Television Commission), BSC (Broadcasting Standards Commission), the Radio Authority, Oftel and RA (Radiocommunications Agency). Ofcom's specific duties fall into six areas:

1 ensuring the optimal use of the electromagnetic spectrum
2 ensuring that a wide range of electronic communications services – including high-speed data services – is available throughout the UK

3 ensuring a wide range of TV and radio services of high quality and wide appeal

4 maintaining plurality in the provision of broadcasting

5 applying adequate protection for audiences against offensive or harmful material

6 applying adequate protection for audiences against unfairness or the infringement of privacy.

Ofcom's regulatory principles:

- Ofcom will regulate with a clearly articulated and publicly reviewed annual plan, with stated policy objectives.

- Ofcom will intervene where there is a specific statutory duty to work towards a public policy goal which markets alone cannot achieve.

- Ofcom will operate with a bias against intervention, but with a willingness to intervene firmly, promptly and effectively where required.

- Ofcom will strive to ensure its interventions are evidence-based, proportionate, consistent, accountable and transparent in both deliberation and outcome.

- Ofcom will always seek the least intrusive regulatory mechanisms to achieve its policy objectives.

- Ofcom will research markets constantly and will aim to remain at the forefront of technological understanding.

- Ofcom will consult widely with all relevant stakeholders and assess the impact of regulatory action before imposing regulation upon a market.

Ofcom is a 'super regulator'. So wide is its remit and the range of its regulatory powers that there must be some concern that it could become overly bureaucratic. Its concerns include the level of media literacy in the UK and it has organised consultation to discover what various parties think media literacy might be and how it might best be promoted. This means Ofcom, which for most of its activities will be in consultation with the Department for Culture, Media and Sport and the Department for Trade and Industry, will also need to liaise with the Department for Education and Skills. Website: www.ofcom. org.uk.

The Communications Act which established Ofcom was not universally welcomed. One of its most trenchant critics was the Campaign for Press and Broadcasting Freedom (CPBF) which argued against the shift to support markets and the concomitant assumption that plurality and diversity will be served by 'a competitive free market'. The CPBF saw two problems with this:

- The loosening of ownership controls is likely to reduce the number of providers (one owner of ITV, one cable provider, etc.). This has indeed happened.
- Whichever global media corporations remain in the newly consolidated UK market, they will be likely to share the same editorial 'lines' (see Chapter 4) on major issues and the same basic attitudes towards broadcasting services. If free market competition is encouraged, the public service providers will be marginalised and plurality will be reduced.

In addition:

- The White Paper suggested a 'negative view' of regulation, especially in relation to 'protecting consumers' and ensuring competition. Previously regulation had supported the promotion of public service broadcasting with its positive aims. Media studies teachers are also likely to want to move media literacy policies away from 'protection' towards 'enabling' activities.

ACTIVITY 16.3

CPBF

Check the website at www.cpbf.org.uk. What kinds of arguments about the work of Ofcom is CPBF making now?

'Ofcomwatch is an informal group blog (www.ofcomwatch.co.uk) commenting on the processes and practices of the Office of Communications (Ofcom) and related media and communications regulation issues both in the United Kingdom and around the world.'

The US regulator is the Federal Communications Commission (FCC), an independent agency funded by the US government 'working to make sure the nation's communications systems are working seamlessly and competitively in your best interest' (website www.fcc.gov). Although by UK standards the FCC appears a very 'light touch regulator', there are several campaigns fighting against its actions to 'curtail free speech'. See, for example, www.firethefcc.com and www.stopfcc.com.

What might a 'free market' mean for the UK?

Television and the price mechanism

As we have indicated above, the test for US-style free markets in media goods and services is likely to be television in the UK and other parts of Europe. The arrival of **multi-channel television** has been embraced by large sections of the UK population giving the UK the highest 'penetration' of digital television services in Europe. This development might at first glance look like a triumph for the new market freedoms and 'increased choice' in television services. But we need to look a little closer to understand fully the complexity of what is happening. (Some of these issues are also addressed in 'Case study: Television as institution'.)

The basis for the free market model is the price mechanism. In a truly 'free' market, there would be many sellers and many buyers. Some sellers would fall by the wayside, but new sellers would emerge through free access to trading. This would deliver 'freedom of choice'. Let's consider the 'real' rather than the theoretical market. In most European countries, there are at least five ways of paying for television:

- via some form of taxation (e.g. the licence fee)
- higher prices for goods in order to support advertising
- subscription to receive a cable, satellite or encrypted broadcast system
- pay per view per programme
- direct payment for 'interactive services'.

Let's consider each as a payment mode. The UK *licence fee* has several advantages:

- Everyone pays but some groups have concessions (visually impaired, over-75s, etc.).
- It is efficient to collect, so revenue is not wasted.
- In 2005 all BBC programmes were available for a charge of £126.50 or less than £2.50 per week.

But the main advantage is that universal payment means the possibility of broadcasting remaining as a 'public good' – a service to provide something we could not buy ourselves (or perhaps would not consider buying, but may still need).

The weakness of the licence fee is that under the new orthodoxy it is increasingly open to attack by the 'free market' lobby because it is compulsory. This lobby can (and does) argue that people are forced to pay for a service that they do not want to use. The main defence against this charge is the popularity of BBC programmes. If the BBC's share of the broadcast market falls below a certain figure, the licence fee could become difficult to defend on this basis. The actions of Ofcom as a regulator are crucial here. In order to maintain popularity, the BBC must be allowed to make popular entertainment programmes. A policy that encouraged the BBC to concentrate on news, current affairs and arts programming at the expense of *EastEnders*, *Strictly Come Dancing* and *Match of the Day* could be very damaging.

Advertising is losing ground as a source of television funding:

- It is increasingly difficult for ITV to deliver large audiences.
- Technology is beginning to offer simple ways of avoiding advertisements.

ITV programmes have never been 'free'. Advertisers have effectively paid for the programmes and these costs have to be covered by profits from sales. However, most of us have accepted this system without making direct connections between the programmes we watch and the goods we buy (most of us like to think that we aren't influenced by ads, but the advertisers must have been convinced that we are, because they have funded ITV for fifty years). Note that the regulation of advertising on ITV

It is often forgotten that the licence fee also pays for BBC radio programming, which because of the strength of national BBC Network Radio, still gains the majority share – but as new broadcast franchises are awarded this too may shrink. (In 2005 it appeared much stronger in market terms than BBC Network Television.)

See 'Case study: Selling audiences'.

(a limit on minutes per hour, a clear distinction between ads and programming, etc.) has arguably helped to maintain ITV as a watchable service. A looser regulatory structure risks an advertising environment in which the narrative flow of a programme is constantly interrupted by commercial breaks, some of which may be difficult to distinguish from the programme itself. Rick Instrell (2005) examined a US broadcast of an episode of *Friends* and counted three advertising breaks, lasting over eight minutes in total, in a programme of less than twenty-two minutes. Regulation has helped to restrain the excesses of advertising-funded television and certainly until the 1990s the lack of any direct connection between advertisers and programmes allowed ITV, as well as the BBC, to be 'producer-led' – i.e. to make a range of interesting programmes that would attract significant audiences, large enough to satisfy advertisers. This situation ended with the new offers from satellite and cable.

One of the ways that ITV has tried to counteract the 'avoidance' of ads has been through programme sponsorship, which allows a closer connection between the programme and the ad, so that the brand appears as part of the programme title card. (See Chapter 8 'Case study: Selling audiences'.)

Subscription television implies a willingness to pay for extra television services. In one sense this is similar to the purchase of consumer goods such as a DVD player etc. It is a willingness to pay not for a specific programme, but for a new technology.

Perhaps a majority of BSkyB and cable subscribers will purchase 'premium channel' subscriptions on top of a basic package. This has been the basis for the growth of BSkyB's business with the following outcomes:

- Families with children are more likely to be in 'multi-channel homes'.
- Sport and movies have been the main premium services.

Children are important to advertisers and to the new television service providers. They don't have any prior experience of 'public service broadcasting'. They don't have expectations of 'quality dramas' and educational programming. But are they happy simply to choose from a range of animation programmes? BBC children's programming has not capitulated completely in the new environment and when new BBC digital channels became available, children's programming on CBBC and CBeebies was the most successful element of the new offer. In June 2005, CBeebies, the channel for younger children, was one of the most watched channels on multi-channel television, competing well with Sky 1 and Sky Sports 1 (source: BARB). On the other hand, the availability of so many channels to young consumers introduces the idea of choice as 'natural' and as these television viewers grow up they will likely not think about the subscription payment. Will they resent the licence fee?

For older viewers, paying a monthly subscription will also be a reminder of a period, up to the 1980s, when many people rented rather than bought televisions and VCRs. This rental culture helped VCRs take off in the UK before most other countries.

The 'market value' of a new movie on DVD rental or retail is indicated by the 'window' in which a premium price is attached. After a few months, the purchase or rental price will drop. Later still, in the next release window, the film will appear on subscription or PPV at a lower price. Finally it will appear free on terrestrial television.

In December 2003, BSkyB earned an average of £369 from each 'User' or 'Subscriber'. With the licence fee, the average Sky subscriber is paying out around £500 per year, or around £10 per week, on television services. This isn't a particularly large sum compared to the average cost of a cinema ticket, a DVD purchase or a premiership football ticket – especially since the television set can be watched by anyone in the family.

Pay per view television (PPV) hasn't yet taken off in the UK or the rest of Europe to the same extent as in North America. Once again, it is primarily concerned with entertainment (movies or music events) or sport, with a focus on unusual high-profile events such as boxing matches (for which US viewers are willing to pay upwards of $40 per event). The important point to note in the context of this chapter is that PPV offers the clearest sense of 'paying for television' just like any other product. Assuming you have already bought/rented the necessary equipment, a decision to 'pay to view' is no different from purchasing a ticket to go to the live event. This should give the clearest indication of what a 'free market' in television might look like – at least in terms of sports or music events.

Figure 16.2 The PPV offer from Irish broadcaster Setanta available to UK viewers via Sky's Astra satellite (from www.setanta.com).

In 'Case study: Television as institution', we also noted that the willingness of viewers to pay something to 'participate' in forms of interactive television, texting or phoning in to programmes to vote, etc. is another example of a direct decision to pay (although of course most people don't think of the payment as such). Nevertheless it is an indication of 'willingness to pay' and in future it is likely that more

PPV opportunities will be available on computer screens and mobile phones, along with subscription packages.

Paying for interactivity is a relatively recent development in which viewers choose to spend money on extra services such as voting for gameshow contestants or entering competitions (gambling really, since many competitions require little skill) or telephone shopping. It could be argued that this moves television more towards the casino or a general leisure activity.

Controlling the television market

With all of these payment methods, the television market in Europe is a 'mixed economy', with the intervention of the regulator having an impact on pricing. We can't simply look at the US experience and decide what would happen without the current level of regulation. Because of the existence of a large public service provider like the BBC, companies like BSkyB have adopted certain strategies which have had consequences outside television:

- Sky Sports has spent heavily on acquiring rights to football, cricket, rugby, etc. This has helped Premiership football clubs buy world-class players – and created a divide between rich and poor clubs in English football. Sky's expenditure on sports, at £723 million in 2003, is the largest element of its programming budget. The second largest element is the purchase of rights to movies.

- BSkyB has become a dominant player in UK television through concentration on sport and movies and a schedule of mainly acquired (rather than commissioned) programming, apart from news. Some sports fans fear that in future BSkyB may be able to reduce the payments it makes to sports bodies now that other potential bidders have fallen away (e.g. with the monopoly position re Sky and live test cricket in 2006).

In theory, the existence of other commercial television operators on terrestrial/analogue (i.e. ITV, Channel 4 and Five) and digital cable (NTL and Telewest) should ensure a competitive television market in the UK. But this cannot be a 'free market'. Besides the BBC, the other terrestrial broadcasters also have public service commitments to varying degrees, constraining them from direct competition with BSkyB. So far, BSkyB has remained ahead of the others, but the gradual relaxation of ownership rules may eventually lead to larger multinational corporations moving in. (See 'Case study: Television as institution' for some of Ofcom's conclusions about PSB and competition in the digital television future.)

Payments via voting for 'Great Britons' etc. on BBC channels is a move towards another US model which sees 'public broadcasting channels' supported by donations from audiences who want to see the channels continue to broadcast. We might call this a 'charity model' of funding – going back to the world before the Welfare State and public services funded via taxation.

Classification, censorship and sex and violence

As we've argued, the price mechanism and the free market are associated with 'value-free' economics. This means an economics which deals only with the effects of a change in prices on supply and demand and not with questions about what economic policy should be or what would be a price that was 'good for society'. The importance of this distinction is clear when we consider issues of classification and censorship.

'We stand for less government, lower taxes, free enterprise and solid family values . . . we are guided by the principles, which limit government, promote free enterprise and Judeo-Christian values' (from the website of the 'Free Market Foundation' in Texas, www.freemarket.org). By contrast, the British Labour movement, which helped create the Welfare State and other forms of socialist enterprise for working people, was strongly supported by Nonconformist churches in the nineteenth and twentieth centuries.

In a 'free market' we might expect to see a thriving trade in pornographic material, as in many other European countries, if that is what people wish to buy. Indeed, developments in media technologies (video, DVD, the internet, etc.) have nearly always been adopted first within the porn industry – since it is the least regulated and most market-driven media industry. However, the very advocates of the free market are often among those who wish to control access to the marketplace for certain kinds of products. The result is that in terms of 'sex and violence' we expect to see the development of some form of self-censorship in all media, whereby the distribution companies in that medium agree to set standards for acceptable products. This has happened with film, magazines and, more recently, video and computer games.

The oddity of the debate about sex and violence in broadcasting (or in print or on film) is that the issue is rarely put to the market test. We don't know what would happen if 'hard' material were freely available – if it is unacceptable to a large number of media consumers, perhaps 'the market' would drop it from general release when it didn't sell? There are many pressure groups arguing for censorship but few actively campaigning against. The libertarian might argue that the current attitude to self-censorship is patronising towards the audience. If someone is capable of making a decision about whether a media product represents 'value for money', why can't they also decide whether or not it is offensive and 'liable to corrupt'? And if they can't decide, what makes a programme-maker better qualified to decide? This is a complete refutation of public service broadcasting, without the qualifications of the social market position.

In some respects this libertarian position looks acceptable (assuming that children are protected from 'offensive' material). However, 'freedom to choose' is also the freedom to be assailed by fierce marketing. With that comes the possible acceptability of more explicit sex or violence, leading to more of such programming and less overall variety of material.

ACTIVITY 16.4

Offensive material

How do you think offensive material should be handled in the media? How would you define 'offensive material'?

- What would be the consequences of a media environment without any classification of offensive material? What do you think would happen in a free market?
- What are the arguments for and against such material being available only through licensed outlets at premium prices (could it be taxed like cigarettes and alcohol)?
- What are the arguments for banning such material altogether?
- Why is self-censorship preferred to an 'official censor' in non-broadcast media industries?

This topic is a good one to choose if you want to try producing a video or audio 'debate'-style programme. You should quite easily find people prepared to adopt specific positions. But first you will have to decide whether it is going to be a 'balanced' programme, or whether as producer you want to slant it in any particular way. In other words, you need to think about the institutional factors.

(See the BBFC website at www.sbbfc.co.uk for thoughtful discussion of 'classification'.)

In March 2002, a court found against the BBC after an election campaign broadcast for an anti-abortion group was not broadcast because it contained 'offensive material'.

The public gets the media it deserves?

Much of the UK debate about television (and radio and, possibly, newspapers) is about the 'level' or 'seriousness' of programming and scheduling. Public service broadcasting in the period up to the 1980s was heavily geared to ensuring that certain kinds of programme were scheduled on all channels in peak time. Current affairs and news and arts programming were all prescribed, as well as education during the day and at other times. The loosening of such requirements allowed ITV and then Channel Five and the satellite and cable companies to target BBC programmes in the schedule with more 'ratings-friendly' shows. The BBC struggled within its remit to compete, and towards the end of the 1990s various 'test cases' were widely discussed in the press and by regulators:

- the disappearance of current affairs and arts programmes from peak time
- reduction of news programmes on ITV and the move to 10 p.m. by the BBC for its main evening news.

In the 'free market', are these changes inevitable? The market is reflected in ratings and these in turn are used in negotiations with advertisers. Scheduling is a strategy game in which the scheduler makes an 'educated guess' about how well a programme will fare in a particular time-slot. Because an instant response is important in ratings terms, the scheduler is likely to:

- risk only those programmes which are formulaic (have worked before)
- take off very quickly any programmes which don't achieve the target rating.

In the regulated market with strong support for the public broadcaster, the scheduler would often allow a programme to 'build' an audience – especially if it was a new kind of programme. This was 'production-led' scheduling rather than 'ratings-led' television. How do you see the current schedule on BBC1 and BBC2 compared to ITV, Channel 4 and Five? Is it full of programmes looking for 'easy acceptance'? The proponents of the free market in broadcasting are likely to offer these observations:

- People want popular programmes: why shouldn't they have what they want? (This argument is often couched in class terms, with the public service supporters represented as being a middle-class elite and out of touch with the tastes of the majority.)
- The market is very conscious of 'niche audiences' who want very different kinds of programmes. These audiences are often ABC1 and attractive to advertisers. As such they are targeted by schedulers.
- The market makes producers more focused and more efficient (an argument often made to explain the success of some imported US programming).
- Were the majority of programmes any better under the old system? Yes, there were some great television plays and some classic sit-coms, but what about the rest?

ACTIVITY 16.5

Comparing schedules

Compare the schedules shown in Figure 16.3 with those for a Saturday evening on the same three channels today.

- How do the arguments above work out?
- Which specific programmes from 1980 are unlikely to appear now?
- Was there a greater diversity in 1980 with evidence of the public service requirement?
- Or are the free marketeers right?

BBC1	BBC2	ITV
5.50 Wonder Woman (US series)	5.50 Mr Smith's Indoor Garden	6.00 Happy Days (US sitcom)
6.40 Jim'll Fix It (Jimmy Saville gameshow)	6.15 Open Door (Community access programme)	6.30 Film: *The Valley of Gwangi* (US 1969)
7.15 All Creatures Great and Small (UK comedy drama series)	6.45 Test Cricket (Australia v. West Indies)	8.15 The Faith Brown Chat Show
8.05 Dick Emery Show (UK comedian)	7.15 News and Sport	8.45 Enemy at the Door (UK WWII drama series)
8.40 Dallas (US series)	7.30 International Table Tennis	9.45 News and Sport
9.10 News	8.05 Film: *The Petrified Forest* (US 1936)	10.00 *Heartland: Family* (UK single drama)
9.40 Match of the Day	9.25 Animated Conversation	11.00 Film: *Licensed to Kill* (UK 1965)
10.50 Parkinson (Chat Show)	9.30 Playhouse: *Lifelike* by John Challen (single drama)	12.35 Closedown
11.50 Weather and Closedown	10.25 Something of a Miracle: 1979 Eisteddfod at Llangollen	
	11.15 News on 2	
	11.20 Film: *Rosemary's Baby* (US 1968)	
	1.35 Closedown	

Figure 16.3 The evening television schedules for Saturday, 26 January 1980, when there were only three channels.

'Free choices'?

'Freedom of choice' is seen by the free marketeers as a winning slogan. But what does it mean? As a traveller walking down an alley in Baghdad a thousand years ago, you might well have been able to buy a carpet or a sack of dates from one of many sellers, making your choice based on knowledge of all the prices and a chance to see all the goods. Your purchase decision may even have led to another buyer lowering prices. Go to the 'media bazaar' anywhere in today's global media marketplace and your choice isn't quite so simple. The chances are that you will know most about the products with the biggest marketing budgets. Products from smaller independent products may not even be 'on sale' at all if the producers can't afford to hire a stall. What kind of choice is being offered?

In Chapter 13 we refer to the way in which modern distribution methods have increased access to books, DVDs, CDs, etc. Although your chance of seeing a wide range of films at your local multiplex is not very good (i.e. the same nine or ten films play at most multiplexes), you have the opportunity via internet shopping (as long as you have a home connection and a credit card) to buy any one of thousands of DVDs to be delivered to your door. That is the power of 'the market'. Of course, you

'Free markets' are supposed to appeal to sellers as well as buyers. In August 2005, an 'amateur' cameraman had some exclusive footage of suspects for London bombings being arrested. He sold it to ITN, despite a higher price offered by Sky News – because he didn't approve of Rupert Murdoch's domination of the media (broadcastnow.co.uk, 8 August 2005).

'Choosing' your computer

How did you choose your computer? If you haven't yet bought one, what would influence your choice?

Worldwide, 96 per cent of people use a Windows PC, made from widely available components. Was it price or familiarity that led consumers to make this choice? In fact, we don't choose a computer, but an operating system (OS). Most computers are manufactured from standard components, so it is Microsoft's Windows OS that makes the difference.

Less than 3 per cent worldwide chose an Apple Macintosh with its distinctive OS. Was it because Macs were more expensive or because most people have to use PCs at work or at school? In 2005, the price of Macs fell and the new OS, 'Tiger', was agreed by most commentators to be far superior to the latest Windows software. Yet when Mac sales did rise, it was the 'fashion icon', the iPod, that was credited with revitalising Apple, not the price competitiveness and operating efficiency of its laptop or desktop computers. Free software that does everything that Microsoft's packages do has been available for some time, based on 'open source' coding and running in Windows. Price does not seem to be the issue – this is clearly not a 'free market'.

Since 1998, various government agencies in the US and in Europe have fought Microsoft in court, attempting to curtail the company's 'monopoly power' over PC operating systems and 'utility software' such as word processing and web browsing. In 2005 the legal action was still ongoing. The defenders of Microsoft claim it got to its position of such domination because it was a successful 'competitor' in computer software markets. The prosecutors of the case believe Microsoft distorted the market (by 'bundling' its software in complete packages sold with computers). Can they both be right? We might conclude that the crucial issue here is lack of knowledge or 'fear of the unknown' which prevents consumers 'risking' software from companies other than Microsoft.

In order to determine whether the consumer has benefited from this domination of the software market since 1995, try one of the free competitors to Microsoft's web browser (e.g. Firefox from GetFirefox.com) and decide for yourself.

may help to put your local video shop, bookshop and record shop out of business. That is the power of 'the market' as well. Are there any social benefits in having a record shop manager to talk to or to sell tickets for concerts or copies of your band's CD? If you think there are, keeping them might require some 'intervention' in 'the market'.

See Case study: 'Music industries' for more on this.

References and further reading

Gripsrud, Jostein (2002) *Understanding Media Culture*, London: Arnold.

Instrell, Rick (2005) 'The economic shaping of US television drama',
Media Education Journal, 37.

Küng-Shankleman, Lucy (2000) *Inside the BBC and CNN*, London:
Routledge.

Nowell-Smith, Geoffrey (ed.) (1996) *The Oxford History of World Cinema*,
Oxford: Oxford University Press.

Websites

www.cpbf.org.uk
www.ofcom.org.uk

Part IV
Reference

Jim Carrey and Kate Winslet in *Eternal Sunshine of the Spotless Mind* (US 2004). Credit: Focus Features

Glossary of key terms

Listed below are some of the key terms we have used (and one or two others you may come across), and which you will need to know, with short 'thumbnail' definitions. Some common words are referenced only when they have special meanings in media studies. Use this glossary in conjunction with the index, contents page and chapter 'menus' to find the material you want. In many cases, you could use **Wikipedia** to find a fuller definition.

180-degree rule narrative continuity 'rule' on the placement of the camera in film-making (also known as 'not crossing the line')

3G 'third generation' mobile phone systems, developed to allow more media applications to be accessed via mobiles

A&R 'Artists and Repertoire' represent the main assets of companies in the music industry. Performers are signed on contract and rights are held on recordings

ABC Audit Bureau of Circulation – independent body which provides circulation figures of newspapers and magazines for advertisers

access media slots or opportunities enabling audiences either to become producers or to have some form of right to reply to dominant media producers, e.g. UK Radio 4's *Feedback* programme

acoustics the science of sound – here, a consideration of the environment for sound recording

Acrobat Adobe software that allows **pdf** files to be produced and read on any computer

ADR Automatic Dialogue Replacement – a process during feature film production, also known as 'looping', which allows actors to rerecord dialogue for greater clarity while watching themselves on screen

advertising agencies organisations which create and manage advertising campaigns, from conception to placement

aesthetics activities which try to understand or evaluate the sense of beauty or of form in a text

age profile the audience for a particular media text, classified according to age group

agenda prioritised list of items dealt with by a meeting, and by extension a media text, especially in news. Hence the term 'agenda setting', suggesting a **public sphere** whose 'meetings' are more likely to discuss topics 'at the top of the agenda'

analogue any device which represents a quality or value by a physical change in a measuring agent, e.g. the silver nitrate on photographic film which changes colour in response to light.

anamorphic lens distorting lens which 'squeezes' or 'unsqueezes' an image – used in widescreen film projection

anchoring (1) written or spoken text (e.g. caption, voice-over) used to control or select a specific reading of a visual image; (2) also refers to a person ('anchor') who introduces news items and often conducts interviews – both roles which can try to secure interpretation of them, one way or another

ancillary market refers to subsequent or 'additional' markets for a film or television programme after a first release in the primary market. DVD markets are now often more valuable than cinema or television markets, so perhaps the term is becoming problematic

anthropology study of the human species – applied in audience studies

anti-aliasing a computer software feature that reduces the effect of visible pixels in computer/video graphics

anti-trust legislation US government action taken to break up the monopoly power of large producers, e.g. the Paramount decision in 1948 forcing Hollywood studios to sell their cinema chains

arbitrary signifiers term used in semiotics; signifiers with no resemblance to the referent or the signified; see **iconic**, **indexical** and **symbolic**

archive any collection of similar material which can be used in future media productions, e.g. a film archive

artwork term used in printing to describe any material which will be used to make a printing plate – could be text or illustrations

ASA Advertising Standards Authority: regulator of advertising in newspapers, magazines, cinema, outdoors and, since November 2004, broadcasting (contracted by Ofcom)

aspect ratio the ratio of height to breadth of a cinema screen (e.g. 1:1.85) or breadth to height of a television screen (e.g. 16:9)

audience ethnographies research using ethnographic approaches; joining a specific audience group and working 'from the inside' as far as possible

auteur French term for author, used in '*la politique des auteurs*', a debate from 1950s–1960s film theory (see **authorship**)

authorship approach originating in film studies which places emphasis on an individual author (usually the director) rather than the collective and collaborative nature of production; see **auteur**

avant-garde an artistic movement which is 'ahead of the mainstream' and usually experimental

AVID name of the early market leader in provision of non-linear (digital) editing equipment. Often used as a generic term for computer editing of video or film, but now being challenged by **Final Cut Pro**.

'B' picture in the studio era, the shorter and less important feature in a cinematic double bill

back light the third light source in a conventional three-point lighting set-up for film and video. The back light helps the subject to stand out from the background

bandwidth referring to the amount of data that can be carried by a cable or a wireless transmission

BARB Broadcasters' Audience Research Board, the body in Britain which produces television viewing figures for the TV companies

base–superstructure critical term from early Marxism referring to the economic base on which is built the 'superstructure' of cultural and ideological institutions and assumptions

BBFC British Board of Film Classification

behaviourism/behaviourist movement in psychology which sees human behaviour as s omething which can be moulded by punishment and reward

Berliner a newspaper format, smaller than broadsheet, bigger than tabloid, adopted by the *Guardian* in 2005 and *Observer* in 2006

best boy assistant to the **gaffer** on a film shoot

bias/biased ideological 'slant' in debates around factual reporting. Has been questioned due to the rise of pluralist rather than binary ('two sides to every question') models of news, within a global and multimedia environment

bi-media journalism a BBC policy to train journalists for television and radio under the same scheme

binary oppositions sets of opposite values said to reveal the structure of cultures and, by extension, media texts; see **structuralism**

bit corruption of 'binary digit', the '0' or '1' in a stream of binary data. Often used as an indicator of 'quality' or 'resolution', e.g. '24-bit colour image' implies a palette of millions of colours described by different combinations of primary colours, whereas a '1-bit' image can be only black and white

bitmap an image stored on a computer in the form of a matrix of '**bits**'. Bitmaps cannot be enlarged without losing quality

blog shortened form of 'web log': a web-based publication consisting primarily of periodic articles (normally in reverse chronological order). Can often be in diary form, or exist as coverage of news

blonde a portable light (2000 watts) used for television interviews, low-budget film shoots, etc. – see **redhead**

Bollywood contentious term, sometimes wrongly used in the UK to refer to any form of Indian cinema (which has many 'regional cinemas' making films in regional languages). A corruption of 'Bombay Hollywood' – Hindi films made in Mumbai (Bombay)

branding attaching powerful meanings or associations to products, especially in markets where one or more other products might be as good as each other. Involves work on the reputation or image of the producing company

bricolage French term for 'putting together different articles', as in punk fashion

broadband cable modern telecommunications and television cable which allows more separate signals (channels) to be transmitted

broadcaster-publisher a television broadcasting organisation that doesn't make its own programmes, but instead commissions from other companies (e.g. Channel 4)

broadsheet type of 'serious' newspaper with larger, less square pages than **tabloids**

browser computer software used to look at pages on the World Wide Web

burden of representation the problem arising when a previously under- or misrepresented group begins to be imaged in the media, and too few characters and producers have to bear the burden of being seen to represent the whole group – as 'positive role model' etc.

byte computer term (not the same as **bit**), referring to the basic unit of data storage for characters. File sizes and the capacity of computer memory are measured in kilobytes (a thousand bytes – KB), megabytes (MB) or gigabytes (GB)

camp a sensibility, emerging from male gay culture, which revels in surface, style, theatricality and exaggeration or parody of 'straight' ways of being

capitalism a competitive social system which emerged in seventeenth-century Europe, involving private ownership of accumulated wealth and the exploitation of labour to produce the profit which helps create such wealth

cartel a group of organisations in an industry which secretly agree on maintaining high prices and effectively killing competition; see also **oligopoly**

CCCS Centre for Contemporary Cultural Studies at Birmingham University, 1964–2002

CD compact disc (or disk), a digital data storage medium. CD-Rom is a 'read-only' disk. CD-R is 'writable', CD-RW is 're-writable'

celebrity someone seen as having the same access to fame as stars, and with a constructed 'parallel media narrative' of their life, but arguably without the same level of achievement in the sphere which initially made them famous

censorship decisive acts of forbidding or preventing publication or distribution of media products, or parts of those products, by those with the power, either economic or legislative, to do so

CGI (1) Computer Generated Imagery, a term sometimes used for digital special effects; (2) Common Gateway Interface, an agreed standard that defines how a web page can allow users interactivity with an external program, e.g. using a search engine or shopping over the internet

churn measure of the rate at which media service providers lose customers compared to the number of new customers signed up

cinéma vérité literally 'cinema truth' – an approach to documentary film-making aiming to get as close to events as possible, often producing very high **shooting ratios** of footage shot to that used in the final edit. Sometimes describes fiction narratives which attempt to resemble documentaries through use of hand-held cameras etc.

CinemaScope trade name for the **anamorphic** widescreen process introduced by 20th Century-Fox in 1953

cinematography the art of lighting the set and photographing a film

class (1) one of the groups into which people are divided as a result of socio-economic inequality; (2) a specific group of consumers as recognised by advertisers, six classes now usually grouped into ABC1 ('upmarket') and C2DE ('downmarket'); (3) one of the groups assigned to occupational categories for statistical purposes as defined by the UK Registrar-General

classification placing into categories. Used along with 'censorship', e.g. by the BBFC. Scheduling and ideas of a watershed, prime time, the supposed characteristics of different age groups, etc. are ways in which understandings of texts are prepared by different ways of classifying them

classified advertising advertising expressed in a few lines of text with ads grouped according to subject matter, also known as 'small ads' (cf. **display advertising**)

clipart commercially produced artwork, available at low cost to enhance business and semi-professional print and electronic publications

closed term used of a narrative which is 'resolved' or comes to a conclusion, as opposed to an *'open'* or more ambiguous narrative ending

codes systems of meaning production, both textual and at production levels

coding that part of content analysis (also known as quantitative analysis) which applies a set of categories (and sometimes sub-categories) to the chosen sample, e.g. 'images of disability' which might be broken into 'mental and physical disabilities'

COE advertising acronym, 'country of origin effect' whereby consumers' awareness of the country of origin, whether of manufacture or ownership, affects the product or brand image. Most recently applied to major US brands, such as McDonald's.

cognitive psychology movement in psychology (opposed to **behaviourism**) which argues that human behaviour is changed by appeals to thought processes

colour grading final process in preparing a feature film print for screening

colour temperature a measure of the lighting source on a film or video shoot, which affects the colour cast of white parts of the image and needs correction via filters (see **white balance**)

commissioning the process by which large media producers (usually television broadcasters) agree to

contract individuals or smaller independents to produce new programme material, increasingly important since many broadcasters are now **'publisher broadcasters'**

commodification a commodity is anything which can be bought and sold, usually within capitalist relations; **commodification** and the idea of commodity fetishism are terms used, often in Marxist theory, to argue against the undue spread and unnecessarily high valuation of certain services, items, values

common sense in discussions of ideology especially from Gramsci, a set of assumptions that the world's meanings are obvious and can be understood without recourse to analysis or theory. Opposed to 'good sense' which would combine theory and experience

commutation test a critical test used in semiotics, involving the substitution of one element in a complex sign

compact term adopted by former broadsheet newspapers in the UK which have converted to tabloid size

composition concept used in analysis of visual images referring to the position of objects in the image, their shape and the use of various devices to divide up the available space

conglomerate large industrial corporation, usually involved in several different industries

connote/connotation in semiotics, the meanings interpreted from a sign which link it to other concepts, values, memories

consolidation in media markets, the trend for large corporations to acquire smaller companies, producing an **oligopoly** of large **media conglomerates**

construct/construction semiotic term used to emphasise that media texts are 'made' and not simply 'taken from the real world'

consumers term for media audiences which emphasises the commercial aspects of distribution and exhibition, thus production and consumption of media texts

content analysis see **quantitative analysis**

content provider a media company which produces programme material for delivery on distribution systems, especially cable, satellite and internet

continuity editing editing techniques which are said to disguise the ways that narratives are constructed filmically. Sometimes called the 'continuity system' or 'continuity rules'

conventions 'unwritten rules' in the production of texts. Conventions are the dominant codings in any media

convergence the 'coming together' of previously separate industries (computing, printing, film, audio, etc.) which increasingly use the same or related technology and skilled workers. A feature of the contemporary media environment, convergence is a product of mergers between companies in different sectors as well as a logical outcome of technological development

copy (1) text written to support an advertisement; (2) the 'raw material' for journalism

copy-editing checking the accuracy and legality of text intended for publication and its adherence to house style

copyright the rights to any creative work, held by an individual author or a production company

CPT advertisers' term standing for 'cost per thousand' or the cost of reaching each thousand people in the target audience

critical pluralism a theoretical approach which acknowledges the coexistence of different sets of ideas (as in pluralism) but recognises that some are more powerful than others

cropping resizing or reshaping an image by removing material from one or more sides

cross-cutting technique of sequencing images from different narrative spaces so that stories run in parallel, e.g. 'meanwhile, back at the ranch . . .'

cross-generic blending different genre elements, e.g. horror and comedy in the *Scream* series. Arguably only a very few films do *not* combine different generic elements

crossing the line 'rule' for ensuring narrative continuity – 'not crossing the line (of action)' (also known as the **180-degree rule**)

cross-over a media text which gains acceptance in a different genre market, e.g. *Touching the Void* (UK 2004) which became a mainstream hit even though originally produced for TV and art cinema distribution.

cult term used of media texts around which 'cults' or communities of enthusiastic users have developed. Often now used to signal the virtual communities possible via the internet

cultural codes meanings derived from cultural differences; see **codes**

cultural competence from Bourdieu, the idea that ease of access to media texts depends on cultural difference and experience

cultural imperialism position that the globalisation of communication has been driven, particularly since the Second World War, by the 'military industrial complex' of the large US-based corporations and state. Sometimes used interchangeably with **media imperialism**

cut a transition between two different visual or audio images in an edited sequence in which one image is immediately replaced by another (see **fade, dissolve, wipe**)

cutaway an extra shot inserted between two visual images in a sequence which prevents a jarring transition (see **jump cut**)

cycle related to genre, a series of films with very similar content or themes, often quite clearly referring to each other, produced over a short period

DAT Digital Audio Tape. Compact cassette housing tape suitable for digital recording. Used for some forms of professional audio recording and also for computer data storage

DBS Direct Broadcasting by Satellite

decoding semiotic term for 'reading' the codes in a media text. Now seen as problematic since it implies a single, clear-cut meaning, waiting to be 'decoded'

deep-focus technique in photography or cinematography, producing 'depth of field' – everything in shot in focus

default settings settings or 'preferences' provided with computer software, usually adjustable to 'user settings'

demographics (1) measurement of a population (from Greek *demos* = people) in terms of occupational class, age, sex and region (usually to ascertain their values and assumptions about spending); (2) a 'demographic' is a specific target audience identified by an advertiser

denote/denotation in semiotics, the work of that part of the sign (the signifier) which is immediately recognisable to the reader and which has a direct relationship to a real-world entity (the referent)

deregulation removal or 'lightening' of government restrictions on media industries

de-rig the final part of a film or television shoot when the set, scaffolds, power cables, etc. are taken down

design grid the page layout design in a magazine

desktop reference to the way in which traditional media activities have been simulated on the computer screen, as in desktop publishing (DTP) or desktop video (DTV)

development money funds provided to writers to work on script ideas

Dewey decimal system the cataloguing system used by the majority of libraries in organising how books and other material are displayed and stored

dialectical montage juxtaposition of sequences in Soviet cinema representing the 'struggle' of opposing ideas

dialectics Marxist term to describe the process of change: the struggle of opposing ideas (thesis and antithesis) produce synthesis

diaspora dispersal, often forced, across the globe of peoples who originated in a single geographical location, e.g. the dispersed African communities formed as a result of the slave trade

diegesis the 'fictional world' of the audio-visual narrative. Most useful in distinguishing between **diegetic** and **non-diegetic** sound

diegetic part of the **diegesis**

difference key part of structuralist and semiotic emphases, arguing that meaning is produced largely in the difference between units such as words, rather than what they have in common. Has important (often destructive) consequences for thinking about interest

in shared 'sameness', important for social and political struggles

differential pricing means of accumulating maximum profit on a product by differentiating its price depending on what different markets (i.e. the wealth of potential consumers) will allow

digital based on numerical information, distinguished from **analogue**

digital editing editing using audio and/or video images which have been *digitised* (converted into computer data). Digital audio editing is sometimes called 'hard disk recording'. Digital video editing is usually termed **nonlinear editing**

digital imaging used to describe 'photography' which involves capture, manipulation or exhibition of images using a computer or other digital device. Some critics argue that this term should replace 'photography' altogether

Direct Cinema documentary movement in 1960s US using new lightweight cameras and microphones, kept as close to events as possible, with nothing rehearsed or scripted, no voice-over or music track, and a high **shooting ratio**

direct sound sound recorded 'in sync' with the image, on location (i.e. not **dubbed** in a recording studio later)

discourse any regulated system of statements or language use (e.g. in the law or medicine) which has rules, and therefore exclusions, and connections to power

display advertising advertising using a substantial area of a newspaper page (including graphics) (cf. **classified advertising**)

display font font used for posters, signage or in display advertising (i.e. not for 'body text')

dissolve film term for the transition between two images in which one fades out as the other fades up (usually called a **mix** in television)

diversity (1) the range of different types of programmes available on broadcast networks; (2) policy target for equality of employment or access to media for people of different ages, genders, ethnicities, etc.

division of labour work organised in specialist roles – traditional in the Hollywood studio system

docudrama fiction narrative using documentary techniques. See also **drama-doc**

documentary media text which sets out to deal, and is seen as dealing, primarily with 'real-world' events

docusoap a broadcast hybrid blending elements of soap (serial nature with character-driven narratives and a focus on emotional or 'gossipy' aspects of everyday life) with the codes and conventions of one kind of documentary (*vérité* camera work; real people not actors; real places not locations)

domestic market special use in the film industry to refer to the North American (Canada and US) market; more generally to refer to the 'home' market as distinct from overseas

dominant referring to the most powerful ideas in a social order at any time – expressed in **discourse** and **ideologies**

download transfer of a file from a remote website to a desktop computer

DP director of photography – the person responsible for camerawork and lighting on a film shoot. British term used instead of 'cinematographer'

dpi 'dots per inch', a measure of the resolution of an image or '**pixels** per inch' in **Photoshop** (72 dpi is appropriate for images on a computer screen, 300 dpi for high-quality print publications)

drama-documentary, 'drama-doc' a re-enactment of 'real' events presented using techniques from fictional drama narratives

DSN Digital Screen Network, plan by the UK Film Council to place digital screens in cinemas to boost specialised cinema presentations

DTH Direct to Home satellite broadcasts to domestic receivers

DTT Digital Terrestrial Television

dub, dubbing (1) the process of adding (or replacing) sound on a finished image sequence; (2) making a copy of a sound recording; (3) a style of Jamaican music (a form of reggae)

duopoly an industry in which two companies control the market

DVD digital video disc. A storage device for digital data which through **MPEG** compression allows video copies of feature films to be carried on a single 'compact' disc. Also used as a removable storage device for computer data. Attempts have been made to market DVD as 'digital versatile disc' to emphasise the different uses

dystopia term used in science fiction; a dreadful future society, the opposite of **utopia**

economic determinist theory in political economy which looks for economic conditions as the basis for explanations of the social, cultural, etc.

economies of scale cost savings which can be made by large organisations on the basis of the size of the operation, e.g. 'bulk buying'

editing (1) sequencing of text, images and sounds, the 'shaping' of a narrative; (2) the overall control and direction of fact-based publications in print and broadcasting

editorial either a statement in a publication by the editor or any feature material (i.e. not advertising)

effects model model concerned with how the media 'does things to' audiences

empirical relying on observed experience as evidence for positions. A controversial term, often caricatured by opponents to imply an approach opposed to any kind of theory and relying on sense experience or simplistic facts alone

encrypted service a television broadcast that requires both a decoder (set-top box) and a specific subscriber number to unlock the signal

EPS Encapsulated Postscript – a computer image format used for placement of images in print documents

equilibrium the initial status quo which is 'disrupted' in a narrative

escapist seeking escape, especially from reality, a term used disparagingly of mass cultural forms. Often used as synonymous with 'entertainment'

establishing shot the opening shot of a conventional visual narrative sequence showing the geography of the narrative space

ethnography a method of deep research, involving spending considerable periods of time with a particular community or group of people. Audience ethnography was important in establishing cultural studies, and then in developing work on audiences

evaluation the process of reflecting on how well a media production has met its original aims. Often required by public sector funders as a condition of grant aid and by examiners as part of student assessment

expressionism aesthetics in which ideas and feelings are shown through exaggerated elements in the image (lighting, decor, sound, etc.). Originated in Germany in years following the First World War (1914–18)

fade a production direction in audio and video editing in which an image gradually disappears

fan from 'fanatic': term for one who is passionately attached to a media text or performer. Originally often used derogatorily, it now signals an interest in the varied activities of fans, especially over the internet

feminist belonging to movements and ideas which advocate the rights of women to have equal rights and opportunities to those possessed by men

fibre optic technology using glass fibres to carry data

fill light one of three lighting sources on a film **set-up**, used to 'fill' shadows created by the **key light**

Final Cut Pro software from Apple, now gaining ground as a standard application for digital video editing in competition with **AVID**. A 'light' version, Final Cut Express, is also available

fixed assets/fixed costs anything owned by a company (buildings, heavy equipment, etc.) that incurs costs even if it isn't used – many media producers prefer to 'buy in' facilities as they need them

flightchecking analogous to preparing an aircraft for take-off, computer files to be used in printing are checked as 'all present and correct' before being sent to the printer

flow term coined by Raymond Williams, after his first experience of US television in the 1950s, to suggest that broadcast media are experienced not as separate items but as a flow of similar segments

focal length the distance between the lens and the sensing device in a camera

focus groups small, representative groups whose fairly informal discussions are facilitated, taped and analysed by, e.g., the producers of a television series seeking guidance on how to increase viewing figures or by advertisers researching associations for the launch of a new product

Foley refers to technology used in feature film production to create sound effects. Foley artists work with a variety of materials to produce sounds mixed by a Foley editor

footprint (1) the area covered by a satellite broadcaster in which a clear signal can be decoded; (2) the physical size of a piece of equipment, e.g. a computer on a desk or table

Fordism ideas about industrial production (including film etc.) derived from the concentrated large-scale assembly line established by Henry Ford in Detroit and then internationally from the 1920s

formal referring to the characteristics of a media text concerned with shape, colour, length, etc., rather than content. In practice the distinction is tricky to maintain.

formalist theoretical approach which privileges form over content

format (1) different size or shape of common media products (video is formatted as Betacam or VHS; newspapers as tabloid or broadsheet; film as 35 mm or 16 mm etc.); (2) a TV category allowing for the international trading of TV show concepts and set-ups: e.g. both *The Weakest Link* and *Who Wants to Be a Millionaire?* belong to the genre 'quiz show' though their formats differ; (3) 'format radio': station using only one kind of music or speech

fragmented audience the result of the spread of **multi-channel television** – smaller audiences for many channels rather than four or five large audiences

framing (1) composing an image by selecting the size and position of an object or the human figure within the frame, e.g. a medium shot showing a person from the waist up; (2) the power of media to shape and set the limits to how audiences are invited to perceive certain groups, issues, stories, especially in news forms.

franchise generally a licence to use a brand name in retailing or the service sector. Now used in Hollywood to describe a successful film title that can be developed into new films and associated products, e.g. *The Matrix*

Frankfurt School German critical theorists of mass culture working from the 1920s and 1930s, and later in the US in exile from German fascism

freelance a self-employed worker who works for different employers, often at the same time on specific contracts

ftp internet **protocol** controlling file transfers between computers

gaffer the person responsible for lighting equipment on a film or television shoot. Gaffer tape is used to secure cables (i.e. by taping them to the floor) on set as part of safety procedures

gatekeeping process of choosing certain items for inclusion in news programmes and rejecting others

genre theoretical term for classification of media texts into type groupings

GIF Graphics Interchange Format: originally developed by Compuserve, GIF was the first standard format for non-photographic images on web pages, offering high compression and small file size

globalisation a process in which activities are organised on a global scale, in ways which involve some interdependence, and which are often instantaneous around the world

greenlight (verb) film industry jargon for giving the 'go ahead' for a production by a studio executive

grid basic design of a 'page' in a print or electronic publication, showing columns, margins, etc.

grip a film crew member working on rigging, moving lights, dollies, props, etc.

gutter in DTP, the distance between two columns of print on a page

hard money film industry term for money actually invested in a film production (cf. **soft money**)

hardware the physical equipment used to produce, distribute and exhibit media products

HDTV High Definition Television. Standard for video images with a resolution in 'lines' which is double current norms (i.e. 1250 lines in the UK, 1050 lines in Japan and the US)

hegemony, hegemonic concept from Gramsci suggesting that power is achieved by dominant groups through successful struggles to persuade the subordinate that arrangements are in their interest

high-concept movie the modern high-budget Hollywood film, based on a single strong idea which is easily 'pitched' and can be effectively marketed

high-res high-resolution image with sufficient data to produce an acceptable image on broadcast television, glossy magazines, etc.

holding company company set up simply to own shares in other companies – some media companies are majority-owned by holding companies

horizontal integration when an organisation acquires or merges with competitors in the same industry sector

hybrid (n. hybridity) combining differences, of style, or technologies or cultural form (e.g. *Men in Black's* combination of horror and comedy)

hypertext computer language allowing readers options to read documents in any order, hypertext mark-up language (*html*) is used to write pages on the **World Wide Web**

hypodermic model critical term for a model of media effects on audiences which it characterises as over-simple, seeing meaning as resembling the injection of a drug, with guaranteed effects

iconic (from semiotics) resembling real-world objects (of signs) – see also **arbitrary**, **indexical** and **symbolic**

iconography art history term, used to describe the study of familiar iconic signs in a genre

ident a logo or sound image used on television or radio to identify the station

identity the characteristics of an individual human being which are most central to that person's self-image and self-understanding

identity politics the values and movements which have developed since the 1960s around issues of identity, in particular gender, race, sexuality and disability. Class is not usually included as one of these key identities

ideology, ideological complex term relating to ideas, values and understanding in the social world, and how these are related to the distribution of power in society. Also involves how such values come to seem 'natural'

image a 'representation' of something expressed in visual or aural terms

imperfect competition in economics, a theoretical 'market' in which a group of buyers or sellers is able to influence market forces; the basic condition for **oligopoly**

independent any company in a media industry which is not seen as a major

InDesign DTP software from Adobe, now challenging Quark Xpress as the industry standard

indexical (in semiotics) referring to concepts via causal relationships (e.g. heat signified by the reading on a thermometer)

institution complex term, used in media studies to refer to the social, cultural and political structures within which media production and consumption are made

institutional category a classification of media texts based on institutional practices, e.g. photographs for passports, court cases, industrial research, etc.

institutional documentary common genre type, a documentary about school, hospital life, etc.

international theatrical the cinema market outside North America

internet the global 'network of networks' offering a range of services governed by different protocols, such as the World Wide Web, email, **IRC**, etc.

intertextuality the variety of ways in which media and other texts interact with each other, rather than being unique or distinct

IRC Internet Relay Chat: software which allows internet users to join 'conversations' organised in an ad hoc way around particular topics

ISDN Integrated Services Digital Network – a high-speed digital version of the familiar telephone system

ISP Internet Service Provider: a company that provides individual users with access to internet services through its 'server' computers

Italian neo-realism national film movement of the 1940s and 1950s, characterised by use of non-actors, location shooting, stories from everyday life, etc.

jargon derogatory word for specialised terms within any subject area

JICREG Joint Industry Committee of Regional Newspapers – industry body researching readership of the regional press in the UK

JPEG Joint Photographic Experts Group: a standard for compression of data in a computer image file. JPEGs use 'lossy' compression – some quality is lost. Used for photographic images on the internet

jump cut a very noticeable edit between two images with the same subject and roughly the same framing. Can be avoided by use of **cutaways**

justification in typesetting, alignment of text to right or left or both ('flush'). Text which is not justified right is known as 'ragged'

key light the main light source in a film **set-up**, a bright hard light producing deep shadows

lamp a general term for a light on a film set, different types of lamp are often referred to either by their function (e.g. **key light**) or their power (e.g. **blonde**)

landscape an image that is wider than it is high (cf. 'portrait')

leader (1) another name for the main editorial statement in a newspaper; (2) coloured tape at the beginning of an audio tape reel

leading the space a typesetter creates between lines of text, derived from strips of lead placed on the frame when text was set in trays of metal type

liberalisation the loosening of controls over media markets by governments – a contentious term since this also involves new forms of regulation

light-touch regulation a loosening of regulatory controls associated with 'free market' policies in the 1980s and 1990s

linear editing analogue video editing with shots copied from one tape to another in a linear sequence that cannot subsequently be re-edited. See **nonlinear editing**

long shot shot size or framing which shows the full human figure

long take shot lasting twenty seconds or more

looping rerecording of dialogue by actors watching a film sequence in a recording studio (see **ADR**)

low-res a 'low-resolution' digital image with only a small amount of image data, subject to pixellation if enlarged

mainstream the most highly commercialised areas of media production, ones in which dominant cultural and industrial norms operate

majors the most powerful producers in any media industry, e.g. the Hollywood studios

market the total of all the potential sellers and buyers for a particular product (and the number of products likely to be exchanged)

market penetration the extent to which a product captures the potential sales in a market – expressed as market share

marketing the process of presenting a product to its target audience; the ways in which it is positioned in its particular market

matte a 'mask' used in traditional cinematography to create special effects (e.g. a skyline painted on glass), now also referring to digital techniques that serve the same purpose

media buying the function of an advertising agency in buying 'space' in a media product in which to place an advertisement

media conglomerates the major media corporations which combine several different activities under a single brand

media imperialism (also called **cultural imperialism**) the argument that rich and powerful countries (or 'military industrial complexes'), especially the US, dominate poorer ones through control of globalised media industries

mediate, mediation changing the meaning of any 'real' event through the application of media technology

melodrama often used to mean 'exaggerated', 'hysterical' or 'extreme'; originally a kind of drama which, coming out of censored theatre in the seventeenth century, developed an elaborate language of gesture and used highly polarised scenarios often pitting 'vice' against 'virtue'

merchandising the exploitation of a film, television, etc. character or title through the marketing of a range of 'branded' non-media products, especially for children. Has a long history, but increased dramatically after the success of *Star Wars* in 1977

metropolitan bias the argument that too much of the UK media is based in London and takes little interest in affairs outside the capital

mid-market in classifications of media texts (especially newspapers), the middle position between **tabloid** and **quality**

MiniDisc format designed by Sony to provide both a smaller CD for consumer playback and a recording medium for the audio industry. Only the latter use has been taken up widely

mise en scène literally 'putting into the scene' or staging the events of the script for the camera. Usually refers to visual processes at pre-edit stage (lighting, set design, etc.) though, confusingly, some critics include sound in this term

mix in video, a transition between scenes in which one image fades up as another fades down; see **dissolve**

MMS Multimedia Messaging System, the protocol for sending sound and moving images via mobile phones

mode of address the way a text 'speaks' to its audience

model in social sciences, a way of imagining how a system might work

modernism innovative, often self-reflexive artistic movements which ran roughly from the 1920s to the 1970s

modernity an alternative to 'postmodernity' as a way of describing the 'contemporary', emphasising attempts to rethink Enlightenment values such as belief in progress, rationality, etc.

monopoly any market situation where one seller controls prices and the supply of product. In the UK a 25 per cent share will attract the interest of the Office of Fair Trading (OFT) and the Competition Commission.

moral panics a sudden increase in concern about the possible 'effects' of media products, e.g. 'video nasties' in the 1980s; mobile phones more recently

morphing the process of presenting a change in shape from one object to another as a single, continuous movement

MPAA Motion Picture Association of America is the trade association formed by the major Hollywood studios to protect their interests. The Motion Pictures Association (MPA) is the international arm of the organisation which has successfully defended the studios' rights to their exploitation of international markets

MPEG Motion Picture Experts Group: MPEG-2 is a standard for compressing video data for editing and playback

MP3 (MPEG-1 Audio Level 3) the standard format for compressing music files

multi-channel television a television environment with the capacity for many different channels to be received by any household – a significant change from the era of **spectrum scarcity**

multimedia referring to several traditionally separate media being used together, e.g. sound, image and text on computers

multiplex (1) multi-screen cinema complex, often located in a shopping mall or leisure park; (2) in digital broadcasting, the capacity for several different television or radio channels to be broadcast on the same waveband width as a single analogue channel

myths traditional stories through which societies reinforce and explore their beliefs about themselves; in media studies, associated with the work of the anthropologist Lévi-Strauss, and then Roland Barthes, who uses it to mean almost the same as **ideology**

narration the process of telling a story, the selection and organisation of the events for a particular audience

narrative complex term referring to a sequence of events organised into a story with a particular structure

narrowcasting term which contrasts itself with 'broadcasting' to draw attention to the assumed fragmentation of audiences addressed by much television now

national identity the sets of ideas constructed around the concept of 'nation' and the ways in which individuals and groups relate to them

negotiated in audience theory, the idea that a meaning is arrived at as a result of a process of give and take between the reader's assumptions and the 'preferred meaning' offered by the text

news agencies organisations such as Reuter's which gather news stories and sell them to broadcasters and newspaper publishers

news professionals the media workers who are trained to process news stories according to institutional norms

news values the criteria used by editors, not always consciously, to select and prioritise news stories for publication

niche marketing the idea that there are very small but highly profitable markets which could support specialist advertising-led media products

noise usually refers to extra, unwanted, data in a video or sound image; a filter in Photoshop reduces the visibility of such 'interference'

non-diegetic not part of the diegesis, the fictional world of the text, 'theme music', credits, unattributed voice-over in a film

nonlinear editing (NLE) editing on a computer allowing digitised sounds and images to be 're-sequenced' as required before producing a 'master edit'. See **linear editing**

NRS National Readership Survey is the organisation supplying information on UK readership of national newspapers and magazines

NTSC the television and video standard in North America and Japan (525 lines, 30 frames per second)

objectivity an idealist aim for journalists – to report events without becoming involved in them (i.e. not being 'subjective'); see **bias**

Ofcom statutory regulator for the UK broadcasting and telecommunications industries

oligopoly an industry controlled by a small number of producers

opinion polls quantitative polls, whose results are highly structured by editorial decisions about which results to emphasise, which give a 'snapshot' of how a supposedly representative sample of people feels about an issue (e.g. '60 per cent of UK voters would support a 1 per cent tax on incomes over £100,000 to support public services')

oppositional actively opposed to the dominant; in audience theory describes a reading which rejects the 'preferred meaning' offered by the text

option a purchased right to develop a property such as a novel for a new film

outline (1) term for an idea forming the basis for negotiating a production commission; (2) a drawing or a font used in desktop publishing based on a mathematical formula describing the shape, also sometimes known as 'vector graphics' (cf. **bitmap**). Outline drawings and fonts maintain the same quality if enlarged

P&A 'prints and advertising' is the industry term for the distribution budget for a feature film (cf. **production budget**)

package unit system the basis for Hollywood film production which replaced the studio system in the 1950s. Each film is treated as a 'one-off' and a package of director, stars and crew brought together for a specific production

PAL the television and video system standard as used in the UK, Germany and other parts of Europe (625 lines, 25 frames per second)

pan and scan technique for showing widescreen films on a standard-shape television set

paradigm/paradigmatic a class of objects or concepts. Defined along with **syntagm**: an element which follows another in a particular sequence. For example, in choosing from a menu, the paradigms (starters, main courses, desserts) are elements from which you choose, and the syntagm is the sequence into which they are arranged (soup/fish/ice cream)

pattern of ownership the way in which ownership and control of media companies is organised in a particular industry sector, e.g. the ownership of UK cinema chains is mainly via venture capital groups

PCC Press Complaints Commission

pdf portable document format, a computer file format that allows a document to be viewed correctly and printed out on any computer using **Acrobat** Reader software

perfect-bound magazines with pages glued to a flat spine; alternatives are stapling or 'stitching' or spiral binding

permissions agreements to film on specific locations; or, by rights holders, that images, sounds and text may be used in a media production

photo opportunity part of the promotion of any media figure which allows photographs or video footage to be secured for news broadcasts etc.

photographic truth the belief that photography can produce documentary 'evidence' – now challenged by **digital imaging** and always subject to arguments that the photograph is always structured in some way or another

photorealistic referring to the realist effect achieved by photography

Photoshop computer software from Adobe used for image manipulation

pitch (verb or noun) the process of 'selling' a production idea to a studio or television broadcaster

pixel the smallest element in a digital image, which can be given a colour (depending on the image format); in a low-res image individual pixels (square-shaped) may become visible, a condition known as **pixellation**

pixellation see **pixel**

pixilation a form of film animation in which action is recorded as single frames ('stop motion photography')

planned obsolescence concept that suggests manufacturers deliberately 'build in' to certain products (especially cars) features that prevent them lasting for as long as they could, thus encouraging (unnecessary) repeated purchases

platform release initial release of a film to only a handful of cinemas in order to gain attention, followed by a gradual 'opening' to a wide release

plot defined in relation to '**story**' as the events in a narrative which are presented to an audience directly

pluralist used to describe a political position which allows for several competing ideologies to all be accepted as valid

PMP portable media player, generic term for hand-held devices that can play one or more media formats

PNG Portable Network Graphics, a file format for images, beginning to replace GIFs on web pages

podcast a form of broadcasting in which a radio programme is stored as an MP3 file and can be downloaded (possibly automatically by subscription) and played by listeners at a convenient time on any MP3 player

point size measure of the size of text characters in typesetting: 72 points is roughly one inch

political economy study of the social relations, particularly power relations, that together constitute the production, distribution and consumption of resources

polysemic literally 'many-signed', a text in which there are several possible meanings depending on the ways its constituent signs are read. Often now abandoned in favour of the position that audience activity as part of meaning production means that no sign can secure only one meaning

popular widely used term, literally meaning 'of the people'. Used negatively, in contrast to 'high culture', 'art', etc. and also as synonymous with 'mass'

portal an internet term for a website which acts as a 'gateway' to many other websites offering material on related topics, or as a shopfront for commercial websites

portrait an institutional category of photography or journalism, focusing on an individual; the tall vertical shape of a photographic portrait (cf. **landscape**)

post-feminism position which argues that the condition of women 'after' the successes of 1960s and 1970s feminist struggles means that they can take for granted respect and equality and enjoy ironic pleasures and playfulness around traditional 'femininity'

post-Fordism method of commodity production which subcontracts part of the production process to a number of firms and uses new technology to make production more responsive to consumer demand

postmodernism complex term used with several meanings, usually involving emphasis on the self-reflexity of contemporary culture and media

Postscript 'page description language' used in print publishing which is 'platform-free' – not dependent on the type of computer used

PPV pay per view: method of charging television viewers for a single viewing of a programme, rather than subscribing to a channel for a set period. Used first for sports events and concerts, now also for some film screenings

preferred reading (from Hall's encoding/ decoding theory of audience readings): the most likely reading of a text by audiences, given the operation of power structures and dominant values both in the institution producing the text and in audiences

pre-press that part of the print publishing process in which final checks are made to prepared text and images before printing. A crucial stage in the 'digital work-flow', in which '**flightchecking**' software is used to ensure that all computer files are present and compatible with the print software being used

pre-sale the possibility of selling the distribution rights to a product before production is completed, giving some security to the production

price mechanism the movement of prices in any market that some economists argue operates the 'laws of supply and demand'

primary research research into the original source of a media story – an interview, personal letters, government records, etc.

prime time that part of a radio or television schedule expected to attract the biggest audience, usually around 19.30 to 22.30

principal photography the production phase on a film shoot

privatisation process by which services or utilities in the **public sector** are transferred to private ownership

producer choice BBC policy encouraging producers to consider less expensive non-BBC facilities

product placement an unofficial form of advertising in which branded products feature prominently in films etc.

production budget the cost of actually making a film (as distinct from the overall cost of producing and marketing the film)

production cycle in the Hollywood studio system, the constant film production process involving strict division of labour

production quota public service broadcasting requirement that all terrestrial UK broadcasters commission 25 per cent of programmes from 'independents' and make 25 per cent of programmes in UK regions

promotion process of using the media to put a celebrity or media product in front of potential consumers

proofing process of checking the text in the final version of a media product before publication for errors in placement, spelling, etc.; test printing a colour image on paper (because colours on a computer screen are not reliable guides)

propaganda any media text which seeks openly to persuade an audience of the validity of particular beliefs or actions

property any original story, the rights to which have been acquired by a production company

proposal idea for a new media product submitted speculatively by a freelance to a major producer, including an outline and an argument that a market exists

protocol software controlling the interface between computers in a network. Protocols cover every aspect of using the internet

public domain (1) describes any media product for which copyright has expired or has never been claimed, implying that no payment to a rights holder is required. This applies only to the work itself and not to a particular publication of it – i.e. the text of a Dickens novel, but not the Penguin printed version; (2) also used in a sense close to '**public sphere**'

public relations professional services promoting products by arranging opportunities for exposure in the media

public sector the part of the economy comprising organisations funded by central or local government. A public limited company (*plc*), however, is in the private sector, being owned by shareholders (it is listed on the stock exchange with shares available for sale to the public)

public service a service provided with a prime aim of meeting perceived social needs, rather than private profit. In broadcasting can be a requirement of a license granted to private sector companies (see **PSB** and **PSP**)

public service broadcasting (PSB) regulated broadcasting which has providing a public service as a primary aim

public service publisher (PSP) proposal by Ofcom to fund a new form of electronic publishing, embracing internet and telephone media as well as broadcast television

public sphere that part of social life, outside government, where citizens can democratically share views and attempt rational discussion

publisher broadcaster Channel 4 was the first UK broadcaster to commission all programming from other companies, i.e. not to make any programmes itself

PVR personal video recorder, an 'intelligent' recorder that can automatically record certain types of programme, cut out adverts, etc.

qualitative research audience research based on discussion groups or one-to-one interviews with interaction between researcher and subject

quality (film and television) subjective term used by critics and commentators to describe certain types of films and television programmes. Although there are no strict guidelines, the concept has been used in the licensing of UK television channnels in the form of the 'quality threshold' – a commitment to broadcast a specified amount of 'quality programmes'. Could refer to high production values, popular appeal or unusual programmes

quality document an audit document showing how an organisation maintains the integrity of its administration systems

quality press 'serious' national newspapers in the UK, once synonymous with **broadsheet**, now changing as various titles 'downsize', e.g. the **Berliner**

quantitative analysis also called **content analysis**, based on counting the frequency of certain elements in a clearly defined sample, by applying categories to them (called 'coding') and then analysing the results. The categories chosen (e.g. 'headlines involving the word "terrorist" ') should be unambiguous, so that different researchers at different times using the same categories, would produce the same results

quantitative audience research audience research based on anonymous data with **samples** constructed to represent larger 'populations' of viewers, listeners and readers in order to estimate the size of the audience

Quark Xpress industry standard DTP software used in page layout, now challenged by **InDesign**

quota a designated amount of production, minimum or maximum, which is specified for purposes of regulation or to protect specific producers from competition, e.g. attempts to limit Hollywood's share of film markets by insisting that cinemas show a percentage of 'home' nation product

R&D Research and Development. The section in any organisation working on future products or services

racism the stigmatising of difference along the lines of 'racial' characteristics in order to justify advantage or abuse of power, whether economic, political, cultural or psychological

RAJAR Radio Joint Audience Research, the industry body which collects and publishes data on radio audiences in the UK

ratings viewing and listening figures presented as a league table of successful programmes, depending on audience size – see TVR

reader panels groups of readers who can be questioned about their responses to a media product

reader research research into who 'reads' a media product

real time time taken for an event in an audio-visual text which exactly matches the time taken for the same event in the real world

realism a fiercely contested term which emphasises the need to take seriously the relationship between media texts and the rest of the 'real world'

realism effect the real-seemingness of a text, paradoxically always achieved through artifice

realist aesthetic an approach to presenting an image which seeks to achieve realism

'reality TV' form of factual television on UK screens from about 1989. First applied to magazine format

programmes based on crime, accident and health stories or 'trauma television' (*Crimewatch UK* etc.). Now used loosely of television which is largely unscripted, making substantial use of ordinary people, and mixing information and entertainment forms. *Big Brother* is often cited, but the term covers a range of different forms

ream standard measure of paper – 500 sheets

recce 'reconnaissance' – part of pre-production, checking out venues for performances or locations for recording

recto the right-hand page in a print publication

redhead a portable light (600–1000 watts) used on low-budget film and television shoots; may be found in education and training productions

red-top UK term for a 'downmarket' **tabloid** newspaper (as distinct from 'midmarket' tabloids and **compacts**, argued to be less sensationalist)

referent in semiotics, the 'real world' object to which the sign or signifier refers

regional press newspapers (morning or evening dailies and/or Sundays) published outside London with a distinct regional circulation. 'Local' papers (daily or weekly) are included in the industry definition of the regional press

regional production obligation by the BBC (and other national broadcasters) to spread production around the regions and nations of the UK

regulation the process of monitoring the activities of industries. Some media industries regulate themselves and others are regulated by bodies set up by legislation

release patterns the geographical patterns of the release of media texts, especially feature films

repertoire (music) see **A&R**

repertoire of elements the fluid system of conventions and expectations associated with genre texts

repetition and difference the mix of familiar and new characteristics which offer pleasures and attract audiences to generic media texts

replicability unambiguity of research findings such that different researchers at different times would interpret the evidence in exactly the same way (see **quantitative analysis**)

resolution refers to image quality (see **low-res, high-res**)

rigging process of building scaffolding, setting up power supplies, etc. for a film or television shoot

right of reply the idea that persons who feel they have been misrepresented should have the right to challenge media producers on air or in a newspaper

romance fiction genre in which intimate personal relationships related to love are the central focus. Originally a medieval form – tales of knights, honour, battle and the (often adulterous) love of characters like Lancelot and Guinevere. 'Romantic' now often inherits feelings (of longing, of unrequited or troubled love, etc.) from the love strands in these earlier 'romances'

royalties payments made to a copyright holder each time a media product is bought (e.g. novel), broadcast (play) or performed (song), etc.

RSL restricted service licence, granted to radio (and more rarely televison) broadcasters in the UK for local broadcasts over a set period (usually twenty-eight days) or in a restricted community

samples (1) in digital audio production, sounds or sequence of sounds 'captured' by a computer for use in future productions; (2) carefully selected groups of people chosen in audience research to represent larger populations

sans-serif any typeface or font 'without a **serif**'

schedule as in 'production schedule', the careful planning of the production process

scheduling strategies adopted to place programmes in radio and television schedules to most effect

script (1) dialogue and production directions for a radio, film or television production; (2) arrangement of sounds, images and effects placed in sequence on a computer for presentation; (3) a typeface designed to resemble handwriting; 4) more broadly, 'shared expectations about what is likely to happen in certain contexts, and what is desirable and undesirable in terms of outcome', often derived from repeated fictional shapes, e.g. 'the happy ending'

search engine computer software used to find a specific word or phrase in a database or across a network such as the internet

secondary research research using reference books or previously annotated or published sources (cf. **primary research**)

segment (verb) to divide up a target audience into even more specialised groups which can be addressed by advertisers

self-reflexive applied to texts which display an awareness or a comment on their own artificial status as texts

self-regulation cinema and the press are regulated by bodies set up by the industries themselves

semiotics/semiology the study of sign systems

serif the bar across the ends of the main strokes of a text character in a typeface

service provider see **ISP**

set-top box computer which sits on top of a television set and controls the variety of possible incoming signals (e.g. satellite, cable or **DTT**)

set-ups term for the separate camera, lighting and sound positions necessary for shooting a feature film

shooting ratio the amount of filmed footage used in the final edited film compared to the actual amount of film shot during the production

shot the smallest element in any film sequence, a single 'take' during shooting which may be further shortened during editing

shot/reverse shot term for the conventional way of shooting an exchange between two characters in a film or television programme

sign/signified/signifier the sign, in semiotics, is divided into the signifier or physical form taken by the sign, and the signified, which is the concept it stands in for

slate film industry term for the list of major features to be produced during a production period

SMS short message service (see **text**)

soap, soap opera the radio and television multi-strand continuous serial narrative form originally designed as a vehicle for sponsorship by soap powder manufacturers

soft money film industry term for funding that derives from various forms of public revenue support such as tax breaks, grants, etc. (cf. **hard money**)

software the programs written for computers, or the films, music, etc. which could be played on them

sound effect frequently used to refer to artificially created 'sounds' produced for audio-visual texts; can also be extended to refer to all aural material in a production apart from dialogue and music

sound image term used to emphasise the possibility of analysing or reading sounds in the same way as 'pictures'

sound stages term describing the individual buildings available for shooting in a film studio – the name implies that they can be used for recording sound

specialised/specialist cinema term used by UK Film Council to describe any film not seen as 'mainstream' (i.e. unlikely to play in a multiplex)

spectrum scarcity description of the environment of analogue television broadcasting with a limited number of channels

spin activities of press or PR officers (also called 'spin doctors') employed to put a positive 'spin' or angle on stories about their employer or client. It suggests an unjustifiable degree of intervention in the construction of news, though it could be seen as a necessary part of any institutional communication

SPV (single-purpose vehicle) term used by UK Film Council to describe a film production company set up to make just the one film

standardisation has a double meaning: it can signify 'sameness' but can also denote the maintenance of standards, in the sense of quality

standard lens for a 35mm or still camera, a lens of 50mm focal length gives an image thought to be similar to the perspective of the human eye. **Wide angle** is 'shorter' than this and **telephoto** is 'longer'

star actor whose image, via accumulated publicity, debate, etc., is strong enough to be valued as an added component of any performance, and acts as a parallel narrative for audiences

star image the constructed image of the star, usually in relation to film and associated 'secondary circulation'

statutory regulation regulatory powers established by law (e.g. the Broadcasting Acts of 1990 and 1996)

Steadicam trade name for a stabilising device allowing a camera operator to move freely without jerking the image

stereotypes, stereotyping originally a term from printing, literally a 'solid' block of metal type; then, a representation of a type of person, without fine detail

story all of the events in a narrative, those presented directly to an audience and those which might be inferred – compare with **plot**

structuralism an approach to critical analysis which emphasises universal structures underlying the surface differences and apparent randomness of cultures, stories, media texts, etc.

structuring oppositions see **binary oppositions**

studio system Hollywood production system from about 1930 to the 1950s, in which 'vertically integrated' film companies produced, distributed and exhibited a constant stream of new films. Other countries also had 'studio systems' and the concept could also be applied to television studios

sub-editing process late in the production of a newspaper in which stories are shortened or rewritten to fit the space available and headlines and picture captions are written – also evident in television news

subliminal advertising kind of advertising associated with hypnosis. Said to work by flashing barely perceptible messages to audiences in between frames of a film or television advertisements. The idea still fascinates, though it is now discredited

superstructure ideological structures built on an 'economic base', according to Marxist theory

switchover the planned 'switch-off' of analogue television in the UK in 2012, when all viewers will need to have access to digital television

symbolic used in semiotics of a sign (usually visual) which has come to stand for a particular set of qualities or values, e.g. the 'Stars and Stripes' for the US; see **arbitrary**, **iconic** and **indexical**

sync 'synchronised', usually refers to sound and the coordination of sound and image, e.g. sound matched to action later is 'post-sync' and if it involves dialogue may need to be 'lip-synced'

synergy the benefits to large corporations that are said to accrue from developing, producing and marketing media 'products' and associated merchandising (in film, music, toys, internet and television programmes, T-shirts, theme park rides and so on) in such a way as to share costs and maximise potential profits – the 'interconnectedness' of these products produces more than the sum of their parts

syntagmatic see **paradigm**, with which it is often used in combination

tabloid the size of a newsprint page, half that of the 'broadsheet'; by extension: sensationalist media form (television and radio as well as the press)

talent anyone appearing in front of the camera or microphone, the performers

target audiences the specific audiences to be addressed by a particular media text

Technicolor colour film process developed for cinema in the 1930s, often used as a synonym for 'colour' in cinema

technophobia fear of machines or technology, especially in science fiction narratives

telcos telephone companies, increasingly important in media markets as distributors of media products

telephoto 'long' camera lens (with long **focal length**) which enables distant objects to be shown in close-up – has the effect of 'flattening' the image

tentpole movie a major film which a studio hopes will provide the support for its annual slate and almost guarantee box-office returns

territories geographical areas for which the rights to a media product are negotiated

text (1) any system of signs which can be 'read' – a poster, photograph, haircut, etc. (2) text message: short written message sent via use of a service on most mobile phones (see **SMS**). Verb: to text. Often uses a specialised, abbreviated language

tie-ins corporate products which accompany and help publicise a major film or television release, e.g. cereal pack toys of animation characters

TIFF tagged image file format – the standard format for images in commercial publishing

time-based media term used to refer to film, television, radio. 'Lens-based media' is used to link film and television with photography

transparency the way in which media texts present themselves as 'natural'; their construction is invisible to casual readers

treatment document in the pre-production process for television and video which describes how the ideas in the outline will be developed into a programme, referring to genre, style, etc.

turn-around film industry term for a script dropped by one studio and waiting for another to pick it up

TVR television rating – a measure of television audiences used in selling advertising space, usually expressed as a percentage of the potential audience ('universe')

typeface a complete set of text and numeric characters plus symbols and punctuation marks with common design features. A typeface may be available in different weights (bold, light, etc.) or styles (italic, condensed, etc.)

typesetting now completely computerised, the process of arranging text in precise positions on the page

unit production system, unit-based production way of organising production under the Hollywood studio system

universal service (in relation to public service broadcasting) a service available to everyone at the same price

upload to transfer data to a website on a remote computer (or to a satellite for broadcasting)

uses and gratifications model 'active' model of audience behaviour, emphasising the uses to which audiences put even the most unlikely texts

USP unique selling proposition, term used in brand advertising for the supposedly unique quality of products which advertisers seek to communicate to potential buyers

utopian associated with an ideal, if not impossible, social world

vector graphics see **outline** (2)

verisimilitude quality of seeming like what is taken to be the real world of a particular text; see entries around **realism**

verso left-hand page in a print publication

vertical integration business activity involving one company acquiring others elsewhere in the production process

violence debate recurring debates over assumed audience behaviour, focusing on the possible 'effects' of representations of violence

virtual something which is a representation rather than the 'real' thing, thus 'virtual reality'

voice-over voice used in sound track as encouragement to viewers to interpret the visual images in particular ways; a kind of '**anchoring**' in semiotic terms

voyeurism the pleasure of looking while unseen; often used in sexualised contexts

West pre-eighteenth century simply signified a direction on a map – the opposite of east. As West European power spread, it came to signify a group of people supposedly unified by residential geographies, traditions and 'shared civilisation'. Now highly contested

white balance the process of correcting the sensitivity of a video camera to match a specific lighting source (see **colour temperature**)

white space the blank spaces on a printed page – considered to be an important component in the overall design and 'look' of the page

wide angle a 'short' camera lens (a short **focal length**) which enables more of a scene to be included in the framing than a standard length lens – the opposite effect to **telephoto**. Can produce distorted images of objects close to the camera

wide release distribution of a film to many cinemas simultaneously, in the UK more than fifty prints in circulation

Wikipedia web-based encyclopedia created and edited by users

window a period of time during which a film will be promoted in a specific market, e.g. on DVD rental or PPV television

wipe transition in video editing in which one image replaces another according to a specific pattern such as the appearance of a page being turned

word of mouth informal way in which media products become known about by audiences

World Wide Web the network of 'pages' of images, texts and sounds on the internet which can be viewed using browser software

wrap industry jargon for the completion of a film shoot

zapping rapidly cutting between television channels using a remote control device

zoom an arrangement of camera lenses, allowing the operator to change the focal length and move between **telephoto** and **wide angle** settings

Bibliography

For detailed lists of sources and ideas for further reading on specific topics, as well as for DVDs and other non-book resources, see individual chapters. The titles below provide general introductions to the major debates in the book. You can use them as starting points for background reading and consult their bibliographies for further ideas.

Abercrombie, Nicholas (1996) *Television and Society*, Cambridge: Polity.

Alasuutari, Pertti (1999) *Rethinking the Media Audience: The New Agenda*, London: Sage.

Allan, Stuart (2000) *News Culture*, Buckingham: Open University Press.

Allen, Robert C. and Hill, Annette (eds) (2004) *The Television Studies Reader*, London and New York: Routledge.

Andermahr, Sonya, Lovell, Terry and Wolkowitz, Carol (2000) *A Glossary of Feminist Theory*, London and New York: Hodder Arnold.

Ang, Ien (1996) *Living Room Wars: Rethinking Media Audiences for a Postmodern World*, London and New York: Routledge.

Angelini, Sergio (2005, 7th edition) *The Researcher's Guide: Film, Television, Radio and Related Documentation Collections in the UK*, London: BUFVC.

Appadurai, Arjun (1996) *Modernity at Large: Cultural Dimensions of Globalization*, Minneapolis: University of Minnesota Press.

Barker, Martin and Austin, Thomas (2003) *Contemporary Hollywood Stardom*, London: Hodder Arnold.

Barker, Martin and Beezer, Anne (eds) (1992) *Reading into Cultural Studies*, London and New York: Routledge.

Barker, Martin and Petley, Julian (eds) (2001, 2nd edition) *Ill Effects: The Media/Violence Debate*, London and New York: Routledge.

Barker, Martin with Austin, Thomas (2000) *From Antz to Titanic: Reinventing Film Analysis*, London: Pluto Press.

Barthes, Roland (1972; first published 1957) *Mythologies*, London: Paladin.

Bennett, Tony, Grossberg, Lawrence and Morris, Meaghan (eds) (2005) *New Keywords: A Revised Vocabulary of Culture and Society*, London: Blackwell.

Berman, Edward S. and McChesney, Robert W. (1997) *The Global Media: The New Missionaries of Corporate Capitalism*, London and Washington, DC: Cassell.

Bignell, Jonathan (1997) *Media Semiotics: An Introduction*, Manchester: Manchester University Press.

Bignell, Jonathan (2004) *An Introduction to Television Studies*, London and New York: Routledge.

Billig, Michael (1995) *Banal Nationalism*, London: Sage.

Blandford, Steve, Grant, Barry Keith and Hillier, Jim (2001) *The Film Studies Dictionary*, London: Arnold.

Bogle, Donald (2003, anniversary edition) *Toms, Coons, Mulattoes, Mammies and Bucks: An Interpretative History of Blacks in American Films*, New York: Continuum.

Bordwell, David and Carroll, Noel (eds) (1996) *Post-theory: Reconstructing Film Studies*, Madison and London: University of Wisconsin Press.

Bordwell, David and Thompson Kirstin (2004, 7th edition), *Film Art: An Introduction*, Maidenhead and New York: McGraw Hill.

Born, Georgina (2004) *Uncertain Vision: Birt, Dyke and the Reinvention of the BBC*, London: Secker and Warburg.

Bourdieu, Pierre (1984) *Distinction: A Social Critique of the Judgement of Taste*, London: Routledge and Kegan Paul.

Branston, Gill (2000) *Cinema and Cultural Modernity*, Buckingham: Open University Press.

Branston, Gill (2006) 'Genre' in Gillespie, Marie and Toynbee, Jason (eds), *Analysing Media Texts*, London: Sage and the Open University Press.

Brierley, Sean (2001, 2nd edition) *The Advertising Handbook*, London and New York: Routledge.

Briggs, Adam and Cobley, Paul (eds) (1998) *The Media: An Introduction*, Harlow: Longman.

Bromley, Michael and O'Malley, Tom (eds) (1997) *A Journalism Reader*, London: Routledge.

Brooker, Peter (2003, 2nd edition) *A Glossary of Cultural Theory*, London: Hodder Arnold.

Brookes, Rod (2003) *Representing Sport*, London: Hodder Arnold.

Brunsdon, Charlotte (1997) *Screen Tastes: Soap Opera to Satellite Dishes*, London and New York: Routledge.

Bruzzi, Stella (2000) *New Documentary: A Critical Introduction*, London: Routledge.

Buscombe, Ed (ed.) (1988) *The BFI Companion to the Western*, London: André Deutsch/British Film Institute.

Carter, Cynthia, Branston, Gill and Allan, Stuart (eds) (1998) *News, Gender and Power*, London: Routledge.

Chambers, Deborah, Fleming, Carole and Steiner, Linda (2004) *Women and Journalism*, London: Routledge.

Coakley, J. (1998, 6th edition) *Sport in Society: Issues and Controversies*, New York: McGraw Hill.

Cohen, Stan (2002, 2nd edition) *Folk Devils and Moral Panics*, London and New York: Routledge.

Connell, Robert W. (2000) *The Men and the Boys*, Cambridge: Polity.

Cook, Pam and Bernink, Mieke (1999, 2nd edition) *The Cinema Book*, London: British Film Institute.

Cooke, Lez (2003) *British Television Drama: A History*, London: British Film Institute.

Corner, John (1996) *The Art of Record: A Critical Introduction to Documentary*, Manchester: Manchester University Press.

Corner, John (1998) *Studying Media: Problems of Theory and Method*, Edinburgh: Edinburgh University Press.

Corner, John (2003) *Media and the Re-Styling of Politics: Consumerism, Celebrity and Cynicism*, London: Sage.

Corrigan, Timothy and White, Patricia (2004) *The Film Experience: An Introduction*, Basingstoke: Palgrave Macmillan.

Creeber, Glen (ed.) (2001) *The Television Genre Book*, London: British Film Institute.

Crisell, Andrew (1994, 2nd edition) *Understanding Radio*, London: Routledge.

Crisell, Andrew (1997) *An Introductory History of British Broadcasting*, London: Routledge.

Croteau, David and Hoynes, William (2001) *The Business of Media: Corporate Media and the Public Interest*, London: Sage.

Curran, James and Gurevitch, Michael (eds) (2005, 4th edition) *Mass Media and Society*, London: Arnold.

Curran, James and Morley, David (2005) *Media & Cultural Theory*, London: Routledge.

Curran, James and Park, Myung-Jin (eds) (2000) *De-westernizing Media Studies*, London: Routledge.

Curran, James and Seaton, Jean (2003) *Power Without Responsibility: The Press and Broadcasting in Britain*, London: Routledge.

Curran, James, Morley, David and Walkerdine, Valerie (eds) (1995) *Cultural Studies and Communications*, London: Arnold.

Dunant, Sarah (ed.) (1994) *The War of the Words: The Political Correctness Debate*, London: Virago.

During, Simon (2005) *Cultural Studies: A Critical Introduction*, London: Routledge.

Durkin, Kevin (1985) *Television, Sex Roles and Children*, Milton Keynes: Open University Press.

Dyer, Richard (2002, 2nd edition) *Only Entertainment*, London: Routledge.

Dyer, Richard (2003, 2nd edition) *Heavenly Bodies*, London: Routledge.

Dyer, Richard (1997) *White: Essays on Race and Culture*, London: Routledge.

Eagleton, Terry (1983) *Literary Theory: An Introduction*, Oxford: Blackwell.

Eldridge, John (ed.) (1995) *The Glasgow University Media Reader*, vol. 1, London: Routledge.

Ellis, John (2000) *Seeing Things: Television in the Age of Uncertainty*, London: I.B. Tauris.

Evans, Harold (1997) *Pictures on a Page: Photo-journalism, Graphics and Picture Editing*, London: Pimlico.

Franklin, Bob and Murphy, David (1998) *Making the Local News: Local Journalism in Context*, London: Routledge.

Gamman, Lorraine and Marshment, Margaret (eds) (1998) *The Female Gaze: Women as Viewers of Popular Culture*, London: Women's Press.

Ganti, Tejaswini (2004) *Bollywood: A Guidebook to Popular Hindi Cinema*, London: Routledge.

Gauntlett, D. (2004, 2nd edition) *Web Studies: Rewriting Media Studies for the Digital Age*, London: Hodder Arnold.

Geraghty, Christine (1991) *Women and Soap Opera: A Study of Prime Time Soaps*, London: Polity.

Geraghty, Christine and Lusted, David (1998) *The Television Studies Book*, London and New York: Arnold.

Gill, Ros (2006) *Gender and the Media*, Cambridge: Polity Press.

Glasgow University Media Group (1993) *Getting the Message: News, Truth and Power*, London: Routledge.

Gledhill, Christine (ed.) (1987) *Home Is Where the Heart Is*, London: British Film Institute.

Gledhill, Christine (1991) *Stardom: Industry of Desire*, London: Routledge.

Gledhill, Christine and Williams, Linda (eds) (2000) *Reinventing Film Studies*, London and New York: Arnold.

Glynn, C., Herbst, S., O'Keefe, and Shapiro, R. (1999) *Public Opinion*, Boulder, Col.: Westview Press.

Goffman, Erving (1976) *Gender Advertisements*, London: Macmillan.

Golding, Peter and Elliott, Philip (1979) *Making the News*, London: Longman.

Gomery, Douglas (1992) *Shared Pleasures*, London: British Film Institute.

Goodwin, Andrew and Whannel, Gary (eds) (1990) *Understanding Television*, London: Routledge.

Gramsci, Antonio (1994) *Selected Writings from the Prison Notebooks*, London: Lawrence and Wishart.

Gripsrud, Jostein (ed.) (2002) *Understanding Media Culture*, London: Arnold.

Hall, Stuart (1996) *Race, the Floating Signifier*, videotape available from the Media Education Foundation.

Hall, Stuart (ed.) (1997) *Representation: Cultural Representations and Signifying Practices*, London: Thousand Oaks and New Delhi: Sage.

Hawthorn, Jeremy (1998) *A Glossary of Contemporary Literary Theory*, London and New York: Arnold.

Herman, Ed and McChesney, Robert (1997) *The Global Media: The New Visionaries of Corporate Capitalism*, London: Cassell.

Hesmondhalgh, David (2002) *The Cultural Industries*, London: Sage.

Hill, Annette (2004) *Real TV Factual Entertainment and Television Audiences*, London: Routledge.

Hill, John and Church Gibson, Pamela (eds) (1998) *The Oxford Guide to Film Studies*, Oxford and New York: Oxford University Press.

Hillier, Jim (ed.) (2001) *American Independent Cinema: A Sight and Sound Reader*, London: British Film Institute.

Hills, Matt (2002) *Fan Cultures*, London and New York: Routledge.

Hochschild, Arlie and Ehrenreich, Barbara (eds) (2003) *Global Woman: Nannies, Maids and Sex Workers in the New Economy*, London: Granta.

Holland, Patricia (2000, 2nd edition) *The Television Handbook*, London and New York: Routledge.

Holland, Patricia (2003) *Picturing Childhood: The Myth of the Child in Popular Imagery*, London: I.B. Tauris.

Jameson, Fredric (1991) *Postmodernism, or, The Cultural Logic of Late Capitalism*, Durham, NC: Duke University Press.

Jancovich, M. (1996) *Rational Fears: American Horror in the 1950s*, Manchester and New York: Manchester University Press.

Jeffreys, Sheila (2005) *Beauty and Misogyny: Harmful Cultural Practices in the West*, London: Routledge.

Keeble, Richard (1998, 2nd edition) *The Newspapers Handbook*, London: Routledge.

King, Geoff (2002) *New Hollywood Cinema An Introduction*, London: I.B Tauris.

Klein, Naomi (2001 edn) *No Logo*, London: Flamingo.

Kramer, Peter (2002) *The Big Picture: Hollywood Cinema from Star Wars to Titanic*, London: British Film Institute.

Lacey, Nick (2002) *Media Audiences and Institutions*, Basingstoke: Palgrave.

Lacey, Nick (2005) *Introduction to Film*, Basingstoke: Palgrave Macmillan.

Lacey, Nick and Stafford, Roy (2000) *Film as Product in Contemporary Hollywood*, London: British Film Institute; Keighley: ITP Publications.

Langham, Josephine (1996, 2nd edition) *Lights, Camera, Action!: Careers in Film, Television and Radio*, London: British Film Institute.

Lewis, Justin (2001) *Constructing Public Opinion: How Political Elites Do What They Like and Why We Seem to Go Along with It*, New York: Columbia University Press.

Lister, Martin (ed.) (1995) *The Photographic Image in Digital Culture*, London: Routledge.

Littler, Jo and Naidoo, Roshi (eds) (2005) *The Politics of Heritage*, London: Routledge.

Lovell, Alan and Kramer, Peter (1999) *Screen Acting*, London: Routledge.

Lovell, Alan and Sergi, Gianluca (2005) *Making Films in Contemporary Hollywood*, London: Hodder Arnold.

Macdonald, Myra (1995) *Representing Women: Myths of Femininity in the Popular Media*, London and New York: Arnold.

McGuigan, Jim (1992) *Cultural Populism*, London: Routledge.

McGuigan, Jim (1999) *Modernity and Postmodern Culture*, London: Open University Press.

McKay, Jenny (2000) *The Magazines Handbook*, London: Routledge.

McRobbie, Angela (2005) *Uses of Cultural Studies*, London: Sage.

Malik, Sarita (2001) *Representing Black Britain: Black and Asian Images on Television*, London: Sage.

Maltby, Richard (2004) *Hollywood Cinema*, Oxford: Blackwell.

Medhurst, Andy and Lunt, Sally R. (eds) (1997) *Lesbian and Gay Studies: A Critical Introduction*, London: Cassell.

Miller, Daniel (ed.) (1998) *Material Cultures: Why Some Things Matter*, London: UCL Press.

Miller, Daniel and Slater, Don (2001) *The Internet: An Ethnographic Approach*, Oxford: Berg.

Miller, Toby (ed.) (2002) *Television Studies*, London: British Film Institute.

Miller, Toby, Govil, Nitin, McMurria, John and Maxwell, Richard (2005) *Global Hollywood 2*, London: British Film Institute.

Moores, Sean (2000) *Media and Everyday Life in a Modern Society*, Edinburgh: Edinburgh University Press.

Neale, Steve (2000) *Genre and Hollywood*, London: Routledge.

Neale, Steve (ed.) (2002) *Genre and Contemporary Hollywood*, British Film Institute Publishing.

Neale, Steve and Smith, Murray (eds) (1998) *Contemporary Hollywood Cinema*, London: Routledge.

Nelmes, Jill (ed.) (2006, 4th edition) *An Introduction to Film Studies*, London: Routledge.

Norden, Martin (1994) *The Cinema of Isolation: A History of Physical Disability in the Movies*, New Brunswick, NJ: Rutgers University Press.

Nowell-Smith, Geoffrey and Ricci, Steven (eds) (1998) *Hollywood and Europe:*

Economics, Culture, National Identity 1945–1995, London: British Film Institute.

O'Sullivan, Tim and Jewkes, Yvonne (eds) (1997) *The Media Studies Reader*, London and New York: Arnold.

O'Sullivan, Tim, Dutton, Brian and Rayner, Philip (2003, 3rd edition) *Studying the Media: An Introduction*, London, New York, Melbourne and Auckland: Arnold.

Philo, Greg (1990) *Seeing and Believing: The Influence of Television*, London and New York: Routledge.

Philo, Greg and Berry, Mike (2004) *Bad News from Israel*, London: Pluto Press.

Poole, Elizabeth (2002) *Reporting Islam: Media Representations of British Muslims*, London: I.B. Tauris.

Rose, Gillian (2001) *Visual Methodologies*, London: Sage.

Rosenbaum, Jonathan (2000) *Movie Wars: How Hollywood and the Media Conspire to Limit What Films We Can See*, Chicago: A Cappella Press.

Rosenthal, Alan and Corner, John (eds) (2005, 2nd edition) *New Challenges for Documentary*, Manchester: Manchester University Press.

Schatz, Thomas (1989, 1998) *The Genius of the System: Hollywood Filmmaking in the Studio Era*, London: Faber & Faber.

Schechter, Danny (2003) *Media Wars: News at a Time of Terror*, New York: Rowan and Littlefield.

Schiller, Herbert I. (1996) *Information Inequality*, London and New York: Routledge.

Schlesinger, Philip (1987) *Putting 'Reality' Together*, London: Methuen.

Sergi, Gianluca and Lovell, Alan (2005) *Making Films in Contemporary Hollywood*, London: Hodder Arnold.

Shohat, Ella and Stam, Robert (1994) *Unthinking Eurocentrism: Multiculturalism and the Media*, London and New York: Routledge.

Silverstone, Roger (1999) *Why Study the Media?*, London: Sage.

Slater, Don (1997) *Consumer Culture and Modernity*, Cambridge: Polity.

Sparks, Richard (1992) *Television and the Drama of Crime: Moral Tales and the Place of Crime in Public Life*, Milton Keynes: Open University Press.

Sreberny-Mohammadi, Annabel, Winseck, Dwayne, McKenna, Jill and Boyd-Barrett, Oliver (eds) (1997) *Media in Global Context*, London and New York: Arnold.

Stacey, Jackie (1993) *Star Gazing: Hollywood Cinema and Female Spectatorship*, London: Routledge.

Stafford, Roy (2001) *Representation: An Introduction*, London: British Film Institute; Keighley: ITP Publications.

Stafford, Roy (2003) *Audiences: An Introduction*, London: British Film Institute; Keighley: ITP Publications.

Stam, Robert and Miller, Toby (eds) (2000) *Film and Theory: An Anthology*, Oxford: Blackwell.

Stokes, Melvyn and Maltby, Richard (eds) *Identifying Hollywood's Audiences: Cultural Identity and the Movies*, London: British Film Institute.

Strinati, Dominic (2004, 2nd edition) *An Introduction to Theories of Popular Culture*, London: Routledge.

Stringer, Julian (ed.) (2003) *Movie Blockbusters*, London: Routledge.

Tasker, Yvonne (2004) *Action and Adventure Cinema*, London and New York: Routledge.

Thompson, John B. (1997) *The Media and Modernity: A Social Theory of the Media*, Cambridge: Polity.

Thompson, John B. (2000) *Political Scandal: Power and Visibility in the Media Age*, Cambridge: Polity.

Thompson, Kenneth (1998) *Moral Panics*, London and New York: Routledge.

Thornham, Sue (2000) *Feminist Theory and Cultural Studies*, London: Arnold.

Thussu, Daya and Freedman, Des (2003) *War and the Media; Reporting Conflict 24/7*, London: Sage.

Tolson, Andrew (1996) *Mediations: Text and Discourse in Media Studies*, London and New York: Arnold.

Van Djik (2005, 2nd edition) *The Network Society*, London: Sage.

Van Zoonen, Lisbet (2004) *Entertaining the Citizen: When Politics and Popular Culture Converge*, Boulder, CO: Rowmand and Littlefield.

Wasko, Janet (2001) *Understanding Disney: The Manufacture of Fantasy*, Cambridge: Polity.

Wasko, Janet (2004) *How Hollywood Works*, London: Sage.

Wells, Liz (ed.) (2000, 2nd edition) *Photography: A Critical Introduction*, London and New York: Routledge.

Wheen, Francis (2004) *How Mumbo-Jumbo Conquered the World*, London: Fourth Estate.

Wilby, Peter and Conroy, Andy (1994) *The Radio Handbook*, London: Routledge.

Williams, Raymond (1976) *Keywords: A Vocabulary of Culture and Society*, London: Fontana/Croom Helm.

Williams, Raymond (1979) *Politics and Letters: Interviews with New Left Review*, London: Verso.

Wilson, Elizabeth (2003) *Adorned in Dreams: Fashion and Modernity*, London: I.B. Tauris.

Wright, Terence (2004) *The Photography Handbook*, London: Routledge.

Wyatt, Justin (1994) *High Concept: Movies and Marketing in Hollywood*, Austin: University of Texas Press.

Wyatt, Justin (2002) *Marketing, The Film Reader*, London: Routledge.

Zelizer, Barbie and Allan, Stuart (eds) *Journalism after September 11*, London and New York: Routledge.

For specific technical manuals, please see the catalogues published by Focal Press obtainable via http://books.elsevier.com.

Useful information

Magazines

The following magazines are useful sources of specialist material on the industries concerned. The North American magazines are all available in the UK, although outside major city centres they would need to be ordered. Trade magazines are expensive, but access to only one or two copies can give you a valuable insight into industry concerns, unavailable elsewhere. Many university libraries will carry the full range.

Billboard (www.billboard.com) American music and related entertainment industry trade paper.

Broadcast (www.broadcastnow.com) the trade magazine for the UK broadcasting industry.

Campaign (www.brandrepublic.com) the trade magazine for the UK advertising industry.

Free Press (www.cpbf.org.uk) newsletter of the Campaign for Press and Broadcasting Freedom (CPBF), available from 8 Cynthia Street, London N1 9JF.

Hollywood Reporter (www.hollywoodreporter.com) American film industry paper.

The Journalist (www.nuj.org.uk) magazine of the National Union of Journalists.

Marketing Week (www.mad.co.uk) the trade magazine for the UK marketing industry.

Media Week (www.mediaweek.co.uk) the trade magazine for UK media buyers.

Music Week (www.musicweek.com) trade paper of the UK music industry.

Screen (www.screen.arts.gla.ac.uk) academic journal for film and television studies in higher education.

Screen Digest (www.screendigest.com) monthly international television industry news magazine.

Screen International (www.screendaily.com) the international trade magazine for film production, distribution and exhibition (includes video and television films).

Sight and Sound (www.bfi.org.uk/sightandsound/) monthly magazine from the British Film Institute, giving details of film and video releases plus critical writing and features.

UK Press Gazette (www.pressgazette.co.uk) trade paper of the UK Press.

Variety (www.variety.com) the American trade paper for the entertainment industry generally.

Yearbooks

Guardian Media Directory, London: Guardian Books.
The Writers' and Artists' Year Book, London: A.C. Black.
Writers Handbook, London: Macmillan.

Doing your own research

To assist in your own research for essays, projects and seminars, we have listed organisations which offer useful advice and information for media students. Most organisations now have an easily accessible internet presence. Because web addresses change, you may need to search for sites. Postal and telephone contact details should be available via the website.

Advertising Standards Authority (ASA) (Advertising regulator)
www.asa.org.uk

Arts Council of England (Development agency supporting arts activities)
(see website for details of regional offices)
www.artscouncil.org.uk

Arts Council of Northern Ireland
www.artscouncil-ni.org

Arts Council of Wales
website: www.artswales.org.uk

BBC
www.bbc.co.uk

British Board of Film Classification (BBFC)
www.bbfc.co.uk

British Film Institute (BFI)
www.bfi.org.uk

Broadcasting, Entertainment, Cinematograph and Theatre Union (BECTU)
www.bectu.org.uk

Campaign for Press and Broadcasting Freedom (CPBF)
www.cpbf.org.uk

Channel 4 Television
www.channel4.com

Community Media Association
www.commedia.org.uk

Film Education
www.filmeducation.org

Institute of Practitioners in Advertising (IPA)
www.ipa.co.uk

ITV plc
www.itvplc.com

Mechanical-Copyright Protection Society (MCPS)
www.mcps.co.uk

Media Education Wales
www.mediaedwales.org.uk

National Union of Journalists
www.nuj.org.uk

Northern Ireland Film and Television Commission
www.niftc.co.uk

The Performing Right Society (PRS)
www.prs.co.uk

Press Complaints Commission
www.pcc.org.uk

Royal Photographic Society
www.rps.org

Scottish Arts Council
www.scottisharts.org.uk

Scottish Screen
www.scottishscreen.com

Sgrin (Media Agency for Wales)
www.sgrin.co.uk

Skillset (Sector Skills Council for Audio-Visual Industries)
www.skillset.org

UK Film Council
www.ukfilmcouncil.org.uk

Useful websites

www.aber.ac.uk/media/medmenu.html – Daniel Chandler's Media and Communication Studies site, highly recommended for media students

en.wikipedia.org – the web encyclopedia being constructed by its users (see Chapter 10)

www.mediauk.com – starting point for researching information about all UK media organisations

www.newmediastudies.com – David Gauntlett's interesting and entertaining website, looking at how the web has changed ways of thinking about media studies, also links to www.theory.org.uk with equally entertaining introductions to popular culture and social theory

uk.imdb.com – the Internet Movie Database, starting point for research on films and television programmes

Index

This index lists page references to four different kinds of information: key terms, media organisations, people and titles of films, radio and television programmes etc. It isn't exhaustive but, used in conjunction with the Glossary, should help you find out what you want. Definitions (either in the chapter or in the Glossary) will sometimes be signalled by **bold numbers**, illustrations by *italic numbers* and margin entries by '(m)'.

Related titles from Routledge

Media Studies: The Essential Resource
Edited by Philip Rayner, Peter Wall and Stephen Kruger

A unique collection of resources for all those studying the media at university and pre-university level, this book brings together a wide array of material including advertisements, political cartoons and academic articles, with supporting commentary and explanation to clarify their importance to Media Studies. In addition, activities and further reading and research are suggested to help kick start students' autonomy.

The book is organized around three main sections: Reading the Media, Audiences and Institutions and is edited by the same teachers and examiners who brought us the hugely successful *AS Media Studies: The Essential Introduction*.

This is an ideal companion or standalone sourcebook to help students engage critically with media texts – its key features include:

*   further reading suggestions
*   a comprehensive bibliography
*   a list of web resources.

ISBN10: 0-415-29172-0 (hbk)
ISBN10: 0-415-29173-9 (pbk)

ISBN13: 9-78-0-415-29172-9 (hbk)
ISBN13: 9-78-0-415-29173-6 (pbk)

Available at all good bookshops
For ordering and further information please visit:
www.routledge.com

Related titles from Routledge

Print Journalism
Edited by Richard Keeble

Print Journalism: A critical introduction provides a unique and thorough insight into the skills required to work within the newspaper, magazine and online journalism industries. Among the many highlighted are:

- Sourcing the news
- Interviewing
- Sub-editing
- Feature writing and editing
- Reviewing
- Designing pages
- Pitching ideas

In addition separate chapters focus on ethics, reporting courts, covering politics and copyright whilst others looks at the history of newspapers and magazines, the structure of the UK print industry (including its financial organisation) and the development of journalism education in the UK, helping to place the coverage of skills within a broader, critical context.

All contributors are experienced practising journalists as well as journalism educators from a broad range of UK universities.

ISBN10: 0-415-35881-7 (hbk)
ISBN10: 0-415-35882-5 (pbk)

ISBN13: 9-78-0-415-35881-1 (hbk)
ISBN13: 9-78-0-415-35882-8 (pbk)

Available at all good bookshops
For ordering and further information please visit:
www.routledge.com